Mount Vernon

Port Angeles

Port Townsend

Oak Harbor

OLYMPIC
NATIONAL
PARK

Everett

Shoreline

Lynnw

Park

Bremerton

405

101

SEATTLE

Belle

Tacoma

Renton

Aberdeen

5

Kent

12

Puyallup

101

Olympia

ond

Centralia

Mt. Rainier

Chehalis

14,411 ft

MOUNT RAINIER
NAT'L PARK

30

Longview

Packwood

Mt. St. Helens

The Amplified Come as You Are

The Story of Nirvana

MICHAEL AZERRAD

HarperONE
An Imprint of HarperCollinsPublishers

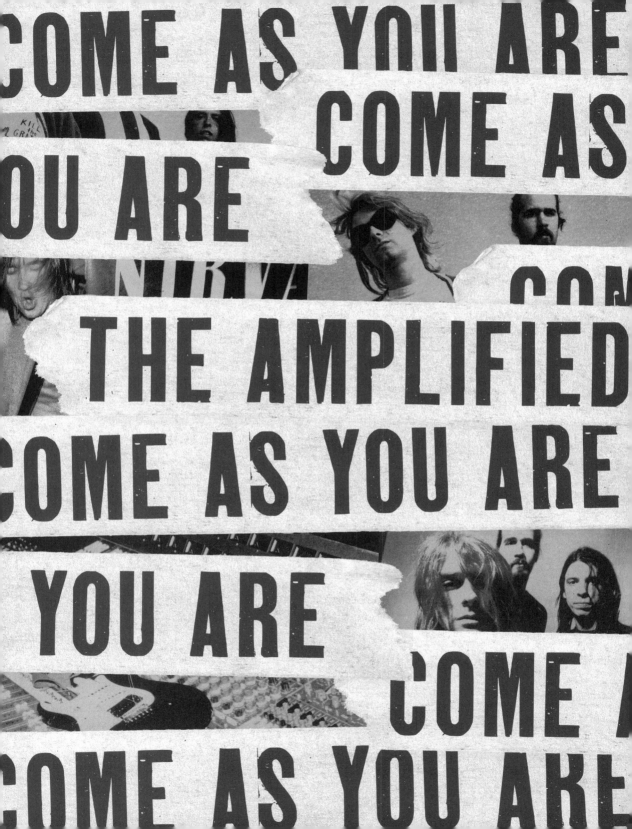

THE AMPLIFIED COME AS YOU ARE. Copyright © 2023
by Michael Azerrad. All rights reserved. Printed
in the United States of America. No part of this
book may be used or reproduced in any manner
whatsoever without written permission except in
the case of brief quotations embodied in critical
articles and reviews. For information, address
HarperCollins Publishers, 195 Broadway, New
York, NY 10007.

HarperCollins books may be purchased for
educational, business, or sales promotional use.
For information, please email the Special Markets
Department at SPsales@harpercollins.com.

FIRST EDITION

Designed by Janet Evans-Scanlon

Library of Congress Cataloging-in-Publication
Data has been applied for.

ISBN 978-0-06-327993-3

23 24 25 26 27 LBC 5 4 3 2 1

What could be put up against the noise
of time? Only that music which is inside
ourselves—the music of our being—which
is transformed by some into real music.
Which, over the decades, if it is strong
and true and pure enough to drown out the
noise of time, is transformed into the
whisper of history.

—Julian Barnes, *The Noise of Time*

THAT WOULD BE TOO GUNS N' ROSES

ery late one night in the autumn of 1992, the phone rang. It was Courtney Love. She wanted to know if I would like to write a book about Nirvana. Of course I did, even though I'd never written anything longer than the 4,895-word Nirvana cover story I'd done earlier that year for *Rolling Stone*. "That sounds interesting," I said, playing it as cool as I could manage, "but could I talk to Kurt about it?" She handed the phone to Kurt Cobain.

"Hey," he said in his cigarette growl. I asked Kurt why he wanted to do the book. And he said it was because the truth, as unflattering as it might be, would be better than all the lies that were being printed about him and Courtney and the band—this was shortly after the *Vanity Fair* story that was used as some of the evidence to briefly take away custody of their infant daughter Frances. He promised me access to anyone I wanted to talk to. "Just tell the truth," he said. "That'll be better than anything else that's been written about me."

"But I don't want it to be an authorized biography," I said. Kurt was savvy—he knew the journalistic meaning of that term, which is that the subject has final approval over the manuscript. I'll never forget his reply. "No way," he said. "That would be too Guns N' Roses."

OK, I was in.

###

When I first met Kurt, in early 1992, he and Courtney were living in a little apartment in a two-up, two-down apartment building on an anonymous stretch of street in the Fairfax section of Los Angeles. They'd moved to Los Angeles to get out of the hermetic atmosphere of Seattle and live in a place where it was more comfortable to be a celebrity. I guess that it was also easier to get drugs there—and seek treatment for them. I was there to interview Kurt for a *Rolling Stone* cover story, the one with him on the cover wearing a homemade T-shirt that said "Corporate Magazines Still Suck."

I was really nervous. Not a whole lot was known about Kurt at that point. He was the guy from Seattle who screamed in his songs, smashed his guitars, and might be a heroin addict. I had never knowingly met a heroin addict. I knew he had already done the photo shoot wearing a handmade T-shirt that insulted the magazine I was writing the article for, so that was kind of daunting. He was also the most celebrated rock musician on the planet. I really did not know what I was going to encounter. And I was there to write a cover story for *Rolling Stone*, which was a really big deal back then. I was nervous.

It was dusk when my taxi dropped me off at the address. Courtney greeted me at the door and graciously offered me a plate of green grapes. I'd never met the obscure and yet somehow already notorious Courtney Love, only heard her paint-peeling shriek over Hole's cantankerous racket, and now she was standing right in front of me, looking artfully disheveled, barefoot, in a vintage slip. I'd never met her before, and, going sheerly by her reputation, I was expecting someone approximating a feral child. Instead, as I say, she quietly welcomed me with a plate of grapes and invited me into her home.

First, there was a tiny, dimly lit living room with no furniture in it, LPs and guitars strewn around the bare floor, and against one wall a small Buddhist shrine with burning candles. (I don't think I'd ever knowingly met a Buddhist either.) "Norwegian Wood (This Bird Has Flown)" was playing on the crappy little stereo.

And then there was the very long walk down a very short hallway to the bedroom—it couldn't have been more than fifteen feet, but it just seemed to elongate as I walked down it, kind of like at the end of *The Graduate* when Dustin Hoffman runs down the sidewalk toward the church. Eventually, I got to the door and opened it to find Kurt lying in a little bed in a little room, his back against the wall, facing the doorway, his shocking blue eyes laser beaming through the subdued lighting. His bare feet were sticking out past the bedsheets, and his toenails were painted a rosy hue. The smell of jasmine flowers wafted through the screen on the window above his head, and to this day, when I smell jasmine, it shoots me straight back to that moment.

"Hi," he said. And two things struck me instantly. And I mean in an instant. The first was: oh wow, I *know* this guy. He wasn't some sort of rock & roll space alien; he was actually like a lot of the stoners I went to high school with. Hell, *I* was a stoner in high school. He was a little bit like *me*.

A year or so later, I told Kurt about the moment we met, about how I instantly felt comfortable with him. And he said something like, "That's how I felt about you, too! I was nervous about it, but the second you walked in the door, I thought, this is going to be OK." Because, as huge as Nirvana was, Kurt had been relatively unknown only a few short months before, a one-time small-town deadbeat—and now, a guy whose articles he'd been reading for the past few years had flown out from New York City to interview him for a cover story in *Rolling Stone*. Kurt had been dreaming of this for most of his life: from when he was a little kid, he wanted to "play in a rock band and be on the cover of magazines and stuff." As I said, this was a really big deal. For both of us.

I just played it cool about the fact that he was doing an interview while lying in bed—hey, maybe he often did interviews this way, and besides, it provided a nice bit of color. So I sat down on a little footstool next to him and started asking questions. I asked Kurt about what he was like as a kid, and he said something about being small for his age, and I stood up from my footstool, unfurled my wiry five-foot-six frame, and said, in a theatrically manly voice, "I don't know what you're talking about!" And we exchanged smiles, and that was that: we understood each other.

He said he was an artistic, sensitive kid. So was I! OK, maybe not as artistic as Kurt was. And he said his parents were divorced by the time he was ten years old and he was melancholic ever since. Same here! And somehow I got to talking about Arlo Guthrie's "The Motorcycle Song" and how I'd play the song on the family record player and run around the house pretending I was a motorcycle. And Kurt said, "I did that, too!" We grew up on the same music that so many American kids did: Kiss, Cheap Trick, Queen, Black Sabbath, and so on. We even became stoners around the same age, too. It was kind of uncanny.

So here I was, the bespectacled college-boy *Rolling Stone* journalist from New York City, connecting with this guy from clear across the country, from a very different background, a rural high school dropout whose dad had worked counting logs in a lumber mill.

Now, I'm not saying I was unique or special about any of this—literally millions of people have a similar story and would have had a similar experience with Kurt if they'd met him—but it was amazing how much we had in common. We hit it off.

(A couple of years after Kurt passed, I asked Courtney why Kurt had connected with me so well. And she said, "He thought you had a similar kind of melancholy." I told this to my father and it made him a little worried.)

Turns out Kurt was very much like a whole lot of people, actually. He just had a genius for conveying that in song and in the most ineffable way.

But the second thing I realized in the first few moments of meeting Kurt is really uncomfortable to say: I sensed that he was one of those rock musicians who dies young. I'd never met one of those people before, or even known many people who died at all. I just sensed it. He was more than enough of a student of rock paradigms that he probably realized it himself. (Frequent Nirvana photographer Ian Tilton once said, "He had this sort of fascination with dead pop stars.") Other people around him felt this same feeling, but maybe they ignored their intuitions; a lot of people do. Then again, maybe they just wouldn't say such a horrible thing out loud.

Dave Grohl knew though. In 2009, he told the BBC, "There are some people that you meet in life that you just know that they are not going to live to be a hundred years old. . . . In some ways, you kind of prepare yourself emotionally for that to be a reality."

Courtney knew, too. "How could I not when he talked about it every single day?" she told *Spin* magazine's Craig Marks in a remarkable 1995 story. "If there were ninety-nine dots on the wall, he was going to kill himself. If such and such happened that day, he was going to kill himself." And, as she said in her taped message to the crowd gathered at the public memorial for Kurt in Seattle, "I mean, it was going to happen."

Even Kurt's mom, Wendy, felt it: "I said if he ever lived to be thirty," she told *Spin*, "I'd be surprised."

"When you see the way he was," Neil Young once said of Kurt, "there's no way he could ever get through the other end of it. Because there was no control to the burn. That's why it was so intense. He was not holding back at all."

At the time, there was so much phoniness in popular music. It was frustrating. The feeling in the air was, in the exasperated words of John Lennon, "just gimme some truth." And then, suddenly, there was Nirvana. They were for real. There was no artifice in the music; they meant every millisecond.

At the very moment I was talking with him, Kurt was detoxing from heroin. He said he was in bed because he had a cold or something, which made sense—he was just coming off a tour that went from Australia to New Zealand to Singapore to Japan to Hawaii, and all those shows and air travel would naturally take a toll on anybody, even someone who had just turned twenty-five. It didn't really seem like he had a cold, though, but I just partitioned it in my mind. In retrospect, it was obvious what he was going through. But I was so naive. I just didn't know. Or maybe I just didn't *want* to know. I've always considered that inclination to be one of my weak points as a journalist. With the sketchy stuff, I tend to look the other way.

And maybe Kurt, Courtney, and the whole apparatus around them realized that too when they asked if I'd like to write this book. I was a pretty nice person. And maybe it was obvious that I was pretty green. Or they thought they could successfully hide the bad parts from me. Probably all those things were true. So they took a chance on me for this book. It was quite a risky gamble for them but a canny one.

#

The *Rolling Stone* cover story came out that April. I was mostly a pretty mediocre writer up until then, but somehow I rose to the occasion, and I'll forever be grateful to *Rolling Stone* for taking a chance on me. It was a professional and artistic breakthrough for me. And I think it was the first coverage that connected Kurt's personal story to the music that he made.

#

A few months later, *Rolling Stone* assigned me to cover the 1992 Reading Festival, the final day of which featured a bill almost entirely composed of grunge bands, with Nirvana headlining.

The Amplified Come as You Are

I was staying at the Reading Ramada, where a lot of the bands were staying too, and many musicians congregated at the ground floor bar, making it quite the scene. Late one evening, I was standing in the lobby, just spacing out for a moment. And I felt something pass just over the top of my head, like maybe someone's hand just an inch away but not touching. I figured someone was goofing on me, so I ignored it and waited for whoever it was to give up and introduce themselves. But there wasn't anyone anywhere near me. So finally, I just turned around to see what was going on. And there, some twenty feet away, was Kurt Cobain, staring directly at me with those laser beam eyes.

(I've had that sensation only once since: I was at a memorial gathering for Lou Reed, and again I thought it was someone playing a trick on me, and again I played it cool and took my time to turn around. There was no one there. But maybe fifteen feet behind me, David Bowie was, for some reason, staring right at me.)

I walked up to Kurt, and he was glad to see me. He said he liked my *Rolling Stone* story. In retrospect, I can see how the article served his purposes: I quoted his anti-drug speech; I acknowledged that he was truly in love with Courtney, who was starting to get a lot of grief from the media; I took his stomach pain seriously, which few people did; and I let him plug a bunch of his favorite bands, which helped him feel a little better about his exploding fame.

There, in the hotel lobby, we continued the connection we'd made during the interview; we just talked really easily with each other. I bought him a vodka-and-orange at the crowded bar, which, looking back on it, means he wasn't using at the time—like any other heroin user, he knew very well that mixing alcohol and opiates is potentially fatal. We chatted a little bit before the swirl of fellow musicians and the gawking of onlookers got to be too much and Kurt retreated to his room.

And then there was that fateful late-night phone call from Courtney, when she asked if I'd like to write a book about Nirvana.

From there, it was pretty easy to get a book deal. I signed a contract with Main Street Books, an imprint of Doubleday. The next Nirvana album was due out the following September, which was when Doubleday wanted to publish. And so I had a little less than seven months to write my first book. After that, it was nothing but pedal to the metal.

#

Before I began writing, Courtney would sometimes call me, I think partly to try to frame the narrative for me, partly to ingratiate herself with the guy who was going to write the book, and maybe just because she and Kurt liked and trusted me. Her conversations were routinely peppered with references to various pharmaceuticals that I'd never heard of, like Klonopin and Diazepam and Vicodin, as if everybody knew what they were; that's how Courtney talks, as if you're intimately familiar with all the arcane things and people she's analyzing at such high velocity. The pharmaceutical thing was so relentless that one day I walked over to downtown Manhattan's cavernous, beloved Strand Bookstore—remember, this is basically pre-internet—and bought a used copy of the *Physicians' Desk Reference*, a big, fat book that lists all prescription drugs and their uses and effects, so I could try to keep up with Courtney.

On the way home from the Strand, I happened to bump into someone from Nirvana's management team who was extremely distrustful and controlling. This was before any of the interviews for the book started, and if this person suspected that I was going to write a lurid exposé about Kurt and Courtney's drug use, they might well cancel the book. But I really just wanted to know what Courtney was talking about. And, of course, right away this person noticed the telltale Strand book bag and asked the very question I was dreading: "Oh, what book did you buy?" I mumbled something and quickly changed the subject, dangling the bag behind my back. I can laugh about it now, but at the time, I was practically shaking with fear.

The next six months went by quickly. All I did was fly back and forth to Seattle (and once to Los Angeles) to do interviews and then come back home to transcribe, research, and write.

Being around such high-voltage people like Kurt and Courtney, with all their drama and just the powerful ambient electricity coursing around them, was exciting, but it was also stressful and exhausting—getting close to really charismatic people is kind of exciting but it's easy not to notice that it's also sucking the life out of you. That, and traveling so much and then working day and night for weeks on end, took a heavy toll on my health and my personal relationships. The day I turned in the manuscript, my dad took a photo of me: I still can't even look at it; I look pale and gaunt, almost sickly, but also really proud.

Many rock memoirs are done to settle one particular score, and to the writer, the rest of it is just sandwich bread. Look at Morrissey's 2013 *Autobiography*, for instance: there's lots of juicy stuff, but really it's all just a delivery system for a lengthy screed about his former Smiths bandmates and their lawsuits against him. Likewise, in light of the debacle with their custody of their baby, Kurt and Courtney mainly just wanted *Come as You Are* to clear their name as parents; everything else in the story was window dressing.

Yes, both of them were substance abusers, but parental love is an extremely powerful force, and Kurt and Courtney dearly loved Frances. I knew that keeping their child was the real point of the book, but that didn't bother me—I wanted them to keep their kid, and besides, I was excited to tell the Nirvana story with no interference.

The subtitle of the book is very pointedly *The Story of Nirvana*. It's not, as people sometimes say to me, "your book about Kurt Cobain." That subtitle gave me a good reason, or was that excuse, not to go too deeply into dark, dark places. I just wasn't interested in that stuff—I'm interested in how bands form, their internal dynamics, how they make the music that we all love. And I think that, as a lifelong drummer, maybe I was a little biased toward emphasizing that Nirvana was a *band*, that everybody in it made a meaningful, invaluable contribution. I took care to tell Krist's and Dave's pre-Nirvana stories and discuss their indispensable roles in the band, both on- and offstage, and I delve deeper into that here.

I began doing interviews during some precious downtime: touring for *Nevermind* was done, and Kurt was ostensibly working on songs for the next album. The fallout from the *Vanity Fair* story was ongoing, and so there was a lot of very understandable turmoil, but everyone had plenty of free time to talk and reflect on what had just happened. It all came together. I was very lucky.

Rereading the book for this annotated edition, I began to notice some patterns that I hadn't noticed when I was in the thick of writing the original version. Maybe I was too young to see them; maybe I was looking the other way because I was smitten by my subject; maybe I had to work too fast to notice such things. But thirty years can give you some objectivity.

In journalist Janet Malcolm's essential book *The Journalist and the Murderer*, published in 1990, she notes that every journalist "is a kind of confidence man, preying on people's vanity, ignorance or loneliness, gaining their trust and betraying them without remorse." But the subject can also play the journalist exactly the same way.

Kurt, being a student of rock history, knew that the story of a rock band is essentially a legend—in the sense that there's some wiggle room in the truth as long as it serves the overall myth. So Kurt was an unreliable narrator of his own story. And that's nothing new—everyone does it. It's on the journalist to determine what's true and what isn't. But sometimes the journalist just plays along because they're naive, lazy, overworked, or they just want to be in on the game because it makes for sensational copy. Or maybe they want to ingratiate themselves with the subject so they can work with them again. Whichever way, it works to the artist's advantage.

Which is to say that I wish I could have brought more skepticism to the project and done more reporting, but there just wasn't time—I had to finish the manuscript quickly so it could be published around the release of *In Utero*.

Remember, too, that I was pioneering a lot of this stuff—Kurt and the band are extremely well-documented now, but this was the first book about Nirvana. Later journalists would have the benefit of hindsight and piles of articles, not to mention the internet, but in 1993, I enjoyed none of those things.

As a narrator, Kurt also knew that every good legend has a protagonist and an antagonist. There's a Greek word for this timeless conflict: *agon*. Not coincidentally, it's the root of the word "agony."

Kurt just before his second birthday.

The protagonist of this particular legend is Kurt Cobain. Over the course of his story, there's a long litany of antagonists: Aberdeen bullies, Aberdeen itself, Kurt's parents, various drummers, homophobes, misogynists, racists, Sub Pop, his own body, "the grown-ups," Pearl Jam, heroin addiction, Geffen/DGC, and so on. For every setback, there was someone or something to blame. When one antagonist left the stage, he found a new one. There was always, as one of his songs puts it, something in the way.

It's funny, this may have started young: when Kurt was very little, he had some imaginary friends. "There was one called Boddah," his mother, Wendy, told me for the *Rolling Stone* cover story. "He blamed everything on him."

Another antagonist was himself: the self that hated itself. And wanted to die. In legends, the protagonist is supposed to vanquish the antagonist. That didn't happen this time. Or, actually, it did.

###

"Passionate" was the word Kurt reserved for his highest praise: the best thing he could say about someone was that they had passion for what they were doing, whatever it was. Nirvana walked that walk: after several years of fluffy boy bands and fluffy metal acts, Nirvana was indisputably passionate: intensely emotional and fully committed, with no control to the burn.

Besides passion, another really key concept for Kurt was empathy. "I've always had enough empathy in people to realize that everybody has a good side to them," he told me, "no matter how much of an asshole they are." Which is kind of surprising, given his avowed disdain for so many of the people around him. How much empathy did he have

The Amplified Come as You Are

when he hit a man on the head with his guitar during a show in Dallas in 1991? Well, nobody's perfect, and maybe incidents like that reminded him of how far he still had to go.

Maybe, as he claimed, opiates really did still that hostility and help him experience empathy in his everyday life. The thing is, there are much better, healthier ways to develop the ability to feel what others are feeling. And Kurt was quite empathetic, almost painfully so. Maybe his outspokenness about empathy was really a plea for people to have empathy for *him*.

At any rate, Kurt avowedly revered the ability to imagine what other people are feeling, and he did so right down to his last moments. In his suicide note, the word "empathy" was underlined twice. His name was in the smallest lettering on the whole page.

I wrote this book with a lot of passion and, I hope, empathy as well.

#

The idea behind *The Amplified Come as You Are* is to illuminate my 1993 book *Come as You Are: The Story of Nirvana*, and mine it for insights on Nirvana, its members, and the time in which the band existed.

My intention isn't to track down every gory detail, find every skeleton in every closet. It's to shed additional light on Nirvana's story, and help Nirvana fans, people interested in the cultural history of the '90s, and yes, myself get a better understanding of what the hell happened.

#

NB: This book was written before Chris Novoselic became Krist Novoselic—he decided to acknowledge his Croatian heritage and began going by his given name. So while the original text refers to him as Chris, he's Krist in the annotations.

NB II: A note about the occasionally wacky chapter numbers. I started writing *Come as You Are* at chapter 1. But later I realized I should write an introduction, so rather than renumber all the chapters, I just made the introduction chapter 0. Chapter 8.5 was originally part of chapter 8, but eventually, it became its own chapter and I already had a chapter 9. I didn't know where I was going to put chapter X, so that's how it got that name. I am pleased to finally clear up these deep and enduring literary mysteries.

NB III: Scattered throughout the book, you will encounter some language that is unacceptable today. Remember, this was the early '90s and, as cool and visionary as the members of Nirvana were about so many things, they were still very much of their time and not as enlightened as they could be. I'm guilty of a sin here and there, too.

I DON'T CARE IF YOU LIKE ME, I HATE YOU

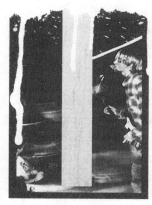

t's April 9, 1993, at the Cow Palace in San Francisco. Eleven thousand people—grunge kids, jocks, metalheads, mainstreamers, punks, little kids with their parents, hippie-types—have come from as far away as Los Angeles and Seattle to see Nirvana's first American show in seven months, a benefit for Bosnian rape victims. Besides a seven-week club tour in late 1991, the closest most American fans had come to seeing the band in concert was their appearance on *Saturday Night Live* over a year before. So much has happened in the meantime: drug rumors, breakup rumors, lawsuits, and about five million more copies of the *Nevermind* album sold worldwide. And much *hasn't* happened—a US arena tour, a new album. It's a crucial show.

This really was an important show for Nirvana. In some ways, it was similar to the atmosphere around the Reading Festival concert they'd played ten months before: no one was quite sure what shape Kurt was in or what the internal state of the band was. Nor did anyone know how the audience would receive the songs from their upcoming album, *In Utero*, an intensely raw, stark, and bristling screed with no obvious hit singles. A lot was riding on this show at the Cow Palace, the funky, 16,500-capacity Daly City arena that, since the '60s, had hosted legends such as the Beatles, the Rolling Stones, Elvis Presley, the Who, U2, Prince, and many other legends. But it wasn't as if the band was in top form in the middle of a tour—they were playing a one-off gig after considerable time away from the road. The Cow Palace show could have been a mess; Nirvana was certainly capable of that, and worse.

From what members of the band told me, as well as off-the-record comments from others, I knew that "the grown-ups"—Kurt's sarcastic term for the higher-ups at their label and management company—were hardly gung ho about *In Utero*. They weren't hearing *Nevermind II*. They thought the whole album was a self-sabotaging punk rock folly, a gigantic missed opportunity to shift some serious units, and Steve Albini's rigorously unadorned recording was a disservice to Kurt's towering genius. I'm sure most of them would dispute that now, but that's how I remember it, and I'm not the only one. This would be the debut of many songs from the upcoming album, and everyone was going to scrutinize how the crowd reacted.

I flew to San Francisco for the occasion and arrived at the backstage of the Cow Palace long before showtime to find Krist attired in some sort of clerical vestments, doing a photo shoot in the cinder-block hallway. (The photo wound up on the cover of a single Kurt did with William S. Burroughs called "The 'Priest' They Called Him.") I found the band, the crew, and a few friends hanging out in the bare-bones, white-walled dressing room. Eddie Vedder was there; Nirvana and Pearl Jam did have some beef, but it's difficult to have beef with Eddie Vedder; he's a great person. It was a pretty jovial atmosphere considering the pressure of the show.

At one point, I was sitting down and chatting with Kurt, who had little baby Frances on his knee, when Courtney asked to take a photo of us and said I should hold the baby. Kurt handed Frances to me, but I had no idea how to hold a baby, so she squirmed and whined. Kurt stuck his cigarette near Frances's mouth so it looked like he was making her smoke and got Courtney to snap the photo. That was a classic Kurt thing to do, mocking all the publicity about what terrible parents he and Courtney were supposed to be. He was making light of it, but it was still a really painful thing for them.

A couple of years later, I met up with Courtney after a Hole show in New Orleans. We were sitting in the tour bus, catching up, when she said, "I have something for you." And she went somewhere back in the bus and returned with something in her hand. It was the photo of Kurt, Frances, and me. Courtney can be exquisitely thoughtful.

At the Cow Palace, showtime finally rolled around and Kurt, Krist, and Dave made their way down to the area behind the stage. A few of us followed, just standing around in a dim gray concrete and cinder-block corridor, separated by a small curtain from the arena teeming with light and crowd noise. I could tell Kurt was a little nervous. Maybe this was dumb, but I walked up to him as he stood next to the curtain, guitar in hand, and I jumped up and down in an excited little pogo. I wasn't being punk rock; I was imitating the Beatles in that famous playground scene in *A Hard Day's Night*, or maybe Snoopy. He smiled a little smile, and then I backed off, maybe a little embarrassed about being so dumb and uncool, and watched him part that curtain and walk onto the stage for one of the most important shows of the band's career.

There were some seats by the side of the stage where "the grown-ups" and Nirvana's friends were. I was in front of some of "the grown-ups" and made sure to bop extra hard during the new songs. This was before I'd finished writing the book. So you can see how I had lost my objectivity.

The band walks out on stage. Kurt Cobain, sporting an aqua cardigan, an inside-out Captain America T-shirt, and decomposing blue jeans, gives a nervous little wave to the crowd. He's dyed his hair blond for the occasion; a mop of it obscures his eyes and indeed the entire top half of his face.

From the opening chords of "Rape Me," the band plays with explosive force,

The Amplified Come as You Are

salvos of sound catapulting off the stage and into the crowd—"Breed," "Blew," "Sliver," "Milk It," "Heart-Shaped Box." Toward the end, they play "The Hit" and even though Kurt mangles the opening chords, the moshers on the floor go berserk. As matches and lighters are held aloft during "Lithium," everyone in this cavernous barn is reminded of exactly why they love Nirvana.

That was Captain America, the band, not the comic book superhero. They were led by one of Kurt's favorite songwriters, Eugene Kelly, one half of the Vaselines. After legal warnings from Marvel Comics, they changed their name to Eugenius and released 1992's wonderful *Oomalama*.

The reason for the quotation marks around "The Hit" was because nobody in the Nirvana touring party ever uttered the title "Smells Like Teen Spirit." It was always, sarcastically, "The Hit." That was to show that you were down with the program and had disdain for commercial success, a sentiment that trickled down from the top. Kurt would often intentionally screw up the song just to show he didn't care, that he wasn't a performing monkey. It was embarrassing to have a hit—almost by definition, punk rockers weren't supposed to have them. Then again, Kurt had grown up on musicians who had many, many hits and enjoyed them very much.

Although Chris Novoselic and Kurt are at least thirty feet apart, they move and react to each other as if they are much closer; the communication is effortless. Midway through the set, Kurt calls over to Chris, "I feel great! I could play another hour!" And they do, packing twenty-four songs in an hour and a half, including eight songs from the upcoming album. The crowd applauds the new stuff enthusiastically, especially the ferocious assault on "Scentless Apprentice" and the majestic "All Apologies," which dissolves in a haze of mantra-chant and feedback.

Eddie Vedder from Pearl Jam watches from the side of the stage; not far away is the Melvins' Dale Crover. Frances Bean Cobain is upstairs in her dad's dressing room with her nanny; Courtney comes down just in time to dodge a plastic bottle of mineral water that Kurt has thrown without looking. She waves at him sarcastically.

At the end of the set, Kurt, Chris, and Dave Grohl disappear behind the drum riser and pass around a cigarette as they discuss what songs to play, then return for a seven-song, half-hour encore climaxing with "Endless, Nameless," the mystery track that closes *Nevermind*. As the band accelerates the song's main riff, it becomes a trance. Kurt walks across the top of his amp stack. It's not that high off the ground, but he's riveting anyway, like a potential suicide walking along the ledge of a building. The music speeds up even more. The guitars are squalling, Chris has unstrapped his bass and is waving it in front of his amp; Dave flails with precise abandon. As the music peaks, Kurt falls hard onto the drum set and drums and cymbal stands fall outward, like a carnivorous flower opening up and swallowing its prey. Show over.

That line about the potential suicide makes me wince. But obviously I was picking up on something—I just couldn't connect the dots. Kurt had done the ledge walk thing much more frighteningly during a scary freak-out at a show in Rome a few years before. In retrospect, both times, it was as if Kurt was rehearsing something, or foreshadowing it, the proverbial cry for help from someone who may or may not have wanted to be helped but certainly wanted to threaten the world with the prospect of his demise. Almost exactly a year later, Kurt would take his own life. Things like that have a way of focusing one's hindsight.

People ask each other if he's all right. It's not showmanship. If it were, they'd put down padding first. Maybe it's a geek stunt, like the kid in grade school who would make his nose bleed and smear the blood on his face so the bully would leave him alone, a case of "I'll hurt myself before you can" from a guy who opened the set with a song called "Rape Me." Perhaps it's an homage to two of Kurt's favorite stuntmen, Evel Knievel and Iggy Pop. Or is it that he's so jazzed up from the music that he's impervious to all physical harm, like a psyched-up swami who can walk across hot coals? Judging by the audience, all agog and aglow, that last explanation seems to fit the best.

That was the whole point of Nirvana's music: to transcend pain of all kinds. For Kurt, the pain was depression, his scoliosis, his mysterious chronic stomach condition, the overwhelming pressures of fame. Kurt's ritual end-of-show self-harm was proof of concept: the music had made him immune to suffering. But it was also, as I say, hurting himself before anyone else could.

Afterward, the entire entourage celebrates the triumphant gig in the courtyard of the trendy Phoenix Hotel—except for Kurt and Courtney, who have retired to a fancy hotel across town. The Phoenix, Courtney says, holds some bad memories for them. And besides, the bath towels are too small. Even without them, the place has turned into a little Nirvana village. Dave and his mother and sister are there, Chris and [his wife] Shelli are there, so is smiling Earnie Bailey the guitar tech and his wife Brenda, tour manager Alex Macleod, lighting designer Susanne

The Amplified Come as You Are

Sasic, folks from Gold Mountain Management, Mark Kates from Geffen/DGC, even members of Seattle's Love Battery who happen to be in town. Chris goes down to the grocery store and gets a couple of armloads of beer and the party lasts into the wee hours of the morning.

Everybody was in great spirits after the triumphant show, just really relieved, and we all laughed and horsed around deep into the night. The Phoenix is pretty famous for being a rock hotel, the courtyard the site of many an epic rocker bash. Later that evening, I think a few people might have jumped into the pool with their clothes on.

But Kurt was notably absent. There was now a divide in the band; Krist and Dave were simply enjoying the fame and money and acclaim, not to mention the sheer overwhelming rush of playing in a truly magical band. They'd get recognized on the street, but it was never a hassle—the perfect kind of fame. Kurt, though, had become a tabloid celebrity. He'd begun to sequester himself with Courtney, who didn't mix well with the rest of the organization anyway. It was the only cloud over an otherwise joyous evening.

The next day, Chris makes a pilgrimage to the fabled Beat landmark, the City Lights Bookstore. He goes outside to a cash machine, where a homeless man announces, "Good news, people! We are pleased to accept twenty-dollar bills for Easter!" Chris gives him one.

Krist wasn't just a punk—he identified with the generations of bohemian culture that preceded punk, so he was also kind of a hippie, as well as being interested in the direct predecessors of the hippies: the Beat generation, the fabled American bohemian community of the '50s that included Allen Ginsberg, Jack Kerouac, William Burroughs, and others.

Early in Nirvana's career, Krist moved to Tacoma to be closer to his day job as an industrial painter and built a practice space in the basement of the house he was renting. Then he read Jack Kerouac's 1957 Beat classic *On the Road*. As Krist later wrote in his 2004 book *Of Grunge and Government: Let's Fix This Broken Democracy!*, after reading Kerouac, "I figured all I needed in life was a bass guitar and the promise of the open road." He quit industrial painting to pursue the band full-time.

Many of the Beats gravitated to San Francisco and the City Lights Bookstore, which became a literary landmark. So that's why Krist and I went there. When I paid the taxi fare, I gave a decent tip, but then Krist boomed, "Sorry, driver, this man is from New York and they're cheap there!" and handed him a twenty, which was more than the fare. I think maybe Krist was still getting used to having a lot of money.

The Cow Palace show was a victory. It seemed like a confirmation that a punk rock band that hit the mainstream jackpot wasn't a fluke after all. That victory had repercussions for the band, all the bands like them, and maybe even the culture at large. As Sonic Youth's Kim Gordon said recently, "When a band like Nirvana comes out of the underground, it really expresses something that's going on in the culture and it's not a commodity."

Of course, it *was* a commodity, which was something the members of Nirvana had difficulty grappling with. But the band did express something happening in mainstream culture, a generational shift that just couldn't be ignored any longer, if only because it was such a commercial juggernaut. Nirvana might have been the last rock band to exemplify societal change. But no one could have known that at the time—gangsta rap had yet to conquer the charts, alternative rock was exploding, and Nirvana would surely be huge for years to come. That's how it appeared in the spring of 1993.

What was going on in the culture was reflected not only in the sound of the music but just as importantly, how it became popular. The punk rock phenomenon started practically the moment Johnny Ramone first put pick to string, inspiring a decade and a half's worth of hard work by countless bands, independent record labels, radio stations, magazines and fanzines, and small record stores that struggled to create some sort of alternative to the bland, condescending corporate rock which was being foisted on the public by the cynical major labels, the impersonal arenas, the mega-sized record stores, the lowest-common-denominator radio stations and the star-struck national rock magazines.

Galvanized by the punk rock revolution, the music underground formed a worldwide network, a shadow music industry. It grew and grew until not even the best efforts of the baby boomer—controlled music industry could hold it back. R.E.M. was the first explosion, Jane's Addiction came later, and then came the Big Bang: *Nevermind* has sold over eight million copies worldwide to date. It defied the best efforts of the likes of Michael Jackson, U2, and Guns N' Roses, and hit #1 on the Billboard album chart.

I later exploded those preceding two paragraphs into an entire book called *Our Band Could Be Your Life: Scenes from the American Indie Underground 1981-1991*. Writing *Come as You Are*, and the book's success, changed my life in many ways, and I wanted to repay the debt by doing the journalistic equivalent of the way Kurt would wear

T-shirts of obscure indie bands who inspired him. So I wrote a book about the musical community that birthed and inspired Nirvana and so many of their peers.

After this, everything was either pre- or post-Nirvana. Radio and press started taking the "alternative" thing seriously. Suddenly, record labels were rethinking their strategy. Instead of heavily promoted lightweight pop that would sell well at first and never be heard from again, they decided to start signing acts with long-term potential. And they were promoting them from a more grassroots level, instead of throwing money at them until they started selling. This was an imitation of the way Nirvana broke—a small core group of grassroots media and music fans whose valuable word of mouth expanded the group's base little by little at first, and then by leaps and bounds. Minimum hype, just good music.

The investigative zeal required in order to make one's way through the morass of independent music was in effect a rebuke of herd consumerism. It was a pesky development for the major labels, who had come to depend on promotional dollars to make the public see their way. Independent music required independent thinking, all the way from the artists who made the music to the entrepreneurs who sold it, to the people who bought it. It's a lot harder to track down that new Calamity Jane single than it is to pick up the latest C+C Music Factory CD.

Back then, you had to read fanzines to find out about the latest grassroots indie music, and then to get the music—and if you didn't live in a college town with a hip record store—you had to send away for it. That active, investigative sense and the obscure musical niches it enabled were a crude precursor to what happened in the following decade, when the internet provided online communities for even the most arcane sub-sub-genres.

###

In 1990, not one rock album hit the #1 spot, prompting some industry pundits to prophesy the end of rock. The audience for the music had been systematically fragmented by radio programmers looking for the perfect demographic, and it appeared unlikely that rock fans could unite around one record in large enough numbers to put it at the top of the charts. And while rock degenerated into a blow-dried, highly processed *faux* rebellion, genres such as country and rap more directly addressed the mood and concerns of the masses. Although several other rock albums hit #1 in 1991, *Nevermind* united an audience that had never been united before—the twentysomethings.

Tired of having old fogies such as Genesis and Eric Clapton or artificial creations such as Paula Abdul and Milli Vanilli rammed down their throats, the twentysomethings wanted a music of their own. Something that expressed the feelings *they* felt. A staggering number are children of divorce. They had the certain knowledge that they were the first American generation to have little hope of doing better than their parents, the generation that would suffer for the fiscal excesses of the Reagan '80s, that spent their entire sexual prime in the shadow of AIDS, that spent their childhoods having nightmares about nuclear war. They felt powerless to rescue an embattled environment and spent most of their lives with either Reagan or Bush in the White House, enduring a repressive sexual and cultural climate. And they felt helpless and inarticulate in the face of it all.

The most popular artists of 1990 included: middle-of-the-road maestro Phil Collins, videogenic dance-pop queen Paula Abdul, and pop-rappers MC Hammer and Vanilla Ice, as well as Janet Jackson, Michael Bolton, Don Henley, and Billy Joel. True, there was also Aerosmith and Mötley Crüe, but rock was certainly in the commercial minority.

Countless articles were written about Generation X at the time. These pieces enumerated how miserable their lives were and then castigated them for being lazy and living with their parents long after they should have been living on their own. They were called "slackers."

As Kurt wrote in his journals, the relationship of the record industry to the pop music audience had gone topsy-turvy: once, the industry catered to trends in youth culture music, but now, "record store chains and radio play it safe, target audience, what sells, were [*sic*] completely at their mercy it used to be the other way around." Thanks in no small part to Nirvana and their alternative rock peers, that would soon change.

Throughout the '80s, many musicians were protesting various political and social inequities, but most of them were boomers like Don Henley, Bruce Springsteen, and Sting. And many fans saw this protest for what it essentially was: posturing, bandwagon-jumping, self-righteous self-promotion. Exactly why *did* Duran Duran appear on Live Aid, anyway? Kurt Cobain's reaction to bad times was as direct as can be, and a hell of a lot more honest. He screamed.

It's a mistake to call Kurt Cobain a spokesman for a generation, though. Bob Dylan was a spokesman for a generation. Kurt Cobain isn't supplying any answers and he's barely even asking the questions. He makes an anguished wail, reveling in negative ecstasy. And if that is the sound of teen spirit these days, so be it.

I don't know why I singled out Bruce Springsteen. He had always been super cool.

Bob Dylan always denied that he was a spokesman for a generation, but then who in their right mind would actually say they were? The thing is, Dylan really might have been—in the same way Kurt might have been, which is to say, without trying to be.

"I'm just as confused as most people," Kurt protested to me for the *Rolling Stone* cover story. "I don't have the answers for anything." But if he hadn't been confused then all those kids wouldn't have related to him. And a spokesperson doesn't have to have answers—they just have to be able to convey how their people feel. Kurt could do that very effectively even if you couldn't quite put your finger on exactly what he was saying. "He doesn't necessarily know what he wants, but he's pissed," added *Nevermind* producer Butch Vig. Obviously, young people in particular have felt that way ever since there have been young people, but Nirvana's expression of it was rooted in the particular cultural moment of the early '90s, and it was overwhelmingly powerful in the most ineffable way.

Nirvana's music is very ecstatic. That was on purpose, to liberate Kurt, and anyone else who needed it, from worldly hurt. As Kurt wrote in his journals, "Nirvana means freedom from pain and suffering in the external world and thats [*sic*] close to my definition of punk rock." Freedom from pain and suffering *was the whole idea*.

The songs on *Nevermind* might have been about alienation and apathy, but alienation and apathy about things that didn't mean much anyway. By contrast, the band has expressed strong feelings about feminism, racism, censorship, and especially homophobia. And any hint of passivity was blown away by the awesome force of the music (particularly Dave Grohl's explosive drumming) and the undeniable craft of the songwriting. This was passionate music that didn't pretend. Getting into Nirvana was empowering for a generation that had no power.

It can't be emphasized enough how socially visionary Kurt was. Sure, some musicians had campaigned against things such as apartheid and nuclear power, and other musicians had embraced various causes, but in the early '90s it was extremely rare for straight white male rock stars to so outspokenly call out racism, homophobia, and sexism.

Perhaps Kurt's most famous nemesis was Guns N' Roses lead singer, Axl Rose, who represented many things that Kurt abhorred. While Rose had spouted horribly racist, xenophobic, and homophobic slurs in one of the band's songs, Kurt was wearing dresses on national television and singing "everyone is gay." And more than a quarter century before a January 2019 *New York Times* article hailed "The New Angry Young Men: Rockers Who Rail Against 'Toxic Masculinity,'" Kurt wrote in the *In Utero* liner notes, "If you're a sexist, racist, homophobe or basically an asshole, don't buy this CD. I don't care if you like me, I hate you."

It can't be emphasized enough that Kurt got introduced to these ideas by the underground community in Olympia, Washington, and many of them specifically and very directly from the riot grrrl movement.

###

The early lives of the band members echo that of their generation. All three come from broken homes. All three (and even their previous drummer) led painfully alienated childhoods; two are high school dropouts.

This was a very fashionable point at the time: this was the first generation that wasn't going to do as well as their parents, which was widely viewed as a failure of the American dream. This idea inspired reams of opinion columns. At the same time, the national divorce rate was rising dramatically: for instance, it doubled between the year Kurt was born (1967) and the year his parents split (1977). Unprecedented numbers of kids had divorced parents. Things like this were some of the key reasons why Nirvana was viewed as a cultural bellwether.

Although they're considered part of the "Seattle sound," they're not a Seattle band—Kurt Cobain and Chris Novoselic come from the isolated coastal logging town of Aberdeen, Washington. The band came of age there and in nearby Olympia, home of K Records and the "naive pop" band Beat Happening, both major philosophical, if not musical, influences on Nirvana. When Kurt talks about punk rock, he doesn't mean green hair and safety-pinned nostrils. He means the do-it-yourself, be-yourself, low-tech ethos of K, Touch & Go, SST, and other fiercely indie labels. It's an effort to reclaim music from the corporate realm and bring it back to the people, to make it electronic folk music.

Kurt didn't invent this redefinition of punk rock—that it wasn't just safety pins, pogoing, and jackhammer tempos and instead could be something much broader, a worldview—but he was instrumental in popularizing it. Major influences on Kurt such as "Beat Happening and K [Records]," I wrote in *Our Band Could Be Your Life*, "were a major force in widening the idea of a punk rocker from a mohawked guy in a motorcycle jacket to a nerdy girl in a cardigan."

The members of Nirvana clearly weren't corporate employees (they've visited their label's L.A. headquarters exactly once)—the band carefully defined themselves as being outside an idealized generic mainstream as concocted by Madison Avenue, television executives, the major record labels, and Hollywood. To use a now co-opted term, Nirvana presented an alternative. When eight million people said they felt the same way, the mainstream was redefined.

Many bands in the charts made good enough music, but it was merely entertainment. This music had *resonance*. It wasn't slick, it wasn't calculated. It was exhilarating, frightening, beautiful, vicious, vague, and exultant. And not only did it rock, but you could hum along to it.

Fame was not something the band wanted or was equipped to deal with. It was a surprise. It was embarrassing to them. It was too much too soon. Chris and Dave took it hard enough, but Kurt took it harder. They lay low for much of 1992, and by the early spring of the following year, Kurt, Chris, and Dave could look back on everything that had happened with 20/20 hindsight.

Dave told his side of the story at the Laundry Room, the modest Seattle recording studio he co-owns with his old friend and drum tech Barrett Jones. Sitting on the floor amid instruments, amps, and cables, he wore a K Records button on his button-down shirt and wolfed down a toxic meal from the nearby 7-Eleven. Dave is articulate, poised well beyond his twenty-four years. He is extremely self-possessed; he harbors no delusions of grandeur, nor will he sell himself short. "He's the most well-adjusted boy I know," Kurt is fond of saying.

Kurt would often say "He's the most well-adjusted boy I know" in the same fluty, singsong falsetto, imitating a wholesome girl with a crush. The subtext of that little routine was that Dave wasn't a misfit like Kurt and Krist were—he was relatively normal, the popular kind of guy who really did get elected vice president of his freshman high school class. So that was kind of a snipe at Dave, but it was also said with admiration—or maybe jealousy.

It was very gracious of Dave to agree to an interview. In the *Rolling Stone* story, I had quoted a friend of the band as saying that Dave was enjoying one of the more well-known perks of being a rock star. I didn't think through the impact of including that in the piece, but it obviously made Dave really angry. It remains a great journalistic regret; there was no need to put that in there.

So when I called Dave to set up the interview, he was clearly reluctant, but Kurt wanted him to do it, so he agreed. But Dave told me, "I'll do this but: Don't. Fuck. Me. Over." He didn't raise his voice, but I could hear the hostility down the phone line; he didn't need to spell out what he was referring to. When we sat down on the floor of the Laundry Room on March 9, 1993, to do the interview, the first thing Dave did was wag his finger at me—actually, it was more like a clenched fist with an index finger poking out—and say again, "Don't. Fuck. Me. Over." Message received, sir, loud and clear.

Dave, the son of a Washington, DC, journalist/speechwriter and a high school English teacher, was well-spoken. Our sole interview for this book lasted about two hours, and I used almost everything he said.

Dave is the least visible of the three—after all, he's not six foot seven like Chris and he's not the frontman like Kurt. Like Chris, he goes to shows in Seattle all the time and can be found standing in the crowd just like everyone else. He's in an ideal position and he knows it—he's in one of the most successful rock bands on the planet, yet he can go out on the town for the evening and count the number of people who even recognize him on one hand.

"Chris has a heart of gold," says a family friend. "He is a good soul." Chris speaks slowly, cautiously, and although he's not a book-learned intellectual type, he's a genius of horse sense, always ready with plain-spoken perceptions that cut through the bullshit. A self-described "news junkie," he is deeply concerned and deeply knowledgeable about the situation in what was once Yugoslavia, where his family comes from.

He and his gracious and levelheaded wife Shelli own a modest house in Seattle's quiet, suburban University District. It's a communal sort of place—his sister Diana lives with them, as does tour manager Alex Macleod, a bright, pony-tailed Scot so loyal he'd probably step in front of a bullet for any member of the band. Chris's brother Robert stops by all the time. Early in March, Sonic Youth's Kim Gordon and Thurston Moore stay there while they're in town to finish up a world tour. Gordon, Moore, and Mudhoney's Mark Arm stop by after a day of buying records, one of which is an old Benny Goodman 78. As "Royal Garden Blues" emerges from the crackles and hisses of his old Victrola, Chris jokes to Moore, "Yeah, man, low-fi. This is what our new record sounds like!"

Sonic Youth was a crucial hub of the American underground music community. They knew everybody and everything. They'd even shepherded Nirvana to both their management company and their label. Sonic Youth had been plugged into the Seattle scene since 1985, when they befriended Sub Pop founder Bruce Pavitt, who included Sonic Youth on the first Sub Pop LP, the *Sub Pop 100* compilation. In 1988, Pavitt sent them a five-song Mudhoney tape to see what they thought about it—Sonic Youth's blessing was priceless—and they immediately responded by proposing a split single with Mudhoney, who at that time had only released a single. The split single, with Sonic Youth covering Mudhoney's now-classic "Touch Me I'm Sick" and Mudhoney covering Sonic Youth's "Halloween," was released that December.

No-nonsense, wonderfully sardonic, and about two heads shorter than Krist, Shelli was an important part of the Nirvana equation, very much unsung. She was a great reality check, completely immune to the insanity of the Nirvana phenomenon. She was a great ground for Krist and everyone around them, just a very sensible person who saw through the bullshit and was not shy about calling it out. (They divorced in 1999.)

Krist had a small office room in his house where he took care of Nirvana business—it had a fax machine and everything. I gather he did a lot of that sort of work before the band really took off and they acquired a phalanx of managers and lawyers and accountants. Taped to the side of one file cabinet was a mailing from the Publisher's Clearinghouse sweepstakes: "KURT COBAIN, YOU MAY ALREADY HAVE WON $1,000,000!"

A huge jukebox dominates the living room, which is decorated with funky old thrift shop furniture, but mostly everyone—including the cats Einstein and Doris—hangs out in the kitchen. The refrigerator is stocked with organic this and preservative-free that. Recycled paper is used wherever possible. A vintage late-'50s dry bar and three pinball machines—Kiss, the Addams Family, and Evel Knievel—are down in the basement, where Chris threw a party the night before the band left to record *In Utero*. Old friends like Matt Lukin from Mudhoney, Tad Doyle from TAD, and Dee Plakas from L7, new friends like Eddie Vedder, folks from Nirvana's extended family like Earnie Bailey and Geffen/DGC A&R (Artists and Repertoire) man Gary Gersh all partied into the wee hours. Shelli whipped up some vegetarian hors d'oeuvres.

That was a really nice evening. Krist was kind of the social ambassador for the band, and he attracted some good folks, like Eddie Vedder. Vedder and I chatted about the Who and battled each other on the Kiss pinball machine. The day before the party, Krist and I headed up to Al's Guitarville, in Edmonds, where he found the bass he played on *In Utero*. I was trying to learn how to play guitar and was shopping for an instrument, too—Krist advised me to get a really cool cream-colored 1963 Fender Musicmaster. It sounded great; I still have it. But I needed a case for it. "Don't worry," Krist said, "I've got one at home." And when we got back to his place, he pulled a few cases from some closet somewhere. "I've got a ton of these," he said. "Kurt smashes so many guitars, and I keep the cases." He gave me a case with a piece of duct tape that said "UNIVOX" in Kurt's handwriting. I still have that, too.

Chris lives low to the ground, spends his money wisely. This is hardly a high-living rock star—the door falls off his aged tape deck.

OK, that last bit contradicts what I said earlier about overtipping the cabbie, throwing money around like a newly wealthy person. But Krist did eventually move to a nicer house.

After a quick preliminary interview just before Christmas of 1992, the first round of more than twenty-five hours of interviews with Kurt took place in early February. They began very late at night, after Kurt would return from rehearsals for *In Utero*, lasting until four or five in the morning. In the midst of moving into a temporary home in Seattle, Kurt padded around his and Courtney's hotel suite in mismatched pajamas, chain-smoking as he peppered his story with a supremely dry and sarcastic wit. Once, he strapped on a virtual reality machine—something between a Walkman and a private psychedelic light show—that he was experimenting with to control his chronic stomach pain. Various settings supposedly stimulate memory, creativity, energy, and relaxation.

Additional interviews took place on February 8, 9, and 11, and March 6, 7, 25, and 31. We did some phoners, too.

During this time, Kurt was very nocturnal: his day was almost completely upside down. That couldn't have been very good for his mental health, but it was great for doing interviews: by the time we'd get to talking, Courtney and the baby would be fast asleep, and if the TV wasn't on, the loudest sound in the house would be the hum of the refrigerator. It was very intimate. By the time we were done talking, the sun would be coming up, and we'd stand at the floor-to-ceiling kitchen windows and look out at Lake Washington as the occasional seaplane skidded for a landing on the water. Those were great, peaceful moments, both of us completely talked out, just quietly gazing out the window together. We'd do that again after the book was finished, looking out a different window.

Sometimes while we talked, Kurt would eat—TV dinners or premade meals in plastic containers that he'd heat up in the microwave. Neither he nor Courtney cooked, and they didn't want household help—anyone like that could have been co-opted by the tabloids—and going out wasn't really an option, so they had to do this rich people thing with premade meals that someone dropped off every few days.

One evening, Kurt went off on a rant about how much he hated journalists and they were all lying scum. He'd completely forgotten that he was sitting across the kitchen table from a journalist. So I said, with a smile, "Um, well, I guess I'll be going then . . ." And he got all flustered and said I wasn't like the rest of them. It was a moment.

That device he wore wasn't actually a "virtual reality machine"—this was 1992 and not many people fully understood the term yet (including me, apparently). In fact, it was a pair of special goggles with blinking lights inside, with a little Walkman-sized controller, and the patterns allegedly could induce different kinds of brain waves. That machine was kind of controversial—some people claimed it exacerbated depression rather than curing it. But I never saw Kurt use it again.

It was a high-tech version of the Dreamachine, which was cocreated by one of Kurt's literary heroes, the poet, sound artist, and painter Brion Gysin, a pivotal figure who spanned the Surrealists and the Beats. One day in 1958, Gysin had a mystical-psychedelic experience from closing his eyes while the sunlight flickered through the trees as he rode on a bus to Marseilles. "An overwhelming flood of intensely bright colors exploded behind my eyelids: a multidimensional kaleidoscope whirling out through space," he later wrote. "I was swept out of time." And so he built the Dreamachine, the first known work of art meant to be seen with the eyes closed.

In the 1985 movie *Perfect*, John Travolta plays a *Rolling Stone* reporter and delivers a pretty famous line about how *Rolling Stone* writers acted toward their subjects: "Always treat a famous person as if they're not. And a person who's not as if they were." I had written many pieces for *Rolling Stone* before writing *Come as You Are*, and maybe I absorbed that philosophy from the magazine's culture, but I think I came to it naturally. It was the only way I could cope with someone's fame—pretend it didn't exist. And so, as struck as I was, like everybody else, by Kurt's almost palpable charisma, not to mention being deeply moved by his music, I managed to ignore all that and treat him like a normal person, which put him at ease with me, since so many other people freaked out around him, which in turn freaked him out. Aside from the formative childhood experiences we had in common, I guess that's another reason why he opened up to me. I'm not a great interviewer, really, but I'm good at having long conversations.

For internationally famous celebrities, Kurt and Courtney live a pretty no-frills lifestyle. There are no minders, no beefy bodyguards around them. Kurt takes a taxi around town, stops in the McDonald's for a burger, wearing a ridiculous Elmer Fudd hat pulled down on his head for a disguise. A visitor to their hotel room one night walked into the hotel, took the elevator to their floor, and walked right through their open door to find Kurt and Courtney in their pajamas and nestling together on the bed, watching a trashy Leif Garrett TV movie in the dark. "Oh hi," Courtney said, not even startled.

Present-day readers might not appreciate the significance of Leif Garrett—and neither did I. But Kurt and Courtney were a little fascinated by Garrett, a '70s teen idol who went on to experience some very high-profile substance abuse problems, not to mention being the driver in a tragic car crash. In retrospect, they were clearly studying someone else who had grappled—not very successfully—with drugs and the bizarre experience of sudden money and fame.

And then it went full circle: the Melvins got Garrett to sing on their faithful cover of "Smells Like Teen Spirit" for their 2000 album *The Crybaby*. The *Dallas Observer* wrote that "the band's intent was only to draw an ironic parallel between two teen-idol pop stars ruined by the music industry that exploited them."

"It's one of the best, most fucked-up ideas I've ever come up with," said the Melvins' ever-sardonic singer-guitarist Buzz Osborne, who had been a formative musical influence on Kurt when both were in their teens. "Especially with Leif's obvious drug past and Kurt's public drug use."

Kurt appears frail, rail-thin. He speaks in a sort of deadpan singsong, abraded by too many cigarettes into a low growl. It makes him seem sad and spent, as if he's just finished a crying jag, but that's just the way he is. "Everyone thinks of me as this emotional wreck, this total negative black star—*all the time*," Kurt says. "They're always asking 'What's the matter?' And there's nothing wrong with me at all. I'm not feeling blue at all. It got to the point where I had to look at myself and figure out what people are seeing. I thought maybe I should shave my eyebrows. That might help."

Although Kurt's charisma is almost palpable, he is profoundly low-key. It helps to mentally amplify his every reaction: a distracted "hmph" translates into "Wow!"; a quick chuckle is a guffaw; a dirty look is murder.

As in photographs, his face takes on many different aspects. Sometimes he looks like an angelic boy, sometimes like a dissipated wastrel, sometimes like the guy who fixes your transmission. And sometimes, in certain lights, he even looks eerily like Axl Rose. His pale complexion is lightly veiled by scruffy stubble. An angry red patch on his scalp shows through the trademark unwashed hair, which is strawberry blond for the time being. He usually wears pajamas and is perpetually unkempt. Although the time of day has very little to do with his schedule, he always wears a watch bearing the likeness of Tom Peterson, the owner of a chain of appliance stores in Oregon.

Kurt's eyes are so extremely blue that they give his face a perpetually startled expression. In his pajamas, he gives the impression of a shell-shocked young private padding around a veteran's home. But he doesn't miss a trick.

By early March, after the recording of the band's new album, *In Utero*, Kurt, Courtney and their baby Frances moved into a largish rented house overlooking Lake Washington. At the kitchen table, Kurt would play at disemboweling a

plastic anatomical model, chain-smoking the whole time. "I like the idea that you can take them all apart and just see the guts," he said. "Organs fascinate me. They work. And a lot of times they fuck up, but it's hard to believe that a person can put something as poisonous as alcohol or drugs in their system and the mechanics can take it—for a while. It's amazing they take them at all."

The new house was in the Matthews Beach neighborhood of Seattle. It wasn't particularly fancy, and Kurt and Courtney barely even had any furniture in there, even though Courtney has sophisticated taste and could have decorated it very handsomely. It was just a nice house with a few bedrooms and a two-car garage. The most luxurious aspect of it was the deck that overlooked Lake Washington.

The place is sparsely furnished—there's beige wall-to-wall carpeting and nothing on the walls—but this is just temporary. They'll be moving to a remodeled house in a small town a few dozen miles out of Seattle later this year, and they're looking for a *pied à terre* on Seattle's hip Capitol Hill. Upstairs is the bedroom, the baby's room, and Kurt's painting room, where an easel holds a portrait of a withered, forlorn creature with skeletal arms and lifeless black eyes. In the downstairs bathroom sits an MTV Award for Best New Artist, the little silver astronaut keeping a close watch over the toilet. Frances's nanny, Jackie, has a room down in the basement. In the dining room off the kitchen, a model-car track is set up.

It's funny how famous people often put their awards in the bathroom.

One room of the house is designated "the mess room." The floor is covered with old letters, notes, work tapes, records, photographs, and posters dating back to the earliest days of Kurt's musical life. Against one wall is Courtney's Buddhist chanting shrine, which she doesn't use much anymore, probably because she can't get to it through the clutter. A brown paper bag has tipped over, disgorging a score or so of plastic Colonel Sanders and Pillsbury Doughboy dolls.

"The mess room" was the house's dining room, which adjoined the kitchen where Kurt and I did most of our interviews. It was also where Kurt arranged all the doll parts and various other objects that Charles Peterson photographed for the back cover of *In Utero*.
    The Matthews Beach house was disheveled just like all Kurt's homes were. Looking back on it, that might well have been a reflection of never having lived in a place for very long since he was a little kid. Or just rebelling against his mom's pristine approach to keeping house.

Guitars are everywhere, even in the bathroom. A sonorous old Martin sits in the living room alongside a more modest instrument painted red and covered with appliqués of flowers.

Seven-month-old Frances Bean Cobain is a beautiful baby with her father's piercing blue eyes and her mother's jaw line. Although her parents seem to dote on her for the benefit of the visitor, they are clearly loving. Kurt seems a little more graceful with children than Courtney, but both do a fine job of making the usual goo-goo noises for the obvious amusement of the baby.

So I was savvy enough to pick up on how "her parents seem to dote on her for the benefit of the visitor"—again, for Kurt and Courtney, that was the whole point of the book. But they didn't have to do that—once they relaxed, they always wound up playing with the baby in a more natural way, with Courtney singing little bits of nonsense to her in a surprisingly sweet voice, or Kurt making her laugh with his ridiculous Donald Duck impression. It wouldn't be the last time that Kurt and Courtney doted on their child for the benefit of the press.

By all accounts, Frances did wonders for Kurt. "He looks at Frances all the time and he says, 'That's the way I used to be! That's the way I used to be!'" Courtney says. "You can't change a person, but my goal in life is to make him that happy again. But it's hard because he's always dissatisfied with stuff."

One night, Courtney quietly strums an acoustic guitar into a boom box in the living room upstairs while down in the garage next to their used Volvo, Kurt bangs on a dilapidated drum set left over from some long-forgotten tour. The garage is filled with boxes and boxes of papers, artwork, guitar guts, and years of thrift shop purchases. Two boxes are crammed with transparent plastic men, women, and even horses. Close by are an amplifier, a bass guitar, and the one thing in the house that could conceivably be called an indulgence—a Space Invaders–type video game that Kurt picked up for a couple of hundred bucks. He records high scores on it with initials like "COK" and "POO" and "FUK."

Kurt was proudly demonstrating that he could play the very cool drum beat of Public Image Ltd.'s "Four Enclosed Walls" from 1981's *The Flowers of Romance*.

Our conversations were extremely frank. Kurt has a simple explanation for his candor. "I'm caught," he says, referring to his widely-publicized problems with heroin, "so I may as well fess up to it and try to put it in a little bit more perspective. Everyone thinks I've been a junkie for years. I was a junkie for a really small amount of time."

That wasn't true—he had been a junkie for several years and would essentially continue to be until the day he died. Junkies, I learned, are very comfortable with being deceptive. But Kurt had to say that so he could keep his child. And I knew that, and he knew that I knew that. Perhaps he was also a shrewd enough judge of character to know that I wouldn't challenge him on it.

Furthermore, he's not worried about exploding the band's—or his own— formidable myth. Quite the opposite. "I never intended to have some kind of a mystery about us," he said to me once. "It's just that I didn't have anything to say in the beginning. Now that it's gone on long enough, there's a story, in a way. Still, every night after you leave, I think, 'God, my life is so fucking boring compared to so many people that I know.'"

Kurt is eager to set the record straight. There have been so many rumors about him, his wife, and even his infant daughter that he figures the best way he can cut his losses is just to tell exactly what happened. His tales are sometimes self- serving, full of rationalization and self-contradiction, but even his distortions are revealing about his life, his art, and the connections between the two.

Yes, he was keen on *expanding* his myth, not demolishing it. I kick myself for how naive I was about Kurt and his lies and manipulations. Kurt's legendary tale of sleeping under the bridge near his childhood home is a good, if fairly benign, example. Others have done some good sleuthing about that particular story and determined that it wasn't true. Looking back on it, it's a typical fiction on Kurt's part, intended to spite his parents and exalt his own victimhood.

As Kurt says later in this book, his real life was so boring that "I pretty much like to make it up." He probably didn't run away and catch fish in the Wishkah River; it was probably more like shoplifting corn dogs from a local convenience store or going over to his friends' houses for his lifelong favorite, mac and cheese.

Although I did recognize that Kurt's stories were "sometimes self-serving, full of rationalization and self-contradiction," I still missed a lot of stuff, and that was partly because I was just kind of green—I wasn't skeptical enough, took a lot at face value. And because of the tight deadline, I just didn't have time to track down everything.

chapter one

A GREASY-HAIRED LITTLE REBELLIOUS KID

berdeen, Washington (pop. 16,660), is 108 long miles southwest of Seattle, way out on the remote Washington coast. Seattle has a lot of rain, but Aberdeen has more—up to seven feet a year—casting a constant, dreary pall over the town. Far from the nearest freeway, nothing comes in and rarely does anything come out.

Art and culture are best left to the snooty types over in Seattle—among the "fascinating activities" listed in a brochure from the Grays Harbor County Chamber of Commerce are bowling, chain-saw competitions, and video arcades.

While Aberdeen definitely had more than its fair share of rednecks, violence, booze, guns, and drugs, and thanks to the decline of its once-thriving logging industry, not much did come out of the town anymore, I had fallen under the spell of Kurt's disdain for the place, his need to paint it as worse than it actually was. In truth, the town is near a beautiful stretch of Pacific coastline and many state parks; the scenery is spectacular; the lakes, streams, and air are pristine. And in 1992, there was a center for the performing arts, a community theater company, a county choir and a symphony orchestra, a jazz festival, and one of the best library systems in the area. Aberdeen had a nice side—if you wanted to see it. But, to coin a phrase, Kurt Cobain will have his revenge on Aberdeen.

Many years later, that condescending remark about Aberdeen not caring about art and culture became kind of interesting. In 2007, I went to a small restaurant in the East Village for a performance by the excellent avant-garde cellist Erik Friedlander on the occasion of the release of his album *Block Ice and Propane*. Recently, I'd discovered not only that Friedlander's father is the great photographer Lee Friedlander, but that Lee Friedlander, the celebrated choreographer Trisha Brown, and the truly iconic abstract expressionist painter Robert Motherwell all came from Aberdeen. So, counting Kurt, four of the most renowned artists of the twentieth century all came from this one small, remote, beyond-unassuming place. (Another notable Aberdonian: Dr. Douglas Osheroff, who won the 1996 Nobel Prize in physics.)

After Erik Friedlander's set, I walked up and asked him if he had any idea why four artistic giants all came from this one little roughneck town.

"Huh, I don't know," Friedlander replied and then called over to some people at a table in the corner. "Hey, Dad, come here."

And up strides *the* Lee Friedlander, a certifiable giant of American art photography. And we got to talking. Friedlander reminisced about the town's early days, all logging and brothels, and said that Motherwell was renowned around town as "a big jock." In the end, he couldn't answer my question, but the moral of the story is that great artists can come from anywhere—not just New York or Los Angeles.

But maybe not all of them should *stay* in places like Aberdeen. The great music journalist Mikal Gilmore wrote a masterly *Rolling Stone* piece about Kurt a week or so after Kurt's death. Gilmore happens to be the brother of Gary Gilmore, the infamous convicted killer who demanded the death penalty for his crimes in 1976; Mikal's powerful 1994 memoir about growing up with Gary, *Shot in the Heart*, shows his all-too-intimate familiarity with guns, darkness, and death wishes. For the *Rolling Stone* piece, Gilmore visited the North Aberdeen Bridge, where Kurt claimed he had camped out when he was homeless. Under the bridge, Gilmore noticed a graffito that he thought might have been in Kurt's handwriting. It read: "WELL, I MUST BE OFF. IT'S TIME FOR THE FOOL TO GET OUT."

"To save yourself from a dark fate," Gilmore writes, "you have to remove yourself from dark places. Sometimes, though, you might not remove yourself soon enough, and when that happens, the darkness leaves with you. It visits you not just in your worst moments but also in your best, dimming the light that those occasions have to offer. It visits you, and it tells you that *this* is where you are from—that no matter how far you run or how hard you reach for release, the darkness, sooner or later, will claim you."

Kurt tried to leave Aberdeen in many ways, not just physically. It was a macho place, so he embraced feminism. It was homophobic, so he stuck up for gay people. Aberdonians loved heavy metal, so he renounced heavy metal. His mom made him wear nice clothes, bathe, and have a nice haircut, so he cultivated the grunge look. Aberdeen, to him, was an uncouth, uneducated place, so he sought out people who were more cultured and intellectual than he was, starting with Buzz Osborne and Krist Novoselic.

Motherwell, Brown, and Friedlander all got out of Aberdeen in time, but Kurt didn't. "I always wanted to move to the big city," he told Jonathan Poneman in a December 1992 *Spin* interview. "I wanted to move to Seattle, find a chicken hawk, sell my ass, and be a punk rocker, but I was too afraid. So I just stayed in Aberdeen for too long, until I was 20 years old." So Aberdeen stayed within him. And it claimed him.

Route 12 into Aberdeen is bordered by an endless succession of trailer parks; beyond them are hundreds of thousands of acres of timberland, often marred by vast stubbly scars where the loggers have been clear-cutting. Coming in from the east, the first thing a visitor sees of Aberdeen is the sprawling, ugly Weyerhaeuser lumberyard fronting the Wishkah River, where the limbless carcasses of once proud trees lie stacked like massacre victims. Surveying the scene from the other side of the river is a long strip of plastic fast food joints.

Logging dominates the town; or rather, it once did. Business has been falling off for years and layoffs are turning Aberdeen into a ghost town. These days, the streets downtown are slowly filling with empty or boarded-up storefronts. The only places that are doing good business are taverns like the Silver Dollar and the aptly named Pourhouse, as well as the local pawnshop, which overflows with guns, chain saws, and electric guitars. The suicide rate of Grays Harbor County is one of the highest in the nation; alcoholism is rampant and crack came to town years ago.

People hate the spotted owl—recipes for cooking the endangered creature pop up on local bumper stickers—even though decentralization of the timber industry, rising labor costs, and automation are really what's putting people out of work. One of the biggest mills in town used to employ scores of workers and now it has five: four men and a laser-guided computerized cutting machine.

In Nick Soulsby's 2015 oral history of Nirvana, *I Found My Friends*, Steve Moriarty, from early-'90s Seattle punk band the Gits, had a very evocative take on Aberdeen: "It's like logging trucks and the smell of low tide—a pretty depressed area."

In Kurt's journals, he called Aberdeen and nearby Montesano "coastal logging slums." And in one of Nirvana's earliest bios, well before they got signed, Kurt wrote, "Aberdeens [*sic*] population consists of Highly bigoted Redneck snoose [*sic*] chewing deer shooting, faggot killing logger types who 'ain't to [*sic*] partial to weirdo new wavers!'" (Snus is a brand of chewing tobacco.)

In 1992, clear-cutting of old-growth forest was destroying the habitat of northern spotted owls, which had recently been designated a threatened species. To save the ecosystem in which the owl thrived, environmentalists proposed protecting huge swathes of land from logging—which would cost many jobs in an economically strapped region that, as stated, was already suffering.

In fact, lumber companies were breaking unions, severely automating the work, and shipping raw logs to be processed in Japan. But the industry managed to shift the blame onto the spotted owl.

People in lumber-dependent Washington towns such as Aberdeen were outraged that someone would seem to value a bird over their ability to support themselves, and Republican president George H. W. Bush was more than happy to side with big business on this issue, proclaiming to a group of rural Washington lumber workers in 1992, "It is time to make people more important than owls!"

"The Timber Wars" constantly made the nightly news all over the Northwest; the spotted owl even made the cover of *Time*. It was emblematic of a culture war—big business and the people who love it versus science-based progressive ideals—that continues to this day.

In 1992, the US Fish and Wildlife Service dramatically reduced the spotted owl's critical habitat. Today, the species remains in imminent danger of extinction.

One of the biggest growth industries in the county is the cultivation of marijuana and psychedelic mushrooms, which people grow in order to supplement their meager or nonexistent incomes.

Things didn't used to be so rough. Aberdeen was once a bustling seaport where sailors stopped off for rest, food, and some rented female companionship. Fact is, the town was once one big whorehouse, centered on the notorious Hume Street (which the town fathers renamed State Street in the '50s to try to bury the memories). Later, the town became a railroad terminus and the home of dozens of sawmills and logging operations. Aberdeen teemed with single young men making plenty of money in the wood industry and prostitution thrived, with as many as fifty bordellos ("women's boardinghouses," they were called) in the downtown area at one point. Prostitution lasted as long as the late '50s, when a police crackdown finally put an end to it. Some say Aberdeen's unsavory past gives its residents an inferiority complex.

Around the turn of the twentieth century, thanks to all the sailors, fishermen, and loggers in town—and the saloons, gambling joints, and brothels that catered to their vices—Aberdeen earned the nickname: "The Hellhole of the Pacific." The town's alarming murder rate also inspired another unsavory sobriquet: "The Port of Missing Men."

Prostitution was prevalent in Aberdeen almost from the time of its founding in the 1890s and continued into the early '60s, still well within the collective memory of the town in the mid '80s. Aberdeen "was mainly just a whorehouse," Kurt told Chris Morris for *Musician* in January 1992. "The sailors would come and screw the women.... So there's also this overall sense that we're a little ashamed of our roots."

This is where Kurt Donald Cobain was born on February 20, 1967, to Wendy Cobain, a homemaker, and her husband Donald, a mechanic at the Chevron station in town. The young family started out in a rental house in nearby Hoquiam, then moved to Aberdeen when Kurt was six months old.

Kurt grew up not knowing where his family name came from. His maternal grandfather is German, but that's all he knew. Only recently did he discover that his father's side of the family is full-blooded Irish, and that Cobain is a corruption of the name Coburn.

Although the Cobains were of humble means, life started out very well for their golden-haired son. "My mom was always physically affectionate with me," says Kurt. "We always kissed good-bye and hugged. It was really cool. I'm surprised to find out that so many families aren't that way. Those were pretty blissful times."

Looking back on it, that's one of the most pivotal quotations in the whole book. That equation of motherly love and "bliss" and the yearning for those things, that explains a lot about Kurt. It ran very deep in him.

Later on, as an adult, how do you recapture that childhood bliss, of being cradled in your mother's soft, gentle arms, feeling safe and loved? Sex is one way— "Sex, to him, was incredibly sacred," Courtney told *Rolling Stone* in December 1994. Another way is to take heroin. Then you get a euphoric contentment, and all your troubles seem so far away. Kurt wrote a great song about that childhood bliss. It was his Rosebud.

Kurt just before his second birthday.

Kurt's sister Kim was born three years after he was, but Kurt and his mother had already established a tight bond. "There's nothing like your firstborn—nothing," says Wendy, now remarried and still living in the same house in Aberdeen with her husband and eight-year-old daughter. "No child even comes close to that. I was totaled out on him. My every waking hour was for him."

Kurt was obviously a bright child. "I remember calling my mother," Wendy recalls, "and telling her it kind of scared me because he had perceptions like I've never seen a small child have."

Kurt had started showing an interest in music when he was two, which is not surprising since his mother's side of the family was very musical—Wendy's brother Chuck played in a rock & roll band, her sister Mari played guitar, and everyone in the family had some sort of musical talent. At Christmas, they would all sing or act out skits.

Wendy's uncle changed his name from Delbert Fradenburg to Dale Arden, moved to California to become an operatic balladeer, and cut a few records in the late '40s and early '50s. He became friends with actor Brian Keith (who later starred in the '60s sitcom *Family Affair*) and Jay Silverheels, who played Tonto in the *Lone Ranger* TV series. So, as Wendy jokes, "this celebrity thing is nothing new to the family."

Uncle Delbert was a real entertainer—in the late '20s, he appeared in Florenz Ziegfeld's landmark musical *Show Boat* and had a solo spot in one of the first color films, *King of Jazz*, a 1930 revue that also featured a couple of appearances by an up-and-comer named Bing Crosby. The June 13, 1930, issue of the *Grays Harbor Daily Washingtonian* mentions the "well known Aberdeen singer" and that "the youthful promise his voice held when he delighted Harbor audiences with his singing a few years ago is fully realized by his performance in 'King of Jazz.'" But the movie was a terrible flop and actually prompted Hollywood to stop making musicals for several years.

Aunt Mari gave Kurt Beatles and Monkees records when he was seven or so. She would invite Kurt over to her house to watch her band practice. A country musician who had actually recorded a single, Mari had played in bar bands around Aberdeen for years, sometimes appeared solo at the Riviera steak house, and once placed second on a local TV talent contest called "You Can Be a Star."

So Kurt gets introduced to some very tuneful, extremely popular rock music at a very impressionable age; the Beatles would turn out to be a huge influence on his music. And one of his first musical heroes was someone he actually knew—his mom's sister— who had played shows and even recorded, which made such things seem really achievable. And, of course, this musical hero happened to be a woman.

Mari tried to teach Kurt how to play guitar, but he didn't have the patience—in fact, it was hard to get him to sit still for anything. He had been diagnosed as hyperactive.

Like many kids of his generation, Kurt had been given the drug Ritalin, a form of speed, which counteracts hyperactivity. It kept him up until four in the morning. Sedatives made him fall asleep in school. Finally, they tried subtracting sugar and the infamous Red Dye #2 from his diet, and it worked. It was hard for a hyperactive kid to stay away from sugar because, as Wendy puts it, "They are, like, addicted to it."

In 1961, the US Food and Drug Administration (FDA) approved the use of Ritalin to treat hyperactive children, and its use skyrocketed so much that, in 1970, the *Washington Post* raised the alarm about the use of "behavior modification" drugs to control unruly children, prompting congressional hearings. A few years later, when Kurt was in grade school, more than one million US children had been diagnosed with ADHD and given powerful, aggressively marketed pharmaceuticals such as Ritalin. (There has been speculation that several artificial colors cause hyperactivity in children, but the FDA has never found a link.)

But Kurt's cousin Bev Cobain, a registered nurse with certifications in psychiatric and mental health nursing, has been quoted as saying Kurt really had been diagnosed with ADD. Kids with ADD are far more likely to go on to abuse drugs and alcohol.

But not being able to have a candy bar hardly dampened Kurt's spirits. "He got up every day with such joy that there was another day to be had," says Wendy. "He was so enthusiastic. He would come running out of his bedroom so excited that there was another day ahead of him and he couldn't wait to find out what it was going to bring him."

"I was an extremely happy child," says Kurt. "I was constantly screaming and singing. I didn't know when to quit. I'd eventually get beaten up by kids because I'd get so excited about wanting to play. I took play very seriously. I was just really happy."

The first kid of his generation, Kurt had seven aunts and uncles on his mother's side alone who would argue over who got to babysit for him. Used to being the center of attention, he entertained anybody who wanted to watch. "He was so dramatic," says Wendy. "He'd throw himself down on the floor at the store for this old man because this old man would just love to have Kurt sing for him." One of Kurt's favorite records was *Alice's Restaurant* by Arlo Guthrie. Often, he'd sing Guthrie's "Motorcycle Song": "I just want to ride on my motorcycle / And I don't want to die!"

There's probably no need to point out the irony of Kurt singing that last line; I included it pointedly because of the dark intimation I felt when I first met him. That Arlo Guthrie album, released in 1967, also features the eighteen-minute "Alice's Restaurant Massacree," a quintessential classic of the '60s counterculture. It's funny to think that Kurt was familiar with it.

His aunt Mari gave him a bass drum when he was seven. Kurt would strap it on and walk around the neighborhood wearing a hunting hat and his dad's tennis shoes, beating the drum and singing Beatles songs like "Hey Jude" and "Revolution."

Kurt was ever image-conscious, even in jest. One day I was doing a phone interview with Courtney, and since I knew Kurt was also in the house, I asked her if she could ask him what Beatles songs he sang when he was a little kid, blissfully banging on his little bass drum. She hollered the question at him, a couple of rooms away.

There was a pause. I couldn't hear what he said, but Courtney hollered back, "YOU DID NOT SING 'REVOLUTION #9'! C'MON!"

Another pause. "NO, YOU DID NOT SING 'WHY DON'T WE DO IT IN THE ROAD'!"

Eventually, she got it out of him. Interviewing can be very trying.

Kurt didn't like it when men looked at Wendy, a very attractive woman with blond hair and pretty blue eyes. Don never seemed to care, but Kurt always got angry and jealous—"Mommy, that man's looking at you!" he'd say. Once, he even told off a policeman.

Even at age three, Kurt didn't much like policemen. When he'd spot one, he'd sing a little song. "Corn on the cops, corn on the cops! The cops are coming! They're going to kill you!" "Every time I saw a cop I'd start singing that at them and pointing at them and telling them that they were evil," says Kurt, grinning. "I had this massive thing about cops. I didn't like them at all." When he was a couple of years older, Kurt would fill 7-Up cans full of pebbles and heave them at police cars, although he never actually hit one.

In the 2015 documentary about Kurt, *Montage of Heck*, Kurt's sister Kim confirms this little bit of wordplay, "corn on the cops," adding that her earliest memory—she was about three and Kurt was about six—is of Kurt getting her to give the middle finger to members of the local constabulary.

I asked Kurt how he got the feeling that cops are evil. "It was just a gut feeling I had," he said. "They just seemed real intimidating. I was really into this television show called *SWAT*, and they were cops. But the reason I liked them was they had M16s." So the fascination with guns started early, too.

That was also about the time that Kurt somehow learned how to extend his middle finger in the time-honored manner. While his mother drove around town doing errands, he'd sit in the backseat of the car and flip the bird to everyone they passed by.

By the time Kurt was in second grade, everybody had noticed how well he could draw. "After a while," says Wendy, "it kind of got crammed down his throat. Every present was a paintbrush or an easel. We kind of almost killed it for him."

Everybody thought Kurt's drawings and paintings were great. Except for him. "He would never be happy about his art," says Wendy. "He would never be satisfied with it, like typical artists are." One day around Halloween Kurt came home with a copy of the school paper. It had a drawing Kurt had done on the

cover, an honor usually reserved for kids who were at least fifth-graders. Kurt was really mad about it when he came home, because he didn't think his picture was that great. "His attitude toward adults changed because of that," says Wendy. "Everybody was telling him how much they loved his art and he was never satisfied with it."

Another prophetic anecdote. One of the things that wounded Kurt deeply was when the band would play a bad show and people loved it anyway. To him, that meant that they weren't really paying attention, they weren't really as deeply invested in the music as he was. Of course, people think that's what the artist wants to hear: "Hey, man, that was awesome!" But musicians know all too well when they've played a bad show. And nobody can convince them otherwise.

Up until third grade, Kurt wanted to be a rock star—he'd play Beatles records and mime along with his little plastic guitar. Then, for a long time, he wanted to be a stuntman. "I liked to play outside, catch snakes, jump my bicycle off the roof," he recalls. "Evel Knievel was my only idol." Once, he took all the bedding and pillows out of the house, put it on the deck, and jumped onto it from the roof; another time, he took a piece of metal, duct-taped it to his chest, and put a bunch of firecrackers on it and lit them.

The early rock star dreams and stuntman fantasies collide in the spectacle of Kurt hurling himself into the drum set at the end of so many shows, demonstrating that music could literally be an anodyne. The attraction to intense sensation, danger, potential self-destruction, taking play very seriously, freedom from pain, it's all there from the start.

Sometimes Kurt would visit Uncle Chuck, Wendy's brother, who played in a band. Chuck had built speakers for his basement studio that were so big he couldn't get them out of the room. He'd put Kurt downstairs, give him a microphone, and roll some tape. Wendy still has a tape he made when he was four or so. Kurt sings and then, when he thinks no one's listening, he starts saying dirty words. "Poo-doo," he says. "Poo-doo!"

Don and Wendy got Kurt a little Mickey Mouse drum set. "I kind of pushed drums on him because I wanted to be a drummer," Wendy admits. "But my mother thought that was so unfeminine, so she never let me play." Kurt didn't need to be pushed—as soon as he could sit up and hold things, he had been banging on pots and pans. He thrashed his Mickey Mouse drum set every day after school until it was broken.

Although it wasn't in the best section of Aberdeen—in fact, the neighborhood is quite run down—the Cobain home was always the nicest on the block. Don kept it in tip-top shape, installing the wall-to-wall carpeting, the fake-brick fireplace, the imitation-wood paneling. "It was white trash posing as middle class," Kurt says of his upbringing.

Wendy came from a family that was hardly well-to-do, but her mother always made sure that her children looked like they had a lot more than they did. Wendy was the same way. Every morning, she would diligently feather Kurt's hair for that Shaun Cassidy look, make sure he brushed his teeth, and dress him in the nicest clothes they could afford, and he would trudge off to school in his wafflestomper hiking boots. She even made Kurt wear a sweater that he was allergic to, because it looked good on him. "Both my kids were probably the best-dressed kids in Aberdeen," says Wendy. "I made sure of that."

Wendy tried to keep her kids away from what she calls "certain friends from certain kinds of backgrounds that lived in certain situations." Kurt says she basically told him to stay away from poor kids. "My mom thought that I was better than those kids, so I picked on them every once in a while—the scummy kids, the dirty kids," says Kurt. "I just remember there were a couple of kids that stunk like pee all the time and I would bully them around and get in fights with them. By fourth grade I realized that these kids are probably cooler than the higher-class children, more down to earth, down to the dirt." Later on, Kurt's unwashed hair, ever-present stubble, and tattered wardrobe would become world-famous trademarks.

Wendy was very conscious of appearances. When I first went out to Aberdeen to speak with her, no one answered the door even though we'd made plans to talk. I figured no one was home, so I walked into town and killed an hour or so, then came back, and she answered the door. Months later, I asked her why she hadn't been there at the appointed time. She admitted she *was* there—she just hadn't gotten her makeup on yet.

"Both my kids were probably the best-dressed kids in Aberdeen. . . . I made sure of that." As Kurt put it, that was part of being "white trash posing as middle class." He later rebelled against that with the threadbare cardigans, the sneakers scrawled with Magic Marker, the ripped jeans (basically a new thing back then), the messy and unwashed hair, the stubble, and so on. And despite all that, Kurt was, in his own way, just as conscious of appearances as his mom was: yes, he was unkempt, but he was *meticulously* unkempt.

Kurt started taking drum lessons in third grade. "Ever since I can remember, since I was a little kid," says Kurt, "I wanted to be Ringo Starr. But I wanted to be

John Lennon playing drums." Kurt played in the school band in grade school, though he never learned how to read music—he'd just wait for the kid in the first chair to learn the song and then copy what he was doing.

By the Christmas of 1974, when he was seven, Kurt got the idea that his mom thought he was a problem child. "The only thing I really wanted that year was a five-dollar *Starsky and Hutch* gun," Kurt says. "I got a lump of coal instead."

Regardless of whether that really happened, it's an example of the "tough love" approach to parenting problem children that was then in vogue. Either way, it's a telling little story, especially since it involves a gun.

Kurt says he was ambidextrous, but his father tried to force him to use his right hand, fearing Kurt would have problems later in life as a lefty. He became a lefty anyway.

For most of his life, Kurt has been plagued by one health problem or another. Besides his hyperactivity, he's always suffered from chronic bronchitis. In eighth grade, Kurt was diagnosed with a minor case of scoliosis, or curvature of the spine. As time went by, the weight of his guitar actually made the curvature worse. If he had been right-handed, he says, it would have corrected the problem.

In 1975, when Kurt was eight, his parents divorced. Wendy says she divorced Don because he simply wasn't around very much—he was always off playing basketball or baseball, coaching teams or refereeing. In retrospect, she wonders if she ever really loved him. Don bitterly opposed the divorce. Both Wendy and Don admit the kids were later used in a war between their parents.

Kurt took the divorce and its aftermath very hard. "It just destroyed his life," says Wendy. "He changed completely. I think he was ashamed. And he became very inward—he just held everything. He became real shy.

"I think he's *still* suffering," she adds.

She was right. Even though he would later sing, "The legendary divorce is such a bore," that was a false protest—it was a pivotal point in Kurt's life, as he would sometimes acknowledge.

Instead of the sunny, outgoing kid Kurt once was, "He became real sullen," Wendy says, "kind of mad and always frowning and ridiculing." On the wall in his bedroom, Kurt wrote, "I hate Mom, I hate Dad, Dad hates Mom, Mom hates Dad, it simply makes you want to be sad." A few feet over he drew caricatures of Wendy and Don along with the words "Dad sucks" and "Mom sucks." Below he drew a brain with a big question mark over it. The drawings are still there to this day, along with some nifty Led Zeppelin and Iron Maiden logos that he drew. (He denies he made them, but sisters don't lie.)

Kurt was like a lot of kids of his generation—in fact, everyone who has ever been in Nirvana (but one) has come from a broken home. The divorce rate skyrocketed in the mid 70s, more than doubling in ten years. The children of these broken marriages didn't have a world war or a Depression to contend with. They just didn't have a family. Consequently, their battles were private.

Kurt says it was like a light went out in him, a light he's been trying to recapture ever since. "I just remember all of a sudden not being the same person, feeling like I wasn't worthy anymore," he says. "I didn't feel like I deserved to be hanging out with other kids, because they had parents and I didn't anymore, I guess."

It's essential to remember that the sudden fame that happened to Kurt years later happened to someone with low self-esteem. Because I underwent a similar change when my parents got divorced, and all biography is, to some extent, autobiography, I consciously focused on the effect of Kurt's parents' divorce. It just happened to be very pertinent.

While the divorce rate in the United States was rising, it was still a pretty rare thing in staid Aberdeen, according to Kurt's sister Kim in *Montage of Heck*. So that probably made Kurt feel extra weird about it.

Children of divorce often experience shame: their family is screwed up and different from most other people's families, and it's something they want to hide. "I remember feeling ashamed for some reason," Kurt told the great UK music journalist Jon Savage in 1993. "I was ashamed of my parents for. . . . I couldn't face some of my friends at school anymore because I desperately wanted to have the classic typical family: mother, father. I wanted that security. I resented my parents for quite a few years because of that."

Shame, as we'll see, was a recurring aspect of Kurt's life and art.

"I was just pissed off at my parents for not being able to deal with their problems," he continues. "Throughout most of my childhood, after the divorce, I was kind of ashamed of my parents."

But Kurt had begun to feel like an outsider even before the divorce. "I didn't have anything in common with my dad especially," says Kurt. "He wanted me to be in sports and I didn't like sports and I was artistic and he just didn't appreciate that type of thing, so I just always felt ashamed. I just couldn't understand how I was a product of my parents because they weren't artistic and I was. I liked music and they didn't. Subconsciously, maybe I thought I was adopted—ever since that episode of *The Partridge Family* when Danny thought he was adopted. I really related to that."

It's difficult to overstate the importance *The Partridge Family* had for kids of a certain generation. On one hand, it was basically just a wholesome sitcom about a family that also happened to be a pop group. But, years before MTV, it was also one of the extremely few opportunities to see rock music portrayed on television, especially in prime time. And this was in the pre-punk era when rock stars were otherworldly quasi-royalty—by contrast, the generic suburban setting of *The Partridge Family* gave the (admittedly illusory) sense that life as a successful professional rock musician was somehow achievable.

Kurt probably related to the character Danny because Danny was the misfit of the band—a moody, wisecracking redhead who was as alienated as a kid in a fluffy '70s family sitcom could be. Later, Kurt surely became aware that, like Leif Garrett, Danny Bonaduce was a child star gone bad. In her memoir, *Partridge Family* mom, Shirley Jones, wrote that "Danny was a wild child who came from an unhappy home. At eleven, he started smoking." Later in life Bonaduce acknowledged some substance abuse problems, including multiple drug arrests as well as a conviction for the 1990 beating and robbery of a cross-dressing sex worker.

Earlier, Kurt revealed his fantasy that he was actually a space alien; now he says he thought he might have been adopted. In other words, he felt alienated from his parents. Kurt's father, for instance, was keen on sports, unartistic, and perhaps not the most sensitive man—in other words, the polar opposite of his son.

Kurt's creativity and intelligence—and the early realization that he was an artist—compounded the problem. "Until I was about ten or eleven, I didn't realize that I was different from the other kids at school," he says. "I started to realize that I was more interested in drawing and listening to music, more so than the other kids. It just slowly grew on me and I started to realize that. So by the time I was twelve I was fully withdrawn." Convinced he'd never find anyone like himself, he simply stopped trying to make friends.

"This town—if he would have been anywhere else he would have been fine," says Wendy. "But this town is just exactly like Peyton Place. Everybody is watching everyone and judging and they have their little slots they like everyone to stay in and he didn't."

Peyton Place was a popular soap opera in the '60s, set in a claustrophobically small town. It helped to make stars of Mia Farrow and Ryan O'Neal, among others.

Kurt lived with his mother for a year after the divorce. But he didn't like her new boyfriend, whom he calls "a mean huge wife-beater." At first, Wendy attributed

Kurt's dislike of her boyfriend to mere jealousy. Five years later, she realized her boyfriend was "a little nuts"—a paranoid schizophrenic, in fact. Kurt was extremely unhappy and would take out his anger on everyone from Wendy to his babysitters, whom he would usually lock out of the house. Wendy couldn't control him anymore, so she sent him to live with Don at his trailer home in Montesano, an even smaller logging community about twenty miles east of Aberdeen.

Don's place wasn't a mobile home, but a prefabricated house that is towed in sections behind a truck to a trailer park and assembled. "It wasn't one of the more luxurious ones—the double-wide ones that the *rich* white trash got to live in," Kurt says.

At first it was great. Don bought Kurt a minibike and they did things together like go to the beach for the weekend or go camping. "He had everything," says Don. "He had it made. He had the run of the whole house, he had a motorcycle, he got to do whatever *he* wanted to do, we were always doing stuff. But then when two other kids and a new mother comes in . . ."

Don once offhandedly told Kurt that he'd never get married again. He soon remarried in February of 1978. His new wife brought along her two kids, and they all moved into a proper house in Montesano. Kurt didn't get along with his new family at all, especially his new stepmom. "Still, to this day, I can't think of a faker person," he says. "She's one of the most nicest people," Don protests. "Treated him perfect, tried stuff, she got him jobs and tried to cope with everything but it was just screwing up the whole family, just the way he was acting and things that he was doing—and not doing."

Don Cobain.

I interviewed Don Cobain over the phone. What a tough deal he got. Kurt just wanted to be with his mom, who had rejected him, and resented his dad, even though he was the one who took him in. And Don wasn't, as he acknowledged, emotionally equipped to deal with any of it. Many men of his generation weren't very emotionally savvy; it's part of what Kurt was rebelling against, although Kurt was acting out badly. Years later, Don was an easy target for Kurt, who by this time had a massive megaphone and millions of acolytes, whereas Don was just a working guy in rural Washington State. I wish I'd been more sympathetic to Don.

Kurt skipped school and refused to do household chores. Don says he didn't even show up for the table-bussing job he arranged for him. He began picking on his younger stepbrother and didn't like his stepsister much, either—even though she was four years younger than Kurt, she was assigned to babysit for him when their parents went out.

Then he noticed that his dad started to buy lots of toys for his stepsister and brother. While he skulked around in his basement room, they would go out to the mall and come back with a Starhorse or a Tonka truck.

"I tried to do everything to make him feel wanted, to be part of the family and everything," says Don, who maintains he got legal custody of Kurt just to make him feel more a part of the family. "But he just didn't want to be there and wanted to be with his mom and she didn't want him. And then here she is the goody-goody and I'm the big bad guy."

But there may be more to it than that. "I'm emotional at times, but other times I'm not and I just don't know how to express myself," Don admits. "Sometimes my smart-ass stuff hurts people's feelings. I'm not trying to hurt somebody's feelings but I don't know I'm doing it, I guess." Maybe something like that happened with Kurt. "Maybe," says Don. "Definitely."

Oddly, Don seems to have genuine amnesia about his years with Kurt. Although he comes across as a sweet and simple man these days, the strain of the divorce may have brought out a darker side. "Did I rule with a strong arm?" he says. "Okay, my wife says I do. I do probably blow up before I think. And I hurt people's feelings. And I get over it, I forget about it and nobody else does. Yeah, my dad, he beat me with a belt and stuff, give me a black eye and stuff, but I don't know, I spanked him with a belt, yes."

In *Montage of Heck*, Kim Cobain recalls the time that Kurt forgot to feed the dog, and Don grounded him for a year, which included not being able to watch television during that time. So when Don, his wife, and his new family would watch TV after dinner, Kurt had to go up to his room. For a year.

"Everything that Kurt did was a reflection on Don," says Wendy. "If he was bad at a baseball game, he would be just infuriated after that game to the point where he'd just humiliate Kurt. He would never allow Kurt to be a little kid. He wanted him to be a little adult and be perfectly behaved, never do anything wrong. He

would knuckle-rap Kurt and call him a dummy. He'd just get irritated really quickly and—whack, over the head. My mom says she remembers a time when he actually threw Kurt clear across the room when he was like six." Don says he doesn't remember any of this.

"It's called 'denial,'" Wendy replies.

After the divorce, Don had begun working at Mayr Brothers, a logging company, as a tallyman. "Basically," says Kurt, "he just walked around all day and counted logs.

"His idea of a father-and-son day out would be to take me out to work on Saturdays and Sundays," Kurt continues. "I would sit in his office while he went and counted logs. It's really a quite exciting weekend." In his dad's office, Kurt would draw pictures and make prank phone calls. Sometimes he'd go out into the warehouse and play on top of the stacks of two-by-fours. After all that excitement, he would get into his dad's van and listen to Queen's *News of the World* over and over again on the eight-track. Sometimes he'd listen so long that he'd drain the battery and they'd have to find someone to jump-start the engine.

Later in life, Kurt staunchly advocated for punk rock, but it's important to remember that he grew up on stuff like Queen. There simply wasn't much else to listen to at that time and in that place. The funny thing is, Queen was actually formative for a whole lot of punk musicians: listen to the ferocious "Sheer Heart Attack" from 1977's *News of the World*, the very album Kurt listened to so obsessively.

During my research for *Our Band Could Be Your Life*, Fugazi's Ian MacKaye told me that Queen was a big influence on his very influential, very iconoclastic, and definitively underground band. One of the reasons the members of Fugazi loved Queen, he said, was because "they served up their riffs on a platter." In other words, they didn't gussy up the riffs with a lot of fancy stuff. That's what Fugazi did, too, and so did Nirvana.

Don used to run around with the jock crowd in high school, but he never excelled in sports, perhaps because he was small for his age. Don's father expected a lot from him, but he just couldn't compete. Some believe that's why Don pushed Kurt into sports.

Don got Kurt to join the junior high wrestling team. Kurt hated the grueling practices and worse yet, having to hang out with jocks. "I hated it—every second of it," says Kurt. "I just fucking hated it." He'd come home in the evening from practice, "and there'd be this disgusting, shriveled-up, dry meal that my stepmom had cooked with a lot of love and preparation and it had been sitting there since

The Amplified Come as You Are

dinnertime and the oven on low heat and everything was totally dried up and awful. She was the worst cook."

Nevertheless, Kurt says he did pretty well at wrestling, basically because he could vent his anger on the mat. But on the day of a big championship match, Kurt decided to get back at his dad. He and his opponent walked onto the mat and got in position while Don sat in the bleachers, rooting for his son. "I was down on my hands and knees and I looked up at my dad and smiled and I waited for the whistle to blow," says Kurt, "just staring straight into his face and then I just instantly clammed up—I put my arms together and let the guy pin me. You should have seen the look on his face. He actually walked out halfway through the match because I did it like four times in a row." Don doesn't remember that episode either, but Kurt says the incident resulted in one of the times he had to move out of the house and live with an aunt and uncle.

That story now sounds like a revenge fantasy, a tale Kurt intended to mythologize himself at an antagonist's expense.

The guitar was another reason why Kurt had to leave Don's house. Kurt's uncle Chuck Fradenburg (Wendy's brother) gave Kurt a used Japanese electric guitar for his fourteenth birthday. In the '60s, Uncle Chuck had played drums in a local band called the Beachcombers and now played in a band with Kurt's guitar teacher Warren Mason. Kurt became much more interested in playing guitar than doing homework, so Don cut off his music lessons. And Kurt moved out. Eventually, he moved in with Jesse Reed's family; Reed's father, Dave, had been the singer-saxophonist with . . . the Beachcombers.

Don also took Kurt hunting once, but once they got to the woods, Kurt refused to go with the hunting party. He spent the whole day, from dawn to dusk, in the truck. "Now that I look back on it," Kurt says, "I know I had the sense that killing animals is wrong, especially for sport. I didn't understand that at the time. I just knew that I didn't want to be there."

Meanwhile, Kurt began to discover other kinds of rock music besides just the Beatles and the Monkees. Don had begun to develop a pretty serious record collection after someone talked him into joining the Columbia House record and tape club. Every month, records by bands like Aerosmith, Led Zeppelin, Black Sabbath, and Kiss would come in the mail. Don never got around to opening them, but after a few months, Kurt did.

The Columbia House record and tape club used to be a pretty big deal. You'd sign up for this once-popular service and get a bunch of records of your choice for some absurdly low fee, like $1.97—but then you had to buy a set number of other records at the usual prices. It was a boon to people in out-of-the-way places like Aberdeen, which didn't tend to have record stores, especially ones that carried cool stuff like Black Sabbath.

Kurt had begun hanging out with a bunch of guys who sported puka shells and feathered hair and Kiss T-shirts. "They were way older than me—they must have been in junior high," says Kurt. "They were smoking pot and I just thought they were cooler than my geeky fourth-grade friends who watched *Happy Days*. I just let them come over to my house and eat my food, just to have friends." These stoner guys soon noticed Don's awesome record collection and urged Kurt to play the records. "After they turned me on to that music," says Kurt, "I started turning into a little stoner kid."

"He never came out and said anything, even in his early years, about what was really bothering him or what he wanted," says Don. "He's like me—don't say anything and maybe it'll disappear or something. And don't explain. You just bottle it all up and it all comes out at one time."

For all of Kurt's sensitivity, Don was right about that. Kurt was often very subdued, as I note elsewhere in this book, and wouldn't express himself, passive aggressively expecting the other person to intuit his feelings. But when Kurt did get angry, it was volcanic. I was in the house when he and Courtney had a few arguments, and Kurt's yelling practically rattled the windows. (And so did Courtney's.) But most other times, they were very sweetly lovey-dovey. It's tempting to compare this to the dramatic loud-soft dynamic leaps that typified Nirvana's music.

"He got married and after that I was one of the last things of importance on his list," Kurt says. "He just gave up because he was convinced that my mom had brainwashed me. That's a real pathetic weak thing to base your son's existence on."

"I don't really think of my dad as a macho jerk," Kurt says. "He isn't half as extreme as a lot of fathers I've seen." So exactly what is Kurt's beef with his father? "I don't even know," he confesses. "I wish I could remember more. I never felt like I really had a father. I've never had a father figure who I could share things with."

Ultimately, Don couldn't deal with his son either, so Kurt was shuffled through the family, eventually living with three different sets of aunts and uncles, as well as his grandparents on his father's side. He moved at least two times a year between Montesano and Aberdeen, switching high schools as well.

Wendy knew she should take Kurt back, but she had been going through her own traumas—she had finally gotten rid of the paranoid schizophrenic, who had mentally and physically abused her, even putting her in the emergency room at one point. She had since lost her job and asked her brother Chuck, the musician, to take care of Kurt.

For Kurt's fourteenth birthday, Chuck told Kurt he could either have a bicycle or a guitar. Kurt took the guitar, a secondhand electric that barely played, and a beat-up little ten-watt amp. "I don't think it was even a Harmony," Kurt says of the guitar. "I think it was a Sears." He dropped the drums and took guitar lessons for a week or so, just long enough to learn how to play AC/DC's "Back in Black." "That's pretty much the 'Louie, Louie' chords," says Kurt, "and that's all you need to know." After that, he started writing his own songs. His guitar teacher, Warren Mason (who played in a band with Chuck), remembers Kurt as "a quiet, little nice kid." Kurt vehemently denies it, but Mason says he really wanted to learn how to play "Stairway to Heaven."

Of course, "Smells Like Teen Spirit" is based on the "Louie, Louie" chord progression, too.

I have to believe Warren Mason about Kurt wanting to learn "Stairway to Heaven." After all, Kurt was so into Led Zeppelin that he inscribed their name on his bedroom wall. He probably denied this story not just because Led Zeppelin was metal and therefore uncool, but because "Stairway to Heaven" had since gotten so wildly overplayed that it had become a cliché. And then, just before these interviews, the song became a punchline. In a scene from *Wayne's World* (1992), Wayne stops by a music store and begins to try out a guitar, only managing to play a few notes before the clerk stops him and points indignantly to a sign on the wall: "NO STAIRWAY TO HEAVEN."

Kurt found Aberdeen intimidating. Compared to Montesano, Aberdeen was like the big city. "I just thought these kids were a higher class of people and I wasn't quite worthy of being in their group," he says.

In class, he'd read S. E. Hinton books like *Rumble Fish* and *The Outsiders* and avoided speaking to anybody. He says he didn't make a single friend that year. Instead, he'd come home every day and play guitar until it was time for bed. He already knew how to play "Back in Black" and he figured out a few more covers— the Cars' "My Best Friend's Girl," "Louie, Louie," and Queen's "Another One Bites the Dust."

S. E. Hinton pretty much invented the YA novel with *The Outsiders* (1967), a book that has been a staple of American coming-of-age literature ever since. *The Outsiders* remains controversial: at some schools, it's part of the middle or high school curriculum, while others have banned it for its depictions of abusive alcoholics, underage smoking and drinking, lethal gang violence, and general juvenile delinquency—and perhaps also for its depiction of literal class warfare. Kurt surely related to the book's sensitive, poetry-reading outcast protagonist, and it's easy to see how both *The Outsiders* and Hinton's *Rumble Fish* (1975), another perennial staple of American youth culture, primed him for one of his favorite movies, *Over the Edge*.

Remember "My Best Friend's Girl": it'll come up later.

Early in 1980, when Kurt was twelve, he and his friend Brendan had seen the B-52's on *Saturday Night Live*. They got bitten by the new wave bug and Brendan got his parents to buy him some checkered Vans. Kurt's dad couldn't afford that, so Kurt just drew a checkerboard pattern on his regular sneakers.

They never enjoyed the prestige or mystique of peers such as Talking Heads or Blondie, but it really can't be said enough how influential the B-52's were. Their music was the musical equivalent of a thrift store: cast-off culture pieced together from scraps of Motown, garage rock, '60s film scores, novelty records, Yoko Ono, and surf music, all stuff that was pretty passé in the late '70s. The B-52's sounded like no one else—which had a huge impact in itself because it opened up the possibility of a new kind of music taking the place of the hoary classic rock paradigm. It was music by, for, and about outsiders—as the band's Fred Schneider hollered on "There's a Moon in the Sky (Called the Moon)," "If you're in outer space, don't feel out of place / 'Cause there are thousands of others like you."

Significantly, the music was bone-simple—it seemed like anybody could play it, although that was actually deceptive—and one of the singers didn't even sing; he just kind of hollered!

The January 26, 1980, episode of *Saturday Night Live*, in which the B-52's played "Dance This Mess Around" and the juggernautic "Rock Lobster," electrified not just Kurt but an entire generation of kids, including ten-year-old Dave Grohl of Springfield, Virginia. "I somehow felt empowered by their weirdness," Dave wrote in his 2021 memoir *The Storyteller*. "I knew I wanted to break out, too."

Somewhere around the summer before tenth grade, Kurt began following the exploits of the Sex Pistols in *Creem* magazine. The idea of punk rock fascinated him. Unfortunately, the record store in Aberdeen didn't stock any punk rock records, so he didn't know what it sounded like. Alone in his room, he played what he *thought* it sounded like—"Three chords and a lot of screaming," says Kurt. Not so far off the mark, as it turned out.

For American kids who didn't live in cities, it was far easier to see photos of punk rock musicians than to hear their music. "There was pictures of these guys for a few months before we heard the records," former Minutemen bassist-singer Mike Watt told me for *Our Band Could Be Your Life*. "And it blew our minds when we first heard the actual music . . . It turned out to be guitar music like the Who! That's what blew our minds. When we heard that, we said, 'We can do this!'"

A few years later, he finally tracked down a "punk" record, the Clash's sprawling, eclectic three-album set, *Sandinista!*, and was disappointed when it didn't sound like what he thought punk should sound like.

The first time I interviewed Kurt for this book was December 23, 1992. We spoke in my room at the Inn at the Market, a hotel in Seattle's Pike Place Market. Kurt, Courtney, and Frances were between homes and staying at the same hotel.

I stopped by Kurt and Courtney's room to retrieve Kurt. The TV was blaring but no one was watching it, clothes and other belongings were draped over various surfaces, and miscellaneous baby paraphernalia was scattered about. Courtney, in thoughtful mode, asked if I wanted to join them for Christmas. That was very kind, and it sure would have been interesting, but I had family obligations. Kurt's close friend Dylan Carlson was there, too, and we chatted for a bit as I waited for Kurt.

It's easy to see why Kurt and Dylan Carlson got along: both were misfits, artists, and people who wanted to learn a whole lot more about art and the world in general. And they were drug buddies. Carlson is kind of renowned as a nice person, as well as an avid autodidact in the tradition of many fellow musicians, such as Peter Buck, Grant Hart, and Mike Watt. As I was talking with him, he kept mentioning an "eppy-fanny." It took me a minute to realize he meant "epiphany." People who mispronounce fancy words deserve respect—they discovered those words by reading them, not by being taught them by someone else.

Kurt and I headed to my room to talk, and he began by professing his love of the Clash's 1982 album *Combat Rock*. Considering how excellent the Clash's first three albums are, that was a strange choice—it does have "Should I Stay or Should I Go" and "Rock the Casbah," but with its ill-advised excursions into rap and reggae, *Combat Rock* is often derided as the beginning of the end for a once-great band. But this was at the peak of the Age of Irony, and I couldn't tell if Kurt was kidding. *Combat Rock* does turn up in some of the favorite albums lists in his journals, so I guess he was actually serious. He must have forgiven the Clash for *Sandinista!*

I gave him a present that evening: a yellow-and-orange-striped vintage cardigan. He was really appreciative—when I offered it to him, he snatched it away from me and held

Nirvana at the Crocodile. © Charles Peterson

it close to his chest as if he was afraid I was going to grab it back. I'm pretty sure he was cremated in it, along with a Breeders T-shirt. That is very strange to think about.

But Krist was the first member of Nirvana I interviewed for the book. I got a call from the lobby that he was coming up, so I left the door open for him. I was sitting in a low comfy chair between the door and floor-to-ceiling windows that looked out on Puget Sound when suddenly Krist burst in the door, all six-foot-seven of him, ran straight at me, jumped right over my head, and stopped right at the window, theatrically slamming his palms on the glass to stop himself. What an entrance! That was Krist back then— just slightly dangerous in the most goofy, irreverent, hilarious, and charmingly icebreaking way.

Kurt describes his early music as "really raunchy riff-rock." "It was like Led Zeppelin but it was raunchy and I was trying to make it as aggressive and mean as I could," he says. "I was thinking, 'What would punk rock really be like? What is it? How nasty is it?' And I would try to play as nasty as I could. Turn my little ten-watt amplifier up as loud as it could go. I just didn't have any idea what I was doing."

His early music was "like Led Zeppelin," and yet he didn't want to learn how to play "Stairway to Heaven." OK!

"It was definitely a good release," says Kurt. "I thought of it as a job. It was my mission. I knew I had to practice. As soon as I got my guitar, I just became so obsessed with it.

"I had this feeling all the time—I always knew I was doing something that was special," says Kurt. "I knew it was better, even though I couldn't prove it at the time. I knew I had something to offer and I knew eventually I would have the opportunity to show people that I could write good songs—that I could contribute something musically to rock & roll."

So far, we've learned that Kurt was a fan of blockbuster rock bands such as Kiss, Queen, Led Zeppelin, and the Beatles. Bands who unabashedly sought fame and fortune were Kurt's early role models, and that kind of thing doesn't just completely disappear. And, as Kurt said, he wanted to "contribute something musically to rock & roll," a lofty goal. Soon, though, that ambition would collide with a very different set of values held by a group of people whose approval he craved—such as the Olympia crowd, Mudhoney, Sonic Youth, Matador Records co-founder Gerard Cosloy, Steve Albini, Fugazi—and still craved even at the height of his fame. It was a massive conflict that he never managed to resolve.

Kurt was desperate to take the next logical step and form a band. "I wanted to see what it was like to write a song and see what it sounded like with all the instruments at once," Kurt says. "I just wanted that. At least to practice. That's all I wanted." It would be four years before he would find a band, but it wasn't for lack of trying.

In school, he met two kids named Scott and Andy who played bass and guitar and jammed out in an abandoned meat locker way out in the woods. Kurt went out there and played one day and the three decided to form a band. Kurt agreed to leave his guitar out there because after all, he was going to come back the very next day and rehearse again. But Scott and Andy kept putting off practice and days turned into weeks, weeks into months. Kurt couldn't get his instrument back because he didn't have a car, and his mom wouldn't drive him. He made do with a right-handed guitar owned by a kid whose mother had died and was staying at the Cobains' house. "He was just this stoner guy who was really stump dumb," says Kurt. "I liked him because he was a real depressed person." Eventually, Kurt got a friend to drive him out to the woods where his guitar was and they found it in pieces—just a neck and some electronic guts. Kurt painstakingly made a new body in wood shop, only to find that he didn't know the correct proportions to make it stay in tune.

"When I was a lot younger, around seven years old, I thought for sure I could be a rock star," says Kurt. "There was no problem because I was so hyperactive and the world was in my hands—I could do anything. I knew I could be the president if I wanted to, but that was a stupid idea—I'd rather be a rock star. I didn't have any doubt. I was really into the Beatles and I didn't understand my environment, what was lying ahead, what kind of alienation I would feel as a teenager."

That was a recurring theme for Kurt: the idea that there was a blissfully innocent, idyllic phase of his life that was destroyed by his parents' divorce. He would later dread the same thing happening to his daughter.

"I thought of Aberdeen as any other city in America," Kurt continues. "I thought they were all the same—everyone just got along and there wasn't nearly as much violence as there actually was and it would be really easy. I thought the United States was about as big as my backyard, so it would be no problem to drive all over the place and play in a rock band and be on the cover of magazines and stuff.

"But then when I started becoming this manic depressive at nine years old, I didn't look at it that way. It seemed so unrealistic."

Both Kurt and Courtney mentioned manic depression in conversation. A lot. Kurt even wrote a song called "Lithium"—lithium carbonate is often used to treat bipolar disorder. And it could be said that Nirvana's defining loud-soft dynamics were truly bipolar. But the way he talked about it, I never got the sense that Kurt meant he was literally manic-depressive; I thought he was just being melodramatic and a bit of a hypochondriac. He talked about suicide the same way. But it turns out that he might really have been manic-depressive. And, sadly, he did commit suicide. Even decades later, it's very difficult to make peace with the fact that these things were right there in the open.

By tenth grade, Kurt had abandoned all fantasies of fame. "I was so self-conscious at that time," he says. "I had such a small amount of esteem that I couldn't even think of actually becoming a rock star, never mind dealing with what they would expect a rock star to be. I couldn't imagine being on television or doing interviews or anything like that. Stuff like that didn't even seep into my mind at the time."

Kurt's father had made him join the Babe Ruth League baseball team. Basically, Kurt just warmed the bench, and whenever he was called to bat, he'd strike out on purpose, just so he wouldn't have to get into the game. On the bench, he hung out with a guy named Matt Lukin and they talked about Kiss and Cheap Trick. The two had met before in electronics class at Montesano High. Lukin remembers Kurt as "this greasy-haired little rebellious kid."

Lukin played bass in a local band called the Melvins, whom Kurt had actually seen rehearse one night the summer before ninth grade. Kurt's friend Brendan knew someone who knew the drummer for the Melvins and they wangled an invitation to the Melvins' practice, which was then an attic in someone's house. The Melvins had not gone punk yet, and were playing Hendrix and Who covers.

The Melvins, soon to become one of the most original and influential rock bands in the Northwest, started out playing Hendrix and Who covers—again, their roots were classic rock. Along with metal, that type of stuff was just what rocker kids of that era listened to until they found punk. There just wasn't anything else.

Matt Lukin went on to be the bass player in Mudhoney, Sub Pop's flagship band before Nirvana exploded. Lukin used to hand out a business card with his phone number and the words "Matt Lukin . . . all around good guy. Invite him over for a beer." And I bet a lot of people took him up on it. Everybody loves Matt Lukin.

It was the first time Kurt had seen a real rock band up close and he was terrifically excited. "I'd been drinking wine all night and I was really drunk and

obnoxious and I remember complimenting them about a million times," says Kurt. "I was so excited to see people my age in a band. It was so great. I was thinking, 'Wow, those guys are so lucky.'" Disgusted with this fawning little squirt, they kicked Kurt out. Still drunk, he fell down the attic ladder as he left.

In art class at Montesano High that year, Kurt again met Melvins leader Buzz Osborne, a stocky, wild-looking kid a couple of years his senior. At the time, Osborne was a big Who fan, but soon moved into punk rock. He had a photo book on the Sex Pistols, which he let Kurt borrow. Kurt was riveted. It was the first time he had gotten to see punk rock other than those precious few spreads in *Creem*. "This was the Sex Pistols in all their wildness," says Kurt, "and I got to read about them and everything. It was really cool." Soon he was drawing the Sex Pistols logo on his desk in every class and all over his Pee-Chee folder. Then he began telling anyone who would listen that he was going to start a punk rock band and that it was going to be really popular, still not having any idea what punk rock sounded like.

"He struck me as a freak," says Kurt of Osborne. "Someone who I definitely wanted to get to know." Kurt envied Osborne because he had a punk rock band that actually played sometimes in Seattle and Olympia. "And that's all I ever really wanted to do at that point," says Kurt. "I didn't have any high expectations for my music at all. I just wanted to have the chance to play in front of some people in Seattle. The thought of being in a band that was successful enough to actually go on tour was too much to ask for at that time."

A few years earlier, Seattle had been officially nicknamed the Emerald City, ostensibly for its greenery. But the name also fit because, like the city in *The Wizard of Oz*, it was a regional mecca. Seattle was a magnet for ambitious, creative people, or folks who just plain didn't fit in with small-town America; they made the pilgrimage to Seattle not just from places in Washington State but from as far away as Idaho and Montana.

Kurt had been to Seattle only a few times at that point; for a kid from a provincial town like Aberdeen, Seattle, a couple of hours' drive to the northeast, was a sophisticated place that could confer validation—and provide an escape from the stifling claustrophobia and regressive social values that Kurt so despised. And this was while Seattle was still a relative backwater, long before Microsoft and Amazon dominated the town. Later, Kurt would be impressed by a couple of hip, worldly college boys who ran a record label in Seattle.

Buzz Osborne was a pretty sophisticated person, too: extremely bright, fundamentally rebellious, with a quick, sardonic wit, he somehow found out about a lot of cool stuff, like punk rock, long before anyone else in town did. For a kid like Kurt, who was starving for information about the world beyond Aberdeen, Buzz was a priceless early lodestar.

The Melvins also included original drummer Mike Dillard, who was later replaced by Dale Crover. In their first punk phase, they played faster-than-light hardcore. Then, when everyone began doing the same, they played as slow as they possibly could, just to piss everybody off. And to *really* piss them off, they injected heavy metal into the mix. With 1987's influential *Gluey Porch Treatments* album, the Melvins would become one of the founding fathers of what eventually became known as "grunge"—a new, mutant form of punk rock that absorbed heavy metal as well as proletarian '70s hard rock bands such as Kiss and Aerosmith. Their sound revolutionized the Seattle music scene, which had previously been dominated by art-rock bands.

The Melvins had already played in Seattle when Kurt first saw them, and by 1985, had appeared on the protean *Deep Six* collection along with the U-Men, Soundgarden, Green River, Malfunkshun, and Skin Yard. Except for the art-rock U-Men, all mixed varying amounts of punk, '70s-style hard rock, and heavy metal into a crude but effective musical mongrel.

Kurt would sometimes help the Melvins haul their equipment to Seattle for gigs. Aberdeen didn't have much of a musical history—although half of platinum-selling speed-metalers Metal Church hailed from the town—and a band that played in Seattle was big news.

###

Kurt was very unhappy about getting shuttled from relative to relative. In May of 1984, Wendy had married Pat O'Connor, a longshoreman. Pat was drinking heavily then and Wendy had her hands full with that—she didn't feel she could also deal with Kurt, but Kurt eventually convinced her to have him back. "It took months of being on the phone crying every night, trying to talk her into letting me live with her," says Kurt.

There's that tough love again.

Pat went out one night and didn't come back until seven in the morning, drunk and, as Wendy puts it, "reeking of a girl." She was furious, but she still went to work at the department store. Then a couple of townies walked through the store just to taunt her. "Hey, where was Pat last night?" they cackled. Wendy got so mad that she went out and got drunk with a friend, then came home and exploded at Pat. In front of both the kids, she grabbed one of his many guns out of the closet and threatened to shoot him—but she couldn't figure out how to load the gun. Then she took all his guns—shotguns, pistols, rifles, antique guns—and dragged them down the alley, with Kim hauling a big bag of bullets, to the Wishkah River and dumped them in.

Kurt was watching from his bedroom window. Later that day, he paid a couple of kids to fish as many guns as they could find out of the river and then sold them. Kurt bought his first amplifier with the proceeds. Then he drove the guy who sold the amp to him to his pot dealer's place and the guy spent all the money on pot.

Some stories are just too good to be true—but apparently this is not one of them. Not only does it perfectly capture the rural lower-middle-class stoner milieu of that time and place, but what a metaphor for Kurt's preternatural gift for alchemizing anger and anguish into music.

Kurt played his guitar very loud. The neighbors complained. Wendy marked up the ceiling with her broom handle. Kurt loved it when the family left to go shopping or something, because that meant he could crank. "We'd come home hoping we had windows left," says Wendy. Kurt tried to get his friends to play with him, but no one had any musical talent. He'd be very bossy and direct in his criticism. He knew exactly what he wanted.

Maybe the title of this chapter should have been "The Child Is Father to the Man": as an adult, Kurt controlled every aspect of Nirvana, from T-shirt designs to liner notes to music video treatments to choosing opening bands. And, as it turns out, this trait was evident even in his youth.

Nobody knew he was also *singing* up there in his room. "One day," says Wendy, "Pat and I heard him. He was singing real low. He did *not* want us to hear it. We put our ears to the door and we both looked at each other, wrinkled up our noses, and said, 'Better stick to the guitar.'"

chapter two

WE WERE JUST CONCERNED WITH FUCKING AROUND

round this time, Kurt first noticed Chris Novoselic at Aberdeen High. "I remember thinking he was definitely somebody I wanted to meet," says Kurt. "But we never connected." The two didn't have any classes together—Kurt occasionally saw Chris at pep assemblies, where he would sometimes participate in little skits, only to sabotage them by doing things like spontaneously singing "The Star-Spangled Banner."

That's a foreshadowing of warbling "Get Together" on the intro to "Territorial Pissings."

Krist, Dale Crover told Greg Prato in *Grunge Is Dead: The Oral History of Seattle Rock Music*, "was a popular guy at high school," but from what Krist says about his alienated high school years here, his humor might have served its classic purpose of winning over people while keeping them at arm's length.

"He was a hilarious person who obviously had a different sense of humor," says Kurt. "Everyone was just laughing *at* him but I was laughing *with* him, because he was basically making fools out of everybody else. He was just a really clever, funny, loudmouth person. He was taller than anybody in school. He was *huge*. It was too bad I never got to hang out with him, because I really needed a friend during high school."

Kurt felt like an outcast, but even outcasts can find other outcasts to hang out with. Except, apparently, in Aberdeen. "I wanted to fit in somewhere, but not with the average kid, not with the popular kids at school," says Kurt. "I wanted to fit in with the geeks, but the geeks were sub-geeks in Aberdeen. They weren't the average geek. They weren't the type of kid who would listen to Devo. They were just usually deformed."

It's perhaps worth noting that this was the early '90s, and even among people as enlightened as Kurt, the discourse around disability was not where it is today. Still, I wish I'd noted that after he said that, he chuckled warmly at the memory.

It's kind of striking how Kurt's predicament recalls a line that James Dean utters in the 1955 classic of teen alienation *Rebel Without a Cause*: "Boy, if I had one day when I didn't have to be all confused and I didn't have to feel that I was ashamed of everything. If I felt that I belonged someplace. You know? Then . . ."

Kurt says there were only two other guys in school that he even *thought* about being friends with. Both were at least cool enough to be into Oingo Boingo, the manic new wave band from Los Angeles. "But they were just such geeks—total idiots," Kurt says. "They were the kind of guys who would paint their faces at football games."

High school was a teenage wasteland for Kurt, composed of three castes: the social types, the math nerds, and the stoners. The girls at Aberdeen High had noticed Kurt's dimples and blue eyes, and decided that he was cute. "They kind of liked me," says Kurt, "but I just didn't like any of those girls because they were just stupid." And because girls liked Kurt, their jock boyfriends tried to buddy up to him, but Kurt blew them off, too.

Kurt considered hanging out with the nerdy kids who were into computers and chess, but they didn't like music.

That left the stoners. "Although I hated them," he says, "they were at least into rock & roll." So Kurt donned the typical stoner jacket—the jean jacket with the fleece lining which still finds favor among today's wasted youth—and began hanging out at the traditional stoner hangout, the smoker's shed. Kurt hardly said a word to anybody; he was so quiet that occasionally, someone would ask him if he was a narc.

Kurt had fallen out of touch with the Melvins after his move back to Aberdeen. But then he met a fellow music fan named Dale Crover at the smoker's shed. Chris also knew Crover because Crover used to jam with Chris's younger brother Robert. When the Melvins needed a drummer, Chris suggested Crover, who got the gig. And since Kurt knew Crover, he began hanging out with the Melvins again.

The Melvins began practicing in an extra room at Crover's parents' house. Anywhere the Melvins rehearsed quickly turned into a seemingly permanent haven for a group of Aberdeen stoners dubbed "the cling-ons," and Crover's place was no different. Clad in bell-bottom jeans and quilted pullover jackets with zippered pockets so they could keep their pot safe, "these guys were just the most classic cartoon types of stoner metalhead kids that you could imagine," Kurt recalls. "They were so hilarious—zits, no teeth, reeking of pot."

For the cling-ons, hanging out at the Melvins' practice space was just about the only source of excitement there was. "All there was to do in Aberdeen was drink beer, smoke pot, and worship Satan," quips Crover. "There's nothing there. We watched a lot of TV."

The practice space itself was festooned with posters of Kiss, Mötley Crüe, and Ted Nugent, pages torn out of *Circus* magazine, and pictures of naked women with different faces pasted on them (a similar image would one day resurface on a Nirvana T-shirt). Visitors would go up the stairs of the back porch of the house, through a tiny room, and then into the rehearsal room. Buzz didn't like many people around at practice, so the cling-ons contented themselves with hanging out on the back porch while the Melvins rehearsed. The band's daily practice usually lasted three or more hours, but only because they had to stop playing every twenty minutes or so while one of the members transacted some business with the cling-ons.

Kurt auditioned to become a Melvin, but it didn't work out. "I totally botched it," Kurt says. "I was so nervous that I forgot all the songs. I literally couldn't play a note. I just stood there with my guitar and played feedback with a blushed face."

The mind reels at the thought of the music that might have transpired had Kurt passed the audition. Then again, it's doubtful that one band could contain both Kurt Cobain and Buzz Osborne. Within a year or so, though, Kurt played with Dale Crover, and with life-changing results.

It was just as well, because Kurt was already writing and recording his own material. Matt Lukin recalls a tape Kurt made of his own songs, just guitar and vocals. "They were just some really cool songs," recalls Lukin, "especially for somebody in Aberdeen who played guitar at that point that was our age—most guys just wanted to play Judas Priest. We found it kind of odd that some kid was writing his own songs and would rather play that than Mötley Crüe."

And then Buzz Osborne introduced Kurt Cobain to punk rock. Osborne made a few compilation tapes, mostly Southern California bands such as Black Flag and Flipper, as well as Austin's radical left-wing punk band MDC. The first song on the first tape was Black Flag's "Damaged II," an all-out attack of abrasive guitars and shambling but assaultive drums, brimming with buzzsaw rancor. "Damaged by you, damaged by me / I'm confused, I'm confused / Don't want to be confused" screamed singer Henry Rollins.

Discovering punk rock was a pivotal moment for Kurt. "Punk rock made me realize that you don't have to be professional," he told the BBC2 TV show *Rapido* in November 1991. "You just have to have passion. You can be as sloppy as you want. That's what made me start playing guitar—I was intimidated when I first started playing guitar. I was intimidated by really professional musicians, like heavy metal musicians who were very anal and technical and promoted the fact that they could play 'good.' That made me not ever think of playing rock & roll realistically or ever making any career out of it or actually going for it and doing it. But when I heard punk rock, it made me realize that these people are a lot like me. They're just as sloppy and as bad musicians. But they still like passion and they like energy. So it helped me start a band."

Kurt was floored. "It was like listening to something from a different planet," he says. "It took me a few days to accept it." By the end of the week, though, he was a certified, self-proclaimed punk rocker. "I sensed," says Kurt, "that it was speaking more clearly and more realistically than the average rock & roll lyric."

Getting your head around music that sounds like "something from a different planet" is an intensely gratifying, paradigm-shifting experience. It's as if you've just graduated to another plane of consciousness. In Black Flag, Kurt had finally found music that embodied his anger and alienation: the music "boiled over with rage on several fronts: police harassment, materialism, alcohol abuse, the stultifying effects of consumer culture, and, on just about every track on the album, a particularly virulent strain of self-lacerating angst," I wrote in *Our Band Could Be Your Life*, "all against a savage, brutal backdrop that welded apoplectic punk rock to the anomie of dark '70s metal like Black Sabbath." So, as strange as the music may have sounded, it also had some roots in music (and an entire worldview) that Kurt was familiar with. And it spoke directly to a small community of outsiders who were actively, even aggressively, making music and art.

Soon after that, in September 1984, Kurt, Lukin, Osborne, and others drove up to Seattle to see Black Flag play the Mountaineer Club during the *Slip It In* tour. In order to raise enough money for a ticket, Kurt sold his record collection—which at that time consisted of albums by bands such as Journey, Foreigner, and Pat Benatar—for twelve dollars. "It was really great," says Kurt of the show. "I was instantly converted."

Buzz Osborne told *Revolver* in 2013 that that Black Flag show "really put [Kurt] over the edge. I just remember him saying, 'That's exactly what I want to do. That's it. This is me.'"

The symbolism of selling Journey, Foreigner, and Pat Benatar records to attend a punk rock show is just perfect. Maybe a little *too* perfect. Although maybe those were albums Kurt was practically obligated to buy through Columbia House. Regardless, it makes for some good mythology.

The thing is, the music that Black Flag played on that tour wasn't entirely the ripsnorting cavalcade of hyperactive angst explosions that had originally entranced Kurt. By that time, Black Flag had begun to leave behind the classic hardcore sound and blaze bold new territory: they slowed their new music way down. It was just as aggressive but much heavier. "A lot of other people around the country hated the fact that Black Flag slowed down," Mudhoney guitarist Steve Turner told me for *Our Band Could Be Your Life*, "but up here [in Seattle], it was really great—we were like, 'Yay!' They were weird and fucked-up sounding."

The members of Black Flag had also done something else that was heretical: they'd grown their hair long, which shocked some die-hard punks all along that tour—and galvanized others. "They started growing their hair, and so did Seattle," Turner continued, and "a lot of people secretly were heshers [stoner kids with greasy long hair who listen to metal and wear jean jackets] anyway and just cut their hair once to be punk but secretly liked the metal long hair to begin with." That hesher-punk hybrid would form the basis of what would come to be called grunge.

Somehow both trudging and raucous, like gleefully wading through a lake of filthy molasses, San Francisco punk band Flipper also contributed to the slowing of Seattle punk. Crude, passionate, and revelatory *Generic Flipper* (1982) had an immense impact on Nirvana's music; in fact, Kurt wore a homemade Flipper T-shirt on the cover of the original version of this book. That fandom was reciprocated in 2000, when Flipper recorded a positively cataclysmic cover of "Scentless Apprentice." Krist even joined Flipper from 2006 to 2009 and played on the well-received 2009 *Love* studio album as well as a live album the same year—both recorded by Jack Endino.

"Becoming a punk rocker fed into my low self-esteem because it helped me realize that I don't need to become a rock star—I don't *want* to become a rock star," Kurt says. "So I was fighting this thin line—I was always on the left or right side of not caring and not wanting to and not being able to, yet kind of wanting to at the same time. Still wanting to prove myself to people. It's kind of confusing. I'm so glad that I got into punk rock at the time I did because it gave me these few years that I needed to grow up and put my values in perspective and realize what kind of person I am.

"I'm just really glad I was able to find punk rock," Kurt says. "It was really a godsend."

Black Flag was just one of the many, many underground bands who embraced the then-radical idea of playing in a rock group and yet not trying to be rich and famous. Black Flag thought of their tours as "creepy crawls"—a term borrowed from the homicidal Manson Family cult of the late '60s that referred to their breaking into people's homes and doing nothing but subtly rearranging things so that the occupants knew someone had been there. A Black Flag tour did the same thing: they hit town, did some below-the-radar rearranging (of minds), and then moved on.

By rejecting the jackpot mentality of the major labels, which dictated that bands either hit it big or get dropped, punk bands on independent labels could "jam econo," as the Minutemen put it, and have a sustainable career. These bands had no possibility of true stardom or anything even vaguely approaching wealth, but if they played their cards right, they could make exactly the music they wanted to make for as long as they wanted to make it. This was revolutionary.

It was part and parcel of punk's egalitarian ethos, where nobody was a star. It went far beyond the fact that members of the audience could jump onstage and then dive off: they weren't passive consumers, they were active participants and could not only start their own bands, they could start fanzines and record labels and underground radio stations and venues and record shops, forming a far-flung cooperative community.

But what a tangled web Kurt wove here. As a kid who grew up on Kiss, Cheap Trick, and Queen, Kurt had big rock dreams. And then he discovered punk, whose diminished commercial expectations "fed into [his] low self-esteem." So now what? As Kurt acknowledged with no small degree of understatement, "It's kind of confusing."

Osborne also showed him a way to deal with his environment. "He just had a really awesome attitude toward the average redneck," says Kurt. "I was really inspired by his attitude. It was 'Fuck with them as much as you can get away with.' We would go to jock parties and follow the big muscle men around and spit on their backs. And write dirty sayings on the walls of their houses and take the eggs out of the refrigerator and put them in the host's bed. Just try to get away with as much damage as we could."

Eventually, Kurt met a guy named Jesse Reed, who "was the only nice friend that I could find in Aberdeen." Besides a handsome kid named Myer Loftin.

Kurt met Loftin in art class and the two hit it off after discovering they were into the same music—everything from stuff like AC/DC, Aerosmith, and Led Zeppelin to punk rock. To Loftin, Kurt "looked like your average blue-jeans-and-nice-neat-haircut, kind of straightlaced kid." It really surprised him that Kurt was a musician. "He was kind of mild-mannered and quiet," says Loftin. "Very nice, very sincere." They became good friends.

What Kurt didn't know at first was that Loftin was gay. Loftin mentioned it to Kurt soon after they started hanging out. "He said, 'Well, that's okay, you're still my friend, I still love you, it's no problem,'" says Loftin. "And we hugged."

It's not as big of a deal now, but in the '80s, a teenager coming out, even privately, could be downright dangerous, even fatal—especially in a violent and conservative

The Amplified Come as You Are

place like Aberdeen. Especially at the height of the HIV/AIDS epidemic and the ignorance, fear, and loathing that surrounded it. That was so brave of Loftin.

I interviewed Loftin by phone, and he was a really solid, kind person who clearly had the emotional equipment to stand up for himself. I imagine he was a great influence on Kurt.

Loftin would sometimes stay over at Kurt's house and Wendy, a "cool mom," let them "party" in the house as long as they didn't drive anywhere until the next morning. Once, Wendy came home drunk and caught them smoking pot. In a futile attempt to psyche Kurt out of smoking pot, she ate his stash and got terribly stoned and sick afterward. On less eventful nights, they'd hang out in Kurt's room and Kurt would teach Loftin Led Zeppelin licks on the guitar.

But hanging out with an openly gay friend was a little more risky than Kurt had anticipated. Soon, says Kurt, "I started to realize that people were looking at me even more peculiarly than usual." He started to get harassed. It always seemed to happen in P.E. class. After everybody got dressed, somebody would inevitably call Kurt a "faggot" and push him up against a locker. "They felt threatened because they were naked and I was supposedly gay," says Kurt. "So they either better cover up their penises or punch me. Or both."

Life in high school just got harder for Kurt. Often, jocks would chase him on the way home from school. Sometimes they caught him. "Every day after school," says Kurt, "this one kid would hold me down in the snow and sit on my head."

It should be noted that it doesn't actually snow very much in Aberdeen, so once again, Kurt might have been exaggerating a real or perceived antagonist.

There was surely at least a grain of truth in the story though. In July 1993, Jon Savage interviewed Kurt for *Guitar World*.

Savage: Tell me about your high school experience. Were people unpleasant to you?
Kurt: I was a scapegoat, but not in the sense that I was picked on all the time. They didn't pick on me or beat me up because I was already withdrawn by that time. I was so antisocial that I was almost insane. I felt so different and so crazy that people just left me alone. I wouldn't have been surprised if they voted me Most Likely To Kill Everyone At A High School Dance.
Savage: Can you now understand how some people become so alienated that they become violent?
Kurt: Yeah, I can definitely see how a person's mental state could deteriorate to the point where they fantasized about it, but I'm sure I would opt to kill myself first.

"After that," says Kurt, "I started being proud of the fact that I was gay even though I wasn't. I really enjoyed the conflict. It was pretty exciting, because I almost found my identity. I was a *special* geek. I wasn't quite the punk rocker I was looking for, but at least it was better than being the *average* geek."

It's tempting to look at gayness as being Kurt's metaphor for any attribute that marginalizes someone.

But the social pressures eventually became too strong and one day, Kurt walked up to Loftin, visibly upset, and told him that he couldn't hang around with him anymore. He was just getting too much abuse for being the friend of a "faggot." Loftin understood completely, and they parted ways.

Kurt had started smoking pot in ninth grade and got high every day until senior year, when he at least waited until nightfall. "I was getting so paranoid from it that I couldn't be as neurotic as I already naturally was and have it intensified by pot," Kurt says.

Kurt was self-medicating, which he would continue to do until the very end. "One day I discovered the most ultimate form of expression ever: *marijuana*," he said on a tape recording that was featured in *Montage of Heck*. "Oh boy, *pot*. I could escape all day long and not have to have routine nervous breakdowns once a week. . . . I claimed [it] as something I will do for the rest of my life."

He did badly in school and began skipping classes in eleventh grade; moving around so much between schools was only part of the problem. "The biggest reason I flunked out of certain classes was because I hated the teachers so much," says Kurt. "There was this one guy who was a religious fanatic, an apocalyptic racist. He taught social sciences and he would do nothing but waste our time by incorporating Revelations into history. He was part of the mid-'80s Cold War scare—*the Russians are coming*—one of the crusaders for that Reagan mentality. Son of a bitch. I wanted to kill him every day. I used to fantasize how I'd kill him in front of the class. Because the rest of the class were completely buying it hook, line, and sinker. Totally swallowing this garbage. I couldn't believe so many people were just taking it."

It's probably worth explaining that in the mid '80s, when the Soviet Union still existed, it was the right wing, not mainstream Democrats, who loathed Russia. The resulting fear was used to dramatically ramp up military spending, as it is today.

Kurt was a remarkably independent critical thinker, even as a teen. No wonder he didn't fit in.

Kurt was rebelling at home, too. "He didn't want to be part of the family but he wanted to live in the family house," says Wendy. "He complained about everything I asked him to do, which was very minimal." Meanwhile, Wendy acknowledges that her patience with Kurt wore thin because she was also angry at Pat for his drinking. She often transferred some of her anger to her kids.

By all accounts, Kurt just wanted to be back with his mom after being asked to leave by virtually every relative who'd been kind enough to take him in. And then once he was back, he deliberated sabotaged everything. "He wanted normalcy," his sister Kim says in *Montage of Heck*. "He wanted the mom, the dad, and the kids and everything happy. But then he didn't. 'Cause he kind of fought against it. So he fought against what he really wanted." That turned out to be a pattern for Kurt: fighting against things he really wanted.

For a few months, Kurt went out with "a stoner girl," a very pretty young woman named Jackie. According to Kurt, "she was basically using me until her boyfriend got out of jail."

One night, Kurt sneaked Jackie up to his room. Kurt was psyched—he was about to lose his virginity. They had just gotten their clothes off when Wendy suddenly burst into the room, flicked on the lights, and hissed, "Get that *slut* out of here!" Kurt ran away to a friend's house and stayed until his friend's mother called up and said, "Wendy, I think your son's living at my house."

Kurt stopped smoking pot "in an attempt to try to turn my life around." Then Kurt's stepmother called up and asked Kurt to live there again. Right away, Don said that if Kurt were to stay there, he'd have to stop doing music and start doing something constructive with his life. He somehow persuaded Kurt to pawn his guitar, then got him to take the Navy entrance exam. Kurt got a very high score and an excited local recruiter came by the house two nights in a row. But on the second night, right on the brink of signing up, Kurt went downstairs to his basement room, found some pot, smoked it, came back upstairs and said "No thanks," then packed up his stuff and left. He'd been there only a week. He wouldn't see his father again for another eight years.

To this day, Don collects all the magazine articles on Kurt that he can find. He's got a big scrapbook and a cupboard full of memorabilia. "Everything I know

about Kurt," says Don Cobain, "I've read in newspapers and magazines. I got to know him that way."

#

Wendy sent Kurt off to live with his buddy Jesse Reed, whose parents were born-again Christians.

During a January 1994 video interview the ingenious Canadian music journalist/ performance artist Nardwuar did with Kurt, Nardwuar mentioned me—and Courtney announced, "He's obsessed with Jesse Reed," which was *sort of* true: I wouldn't say I was "obsessed" with Jesse Reed, but I knew there was something interesting there—unfortunately, I just never got the opportunity to delve into it because Reed was somewhere at sea with the US Navy. My hunch was right, though—it later turned out that Kurt briefly became a born-again Christian while living with the Reeds, which would explain, among other things, "Lithium." But it also reveals that this perpetual pariah devoutly wanted to belong somewhere, to something—note that Kurt also seriously considered enlisting in the military. Maybe that impulse was to compensate for his fragmented family life. But Kurt also had an equal and opposite disdain for authority—"Corn on the cops!"—that eventually won out. Soon, though, he would arrive in Olympia and find a close-knit community that he could (sort of) belong to.

Kurt was broke and told a local drug dealer that he would sell him his guitar and left it at his house on good faith. After a week Kurt changed his mind, but the dealer kept the guitar anyway and Kurt went without it for months until he and Reed snatched it back.

Kurt wasn't quite the ideal house guest at the Reeds'. "I was a bad influence on Jesse," Kurt says. "I smoked pot and I didn't like to go to school." Once, Kurt spent a long phone conversation insulting Mrs. Reed, then hung up the phone only to realize she had been listening in on an extension. The final straw came one day when Kurt, locked out of the house, did the only logical thing and kicked in the door. Kurt says that Reed's father hit the roof and told him, "Kurt, we've tried really hard to turn you into a good citizen but it's just not going to work. You're a lost cause. So I'd appreciate it if you packed up your stuff and left." Mrs. Reed explained to Wendy that "Kurt was leading Jesse down the wrong road."

A special remedial program for school didn't work out. Six months before graduation, Kurt realized he had almost two years of credits to make up. Mr. Hunter, his art teacher, had entered him in some college scholarship competitions and Kurt had won two, but he still decided to drop out in May 1985, just a few weeks short of what should have been his graduation.

Kurt had decided to make music his life's work, but Wendy felt he was wasting his time. "I told him he better get his life going," says Wendy. "If you're not going to finish school, you better get a job and get your life going, because you're not going to stay here mooching off of us."

But Kurt did continue to mooch off his mom and one day, she laid down the law. "I told him 'If this doesn't get better, if you don't get a job, you're going to be *out*,'" says Wendy. "'You're going to come home one day and you're going to find your stuff in a box.'" Sure enough, Kurt came home from hanging out at the Melvins' practice space one day to find all his belongings packed in cardboard boxes stacked on the dining room floor. "I played the 'tough love' thing," says Wendy. "That was when 'tough love' was first coming into being and I thought 'Well, I'm going to try this on him.'"

Kurt was just seventeen at the time.

Using some of Don's child support money as a deposit, Kurt moved into an apartment in Aberdeen with Jesse Reed, paying his rent with money he earned working at a restaurant at one of the resorts on the Washington coast. He tried to enlist Reed to play with him. They would talk about guitars all the time when they first met, and Reed's dad used to play in a surf band that had actually put out some singles. When Reed mentioned that he had just got a bass guitar, Kurt got very excited. "We started playing together one night and it turns out he's one of the most musically retarded people I've ever met," says Kurt, the disappointment still plain in his voice. "He couldn't even play 'Louie, Louie.'"

As enlightened as Kurt was about racism, feminism, and homophobia, he wasn't quite hip to the problem with using the word "retarded." (But then few people were at the time.) In his more self-deprecating moods, he would refer to himself as "retarded" and in concert would sometimes change a line in one of the verses of "Lithium" to "I'm so retarded, I can't take a sedative." The thing is, he was kind of fascinated with intellectually disabled people; I think it had to do with his leitmotif of childlike innocence and the idea that, like children, intellectually disabled people are pure and blameless, too.

Kurt was a big fan of a 1989 album called *Special Music from Special Kids* by the Kids of Widney High—songs composed and sung by a class of Los Angeles students with disabilities, backed by studio musicians and a drum machine. Maybe Kurt got the same thing out of this music that pop music icon Smokey Robinson described in his blurb about the Widney High record: "Listening to this album proves to me that music is the universal language that transcends everything."

The Kids of Widney High enjoyed a bit of cult status among underground musicians and opened for the Melvins, Fantômas, and Mr. Bungle (whose singer Mike Patton released a second Widney High album on his Ipecac label), as well as playing some dates on the Warped Tour.

In the liner notes for *Special Music from Special Kids*, the class's teacher Michael Monagan wrote, "As a result of the project, many of the behavior problems decreased and the kids experienced a boost in self-esteem and a feeling of success and accomplishment too rare in their lives." Sound familiar?

Soon, Kurt got a job as a janitor back at Aberdeen High, spending most of his days scraping gum off the bottoms of desks. It was the last place on earth he wanted to be. One day, he smuggled home a sample case of shaving cream and decorated a doll with it so it looked like something out of *The Exorcist*, with the green, slimy goo hanging out of its mouth. He hung the doll by its neck in the window that overlooked the sidewalk, just to freak out the rednecks.

"I had the apartment decorated in typical punk rock fashion with baby dolls hanging by their necks with blood all over them," says Kurt. "There was beer and puke and blood all over the carpet, garbage stacked up for months. I never did do the dishes. Jesse and I cooked food for about a week and then put all our greasy hamburger dishes in the sink and filled it up full of water and it sat there for the entire five months I was there." People would party at Kurt's place all the time and the bash would invariably peak with an all-out shaving cream war.

While hanging out at the Melvins' practice space, Chris Novoselic and Kurt had struck up a friendship. Chris mentioned that he played guitar and they would hang out and listen to music, drink, and make little movies with Chris's Super 8 camera. Sometimes Chris's girlfriend Shelli would come over to the apartment and party, too. They were outcasts and weirdos, but at least they were outcasts and weirdos together. "We all had so much in common," Shelli recalls. "It was like us against everybody else. It was great to have our own circle and we were really close-knit and nothing bugged us. If one person would do something, we wouldn't hold grudges and we were less jaded and more accepting of other things. It was really fun."

After three months, Jesse Reed moved out to join the Navy.

One day, Kurt was acid tripping with a friend who had come over to Kurt's place on a scooter. When the friend went downstairs to get something from his scooter, Kurt's redneck neighbor began beating up his friend because he had parked the scooter on his property. Kurt heard the commotion and dashed downstairs as his friend ran away. The neighbor settled for Kurt instead, eventually pushing Kurt into his apartment and punching and manhandling him for two hours like a cat playing with a mouse.

Eventually he stopped punching Kurt and sat down to rest. Then he looked around the room and noticed the mutilated Barbie dolls and the paintings of the three-headed babies and the graffiti and the garbage. And a flicker of fear and confusion crossed his face. "He started asking me questions," says Kurt. "Why did I do all that stuff to my room?" He started to shove Kurt around again and Kurt screamed until the landlady hollered upstairs that she was going to call the police. The bully ran away. Eventually the police came, but they advised Kurt not to antagonize his neighbor by pressing charges.

Kurt got his revenge. For a month afterward, his friends would come over and pound on the neighbor's walls and scream obscenities and death threats while the bully cowered in his apartment. Kurt says he left little presents on his doorstep, like a six-pack of beer with acid in it or a painting of a redneck hanging from a tree.

In retrospect, that whole story seems, shall we say, heavily embroidered. And it would be quite a feat to insert LSD into unopened cans of beer. Once again, it's apparently a dubious, self-serving account of Kurt retaliating against an antagonist.

Kurt stayed on for a couple of months after Reed left. At first he could sweet-talk the landlady into letting him pay his rent late, but she began to notice the condition of the apartment. Kurt's friends would write all over the walls in the stairway. The apartment itself was a shambles.

Kurt couldn't keep up with the rent and eventually moved out in the late fall of 1985, owing several months' rent. Unemployed and virtually penniless, he passed the time that winter by hanging out in the library reading books and writing poetry. At the end of the day, he'd buy a six-pack of beer and bring it over to a friend's house, where they would drink and eventually Kurt would crash on the couch. Other times, he'd sleep in a cardboard box on Dale Crover's porch, Chris and Shelli's van, or sneak back into his mother's house while she was at work and crawl up into the attic or sleep on the deck of the house overnight. And sometimes he'd sleep under the North Aberdeen Bridge, which crosses the Wishkah River near Wendy's house.

In fact, the whole sleeping-under-the-bridge scenario never happened. It was yet another fiction invented as a way of getting back at yet another antagonist: this time, his mother, for banishing him from the house.

As Wendy told me, "I don't think he was really *living* under there. He just wanted everybody to think he was." I fell for Kurt's version, and why not—it was a great story, told with unblinking earnestness, and it fit with "Something in the Way."

As a single male, Kurt qualified for forty dollars' worth of food stamps a month, but he rarely bought food with them. Instead, he and his friends would fan out around town and buy Jolly Rancher penny candies with the food stamps and use the change to buy a case of beer. The operation was an entire day's work.

He was rather proud of himself for being able to survive without having to have a job or a home. His only worries were being able to steal food, catch fish from the river, and get food stamps. And bum the occasional macaroni and cheese from his friends. "I was just living out the Aberdeen fantasy version of being a punk rocker," says Kurt. "It was really easy. It was nothing compared to what most kids are subjected to after they run away to the big city. There was no threat of danger, ever." Kurt would have moved to Seattle, but he was too intimidated by the big city to do it alone—he'd barely been out of the Aberdeen-Montesano area—and nobody else in Aberdeen was brave enough to make the move.

Sometimes he'd stop by Wendy's house and she'd make him lunch. "For my guilt over letting Kurt go and live with his dad," says Wendy, "I have always pampered Kurt. He would come to visit—'You want some lunch?' Fix, fix, fix. Because I was guilty, I was feeling horribly guilty."

Wendy became pregnant and was feeling depressed about what had become of Kurt. "I've really screwed up my first kid, so what am I doing having another one?" she remembers thinking to herself. "And he came home at one point when I was very pregnant and I was crying about it," she says. "He asked me what was the matter and I told him I felt so awful having one in the oven and one out on the streets and he just knelt down and put his arms around me and said he was doing fine and not to worry about him and that he was going to do just fine."

That winter, Kurt got together with Dale Crover on bass and Greg Hokanson on drums and began rehearsing some of his material. Once, the trio, which Kurt dubbed Fecal Matter, opened for the Melvins at the Spot Tavern, a beach bar in Moclips, a remote little town on the Washington coast. After a while, they ditched Hokanson, whom they didn't like much anyway. The two began rehearsing intensively in preparation for recording a demo tape. With Matt Lukin behind the wheel of the trusty blue Impala, they set out for the Seattle home of Kurt's aunt Mari the musician, who had a four-track tape recorder.

Mari was taken aback by the aggressiveness of Kurt's vocals. "She didn't have any idea that I was such an angry person," says Kurt. He recorded the guitars directly into the tape machine, a classic low-budget punk rock technique that he used again years later on *Nevermind*'s "Territorial Pissings." They recorded seven tracks with titles like "Sound of Dentage," "Bambi Slaughter" and "Laminated Effect," which sounds like a cross between *Nevermind*'s "Stay Away" and the MTV theme, as well as a slowed-down, instrumental version of "Downer," which would later appear on the *Bleach* album. The Fecal Matter tape contained some of the ingredients that would distinguish Kurt's later music—mainly the ultra-heavy riffing sparked by an ear for the hook, but it also had thrashworthy tempos and a gnarled sense of song structure as reminiscent of the Melvins as it is of Metallica. There were not yet any strong melodies to speak of and Kurt's vocals ranged from a gruff bark to a blood-curdling howl.

Some of the lyrics—difficult to decipher because of Kurt's garbled singing style, as well as the crudeness of the recordings—are metal nonsense, some are the typical know-it-all social commentary of a teenager. "Laminated Effect" pronounces that "We're living in a time of change" and reviles religious fundamentalists ("Maybe someday soon they'll realize they're wrong") while "Class of '86" rips on his stupid classmates. Throughout, you can hear odd-meter riffs and elements of Bay Area speed metal of the time; Kurt would soon drop those affectations like the proverbial hot potato.

Later, Kurt rehearsed the Fecal Matter songs for a while with Buzz Osborne on bass and former Melvins drummer Mike Dillard, but then Dillard lost interest and the project evaporated completely when, as Osborne remembers it, "Kurt got disgusted with it because I wouldn't buy a bass system and so he said that I wasn't dedicated enough."

#

Kurt had met a hardcore partyer named Steve Shillinger at Aberdeen High, where his father Lamont was (and still is) an English teacher. Shillinger had first noticed Kurt because he had written "Motörhead" on his Pee-Chee folder. Shillinger remembers tapes Kurt would make of his music—"Really cheesy heavy metal songs," as he recalls—with titles like "Suicide Samurai." The first time Shillinger and Kurt made plans to hang out together—at a Metal Church concert—Shillinger ditched him because "there wasn't enough booze to go around and I didn't know him that well."

Shillinger's friends had worn out their welcome with his parents, so when Kurt needed a place to stay, he befriended Shillinger's brother Eric. The Shillingers had five sons and one daughter, so another mouth to feed wasn't a big deal. Kurt wound up staying there for about eight months, beginning late that winter of 1985, and faithfully did his chores just like everyone else.

Eric also played guitar, and Steve Shillinger swears that Eric and Kurt would plug their guitars into the family stereo and play a particularly tasty section of Iron Maiden's "Rime of the Ancient Mariner." Both Eric and Kurt totally deny this, but as Shillinger says, "People often deny their past."

Hey, we all have musical skeletons in our closet. These days, it's pretty difficult to get mocked for a musical influence, but in the early '90s, it just wasn't cool for punk rockers to admit they used to be into Iron Maiden. Even at the height of his fame, Kurt didn't feel secure enough to acknowledge these things. He didn't want the cool kids to laugh at him. He didn't want to be shamed.

The Shillingers had taken in several "strays" over the years, and usually a day or two later, a concerned parent would call the house and ask whether the kid was there. Not this time. "We didn't hear word one from Kurt's mom the whole time he was there," says Lamont Shillinger.

And here, when Kurt was seventeen or eighteen, was some more "tough love."

That summer, Kurt intensified his long career as a graffitist. He'd been a vandal ever since he started getting drunk in seventh grade, but this summer's work was, as Kurt says, "the focused statement." He'd play the Bad Brains' *Rock for Light* album over and over by day, then drink and eat acid by night throughout that summer. He, Osborne, Steve Shillinger, and others started with marker pens, prowling the alleys behind the main streets of Aberdeen, writing provocative things like "ABORT CHRIST" and "GOD IS GAY" or spray-painting "QUEER" on four-by-four pickups (preferably with rifle rack) to annoy the rednecks. Other times they wrote deliberate nonsense like "AMPUTATE ACROBATS" or "BOAT AKK," just to baffle people.

One night they noticed a huge, ornate Pink Floyd mural which someone had painstakingly painted in one of the alleys. Its minutes were numbered. "We were freshly punk," Shillinger explains. "And we had spray paint."

Kurt had silver spray paint and Shillinger had black, and right over the "Pink,"

Shillinger wrote "Black"; over the "Floyd," Kurt wrote "Flag." "We had hippies who just wanted to kick our fuckin' asses the whole rest of the summer," says Shillinger, still gleeful. "We were like hunted underground figures."

About a decade earlier, Pink Floyd had been *détourned* by another soon-to-be-famous punk singer. In the summer of 1975, London clothing shop owner Malcolm McLaren and his friend Bernard Rhodes spotted a scrawny, intense-looking kid with green hair and a Pink Floyd T-shirt on which he had scrawled the words "I hate" above the band's name. McLaren asked the kid to audition to be the singer of a band they were forming to promote McLaren's new clothing line. Nineteen-year-old John Lydon, soon christened Johnny Rotten, got the gig, and the band became the Sex Pistols.

Kurt was out on a graffiti raid with Osborne and Chris, who had just spray-painted the words "HOMO SEX RULES" on the side of a bank wall when a police car appeared out of nowhere and caught Kurt in its headlights. Chris and Osborne ran away and hid in a garbage dumpster, but Kurt was hauled in to the police station and took the rap. A police report detailed the contents of his pockets: one guitar pick, one key, one can of beer, one mood ring, and one cassette by the militant punk band Millions of Dead Cops. He got a $180 fine and a thirty-day suspended sentence.

Vandalism wasn't anything new to Kurt. While he was still in high school, he and his friends would find an abandoned house, or one that was in the midst of being vacated, break in and destroy everything in sight. Kurt had always wanted to rent one particular house that stood in a field because it was a perfect band rehearsal pad but the owners repeatedly refused to let him rent the place, always renting it to somebody else. Late one night, Kurt was walking home from a party with a friend and they noticed the house was vacant again. They broke in and went berserk, throwing the appliances around the house, taking care to break every single window and smashing everything else to bits with a weight set. "I got my revenge," says Kurt.

Eventually, he took a job as a maintenance man at the YMCA about a block away from the Shillingers' house, mostly so he could afford some musical equipment, should he suddenly find a band. In the morning, he'd walk over to work, check in with his boss, then go back over to the house and sit around and watch TV and drink until quitting time. Sometimes he'd have to clean off the graffiti that he himself had written the night before. A little later, Kurt got the only regular job he's ever really loved—as a swimming instructor for kids age three through seven.

According to Kurt's diaries, that was at the Aberdeen YMCA from May 1986 to September 1986, when he was nineteen.

Kurt's first live performance was with Dale Crover on bass drum, snare and cymbal, Buzz Osborne on bass, and Kurt essentially rapping his poetry over improvised heavy rock at GESCCO Hall, a barnlike performance space in Olympia associated with the Evergreen State College. The trio was originally called Brown Towel, but a misspelling on the poster made it Brown Cow. Kurt was extremely nervous. "I had to get drunk," he says. "I got totally wasted on wine."

Attendance was sparse and the reaction was lackluster, but two people in the audience—Olympia scenester Slim Moon and his buddy Dylan Carlson, a self-made intellectual who played guitar in several bands around town—were blown away. The two knew Kurt as a member of the Melvins entourage, but now he was something more. "That's when our perception of Kurt changed from the dweeby trench coat new waver that hung out with the Melvins," says Slim Moon, "to realizing, 'Wait, this guy has talent.'" Carlson, now one half of the ultra-heavy guitar noise duo Earth, walked up to Kurt afterward and told him the show was one of the best things he'd ever seen. They began bumping into each other at cool shows in Olympia and soon became fast friends, as they are to this day.

Meanwhile, Kurt had begun to hang out with a drug dealer nicknamed Grunt (not his real name). "He was this total drug fiend stoner," says Kurt. "He was like the overlord king of drugs." Grunt was a despicable person, but people hung out with him because he could get practically any drug. No one knew it at the time, but he got his wares by burglarizing pharmacies along with his lover, sidekick, and whipping boy. Grunt began bringing Kurt handfuls of Percodans, an opiate-derived painkiller, each in their little foil and plastic pouches, charging him only a dollar a day. Kurt liked Percodans because they made him feel "relaxed." "It just felt like the best euphoric state that I'd ever been in," he says. "It was just like sleeping. It was as close to sleep as I could get without actually having to sleep."

Kurt was so naive about drugs that he didn't know Percodan was addictive and got hooked without even realizing it. He eventually took up to ten Percodans a day and was "getting real itchy." After about two months, Grunt's supply ran out, and Kurt had to go cold turkey. "It wasn't that bad," he says. "I had diarrhea and I sweated in Eric's bed for a couple of days."

One night that summer, Grunt and Kurt did heroin together. Grunt shot Kurt up. "It was really scary," says Kurt. "I always wanted to do it—I always knew that I

would." He's not exactly sure why he was so sure he'd eventually do it. **"I don't know,"** says Kurt. **"I just knew."**

So here are Kurt's first encounters with opioids. Kurt's experience was a lot like so many people who became addicted to prescription opioids decades later: their supply of pharmaceuticals ran out, so they turned to heroin. Ironically, Kurt was solidly in the rural working-class demographic of so many prescription opioid abusers in the 2000s.

This was long before drug addiction (as well as suicide) was recognized as a "disease of despair."

Note Kurt made no mention of doing heroin to alleviate stomach pain. It was just for the "euphoric state."

But was that the entire reason Kurt did heroin? There was that euphoria, the illusion of a blissful, even loving embrace that heroin provides. But I believe there was more to it than that. Since I met Kurt, I've met a few people who were as exquisitely sensitive as he was—all of them, perhaps not coincidentally, were artists. By exquisitely sensitive I mean that they sense every feeling in the room, things that most people are oblivious to. It's hard for some people to understand that—it's like claiming that someone is able to see a color that no one else can see. But that's really the way those rare people are—they involuntarily pick up on cues from all around the room. It can be torturous to be bombarded by that many signals, a deafening cacophony that can't be switched off. It can make them really cranky—or much worse. All too often, people like that turn to opiates or alcohol to keep it all down to a dull roar. As another drug-abusing visionary, the Fall's Mark E. Smith, once said, "I used to be psychic, but I drank my way out of it." And that never leads anywhere good.

High sensitivity is a bona fide psychological phenomenon. In a November 2021 piece in the *Guardian* about the "highly sensitive," clinical research psychologist Dr. Elaine Aron said it applies to up to 20 percent of the population.

"They tend to take in much more information from lots of different kinds of stimuli," explained clinical psychologist Dr. Genevieve von Lob. "And then they're processing it more deeply than a non-sensitive person—and because they're taking in so much at once they can get much more overstimulated, overaroused and overwhelmed."

A lot of highly sensitive people have low self-esteem, von Lob added, because they've been told all their life that, basically, they're too sensitive.

"They have this great capacity for empathy," von Lob continued. "So that's really good in leadership roles. They often are creative people, so they could be the visionaries of our world—they come up with different ways of thinking from the mainstream. They have a very strong sense of justice and fairness. They're very good listeners, and question rules that don't make sense." That all, of course, describes Kurt to a tee.

The article noted that "it [is] common to report crying at emotional adverts"—which was exactly what I saw Kurt do.

Besides, by then he'd done just about every drug except PCP ("I'd always heard about people freaking out and jumping off of buildings after they did it"). Heroin was the final frontier. Another attraction was the decadent, outlaw glamour the drug had acquired through its association with rockers such as Keith Richards and Iggy Pop. "Iggy Pop, he was my total idol," says Kurt. "I just wanted to try it because I knew that I liked opiates. It was such a scarce thing to find heroin in Aberdeen that I just thought I would try it." Kurt knew there was no chance of getting hooked on the drug because it was impossible to get a steady supply in Aberdeen.

Kurt was probably confusing the jumping off buildings thing with the sad fate of Diane Linkletter, daughter of popular radio and TV show host Art Linkletter. She jumped to her death from a sixth-floor window in 1969. With no supporting evidence, her grieving father blamed an LSD flashback. President Nixon invited Art Linkletter to the White House and used the tragedy to bolster his recently announced "war on drugs." The Diane Linkletter incident became embedded in the popular culture of the time: the word was, if you do acid, you might jump off a building.

Heroin's illusion of euphoria may also have had something to do with it. Euphoria of any kind was in short supply in Kurt's life. Beginning in high school, he had become so angry at his surroundings that he developed nervous tics like popping his knuckles, scratching his face, and flipping his hair compulsively. His eye twitched. He thought he might be becoming schizophrenic.

It's amazing, the different psychological conditions that Kurt feared he suffered from: depression, manic depression, neurosis, hyperactivity, paranoia, and now schizophrenia. I'm not sure how Kurt settled on a diagnosis of schizophrenia, but from the beginning, declarations of mental illness were a staple of punk rock (see Black Flag's "Nervous Breakdown" and "Depression," and the Ramones' "Gimme Gimme Shock Treatment," "Bad Brain," and "Teenage Lobotomy") as a metaphor for not fitting into society.

"It was a mixture of hating people so much because they didn't live up to my expectations and just being so fed up with being around the same kind of idiot all the time," he says. "It was obvious in my face and how I reacted toward people that I couldn't stand them. I had this personal vendetta toward them because they were so macho and manly and stupid. I started to become aware of this—that people were noticing that I had this hatred toward a lot of people."

The Amplified Come as You Are

Kurt was convinced that everyone knew he felt this way, which only made him feel more neurotic. He grew more and more paranoid because he was sure everyone knew he could freak out at any time. "They thought I was the kid who was most likely to succeed—to bring an AK-47 to the school and blow everybody away," Kurt says. "I just had this air about me that I would eventually explode one day. People eventually just stayed away from me."

He said this seven years before Columbine. It's the second reference he makes in this book to school shootings.

"Maybe Kurt was exasperated by humanity itself," Krist said to interviewer John Hughes in 2008. "Exasperated, that weight of, 'Oh, how do I fit in this world?'"

Opiates like Percodan gave Kurt a sense of relief; on opiates, he didn't hate people so much. "I had a little bit of affection for them or at least could see past the superficiality of their personality and think of them as a real person," he says. "Maybe they had a fucked-up childhood or maybe it's their environment that's making them this way. It relieved some of the animosity that I had toward people. I needed to do that because I was tired of hating people so much and being so judgmental toward everyone. It just allowed me to have a few days of peace of mind."

A 2018 *New York Times* article quoted a former heroin addict about the feeling of being high: "I remember feeling like I was exhaling from holding my breath for my whole life. Just intense relief from suffering." In other words, a temporary nirvana.

Meanwhile, although Kurt and Eric had started off as friends, their friendship had begun to disintegrate, perhaps because of a musical rivalry. The antagonism built and built until one night, eight months after Kurt arrived at the Shillingers', when Kurt, Eric, and Steve Shillinger came home from three different parties, all quite drunk. Steve says it was over a frozen pizza pie, while Kurt thinks it was because he wanted to sleep and Eric wanted to watch TV, but for some reason a fight broke out between Kurt and Eric. Kurt declared a cigarette break and then the fight resumed in the backyard. "There was actual blood on the wall," says Steve. "I don't want to get involved in who won the fight—all I'll say is, it was a very bloody and terrible battle."

Kurt beat a hasty exit after it was all over. The next day, he paid Steve Shillinger ten dollars to put his stuff into garbage bags and take it to Dale Crover's house. Kurt stayed at Buzz Osborne's house for a few days, then briefly moved back in with Wendy.

Mr. Shillinger asked Kurt to come back, but he refused and went back to the bridge, where every once in a while he'd catch fish and eat them until one day someone told him they were poisonous. Other times, he slept in the apartment above Chris's mom's beauty parlor.

Yeah, I'm not so sure about this bridge thing. Kurt had gone on fishing trips with Don's wife's family, so he might have been familiar with how to catch, gut, and cook a fish outdoors. But he would have needed some equipment for all that. Also, the Wishkah River has tides, which would surely roust anyone sleeping on its banks.

He'd have to wake up by seven in the morning so he could get out of there before she came to work.

In the fall of 1986, Kurt got Wendy to put down a deposit on 1000½ East Second Street in Aberdeen, a decrepit little shack a few hundred yards from her house. It rented for only a hundred dollars a month, perhaps because the porch was falling off the front of the house. "It was the bottom of houses," Kurt recalls, but at least it was his. It had two small bedrooms and two small living rooms. His housemate was Melvins bassist Matt Lukin, who was also a trained carpenter. Lukin had to do a lot of work on the house before it was even livable.

As usual, hygiene was not a priority. If you drank a beer, you could just throw the can on the floor. And with all the partying going on at the shack, the floor was covered with festive detritus. They didn't have a fridge, so they kept all the food in an unplugged old icebox out on the back porch. They cooked in a toaster oven. Wendy stopped by occasionally with care packages of food.

One day Kurt bought about half a dozen turtles and put them in a bathtub in the middle of the living room; a terrarium attached to the tub took up most of the rest of the room. For irrigation, carpenter Lukin drilled a hole in the floor and drained the smelly hamburger-meat-and-turtle-poop-fouled water into the floor underneath the house. But the foundation was so rotten that water would rise up into the floorboards. "It was, needless to say, a very smelly, very odorous place," says Kurt.

Kurt felt a special attraction to turtles. "There's a fascination with them I really can't describe," he says. "Turtles basically have this 'fuck you' attitude—'I'm stuck in the tank, I'm miserable, I hate you, and I'm *not* going to perform for you.'"

Then there are those protective shells. "Actually those shells really aren't that helpful," Kurt says. "It's part of their spine and it's real sensitive—if you knock on the shell it hurts them, so it really isn't the protective covering that everyone thinks it is. If they fall on their back, it'll split open and they'll die. It's like having your spine on your outside."

"I'm miserable," those turtles seemed to say, "I hate you, and I'm *not* going to perform for you"—and yet they were "sensitive." I'm not sure that even Kurt was aware of how perfect that metaphor was.

Kurt got a job at the Polynesian Hotel in Ocean Shores, a coastal resort about twenty miles from Aberdeen, as a janitor, fireplace cleaner, and "maintenance butt-boy." Once again, he didn't exactly strive to be an ideal worker. Instead of cleaning or fixing things in the hotel rooms, he'd just walk into an unoccupied room, turn on the TV, and take a nap.

According to Kurt's journals, he worked at the Polynesian from September 1986 through June 1987, so he was nineteen going on twenty at this point.

Kurt was always on the lookout for a cheap new high. "Back then, none of us had any money so you don't want to spend a bunch of money on coke and stuff," recalls Lukin. "There was a lot of people who got into cough syrup to get high. I remember this guy I went to high school with who ate handfuls of aspirin and got high off of that."

At the time, a lot of kids in Aberdeen were doing acid, not to mention the powerful local marijuana, inexplicably nicknamed "affy bud." Lukin, Jesse Reed, Kurt, and a few other stoners were sitting around one night bemoaning the fact that they were tired of *all* the usual highs. Then Reed remembered all those cans of shaving cream that Kurt had hung on to ever since they shared an apartment together. The shaving cream came with a little rubber stopper on the bottom of the can where the propellant was pumped in. Inhaling the propellant produced a buzz not unlike that of nitrous oxide. The manufacturers of the shaving cream have since altered the stopper on the can to discourage such abuse.

The problem was, a lot of it would escape, so Reed showed them how to tape a toilet paper roll onto the bottom, poke a hole in the side, and insert a screwdriver in it to pry the gasket loose, then inhale it like a bong. They all ran down to the 7-Eleven and each bought more shaving cream. There was a brief panic when they found the gas lowered their voices—but not permanently—but the high was decent. "We were all yelling at Kurt that he shouldn't have wasted all that shaving cream on decorating the doll that summer," says Lukin. "We could have been getting high off it!"

And then in the wee hours of one winter morning, Kurt came to Wendy's house. "Mom," Kurt called up to her, his voice weak with fear, "I've lost my hand.

I've burnt my hand and it's just gone." He burst into tears. Kurt had been making french fries, his staple food, and severely burned his hand on the hot grease. "It was horrible," she says. "It was burned clear down—it was the most sickening thing I ever saw and I had to bandage it twice a day and peel off the—it was horrible."

Kurt had already been to the hospital, where a doctor had bandaged it up and told Kurt he'd never play guitar again. But then Wendy took him to a specialist she knew from working at the Grays Harbor College nursing program. Now, you can't even see a scar.

While he recuperated, Kurt stayed home and tried to play guitar. Without any income from work, he was forced to live on little else but rice for several months. Every once in a while he'd splurge on a frozen Salisbury steak. "I was starving to death, living in this pigsty," Kurt says, "not being able to play guitar, with the threat of the landlady calling me up every day reminding me that I owed her money. It was just a real sketchy scene." Kurt didn't know where he was going to live pretty soon.

Kurt badly wanted to form a band with Chris, but Chris didn't seem interested. "I kept always making it obvious that I wanted someone to play with in a band," says Kurt, "but still Chris never wanted to." Kurt even lent Chris his amplifier for a week and a half to try to butter him up. But Chris didn't respond to Kurt's overtures and even made Kurt come to his house to retrieve his own amp. "It sounded really nice," says Chris, "but I decided to give it back to him."

Here we have the fabled Northwestern passive-aggressive approach: rather than outright asking Krist if he would like to start a band, Kurt courted Krist by "always making it obvious that I wanted someone to play with in a band." That mentality is crucial to understanding Kurt as a person, as well as the relationships he had with various band members and others around him.

Kurt would slide Chris a copy of the Fecal Matter tape now and then as a not-so-subtle hint, but Chris never said a word about it. Then, a whole year after the demo had been recorded and three years after they first met, Chris told Kurt, "I finally listened to that tape you made. It's pretty good. We should start a band."

Kurt had a guitar and a Peavey amp. Chris used to have an amp, but he had to give it to Matt Lukin in return for bailing him out of jail after a scuffle with some rednecks in the parking lot of the Aberdeen 7-Eleven. For a P.A., they used another guitar amp and a cheap microphone with the diaphragm taped to it—it was a wreck, but it worked. There was an empty apartment above Mrs. Novoselic's beauty shop and they'd play there for hours, with Chris on bass and

Kurt on guitar and someone named Bob McFadden whom Chris recalls only as "some jock guy" who happened to own a drum set. Unfortunately, the place soon became a hangout just like the Melvins' practice space and Chris eventually had to post a sign which read "This is not a big crash pad. So just get out of here because we want to rehearse."

The underground scene was so small in Aberdeen that even Cure fans with their trendy quiffs and goth clothes would hang around the practice space. Chris and Shelli called them the Haircut 100 Club. "We weren't tight with them because they were more concerned with the fashion aspect of it," says Shelli. "We were just concerned with fucking around."

The band worked up a little material but for some reason, the project eventually fell apart after about a month and all three went their separate ways. Chris and Shelli went to Arizona to look for work.

Kurt didn't like the guys who would hang out at the shack. They tended to be underage drinkers who used the house as a place to get trashed. Lukin's work as a cabinet maker was far from steady, so more often than not he and his drinking buddies would be up until all hours, while Kurt had to get up to go to work at the resort. After five months, Lukin realized he should move out.

Dylan Carlson mentioned that he was unemployed, so Kurt told him about these great jobs they could get laying carpet in a hotel out at Ocean Shores. Carlson was going to take Lukin's room at the shack, but he stayed only two weeks because the carpet-laying job never panned out. They went out to Ocean Shores early one morning to find that the boss was so drunk that he couldn't get off the floor to unlock the door. When they went out there a second time, the door was unlocked, but the boss had passed out in front of it, blocking the way. Carlson gave up, but Kurt tried a third time. He got in, but the boss went out to a bar and got falling-down drunk. The great carpet-laying job never materialized.

Kurt had been going more and more frequently to Olympia, about fifty miles east of Aberdeen, with the Melvins. The state capital, Olympia, is the home of the Evergreen State College, a haven for bohemians and misfits of all stripes and a hotbed of adventurous independent music. Kurt went there most weekends to check out bands. Olympia was a small town but it had national indie scene connections that extended from Evergreen's KAOS radio station, *Op* magazine (which has since metamorphosed into *Option* magazine), fanzine publisher Bruce Pavitt, and Calvin Johnson's K Records.

This is pivotal. Evergreen was where kids who were usually several rungs up the socioeconomic ladder from Kurt got a very progressive education. These weren't jean-jacketed stoners with peach-fuzz mustaches: Evergreeners were mostly affluent sophisticates from all over the country, places Kurt had only heard about. Then again, maybe he hadn't even heard about tony places like Darien and Mill Valley and Shaker Heights. Evergreen hipsters weren't into metal and hard rock, or even traditional punk, really—they were into something quite different.

KAOS was the epicenter of Evergreen's bohemian culture. John Foster, the station's visionary director, was one of the first to attach a sociopolitical significance to the idea of music on independent labels. Independent music could be more responsive to regional culture—defying the homogenizing effects of mass media, it was decentralized and egalitarian, and it didn't directly feed multinational corporations. It was kind of like what folk music used to be. Foster instituted a rule that 80 percent of the music the station broadcast had to be on independent labels, a policy that continues there to this day.

The youth culture there wasn't into hard rock, but instead favored a kind of naive music, pigeonholed as "love rock," made by the likes of Jad Fair and the group Beat Happening, led by Calvin Johnson. Johnson dominated the scene and inspired a legion of clones—whom Kurt calls "the Calvinists"—who talked and dressed just like him, aspiring to an innocent childlike state.

It was a whole community of geeks—they were even dismissed by punk rockers. The Calvinists didn't take drugs—at least they said they didn't—and wore their hair short. Everyone played in each other's band, everyone slept with one another. They had their own coffee shop, their own record store, and, practically speaking, KAOS had become their own radio station. "They started up their own little planet," says Kurt.

They also had their own record label. Along with Candice Pedersen, Johnson ran K Records, a small but well-connected indie label which also distributed like-minded foreign bands such as Young Marble Giants, Kleenex, and the Vaselines.

K wasn't just about being what some people might call "twee." John Foster's antipathy for corporate culture was a huge influence on Calvin Johnson, and it became a foundational principle of K. In the label's first newsletter, a comic strip depicts the K logo with arms and legs, facing down a monster: "Our hero battles the many-armed corporate ogre."

Kurt didn't completely buy the K ethos. He liked to wear his hair long and he liked to take drugs. But he did like the music and its message. "It opened up new doors to music that I'd never heard before," Kurt says. "It made me realize that for years I hadn't looked back on my childhood. I tried to forget about it. I'd just forgotten about it. It made me look back on my childhood and have fond memories of it. It was just a nice reminder of innocence." "To try to remind me to stay a child," Kurt got a tattoo of the K logo, a "K" inside a simple shield, on his left forearm.

After years of being trapped in Aberdeen, intensely alienated from nearly everyone, Kurt made it out of town and found a club that he wanted to join. But maybe he didn't feel worthy. His low self-esteem, the shame of being from Aberdeen, and musical and class differences (which were not unrelated) with the Evergreeners made it intimidating for Kurt. He abandoned heavy metal and began to embrace indie rock with the unique zeal of the convert.

The Calvinists' preoccupation with childlike innocence might have been a smokescreen for the sex and drugs that were actually happening in the Olympia scene, but it was also a pointed rebuke to the machismo and obsession with technique and big-ticket production values that permeated popular music and the culture in general. And many Olympia scenesters barely knew how to play their instruments so, in classic punk rock tradition, they made a virtue out of a liability.

The Olympia look was early-'60s nerd, perhaps simply because that was the era of clothing that could be found in thrift stores back then. (Olympia is surely where Kurt picked up his taste for vintage cardigans.) The music also harked to that time: influenced by surf rock and Kennedy-era pop but played with as little technique as necessary, it was the diametric opposite of the loud, aggressive, and highly technical hard rock and metal Kurt dabbled in, which was a more workingman's sound. In other words, Kurt was confronted with the daunting prospect of affluent bohemian college-kid cool.

As far as the K tattoo, creative people often admire the unselfconscious artistry of children. Also, Kurt missed his former self, the one who, as his mother said, "got up every day with such joy that there was another day to be had." And after all the vandalism and drug abuse Kurt had perpetrated, it's easy to see why he'd be attracted to "a nice reminder of innocence." Now think ahead to the cover of *Nevermind*.

Knowing Kurt's outspoken admiration for childhood, one begins to see how withering it was later when he dubbed the executives at his management company and label "the grown-ups." And if they were "the grown-ups," then that made Kurt a kid: pure, blameless, and free from responsibility.

###

Kurt remained at the shack for another two months after Lukin left, owing the landlady back rent.

In the meantime, Kurt started seeing a young woman named Tracy Marander. She wasn't like any of the other girls he knew. She had a zebra-stripe coat and her hair was dyed fire-engine red and she lived in Olympia. Tracy liked to party and had her share of eccentricities, but she was also a placid, nurturing soul. After a few weeks, she became Kurt's first serious girlfriend.

Tracy and Kurt had met a year or so before, in front of the Gorilla Gardens, a barnlike all-ages punk club (now defunct) in the Chinatown section of Seattle. They met through their mutual friend Buzz Osborne. She and her boyfriend were sitting in their car drinking beer and talking to Buzz and Kurt, who were also drinking beer. The meeting was cut short when Tracy noticed a couple of cops heading their way and took off in the car, leaving Kurt and Buzz behind to get busted.

Tracy thought Kurt was nice, if a little young-looking. He was skinny and had short hair. "I was struck by how blue his eyes were," she recalls. "I'd never seen eyes that blue before."

After befriending Chris and Shelli, she became a cling-on and met Kurt again a year later while they hung out at Buzz Osborne's parents' house one day watching Buzz and Chris drink Mad Dog. After Kurt left, Buzz informed her that Kurt was the guy who made the really cool Kiss mural on the side of the Melvins' tour van—known as the Mel-Van—using Magic Markers. Every time a pen ran out, he'd go into the Shop-Rite in Montesano and steal another one. "I thought that was kind of cool," says Tracy.

Tracy is a sweet person, one of the nicest characters in this whole story. Even Courtney liked her. Tracy was the only one of Kurt's ex-girlfriends to be invited to a very small ceremony on Memorial Day 1999, when six-year-old Frances Cobain placed some of her father's ashes in a creek near Kurt's sister Kim's home, a few miles south of Olympia.

Tracy and Kurt were together from early 1987 to mid 1990.

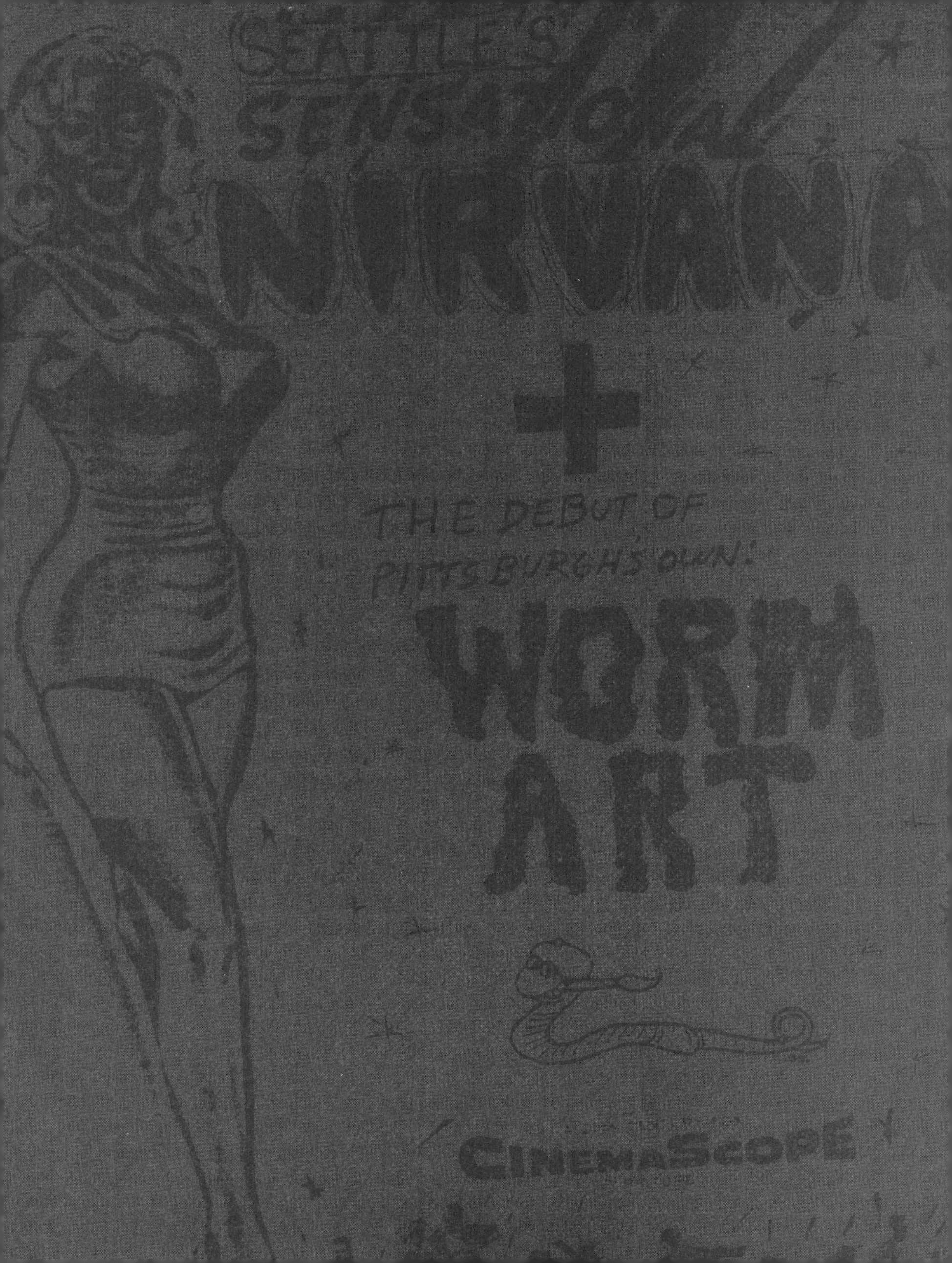

chapter three

THAT'S MY BROTHER CHRIS. HE LISTENS TO PUNK ROCK.

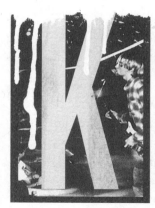

Krist Anthony Novoselic was born on May 16, 1965, in Compton, California. His parents, Krist and Maria, were Croatian immigrants; Mr. Novoselic (the name means "new settler" in Croatian) moved to the United States in 1963, his wife-to-be the following year. They set up house in Gardena, California, and Mr. Novoselic got a job driving a truck for Sparkletts drinking water.

The early '90s were an intense time to be of Croatian descent. In the late '80s, Yugoslavia began to disintegrate into different states, and Croatia declared independence in 1991. Around the same time, the neighboring region of Bosnia and Herzegovina also began to disintegrate along ethnic lines. Serbian rebels, intent on claiming their own territory within the region, began a massive attack on Croatian targets, killing or massacring at least 150,000 human beings, torturing or raping tens of thousands, and displacing hundreds of thousands more. The atrocities popularized the term "ethnic cleansing." Some Croatians were also guilty of such crimes. The horrific fighting continued intermittently until 1995.

For a May 1993 *Spin* feature story, Krist traveled to the region and spoke to young people on the street, as well as explaining the causes and brutality of the conflict. He wound up at the Hard Rock Cafe in Zagreb, a meeting place for the city's privileged young elite. In the piece, people at the next table over openly mocked Krist for ordering the local plum brandy—a "bumpkin" drink—instead of premium Western liquor. "Isn't that what cracked the Berlin Wall," Krist wrote, "the aspirations to go live in the west, to have the 'good life'? But most of the people who will live through this won't even have that dream. Just injustice and pain."

During a band visit to New York in 1993, I went out to a bar with Krist and a couple of people from Nirvana's crew. One of the crew began playing pool with a fellow who had an Eastern European accent. Turns out the guy was Serbian—the mortal enemy of the Croatians. The crew member was fiercely loyal to the band, very much including Krist, and he began taunting the guy: "Hey, chetnik! Chetnik!"—which was a derogatory term for Serbs, sort of like calling someone a Nazi. It got ugly really fast, as you can imagine. A fistfight broke out, and both men essentially punched each other out the front door and onto the street. It was like something out of a Western movie. Typically, Krist—big, physically strong, and a born peacemaker—was the one who broke it up.

After moving around to a series of apartments with Chris and his younger brother Robert, the Novoselics got a modest house and then another, nicer one in 1973 when Chris's sister Diana was born.

Although busing had been instituted in California, in Gardena kids of different races didn't mix—except for one group. "There was the one scene with all of us who were in bonehead math," says Novoselic. "We were totally integrated. Whoever didn't really fit in all bonded together and there was no racial thing. So integration did work.

"Robert and I were kind of big boys and we used to get into trouble," says Chris of his preteen years. "Slash tires, stuff like that. My dad would just have to whip us, because that's all he knew how to do. We were scared of him. But it wasn't like he was an abuser—I don't think he abused us at all. It's not like he would slap us for *anything*. It was action and reaction.

"Like Robert, he got glasses and the first day he got his glasses, he busted 'em," Chris continues. "That's just Robert. We'd just do shit like that. Go throw rocks at houses, throw rocks at cars. There was a time when vandalism was really cool. We really got into vandalism. Throwing eggs . . ."

So: Krist had a tough, working-class father, trouble in school, a lot of youthful vandalism . . . just like Kurt.

Chris says he and his brother straightened out by the time the family moved to Aberdeen in 1979, when Chris was fourteen. Property values in Southern California were getting too high for the Novoselic family and they could get a nice house for a little money in Aberdeen. Besides, there were lots of other Croatian families in the area. Mr. Novoselic got a job as a machinist at one of the town's many lumber mills.

After sunny California, Chris didn't like Aberdeen at all. "It's got everything against it," he says. "It's cloudy and rainy, there's mud in the streets from all the trucks. The buildings are all kind of dirty. It's like an East German town or something. Everything is so damp down there that the wood just gets kind of soft and things fall apart."

Cloudy, rainy, dirty, and damp: there is a compelling argument that Northwest grunge was deeply influenced by the region's terroir. The dank, overcast climate fosters mold and moss everywhere, and all the rain means a thin layer of finely spattered mud tends to settle on things. It's also an incredibly beautiful place with vast, snow-capped mountains and towering pines.

"You gotta understand Seattle," Seattle native and Guns N' Roses bassist Duff McKagan told me for a 1992 *Rolling Stone* piece about the Seattle scene. "It's grungy. People are into rock & roll and into noise, and they're building airplanes all the time, and there's a lot of noise, and there's rain and musty garages. Musty garages create a certain noise." And that noise, as Sub Pop's Jonathan Poneman put it in that same piece, inspired grunge's "backwoods yeti stomp."

Like Kurt, Chris had a hard time at school because he didn't fit in. The California stereotype held true—things really were mellower there. "I was perplexed by the weird, twisted social scene they had in Aberdeen," says Novoselic. "It just seemed like people were a lot more uptight and judgmental."

Some people attribute that uptight, judgmental streak to the area's Scandinavian heritage, some to the fact that the wet weather keeps people cooped up together for much of the year, so they have to keep confrontation to a minimum. But it's a widely acknowledged aspect of Washington mores. And, for outsiders, it takes some getting used to.

Aberdonians wore leather tennis shoes and elephant flares, while Chris sported deck shoes and straight-leg Levi's. You were a geek if you wore straight-leg pants. "Three years later," says Chris, "everybody was wearing straight-leg pants. And I suffered for nothing."

And he was very tall—he was six foot seven by the time he graduated from high school. His parents were hoping he'd become a basketball player but his height only made Chris awkward. "I was just weird and maladjusted more than anything else," Chris says. "I was really depressed when I came up to Aberdeen. I couldn't get along with anybody. I'd go home and sleep all afternoon and listen to music by myself. I couldn't get along with those kids. They were assholes. They treated me really badly. I didn't understand. They just weren't cool."

Chris was into bands like Led Zeppelin, Devo, Black Sabbath, and Aerosmith while his peers were into Top 40, perhaps because that was all the local radio station played. They'd play Top 40 radio on the school bus and Chris was forced to endure the sound of Kenny Rogers warbling "Coward of the County." Over and over again.

Luckily, geography smiled on Chris Novoselic. His family's house was on Think of Me Hill, the tallest hill in Aberdeen (named because at the turn of the century there was a big sign on the hill overlooking the town that advertised Think of Me tobacco), so he got excellent radio reception—on clear days, he could get Portland, Oregon. He'd lie in his room depressed and listen to the hip Seattle rock stations on his clock radio for hours.

That's My Brother Chris. He Listens to Punk Rock.

93

Neighborhoods in the hills tend to be more affluent, and sure enough, Krist's family's place was bigger and nicer than Kurt's mom's place, which was down in the area Aberdonians call "the Flats."

Location and the radio helped make Krist a musical sophisticate. In California, he had heard FM radio stations playing hard rock like Kiss, Aerosmith, and Led Zeppelin— music that was a little precocious for kids his age. Up on Think of Me Hill, he was one of the few people in town who could pick up the cool stations in Portland and Seattle that played new wave and maybe some punk. And when he lived for a year as a teen in Zadar, Croatia, on the twelfth floor of a high-rise apartment, he could tune in Italian stations and, on shortwave, the BBC, and discovered Elvis Costello, Madness, and various other post-punk bands on the Stiff Records label.

By June of 1980, Chris's parents got so worried about his depression that they sent him to live with relatives in Croatia. Chris had picked up Croatian "around the house," and is still fluent in it. He loved living there—he made lots of friends and the schools were excellent. He even heard something there called "punk rock," and discovered the Sex Pistols, the Ramones, and even some Yugoslavian punk bands. It didn't make too much of a dent, however. "It was just music to me," Chris recalls. "It didn't really mean anything to me—it was just music that I liked." After a year, his parents called him back home.

"There were a lot of dysfunctional things that are pretty personal," Krist explained about his move to Croatia to interviewer John Hughes, chief oral historian for the Washington State Legacy Project, in 2008. "I came back [to Aberdeen] because there were some issues with my family. And I don't really want to get into that much more." The bottom line is, there was some turmoil in his life.

"I was just in a weird limbo," Chris says. He began drinking and smoking pot heavily. "I've always been a big drinker," says Chris. "When I drink, I just don't stop. I like to drink because you're in some weird cartoon land where anything goes. Your vision is blurry and nothing and everything makes sense. It's crazy. It's a different reality and a different world of consciousness."

"I guess I've always been maladjusted and a lot of it has to do with just dysfunctional circumstances that I've been in," Krist told John Hughes. "And a lot of times they were out of my control. And so I just needed to sometimes get away and the only way I could do it would be to smoke pot, and alcohol."

So he was doing the same thing as Kurt: self-medicating. But together, Kurt and Krist realized that making music was also an effective antidote to whatever was troubling them.

The Amplified Come as You Are

Chris became well known on the party circuit. "You'd go to parties and people would be like 'Hey, Novie!'" says Matt Lukin. "They always knew him as the big wacky guy because he was always doing weird things. They just thought he was kind of weird. He'd go to parties and jump around."

He had some people to hang out with, but he was hard pressed to call them friends. "I hung out with them because I had nowhere else to go," says Chris. "It was kind of odd and uncomfortable." He finally got a job at the local Taco Bell and threw himself into work, working every night and not socializing, just saving money. By senior year of high school, he had bought a car, some stereo speakers, and a guitar. He took some lessons along with his brother Robert and told his teacher, Warren Mason—the same guy who taught Kurt—that he really wanted to play the blues. He quit after a few months and then woodshedded intensively in his bedroom, patiently working out the licks to old B.B. King records with his brother.

The blues doesn't figure much in Nirvana's music, but if you want to talk about music that exorcises emotional pain, look no further.

Then he met Buzz Osborne.

Chris worked at the Taco Bell with a fellow named Bill Hull, whose principal claim to fame was that he had been expelled from Aberdeen High for planting a pipe bomb in the greenhouse. When Hull got transferred to Montesano High, he met Buzz and Matt Lukin. One day, Buzz and Matt visited Hull at the Taco Bell. "And there was this big tall doofy guy back there singing along to the Christmas carols they're playing on the Muzak," Lukin recalls. Chris mentioned that he played guitar and later Osborne called up and invited him to hang out in Montesano.

They talked politics and Osborne turned him on to some cool music—blazing music from the Vibrators, Sex Pistols, Flipper, Black Flag, Circle Jerks. "It was like wow, *punk rock*," says Novoselic, marveling still. "I just totally disavowed all this stupid metal—Ozzy Osbourne, Judas Priest, Def Leppard, it was just shit, I just could not listen to it anymore. It was crap, it had lost its appeal for me. Sammy Hagar, Iron Maiden, I just didn't like it. I was still into Zeppelin and Aerosmith and stuff." Chris had gone through a prog-rock phase—Yes, Emerson, Lake and Palmer, and their ilk—but, in his favorite phrase, "it never yanked my crank."

Like Kurt, Chris had a delayed reaction to punk rock. "It didn't really grab me right away because it sounded really live," says Chris. "It took about a week into it and it finally grabbed me. I was listening to *Generic Flipper* and the record moved me. It was like, Art. This is *Art*. It was so *substantial*. People pay credence

That's My Brother Chris. He Listens to Punk Rock.

95

to *Led Zeppelin IV* or the *White Album* and this was the same thing. So that turned my life around."

By this time, a lot of those metal and classic rock bands Krist mentioned were either well past their prime or had broken up. So kids his age were essentially left with oldies. That was defining for Nirvana's generation: having no canon of their own, they worshiped at the altar of a previous generation's music—until the alternative rock explosion. As Kurt astutely observed in one of his diaries, sometime in the late '80s, "This is the first decade since the early 1940s that two generations share the same music." That might not seem strange today, when parents buy Ramones onesies for their infants and later send them to rock camp to learn how to play "Seven Nation Army," but it sure was strange in the '80s. Music was still how generations defined themselves, and for Kurt's generation, there wasn't a lot of great popular music they could call their own. For that, they had to dig deep.

"Our parents are in control of the entertainment industry," Kurt told Canadian music television channel MusiquePlus in the summer of 1991, just before *Nevermind* was released. "And there's no generation gap anymore because the kids and the parents like the same music. It's really frightening to us."

That's because of the tyranny of classic rock radio and the baby boomers who controlled it. But the older Generation X got, and the further classic rock receded into history, the more absurd the situation became. There had to be music by, for, and about this new generation of kids. Punk rock to the rescue! It was revolutionary if only because you could get up close to the bands and even meet them afterward if you wanted, and it didn't cost a lot to get into the shows. But punk stayed relatively obscure for a very long time because, for better or worse, the mainstream music industry simply wouldn't embrace it.

It's a little ironic that Krist compared Flipper to the *White Album*, since classic rock is the paradigm he was ostensibly rejecting, but his point was that every culture produces its own art, and Krist's culture could make its own art, in its own way, for its own time, for its own people. It wouldn't need to be validated by mainstream commercial media and older people—the kids could validate it themselves. It was empowering, enacting one of punk's foundational concepts: DIY. Do It Yourself: because no one else is going to do it for you.

Once Krist got his head around punk rock, it fundamentally changed his life. "I felt punk was messianic," Krist wrote in *Of Grunge and Government*. "An alternative vision didn't have to be stuck in the hippie 1960s—it was reborn through punk! A new generation was offered the promise of liberation from the status quo. And we were given community to boot."

He began reading punk fanzines such as *Maximumrocknroll*, discovered political hardcore bands like MDC, and read about everything from anarchism to animal rights. Then he discovered bands such as the Butthole Surfers, Minor Threat, and Hüsker Dü. He and a bunch of friends would pile into Matt Lukin's mammoth blue Impala and drive up to Seattle to see punk rock shows—two hours up, two hours back. Awed by the big city, they kept to themselves.

Around this time, Chris's brother Robert brought his friend Kurt Cobain over to the Novoselic house. When Kurt asked about the racket emanating from the upstairs stereo, Robert replied, "Oh, that's my brother Chris. He listens to punk rock." Kurt thought that was very cool and filed away the information.

Chris graduated from high school in 1983. Soon after, his parents divorced. It was a rough enough time as it was, but he also had some plastic surgery done on his face—doctors cut a small section of bone out of Chris's jaw and moved some teeth forward to correct a severe underbite. ("I looked like Jay Leno," he says.)

Lukin remembers stopping by with Osborne on the day of the operation. They rang the doorbell over and over again, but nobody answered. Then they tossed some pebbles at Chris's window. "Just as we were ready to give up," says Lukin, "the window slides open and he had this huge head, it was totally swollen up—he almost looked like a little fat oriental baby. It was like an elephant man coming up to the window." Chris was mad because they'd woken him up from his anesthetized sleep. His jaws were tightly wired shut, yet he still managed to communicate something to his friends. "You fuckers!" he cried.

Chris's jaw was wired shut for six weeks. He still went out to parties, except he had to carry a pair of wire cutters with him in case he threw up or something got caught in his throat. "He'd go out and get all fucked up," Lukin recalls, "and he'd be puking and it would be draining through his wires. He said he never did have to cut them, but all the food was like milkshakes anyway, no solid food. Still, it was somewhat reckless of him."

"Then the swelling went down," says Chris, "and I had a new face."

One day during his senior year in high school, he had been walking behind two junior girls in the hall who were raving about the album *Never Mind the Bollocks, Here's the Sex Pistols*. "Yeah, they're really great!" he piped up. Shelli remembered him as a "class clown–type guy, always joking." They talked a little and made friends.

Shelli was also friendly with Kurt and remembers him as a "smart-ass" who would delight in riling the redneck who sat next to him in art class. Kurt's mom boarded a friend of Kurt's for a while and Shelli knew his sister, who was old

That's My Brother Chris. He Listens to Punk Rock.

97

enough to buy beer. She'd go over to Kurt's house sometimes to find him and his friends getting very stoned and grooving to Led Zeppelin.

Bands like Led Zeppelin were what stoners listened to back then—Deep Purple and Black Sabbath, too.

It's interesting to note all the boarding of other people's kids that went on in this book. It seems like there was a lot of family strife in Aberdeen but also a lot of kind people who would take in kids who needed a place to stay. So that's another nice thing about Aberdeen.

Shelli dropped out her senior year and took a job at McDonald's and got her own hundred-dollar-a-month apartment on Market Street, across from the fire department. On her way to work, she would walk past the Foster Painting company where Chris worked and she would talk to him. She got his phone number and started calling him up. They had a lot in common—Shelli had been an oddball in school, too—and by March 1985, they had started hanging out as friends at Shelli's apartment, listening to punk rock records and going to shows. Soon they started going out.

Chris and Osborne briefly had a band with original Melvins drummer Mike Dillard, with Chris on guitar and Osborne on bass. Chris played a punked-up version of "Sunshine of Your Love" with members of the Melvins as the opening act of a Melvins/Metal Church bill at the D&R Theater in Aberdeen. Chris became the lead singer for the Stiff Woodies, the Melvins satellite project whose revolving door lineup featured, at various times, Osborne, Crover, Lukin, a fellow named Gary Cole, and others, including drummer Kurt Cobain. ("We sounded just like the Butthole Surfers," Kurt claims.) Chris was a flamboyant frontman, recalls Dale Crover. "He wore this big long purple fringe vest and he'd do all these big high kicks," says Crover. "It was hilarious." The Stiff Woodies played a few parties before going the way of all satellite projects, probably because Chris's vocal talents were at roughly the same level as his cameo at the beginning of *Nevermind*'s "Territorial Pissings."

Chris played bass in another Melvins satellite project, a Mentors cover band. His stage name was Phil Atio.

The Mentors were originally from Seattle—in the late '70s they began dressing up in executioners' hoods, adopted names like Sickie Wifebeater and Dr. Heathen Scum, and played crude punk-metal with spectacularly offensive lyrics. Early on, the band toured around the Northwest, not only smearing their filthy music all over the region but also planting the idea that anybody could start a band, no matter how godawful bad it was. For years afterward, many teenage boys took note.

In 1985, the Mentors were still very obscure. But then came the Parents Music Resource Center (PMRC), co-founded by Democratic Tennessee senator Al Gore Jr.'s wife, Tipper, which inveighed against depraved miscreants such as Prince, Cyndi Lauper, Madonna, and various metal bands who were corrupting the minds of America's youth with album cover imagery such as a circular saw blade erupting from a fellow's crotch. The PMRC somehow managed to unearth the Mentors' music and were duly incensed. A consultant for the center, Pastor Jeff Ling of the Clear River Community Church in Virginia, unintentionally gave a huge boost to the band's popularity when he quoted their song "Golden Shower" in a hearing by the Senate Committee on Commerce, Science, and Transportation: "Bend up and smell my anal vapor / Your face is my toilet paper."

In a demonstration of what a strange and small world it is, years later the Mentors' troubled leader El Duce made the ridiculous claim, parroted by various conspiracy theorists, that he had been paid fifty thousand dollars by Courtney to do a hit on Kurt. Days after he said this, he was decapitated by a train.

[Chris] had been laid off from his painting job by then and was collecting fifty-five dollars a week unemployment. He usually slept in all morning and then hung out at the Melvins' practice space, where the band rehearsed every afternoon. Gradually, Chris moved in with Shelli. Chris didn't hang out with the cling-ons at the Melvins' practice space so much after that, preferring to spend most of his time with his girlfriend.

They didn't have a TV or a phone and they got everything from thrift stores. They had tie-dye curtains and listened to Cream and early Rolling Stones records. "It was one of the greatest times of our lives," says Shelli. "Everything was so new. Everything was so bright for us. It was the first time we'd been away from our parents and the world was ours. It was really cool."

Chris and Shelli moved to a larger but more decrepit house in Aberdeen in December. It was a drafty place, especially in the damp Northwestern winter— you could actually see sunlight streaming through the cracks in the walls.

Thus far, the story is filled with tales of unemployment, substance abuse, poverty, and substandard housing. Kurt and Krist were living very low to the ground at this point. It was touching that Shelli said, "Everything was so bright for us," because they didn't actually have very good prospects. These were not privileged people who fully expected great success in life. So when great success came, they scrambled to adjust to it, or even accept it.

That's My Brother Chris. He Listens to Punk Rock.

Noting that the Melvins were awarded the princely sum of eighty dollars for a night's work, Chris and Kurt started a Creedence Clearwater Revival cover band aptly named the Sell-Outs. They figured CCR was country-rock and therefore would go over well in rural Aberdeen. The band was Kurt on drums, Chris on guitar, and a fellow named Steve Newman on bass. (Newman later lost his fingers in a woodcutting accident.) They practiced at Chris and Shelli's house, but it only got as far as five or six rehearsals. They broke up after Kurt and Newman got into a big fight one day at Chris and Shelli's. They were sitting around drinking when Newman tried to attack Kurt with a vacuum cleaner. Kurt grabbed a two-by-four and brained his much larger opponent.

There's a photo of Kurt in his teens, playing guitar at home. In a bin on the floor is a copy of Creedence's classic 1970 album *Cosmo's Factory*. CCR made sturdy, basic guitar rock, pared down to bass, drums, and guitars, with indelible melodies and a raw-voiced singer—that had to be an important template for Nirvana. Early on, they'd encore with CCR's upbeat and yet foreboding "Bad Moon Rising."

From Creedence's singer-guitarist John Fogerty, Kurt probably learned another trick: not to sing in your normal speaking voice and instead affect a cool, raw timbre—to kind of put a distortion pedal on your voice, as so many great rock singers had, from Little Richard to Johnny Rotten.

Also, Creedence had a lot of indie cred: the Minutemen loved them—and would, on occasion, play an entire set of Creedence covers—and Sonic Youth named one of their albums *Bad Moon Rising*. (Creedence leader John Fogerty was a bit of a fashion visionary: he sported resolutely un-hippielike workingman's plaid flannel shirts, which became a staple of grunge fashion twenty years later.)

It's telling that they called their CCR cover band the Sell-Outs. In other words, making even an exceedingly modest amount of money by playing cover versions of songs by a hugely popular band was an artistic compromise. Even at this early stage, Kurt was well aware of the shame of selling out. Exaggeratedly flaunting the very thing he feared he would be accused of—for example, calling his sell-out band the Sell-Outs—was a frequent preemptive tactic for Kurt, as we'll see.

Although they had left high school behind, they still hadn't escaped Aberdeen and their provincial peers. "It was your basic nowhere town and these people considered it the center of the universe," says Matt Lukin. "There were these bigwigs that were popular in high school who belonged to these little cliques and it kind of carried over out of high school because everybody still hung out. Small-town mentality—real narrow-minded people who looked at something they weren't used to as something bad."

"Kurt was really a victim," says Shelli. "People wanted to beat him up. He was different from them. He wasn't a redneck and he liked his own music and people are afraid of that in a small town—you're different and you're the freak. We got all kinds of shit in Aberdeen. Chris was talking about socialism at a party once and these guys were talking about slitting his throat, these rednecks, because they thought he was a Communist. It was a scary atmosphere, especially back in 1985."

In 1985, Ronald Reagan began his second term as president. Disregarding the policies of the previous three presidents, Reagan escalated Cold War tensions by initiating a massive military buildup and putting tremendous economic pressure on the Soviet people. Infamously, Reagan had taken an unseemly stab at humor and wisecracked into an open mike the previous year, "My fellow Americans, I'm pleased to tell you today that I've signed legislation that will outlaw Russia forever. We begin bombing in five minutes." The year before that, he declared that the Soviet Union was an "evil empire" that would be consigned to the "ash heap of history." Reagan even fought a proxy war with the Soviet Union by funneling billions of dollars, in addition to intelligence support and weapons, to Islamist mujahideen fighters in Afghanistan. (The project backfired: the Taliban and Osama bin Laden both emerged from the Reagan-funded mujahideen.)

That was the political climate at the time—and discussing socialism, especially with people who might not be terribly familiar with what the word means, could be very risky.

In March of 1986, Chris and Shelli moved to Phoenix, Arizona, in search of work. But they soon tired of the stifling, relentless heat and all those Republicans and moved back to the hundred-dollar-a-month apartment. They stayed there for six months before moving to an apartment in nearby Hoquiam (Quinault Indian for "hungry for wood") above a garage.

They became vegetarians. Chris got turned on to the idea by a friend from work named Dwight Covey, a hip older guy who had built a cabin for himself out in the woods and used no electricity or running water. Chris quit eating red meat, then gradually dropped poultry and fish. "I was just looking for a better way to live, I guess," he says. "I started thinking about all the cows slaughtered. It just seemed like a really good thing to do."

Vegetarianism is a good insight into Krist, who is a very thoughtful, very progressively minded person—he's just basically kind of crunchy, which is an interesting extension of being punk. One of American punk's foundational values is to think for yourself. Many punks applied that idea to every aspect of their lives, including the food they ate. So: Why eat meat? Just because it's heavily advertised, available everywhere, and everyone

That's My Brother Chris. He Listens to Punk Rock.

101

else eats it? But what about the colossal waste of resources it requires, the lethal viruses that livestock production unleashes, or the vast environmental destruction it creates? Punk's zest for critical thinking extends far beyond music—it's an entire worldview.

Monk magazine interviewer, 1992: What's teen spirit to you?
Krist: It's something the men in corporations spray in rabbits' eyes.

MELVINS, NIRVANA

AND MACHINE IN:

SATURDAY

TACOMA

BY: RYAN LOISELLE

$7.00

THE 20TH

13TH AND FAWCET
AT LEGENDS

chapter four

THESE GUYS WERE FROM ABERDEEN

ater that winter of 1987, Chris and Kurt found a new drummer—mustachioed Aaron Burckhard, who lived down the street from Kurt. A stoner, Burckhard was one of the cling-ons and would occasionally get to sit behind Dale Crover's drum set and play. "He's a very upbeat, happy person," says Kurt. "Loud but not so obnoxious to the point where you hate his guts or anything. And he's a magnet for trouble." Burckhard was a bit of a rascal-about-town and had been in a car which a friend drove through the front window of the Shop-Rite in Aberdeen, causing fifteen thousand dollars' worth of damage. Not long afterward, his face made the front page of the *Aberdeen Daily World* when another car he was in flipped over a median strip and burst into flames, killing the driver.

Burckhard had his drawbacks, but he was the only person in Aberdeen Kurt and Chris knew who played drums, so he was in. He had a steady job at the Burger King in town, but somehow couldn't find the money for a proper drum set, so they scrounged up a set using a few drums that Burckhard had, bits of Dale Crover's banged-up old Sears kit, and even a sheet music stand to hold up one of the cymbals.

After Chris's parents got divorced, Maria Novoselic had moved into the apartment above her beauty shop, so the fledgling band rehearsed at Kurt's little house. Kurt now had a little Fender Champ and Chris had a PMS brand amp and a clunky old Hohner bass he had borrowed from Greg Hokanson. They started rehearsing in earnest, taking inspiration from the hardworking Melvins.

At first, Kurt sang in an English accent. "When I first heard American punk rock," he says, "it didn't sound punk rock enough to me because the accent was missing." They learned most of the Fecal Matter tape at first, but then started writing new material almost immediately. Within three months they had about a dozen new songs.

It's funny—the early British rockers sang in American accents because they didn't think English accents sounded rock & roll enough. Then the Beatles came along, proudly singing in their Liverpudlian accents, and the tide turned overnight. Later, British classic rockers sang in American accents, so punks such as the Clash and the Sex Pistols rebelliously sang in unabashedly working-class English accents. Years later, American bands like Green Day and Rancid sang with English accents because that was how their favorite British punk rockers sang.

At the time, Chris was big into beads, incense, and psychedelic rock from the '60s—"A full-blown hippie," says Kurt. Chris was raving about a record he had found by Shocking Blue, the Dutch band best known for the classic 1970 pop hit "Venus." Kurt didn't like the album, but just to humor Chris, he agreed to cover one of its songs, a pseudo-trippy wad of bubblegum called "Love Buzz." Kurt rocked it up considerably, dispensing with all but the first verse, essentially because he was too lazy to figure out the rest of the words.

Thrift store culture is an important part of this whole story. Kurt, Tracy, Krist, and Shelli got much of everything they owned from thrift stores, swap meets, and so on. Seemingly every town in the area had a former supermarket that had closed and been turned into a gigantic thrift store that sold secondhand clothes, tools, small appliances, toys, you name it, for dirt cheap, a necessity for an economically downtrodden part of the world. And sometimes they would just have a really fun afternoon traveling from store to store, entertaining each other by trying on the silliest clothes they could find, not spending a dime.

Naturally, these places also sold (very) used records and cassettes—the real no-name stuff might be three for a dollar. Krist might well have picked up a Shocking Blue album because it had "Venus" on it and discovered the rest of the record. Soon, Kurt would write a song called "Swap Meet" about people who sell handicrafts and "seashells, driftwood and burlap" at swap meets (outdoor flea markets), which were very common in places like Aberdeen.

Poverty begat an entire aesthetic. That "grunge" look, with the heavy flannel shirts, came about partly because the whole Northwest was flush with excellent used Pendleton shirt-jackets, which were cheap and sturdy, and specifically designed for staying warm in the penetrating damp of a Northwest winter.

They not only got cast-off clothes and records, they got cast-off musical instruments. Recall Krist's Hohner bass and Kurt's guitars, all secondhand at best, and they virtually never stopped playing used instruments. The title of Mudhoney's debut EP *Superfuzz Bigmuff* came from the names of two distortion pedals the band used (the Super-Fuzz and the Big Muff Pi). By the late '80s, both pedals were out of production, found mainly in thrift stores and pawnshops. Nobody wanted them. But as Mudhoney's Mark Arm told me for *Our Band Could Be Your Life*, "It was like, 'This is cheap, let's buy it!'" The same applied to certain vintage Fender amps, which were disdained by Seattle's many metal bands, making them both inexpensive and plentiful. Those pedals and amps became a key part of Mudhoney's sound, and it was largely due to economics.

Likewise, certain '60s- and '70s-vintage Fender guitar models such as the Mustang and the Jaguar were out of style (and never really popular in the first place), making them very inexpensive even though they were well made (kind of like those Pendleton shirt-jackets), and so those were the instruments that starving young musicians bought. Kurt used both the Jaguar and the Mustang. Both guitars have a distinctive attack and tone, and once again, a sound was born. And now those once-underappreciated guitars are coveted by collectors and cost a fortune.

Early on, some friction developed between Burckhard and the rest of the band. Burckhard was more into mainstream metal than what he calls "the punk shit" and didn't quite grasp Kurt's music, which recalled arty, dissonant bands such as Scratch Acid, early Gang of Four, and the Butthole Surfers. "I was listening more to the mainstream and Kurt was into the underground scene," says Burckhard. "But I dug their music." Looking back on it, it was an early indication of the broad-based appeal Kurt's music would have—heavily influenced by punk and underground rock, it somehow translated into the mainstream.

It was a constant battle to try to get Burckhard to practice. He lived with a divorced mother of two who was on welfare, and when the check came in at the first of the month, she and Burckhard would go out and whoop it up—along with all the other unemployed folks in Aberdeen. "The first is wild around this town," says Burckhard.

"When the welfare check came in," says Kurt, "it was impossible to get him to practice."

In the beginning, even Chris found it difficult to match Kurt's zeal—he'd sometimes miss practice or claim he had something else to do, perhaps because Chris's mother, a proud woman who had started her own successful business, didn't like Kurt very much. "Fuck, she hated my guts," says Kurt. "She called me trash. She hated me. I always heard her talking to Chris, saying he should find other friends, always putting him down and calling him a loser, calling all his friends losers."

Like so many working Americans, the Novoselic family were trying to be upwardly mobile—maybe they felt Kurt was a bad influence on their son.

Kurt brought Chris home a few times. Wendy remembers Chris would accidentally bang his head over and over again on the crossbeams in the house. "Oh don't worry," he'd say matter-of-factly, "that happens all the time." Chris was so shy that he would do anything to avoid Wendy, an admitted "yakker."

Burckhard recalls that Kurt's torn jeans and bohemian attitude set him apart from the usual Aberdeen stoner. "It was just the way he carried himself about—like he didn't give a shit," says Burckhard. "He didn't care what other people thought about him."

Kurt was unstoppable. "I wanted to put out a record or play some shows, instead of having it fall apart like everything else for the past six years," says Kurt. "We would play the set and then I would just start playing the songs again right away without even looking up to see if those guys wanted to play them again. I'd just whip them into shape."

So there's an early example of Kurt's dogged work ethic and leadership skills. Not such a slacker after all—when he put his mind to it.

Kurt's determination came through in a never-aired interview with Seattle TV station KIRO-7 in January 1990:

Interviewer: What advice would you give to someone who's just starting out or wants to have a musical career?

Kurt: Just keep practicing. And don't give up. Just never give up. Play as often as you can and be really dedicated. And try to write good music and don't worry about the material ethics that go with music—it doesn't matter what you look like or anything. It doesn't matter what your "product" looks like, it's what it *sounds* like.

With Burckhard, Krist wrote in *Of Grunge and Government*, "we had the most intense jams. We'd simultaneously orbit inner *and* outer space. It was so serious, if we felt we sucked at rehearsal we were disappointed and we'd sit around bummed out after. . . . If we didn't get that rush, that otherworldly sense of liberation, we were let down." "That otherworldly sense of liberation" was nirvana *and* Nirvana. That's the feeling that Kurt was chasing the whole time.

Eventually, Kurt's zeal won over Chris and the two became so driven that even one bad practice would get them deeply upset. "We'd get really mad," says Kurt. "We took it very seriously." They soon set their sights on getting a gig. "We just had to play a show," says Kurt. "God, if we could just play a show, it would be so great."

At last, they got a gig—a party in Olympia. They loaded up Chris's VW bug with equipment and rode to the gig all keyed up and excited—their first show! But they arrived to find that the party had already been shut down by the police, so they simply turned around and made the hour's drive all the way back to Aberdeen.

Their first real gig was a house party in nearby Raymond, a town even more isolated than Aberdeen, opening for a metal band featuring Aberdeen's then-reigning guitar hero ("this guy knew *all* the Eddie Van Halen licks," says Chris, still semi-impressed). Burckhard recalls the hosts were "these higher-class yuppie people and they had a caseful of Michelob—good beer—and Chris ended up jumping through the window, running around to the front door and repeatedly doing it. He had this fake vampire blood and he just basically made a fool out of himself, but it was fun."

"We had everyone so scared of us that they were in the kitchen hiding from us," says Kurt. "We had the run of the entire living room and the rest of the house." Just to shock the locals, Shelli and Tracy started making out; Kurt would jump on a table mid-solo and they would caress his legs. "Of course, by the end of the evening, most of the girls at the party had talked their boyfriends into wanting to beat us up," says Kurt. "They didn't beat us up, but they let us know we weren't welcome. 'It's time to pack up and leave now, boys.'"

Most people were confused because the band didn't play many covers. "They didn't know what to think," says Chris, who remembers that an adventurous few walked up to the band after the set and raved. "Who knows what happened to the people who thought it was cool," he adds, shaking his head in pity.

By then, their repertoire included originals like "Hairspray Queen," "Spank Thru," "Anorexorcist," "Raunchola" ("That was really raunchy," Chris explains), "Aero Zeppelin," "Beeswax," and "Floyd the Barber," as well as covers such as "Love Buzz," "White Lace and Strange" by the obscure '60s band Thunder and Roses, Flipper's epic "Sex Bomb," and Cher's "Gypsies, Tramps, and Thieves" with Chris on lead vocals.

There's the early Nirvana aesthetic in action: a mélange of thrift store record finds, classic metal, the Melvins, and punk rock. As Skid Row, their summer 1987 cover of "Gypsies, Tramps & Thieves" was done as a spot-on parody of Meat Puppets, complete with Krist on lead vocals, doing a great impression of the band's singer Curt Kirkwood. Turns out their appreciation of that band ran long and deep.

Soon they played their first big gig—closing night of GESCCO Hall in Olympia. They took out the backseat of Chris's Volkswagen bug again and polished off a gallon bottle of wine on the drive up from Aberdeen. There were perhaps ten people at the show, but they all tore down the yards of arty plastic sheeting on the walls and rolled it around them as the band played. It was a good beginning.

Then the band got a show at the Community World Theater, a converted porno theater in Tacoma. Tracy was a friend of the proprietor, Jim May, and helped get them the gig. May charged only a couple of bucks at the door and didn't mind if underaged kids drank beer. Bands with names like the Dicks and Jack Shit played the Community, as well as the Melvins and touring punk bands such as the Circle Jerks.

The band didn't have a name yet and May wanted a name to put on the marquee, so Kurt came up with the name Skid Row (the term had originated in Seattle). None of their friends expected much from the band, but a bunch went to see the show. And surprise—the band was good—they had real songs and Kurt could really sing. And they were not above a little showmanship—for a while, Kurt would put on a pair of outrageous silver-sparkle platform shoes during "Love Buzz," jump five feet in the air, and land in a split. Skid Row soon amassed its own group of "cling-ons."

The phrase *skid row* may not actually have originated in Seattle but it does come from the Northwest: it's the term for a road where gigantic logs get hauled down from the hills on skids and loaded onto boats and trains. So being on Skid Row/Road might mean that you're going downhill fast, or maybe it just referred to the fact that the areas around skid rows were typically very rough; in the old days, Seattle's skid row teemed with poverty, violence, and prostitution. There had surely also been a skid row in Aberdeen, from the forests outside of town down to the Chehalis River.

Of course, a hair metal band later claimed the name Skid Row and achieved great success before becoming precisely the kind of band that Nirvana displaced in the rock firmament.

In April of 1987, the band played a radio show on KAOS, the station at the Evergreen State College in Olympia. Kurt had made friends in Olympia from going to Melvins shows there, and one of them was a KAOS DJ. Their recorded appearance—a live midnight show—became the band's first demo. They did remarkably full-blown versions of "Love Buzz," "Floyd the Barber," "Downer," "Mexican Seafood," "Spank Thru," "Hairspray Queen," and three other songs that even Kurt doesn't remember the names of. Burckhard turned out to be a solid, hard hitter in the John Bonham vein—sort of the hard rock ancestral conscience of the band. (Interestingly, a Bonham maniac would one day become their best drummer.) Kurt sings in a few voices—including a desperate death-metal growl and a strangulated cat-in-heat scream—that sound nothing like he does today.

Later, they went through various names, including Ted Ed Fred, Bliss ("I was on acid one night," Kurt explains), Throat Oyster, Pen Cap Chew, and Windowpane.

And finally, the band settled on Nirvana, a Hindu and Buddhist concept, which Webster's defines as "the extinction of desire, passion, illusion and the empirical self and attainment of rest, truth and unchanging being." That idea of heaven—a place, as David Byrne once put it, "where nothing ever happens"—sounds a lot like the way Kurt felt when he did heroin, but he says that wasn't the idea. "I wanted a name that was kind of beautiful or nice and pretty instead of a mean, raunchy punk rock name like the Angry Samoans," he says. "I wanted to have something different." These days, Kurt isn't so crazy about the name. "It's too esoteric and serious," he says. And later on, he'd have to pay another band fifty thousand dollars for a name he didn't even care for that much.

It's interesting that the band was briefly called Bliss. The word was probably pretty close to the idea of nirvana in Kurt's mind, and not unlike the euphoric state of someone who's nodding out on opiates—or somebody feeling no pain because they're in the ecstatic act of making music. It also recalls Kurt's earlier remark about when he was a kid and his mom was physically affectionate with him, and how those were "blissful times."

Nirvana really is kind of a cheesy band name, perhaps better suited for an upscale Indian restaurant or a little shop that sells incense and essential oils. But it probably sounded cosmic and exotic to a callow Aberdeen teenager yearning to break out of his claustrophobically provincial environment. Of course, the Beatles had a terrible name, too, a corny pun. Bands don't grow into names like that; the names grow with them. So, after a while, a word like "Nirvana" or "Beatles" becomes sort of invisible; we almost don't see it anymore;

Chris and Shelli fall off the veggie wagon at their Tacoma home in the fall of 1990. © Ian T. Tilton

it's just synonymous with a world-famous musical group. At this point, there are one or two generations whose most immediate association with the word "nirvana" is the band, not the transcendent spiritual state. One of the first articles ever written about Nirvana, by Dawn Anderson for the September 1988 issue of her pioneering Seattle music paper *Backlash*, said Nirvana was "a name that signifies both everything and nothing." Yep.

Kurt hadn't paid rent on the little shack in Aberdeen for several months and was being evicted. Tracy asked if he'd like to move into her place in Olympia, and Kurt agreed. It was convenient because Chris and Shelli had decided to move to Tacoma and it was a lot easier to keep the band together if Kurt moved, too. Tacoma was out of the question for Kurt, being, as he describes it, "a more violent Aberdeen." Besides, Olympia was a cool college town.

In the fall of 1987, Kurt moved into Tracy's tiny studio apartment at 114 North Pear Street in Olympia (a "shoebox," according to Kurt), which they rented for $137 a month, including electricity, hot water, and garbage pickup. They stayed there a little over a year, then moved to a small one-bedroom in the same building.

Kurt had escaped from Aberdeen. Tracy remembers that shortly after Kurt moved in with her, he told her that while she was away at work, he had had a meal of cream cheese and crab, and that he felt very cultured sitting in Olympia on a real hardwood floor eating such fancy food.

For about a month that summer, Chris and Shelli lived there during the week, too, to avoid the two-hour commute to their jobs, meaning that four people were now crammed into the little studio apartment. Shelli and Tracy both worked the graveyard shift at the Boeing cafeteria, while Chris worked in Tacoma making six dollars an hour as an industrial painter. Kurt would sleep at night and hang out at the house by day. Chris and Shelli would go back to their place in Hoquiam on the weekends.

The four spent lots of time together, partying or just hanging out at the apartment watching TV or going out tripping. "The acid wasn't what the Beatles took," Chris recalls. "It was more speedy, dirty acid . . . We'd just go wild, raging all night long."

Kurt describes the apartment as "a curiosity shop." Tracy would take Kurt thrift shopping every weekend and come back with carloads of kitsch. "You couldn't even move in that place," he says. The apartment was completely decorated with thrift purchases, including a huge Aerosmith poster on the living room wall and a bunch of transparent plastic anatomical models. The walls were lined with Kurt's paintings, cutouts from the *Weekly World News* and the *National*

Enquirer, and strangely adulterated religious pictures. Always lurking around was one of Kurt's most prized possessions—Chim-Chim, his plastic monkey.

Kurt loved chimps and monkeys—maybe because they were like children, innocent and pure. Chim-Chim was named after the chimp in the late-'60s Japanese cartoon series *Speed Racer*, which Kurt loved.

There were animals everywhere—three cats, two rabbits, some pet rats, and a bunch of turtles. It was as "odorous" as the shack back in Aberdeen. "Rat piss hell" is Kurt's succinct description. By chance, an Olympia punk rock scenester by the name of Bruce Pavitt stopped by one day and one of the pet rats bit him on the finger ("He screamed like a woman," Tracy says with a giggle). Pavitt would go on to co-found Sub Pop Records, Nirvana's first label.

As usual, Kurt stayed indoors, sometimes not venturing outside for weeks at a time, indulging in what he calls his "little art world fantasy." He didn't particularly take advantage of Olympia's cultural scene, but it was nice to know it was there. And he didn't have to worry about having to deal with doltish stoners and rednecks. He let his hair grow long and concentrated on his art.

Kurt began collecting and making dolls. It was the start of a long obsession that continues still. He found a type of clay that turned all sorts of strange colors when it was baked and he made dolls out of it—like the doll on the cover of *Incesticide*, but much more intricate and bizarre. He'd find baby dolls, cover them with clay and bake them in the oven until they looked like ancient artifacts. He also collected antique baby dolls, especially eerily lifelike ones.

Once, when Kurt was working at the resort hotel, he had gone into a room where a gynecologist was staying and lifted a book full of pictures of diseased vaginas. He cut them out and combined them into a collage with pictures of pieces of meat and an illustration of Kiss and put it on the refrigerator door.

That collage is on the back cover of *Nevermind*.

Collage in general was an important part of Kurt's creativity—it was the basis of his cut-up method for lyrics, and he also made collages of sound (one of which was, fittingly, called "Montage of Heck" and included on the Fecal Matter tape). The cover artwork for both *Nevermind* and *In Utero* features collage.

Kurt also made crude video montages. "He had the remote control on the VCR and he would just like watch the most ridiculous thing and he would just compile them," Krist recalled to John Hughes. As Krist wrote in *Of Grunge and Government*, those video montages "were scathing testimonies about popular culture. . . . This wasn't someone who had a hyperactive finger on the record button; those video montages were surreal sociology."

Kurt incorporated one of those montages into a 1990 video performance Nirvana did at Evergreen, where they played "School" in front of a green screen that showed bits of teen movies, inane commercials, pro wrestling shows, footage of people with big late-'80s hair, and other cultural excrescences that Kurt astutely recognized as kitsch even as they were happening.

Kurt went through a brief death rock phase (Black Sabbath—*not* Bauhaus) and started constructing nativity scenes full of decayed bodies, skeletons, and demons.

He'd make psychedelic tapes that strung together Christian records, political speeches, commercials, and music that was slowed down or speeded up. He made collages, but mostly, he painted. His paintings had lots of weird distended figures or fetuses set in thorny landscapes. It's hard not to look at those paintings as autobiographical—helpless children set adrift in hostile worlds.

Kurt also sculpted. "He would make these incredibly beautiful, intricate sculptures out of weird shit he'd buy at thrift stores," says Slim Moon. "Little Visible Man [model kits] and figurines. It would be this weird mixture of pop culture artifacts that you'd get from thrift stores, mixed up with actual clay sculpture of these tortured figures. He'd make a huge four-foot-by-four-foot diorama or he'd make it inside an aquarium and he'd spend weeks on it and anybody who came over would be totally amazed at what a great sculptor he was. We used to try to talk him into getting a show at the Smithfield [Café] and he'd say no and he'd tear it all down. You'd go over the next day and it would be all gone and he'd be starting on a new one."

A lot of artists are fine with destroying their own work: the distinguished list includes Pablo Picasso, Georgia O'Keeffe, Francis Bacon, Agnes Martin, Claude Monet, Jasper Johns, Gerhard Richter, and countless others. This horrifies some people. *But it was so cool! Why did you wreck it?* But if the artist doesn't like it, they simply don't think it should exist, no matter how good other people think it is. The Hindu deity Shiva combines destructive and constructive powers, two sides of the same coin, a force for renewal and recycling. Or, as the 19th century Russian revolutionary anarchist Mikhail Bakunin put it, "The urge to destroy is also a creative urge."

Krist recalled Kurt's home in *Of Grunge and Government*: "What a den of art/insanity that was! He tried to make his own lava lamp out of wax and vegetable oil (it didn't work). He sketched very obscene Scooby Doo cartoons all over his apartment building hallways (they were done very well). . . . He sculpted clay into scary spirit people writhing in agony."

Necessity is the mother of invention, which is how Kurt came up with one of his favorite decorations. "I have this weird magnetic attraction to flies," says Kurt. "Or flies attract to me, actually. I'd wake up in the morning and these flies would keep me awake for hours, buzzing and bouncing off my face. They'd just attack me and this has happened over and over again in my life." Kurt hung up dozens and dozens of fly strips all over the apartment and they soon collected all kinds of dead insects.

Kurt insists that his income from the band paid the meager rent, but occasionally, Tracy would ask him to get a job and Kurt would offer to move out and live in his car, which was enough to keep her from asking again for a while. It seemed as if Tracy was as much Kurt's patron as she was his lover.

And there's some passive-aggressive gamesmanship right there.

So Tracy was one of the first people to recognize Kurt's talent and take him seriously as an artist. Among other things, she truly was a patron, giving him material support so he could develop his work and career. And she was right—during their time together, Kurt turned out reams of visual art and wrote several of the songs that wound up on *Nevermind*.

Kurt insists he was pulling his weight, partly because of something unusual that was happening in Seattle. For a few years before Nirvana arrived, antimaterialistic Seattle punk bands had allowed themselves to be fleeced by the local clubs. But by this time, Seattle musicians had informally united and made it known that they wouldn't play for peanuts anymore. The emerging Seattle record label Sub Pop played a big part in making sure that a lot of their artists got paid well for live gigs. Kurt remembers playing an early show at the Vogue to three hundred people and the band pulling in six hundred dollars, a lot of money even now.

But in order to save up enough money to record a proper demo tape, that fall he took a job at a janitorial company for four bucks an hour. He would ride around town in a cramped van with two "co-workers from hell," as Kurt puts it, "worse than your typical brain-dead Aberdonian." Typically, his workmates would down a couple of sixes each in the course of a night's work while they called Kurt a "fag" and jostled him around the van. Several of their clients were doctors and dentists, and they would show Kurt how to steal pills and inhale nitrous oxide without anyone finding out.

According to Kurt's journals, he held that job from September 1987 to February 1988, when he was twenty.

Dylan Carlson and Slim Moon eventually moved in next door. Since Kurt worked at night and Carlson was unemployed, they hung out a lot, sharing their disdain for the Calvinists ("I think Kurt and I were the only ones not throwing a yo-yo that summer," cracks Carlson). They'd hang up strings of tacky lamps from the '50s (another thrift store purchase) and have barbecues in the backyard. Sometimes Chris would come over and they'd inevitably break out a bottle of red wine and start to act up. The police showed up one time after the three attacked an abandoned Cadillac with some lawn chairs.

Still, Kurt was basically a recluse, and remained so for virtually the entire four years he lived in Olympia. "He was like a hermit in a cave," says Slim Moon. "That was the way we perceived him—the mad hermit who would sit there and play his guitar for twelve hours a day and never leave his house except to go on tour."

Although Kurt was hardly outgoing, he was rather popular around town. He'd go to parties and sit down somewhere and just smile quietly. To most of the Olympia scenesters, he was a blank slate who was whatever they wanted him to be. They liked Kurt, but they really couldn't figure out why, and that mystery seemed to suffuse his music as well.

Imagine how someone who preferred to be "like a hermit in a cave" who, as Kurt himself says a few paragraphs later, "cannot get along with average people" coped with sudden worldwide fame and countless strangers wanting to know him. Some people are suited to that sort of thing, even thrive on it—they're called extroverts. Kurt was not one of those people.

It's not hard to imagine that Kurt was smiling at those parties because, at last, he wasn't surrounded by knuckle-draggers who might try to beat him up. He had found the cool kids, and he was happily absorbing their ways: how they behaved, what they talked about, how they dressed. He might have been quiet because he didn't know what to say to them. But people liked him. It surely didn't hurt that he was good-looking and charismatic, but he was also just really relatable. Maybe he was smiling at those parties because he'd finally found a group of people he wanted to belong to. Or it might simply have been because he was high.

After a while, Kurt was awarded his own janitorial route, but he was far from a model worker. He'd go off in the van to the first building on his route, throw away a few papers here and there, and then go home and nap. Toward the end of his shift, he'd go to a few more places and do the same slipshod job. After eight months of that, he was fired.

Kurt admits he's always been lazy, but he says his dismal employment record doesn't stem from mere lassitude. "I've always had this terrible relationship with co-workers," he says. "I just cannot get along with average people. They just get on my nerves so bad, I just cannot ignore them at all. I have to confront them and tell them that I hate their guts."

Still, Kurt had learned *something* from his workmates: how to steal drugs. His favorites—when he could get them—were codeine and Vicodin, an opiate-derived painkiller. He smoked pot and did heroin again a few times. He tried cocaine and speed but didn't like them. "I felt too confident and too sure of myself," he says. "Just too sociable."

Around this time, he first experienced a terrible, piercing pain in his stomach. "It's burning, nauseous, like the worst stomach flu you can imagine," Kurt says. "You can feel it throbbing like you have a heart in your stomach and it just hurts really bad. I can just feel it being all raw and red. It mostly just hurts when I eat. About halfway through a meal and once it gets up to a certain area, right where it's inflamed and red, once it starts hitting there it starts hurting because the food sits on it and it burns. It's probably one of the worst pains I've ever felt." The condition has dominated Kurt's life—and baffled even the most distinguished specialists—ever since.

From my April 1992 *Rolling Stone* cover story: "'Most of my concentration of my singing is from my upper abdomen, that's where I scream, that's where I feel, that's where everything comes out of me—right here,' Kurt said, touching a point just below his breastbone. It just happens to be exactly where his stomach pain is centered." He literally was singing from a place of pain.

A lot of people were dubious about Kurt's stomach pain, but it was real, it was chronic, and it was excruciatingly painful, and no doctor was ever able to diagnose it. Still, it wasn't a valid excuse to use heroin.

Meanwhile, Aaron Burckhard kept promising to get a new pair of drums, but never did and had trouble showing up for practice, preferring instead to go out partying with his buddies. "They wanted to practice every night," says Burckhard. "Every night. I'm like, give me a break. I didn't show up a couple of times and they got kind of pissed off." For Burckhard, the band was just for fun—"We're not going to make no money off it or anything, you know?"

There may have been some basic incompatibility, too. Although Burckhard now says he's a punk rock fan, he wasn't as committed to it as Kurt and Chris were. "I'm not that much into that kind of scene," Burckhard admits, "where your hair is all different colors and whatnot."

By now, Chris and Shelli were in Tacoma and Kurt was in Olympia, but Burckhard didn't move—his girlfriend was staying in Aberdeen and he himself had hopes of becoming a full manager at the Burger King. Ironically, his cousin married the daughter of the owner of the franchise, and Burckhard never got past production manager. They temporarily lost touch with Burckhard.

For Kurt, it was maybe a half-hour drive from Olympia to Tacoma, but it's about an hour and a half from Aberdeen to Tacoma, which made things difficult for Burckhard.

During this time Kurt and Chris decided to practice with Dale Crover with the intention of recording a demo. It was a way of keeping the band alive. They practiced with Crover three weekends in a row, then went up to Reciprocal Recording in Seattle and recorded a demo on January 23, 1988. "After the demo tape was recorded," Kurt recalls, "we realized that it was actually good music and there was something special about it so we took it a lot more seriously."

Kurt says he happened to choose the most happening studio in Seattle simply by comparison shopping in the *Seattle Rocket*, a free music paper that remains the house organ of the Seattle scene. It was one of the cheapest studios in town, which is partly why it was the hottest studio in town. But others insist that Kurt chose Reciprocal because that was where his favorite new record, the *Screaming Life* EP by Soundgarden, had been recorded for the fledgling Seattle indie label, Sub Pop. "Kurt really wanted to record there because he really liked the sound of the Soundgarden record," says Crover, who set up the studio time. "He was really into it that summer, I remember." Kurt strenuously denies this. At any rate, they were scheduled to work with another engineer, but at the last minute Jack Endino stepped in, probably because he wanted to work with Crover, who was already known as an excellent drummer.

Kurt might have denied being a Soundgarden fan, but on several occasions, Soundgarden guitarist Kim Thayil has mentioned that Kurt took him aside one evening and told him Soundgarden was "our biggest influence." In *Grunge Is Dead*, Tracy Marander revealed that when original Soundgarden bassist Hiro Yamamoto quit the band in mid 1989, Kurt thought about auditioning to replace him, which would have meant dissolving Nirvana. And there are plenty of photos of Kurt with a Soundgarden sticker on his guitar. So yeah, Kurt had been really into Soundgarden.

But long before we did these interviews, Soundgarden had become a bit uncool in some precincts of the underground scene, and so Kurt felt compelled to disavow them. Soundgarden had released their first album on the very hip underground label SST, home of legends such as the Minutemen, Black Flag, Meat Puppets, Dinosaur Jr, and Hüsker Dü, but the whole time, they had been getting ready to move to the major label A&M Records, where they released their next album less than a year later. In the meantime, they had morphed from something kind of dark and arty to being a brilliant neo-metal/alternative rock band with a shirtless lead singer. Perhaps most egregious of all, Soundgarden opened for Guns N' Roses on their *Use Your Illusion* tour in the US and Europe in 1991 and 1992. So Kurt no longer wanted to be seen endorsing Soundgarden. "They used to be great, they were even better in, like, '85 when Chris Cornell had a Flock of Seagulls haircut!" Kurt told the influential *Flipside* fanzine for their May–June 1992 issue. "They were just like the Butthole Surfers, they were amazing." The thing is, Kurt did not see Soundgarden back then.

Jack Endino was the first person I interviewed for *Come as You Are*. He was, and still is, a keystone of the entire Seattle music community, and there are few relationships more intimate than the one between a musician and their producer-engineer, so I figured he'd be a great place to start.

Just going by his name and the sounds he got out of bands, I pictured Jack Endino to be a tough, burly guy with black hair and beard stubble; I imagined he looked and behaved a little like Bluto. But Jack turned out to be a lanky sweetheart of a guy with a kindly baritone and a ponytail, with an easygoing intelligence that made me imagine that he smoked a pipe. He gave me all kinds of details about recording *Bleach*, the band's internal dynamics, and insight into the culture of the Seattle rock community at the time.

If *Come as You Are* is a pearl, my interview with Jack is the grain of sand around which it formed. I'm so grateful to him for that.

Endino, a former Navy engineer, had already become the godfather of the Seattle scene. By recording (he never "produced"—that wasn't punk rock) countless bands for very little money, he fostered the growing scene and made Sub Pop a viable financial proposition. Endino's easygoing, avuncular personal style and rip-roaring sound made him a favorite with the young, raw bands from the area. He founded Reciprocal Recording, a studio in the Ballard section of Seattle, with Chris Hanzsek, who had also produced the *Deep Six* compilation.

Reciprocal was as casual as a band practice room—the paint peeled off the particle-board walls, there were cigarette burns all over every horizontal surface, and it didn't matter a bit if you spilled your beer on the carpet. There are

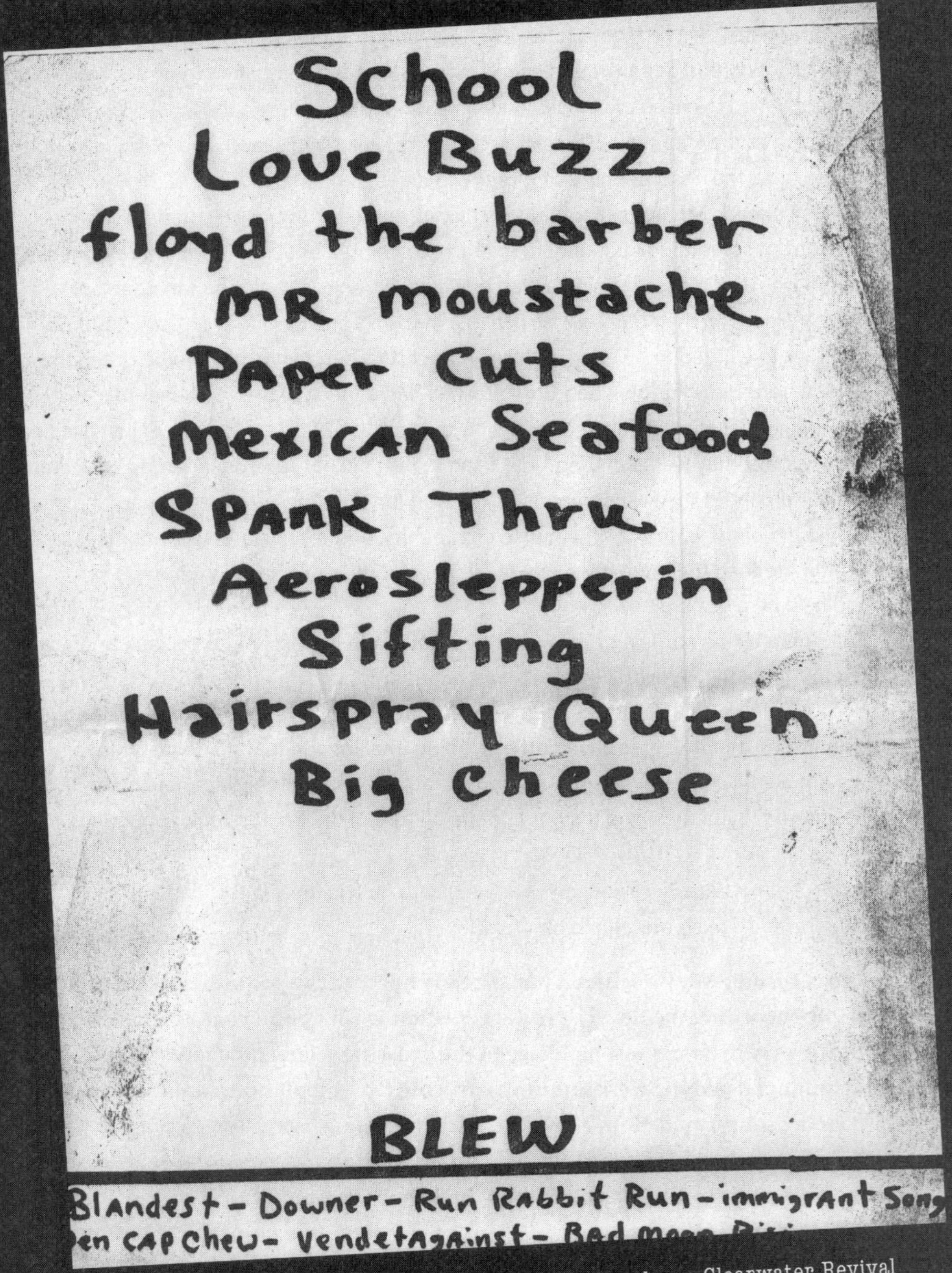

School
Love Buzz
floyd the barber
MR moustache
Paper Cuts
Mexican Seafood
SPank Thru
Aeroslepperin
Sifting
Hairspray Queen
Big cheese

BLEW

Blandest - Downer - Run Rabbit Run - immigrant Song
en CAP Chew - Vendetagainst - Bad moon Risi

An early set list. Note the Led Zeppelin and Creedence Clearwater Revival covers on the reserve list.

few bands in Seattle who haven't seen the inside of Reciprocal (or its latest incarnation, Word of Mouth).

Reciprocal is central to Seattle's musical history. Founded in 1986 by Chris Hanzsek, Reciprocal was in a very small, acutely triangular old building in the Ballard neighborhood. It was a funky space: there was a main door for loading in and a door to the tiny control room that opened right onto the sidewalk.

Major Seattle bands such as Green River, Soundgarden, Mudhoney, TAD, and Screaming Trees all recorded at Reciprocal, usually with Jack Endino, and so did mainstays of the scene such as Blood Circus, Coffin Break, Gruntruck, Seaweed, Malfunkshun, Pure Joy, Skin Yard, the Thrown-Ups, Treepeople, and many more. These days, former Death Cab for Cutie guitarist Chris Walla runs the place, now called Hall of Justice.

Chris's friend Dwight Covey drove the band and their equipment up to Seattle in his beat-up Chevy camper, complete with working wood stove.

After Chris laid down his parts, he decided to party with Dwight and Dwight's son, Guy. "He had this two-paper bomber with all bud and we smoked it in the bathroom," says Chris. "I got so stoned that I had to go outside." They sat in the camper and lit the fire while Kurt did his vocals.

You know what? God bless Krist Novoselic. The fact that he's responsible for some of the funniest parts of this book is just a small indication of how he kept things within the band as light as they could be. That's always important but especially so for Nirvana. A band member's role is far more than just being a musician. A rock band is a sometimes claustrophobically enclosed social unit and the interpersonal dynamics—complex, powerful, and ever-shifting—don't just affect the music, they determine whether the band even exists at all. Krist is an excellent bass player and great onstage, but behind the scenes, he was crucial to keeping Kurt on an even keel, for speaking up for the sensibility of the band when Kurt couldn't, and for providing a big belly laugh for everybody when all around seemed dark. That's priceless.

The band recorded and mixed ten songs in six hours (Endino charged them for only five). All the tracks were basically cut live, and in one or two takes. Kurt did all the vocals in one take. By three in the afternoon, they had finished all the recording. "Floyd the Barber," "Paper Cuts," and "Downer" all wound up on *Bleach*. Two others have never been released: "If You Must" and "Pen Cap Chew," which had a fade ending because the tape ran out. A version of "Spank Thru" was later rerecorded with Chad Channing on drums and released on *Sub Pop 200*. The remaining four tunes—"Beeswax," "Mexican Seafood," "Hairspray Queen," and

"Aero Zeppelin"—can be found on *Incesticide*. Chris had been laid off, so Kurt paid the $152.44 for the recording with money he made as a janitor.

A ponderous waltz-time dirge, "If You Must" would definitely have been an outlier on *Bleach*—with its slow, spacey trudge, it sounds like XTC meets the Melvins. Some of the lyrics seem to suggest Kurt was thinking through how he wanted to portray himself as an artist: "If you want to put off an image / The extremes, the extremes / Act it out / Practicing, perfecting, pressuring."

"Pen Cap Chew" is also very Melvins-y—and also pretty negligible, a very generic riff. It does have one line that reflects something Kurt felt strongly about: "This decade is the age of rehashing." A couple of years later, he wrote in his journals: "Too many compilations of present day bands paying homage to old influential bands. . . . The younger generation never hardly heard of old Aerosmith records or Rod Stewart & Small Faces so they have no sense of pladgerism [*sic*] in the 'now' bands paying homage supposedly or keeping the faith. . . . Rock and Roll: 30 years = Exhausted!" And, as it turned out, he was pretty much correct: thirty years later, rock bands are hard to find on the pop charts.

The evening after they recorded with Jack Endino, Kurt, Krist, and Crover used rough mixes of the session to make a couple of music videos, lip-syncing to "If You Must" and the sludgy monolith "Paper Cuts"—at the Aberdeen Radio Shack. It's absolutely priceless and absolutely weird.

There they are, after closing time, bathed in the cold glare of the store's fluorescent lights, before shelves full of tape decks, VCRs, turntables, miniature TV monitors, and other paraphernalia of '80s home entertainment. For special effects, someone has rounded up some of the blinking colored lights that Radio Shack used to sell for people to put in their rec rooms for parties or getting stoned while listening to *Dark Side of the Moon*, and the TV monitors broadcast the closed-circuit camera trained on the street in front of the store. At one point a smoke machine kicks in—although it might just be someone blowing cigarette smoke in front of the camera.

Krist wields what appears to be a child's bass, probably for sale at that same Radio Shack, comically making him appear even more gigantic than he already is. He barely pretends to play, often just flinging the instrument around, clowning, and crashing to the floor in a pratfall at the end of "If You Must."

By contrast, Kurt is deadly earnest, singing and playing with his usual intensity, although he sometimes strays far from the microphone even while there's singing going on. At the start of "If You Must," he theatrically leaps into frame from a ladder he has placed just out of camera range. There's a groovy strobe light at his feet. Crover also gives it his all, and at twenty years of age, his unique genius is already apparent.

The absurdity of making a music video in a Radio Shack didn't seem to occur to them. (Although it looks like it might have occurred to Krist.) But there was no way they could have known that, less than four years later and five thousand miles away, they'd pull a very similar stunt, miming to their global pop hit on the UK's beloved music show *Top of the Pops*.

Crover had arranged a show for them that night in Tacoma at the Community World Theater. They didn't have a band name again, so Crover suggested Ted Ed Fred, his nickname for Greg Hokanson's mom's boyfriend at the time. Chris finally came down from the effects of a two-paper bomber just before show time.

Kurt was really happy with the demo. Tracy remembers him sitting in her car holding on to the finished tape, with a huge smile on his face. Endino liked the tape, too, so he made a mix for himself that night and gave a cassette to Jonathan Poneman, who had just released the Soundgarden EP on Sub Pop, which had been founded by his business partner, Bruce Pavitt, a few months earlier. There weren't that many Seattle bands that Poneman, a former club booker, didn't already know about but, like Endino says, "These guys were from *Aberdeen*."

Poneman was looking for more bands to fill out Sub Pop's roster, so he asked Endino if he'd heard anything good lately. Endino replied, "Well, there was this one guy who came in—I don't really know *what* to make of it, to tell you the truth. This guy's got a really amazing voice, he came in with Dale Crover. I don't know what to make of it, but his voice has a lot of power. And he looks a lot like an auto mechanic."

Poneman loved the tape. "I was just thoroughly blown away by the guy's voice," he says. "It wasn't like I was listening to any one song that was blowing me away, but at the time, the songs were kind of secondary to the whole feel. The band obviously had a lot of raw power. I just remember hearing that tape and going, 'Oh my God.'"

Poneman excitedly brought the demo in to Muzak, the background music company, where just about anybody who was anybody in the Seattle scene worked at menial jobs like cleaning tape cartridge boxes or duplicating tapes. Green River's Mark Arm (now of Mudhoney), Room Nine's Ron Rudzitis (now of Love Battery), Tad Doyle (an Idaho transplant who would soon lead the band TAD), Chris Pugh of Swallow, Grant Eckman from the Walkabouts, and Bruce Pavitt all worked at Muzak, making it a place where ideas and opinions about rock & roll were developed and discussed. "If anyone wants to get rich," Poneman announced, "this band is looking for a drummer."

But the jukebox jury didn't like it. The music relied too heavily on tortured, complex arrangements for the Muzak bunch, who were getting into more straight-ahead rock such as early Wipers, Cosmic Psychos, and the Stooges. But the guy did have a great voice. On the other hand, the Muzak crowd might not have liked it no matter what. "Everybody wanted their closest friends to be the biggest stars," says Pavitt, "and [Nirvana] was from out of town so people were hedging their bets a little bit." Poneman remembers Mark Arm saying the tape sounded like Skin Yard, "but not as good." "Basically people were pretty much focused on their clique," says Pavitt, "and the music that was coming out of that clique."

The Muzak crew didn't go for the metal elements of Nirvana's music. For them, the Stooges—their economical brutality as finely wrought as a kick to the head—were the gold standard by which all bands were measured.

So if the Aberdeen guys had been intimidated by Seattle, they were right to be. It was the promised land, but it was also daunting—this reaction from the Muzak clique only confirmed an image of a city populated by exclusive sophisticates, cooler than thou and almost inscrutably hard to please.

Pavitt thought it was too "rock"—too much heavy metal and not enough underground. Poneman and Pavitt caught a show at the Central Tavern—eight on a Sunday night—that was sparsely attended, even though hundreds of people now claim to have been there. The band was rough but some of the material was very good. Pavitt agreed the band had potential. Poneman remembers Kurt threw up backstage before the show.

"I wasn't completely swept over by the band," Pavitt admits. "I did not see an interesting musical angle with Nirvana." But Poneman loved the music, and Pavitt, a former journalist, began looking for a hook with which to sell the band to the music press—small indie labels depend on the media to do their promotion for them. Then Pavitt hit on something.

"The more I spent time thinking about who they were and what was going on in Seattle," says Pavitt, "it really started to fit in with this Tad thing—the butcher from Idaho—the whole real genuine working class—I hate to use the phrase 'white trash'—something not contrived that had a more grassroots or populist feel." Up until then (and to a large extent ever since), independent music was dominated by the East Coast circuit of tip sheets, fanzines, radio stations, and clubs. Instead of the pointy-headed college/art school cabal, "We were trying to work with people who were intelligent and creative but weren't necessarily in college," says Pavitt. "And the more I got to know Kurt, they really seemed to fit that picture as well as Tad."

Which was ironic since Tad Doyle of TAD actually had studied music at the University of Idaho and was an accomplished jazz drummer. But a good rule of thumb in marketing is: never let the truth get in the way of a good brand narrative. And while Sub Pop's concept might have been misleading, even condescending, it would nonetheless soon prove to be very, very successful.

When Kurt first moved in with Tracy in Olympia, he complained that he was shunned in Seattle because he wasn't part of a clique. A year later, he didn't want to go to shows because so many people wanted to talk to him. They had all heard the demo tape. Endino would make tapes for his friends, who would make copies for their friends.

The Seattle music community was, at its core, really just a few dozen people. They all played in each other's bands, went to each other's shows, loaned each other equipment, got drunk and did Ecstasy with each other, crashed on each other's floors. And they were hip, often college-educated, and from the cosmopolitan metropolis of Seattle or its suburbs. As with the Olympia scenesters, Kurt really wanted to be accepted by this club—because it was another step on the way to escaping Aberdeen.

Tracy Marander, February 1989.
© 1993 by Alice Wheeler

Kurt dubbed off a bunch of cassettes and sent them to every indie label he could think of, including SST in Lawndale, California, and San Francisco's Alternative Tentacles. But the label he really wanted to be on was Chicago's Touch & Go—home of some of Kurt's favorite bands: Scratch Acid, Big Black, and the Butthole Surfers. He sent about twenty copies to the label, always accompanied by letters and "little gifts," which ranged from little toys and handfuls of confetti to a used condom filled with plastic ants or a piece of paper encrusted with boogers (a stunt which sounds suspiciously similar to what Big Black did with their *Lungs* EP). No one, especially Touch & Go, called back.

He didn't send a tape to Sub Pop because he barely knew it existed. Not a moment too soon, Poneman called Kurt to tell him he liked the tape. Kurt figured

Poneman was cool because he was associated with Soundgarden, his favorite band at the time. They arranged a meeting at the Café Roma on Broadway in Seattle.

Kurt arrived first with Tracy. Tracy was vaguely suspicious and wary of the whole thing—she didn't like the way Poneman kept his hands jammed in the pockets of his long trench coat, or the way he kept nervously sweeping his eyes around the room. "It looked like the police were after him," she recalls.

I'm not sure what was with Poneman's nervousness—he's a very poised and personable fellow. (Full disclosure: over the years, he's become a good friend, as has Bruce Pavitt.) But he was pretty young at the time and maybe a little anxious, even starstruck, about meeting a band that he was so excited about, and they were one of his first signings.

Poneman remembers Kurt as being "very timid, very respectful" and "a very nice, gentle guy." Chris, who came in soon after Kurt and Tracy, was a different story. Chris was nervous about the meeting and had polished off a few Olde English forty-ouncers on the way up to Seattle. He was quite drunk and was swigging from yet another forty-ouncer that he kept under the café table. Throughout the meeting, he would glare at Poneman and insult him, burping loudly and occasionally turning around to bellow at the other customers—"What the fuck are you people looking at? Hey! Hey!" Kurt remembers it as "one of the funniest things I've ever seen."

Krist's drunken antics could have destroyed any chance of fulfilling Kurt's dream of releasing a record. At least Kurt thought it was funny.

This same dynamic would play out countless times during Nirvana press interviews: Krist—physically imposing, loud, voluble, amusing, and sometimes seeming to be a little hammered—dominating the conversation while "very timid, very respectful" Kurt, the leader of the band, let him do all the talking, sitting back and snickering at the absurdity of the scene. Nonetheless, Kurt was torn about this dynamic—on one hand, he knew he didn't have the outgoing nature and gift of gab like Krist did, and yet sometimes, he resented his bass player for dominating the microphone.

Poneman did his best to ignore Chris, and somehow managed to convey the idea that he wanted to put out a Nirvana single in the near future.

Early 1988 was a fallow period for the Seattle scene. Key bands such as the Melvins, Green River, and Feast were either on hiatus or had broken up. Bands such as TAD, Mudhoney, and Mother Love Bone were just getting started. And so was Sub Pop Records.

Sub Pop began in 1980 as a fanzine written by Bruce Pavitt, a Chicago-area transplant who studied punk rock at the free-thinking the Evergreen State College in Olympia. Pavitt soon began making tape compilations which highlighted regional music scenes in the United States and eventually spotlighted Seattle in his first vinyl release, *Sub Pop 100*. In 1986, he released *Dry as a Bone* by Green River, a Seattle band that dared mix the antithetical sounds of metal and punk (the band later splintered into Mudhoney and Pearl Jam). Their mutual friend Kim Thayil of Soundgarden introduced Pavitt to Jonathan Poneman, a college radio DJ and promoter of rock shows in Seattle. They released Soundgarden's *Screaming Life* EP in 1988.

"Pavitt's goal," I wrote in *Our Band Could Be Your Life*, "was to build a national network of like-minded people to fend off what he called 'the corporate manipulation of our culture' by the media centers of New York and Los Angeles." And a key part of establishing that was to demonstrate that there were great bands everywhere, even in the cultural backwater of Seattle. And, lo and behold, there really were: Soundgarden, TAD, Mudhoney, and Nirvana enabled Pavitt and Poneman to pull off one of the great popular culture coups of the late twentieth century.

Canny, articulate, and blessed with good ears, Pavitt and Poneman had a flair for self-promotion, and having closely studied the successes and failures of previous indie labels, rapidly established both the Seattle scene in general and Sub Pop in particular as the coolest thing in indie rock. There were other labels in town, including Popllama (who had the Young Fresh Fellows), but Sub Pop had the promotional moxie. On most of the front covers, Pavitt's friend Michael Lavine took arty, polished studio photographs that created the impression that the label had shelled out big bucks for a fancy photographer. And on the inside and back covers, Charles Peterson created Sub Pop's defining images—grainy, blurry black-and-white shots that often featured more of the audience than the band. Peterson would fearlessly wade deep into the mosh pit, capturing all the violent motion—all sweat, hair, and bare male chests.

Michael Lavine specialized in striking studio photography with loud, saturated colors that embodied a certain '90s visual sensibility; by contrast, Charles Peterson shot his gritty, impeccably composed work in black and white at sweaty, loud nightclubs. They formed the yin and yang of Sub Pop's visual imagery and were a major factor in the label's ascent: if you could supply excellent, free photos, it helped get your band into a magazine or fanzine.

Dave Foster, Kurt,
and Chris.
© 1993 by Rich Hansen

An interesting new band like Nirvana was big news. Kurt's guitar style was jagged, yet had an undeniable metal streak. The riffs were clever. The fact that they could sound so good in so little time amazed Endino, who'd recorded many bands already. Even back then, Kurt was setting his melodies in an unusual way against the rhythms and chord changes. Instead of simply following the guitars, he invented almost contrapuntal melody lines. But what put the band over the top were Kurt's vocals—somehow, he was able to scream *on pitch*, as well as sing in a very accessible and attractive way.

They had crappy equipment and terrible-sounding amps. For a long time, they had to put a two-by-four under Chris's bass cabinet because he was missing a wheel (the problem was remedied only recently).

By that point—early 1988—Crover had left to move to San Francisco with Osborne, but not before recommending Dave Foster from Aberdeen to be his replacement. Foster played bass with Crover in a Melvins satellite band, but was also a fine drummer. Kurt and Chris knew they didn't want Foster in the band permanently—with his souped-up pickup truck and his mustache, Foster was too mainstream, too macho for Kurt and Chris. Still, they played him the Crover demo and Foster seemed to like it.

"They taught me a lot as far as playing," says Foster, who had studied jazz drums in high school. "They just said forget all that shit and just hit 'em hard. That and cutting the size of my drum set in half. When I got in that band, I had a twelve-piece set, and when I got out, I had a six-piece."

They rehearsed in the front room of Chris and Shelli's new house on Pearl Street in Tacoma, near the Tacoma Zoo.

The first party they played was packed with Greeners and hippies and punkers. Kurt was wearing his usual cutoff denim jacket with his plastic monkey Chim-Chim glued to the shoulder and a cut-out section of a Woolworth's tapestry of the Last Supper on the back, while Foster was dressed in his usual Aberdeen metal dude clothes. During their set, a punker grabbed the microphone and said, "Gosh, drummers from Aberdeen are sure weird looking!" "I felt out of place," says Foster, "but I was into what they were doing. I loved to play their music."

That comment from the Olympia punk speaks of the open disdain for the working-class rocker types from surrounding towns. A few years later, another Nirvana drummer would also feel "out of place" in Olympia.

When Rich Hansen sent me the photo of Dave Foster with Kurt and Krist, he included a little note that said, in part, "While I was photographing them they were complaining among themselves about all the mistakes they made. They were perfectionists. This amazed me, because to me it was just loud, obnoxious music. I thought to myself no one would have noticed a mistake in their playing, to me it was comic." Kurt, Krist, and probably Dave Foster were very exacting, with a very clear vision of what they wanted to achieve. It might have been "loud, obnoxious music" at that point, but the people who made it had a very specific idea of how it was supposed to sound.

Poneman got them their first show in Seattle in early 1988 at the Vogue. It was Sub Pop Sunday. Charles Peterson, a key Seattle tastemaker, recalls there were about twenty people there, even though KCMU was playing "Floyd the Barber" regularly. Still, there was a buzz on the band, which reportedly sounded a lot like Blue Cheer. People like Mark Arm were there, scrutinizing this much-ballyhooed new band from the sticks. Kurt later commented that he thought they should have held up scorecards after every song.

The band played sloppily and the malfunctioning P.A. didn't help matters. Peterson, for one, was not impressed with the band's nearly nonexistent stage presence. "They were not particularly engaging," agrees Poneman. And the songs sounded too much like the Melvins. Peterson took Poneman aside and said, "Jonathan, are you sure you want to sign these guys?"

"We totally sucked," says Kurt. "We fucked it up."

Foster lasted only a few months. "He was a really straight guy but I think we really intimidated him because we were just weird," says Chris. "He'd just never seen anything like us before. We were just total counterculture people."

"I think *they* were the ones who were uncomfortable, being around what they thought was probably a redneck or something, I don't know. When all my friends came around, I think that made them uncomfortable. Because they weren't the type of people they hung out with," says Foster. "Everybody's got their own little clique, I guess."

"He also had a problem," says Chris. "He had to go to anger counseling. He'd get in fights and beat the hell out of people. One time we saw him and he was with this friend in his trick truck and the guy spat on his truck and he kicked the guy in the head."

Dave Foster's particular last straw came up when he found out his girlfriend was cheating on him. So he did the manly thing and went out and beat the hell out of the guy she was cheating with. Unfortunately for Foster, his victim happened to be the son of the mayor of nearby Cosmopolis. Foster got a one-year sentence but wound up serving two weeks in jail and getting his license revoked, which meant that he couldn't get up from Aberdeen to Tacoma to rehearse with Kurt and Chris.

It's kind of remarkable, the amount of violence that was around Nirvana. Think about all the fistfights, vandalism, rock throwing, and other violence in the book so far. It makes sense that an aggressive style of music would come from that environment.

Once he got out of jail, Foster would call Kurt, asking when he could come up and start practicing again. Kurt said they were writing new material and would get back to him. What he didn't say was they'd been rehearsing with Aaron Burckhard again, using Foster's drums.

But Burckhard's days in the band were numbered, too. One night after practice, Kurt and Burckhard were drinking at Burckhard's father's trailer home in Spanaway. Burckhard told Kurt he was going to get some more beer and borrowed Kurt's car. But instead of going to the package store, Burckhard hit the taverns instead. After two hours of drinking with his buddies, he left to go back to the trailer and was pulled over on a DWI charge by a Black policeman who happened to be named Springsteen. Burckhard started drunkenly calling out "Hey, Bruce! What's up, Bruce!" and just generally giving the cop "a rash of shit." Officer Springsteen threw the book at him. Kurt's car got impounded.

Since Burckhard's trailer didn't have a phone, Chris got the call to get Burckhard out of jail. Chris says Burckhard had called the cop a "fucking [repugnant racial epithet]," which is really why he got the book thrown at him. "It was just really embarrassing for me to go get him," he says.

"I might have said a few things," Burckhard admits, "but I have the right to remain silent."

Kurt says he called Burckhard the next day and asked him to come to practice. Burckhard said he was too hung over to play and Kurt simply hung up the phone. Burckhard was out of the band for good.

"I loved playing with them guys," says Burckhard. "But I was young and stupid and kind of got carried away, you know?"

If Burckhard hadn't gone to the taverns that night, he might be a millionaire right now. "Yeah," he says. "But it's like playing the Lotto—you can get five numbers and not the sixth and you're like, 'God, one more number!' I don't regret a thing. I'll be like—what's that guy from the Beatles?'"

Nowadays, the Pete Best of Nirvana collects unemployment checks, having been laid off from his job insulating houses. He also plays in a speed metal band called Attica, which boasts tunes such as "Fuck Blister" and "Drunken Hell Thrash." Burckhard recently spent three days in jail because he didn't pay a fine for driving while his license was revoked—apparently, he never did get his license back after that fateful DWI with Officer Springsteen.

Foster still thought he was in the band. Then one day early that summer, he picked up a copy of the *Seattle Rocket* to see if there were any good shows coming up. It said that Nirvana was playing a place in Seattle called Squid Row that very night. Foster called Kurt's house, and Tracy gave him some story. Then he called Chris's and his roommate accidentally spilled the beans. They had another drummer. "I was so fuckin' pissed," says Foster. "It was just like if you caught your girlfriend in bed with someone else." Recall what happened last time Foster felt like that.

Kurt actually wrote a very thorough letter to Foster, explaining why they were firing him, but apparently never sent it. That's another example of his reluctance about confrontation. It was just easier to get another drummer and not tell Foster. So Kurt ghosted him.

Foster was upset for a long time, particularly when he heard that Nirvana had opened for the Butthole Surfers. "Now that that other shit's happened it's even worse," Foster says. But he's philosophical about it. "They did what they thought best, I guess," he says. "I do wish things were different—all I ever wanted to do was play drums for a living."

"He was such a mainstream type of guy," says Chris. "I think we really intimidated him. We'd make him nervous and his beats would be off."

"I wasn't uncomfortable at all," Foster insists. "It seemed like *they* were the ones who were uncomfortable. It didn't bother me a bit."

"And he came from a stable family," Chris half-jokes.

The drummer at Squid Row that night was Chad Channing, a small, pixieish fellow who sounds a little bit like Elroy from *The Jetsons*. "He's an elf," says Kurt. "He should be in the Keebler factory. He's also one of the nicest people I've ever met." Channing lived on Bainbridge Island, an affluent suburb a ferry ride away from Seattle, across Puget Sound. Like Kurt, Chad had also been hyperactive and been given Ritalin.

Chad Channing was born on January 31, 1967, in Santa Rosa, California, to Burnyce and Wayne Channing. Wayne was a radio disc jockey and was forever moving to different jobs all over the country, from California to Minnesota to Hawaii to Alaska to Idaho and back. "Our motto was 'Move every six months,'" says Chad. "So whatever friends I made, wherever I went, I knew they were just temporary. Everything was just temporary. So that was kind of weird. You don't

A sketch of the band by Kurt, with Chad's North drums very much on display.

really hang out with many people because why make a friend if you're not going to be around—you're just going to be gone."

Chad had hoped to be a soccer player but when he was thirteen he shattered his thigh bone in a freak gym accident. It took almost seven years of rehabilitation and surgery for him to fully recover. In the meantime, he discovered music and picked up the drums, guitar, and a few other instruments.

You have to marvel at the fact that everyone who's ever been in Nirvana—at this point, anyway—has been a social misfit with a fairly tough life.

Like Kurt, Chad dropped out of high school during his senior year. He'd lost so much schooling from being in the hospital that he would have had to go through months of summer school and night school to get his diploma. He wanted to be a musician and didn't see the sense of it. When he met Kurt and Chris, he was a sauté cook at a seafood restaurant on Bainbridge Island. By night, he partied with his friends, smoking pot, drinking, and doing the potent local acid, which many swear has fried the brains of an entire generation of Bainbridge Islanders.

When Chad first heard of Kurt and Chris's band, they were called Bliss. Bliss shared a show with Chad's band Tick-Dolly-Row (a sailor's term for "down-and-out") which featured lead singer Ben Shepherd, who went on to play bass in Soundgarden. Kurt and Chris noticed Chad's North drum kit—which was made of fiberglass and had unique flared shells. "They noticed my North kit," says Chad. "It was kind of loud and that's what they hit on there. I remember Kurt telling me a long time ago when they were first checking us out, 'God, man, I wish we could get that guy! Look at those drums! Those are the weirdest things I've ever fuckin' seen!'"

Chad joined a grand tradition of musicians who were drafted into bands in part because they had nice equipment: for instance, Bill Wyman got asked to join the Rolling Stones because he had a cool amp. David Lee Roth (Van Halen) and Ozzy Osbourne (Black Sabbath) both got asked to join their bands because they happened to have a PA system. And those all worked out very nicely. Chad also worked out nicely for Nirvana: having a multi-instrumentalist and fellow songwriter in the band—not to mention a fine drummer who always showed up to practice, shared the band's sensibility, and worked hard—surely upped their game immeasurably.

North drums, with their very distinctive flared plastic shells, like horns or bell-bottoms, had gone out of production in the early '80s, so this was another example of the band using cast-off technology. But the key thing about North drums was, they were specifically designed to be very loud. That was really important to Nirvana, who practiced at extremely high volumes—something their next drummer would find out the hard way.

The name of Chad's band is kind of interesting—like Skid Row, it harks back to the old days of the Northwest. Seattle in those days had a whole lot of regional pride: many musicians had tattoos of Northwest Native American artwork, and they all knew about the region's great garage bands from the '60s, especially proto-punks the Sonics ("Strychnine," "The Witch," "Have Love, Will Travel") and the Wailers ("Tall Cool One" and the first known recorded cover of Richard Berry's "Louie, Louie"), as well as more contemporary regional underground greats like Wipers and Dead Moon.

Kurt and Chris briefly considered asking Tad Doyle to be their drummer, then took out an ad in the *Rocket*: "Heavy, light punk rock band: Aerosmith, Led Zeppelin, Black Sabbath, Black Flag, Scratch Acid, Butthole Surfers. Seeks drummer." Kurt got a bunch of lackluster responses, but in the meantime, their mutual friend Damon Romero introduced Kurt and Chris to Chad at Malfunkshun's farewell show at the Community World Theater. They talked for a bit and agreed to jam soon at Chris's house. Chad liked the band, but he wasn't sure. Then he saw the band play a show

at Evergreen and they talked some more and agreed to jam again. "I just kept on coming over and jamming," says Chad. "They never actually said, 'Okay, you're in.'"

It's funny how this is identical to something Keith Moon said in the documentary *The Kids Are Alright*: he never really joined the Who, he just kept showing up to practices, recording sessions, and gigs. "They never actually told me that I was a part of the band," Moon said. "But I knew by instinct."

Malfunkshun was one of the founding members of the Seattle scene as we know it, appearing on the epochal *Deep Six* compilation. But their glammy, over-the-top hard rock, makeup, and outrageous stage wear didn't fit the Sub Pop template. A local legend in his own time, flamboyant lead singer Andrew Wood went on to form Mother Love Bone with guitarists Stone Gossard and Bruce Fairweather, bassist Jeff Ament, and drummer Greg Gilmore—and then died of a heroin overdose in March 1990, days before the release of the band's major label debut album. The entire Seattle music community was devastated. Gossard and Ament then picked themselves up by the bootstraps and formed Pearl Jam.

In early 1988, Kurt and Chris had built a rehearsal studio in Chris's basement from old mattresses, carpet they got at the Goodwill store, egg cartons that Shelli and Tracy brought home from work, and scrap wood they pinched from construction sites. It was still pretty loud and the neighbors would complain, so they couldn't practice late. One day Chris and Shelli's pet rabbit got out of its cage and chewed through the extension cord that ran down to the basement. The band had to suspend rehearsals for a week until they could get up enough money for a new cord.

After making Chad strip down his mammoth kit just like Dave Foster did, they rehearsed material from the Crover tape as well as new material such as "Big Cheese" and "School." They wrote as a band, with Kurt playing a riff and the other two joining in. They began rehearsing at least two or three times a week and a batch of new songs came together very quickly.

In early May, they played their first show with Chad at the Vogue. Chris sported enormous mutton chop sideburns, while Chad and Kurt's hair hung in long greasy curtains over their eyes. Poneman got them a gig at the Central Tavern in Seattle on a Saturday afternoon at some benefit show. Nobody was in the club at their scheduled six o'clock set time, so they just packed up their gear and drove back to Tacoma. They soon played another show at the Central, opening for Chemistry Set and Leaving Trains. Not many people were there, either.

The following year, cross-dressing Leaving Trains lead singer "Falling" James Moreland would very briefly be married to stripper and aspiring rock star Courtney Love.

The first article ever written about the band, by Dawn Anderson, editor of the free Seattle music paper *Backlash*, noted that the band seemed nervous when playing live. In the piece, Kurt confided, "Our biggest fear at the beginning was that people might think we were a Melvins rip-off," but Anderson bravely ventured that "with enough practice, Nirvana could become . . . *better than the Melvins!*"

The Seattle scene was really starting to bloom around then, with bands such as Skin Yard, the Fluid, Blood Circus, Swallow, TAD and Mudhoney playing the Vogue, the Underground, the Central, the Alamo. Mother Love Bone was gearing up, but the guys in Soundgarden were then the kings of the scene—miraculously, they had just gotten signed to A&M, a full-fledged major label.

Not so miraculously, really—A&M had been courting Soundgarden since before the first Sub Pop record, and Capitol, Geffen, and Slash were all interested in the band.

On June 11, 1988, only a month or two after Chad joined, they did the main session for their first single, "Love Buzz."

"Love Buzz"—a cover tune, after all—may not have been Kurt's first choice for the band's first single, but he eventually came around. It was an accessible, easy-to-listen-to pop song that had become a live favorite of both the crowd and Kurt, who got to run around the stage during the song's extended guitar solo section. They liked the idea of recording a new track instead of rerecording something off the Crover demo. Besides, Kurt had started getting into primitive-sounding, garage-influenced bands like the Sonics, a legendary Northwest band from the early '60s, and Mudhoney, and had begun to abandon the Byzantine arrangements he had favored on the Crover demo. Even though he didn't write it, "Love Buzz," a stripped-down pop song, fit perfectly with the direction Kurt wanted to go.

Around this time, Kurt hand-wrote a bio of the band, presumably aimed at prospective record labels, with a few facts distorted to make the band seem a little more established than it really was. "NIRVANA is a three piece from the outskirts of Seattle WA. Kurdt—guitar/voice and Chris—bass have struggled with too many undedicated drummers for the past 3 years [*sic*] . . . For the last 9 [*sic*] months we have had the pleasure to take Chad—drums under our wings and develop what we are now and always will be NIRVANA.

"Willing to compromise on material (some of this shit is pretty old)," the bio concluded. "Tour any time forever. Hopefully the music will speak for itself."

Aberdeen is hardly on the outskirts of Seattle; it's not even on the outskirts of Olympia. But by this time, Sub Pop had created some value in the association with Seattle, and

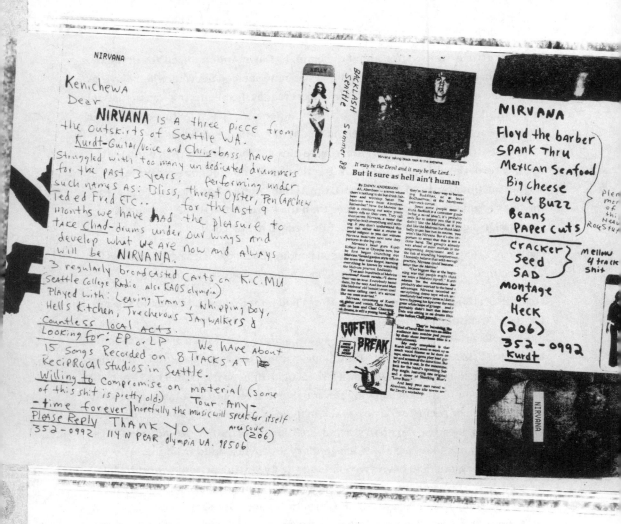

Kurt was astute enough to exploit it. And, as ever, there was an antagonist who had been holding them back: "too many undedicated drummers."

"Willing to compromise on material" is semi-sarcastic, another example of Kurt self-consciously making light of selling out. Ironically, they had compromised on the choice of song for the single, and they would soon compromise on material again, as we see in the very next paragraph.

Realizing that Sub Pop favored straight-ahead rock in the Stooges/Aerosmith vein, they recorded what little material they had that fit that style, instead of the more bizarre Scratch Acid—type songs they had been playing. Kurt regrets the

decision now. "I wish we'd have put 'Hairspray Queen' or something," he says. "But the idea of going into the studio again, instead of using what we had on the demo already, was enough of a challenge."

It's for the best that "Hairspray Queen" didn't wind up on the record—it's much too derivative of Gang of Four and Scratch Acid, and just not as good as anything else on *Bleach*.

Everybody was very excited about putting out their first record. Still, a pattern was already emerging. "For me, recording always went weird," says Chad. "I was there, I did my job, and that was it. I didn't really have any say about how this or that should sound. I might as well have gone up there, did my thing, and then gone out and get a candy bar or something. I'd bang on the drums, get the drum sound down and stuff like that, and then I'd just kick back and wait until they got the bass and guitar sounds and we'd do the song and that was kind of it. The rest of the time, I'd spend listening to see what they did with it. Kurt and Chris were like 'Let's do this and let's do that.' I would have had things to say, but I don't know, it just didn't feel right or something like that. I really had nothing to say or do."

I feel for Chad here, but the recording studio is a prime stage for the "too many cooks" syndrome: everyone in the band has an opinion about how things should sound, but arguing over mixes not only eats up a lot of expensive studio time, it also dilutes the overall aesthetic of the recording. The producer and engineer really do not want to deal with several different viewpoints. It's true that Chad had a lot to do with the way the songs came together in rehearsal, but as founders of the band, Kurt and, to a lesser degree, Krist called the shots. Later, Dave Grohl had a virtually identical experience.

Sub Pop didn't sign its bands to contracts back then. It wasn't done. Poneman simply told Nirvana that he liked that Shocking Blue cover they did, and would they like to do a single? At first, they held out to do their own song, but eventually relented. They recorded for five hours and ended up with several finished songs, including "Love Buzz," "Big Cheese," another stab at "Spank Thru," and "Blandest." It was Chad's first session. He wasn't hitting very hard then, but he'd come around.

In the indie community of the '80s, going without contracts was a matter of honor. Revered labels such as Touch & Go and Dischord didn't use them. "We came from a punk perspective—we did not want to get sucked into a corporate culture where basically you're signing a contract because you don't trust the other person to live up to their word," Big Black guitarist Santiago Durango told me for *Our Band Could Be Your Life*. (Durango later became an attorney.) Big Black figured contracts were worthless anyway—if a record company was going to screw a band, they'd do it with impunity since the band couldn't afford to retaliate. And, added Big Black leader Steve Albini, "If you don't use contracts, you don't have any contracts to worry about."

"Blandest" was going to be the flipside. The song is indeed not nearly as remarkable as what made it to the single, but the track does feature a fairly embarrassing Robert Plant–like falsetto wail toward the end by Kurt. As Endino recalls, the song's title seemed all too fitting, so he convinced Kurt to use "Big Cheese." They returned for more work on June 30 and mixed it all on July 16. Poneman didn't like the vocals on the first mix, so Kurt rerecorded them, although Endino says even he was hard pressed to hear the difference.

Kurt remembers feeling that "Love Buzz" was sounding too lightweight. They blamed Chad, whom they felt was not as good or as hard-hitting a drummer as Dale Crover. "We just couldn't get a good sound out of it," says Kurt. "It sounded really clean and just didn't have any low end. I think it's the wimpiest recording we've ever done."

The intro to "Love Buzz," a forty-five-second sound collage Kurt made from various children's records, was trimmed at Pavitt's request down to ten seconds. It appears only on the original seven-inch single. "They were just constantly having control right away," says Kurt. "Doing exactly what a major label would do and claiming to be such an independent label."

And there's another antagonist: Sub Pop. Kurt railed about this even though, as he himself had said in writing, the band was "willing to compromise on material." But, as he did so often, Kurt revised history as a form of retaliation.

In September, Shelli broke up with Chris. The strain of Shelli's working the graveyard shift at the Boeing cafeteria and Chris's playing with the band got to be too much. She had just turned twenty-one and had never been alone. They decided to live separately. They broke up but saw each other often. They missed each other and were depressed.

As avid students of the indie rock game, Pavitt and Poneman knew that American artists from Jimi Hendrix to Blondie had established a buzz in the UK before anyone in their native country noticed them. So they took the huge financial gamble of flying in a music journalist, *Melody Maker*'s Everett True, all the way from England

LEGGO MY EGO PRESENTS ......
NIRVANA
ALSO KNOWN AS ....
SKID ROW, TED ED FRED, PEN CAP CHEW, BLISS
BRING CANS OF FOOD AND YE'S FEE SHALL BE RE-DUCED
HEY KIDS! Dont Buy A GRAM This week-end, Come see a Revelation IN PROGRESS, it will be A Gosh DARN...
HEALING EXPLOSION.
WITH
LUST
AND OTHER SPECIAL GUESTS YET TO BE ANNOUNCED
$5
SAT. MAR. 19
So. 56th & M st TACOMA
COMMUNITY WORLD THEATRE

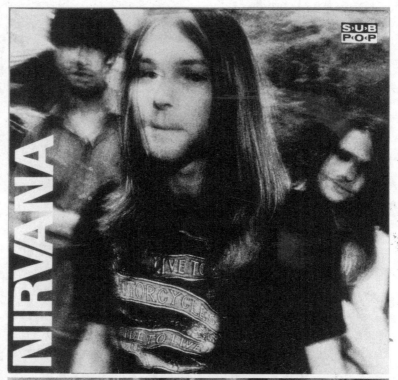

SUB POP

LOVE BUZZ
b/w
BIG CHEESE

KURDT KOBAIN:
VOCALS, GUITAR
CHRIS NOVOSELIC:
BASS
CHAD CHANNING:
DRUMS

RECORDED AT RECIPROCAL STUDIOS,
SEATTLE. PRODUCED BY JACK EN-
DINO & NIRVANA.

PHOTOGRAPHS BY ALICE WHEELER.
INNER LABEL DESIGN BY SUSANNE SASIC.
JACKET DESIGN BY LISA ORTH.
LOVE BUZZ WRITTEN BY ROBBY VAN LEEUWEN.

242 /1000

The cover of the "Love Buzz"/"Big Cheese" single.

to check out a few Sub Pop bands. True raved about the Seattle scene in a series of articles, and soon US press and labels were foaming at the mouth, too.

Mudhoney's *Superfuzz Bigmuff* EP stayed on the UK indie charts for a year, almost unheard of for an American release. Three months later, ultra-influential Radio One DJ John Peel raved about the *Sub Pop 200* box set and basically said it was a testament to regional music not seen since Detroit's Motown label conquered the world in the mid '60s.

That was exactly what Pavitt and Poneman wanted to hear. They had consciously patterned Sub Pop on the model of classic regional American labels with distinct, consistent musical and visual aesthetics, such as Motown, Blue Note, Chess, Sun, and Stax, not to mention contemporaries such as SST and Touch & Go. They set out to do the same thing for Seattle: to establish a Seattle sound and look. "It's a regional chauvinism that you find in sports," Pavitt explained to me for *Our Band Could Be Your Life*. "People relate to that. They get pumped up by that."

They achieved that distinctiveness and consistency not just with the bands they signed, but by having a consistent visual aesthetic. Sub Pop needed Nirvana to fit their template, and that created some tensions.

The Brits went ga-ga over the Seattle scene. "The reason they picked it up was there was a regional identity and flavor to what we were doing," says Bruce Pavitt. "The history of rock music is broken down that way—it comes down to labels or scenes. We understood that from the beginning. Look at the cast of characters—that's how you create a soap opera that people come back into. So all of a sudden, people knew who Mark Arm was, Kurt, Tad, me, and Jon, Jack Endino, Peterson. We tried to introduce in our own way, these celebrities. Like our singles, the only thing that would be on the back was 'Recorded by Jack Endino' and 'Photo by Charles Peterson.' And after you get ten singles like that, with no information other than that, you're going, 'Who's Charles Peterson? Who's Jack Endino?'"

On September 27, Nirvana and Endino mixed "Spank Thru" for the *Sub Pop 200* compilation. A key sonic document, the collection also featured tracks by Soundgarden, TAD, Mudhoney, Beat Happening, and Screaming Trees. The tracks could easily have fit onto two LPs, but Pavitt and Poneman, who always said yes to another excess, decided to release it as a three-EP set with an extensive sixteen-page booklet of photos by Charles Peterson, limited to five thousand copies.

Meanwhile, Kurt and Poneman exchanged countless phone calls, trying to hash out the particulars of the single. So much time elapsed between the time that Poneman agreed to do a single and when it actually came out that Kurt and Chris began to become very suspicious of the deal. Kurt would call and ask about the single and Poneman would promise the record would come out soon. Five months later, Pavitt called up wondering if Sub Pop could borrow two hundred dollars to press the single. Kurt hung up on him and sent out another batch of demo tapes to the various labels. The single came out soon afterward, in November of 1988.

An early Sub Pop catalogue touted the "Love Buzz"/"Big Cheese" single as "Heavy pop sludge from these untamed Olympia drop-ins." It was the first Sub Pop Single of the Month, a clever scheme in which Sub Pop commanded exorbitant prices for limited edition singles for which subscribers paid in advance—"We're ripping you off big-time," the Sub Pop catalogue boasted. Only one thousand hand-numbered copies of the "Love Buzz" single were made. "We were really burned about that," Chris recalls. "We put a single out and nobody can buy it."

Actually, pressing only one thousand copies was a very canny move—like many other of Sub Pop's limited releases, the single sold out quickly, making the record an instant collector's item (it now fetches up to fifty dollars). "It was very effective promotion for the group," says Pavitt. "I do not regret that at all." Word of mouth on the single traveled far and wide.

Today, that single goes for over three thousand dollars.

Kurt wrote the bio that accompanied press mailings of "Love Buzz." The bio speculated about merch the band hoped one day to sell: "dolls, pee-chee folders, lunch boxes, and bed sheets." As ever, Kurt was already acutely aware of both his own ambition and the need to undercut it with sarcasm, so as to preempt criticism.

And significantly, it had won over even the doubting Thomases in the Muzak posse. Pavitt knew something was up when Charles Peterson told him he played the single over and over at his party.

Except for Kurt's songwriting, "Love Buzz" had all the elements of classic Nirvana already in place: the mix of passivity and aggression in the way the song went from an almost hypnotic revelry to screaming, all-out frenzy; the sludgy, pounding drums; the grunged-up pop; and the Scream. With its slow, lurching rhythms and dire, barked vocals, "Big Cheese" showed a heavy Melvins influence. The song's title character is none other than Jonathan Poneman. "I was expressing all the pressures that I felt from him at the time because he was being so judgmental about what we were recording," says Kurt. Although not his finest songwriting hour, the lyrics were typical of Kurt's gift for taking a situation specific to him and turning it into a universal—who hasn't felt resentment at being ordered around by someone else?

To a provincial neophyte like Kurt, Poneman really was a "big cheese" even though in the music industry world at large, Poneman wasn't a big cheese at all—he was small potatoes. Nevertheless, Poneman exerted power over Kurt, and it's easy to understand Kurt's resentment of his barging into the creative process. It wouldn't be the last time a record company questioned Kurt's artistic vision. But Poneman did fulfill an important role for Kurt: another in a long line of perceived antagonists. As Kurt sings in the song, "Need more enemies." (They subsequently reconciled.)

During a visit to Seattle, Kurt heard that the hip community radio station KCMU was playing their single. As he and Tracy were driving back to Olympia from Seattle, they listened to the station for "Love Buzz," but it never appeared. Kurt made Tracy stop the car at a telephone booth, where he called the station and requested the song. They couldn't drive any further or they'd lose the signal, so they waited twenty minutes until they played the single. Kurt was excited.

"It was amazing," says Kurt. "I never thought that I'd get to that point. I just thought I'd be in a band and maybe make a demo, but for them to play it on the radio was just too much to ask for at that time. It was really great. It was instant success and fame beyond my wildest dreams. More than I ever wanted. But once I got a taste of it, I really thought it was cool and I thought I would definitely like to hear my future recordings on the radio. And be able to pay my rent with this band, it would be really great. It made us step up mentally to another level where it was a reality that we could actually live off of this. I didn't think anywhere past ever being able to afford more than a hundred-dollar apartment. That was going to be the rest of my life—to be in a band and tour and play clubs and hear my songs on the radio once in a while. That was about it. I didn't think of ever looking forward to anything more than that."

At the time he told me this, Kurt had sold many millions of records, toured several continents, seen his videos played incessantly on MTV, received all kinds of praise. But he was still visibly awed as he recalled that moment of hearing his song on the radio.

JULY 3 -- the VOGUE

BLOOd CIRCUS
NIRVANA

A Special Sunday show

Around that time, the so-called alternative rock scene was undergoing one of its periodic sea-changes. Although they wouldn't have been caught dead admitting it even a year before, people were now quietly admitting that yes, '70s dinosaurs like Aerosmith and Led Zeppelin and Kiss and Alice Cooper really did rock. But it wasn't like punk rock never happened, either. A new tide of musicians began synthesizing the hard rock they were raised on in the '70s and the American indie punk rock they had embraced in the '80s.

That "drummer wanted" ad that Nirvana took out in the Seattle *Rocket* described them as a "heavy, light punk rock band: Aerosmith, Led Zeppelin, Black Sabbath, Black Flag, Scratch Acid, Butthole Surfers." Today, as streaming music has created musical omnivores out of many people, few would bat an eyelash at a band citing both *echt* classic rock influences such as Aerosmith and Led Zeppelin and gnarly underground punks such as Black Flag and Butthole Surfers. But in the late '80s, that was a new thing. And it was the recipe for grunge.

Some of the dogmatic barriers within the indie rock scene were falling—for a minute. Between the time of recording the demo and *Bleach*, Kurt and Chris were going through a crisis of musical identity. The demo had boasted overt Butthole Surfers and Scratch Acid sounds, yet they were also into cock-rock, as demonstrated by songs like "Aero Zeppelin." "There were a lot of real confused messages going on in our brains," says Kurt. "We just didn't know what we wanted to do at all. We just didn't have our own sound at all. Like everyone else, we were just coming to grips with admitting that we liked all different kinds of music. To be a punk rocker and if you were at a Black Flag show and you said you liked R.E.M. . . . You just couldn't do it."

Actually, "Aero Zeppelin" ripped on a phenomenon of the time, which was mainstream rock bands that sounded like Aerosmith, Led Zeppelin, or both (which was but one reason why Kurt outspokenly disliked Guns N' Roses). "Steal a sound and imitate, keep a format equally," Kurt sang on a chorus that all too fittingly aped Aerosmith and Led Zeppelin. "An idea is what we lack, it doesn't matter anyways!"

Maybe if you were at a Black Flag show, you couldn't say you liked R.E.M., but Nirvana assimilated both those bands.

chapter five

EVERYTHING'S GETTIN' ALL RADICAL

irvana began practicing intensively in preparation for an album, even though Sub Pop, as was their custom for new bands, merely wanted an EP. The rehearsal place had moved from Chris's basement to the space above Maria's Hair Design. Chris's mom didn't close shop until eight in the evening, so practices started then, lasting into the wee hours of the morning, often breaking for Chinese food around midnight. Chad would travel all the way from Bainbridge Island, picking up Chris in Tacoma and then Kurt in Olympia. This went on for two or three weeks. "We'd practice for hours and then we'd go on some trip," says Chris. "One day we went out to the beach and walked around and one night we went out to this water tower." Sometimes they'd just drive around in Chris's van and listen to Celtic Frost and the Smithereens.

That was a two-and-a-half-hour journey each way for Chad, by the way. These guys were committed.

It's uncannily fitting that Celtic Frost and the Smithereens were on different sides of the same cassette tape. Celtic Frost was an influential, groundbreaking Swiss metal band while New Jersey's Smithereens were a notably melancholic power pop trio. (The latter's minor 1986 hit "Behind the Wall of Sleep" was produced by Don Dixon, and it might be more than coincidence that Nirvana would later consider Dixon for *Nevermind*.) In a sense, Nirvana occupied a stylistic middle ground between these two very different bands. And if you're curious about the influence of the Smithereens on Nirvana, listen to "About a Girl" and then the Smithereens' 1986 "Blood and Roses."

On December 21, 1989, about a week and a half before recording, they played a show at the Hoquiam Eagles Lodge. Chris played in his underpants and Kurt painted his neck red.

Shortly before he and Shelli broke up, Chris had quit his job in order to devote more time to the band. He had four hundred dollars saved up and blew it all in two weeks. "I'd go to parties and buy four cases of beer and just give out beer," says Chris. "Once, I gave out a case of beer in two minutes. Next thing I knew, I was broke."

"I was in bumland," says Chris of his bachelor days. "It was awesome." He moved back in with his mom in Aberdeen and it snowed for two weeks while

Nirvana's first photo session, summer 1989. © 1993 by Alice Wheeler

Chris hung around the house and read *One Day in the Life of Ivan Denisovich*. "I felt like I was in a gulag," he says.

Nirvana wanted to record, but Sub Pop, like most indie labels, was having cash flow problems, thanks in part to the exorbitant costs of the cover art for the *Rehab Doll* EP by Green River, who were by then defunct. They went ahead and booked sessions for an album anyway. They began work on *Bleach* on December 24, 1988, and did five hours of basic tracks.

On the twenty-eighth, they played a release party for *Sub Pop 200* at the Underground. Legendary Seattle poet Steven Jesse Bernstein introduced them as "the band with the freeze-dried vocals." The next day, they did another five tracks, then more work on January 24, 1989. When all was said and done, Endino billed them for a total of thirty hours. On the way to recording, Kurt would sit in the front passenger seat, rest a piece of paper on the dashboard, and hastily finish writing down the lyrics to the songs they were about to record.

The Amplified Come as You Are

Kurt may have jotted down the final lyrics on the way to the studio, but he'd been singing those songs with the band for months—the words were probably pretty well set by that time. Maybe he fudged some lines here and there during rehearsal, but there is nothing like a hard deadline, such as studio time, to help you make up your mind. Someone as exacting as Kurt was simply not going to wing it with something as important as lyrics: it's very difficult to sing with conviction if you don't completely believe what you're singing. And Kurt was already extremely demanding about his vocal performances.

Seattle performance poet Steven Jesse Bernstein was a fixture of the late-'80s Seattle scene, opening for Nirvana and other Seattle bands, including Soundgarden, and appearing on the 1988 *Sub Pop 200* compilation. Bernstein also made one of the best albums Sub Pop has ever released: a spoken-word-with-music album called *Prison*, with future Nirvana producer Steve Fisk supplying the music, a kaleidoscopic mélange of trip-hop, sampledelica, spy movie music, and dark ambient sounds.

Bernstein was a very troubled soul who had suffered serious drug and mental health problems; his work is shot through with unsparing self-hatred, exquisitely painful humor, and a sharp, sordid lyricism delivered in a snarling, caustic whine that could cut sheet metal. It figures that Kurt was a fan.

On October 22, 1991, Bernstein took his own life. He was forty years old.

Chad had been in the band six months and they'd been playing a lot. Chad was a more straight-ahead drummer than Dale Crover and the tunes were correspondingly straightforward. They attempted "Floyd the Barber" and "Paper Cuts" again, but they didn't match the Dale Crover versions, so they remixed the Crover tapes and put them on the album. The as yet untitled album was sequenced and edited, but Bruce Pavitt ordered the album completely resequenced. The album was delayed a couple of months, but Sub Pop finally borrowed some money to get it out.

Kurt was very particular about his singing, and would get very angry if he couldn't make the sounds he wanted to make. "He'd start smacking his chest and stuff," says Chad. "Not into it."

If the mixes on *Bleach* sound a little strange, there may be a very good reason. "We were all sick by then," Chris remembers, "and we had this codeine syrup from the Pierce County Health Department. So we were drinking a lot of that for our sickness but we were really on codeine and we were mixing the record and getting really into it."

The album cost $606.17 to record. No one in the band had that kind of money, so a fellow named Jason Everman put up the cash.

For my *Rolling Stone* cover story, Jack Endino very kindly went back through his studio billings and, for the first time, found the precise amount that Nirvana paid to record *Bleach*. That exact $606.17 price tag has since appeared countless times in all kinds of books, articles, and documentaries about Nirvana. It's funny to know that, directly or indirectly, they're all citing my story.

Dylan Carlson had introduced Jason to Kurt, and it soon turned out that Jason had known Chad since they were in fifth grade. The two had even played in several bands together in high school. Jason had spent the past few summers as a commercial fisherman in Alaska and had piled up a lot of money, so lending his old friend six hundred dollars was no big deal—besides, he had heard the Crover demo and knew that the band was destined for bigger things.

He began hanging out with the band.

Kurt didn't have much experience with playing guitar and singing (and remembering the words) at the same time—he'd only been playing in a band for a year and a half, after all. And all of a sudden, they had a tour to do. So one day Kurt mentioned to Jason that they were thinking about getting a second guitar player to thicken up the sound. "We basically were ready to take anybody if they could play good guitar," says Kurt. Jason mentioned that he played, auditioned once, and that was it. "He seemed like a nice enough guy," says Kurt. "And he had long Sub Pop hair." And besides, like Kurt, Chris, and Chad, Jason came from a broken home. He had even lived in Aberdeen for a while as a kid.

Kurt had trouble singing and playing at the same time—which was a big reason why they brought in Jason Everman and, later, Pat Smear—so songs with simple chords and song structures were a necessity. And that necessity mothered the great invention of Kurt streamlining his music.

Although Jason is credited as a guitarist on *Bleach*, he didn't play on it. "We just wanted to make him feel more at home in the band," says Chris.

His first gig with Nirvana was a drunken dorm party at the Evergreen State College. With another guitar player on stage, Kurt didn't have to try as hard; consequently, he became a much better player. Soundman Craig Montgomery recalls that he'd turn Kurt's guitar up much higher than Jason's. Early on, they began to realize what they had gotten into with Jason. Although Jason said he'd been into punk rock for years, Kurt's inspection of his record collection revealed, to his horror, little more than speed metal records.

Meet the Nirvanas: Kurt, Jason Everman, Chad, and Chris. © Ian T. Tilton

Chris found a rehearsal space in Seattle, but they didn't have a place to live in town, so often they'd buy some forty-ouncers and drink in the van until they fell asleep.

In February of 1989, after the album was completed, they did a quick two-week West Coast tour. By leaps and bounds, the band was gaining confidence as a live act. Bruce Pavitt remembers Mudhoney guitarist Steve Turner coming back after his band played with Nirvana in San Jose and raving that "Kurt Cobain played guitar standing on his head!"

The band weathered a devastating flu, visiting the Haight-Ashbury Free Clinic in San Francisco. While riding in their van around San Francisco, the band and Poneman and Pavitt noticed there was a major anti-AIDS campaign going on in town, with signs all over the city urging drug users to "bleach your works," meaning to clean needles with bleach to kill the AIDS virus. There was even a guy dressed up as a bleach bottle walking around downtown handing out bottles of bleach. "We were contemplating how bleach could become the most valuable substance on earth," says Pavitt. And so *Bleach* became the title of Nirvana's as yet unreleased first album.

So, while it began as a tour van in-joke, the title of Nirvana's first album was an oblique reference to doing heroin.

A cover piece in the March 18, 1989, *Melody Maker* on the Seattle scene featured a brief blurb on Nirvana. "Basically, this is the real thing," it began. "No rock star contrivance, no intellectual perspective, no master plan for world domination. You're talking about four guys in their early twenties from rural Washington who wanna rock, who if they weren't doing this, they would be working in a supermarket or lumber yard, or fixing cars." It was a positive little piece, but you could cut the condescension with a knife.

The verbiage followed the Sub Pop party line that their bands were authentic ("the real thing") because they were unpretentious working-class people with "no intellectual perspective." As for the lack of a "master plan for world domination" (a reference to Sub Pop's motto), Kurt had no intention of working in a supermarket or a lumberyard or fixing cars. There was no plan B.

The band came back from their tour and played a lot of area gigs—the Vogue, the HUB Ballroom at the University of Washington, and the Annex Theater, where the crowd paid Kurt the ultimate compliment by passing him over their heads during "Blew." Jonathan Poneman remembers that event as a milestone—only the ultra-cool Mark Arm had enjoyed that honor before.

They played a gig at a community center in Ellensburg, a sleepy cowtown in rural Washington. In the audience was Steve Fisk, who had already made a name for himself as producer of Soundgarden, Beat Happening, and the first four records by Screaming Trees.

"I hated them," says Fisk. "The P.A. system was set up really bad by this jock guy from Yakima. Kurt had broken a string and was really upset and stood in the corner trying to change his guitar string. They were just clowning off and they were all nervous—except for Chris—and they were playing *Ellensburg*. Even when it was obvious that Kurt wasn't playing his guitar they kept playing. Jason started moving his hair, but it wasn't in time with the music at all. I'm sorry—I've seen Black Flag and you move your hair in time with the music or you don't move it at all." Fisk walked out during the first song.

###

Bleach came out in June of 1989. Kurt disavows any personal relevance in the lyrics of the album. "Not much thought went into them at all," he says self-deprecatingly. "It's pretty obvious." But in truth, many of the songs tell a lot about Kurt and various incidents and situations in his life.

Like a lot of artists across all genres, Kurt dismissed his early work. It probably seemed unformed to him, especially once he had written *Nevermind* and *In Utero*. And lots of songwriters disavow any autobiographical nature to their songs, smudging the details so that other people can relate to them or to prevent interviewers and fans from getting

True grunge. Kurt at the HUB. © Charles Peterson

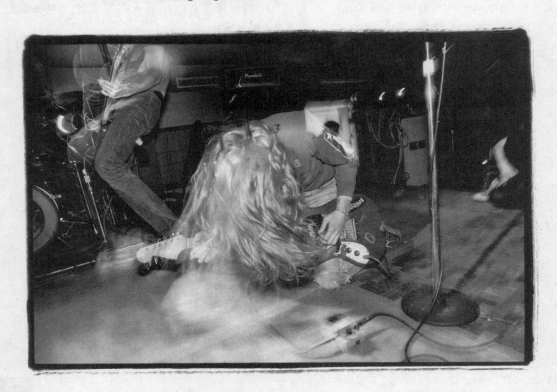

Chris and Kurt at the HUB.
© Charles Peterson

Chris puts his back into it at the HUB.
Note Jason's Soundgarden T-shirt. © Charles Peterson

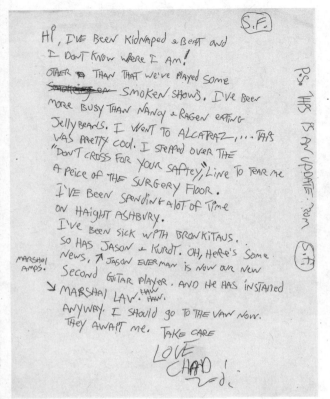

HI, I'VE BEEN KIDNAPED & BEAT and
I DON'T KNOW WHERE I AM!
OTHER THAN THAT WE'VE PLAYED SOME
~~SOMETHING OR~~ SMOKEN SHOWS, I'VE BEEN
MORE BUSY THAN NANCY & RAGEN EATING
JELLYBEANS. I WENT TO ALCATRAZ, ... THIS
WAS PRETTY COOL. I STEPPED OVER THE
"DON'T CROSS FOR YOUR SAFTEY" LINE TO TEAR ME
A PIECE OF THE SURGERY FLOOR.
I'VE BEEN SPENDING A LOT OF TIME
ON HAIGHT ASHBURY.
I'VE BEEN SICK WITH BRONKITAUS.
SO HAS JASON & KURDT. OH, HERE'S SOME
NEWS, JASON EVERMAN IS NOW OUR NEW
SECOND GUITAR PLAYER. AND HE HAS INSTALLED
MARSHAL LAW. HAW. HAW.
ANYWAY, I SHOULD GO TO THE VAN NOW.
THEY AWAIT ME. TAKE CARE
LOVE
CHAD!

S.F.
P.S. THIS IS AN UPDATE. FROM S.F.
MARSHAL AMPS.

Letter from Chad to his mother
from the quickie West Coast tour.

a peek into their personal lives. Then again, maybe Kurt simply didn't have enough objectivity about his own songs to realize how autobiographical they really were, but that's pretty doubtful.

The night before the sessions, the band stayed over at Jason Everman's house in Seattle. Kurt still hadn't written lyrics for most of the songs on the album. "I didn't care about lyrics at all at that time," he says. "I didn't have any appreciation for them. I'd never thought of a song because of its lyrics at that point." But he had to sing _something_, so he sat down and wrote into the wee hours.

One of the remarkable things about _Bleach_ is that the songs often have only one verse, which is repeated two, three, or more times ("School" has only fifteen words). It's barely noticeable because of Kurt's wide range of vocal styles and phrasings, and the hugely catchy riffs which constitute the songs. Kurt chalks up his laconic lyric style to short-term memory loss. "I decided to write songs that I would easily remember the lyrics to so I wouldn't fuck them up during the live show," he says.

The short-term memory loss might have been caused by smoking a lot of marijuana; Kurt often complained in the press about how pot destroys memory. But since Kurt had trouble playing guitar and singing at the same time, the fewer lyrics he had to memorize, the better.

"Swap Meet" comes straight from Aberdeen. A phenomenon of struggling rural America, swap meets take place in drive-ins or parking lots. People come from

miles around to sell baked goods, handicrafts, bric-a-brac and whatever else they can salvage from the darkest recesses of their garages and attics. Some sell their belongings so they can make the rent, others become full-time swap meet merchants. According to Kurt, the latter is usually "a white trash entrepreneur who can't look further than selling junk because they *live* in junk. They're surrounded by it and their whole mentality is based on junk—grease and dirt and poverty."

"Mr. Moustache" would help set a trend in alternative rock—the title is found nowhere in the song. "I've never had any reason to name any of my songs," Kurt says. "That's the only difference between alternative bands and cock-rock bands. Alternative rock bands name their songs with titles that don't have anything to do with the song or the chorus."

"In high school," explains Matt Lukin, "having a mustache was considered a real metal thing to do. Kids who are like eighteen have a real soft peach-fuzz mustache. That was the metal stoner dude mustache. They'd have the jean jacket with the fake wool lining and a mustache and long hair, feathered and maybe an

A 1988 cartoon by Kurt illustrating the true meaning of the term "Mr. Moustache."

earring and usually they'd have pot for sale. You'd say, 'He's got a mustache' and you'd know exactly what kind of guy he was."

That's also a good description of a hesher. Significantly, Aaron Burckhard and Dave Foster had mustaches, an unmistakable signifier that they didn't have a lot in common with Krist and Kurt.

The mustache also symbolized the macho man that Kurt detested so much. But the song, with its refrain of "Yes, I eat cow / I am not proud," is a swipe at self-righteous vegetarians ("poop as hard as rock"), who could be found in Olympia in abundant quantities. Of course, Chris was also a vegetarian, but the song is aimed more at the stridently politically correct types in Olympia, the kind who would walk up to a bare-chested guy and ask him to put his shirt back on in solidarity with women. This kind of thing put Kurt's sarcasm in high gear. "Fill me in on your new vision," he snarls in the opening verse. "Help me trust your mighty wisdom."

This turned out to be a very consistent sentiment on Kurt's part: as he sarcastically put it a few years later, "Forever in debt to your priceless advice." He was a very determined artist with a fully formed conception; he didn't have much patience for people telling him what to do and how to do it.

For "Blew," Kurt tuned down to what's called a "drop-D" tuning, but before recording the song, the band didn't realize they were already in that tuning and went down a whole step lower than they meant to, which explains the track's extraordinarily heavy sound. The leaden, distorted guitars ride a drunken rhythm just this side of plodding, producing a different kind of tension. The thick, gray tone of the track suits perfectly the theme of entrapment and control—"If you wouldn't care I would like to leave / If you wouldn't mind I would like to breathe."

Beyond entrapment and control, many of the songs seem to be about being perceived as a failure. Kurt certainly felt that from his parents, but now he was feeling it from Tracy, who pushed him to get a job, do some domestic chores, and earn his keep. For the rest of his life, there would always be somebody asking, even begging, him to get his shit together.

In the chorus, Kurt sings, "Here is another word that rhymes with shame." It's interesting to speculate about what word he was referring to, but maybe that line was a placeholder—maybe he simply hadn't come up with the right words yet, and this was literally a note to himself to end the line with a word that rhymes with "shame," to go with "stain" and "strain." He did a similar thing in "All Apologies" with "aqua seafoam shame"—perhaps another placeholder for a line he hadn't come up with by the time the tape started rolling. And yes, both lines contained the word "shame." Nirvana also had a song called "Oh, the Guilt." As ever, shame was a feeling that weighed on Kurt's mind.

Standard guitar tuning is E-A-D-G-B-E, but drop-D tunes the low E string down to a D, making a lower, darker, heavier sound. Thanks to bands such as Soundgarden and the Melvins—influenced by Led Zeppelin and Black Sabbath—drop-D was swiftly becoming a grunge staple.

The genesis of "About a Girl" began when Tracy asked Kurt why he didn't write a song about her. So he did. The line "I can't see you every night for free" refers to the fact that Tracy was by then threatening to kick Kurt out of the house if he didn't get a job. The song was indicative of the pop direction that Kurt wanted to go in. It's an anomaly on the record and indeed in the entire Sub Pop scene—no one had written anything so unabashedly melodious and Beatlesque for the label yet (Kurt had also written "Polly" by then, but it fit the Sub Pop format even less).

As the night wore on, Kurt began to make his lyrics simpler and simpler.

> **Blew**
>
> And we were in a garden ~~getting high.~~ wasting time
> ~~So~~ then you add a word-that ends with a Rhyme.
>
> my thoughts had changed a lot by the time we were through — I ~~cannot~~ cannot stand the thought of Hanging with you
>
> is there another Reason for your stain?
> ~~What makes you try to Release A Stain Is there Another Reason for your shame?~~
> What makes- you try so hard for ~~pose~~ impressive stress & strain?
> is there Another Reason for your ~~shame~~?
>
> Now If you wouldn't mind I would like to Blew!
> And if you wouldn't mind I would like to choose.
> ~~I~~ start to feel secure when you go away
> So if you wouldn't mind — ~~I guess I'd like~~ would like to stay
>
> You could do Anything
> decide on Anything
> You could do Anything

Initially, Kurt and Chris disliked the tight-knit, incestuous Seattle scene; at first glance it resembled the exclusive cliques which they had despised in high school. "I just found Seattle so incestuously small and cliquey and everyone knew one another and they just seemed so stuck up and they'd seen it all," says Kurt. He had finally escaped abysmal Aberdeen and arrived in the promised land of Seattle, only to find the same situation all over again. No wonder the refrain of "School," "You're in high school again," sounds so desperate.

When Kurt came up with the basic riff for the song, it sounded so much like a typical Sub Pop grunge-rock riff to them that they considered calling the song "The Seattle Scene." But given Kurt's gift for taking a specific situation and making it universal, it got the broader tag of "School." "We wrote it about Sub Pop," says Kurt. "If we could have thrown in Soundgarden's name, we would have." Still, it's like one of those late-'70s "disco sucks" songs that nevertheless used a disco beat. "It was a joke at first," says Kurt, "and then it turned out to be a really good song."

So there was Kurt ripping on Soundgarden again.

The Seattle community might have been like high school, but then so was the Olympia community. Kurt really wanted to be accepted in that high school. He wanted the respect of the people he hoped would accept him as a peer. He felt validated when a tastemaker like Mark Arm decided his band was pretty good.

"Negative Creep" is a first-person narrative from an antisocial person—"I'm a negative creep and I'm stoned," goes the chanted chorus—the kind that hangs out on the smoker's porch, scowling and sporting long greasy hair and black T-shirts touting dubious metal bands. According to Kurt, that person is himself. "I just thought of myself as a negative person" is his simple explanation. Kurt caught some flak from the Seattle music community for the line "Daddy's little girl ain't a girl no more" because it was dangerously close to Mudhoney's "Sweet Young Thing Ain't Sweet No More." Kurt claims it was merely a subconscious theft.

Those negative, misanthropic feelings were what Kurt said he tried to subdue with heroin. Ironically, though, heroin only served to alienate him from anyone who wasn't doing heroin, too, making a vicious cycle.

In *Grunge Is Dead*, Seattle scenester John Leighton Beezer recalls, "When I first saw [Nirvana] on MTV, I thought, 'Oh my God, that's Mark Arm playing Steve Turner's guitar!' Steve had that trademark baby blue Fender Jaguar, and that was Mark's hair. It wasn't a coincidence—[Kurt] really looked up to Mudhoney, and wanted to be Mudhoney."

The Amplified Come as You Are

By the end, it was very late and Kurt was getting burned out. He wrote "Scoff" and "Sifting" at this point. In "Scoff," Kurt listlessly wails "In my eyes, I'm not lazy. . . . In your eyes, I'm not worth it." It's a little bit of a stretch, but lines like that may be addressed to either Don or Wendy, who didn't consider Kurt's musical aspirations particularly worthwhile. With its mentions of teachers and preachers, "Sifting" seems to take on authority figures of all stripes, but as far as what it's about—it's anyone's guess, including Kurt's.

Two tracks (three on the CD version of *Bleach*) were taken straight from the Crover demo. With its slow, lurching beat, roared vocals, and ponderous chord progression, the eerie "Paper Cuts" is probably the most Melvins-influenced of all the tracks on the album. Part of the lyrics are based on a true story about an Aberdeen family who [had] kept their children locked up in a room with the windows painted over, opening the door only to feed them—or remove the pile of newspapers they used for a latrine. Kurt actually knew one of the kids—he was his old dealer Grunt's sidekick.

But the song is also apparently quite autobiographical—Kurt can only be describing his alienation from Wendy when he sings, "The lady whom I feel a maternal love for / cannot look me in the eyes / but I see hers and they are blue / and they cock and twitch and masturbate." Although it's quite a melodramatic comparison, Kurt seems to be making an analogy between the neglect the imprisoned children endured and the neglect he suffered from Wendy. "And very later I have learned to accept some friends of ridicule," he sings in the last verse, which seems to describe the outcasts he eventually befriended in Olympia. "Nirvana," Kurt moans five times on the chorus.

"Floyd the Barber" is another Melvins-styled number from the Crover demo. Floyd the Barber, of course, is a character from the early-'60s sitcom *The Andy Griffith Show*. It's not hard to divine the claustrophobic provincial theme. "It's just a small town gone bad," says Kurt. "Everyone turns into a mass murderer and they're all in cahoots with one another." But it's more than that—it's a Freudian castration nightmare, as the narrator is tied to a barber's chair and cut with a razor. "I was shaved / I was shamed," Kurt wails. Andy, Barney, Aunt Bee, and Opie all join in on the slashing.

There's shame again. Cutting off hair, by the way, is an age-old ritual of humiliation.

The fictional small town of Mayberry, where *The Andy Griffith Show* was set, is obviously a stand-in for Aberdeen—and towns just like it all over America and indeed the world. In the song, the good citizens of Mayberry sexually assault and then murder the narrator, a psychodramatized version of the abuse Kurt suffered in Aberdeen.

Kurt was a fan of the intense Chicago band Big Black, and "Floyd the Barber" might well be an echo of Big Black's 1986 song "Jordan, Minnesota," based on a purportedly true story of a small-town child sexual abuse ring that allegedly committed a series of gruesome murders. The case was mostly debunked, and twenty-one people had their charges dismissed, but not before the case made national headlines just as child sexual abuse was becoming more widely acknowledged and condemned in American culture.

Kurt would go on to much more explicitly repeat the image of himself as the victim of sexual assault a few years later in "Rape Me." He was very keen on identifying with women, but, as a man, was he right to appropriate a horrific experience virtually unique to women? And of all the despicable things human beings do to one another, why was Kurt fixated on this particular one?

"Downer" was included on the CD version of the album and also came from the Crover tape. It was an old song that Kurt wrote after being politicized by some of the more socially oriented punk rock bands. "I was trying to be Mr. Political Punk Rock Black Flag Guy," says Kurt. "I really didn't know what I was talking about. I was just throwing together words."

The album didn't sound as big and heavy as the band had hoped. It has a strangely claustrophobic, almost implosive feel that apparently unintentionally fits the general cast of the lyrics. Kurt is the first to point out that the album is one-dimensional—mostly slow, leaden, with not much melody. "We purposely made that record one-dimensional, more 'rock' than it should have been," he says.

Kurt purposely suppressed both his more melodic tendencies and his more arty, "new wave" streak because he knew the Sub Pop crowd wouldn't accept either. He figured Nirvana would have to make a grungy Sub Pop–style record to mobilize a fan base before he could get to do what he really wanted to do. "There was this pressure from Sub Pop and the scene to play 'rock music,'" says Kurt. "Strip it down and make it sound like Aerosmith. We knew that that was the thing to do. We had been doing it and we started doing that stuff on our own and now that it's a popular thing, we might as well cash in on it and become popular that way, because eventually we'll be able to do anything. We wanted to try to please people at first, to see what would happen."

So Nirvana was kind of selling out on *Bleach*, even if there wasn't actually much cash to cash in on: they were playing down their more melodic side and calculatedly making

The Amplified Come as You Are

the music they knew the label and its constituents wanted to hear. It was indisputably a careerist move, ironic considering Kurt's condemnation of Seattle musicians who had done similar things.

It was wildly optimistic to foresee that, at some point, Nirvana would be so successful and powerful that they'd "be able to do anything." Extremely few bands get struck by that particular lightning. So either Kurt was really prescient when they recorded *Bleach*—or he was going for some revisionist history here.

Kurt was *driven*: he just wanted everything he did to be really good. That has a way of leading to material success, but material success wasn't necessarily the goal, which can be a difficult nuance to understand: as a fan put it to MTV at a 1992 Nirvana show in Seattle, "Why'd they even start playing if they didn't want to be big, y'know?"

Kurt had written a Vaselines-influenced song called "Beans," based on the Jack Kerouac book *The Dharma Bums*. "Beans, beans, beans / Jackie ate some beans / And he was happy and naked in the woods" went the chorus. He wanted to put it on the upcoming album, but Poneman didn't. "He thought it was stupid," says Kurt, who adds that the band wanted to be more diverse and experimental on their debut album, yet met with heavy resistance from Sub Pop, both stated and unstated. Since the band had no contract, they just didn't know how much they could ignore Poneman's wishes and still get to put their record out.

"Beans" was part of a four-song demo of "weird, quirky songs" that the band wanted to include on the record. Says Kurt, "[Poneman] thought we were retarded."

"Beans" later surfaced on the *With the Lights Out* box set. And Poneman was right: it would have been a mistake to include it. But the track does hint at some artistic approaches Kurt might eventually have taken as a solo artist, as well as showing his playful side; if only for that, it's worth a listen. But maybe only one listen.

Ironically, the restrictions of the Sub Pop sound helped the band find its musical identity. Nirvana's new wave sound—Scratch Acid, Butthole Surfers, and the like—was derivative. It wasn't until they acknowledged the fact that they had grown up on Aerosmith and Black Sabbath that their music found its voice. "We just found ourselves reestablishing our songwriting within a couple of months," says Kurt. "It really was a great learning experience because that's really more where my roots are at anyhow—in rock, rather than the weird quirky new wave stuff that we were trying to do." This took a lot of nerve, especially in a climate where even the Sex Pistols were considered an oldies band.

In the late '70s and early '80s, "new wave" was the term for music that had picked up on punk's economy and energy but was much more commercial, polished, and melodic, like the Police, the Cars, and the Pretenders; it was instantly championed by the major record labels. But Kurt usually meant something different by "new wave": he wasn't talking about skinny ties and thin lapels and "Turning Japanese." His idea of new wave was the adventurous underground rock music that arrived in the wake of early-'80s punk bands like Black Flag and the Dead Kennedys: the aforementioned Scratch Acid and Butthole Surfers, as well as Rites of Spring and others. One might more accurately call it American post-punk.

But if we're talking about a relatively accessible post-punk music that was almost immediately co-opted by the major labels, then maybe grunge was the new wave of American indie rock.

Fessing up to liking working man's hard rock was an act of uncommon honesty in a world where arty poses were the norm, but it was something that needed to be said. When punk rock first erupted, it was necessary to play punk rock and only punk rock—that was the point. Once punk had made that point, it was ripe for assimilation, like any other source music.

The classic rock element of Nirvana's music was a big reason why the band attracted a large mainstream audience—deep in the music's core, those people heard things they were already familiar with.

Kurt saw only one hitch. "At that point I didn't think we had a unique sound," he says. "I didn't think we were really original enough to pull it off."

Bleach **certainly has its moments, but there's no question that Kurt's songwriting is mired in grunge. That attracted a slightly different audience from the one the band expected—a relatively mainstream hard rock audience—a problem which dogs them to this day. "We were never that alternative," Chris says in retrospect. "*Bleach*, all the hair on the front of that record and all those fuckin' rock riff songs—people always knew we had a pretty accessible appeal. We were just basically a rock band."**

Krist was being a little disingenuous there—Nirvana was "just basically a rock band" like Black Flag and Hüsker Dü were just basically rock bands: a singer, electric guitarist, bassist, and drummer playing more or less standard song structures. But Nirvana synthesized a lot of things in a way that was palatable to the masses—as Kurt famously explained in the following paragraph.

Like many Seattle bands, Nirvana sported a serious Black Sabbath streak. Kurt dug Black Sabbath, but he dug the pop side as much as the heavy side. Sabbath classics like "Paranoid" and "Looking for Today" have a catchy verse-chorus structure; they even have bridges. "I remember years ago asking Eric Shillinger, 'How successful do you think a band could be if they mixed really heavy Black Sabbath with the Beatles? What could you do with that?'" says Kurt. "I wanted to be totally Led Zeppelin in a way and then be totally extreme punk rock and then do real wimpy pop songs." He'd have to wait four years to do that.

Maybe mixing Black Sabbath and the Beatles is another example of Kurt's propensity for collage; juxtaposing different things and seeing if some synergy happens. (Interestingly, Soundgarden took that same Beatles-Sabbath formula and interpreted it differently, coming up with, among other great things, "Black Hole Sun" from 1994's *Superunknown*.)

That alternation of "extreme punk rock" and "wimpy pop songs" also echoes Nirvana's manic-depressive loud-soft dynamic. And what a natural segue into the Pixies that is.

Kurt first heard the Pixies' classic 1988 *Surfer Rosa* album after recording *Bleach*. An amalgam of blood-curdling screams, grinding guitars, and nascent but clearly discernible pop-style melodies, it sounded exactly like what he had been wanting to do, but had been too intimidated to attempt. Up until then, it just wasn't cool to play pop music if you were a punk rock band. "I heard songs off of *Surfer Rosa* that I'd written but threw out because I was too afraid to play them for anybody," he says. The Pixies' popularity both in the UK and on American college radio helped give Kurt the encouragement to follow his instincts.

I was just dead wrong there: it absolutely *was* cool to play pop music if you were in a punk band: there were the Ramones, Buzzcocks, and Hüsker Dü, among countless others, and they were indisputably cool.

Bruce Pavitt and the band haggled for weeks over the cover shot. The band wanted a photo Tracy had taken of them at a show at Reko/Muse, a tiny club/art gallery in Olympia. It had been a very eventful night. Ben Shepherd induced the audience to do the Worm, a punk "dance" in which the participants roll around on the floor, trying to knock over everyone else. At that same gig, Chris threw his bass up in the air and it came straight down on Chad's head. "I was sitting there," says Chad, "and boom, it sent me right to the floor immediately. I don't remember

Photos for the proposed *Bleach*
cover taken backstage after
a February 1989 show at the
HUB Ballroom. "We looked like
mutants," Kurt says.
© 1993 by Alice Wheeler

anything. I came out of it and I was like, 'Whoah, everything's gettin' all radical.'".

That's a great example of Chad's good nature. Instead of getting angry at Krist for braining him with a heavy bass guitar, his first thought was, "Whoah, everything's gettin' all radical." Krist would get some solid karmic payback three years later when he tossed his bass high up in the air at the 1992 MTV Video Music Awards and it came down and clocked him hard on the head in front of tens of millions of television viewers.

Reko/Muse, a feminist art space in a converted garage, was co-founded by future Bikini Kill singer and riot grrrl co-founder Kathleen Hanna. The riot grrrl/Nirvana connection began very early.

It was also a big night for Chris and Shelli. All the time they had been apart, Shelli missed Chris terribly. She realized she loved him. Chris had gotten a new girlfriend, but he still couldn't keep Shelli off his mind. So when Shelli heard that Chris's girlfriend had just gone to college in Montana, she swooped right in. She called him up and asked what he was doing, and he said they were playing a show that night and to come on over. They got back together after the show and moved in together for good.

Pavitt, Sub Pop's image czar, wanted a series of intimate, unflattering shots that photographer Alice Wheeler had taken of the individual band members backstage under fluorescent lights after a show. Pavitt liked the shots because they fit with Sub Pop's populist theories. "You could really see the acne and the stubble and it was so *real*," says Pavitt. "These guys were *ugly*—this was the most un-L.A. look you could come up with. I really wanted to use these photos to dramatize the fact that these people are real."

"We looked like mutants," says Kurt.

"But to me that was part of the story," Pavitt replies. "If you look at it in context, everything was Spandex and hairspray and we were trying to create something that was the polar opposite to that, something that we felt people could relate to. The major labels were going the exact opposite way. To me, that's folk music—when you have common folk making music."

Alice Wheeler is, in fact, a very accomplished photographer, as well as a mainstay of the Olympia and Seattle music scenes in the '80s and '90s and a good friend of Kurt. For an evocative blast of Northwest flavor, see her photo book *Outcasts and Innocents: Photographs of the Northwest*, with an introduction by Kathleen Hanna.

One of the foundations of the punk ethos is democratizing media, that media shouldn't be controlled only by huge corporations and some distant elite: you can Do It Yourself. By starting your own band—or magazine or record label or recording studio or venue or record store or whatever—you proactively create what others leave to "the experts." You might not have a whole lot of skill at first, but who cares: as the poet Anne Carson told the *Guardian* in 2006, "Not knowing what one is doing is no prohibition on doing it. We all grope ahead."

That's hardly a new concept—as Pavitt implied, folk music got there long before punk. But the same idea will flourish differently at different cultural moments or within different technologies. For instance, the DIY ethos existed long before the Ramones and the Sex Pistols, but it was uniquely empowered by technological innovations of the '80s such as inexpensive photocopying, the popularity of easy-to-manufacture cassette tapes, the fax machine, and the decreasing cost and increasing simplicity of recording. Doing it yourself got vastly easier as the '80s wore on, allowing underground culture to flourish in new ways.

Pavitt and Poneman's big idea was that "common folk" authenticity could be a marketing strategy, even if it was sometimes deceptive or even hurtful, as when TAD leader Tad Doyle deeply regretted posing for a publicity photo while wielding a chain saw. But it was an effective antithesis to what was happening in rock music at the time, the height of mainstream metal's "hair farmer" phase: high-gloss bands such as Mötley Crüe, Bon Jovi, Warrant, and Cinderella, all renowned for their bounteous, well-tended coifs and clingy nylon trousers. The polar opposite of Spandex was ripped jeans; the flip side of fussy Aqua Net bouffants was hair that hung, as I put it earlier, in "greasy curtains."

Pavitt and Poneman correctly guessed that the British music weeklies, clearly nearing burnout on the effete English new wavers who had readily provided amusing column inches for many years, would not only buy the idea of rough-hewn Americans making burly, primal rock music, they'd enthusiastically sell it to their readers. "Our bands were all lumberjacks," Poneman falsely declared to the *Los Angeles Times*' Jonathan Gold in 1990. "Or they painted bridges."

Sub Pop bands "weren't trying to be really conceptual or pretentious or anything," Pavitt told me for *Our Band Could Be Your Life*. "They just went out there and rocked." The thing is, Sub Pop bands like Nirvana, TAD, Mudhoney, and Soundgarden actually *were*, to varying degrees, kind of conceptual and pretentious. But that just confused the issue, so Sub Pop didn't talk about it.

For the back cover, Pavitt wanted a photo that Charles Peterson had taken of Jason with his hair swinging in textbook Sub Pop style. Kurt didn't like that idea,

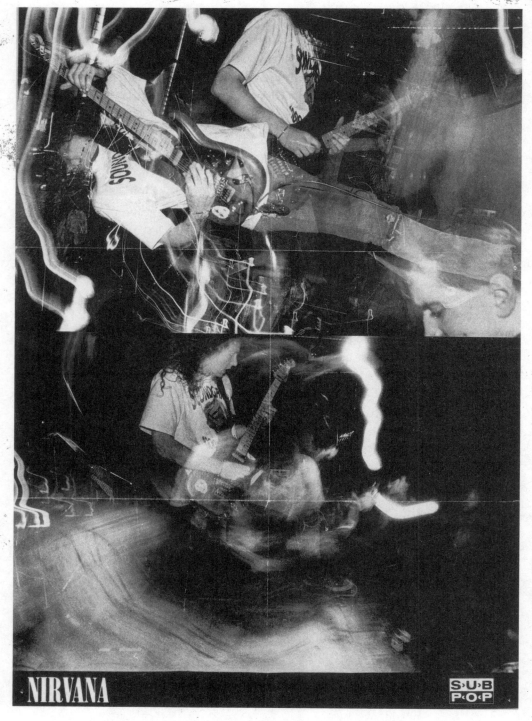

A limited edition poster included in early LP copies of *Bleach*.

so a compromise was reached, with the Jason shot featured on a limited edition poster which was included in the first two thousand copies of *Bleach* to be produced after the initial run of one thousand white vinyl pressings.

The shot on the inside of the CD version of Kurt splayed all over Chad's drum set was taken at the L.A. club Raji's in February of 1990. The shot was part of a sequence that also yielded the photo on the back of the "Sliver" single. *Bleach* also marked the debut of the Nirvana logo—set in Bodoni Extra Bold Condensed type. Because the typesetter was so rushed, the spacing was not graphically correct— there are large gaps on either side of the "V," for instance, that never did get fixed.

Tracy Marander's photo did wind up on the cover of *Bleach*, incorporating Kurt's suggestion that the photo be presented as a negative.

According to *Taking Punk to the Masses: From Nowhere to Nevermind*, which documented the 2011 Nirvana exhibition at Seattle's Museum of Pop Culture, the typeface is actually Onyx, which is very similar to Bodoni Extra Bold Condensed. It was chosen at random: Sub Pop art director Lisa Orth told the typesetter to use whatever font was already set up on their typesetting machine. And that's the logo the band has used ever since.

The combination of the very "rock" image and the very non-rock typography was accidental, but it's a very significant contrast: an intimation that Nirvana was trying something just a little different.

It's telling that Kurt wrote Nirvana's bios and such in-depth ones at that. Even at this early stage, he was thinking carefully about the band's brand, in today's parlance, and how it was reflected in every aspect of what they did. He also knew about rock music paradigms—it seems like he read a fair amount of music journalism—and that he should drop the right influences and flatter his label.

That's a very creative list of influences. *Marine Boy* was a Japanese anime action cartoon from the late '60s that was rerun on local TV stations for many years, a sort of aquatic version of *Speed Racer. H.R. Pufnstuf* was a deeply trippy kids' TV series from the late '60s and early '70s; definitely for stoners, it has to be seen to be believed.

With the mention of Slayer, Kurt was still openly listing metal as an influence, but not for much longer.

Note also that drugs and divorces were listed as influences.

The credits on *Bleach* listed "Kurdt Kobain" on vocals and guitar, the first of several variations that Kurt made on his name. "I think I wanted to be anonymous at first," he explains. "I was really thinking about changing my name for the *Nevermind* record. But then I just decided to spell it the right way. I just wanted it to be confusing. I wish I would have done the same thing that Black

Francis did. He's changed his name so many times that nobody really knows who he is. I wish nobody ever knew what my real name was. So I could some day be a normal citizen again. I have no real reason. I just didn't bother with spelling it correctly. I didn't care. I wanted people to spell it differently all the time."

A Sub Pop bio at the time listed the band's influences as "*H. R. Puffnstuff, Speed Racer,* divorces, drugs, sound effects records, the Beatles, rednecks, hard rock, punk rock, Leadbelly, Slayer and of course, the Stooges."

"Nirvana sees the underground scene as becoming stagnant and more accessible to big league capitalist pig major record labels," the bio continued. "But does Nirvana fell [*sic*] a moral duty to fight this cancerous evil? NO WAY! We want to cash in and suck up to the big wigs in hopes that we too can GET HIGH AND FUCK. GET HIGH AND FUCK. GET HIGH AND FUCK."

Even though he wasn't politically outspoken or particularly knowledgeable about politics, Kurt apparently figured he could score some indie cred points by paying lip service to bashing capitalism and big corporate labels. And then he unleashed a gust of hipster irony, once again mocking the desire to "cash in." All the coy posturing about selling out only served to reveal that Kurt was a callow, provincial kid who didn't actually grasp the realities of fame and fortune. He'd find out soon enough.

On June 9, Nirvana played "Lamefest '89" at the Moore Theatre, opening for TAD and Mudhoney. It was a landmark event—local bands had never packed such a large place before. The Seattle scene was starting to explode. The reviewer for *Backlash* bemoaned the bad sound treatment Nirvana received, because "the band utilizes a lot of melody within their grunge." "As for their performance—totally intense," the review continued. "Hair explosions, prat falls, jumps, body writhing and a trash-a-thon finale that left instruments and bodies strewn about the stage."

In an article in the University of Washington newspaper, Kurt said the band's music had a "gloomy, vengeful element based on hatred." The piece added that Kurt's outlook had improved of late, leading to what Kurt called "a gay pop song phase that will eventually die," although there would probably be more such tunes on the next album. "I'd like to live off the band," Kurt added. "I can't handle work."

They did a session at the Evergreen State College which yielded an early version of "Dive" and a cover of Kiss's "Do You Love Me," which wound up on a tribute album, on the Seattle indie label C/Z Records, called *Hard to Believe.*

Greetings,

NIRVANA is a three piece spawned from the bowels
of a Redneck logger town called ~~of~~ Aberdeen WA. and ~~the~~ a hippie Commune ~~from~~ on Bainbridge ~~Is.~~
Island.   Only together for 7 months Kurdt – Guitar vocals – Chris bass
& Chad – Drums have acquired   a single on Sub Pop Records (
) A Demo, a song in sub pop 200 comp, success & fame & A following of millions. Selling
their bottled Sweat & locks of hair have proven to be the largest
money maker so far, but future: dolls, peechees, lunch boxes &
bed sheets are in the works.   AN LP is due this April
from the wonderful ~~head~~ offices of Sub Pop World headquarters.
talent agents bruce PAVitt (Alias Henry Mancini) And Jonnathan
poneman (Alias fred flintstone) have "treated the boys good". and hope the boys
to work on more projects in the future.   will from them

NIRVANA sounds like black sabbath – playing the KNACK,
Black Flag, Led Zeppelin, & the Stooges; with a pinch of BAY CITY
Rollers.   their musical influences are: H.R. Puffnstuff,
~~Stevie~~ Marine Boy, Divorces, Drugs, Sound effects Records,
the Beatles, young marble Giants, Slayer, leadbelly, IGGY,
NIRVANA sees the underground music SEEN As becoming, stagnant
And more Accessible towards commercial MAJOR LAbel interests.
Does NIRVANA want to change this? No WAY! We want to
CASH IN & suck butt up to the big wigs in hopes that
we too ~~can~~ get High & fuck WAX figure-hot babes, who
will be required to have A certified Aids test 2 weeks prior to
the day of handing out back stage passes.   Soon we will
need chick spray Repellant. Soon we will be coming to your
town & Asking if we can stay at your house & use your stove.
Soon we will do encores of Gloria & louie louie At benefit
concerts with All our celebrity friends.
We Realize that there WAS once A 60's band called NIRVANA
but dont get us ~~confused~~ with them because they totally
Suck Big fucking DICK.
                                    114 N pear olympia wa
Good Bye.   98500
              (206) 352-0992

From a publicity photo session with Charles Peterson. © Charles Peterson

"Do You Love Me" was a hilarious choice for Nirvana. It's a terrible song, and they chose it specifically to lampoon the subject matter: "You like the hotels and fancy clothes / And the sound of electric guitars," wails Paul Stanley. "But do you love me?" Just like the sarcasm in their bio about living the rock star life, it was a poke at bands who do it for all—in Kurt's opinion, anyway—the wrong reasons: wealth, fame, and women.

Around this time, Nirvana decided that they needed a contract with Sub Pop. They wanted to make sure they would get accurate and timely accounting statements. "We thought if we signed a contract," says Kurt, "we'd be able to hold it up against them in the future if we wanted to get out of their contract." Ironically, the contract eventually had the opposite effect.

As it happened, Sub Pop had been thinking along the same lines, and Poneman had been reading *This Business of Music* for tips on a standard contract for all of the label's roster (only Soundgarden had signed one at that point). Poneman had not yet drafted anything when one summer night, Pavitt had thrown a "wild disco party" for the visiting Babes in Toyland. As Pavitt recalls, the party got a

The Amplified Come as You Are

little out of hand so he booted everybody out and they all went next door, where the Babes were staying. Meanwhile, an inebriated Chris Novoselic walked up to Pavitt's house, banged on the window, hollered, "You fuckers, we want a contract!" and fell backward into some bushes. He got up to leave and by sheer coincidence, bumped into Pavitt, who was going back to his house. "I often wonder," says Pavitt, "what if I had stayed next door one more minute."

They talked for about forty-five minutes or so, after which Pavitt called Poneman and told him Nirvana wanted a contract. Poneman stayed up all night typing a document. Legally speaking, it was a blunt instrument, but it would serve the label in good stead soon enough. Soon, Kurt, Chris, Chad, and Jason were up at Sub Pop's offices signing the contract, making them the first band to sign an extended contract with the label. "I remember thinking, 'This could be important,'" says Pavitt.

Kurt, Krist, Chad, and Jason signed the two-page contract on June 3, 1989, agreeing to record one album a year for three years. It offered an advance of $600 for the first album (to cover the cost of recording *Bleach*), a whopping $12,000 for the second, and then $24,000 for the third, an absolutely astronomical, unheard-of amount for Sub Pop. Pavitt and Poneman were sure the band was going to be huge.

At first, the album didn't make a seismic impact on the indie scene or even on Sub Pop, for that matter. "*Bleach* sounded really good, but all [our] stuff sounded really good to me," says Poneman. "I was caught up with a lot of stuff we were putting out," adds Pavitt. "We were putting out a lot of really good records."

But then people started buying it. "We put out *Bleach*," says Pavitt, "and gosh, it just kept selling. Never ever in the history of our company have I seen a record just sell and sell and sell. They did tour, but a lot of bands tour. The word of mouth was there. There was something special there."

After *Bleach* was released in June of 1989, they went on their first US tour, "a total hungry punk rock tour," says Chris, of twenty-six dates, starting June 22 at the Covered Wagon in San Francisco. This was the inaugural run of their trusty white Dodge van, soon nicknamed "The Van." Through three US tours and seventy thousand miles, it never did break down. When it got too hot to drive, they'd pull into a parking garage and just hang out in the van until sundown.

What a lame joke: "soon nicknamed 'The Van.'" Sorry, everyone.

The first part of Umberto Eco's 1980 novel *The Name of the Rose* is about how tedious it is to live in a monastery—and to illustrate that, Eco duly makes that section very long and tedious. I wish I could have done something similar to illustrate those early Nirvana tours because touring isn't all sex, drugs, and rock & roll; it's mostly an exhausting grind: driving for endless hours on boring interstates; stopping for gas at identical service stations and eating the awful food they sell there; hauling heavy, bulky black boxes out of your van and into the club; playing mind-numbing soundchecks; passing the dead hours between soundcheck and show; meeting local bands whom you might never see again or who might become lifelong friends; playing the same songs night after night, sometimes to a handful of people, mostly the other bands and the bartender; hauling those same heavy, bulky black boxes back into your van at the end of the night while you're still buzzing from the show and whatever you've ingested; sometimes getting paid in little more than free beer, or not at all; being cooped up with the same three or four goddamn people for weeks on end, far away from anyone else you know; waking up much too early the next day after (barely) sleeping on strangers' floors and doing exactly the same thing all over again . . . for weeks on end.

But maybe the preceding long and tedious sentence managed to convey even just a fraction of what I'm talking about.

Kurt, Chris, Chad, and Jason were their own road managers—they decided where they'd stay, when they'd leave. Of course, the accommodations weren't that great—most of the time, they'd end up sleeping outside or in the van, and if they were lucky, some fan gave them a floor to sleep on. A few dates into the tour, they were deep in the heart of Texas. They parked near a national park, which Chris recalls was essentially a swamp. A sign near their parking spot read "Caution: alligators," so they dug up a baseball bat and some two-by-fours that were kicking around the back of the van and kept them close by in case of reptilian attack. But eventually, they got hungry and decided to eat some of their canned soup. So they doused the bat and the two-by-fours in motor oil, set them on fire, and cooked the soup over the flames.

They were excited about being on tour and going to places like New Mexico, Illinois, and Pennsylvania and playing to new faces. They played the very lowest tier of the underground circuit, mostly bars; the band got a free case of beer and never more than one hundred dollars a night. "Every time we played a show," says Chad, "it seemed like we got just enough money to put gas in the tank and food in our stomach to make it to the next friggin' gig." Despite the marathon drives, the low pay, and often sparse audiences, morale was high. And attendance started to pick up halfway through the tour, when college radio began playing *Bleach* tracks like "School," "About a Girl" or "Blew." By the time they got out to the Midwest, they almost felt famous.

They started to win fans with their live show, too. "There was always people who came up afterward and said 'Wow, I thought you guys were pretty cool,'" says Chad, "but it's not like people got completely out of hand. There were some people who got like that, but they were drunk."

Chris was in charge of getting paid and keeping the books. It was a lot simpler then. "We'd go to a record store and we'd all buy these records," says Chris. "Maybe I could buy six records, Kurt would buy four records, Chad would buy three, and that was fine. It was 'All together, brothers.' And at the end of the tour, whoever got dropped off first, we'd count out all the money—a third for you, a third for you . . .'"

One way of solving the height problem.
© Charles Peterson

That's a great example of being invaluable behind the scenes. Early on, Krist really was the band's tour manager and bookkeeper. Getting paid at the end of the night is often stressful for a band—clubs are infamous for shortchanging bands or not paying them at all. A classic scenario—and many indie bands who played in, for instance, Pittsburgh at the time have a hairy story about this—is going to the club's office to get paid, and the manager says nothing and instead pulls open a desk drawer to reveal not an envelope full of cash but a handgun. That's when you know you're not going to get paid. But Krist was a big guy and could be intimidating when he wanted to be—unscrupulous promoters were less likely to mess with him.

It's easy to caricature Krist as merely Kurt's bluff, goofy sidekick—and he was that to a certain extent—but he was also much more than that. Even with one significant impediment, which we'll get to in a moment, Krist was one of Nirvana's most important saving graces.

Poster from Nirvana's first US tour.

Not that Chris would just fritter away the band's money. In fact, he became such a tightwad that he wouldn't let anyone turn on the air conditioning in the van—even in Texas in July—because it used up too much fuel.

Back home in Washington, Kurt and Chris often went a separate way from Chad socially—Chad stuck with his hippyish Bainbridge Island crowd—but being on tour was different. "When we were in that van, it was way closer," Chad says. "It wasn't like us against each other, it was like us against whatever's outside of the van."

Inside the van, they'd listen to a tuneful but twisted Scottish band called the Vaselines, as well as everything from the teenaged English pop band Talulah Gosh to the aged headbangers in Motörhead. And they'd listen to the Beatles. Chris and Kurt made compilation tapes. Shelli had even made some, too.

The Vaselines and Talulah Gosh were extremely obscure bands at the time; Nirvana found out about them via the Olympia crowd. They also sounded nothing like Nirvana or virtually anything else Kurt had previously listened to; in fact, the female-led Talulah Gosh is a canonical "twee-pop" band.

Chad's comment about "us against whatever's outside of the van" is touching—maybe Kurt finally felt some camaraderie with at least two other human beings.

Chris was hitting the bottle pretty hard. "He'd get pretty crazy, trashing things and stuff," Chad recalls. "When he'd first get wasted, he'd be all, 'Everybody's great! I love everybody!' and then the next moment he's telling everybody, 'You don't know anything about love! You just don't care! You don't understand!' And he'd pick up a chair and maybe toss it a half mile. Then he'd wake up and he'd say to me, 'Don't talk to me, Mr. Sunshine, I don't want to deal with you.' He'd always wake up looking and feeling like shit all the time."

Kurt was more amused than disturbed by Chris's drinking. "It never seemed like a big deal to me at all," he says. "Everyone gets drunk and he didn't get drunk every single night, it was just every *other* night. When he drinks, he drinks to the point of oblivion—he turns into literally a retard. He can't speak, all he can do is gesture and knock things over. I just never thought of it as a problem, although I'm probably more sympathetic to it now, over the last few years. But I've known so many people that drink that it seems like an ordinary thing."

I didn't know it at the time, but alcoholism ran in the Cobain family, which is one big reason why Kurt said he knew "so many" people who drink. It just wasn't a big deal in his world. That was just generally the way it was in Aberdeen—and still is: prepandemic statistics noted that 60 to 80 percent of emergency room care in Grays Harbor County, where Aberdeen is, involved drugs or alcohol, and alcohol use among middle and high school students is the highest in the state. But eventually, Kurt would come to condemn Krist for his drinking, although for self-serving reasons.

At a tour stop in Minneapolis, the band stayed with Babes in Toyland drummer Lori Barbero, a famed hostess of indie bands who were traveling through the Twin Cities. Apparently, Chris thought Barbero had shot him a look and he hollered "Quit yer gawkin'!" flailed his arms, and fell backward into a cabinet full of plates, which all went crashing to the floor.

It would be difficult to name a notable indie band from the '80s or '90s that didn't crash at Lori Barbero's place at some point. She was, and probably still is, the proverbial hostess with the mostest, one of those amazing people who made the indie rock underground railroad run on time. Her home was a dense, vast, and impeccably curated museum of kitschy knickknacks—I bet those plates Krist knocked over were really cool.

"He never meant any harm or anything," says Chad. "If he was in his right mind, he never would have done some of the shit he did. I think drinking brought out some things that he didn't think about much or things he'd like to say to people that he wouldn't when he wasn't wasted."

Pressed for specific incidents, Chad replies, "It's all blurring together now. When I think about it, I just see him wasted, and then something getting broken."

Kurt would do some pretty weird stuff himself. In Chicago he bought a large crucifix at a garage sale. Out on the road, he'd roll down the window of the van, stick out the crucifix at some unsuspecting victim and snap his picture just to get the expression on his face. Yes, life on the road was pretty good. "We were totally poor," says Kurt, "but, God, we were seeing the United States for the first time. And we were in a band and we were making enough money to survive. It was awesome. It was just great. And if Jason wasn't such a prick, it would have been even better."

Chris had noticed Jason's dissatisfaction early in the tour and mentioned it to Chad and Kurt. "We tried to talk to him about it and he wouldn't talk," says Chris. "He got totally introverted."

Chris and Kurt would often go for long strolls and talk. During a walk along Lake Mendota in Madison, Wisconsin, Chris asked, "Do you think the band is kind of weird ever since Jason joined? It's not the same band anymore." The band was looking and sounding more "rock," as Bruce Pavitt would say. They blamed it on Jason. Jason's stage style was more show-biz than the rest of the band—he posed,

The Amplified Come as You Are

© Charles Peterson

swinging his hair in the classic Sub Pop style, doing a rockist rooster strut around his side of the stage. "He was like a peacock on amphetamines," says Kurt. "He was so posey I couldn't believe it. It was embarrassing. It was so contrived and *sexual*. It was gross."

I'll never forget the way Kurt spat out the word "sexual"—it was as if he had just tasted something disgusting. He abhorred the rooster-strut thing; one of his most scathing insults was "cock-rock," which represented a dynamic that, as an avowed feminist and machophobe, he made a point of finding repulsive.

So there was basically no overt sexuality in Nirvana, especially onstage—no hip grinding or pouting or guitar-neck thrusting, and Kurt certainly could have made himself look more attractive. Then again, they did later record a killer song called "Moist Vagina." (Courtney found that title absolutely puerile and chastised Kurt about it, which might be why the chorus wound up being the much more singable "Marijuana"; the track was relegated to a B-side.)

That said, Everman's stage presence simply wasn't sexual—he was just rocking out and tossing around his hair like any good late-'80s rocker. But moves like that signified metal, which Kurt was very determined to distance himself from.

Actually, Jason's incompatibility had been plain from the start. "It was weird because he didn't even want to rehearse any new numbers," says Chris. "He'd go through the set but he didn't want to jam or anything. He'd set his guitar down." (Jason denies this, saying that since the band was so far-flung, they only rehearsed a handful of times before touring and that jamming was out of the question since their time was completely occupied by learning songs that Kurt had already written.)

"We just kind of noticed that yeah, Jason's kind of weird," says Chris, who also sensed a rockist tendency in Jason early on. "The first day we practiced, he brought these girls over, to kind of hang out. That kind of tells you something."

Neither Kurt nor Chris hung out with Jason much socially, and their alienation was only magnified by the rigors of the road. "Things started getting weird," says Chris. "And then *he* started getting weird." The band played a great show at the Sonic Temple in Pittsburgh, so great that Kurt smashed one of his favorite guitars, a sunburst Fender Mustang. Jason got really mad about that. "We said, 'What? It's rock & roll!'" says Chris, who concedes that "we were broke and he was kind of financing the show."

Jason Everman is an intense person. I interviewed him at my apartment, and wow, was he intimidating: a tall, strapping man who just seemed to be seething inside. I was kind of relieved when he left.

A year later, he was training to become, as my friend Clay Tarver wrote in a memorable 2013 profile of Everman for the *New York Times* magazine titled "The Rock 'n' Roll Casualty Who Became a War Hero," "an elite member of the US Army Special Forces, one of those bearded guys riding around on horseback in Afghanistan fighting the Taliban." And Everman's life took another twist or two after that, too.

The band had begun trashing their instruments a few months before. If it was a bad show, they'd get angry and smash everything up. If it was a really good show, they'd smash out of pure glee. There were few merely average shows, so equipment got smashed often.

It all started on October 30, 1988, at a show at a dorm of the Evergreen State College. "It just *started*," says Chris. "It was fun. It seemed like you couldn't end a

show without doing something spectacular or sensational. No matter how good you played, it seemed like you didn't give it enough. So if you smashed all the gear and had this big gala ending, we could say, 'There, we did it.' We couldn't just walk off the stage."

On tour, they'd find cheap guitars at pawnshops—sometimes fans would just give them a guitar or in a pinch Jonathan Poneman would Fed Ex one out to them—and string them left-handed and smash them that night. "It was fun, and if you were doing a shitty show, it kind of made it spectacular," says Chris. "Then it became addictive."

That show took place at a legendary party in Evergreen's K dorm. The Olympia band Lush played before Nirvana. Lush's lead singer Slim Moon recounts in Nick Soulsby's *I Found My Friends*: "I got mad at Ian [McKinnon] and kicked over his drum set, so he punched me in the face. That was the first night I ever saw Nirvana smash their instruments and I've always suspected that it was partially motivated by Kurt being unwilling to be upstaged by the violent drama of our set just before theirs."

There might have been an additional reason why Kurt smashed his guitars. In March 1992, veteran *Seattle Times* pop critic Patrick MacDonald traveled to Aberdeen in search of Nirvana's roots and found a very plausible theory for why Kurt destroyed one of the very few things that made him happy and fulfilled. "A librarian [at Weatherwax High School] tells me she once saw Cobain when he was very down. She asked him what was the matter and he said his father had smashed his guitar because he was playing too loud. 'Sounds like his father was his first critic,' says [head librarian John] Eko. Maybe that's why he still smashes guitars on stage."

Guitar smashing had not been in vogue since the early days of the Who, in the mid to late '60s—or at least extremely few bands besides Nirvana made a ritual of it the way the Who's Pete Townshend had. A former art school student, Townshend justified guitar smashing in highfalutin terms, calling it "auto-destruction," but it started by accident in 1964, when he inadvertently poked the neck of his guitar through the ceiling at a show. "And the next [time we played]," Townshend recalled to writer Steve Rosen for the April 1980 issue of *Sound International*, "the place was packed." Aside from being cathartic, Townshend realized, smashing guitars was just good showbiz. Kurt surely realized this, too.

Veteran English rock manager Simon Napier-Bell wrote about the Who's instrument smashing in a piece for the *Sunday Times* magazine in 1997: "Most critics saw it as anarchy or an incitement to violence, but it wasn't that at all—it was musical suicide. At the moment when the group had the greatest rapport with their audience, they destroyed their means to communicate with them." I think Kurt might have had a similar thought in mind, and that word "suicide" clangs very loudly. Smashing his guitar, the very thing that gave him life, was an act of self-obliteration and a decisive rejection of other people—in this case, the audience.

Some fellow musicians were appalled by Kurt's guitar smashing. After seeing Kurt heave his squalling guitar over the top of the amps during the 1992 MTV Video Music Awards, revered singer-songwriter John Hiatt wrote a song about it called "Perfectly Good Guitar": "There oughtta be a law with no bail / Smash a guitar and you go to jail."

Kurt smashed a lot of guitars on tour, and they had to be repaired or the band couldn't play. Early on, he and Krist would fix them in the van on the way to the next show, using spare parts they collected. If they were lucky, they'd find a suitable (but dirt-cheap) left-handed guitar in a local pawnshop. Later, the habit was enabled by their brilliant guitar tech Earnie Bailey, who became a particularly essential member of the crew.

MTV's Kurt Loder: How do you keep [your equipment] going?
Dave: Earnie Bailey.
Kurt: Yeah, our guitar friend. He can fix anything—a blender or a guitar.

Earnie went on to work as guitar tech for the Foo Fighters, Brandi Carlile, and a lot of other top bands, and now hand builds his own boutique line of guitars called Wire Instruments.

Chris had recently scrawled the phrase NIRVANA: FUDGE PACKIN, CRACK SMOKIN, SATAN WORSHIPIN MOTHERFUCKERS on a wall and was so pleased with the slogan that he told Kurt about it. Kurt put it on the back of a T-shirt design he had been working on. On the front was a reproduction of an engraving of one of the circles of Hell from Dante's *Inferno*, a book Kurt had discovered during his days passing the time in the Aberdeen library. Jason had all the T-shirts printed up, paid for them, and then sold them after every show. They quickly became a staple of indie rock fashion. Jason probably made a mint.

It was actually the first five Circles of Hell from the *Inferno*—"Upper Hell." The second ring of the seventh Circle, by the way, is reserved for suicides, who are turned into gnarled, leafless trees that bleed painfully when their branches are broken. "They are the image of the self-hatred which dries up the very sap of energy and makes all life infertile," wrote noted *Inferno* translator Dorothy L. Sayers. That ring is also home to those, in Sayers's words, "who dissipated their goods for the sheer wanton lust of wreckage and disorder." Like smashing guitars?

Those *Inferno* shirts were really popular in the indie scene at the time—possibly more popular than the band—and surely contributed to the buzz around Nirvana. As ever, it pays to advertise.

Rather than making "a mint," Everman probably got paid back for the cost of the shirts and then the band split the proceeds from sales.

They were supposed to go up into Canada, but made it only as far as New York City, where they played a lousy show on the eighteenth of July during the New Music Seminar at the Pyramid Club in the East Village. It was Jason's last show with Nirvana. "I don't think Jason really took the pressure of being on tour and being cooped up with us very well," says Chris. "I don't think he was happy with our band because he kind of wanted us to be more rock and we were more punk."

"We started making it toward New York and that's when Jason started getting really quiet," Chris continues. "He wouldn't even talk to us anymore. That's when we first met Anton Brookes, our publicist in the UK. He was like, 'Who's this Jason? Why is he so quiet?' The Mudhoney guys were in New York: 'Why is this Jason so quiet?' We played this show at Maxwell's [in nearby Hoboken, New Jersey]. It was a good show. Still, Jason was quiet. We spent about four days in New York. The New Music Seminar. We watched Sonic Youth and Mudhoney and Laughing Hyenas at the Ritz. Jason went to see the speed metal band Prong at CBGB's. You know what I mean? That said a lot."

Prong was exactly the kind of technical aggro-metal that Kurt had been gradually dissociating himself from ever since he arrived in Olympia, but it wasn't just the musical differences, it was the social differences: favoring a band like Prong over leading indie bands like Sonic Youth, Laughing Hyenas, and their influential Seattle friends Mudhoney spoke of very differing allegiances, values, and communities. It was like Everman went to a different church.

"That's when Chad and I and Kurt got really together," says Chris. "We bonded. We'd go out to eat together, all three, and pitch in for the meal with band money. Without Jason. He would not hang around with us."

They stayed a few days at the Alphabet City apartment of Janet Billig, a factotum at Caroline Records who knew Pavitt and Poneman, and like Babes in Toyland's Lori Barbero in Minneapolis, made her apartment a way station for

needy bands coming through town. One night, Chris and Kurt went down to the street and bought some cocaine. The two of them drank some booze and snorted the coke off Billig's toilet seat. And they decided they were going home and that Jason was out of the band. "We were happy," says Chris. "It was a relief."

"So we went up to him, 'Jason, what's wrong? Is there a problem?' He'd say, 'No, no. Nothing. I'm over it.' We're like, 'What's it? Why is there a problem?'"

Kurt wouldn't confront Jason about it. "He was never in your face," says Chad. "Things would pile up for him underneath and finally it would be, 'Man, I can't take this anymore.' When we were dealing with Jason, because we were all wondering what was up with him, Kurt was always silent about it. Then out of the blue he'd say, 'Man, I can't take this anymore.' It was like, 'Whoa, Kurt's going to say something!' I think it's because he's afraid of talking to the person. He doesn't want to bum them out. He doesn't want to be the one to say, 'This isn't working out and you're out of the band.' He hates that kind of confrontation. He doesn't want to be the executioner or the mean guy."

And there's another example of the stereotypical Northwestern passive-aggressive approach. Or maybe Kurt was emulating his father: remember what Don says earlier in the book: "He's like me. Don't say anything and maybe it'll disappear or something. And don't explain. You just bottle it all up and it all comes out at one time."

At any rate, rather than doing the difficult but productive thing and speaking with Everman about the issue, Kurt said nothing, assuming Everman would get some sort of hint and either mend his ways or quit.

"I always felt kind of peripheral," says Jason. "I don't remember ever being asked for input on songs in that band, which is ultimately why I left." Kurt does concede that Jason may also have taken exception to Kurt's alcohol-fueled "volatile personality" at the time. Kurt also thinks Jason mistook the metallic ring of *Bleach* for the band's true direction instead of the compromise that it was. Even Jason acknowledges that he preferred ponderous songs like "Paper Cuts," "Sifting," and "Big Long Now" to the more melodic material Kurt was getting into. Jason never was afraid to declare that he liked metal. "That was always kind of a burr in Kurt and Chris's side because it wasn't exactly cool," Jason says. "But if there's a band with a cool song and a cool guitar riff I'd listen to it."

Jason, who was also a songwriter, wanted to have more input into the music. "I probably wanted to do things that were not simple enough for them, ideas that were *mine* as opposed to Kurt's," says Jason. "There wasn't a tremendous musical difference—maybe it was just a control thing.

© Charles Peterson

"Basically, anybody besides Kurt or Chris is kind of disposable," Jason continues. "At the end of the day, Kurt could get in front of any bass player and any drummer and play his songs and it's not going to sound that much different."

But there absolutely *was* a "tremendous musical difference"—borne out by the fact that Nirvana was shedding the very influences that Jason liked most about the band. Kurt was leaving behind that kind of music as an unwanted vestige of his Aberdeen years while Everman was stubbornly trying to drag them back into it.

Everman just hadn't acknowledged what he had walked into: it was Kurt's band (with a lot of support from Krist). There simply wasn't room for anybody else's ideas.

He was wrong about Nirvana drummers, too—the band *absolutely* sounded different when a new guy was sitting behind the kit, which would soon be decisively demonstrated.

They abruptly canceled the remaining seven shows of the tour—mostly Midwest dates—and drove home to Washington in fifty hours, not stopping for anything except to get gas, eat a doughnut, or go to the bathroom. The whole time, nobody said a word. Nobody even told Jason that he was out of the band. Jason claims he actually quit. "No, we were just too maladjusted to tell him to his face," Chris says. "We just didn't want to hurt anyone's feelings and that just compounded the problem. I think we're better at it now, more direct, more mature than back then."

"If I would have been in the band when they got huge, I'm sure I would have took my money and said, 'See ya later!'" says Jason. "I would have done whatever I wanted to do. I'd bail and just do whatever."

This attitude would seem to validate the band's decision to let Jason go.

"Artistically, I think it was totally the right thing for me to do," says Jason of his departure from the band. "Economically, maybe not." Two weeks later, Jason got a call from Chris Cornell of Soundgarden, asking him to play bass in the band. He lasted a few months before being replaced by Ben Shepherd and now plays guitar in Mindfunk, a band on Megaforce Records. He says he has no hard feelings about his exit from Nirvana. "Each band is a weird, twisted family," Jason says. "I think I was more the retarded stepchild twice removed."

The band never did repay Jason the six hundred dollars he lent them for *Bleach*. "Mental damages," claims Kurt.

If only Everman had paid the studio directly and gotten a receipt, he would technically own the master recordings and would be a lot wealthier today. As it is, I don't think Nirvana ever did pay him back for the loan.

Kurt had become obsessed with the great Lead Belly, the black folk troubadour of the '30s and '40s whose enduring musical legacy includes "Rock Island Line," "Midnight Special," and "Good Night, Irene." Kurt had gotten into Lead Belly after reading an article by William Burroughs which said something like "To hell with modern-day rock & roll. If you want to hear *real* passion, listen to Lead Belly." Kurt's next-door neighbor, Slim Moon, happened to have *Lead Belly's Last Sessions* (recorded in 1948) and played it for Kurt. He was completely taken. Then he started buying all the Lead Belly records he could find. "It's so raw and sincere," he says. "It's something that I hold really sacred to me. Lead Belly is one of the most important things in my life. I'm totally obsessed with him."

He went out and bought every Lead Belly record he could find, learned how to play his music, and even decorated an entire wall of the apartment with Lead

Belly pictures. It's easy to see Kurt's attraction to the blues—an exorcism of psychic pain—but it's also easy to see why he was especially attracted to Lead Belly, whose work transcended any category, an elegant songwriter who crafted sturdy but melodic music that synthesized several different genres, whose passionate music spoke volumes about the human experience. From Lead Belly and the blues, Kurt got the idea of using recognizable imagery to produce an original, almost mystical, vision.

Lead Belly, born Huddie Ledbetter, actually recorded very few true blues numbers—he played mostly folk songs, cowboy ballads, prison work songs, children's songs, field hollers, and spirituals.

Lead Belly's music is simple, but simple in the way that only a master musician can be, with a grace that comes from economy (the great abstract expressionist painter Mark Rothko called it "the simple expression of the complex thought"), a quality that's easy to admire but extremely difficult to emulate. As a songwriter, Kurt not only aspired to that level of artistry, he actually attained it on a regular basis. (Other Kurt favorites, such as Neil Young and John Fogerty, also have this rare gift.)

There was also Lead Belly's big heart, which produced the quintessential quality of passion, something that Kurt valued above all else, in any field of endeavor. Maybe Kurt also realized that Lead Belly, like himself, blended different sources and traditions into a powerful and distinctly personal sound that appealed to lots of people.

Kurt might also have connected with the fact that Huddie Ledbetter had something in his past that he was ashamed of—Ledbetter was a convicted murderer who had served prison time—and for the rest of his life tried to redeem himself through music.

Kurt had befriended Mark Lanegan, whose band, Screaming Trees, played in Olympia often. In August 1989, Kurt and Lanegan decided to collaborate on some songs for Lanegan's solo album. Unfortunately Kurt couldn't write very well with someone else—he kept worrying that he would come up with something that he'd want to use for Nirvana instead—so they decided to record some songs by Lead Belly with Chris on bass and Screaming Trees' Mark Pickerel on drums.

The sessions were disorganized if only because no one could decide who was in charge. Although Lanegan claimed he led Screaming Trees' practices, "I couldn't bear to do that in this situation, I was too awed by Kurt's genius," he wrote in his harrowing 2020 memoir *Sing Backwards and Weep*. "He was also strangely reticent. Dylan [Carlson] had joined us in the studio just to hang out and ended up offering more direction than either Kurt or me, but in the end not much was accomplished. No one was willing to be the shot-caller."

The group wound up recording but two Lead Belly songs. "Where Did You Sleep Last Night?" wound up on Lanegan's magnificent solo album, *The Winding Sheet*. Kurt sang Lead Belly's "Ain't It a Shame." Both songs were to make up a single, but that fell through and "Ain't It a Shame" was never released. Jonathan Poneman calls it "one of Kurt's greatest vocal performances."

Eventually, the four turned into an informal blues band. Pickerel wanted to call it the Jury; Kurt wanted to call it Lithium.

Kurt got to use the title "Lithium" soon enough.

Kurt surely knew "Ain't It a Shame" from *Lead Belly's Last Sessions*, where it's titled "Ain't It a Shame to Go Fishin' on a Sunday." Lead Belly sings the song a cappella, with some hand claps, and like a lot of his music, it rocks. The Jury's version is a rare example of Kurt singing to such an old-school rock & roll template—you can hear similar chord changes in Chuck Berry classics such as "30 Days" and "Maybellene" and about a million other songs.

The Jury's rip-roaring version of "Ain't It a Shame" has since been released, and it turns out that Poneman wasn't just spouting typical Sub Pop hype—it really is one of Kurt's best vocal performances. The band plays the song as a straight-up rockabilly raver reminiscent of the Cramps (or maybe Kurt favorites Tales of Terror, an excellent mid-'80s Sacramento hardcore band whose ass-kicking cover of "Hound Dog" could well have been an inspiration for this track). Kurt sings the first part in a smooth low register, emulating Lead Belly, then suddenly kicks it up several notches and screams the rest of the song; instead of a guitar solo, Kurt busts out a few soul-searing wails and groans.

The song is a sardonic spin on an old gospel song about the sin of violating the Christian Sabbath: why go fishing, drink, or, very darkly, beat one's wife on a Sunday when there's the rest of the week for that. Remorse for physically abusing a woman seemed to resonate with Kurt; "Shame! Shame! Shame!" he screams, to end the song. So there's that word once again.

Poneman had big plans for an album, but somehow it never happened. Kurt concentrated on guitar, leaving Lanegan to do most of the vocals. Dylan Carlson remembers their best song was "Grey Goose," which they did in a heavy, dirge-blues style. "It was almost like watching one of the great English blues rock bands getting its feet," says Carlson. "It was pretty incredible." Kurt says he'd like to try a blues band again sometime.

Unfortunately, no one could decide who should sing "Grey Goose," Kurt or Lanegan, so it remains a lugubrious instrumental track.

The song is about a goose that gets shot out of the sky by a preacher—with a shotgun, of all things. But the goose is supernaturally defiant: it takes six weeks to fall to the ground, six weeks for the people of the town to pluck it, and six weeks for them to boil it. And despite all that, the goose still lives: knives can't cut it, so they throw it in the hog pen, but it breaks the hogs' teeth, so they take it to the sawmill, and it breaks the saw's teeth, too. That damn bird is just not going to give in.

It's too bad that Kurt didn't sing that song—he might have really connected with it. As his uncle Larry Smith recounted at Kurt's public memorial in Seattle, "I heard from a friend that Kurt was assaulted by a burly 250-pound logger type. Evidently, Kurt did not even fight. He just presented the bully with the appropriate hand gesture every time he was knocked down until the bully gave up."

But it's the ending of the song that really gives it its transcendent power. Here's a few lines from the last verse of "Grey Goose":

> And the last time I seen him,
> He was flying across the ocean
> With a long string of goslings,
> And they were all going quack-quack

The goose has not only prevailed, he's reproduced, and now he's off to a better place, far, far away. As for the preacher, Lead Belly adds in an ad lib, "the goose is still laughing at him."

That laughing goose is how I like to think of Kurt now: flying across the ocean with a bunch of kindred spirits, mocking whoever—or whatever—was trying to bring him down, which was, in the final analysis, probably himself.

Nirvana rehearsed and played a few shows in Seattle that summer as their following began to swell—strictly by word of mouth, since Sub Pop had long ago ceased directly promoting the album. They regularly sold out the Vogue and went on a two-week Midwest tour starting in late September to make up the dates they had missed by coming home prematurely with Jason. Along for the ride was roadie Ben Shepherd, who had been in a couple of bands (Mind Circus and Tick-Dolly-Row) with Chad.

Nirvana was thinking about getting Shepherd in the band, but once word got around that they were thinking about a new second guitarist, members of

Screaming Trees, TAD, and Mudhoney all strenuously advised them to stay a three-piece—another guitarist just cluttered up the sound. "I still kind of regret that because I like that guy a lot—he would have added to the band, definitely," Kurt says of Shepherd. "He was kind of crazy sometimes, but that's okay—I'd rather have that than some moody metalhead." Shepherd later replaced Jason in Soundgarden.

The bigger the city, the bigger the crowd. The best show was at the Blind Pig in Ann Arbor, Michigan. "Everybody was totally into it," says Chad. "They were raging and it was great." It's still one of the band's favorite places to play. In Ann Arbor, they also interviewed comedian Bobcat Goldthwait on a radio show. All Kurt had to do was mention Sylvester Stallone and Goldthwait went on a half-hour riff about why the man who played Rambo fled to Switzerland to avoid the Vietnam War draft.

Surely sensing a kindred spirit in Goldthwait's rage, vulnerability, and penchant for screaming, Kurt was a big Bobcat fan. As Goldthwait is fond of saying, "That's like hearing that Hendrix was really into Buddy Hackett."

The interview happened in early October 1989, after Nirvana played at the Blind Pig. But Goldthwait had a different take on the conversation: "[Kurt had] written a bunch of questions on a paper bag," Goldthwait recalled for the Ringer's Alan Siegel, "and it really just digressed to us making fun of the Grateful Dead."

Later, Goldthwait listened to a tape of *Bleach* and said to a friend, "You know, rock really sucks. It's really a hard business. Because these guys are pretty good, and we'll never hear from 'em again."

Goldthwait stayed friends with Kurt and, to promote *In Utero*, made a really weird thirty-second commercial spot with the band. He plays a midwife, in drag, while Kurt, Krist, and Dave, also in drag, play pregnant women. "Just remember, mothers," hollers Goldthwait, "love your pain!" Then they all simultaneously give birth, pelting Goldthwait with little plastic baby dolls. Just before it fades to black, Goldthwait exclaims, "Did you know the placenta makes really yummy soup?"

Kurt heard that Goldthwait had opened some shows for Cheap Trick, so he invited him on the *In Utero* tour, including a New Year's Eve 1993 show at Oakland-Alameda County Coliseum Arena where, at the stroke of midnight, Goldthwait rappelled from the rafters, naked but for a harness, an oversized hunting hat, and some *In Utero* wings. "Ladies and gentlemen," Kurt quipped, "Pauly Shore!"

Goldthwait not only attended the *Unplugged* taping, but some of the rehearsals, too. Backstage before the show, he huddled with an anxious Kurt, who didn't really want to speak with anyone else. "I definitely did feel often that it would just be him and I," Goldthwait said, "kind of a little bit of padding between him and the world."

In Minneapolis, right at the start of the tour, Kurt had collapsed from stomach pain. Chris was frightened. "His stomach—God, he had nothing to throw up and he was still throwing up," he says. "His stomach hurt so bad. Took him to the hospital and they could do nothing for him."

Once they got back from the tour, Chris and Shelli decided to get married and the band began preparing to record material for an EP.

chapter six

THESE GUYS ARE GOING TO BE BIGGER THAN THE BEATLES!

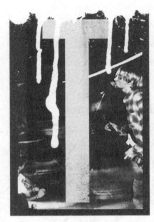

he band recorded the *Blew* EP in late summer of 1989 at the relatively upscale Music Source on Seattle's Capitol Hill, a twenty-four-track studio that specialized in ad jingles and movie soundtrack work. The producer was Steve Fisk. Despite that show in Ellensburg with Jason's out-of-sync hair, Fisk changed his mind about Nirvana after Bruce Pavitt sent him a copy of *Bleach*. "It was obvious," says Fisk, "that it was a very good band."

The band arrived with their instruments in tatters. Fisk recalls Chad and his mammoth North kit. "The smallest guy in the band had the biggest, stupidest drum set in the Northwest," says Fisk. "The kick drum was held together by miles and miles of duct tape because the bass had been used as a hatchet to chop the kick drum in half." The *Blew* sessions were the last appearance, recorded or otherwise, of Chad's North drums.

The rest of the band's equipment was in sad shape, too. Chris's bass had done a lot of aerial work, and had obviously suffered a few too many crash landings. The pickups were nearly shot and one of his two speakers was almost completely destroyed; the other one *was* completely destroyed. They spent a lot of time trying to get everything to sound good, tripling up the guitars. (Kurt was unsatisfied with the recording and later tried to rerecord some of the tracks with their soundman, Craig Montgomery, but they didn't turn out well, either.) "They wanted a Top 40 drum sound," says Fisk. "They were saying that out loud. They knew they were not doing a Top 40 song, but they really liked the idea of having the snare completely jacked up."

It's perhaps telling that the band explicitly wanted to borrow a recording approach from commercial pop music—something they'd do much more extensively on their next album.

They recorded "Even in His Youth," the unreleased "Token Eastern Song," an electric version of "Polly" that went unfinished, "Stain," and "Been a Son." Only the last two made it onto the EP, which also included the title track and "Love Buzz," both culled from *Bleach*.

Like quite a few Nirvana songs, in retrospect "Token Eastern Song" is tough to hear. In one of the verses Kurt appears to sing "Suicide is something mean"—perhaps meant to assure his friends that he would never do such a thing to them. But then why mention it in the first place?

He definitely sings "Hold it in your gut," an apparent reference to his stomach pain; at the end of the song, that line morphs to Kurt wrenchingly screaming "Gut!"—or is it "God!" or "Gone!"? Any of those work.

The instantly catchy two-minute wonder "Been a Son" describes the plight of a girl whose parents would have preferred a boy. "She should have died when she was born," Kurt sings, his vocal draped in most un-Sub Pop-like harmonies ("Total Lennon harmonies, right out of *Rubber Soul*," raves Fisk). Grunge, pop, and feelings of inferiority also merge on "Stain." Self-hatred never sounded so catchy—it's easy to miss the fact that the song is simply the same verse repeated three times. Although a different, peppier version of "Been a Son" (minus Chris's tasty bass solo) wound up on *Incesticide*, the version of "Stain" hails from the Fisk sessions.

"She should have died when she was born . . . She should have been a son," Kurt sings, sarcastically. "Been a Son" is a feminist song, completely counter to the lumberjack image Sub Pop was promoting, as was the music's out-and-out indie pop tunefulness, which could be read as archetypally feminine, especially in the context of that time and place.

The verses of "Stain" are in the third person, about some wretched soul, but the chorus is, tellingly, in the first person: "I'm a stain." So both songs are essentially about shame.

The hypnotic "Token Eastern Song" was a reaction to numerous critical observations that the band often favored Eastern modes, as in "Love Buzz." The back cover shot of the EP, a strangely desolate shot of a doctor's examination table, was taken by Tracy in her gynecologist's office shortly after an examination.

The droning "Love Buzz" is just one chord—like the Beatles' psychedelic masterpiece "Tomorrow Never Knows," with its Eastern influences—which is partly what gives it its "exotic" feeling, as well as being in the Phrygian mode, a type of scale that typically reminds Western ears of the Mediterranean, the Middle East, and beyond.

The title of "Token Eastern Song" surely comes from the effect of the Phrygian mode—the title was obviously a placeholder. Kurt had apparently composed a song in reaction to something critics said about his music, thereby making the classic mistake of reading his press. Then again, he got a cool song out of it.

A musician friend notes that, along with Krist's positively godlike bass playing, "Token Eastern Song" is "pretty bizarre harmonically," and both songs have "weird chromatic stuff going on in the scales their melodies and harmonies are derived from." Kurt didn't know much music theory, and yet he was capable of such uncanny sophistication, even at this early stage. It's one reason why some people call him a genius.

Then came the European tour with TAD. The two bands left Seattle for the first gig, in Newcastle, England, on October 20, 1989. Eleven guys—including the hulking Tad Doyle and all six feet and seven inches of Chris—were crammed into a teeny Fiat van. At first, it was all laughter and smiles, but then little things began to get on people's nerves—some of the guys on the bus smoked, and they weren't always considerate of the guys who didn't. A kind of delirium swept through the van. One of the guys bought some dirty magazines on Hamburg's notorious Reeperbahn. One was a coprophiliac's magazine which got passed around the bus, "Shit on me!" the guy would bellow over and over, collapsing in laughter. But for Kurt and a few others, the joke got old real fast.

The guy in the van may well have been citing the early-'80s Austin punk band the Dicks and their immortal musical composition "Shit on Me."

They played thirty-six shows in forty-two days. Nobody was eating very well and the pace was grueling. It was hard to sleep sitting up in the fiendishly uncomfortable seats. Nirvana was frustrated by their perennially cruddy equipment, hobbled further by the fact that they were smashing it to bits every night and then repairing it on the bus the next day. To make matters worse, the tour manager usually insisted on

Backstage pass from TAD/Nirvana European tour.

going straight to the venue when they arrived in town, meaning that the bands couldn't catch some sleep in their hotel room while awaiting their turn to do soundcheck. Instead, they waited around in the club for hours—cold, hungry, and tired—while the P.A. system was constructed.

 And Doyle had chronic stomach problems. At least once a day, he would have to get the driver to stop on the highway while he got out to throw up. Everyone

TAD and Nirvana. That's Tad Doyle to Chris's right. © Ian T. Tilton

on the bus would watch and do their own imitations of Doyle's hurling style. "He was definitely the puke machine," Chad recalls. "A never-ending vomitron."

Although he didn't smoke hash like most of the other guys on the bus, Kurt got very withdrawn and would react to bad situations either by drinking or retreating behind a wall of sleep. "I used to really enjoy sleep because I could just get away from pain that way," Kurt says. "I used to sleep constantly. On tour, every time we got in the van, I'd fall asleep. Every time we got to a club and we were waiting for soundcheck, we would sleep. Either I'd go back to the hotel and sleep or stay at the club and sleep until right before we went on stage so I didn't have to be in reality."

Doyle wasn't the only one suffering from nausea—Kurt was, too, and the two friends took turns holding each other's puke bucket and evaluating the contents. As Doyle said in Mark Yarm's *Everybody Loves Our Town: An Oral History of Grunge*, "We'd rate it, by chunk size and what the velocity was, what the color was, what the consistency was. . . . He laughed a lot; he loved it. . . . But I was laughing my ass off, too, in between blowing chunks."

Sleeping a lot is, of course, a classic symptom of depression. Although often, Kurt was probably only pretending to sleep so he wouldn't have to deal with anybody.

Increasingly, though, he would not want to be "in reality" and would find a new, more dangerous way to achieve that.

I just hope everybody appreciates the clever double allusion to Black Sabbath's "Behind the Wall of Sleep" and the Smithereens song of the same name, both of which Nirvana knew very well.

Chris was constantly drunk and/or stoned, while Chad, Chris claims, "was kind of out of his mind. He was talking in weird voices and stuff." For his part, Chad says he's *always* talked to himself—once, a waitress in the restaurant where he worked caught him in the walk-in refrigerator talking to a lemon. And he insists that of all the people on the tour, he had the best time—his nomadic childhood was perfect training for touring.

The band was unprepared for the adulation they received in Europe. Although the UK press raved about Nirvana, the band had no idea that they had so many fans over there—they simply weren't getting any sales reports from their UK label. Virtually every show was sold out; the venues were packed, there were lines around the block.

"That was a crazy tour," says Chris with some understatement. During the first gig, Chris slammed his new bass on the stage out of frustration with a malfunctioning amp. The neck snapped off and went right through one of the speakers in Kurt's rented Twin Reverb amp. It went downhill from there.

They played Berlin the day after the wall came down. Kurt smashed his guitar six songs into the set and walked off. "I'm kind of glad he did," says Chris. "I was really, really, really stoned."

Kurt sent Tracy lots of postcards. There was one where he sketched a picture of a typical Italian toilet. "There was no water," Tracy says, "so there's just a toilet with a big stinky pile of shit." Another time he wrote "I love you" over and over again on a postcard and signed his name.

This was probably the first time out of the country for a lot of the musicians, and what with grungemania, it should have been a total blast. But it sounds like it was really unpleasant—the kind of tour where you play places that don't have any water in the toilet bowl—and yet there were also lots of laughs, and the two bands bonded closely, with Kurt even filling in on vocals for a couple of songs with TAD one night when Tad Doyle took ill during their set.

Chad and Krist were apparently much more comfortable with all the traveling: Chad's family had moved around a lot, so he was used to being on the move, and Krist had spent a lot of time in Europe and was bilingual. Kurt, all too provincial, didn't have those advantages.

They did seven shows in the UK, five in the Netherlands, eleven in Germany, then on to Austria, Hungary, and Switzerland before the Sub Pop honchos met up with them in Rome. It was about six weeks—a pretty long tour, with rapid changes of language, currency, food, and so on, and not much rest or privacy. It would have been a test for even the most seasoned road dog.

The way Poneman sees it, that tour was the beginning of the end of both bands' relationships with Sub Pop (TAD eventually signed to WEA-distributed Mechanic Records in 1992). In the midst of one of their (in)famous promotional schmooze tours, Poneman and Pavitt turned up at a show in Rome toward the end of the tour. In retrospect, Poneman realized the message that their arrival sent. "There's TAD and Nirvana riding around in this crummy little van," says Poneman, "and here come the moguls flying in to Rome. We thought that we were lending emotional support, but from their perspective, I can see them thinking, 'These arrogant sons of bitches . . . We don't have any money, we're barely eating, we're riding around in this cramped van, we've got this fat lead singer who's throwing up all over the place, and you've got a crazy drunk bass player, and here come the moguls.'"

Not coincidentally, the Rome show was the nadir of the tour. The P.A. was terrible and so was the rented gear. Disgusted with the sound, the bad food, the cramped bus, the low pay, and the frenetic schedule, Kurt smashed his guitar four or five songs into the set ("Spank Thru"), walked off stage, and climbed onto a speaker stack. "He had a nervous breakdown onstage," says Pavitt. "He was just going to jump off. The bouncers were freaking out and everybody was just begging him to come down. And he was 'No, no, I'm just going to dive.' He had really reached his limit . . . People literally saw a guy wig out in front of them who could break his neck if he didn't get it together."

When the P.A. stack started to sway, Kurt clambered through the rafters, screaming at the audience the whole way until he reached the balcony, where he threatened to throw down a chair until someone took it away from him. He wound up backstage, where someone from the venue was arguing with their tour manager over whether Kurt had broken some microphones. Kurt grabbed both mikes, flung them to the ground, and began stomping on them. "*Now* they're broken," he said, and walked away. Then he told everyone in the entourage that he was quitting and he was going home, then put his hood over his head and burst into tears. Poneman took him out for some air.

"I was walking around the club with him," Poneman recalls, "and he was saying, 'I just want to go home, I don't want to play for these people, these people

are fucking idiots, they're stupid, they expect me to go up there and perform like a trained animal. I don't respect them. I want to be with my girlfriend and I want to quit music. This is not what I'm about.'" Poneman assured him that the next time the band came to Europe, conditions would be far better.

According to Kurt, the first words out of Poneman's mouth were, "Well, now that you're quitting Nirvana, we'd still be interested in you as a solo artist."

The Rome incident, as Bruce Pavitt related in his 2013 photo book *Experiencing Nirvana*, began when Kurt looked out into the crowd and saw "the kind of guys who used to beat me up in high school."

It might be difficult to grasp Kurt's deep emotional investment in his music but there's a well-known photo of him that Ian Tilton took in 1990. Kurt had just finished playing a show and was sitting on the floor backstage, weeping. He wasn't sad, per se—in fact, in a photo taken moments before, he was smiling—he was just overcome with emotion. When you put your innermost self out there for all to see, and the people you're putting it out to just don't get it, it can be devastating.

The episode in Rome was about as close as could be to someone walking out on the ledge of a building and needing to be talked down. (Sure enough, some people in the audience were yelling, "Jump!") It was, very glaringly, an SOS, a more extreme version of the psychodrama Kurt would act out at a lot of Nirvana shows, smashing his guitar and throwing his body into the drums in an orgy of self-harm.

But it's hard to truly see that kind of thing, especially when everyone is young—even Pavitt and Poneman were only in their late twenties.

Besides being close to Kurt at the time, Poneman is a very wise and understanding person and he was probably very comforting. Kurt could not have been more fortunate to have had Poneman at his side at this painful, vulnerable moment. I'm very skeptical that Poneman said anything about a solo career; that was probably Kurt's invention. Pavitt and Poneman took good care of Kurt, taking him sightseeing around Rome the day after the show, then buying him a train ticket to the next stop on the tour, Geneva, so he could get a break from the hurly-burly of the van.

Touring musicians visit many places, but they don't often get to see them: they travel all day, roll up to the club, load in, soundcheck, and play the show. Thanks to Pavitt and Poneman showing him around that day, Rome might have been the only continental European city that Kurt was particularly familiar with. Maybe that's why he fled to it five years later, only to undergo a far more horrific episode of self-harm than this one.

Chris and Chad also quit the band for a moment, but they all reconsidered and played the final two weeks of the tour.

HEAVIER THAN HEAVEN R'N'R FROM SEATTLE

Tad

NIRVANA

Sa 25 Nov. 21h

FRI-SON FRIBOURG FRI-SON

The next day, they took a train to Switzerland and while Kurt was asleep, his shoes, his wallet, and most importantly, his passport were all stolen. "I don't think I have ever seen another human being look as absolutely miserable as Kurt Cobain did at that moment," says Poneman. He somehow got into Switzerland and got a new passport at the American Embassy. Then they went to a music store in Geneva and Poneman bought Kurt a new guitar.

And then Kurt got so sick that they had to cancel a show. "He just needed some time off," says Chris. "I had a crutch—I had booze and hash, but he was straight." Chad, meanwhile, exhibited an almost Buddha-like serenity. No one could tell whether he was some sort of spiritual savant or just oblivious.

Nirvana and TAD met up with the Mudhoney tour for the final gig on December 3 at the Astoria in London, dubbed the Lame Festival. Nirvana had one lousy guitar left, and it kept cutting out throughout the set and Kurt had to keep stopping to fix it. "Nirvana's set was pretty fucked up," says Mudhoney drummer Danny Peters. Chris was so angry that he swung his bass by the strap around his head; eventually, the strap snapped; the guitar flew straight at Danny Peters's head and he only barely managed to bat it out of the way.

"It stunk," is Chris's review of the show. "On a scale of one to ten, that was a zero." The *Melody Maker* reviewer at the concert that night agreed. "It all falls apart when the lanky, rubberlegged, froglike bassist starts making a jerk of himself," went the review. "He'll *have* to go.

"As yet, I'm unmoved," the review concluded.

Others remember the show far more fondly. Bruce Pavitt rates the show as one of the best Nirvana has ever done, while Jonathan Poneman insists, "To this day, it's one of the proudest moments in my life." Journalist Keith Cameron, then with the now defunct UK music weekly *Sounds*, recalls it this way: "It was one of these things where the hall is maybe half full when they started, but by the time they finished, everyone in the hall was listening and getting into this band," he says. "I just ran down the front and freaked out. It was the most amazing band I'd ever seen.

"What impressed me," Cameron continues, "was the complete and utter tension that existed between the three people on stage. They *thrived* upon it. It was uncomfortable watching them sometimes. It was exhilarating and it was exciting because that was the nature of the music but there was also an almost palpable sense of danger, that this whole thing could just fall apart any second but it wasn't. And it was maintained throughout the set—there was never any relaxation from the first note to the last."

At the end of the set, Kurt threw his guitar at Chris, who then smashed it with his bass as if he were hitting a baseball. Kurt's guitar completely disintegrated. "You see bands smash their equipment and it's not a revelation," says Cameron, "but somehow with them, I'd never seen it done with any purpose before. It seemed the perfect way to end that show. You sort of wondered whether Kurt meant to hit Chris with his guitar or was that how they planned it. You got the impression that it wasn't planned at all. That was what was so good about it—you got the impression that they were learning this for the first time and they were as much in the dark as anyone, but it was just perfect."

The baseball-style guitar smash probably *wasn't* planned, but just about any red-blooded American male knows what to do when they're holding a long piece of wood and someone throws something at them.

"This is a key to Nirvana's appeal: At any moment, the group might career out of control or come screeching to a violent halt," wrote Jim DeRogatis for *Request* magazine in 1993, echoing a thought that countless critics wrote about Nirvana. It's a time-honored trope that the greatness of a rock band is embodied by the feeling that it could fall apart at any moment—it's been applied to the Who, the Sex Pistols, the Replacements, Pavement, and many other acclaimed bands—but there's no denying that rock is virtually the only kind of music that can sound great when it seems to be going off the rails. Kurt probably picked up on the power of imminent disaster from Mudhoney's thrillingly disheveled shows; Nirvana took it one giant leap further by insuring that not only did their shows threaten to go off the rails, but so did the very existence of the band.

That tension that Keith Cameron noted was encoded in Nirvana: Kurt was deeply invested in the music, and yet he was always threatening to sabotage it. And when he actively tried to throw it off track, Dave and Krist would usually remain implacable, the music's steel spine. But every once in a while, even they would succumb to chaos and nihilism and destroy the music, and those shows were not just colossal messes, they could be kind of heartbreaking.

If that tension was uncomfortable to watch, imagine what it must have been like to be one of the people actually feeling it—and feeling it night after night for weeks on end in front of hundreds, even thousands, of baying strangers. No wonder they smashed their instruments—it was a good way to defuse that tension . . . at least for the night.

During their visit to London, Nirvana did a session for Radio One DJ John Peel including "Love Buzz," "About a Girl," "Polly," and "Spank Thru."

Peel, a longtime British musical institution, was an uncanny, perennial tastemaker, an early champion of iconic artists such as David Bowie, Pink Floyd, Led Zeppelin, Roxy Music, the Ramones, Siouxsie and the Banshees, New Order, and many more. Playing a four-song Peel Session was the surest sign that a band had "arrived" in the UK, at least on a critical level, and American music media also paid close attention to what got played on Peel's show. This was a really big deal. Nirvana had been anointed.

The British press had really started rolling in by this time, and the articles fed on the idea that the band came from rural, white-trash America. "They're a little bit gross and a little bit awesome," went one profile. "What else would you be if you grew up in the backwoods redneck helltown of Aberdeen . . ." Sub Pop played it

The Amplified Come as You Are

up for all it was worth. "You've got the three-hundred-pound butcher hanging out with Kurt the trailer-trash kid and you've got the moguls—we'd be posing in suits and ties—adding a little theater," says Bruce Pavitt. "People got caught up in it."

Kurt didn't like getting painted as some sort of idiot savant yokel one bit. "To be thought of as this stump-dumb rocker dude from Aberdeen who just blindly found his way up to Seattle and this hip label," says Kurt, "it just felt degrading to be thought of as someone like that when that was something I was fighting against all my life."

Kurt's voice was breaking as he reached the end of that last sentence. He was still really upset about this. He *had* been fighting all his life to leave an Aberdeen of the mind, abandoning the closed-mindedness, violence, and prejudice he felt there, and absorbing as much as he could from whatever music, art, and literature he could discover on his own or through Krist, Buzz Osborne, the Olympia sophisticates, and the Seattle crowd. To go through the painful, arduous process of shedding that old skin, to finally begin to fulfill his artistic and personal vision, only to be marginalized as "this stump-dumb rocker dude from Aberdeen," was frustrating and humiliating.

"They were totally manipulating people in trying to put this package together," says Kurt of Pavitt and Poneman. "They've gotten so much credit for being these geniuses, these masterminds behind this whole thing when it really had nothing to do with them. It really didn't. It had more to do with Charles Peterson's fuzzy pictures than it did with their attempts at making sure we appeared stupid in interviews. I always resented them for that."

And Kurt found Pavitt's professed populism far more condescending than brilliant. "It was just obvious that he thought of himself as an educated white upper-middle-class punk rocker who knows everything and I'm just this idiot from Aberdeen," Kurt says. "That was always something that we sensed and we totally resented him for it." They felt similarly about Poneman, too.

Of course, the explosion of the Seattle scene had *everything* to do with Bruce Pavitt and Jonathan Poneman. Without them, there would have been no platform for the now-familiar constellation of Seattle bands to shine. It was their shrewdness, imagination, resourcefulness, and swashbuckling entrepreneurship that made them and the Seattle music community a worldwide cultural phenomenon.

Besides the bands, Pavitt and Poneman recognized local talent such as Charles Peterson and his "fuzzy pictures," as well as photographer Michael Lavine (a former Evergreen student who had moved to New York City) and Jack Endino. But there were also in-house designers Lisa Orth and Linda Owens; a couple of brilliant publicists in

Nils Bernstein and Jennie Boddy, both of whom began at Sub Pop with zero experience and later rose to the top of their field; Ed Fotheringham, who did illustration work for the label and is now one of the top illustrators in the country (full disclosure: he illustrated one of my books); and the acclaimed art director Art Chantry. So that was proof of concept: Sub Pop's success was a vindication of the idea that talent is everywhere—you just have to recognize and mobilize it. That's what Pavitt and Poneman did so brilliantly, with a huckster's bravado, a gambler's brinksmanship, a student's devotion, and the unbridled zeal of true music fans.

But there's no denying that they broke a lot of eggs to make that omelet.

To be fair, Pavitt and Poneman *had* seized on a bright idea—that art and culture didn't have to be developed and transmitted solely from the media centers of New York and Los Angeles. The indie labels had proved that people in places like Minneapolis and Chicago and Seattle had just as much to say as any New York City media creature. For Poneman and Pavitt, finding someone from a place like Aberdeen who made valid art was like hitting the jackpot. "They thrived on that," Kurt says. "They were excited about it. They'd found these redneck kids from a coastal town that they could exploit, or at least use their image to their benefit. They didn't really want to find out if we were smarter than they wanted us to be, because that would ruin everything."

Kurt might gripe a lot about Sub Pop, but he'll gladly acknowledge the crucial role the label, and Jonathan Poneman in particular, played in their career. "Jonathan was really, really supportive of us from the very beginning," Kurt says. "He wanted us to rule the world."

After the tour, Kurt and Chad went home, while Chris and Shelli flew to what was still called Yugoslavia to see Chris's father.

Chris and Shelli got married soon after they got back home to Tacoma, on December 30, 1989. The ceremony, which was conducted by a woman Shelli knew from work, took place in the couple's Tacoma apartment. It was a small apartment and it was packed. Besides Chris's mom and Shelli's mother and stepfather, there were Kurt and Tracy, Dan Peters, most of the guys from TAD, old friends and some neighbors. Matt Lukin was Chris's best man. "They got married," says Lukin, "and then everybody got drunk." The reception was distinguished by an inebriated three-way wrestling match between Chris, Kurt Danielson, and Tad Doyle.

Kurt at the HUB Ballroom, January 1990. © Charles Peterson

###

After a brief California tour and some local gigs, the band went out on a US tour, Chad's last. They each picked up Pixelvision toy video cameras and shot movies in the van to pass the time. They hired a U-Haul trailer—"It was a total advancement in touring technology," says Chris—and put a loveseat in the back. It was a big step for the band—now they had the whole van to themselves. They also had a T-shirt that reproduced John Lennon and Yoko Ono's infamous nude *Two Virgins* album cover, except sticking Bruce Pavitt and Jonathan Poneman's faces on the bodies. They headlined at clubs with a few hundred capacity, making a few hundred dollars a night.

It must have been whiplash to come home and play small clubs after the grungemania overseas. It would take a little time for American media to pick up the buzz coming over from the English rock weeklies.

The Fisher-Price PXL-2000, or Pixelvision, was an inexpensive, very lo-fi video camera that recorded onto standard audiocassette tapes. They were made for children, but artists snapped them up, too—director Richard Linklater used a Pixelvision camera for a sequence in his essential 1990 debut feature *Slacker*. The PXL-2000 was available

Kurt at Raji's in Los Angeles, February 1990. © Charles Peterson

for only a year, around 1987, and then began popping up in, you guessed it, thrift stores, which was surely where Chad, Krist, and Kurt found them—yet another example of cast-off culture.

They played all the same clubs they used to play, except now they had a tour manager, a roadie, and soundman Craig Montgomery working for them full time. At first, the easygoing Montgomery was a little rattled by all the guitar smashing, but soon came to understand what it was all about. "That's part of the fun of Nirvana, is the unpredictability," he says. "If they didn't have that anger at some times, they wouldn't have that beauty at other times."

By this time, people in important places were beginning to buzz about Nirvana. Indie world demi-gods Sonic Youth had seen the band on the Jason tour and had become big fans and ardent boosters in the press. Bassist Kim Gordon and guitarist Thurston Moore showed up at a gig in New York at the Pyramid Club, along with Geffen A&R (Artist and Repertoire) man Gary Gersh. Besides them, no one in the audience liked the band, except for Iggy Pop, who had been brought to the gig by photographer Michael Lavine. Pop hooted and hollered words of encouragement throughout the set, even though the band played miserably.

The Amplified Come as You Are

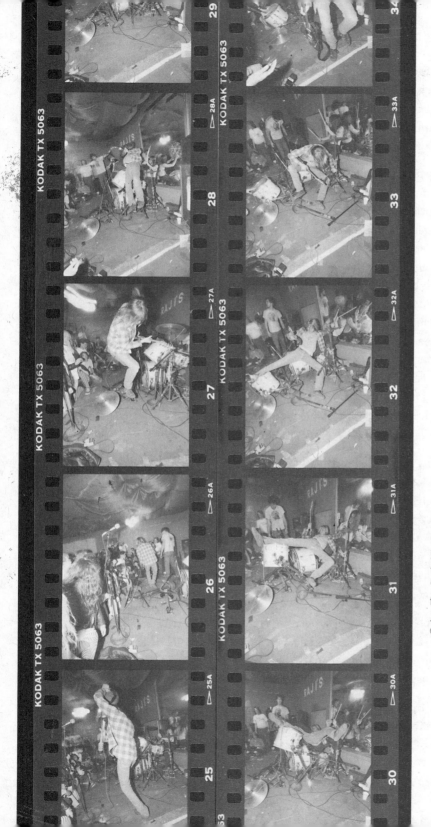

Motor-drive photo sequence
from the February 1990
Raji's show, which yielded
the back cover photo of
"Sliver" (frame 27) and
the inside photo from the
Bleach CD (frame 31).
© Charles Peterson

In penance for the gig, Chris shaved his head in the cheap Jersey City motel the band was staying in, but not before they had started shooting a video for "In Bloom," which can be found on the Sub Pop compilation entitled *Sub Pop Video Network Program One*. In some scenes, Chris has hair and in some, he doesn't. So much for continuity.

The band actually played fine at the Pyramid show, but they'd been rattled by some hecklers, who were none other than Silver Jews' David Berman and Pavement's Stephen Malkmus and Bob Nastanovich. Sub Pop was super-hip, and this show by their buzziest band was, as Nastanovich said in a 2015 interview on the *Kreative Kontrol* podcast, "The see-and-be-seen show of all time." Intent on ridiculing SubPopmania, they decided to taunt Nirvana. Berman really wound up Krist, and they got into a bitter back-and-forth in the middle of the set. Krist kind of lost it. Later, Malkmus joined in. "We were all big fans of Nirvana," said Nastanovich, and after the show, "We were kind of ashamed of ourselves." Krist shaved his head—not unlike the ritual shaming/shaving scenario in "Floyd the Barber."

"In Bloom" was a Sub Pop video: the label was anticipating releasing that song and the rest of the new material. That version of "In Bloom" was from the Butch Vig sessions in Madison, and it's worth noting how close it is to the *Nevermind* version: they'd worked out the parts long before they recorded the album. Chad's drum part has some unique little flourishes that powerfully boost the riffs and the song in general; later, all Dave Grohl did was tweak them slightly.

On April 27, Tracy's birthday, Kurt called her from Amherst, Massachusetts, to tell her that he didn't want to live together, but that he still wanted them to be boyfriend and girlfriend. Tracy knew something like that was coming. "Near the end, we started fighting more and more," she says. "He wanted me to be artistic and I didn't have the time to be artistic. I was driving an hour to work and an hour back from work. I was supporting him and he wasn't doing any housework. He'd say 'Just leave it' and I'd say 'I can't leave it. I can leave it for a week or a few days and then I can't stand it anymore. I have to clean it because you won't do it.'"

So while Kurt appreciated Tracy's support, he wanted someone who would challenge him creatively, an artistic peer he could bounce around ideas with. He soon found one. And then, later, he found another one.

One kind of has to wonder how feminist a guy could be if he won't do any housework.

A few days later in Florida, they met a kid who wanted to be on Sub Pop, and who let them spend the night at his dad's luxury condo. That night they did a lot of acid and drank a lot of Tom Collins drinks. Among other unspeakably strange and bizarre acts, Chris fried mayonnaise in a pan. The next morning, he found himself walking around the driveway stark naked, bald, and yelling, "Cast away your possessions like I have! You're not worth anything!" Kurt hustled him back into the house, got him dressed, and they scrammed out of there before their still-unconscious host discovered all the damage they'd done.

Although Sub Pop didn't promote *Bleach* as heavily as other albums out at the time, it was a steady seller. It was promoted for two months and then, despite Kurt's request that the label stay on top of the record, Sub Pop went on to new projects. The label's relatively low-powered distribution and publicity were beginning to be a problem—their records were hard to find.

Kurt insisted to Jonathan Poneman that *Bleach* could be a million seller. Maybe that was just his way of encouraging Sub Pop to promote it, but back then, indie labels were virtually incapable of selling millions of records; the infrastructure simply wasn't there.

Before the internet, physical distribution was everything: people simply couldn't buy the record if it wasn't in the store. (A relative few plucky souls did send away for records.) Independent labels used independent record distributors—which is, technically, why they're called independent labels—but the indies just couldn't get massive numbers of records into stores even if massive numbers of people wanted them. Independent distributors were also often inept, crooked, or verging on bankruptcy.

The defining advantage of major labels was that they had the ability to press up vast quantities of "product" and then ship it to the big chains. Major labels could also drum up sales with powerful marketing, radio, and publicity departments. It was no contest: if you wanted to sell a lot of records, you had to be on a major.

But Kurt wasn't the only one who thought Nirvana had a shot at selling a lot of records. "If any of the emergent US underground bands are to break through into the mainstream, Nirvana will be the ones to do so," wrote *Sounds*' prescient Keith Cameron in October 1990. "Whatever label it comes out on, Nirvana's next album will undoubtedly bring them to the attention of a far wider audience."

Sub Pop was shopping their own deal with a major—and Nirvana was their sweetest bait for a deal. Nirvana would have had no input on which label Sub Pop signed with, so they decided to take matters into their own hands: if they had to be on a major, at least *they'd* choose which one, not Sub Pop.

Later, independent labels such as Matador, Merge, and, yes, Sub Pop did become capable of selling mass quantities of records, even earning gold records. And that was,

Kurt sees the light in an early Michael Lavine portrait. © Michael Lavine

ironically, in no small part because Nirvana and their peers exposed the record-buying public to an entire parallel universe of music.

"It's the typical story of showing up at gigs and ten to twenty kids coming up to the stage and saying we can't find your record anywhere," Kurt says. "It got real tiring. We didn't do any interviews. We felt we deserved a little bit more than what we were getting. I would have been comfortable playing to a thousand people. That was basically our goal—to get up to that size of a club, to be one of the most popular alternative rock bands, like Sonic Youth." Kurt estimates they did about three interviews while they were on the label.

Again, Kurt was exaggerating as a way of retaliating against a perceived antagonist and justifying his position. Nirvana actually did plenty of interviews while they were on Sub Pop. In 1989 alone, they appeared in *Sounds*, *Melody Maker*, *Flipside*, the *NME*, the *Rocket*, various fanzines, and Dutch, German, Austrian, Swedish, and Italian publications, not to mention a fair number of radio interviews.

And Sub Pop was on the verge of going under. A distribution venture crashed and burned due to mismanagement, Poneman and Pavitt's high-rolling promotional style was draining the company dry, band members were raiding the stockroom and walking off with armloads of vinyl. The label was releasing a record a week while trying to keep too many bands on the road, and now that major labels were offering major label–sized advances to Seattle bands, Sub Pop felt compelled to try to match them. Sub Pop nearly went bankrupt. By the summer of 1990, they were bouncing hundred-dollar checks and owed money to everyone in town. "They hit rock bottom," Chris recalls. "It was just such a mess. They tried really hard to pay us because they really appreciated us and that's cool but it was just too much of a burden."

And further draining the label's coffers were Sub Pop's alleged legal negotiations (neither Pavitt nor Poneman will comment on them to this day) for distribution deals with Columbia Records and Hollywood Records. At one point, Nirvana met with Sub Pop's attorney, who tried to convince them that it was a good arrangement, but the way Kurt and Chris saw it, it simply made more sense for them to choose their own label, instead of someone else choosing it for them. "We decided to cut out the middleman," says Kurt.

Other Seattle bands had preceded Nirvana to majors: Mother Love Bone (Mercury), Soundgarden (A&M), Alice in Chains (Columbia), and the Posies (Geffen's DGC imprint). Pearl Jam and Screaming Trees (both Epic) signed the same year Nirvana did.

The major label distribution deal fell through in the summer of 1990, leaving Sub Pop with nothing but hefty legal bills for the failed negotiations, further crippling the financially struggling label. They were in very bad shape. And then, through a miraculous stroke of luck, they were in very, very good shape.

No indie label could afford to buy Nirvana out of their Sub Pop contract, and besides, Sonic Youth and Dinosaur Jr, both bands of impeccable artistry and credibility, had recently signed to majors, so they began looking for a major label deal. When Poneman and Pavitt found out, they were deeply anguished. "I can think of very few things that have happened in my life that have hurt my feelings more," says Pavitt. "It really fucked with my head for a while."

Through the first half of the '80s, indie bands had largely shunned major labels—partly out of loyalty to the labels who had worked so hard to release their rigorously uncompromising music, and partly because the majors simply weren't interested. And some of them were on indies because they abhorred big corporations.

But indie underground heroes Hüsker Dü had released two major label albums by this point, the Replacements had three, and Soul Asylum had one. In 1988, R.E.M., Jane's Addiction, and college radio darlings Camper Van Beethoven all made their major label debuts with their artistry and integrity intact.

Indie bands enjoyed widely varying degrees of artistic and commercial success on major labels, but the bottom line was that signing to majors had become fairly acceptable. And then it became *really* acceptable: in the summer of 1989, Sonic Youth signed to Geffen's DGC label, becoming labelmates with the likes of Cher, Whitesnake, Aerosmith, and Guns N' Roses. Even Firehose—led by Mike Watt, formerly of archetypal indie underground trio the Minutemen—went to Columbia, one of the majorest of majors. All of this gave Nirvana a big green light of cultural permission.

Pavitt says he and Poneman only found out about the group's plans through the grapevine. "It was so obvious," Kurt replies. "We wouldn't return their phone calls for weeks and weeks at a time. Every time I talked to Jonathan, I feel that I made it clear that there was definitely an uncertainty in our relationship. I just don't understand how you're expected to come right out and tell someone something like that. I suppose it's the more adult thing to do, to tell someone that you don't want to have anything to do with them anymore. It's a really hard thing to do. I've always quit my jobs without any notice. I just quit one day and not show up."

So there's a pattern: Kurt also did that with Dave Foster and Jason Everman.

Kurt admired Pavitt because he had an uncanny instinct for ferreting out great new underground music. Bearing albums by Daniel Johnston and the Shaggs as propitiatory offerings, Pavitt went down to Kurt's apartment in Olympia to try to talk him into a new, stronger contract. "For the first time, Bruce actually seemed like a human being to me," says Kurt. "Every other time I'd see Bruce, our conversation was always real limited and we never got to talk to each other on a human level. I also felt some kind of resentment because why all of a sudden, at that point, did he decide to treat me like a person instead of this casualty every time I came into his office?"

They spoke for five tense hours—"There were just beads of sweat on my forehead and everything," recalls Pavitt—and Kurt couldn't quite bring himself to tell Pavitt that he was sure he didn't want to be on Sub Pop anymore. A few days later, Chris gave Sub Pop the definitive word. They were leaving.

"I felt really bad," says Kurt. "I felt guilty because I wanted to be on their label still because I knew that these are people who share similar thoughts. I kind of felt like the enemy at the time. But still, there was nothing that [Pavitt] was going to do that would change my mind. They were just too risky."

It was the right call, sadly. Sub Pop's checks were bouncing: they couldn't pay their employees, the pressing plant, or even their landlord, not to mention their bands. They laid off most of their staff. The Seattle *Rocket* featured a cover photo of a weary- and dejected-looking Pavitt and the headline "Sub Plop?" With their sense of cheekiness still very much intact, Pavitt and Poneman made up T-shirts that said "Sub Plop" in the style of the Sub Pop logo, with the legend "What part of 'We have no money' don't you understand?" on the back. And then they sold them to raise money.

By August, Soundgarden manager Susan Silver had also introduced them to lawyer Alan Mintz of the powerful Ziffren, Brittenham & Branca firm. Mintz had already engineered outstanding deals for Jane's Addiction and Faith No More. The wining and dining began. Charisma, Slash, and Capitol all wanted the band badly. MCA flew the band down to L.A. and flew a rep up to Seattle. Island A&R man Steve Pross had already been chasing Nirvana, but the band was thoroughly uninterested in Island.

The labels were all excited about a tape the band had recorded in early April of 1990 at Smart Studios in Madison, Wisconsin, the home base of veteran underground producer Butch Vig, an immensely nice man who had become highly regarded for his fierce-sounding but economical production work on albums by Killdozer, the Laughing Hyenas, the Fluid, and Smashing Pumpkins and who had produced records for labels like Touch & Go, Mammoth, Twin/Tone, and Amphetamine Reptile. He'd also produced TAD's excellent *8-Way Santa* album for Sub Pop. Vig started with more pop records but adapted brilliantly to the mid-'80s indie boom with its abrasive sounds and tight recording budgets. Jonathan Poneman had hyped Vig on Nirvana by saying, "These guys are going to be bigger than the Beatles!"

Kurt was very quiet and let Chris do most of the talking. Chris made it clear that the band wanted to sound very heavy. Vig began to sense a tension between Kurt and Chad, who couldn't quite do what Kurt wanted him to.

Once again, Kurt wouldn't communicate and just left it for the other person to figure it out.

They had spent a week recording seven songs for what was supposed to be their second Sub Pop album, but which became, in effect, the demo tape they shopped to the major labels. The arrangements are virtually identical to the *Nevermind* versions—in fact, the version of "Polly" is the one that appears on *Nevermind*, although remixed. "Breed" was then called "Imodium" (after the antidiarrhea medicine Tad Doyle had used on the European tour); "Stay Away" was originally titled "Pay to Play" and featured slightly different lyrics, spectacular feedback, and a screaming kamikaze coda. Also recorded at Smart were "In Bloom," "Dive," and "Lithium," which begins with Kurt playing the same rickety acoustic guitar that features on "Polly" and fades rather than stops. They also made another attempt at the elusive "Sappy," a highly catchy tune about romantic entrapment.

Vig was the perfect producer for the project. He could get nasty sounds, but he was also a self-described "pop geek." In the indie scene, music as melodic and downright catchy as this was anathema. Almost by definition, underground music wasn't supposed to be easy to like. The songs on the Smart sessions were a bold step, as bold and experimental as any noisy angst-fest—perhaps a lot more so. "I think of them as pop songs," Kurt told one UK magazine. "There aren't songs as wild and heavy as 'Paper Cuts' or 'Sifting' on the new record. That's just too boring. I'd rather have a good hook."

It's funny to read a line like "in the indie scene, music as melodic and downright catchy as this was anathema" and think of the tuneful, refined turn indie music took in the following decade with bands such as the Postal Service, Fleet Foxes, the Shins, and Beach House. Before that, the indie world had much more of a Wild West feeling, and the music reflected it. (All the bands listed, by the way, are or were on Sub Pop.)

Both the songwriting and the recording weren't as rushed as *Bleach* had been, so Kurt had a lot of time to hone and polish the songs. "I had finally gotten to the point where I was mixing pop music and the heavy side of us in the right formula," says Kurt. "It was working really well, mostly because of the reports from our friends and other bands. Everyone was saying that it was really good. I could tell that it was definitely more advanced than *Bleach*."

But Kurt and Chris were growing more and more unhappy with Chad's drumming. This time, Kurt had the time to make sure that Chad played the parts that he had taught him—during the low-budget *Bleach* sessions, Chad would change his parts and there was no time to argue or do another take.

"I was really hoping to participate more and become part of what was going on," says Chad, "at least to have a say in how my own drums sounded. I wanted to get more involved in the band and feel like I was actually doing something. I was still happy dealing with the album, but I wanted to be more a part of it. It was

© Michael Lavine

then that I realized that it really is Kurt's show and that what he says goes and that's it, no questions asked."

Chad, who could play guitar, bass, and violin, was also a songwriter and wanted to start contributing material to the band. But even though he was into a lot of the same music that Chris and Kurt were—the Young Marble Giants, the Beatles, Scratch Acid, and the Butthole Surfers—his songwriting style defined the Bainbridge Island sound (which he helped to create before joining Nirvana)— ultra-quirky, pastoral, vaguely prog-rock. "Elfin music," says Kurt. "You just kind of shudder because it's so stupid and dorky." Kurt says they were open to other material, but Chad's music didn't fit the band. "It just wasn't good," says Kurt, "and there was nothing else to be said about it. It was really sad because he felt like he wasn't part of the band because he couldn't really create." And so Chad wound up living out a time-honored rock-biz joke. "Q: What was the last thing the drummer said before he was fired? A: 'Hey, guys, I wrote some songs I want us to play!'"

By late May, after the US tour had ended, Nirvana had started to attract the attention of major labels. Bootlegs of the demo circulated around the music industry, and even though they were hardly as polished as the finished *Nevermind* recordings would be, the buzz was loud. Ironically, Sub Pop had probably helped spread the buzz about Nirvana by touting the band as a valuable property to the labels they wanted to do a distribution agreement with.

And that's when Kurt and Chris chose to fire Chad Channing. Nervous and sad, they took the thirty-five-minute ferry ride from Seattle to Chad's house on Bainbridge Island to give him the news. They told him—Chris did most of the talking—gave him a hug goodbye, and then they left. "I felt like I'd just killed somebody," says Kurt.

Chad's take on the meeting is that he wasn't fired—he quit. "We talked for a while and I just told them this was how I felt and they knew that," he says. "It wasn't like we weren't getting along—we always got along as human beings. It was strictly along the musical line that it just wasn't working anymore. That's where it ended, right there. I never felt like I was totally in the band. I felt like I was just a drummer. I was thinking, why don't they get a drum machine—get it over with. Then they could program it and do anything they damn well wanted."

"Sometimes I just felt sorry for Chad," says Bruce Pavitt. "You could tell that . . . I didn't feel that they treated him with a lot of respect."

Even though Kurt thought Chad was a really nice guy, he never got along with him. Kurt suspects Chad didn't get along with him for some of the same reasons that Jason didn't. Kurt was still prone to being "volatile"—getting drunk and turning into a negative creep. "I was just trying to be 'punk rock' or something," Kurt admits. "I had this terrible Johnny Rotten complex." Chad, used to the mellow, quasi-hippie Bainbridge Island scene, couldn't relate to such a sarcastic pessimist.

Kurt was still openly judgmental, quick to point out people's faults, something Chad frowned upon. Kurt knew he had a problem and tried hard to contain it, but couldn't always, especially when talking about their *bête noire*, crude Seattle sludge-rockers Blood Circus, whose early success baffled Kurt and Chris. "It was almost impossible for me to get along on any level with Chad because I basically couldn't say anything without offending him," says Kurt. "I thought he was judging me for judging other people." Their mutual animosity grew, although they would never say it was. "What an asshole," Chad would think to himself. "What a hippie," Kurt thought.

Kurt had played drums for years, so he was very picky about drumming. He didn't think much of Chad's playing, and that further fueled his animosity. "He really had bad timing and he wasn't a very powerful drummer," says Kurt. Kurt liked Chad much better than any other drummer they'd had, so he encouraged him to take lessons so he could improve. Kurt also says that Chad would tire quickly and start to make more and more mistakes as the set wore on; often, there would be interminable delays while Chad retuned his drums, although Kurt insists he was really resting.

Chad was a powerful drummer who created great parts for himself; he also studied Tae Kwon Do. It's pretty doubtful that he needed to rest between songs. If he needed to tune his drums often, it might have been because they were so damaged from Kurt crashing into them. This sounds like yet more of Kurt's antagonist mythmaking.

"Sometimes there would be weird things," says Chris. "He'd go off in space—there wouldn't even be a drum beat any more. I remember looking over at Kurt and Kurt looking over at me like, 'What the fuck was *that*?'"

"That really is how the instrument smashing came about," says Kurt. "I got so pissed off at Chad that I'd jump into the drum set, then smash my guitar." Early video tapes of the band show that sets often ended with someone hurling a guitar or a guitar case at Chad, soon followed by Kurt and/or Chris sailing into the drum kit.

That's not what Krist said earlier about the roots of Nirvana's guitar smashing, before Chad joined the band: "It just *started*. . . . It was fun. It seemed like you couldn't end a show without doing something spectacular or sensational."

This appears to be yet more revisionism on Kurt's part to justify dismissing Chad.

Chris is still slightly evasive when explaining why Chad got the sack. At first, he chalks it up to good old musical differences. "He kind of wanted to do his own thing," he says, adding that Chad was a "light, jazzy" drummer by nature and had to alter his style in order to play in Nirvana. "We needed a real thumper." But on the Vig demo, Chad hit very hard, and truth be told, Dave Grohl virtually duplicated all his parts for *Nevermind*.

"We've been through a lot with this whole success thing, with all the pressure and stuff," Chris continues. "I'm just glad [Chad] didn't have to go through all that, because . . ." and he trails off. "It was always kind of awkward with Chad. It was weird. I don't regret it at all, though. He just wanted to do his own thing. He had a different perspective than us. A lot of times he had a way better perspective. Way more objective and way more innocent and really good. We were going to make this big step—sign to a major label—and he wasn't right for us. It just wasn't right."

"Even when I look at it now," says Chad. "I don't regret anything. I'd probably be pretty damn wealthy, but would I be happy? That's the question mark there.

"It's kind of weird," he continues. "I mean, I could be there—but I'm not. But at the same time, I'm happy for them. I would have been bummed if it just petered out and the band broke up. I hope they're enjoying themselves and that the pressures aren't too much."

See what a sweet guy Chad is?

So Chad was "way more innocent and really good"—as if he wasn't corrupted enough to come along for the major label sell-out ride and everything that would inevitably come with it.

The bad feelings seem to be few. "Overall, I have massive love for that guy," says Kurt. "I kind of admire him because he's really satisfied with the way that he is. He seems like a really happy person and he always has been."

Chad now plays in a fine band called Fire Ants and made a tidy sum from the royalties of *Bleach* and *Incesticide*.

Without a drummer, they canceled a proposed March 1990 UK tour and asked Dale Crover to fill in on a seven-date West Coast tour with Sonic Youth in mid-August. Crover agreed to play, but on one condition. "I told them—whatever you do, do not jump into my drum set. *Do not.*" Not only did they comply with that request, but they also did not smash one guitar on the tour. "I'm glad they didn't do that stuff," says Crover. "I'd seen them do it before and I just thought it was anticlimactic. Kurt trying to break a guitar—it takes him fifteen minutes. By the time it's over, it's like, big deal. I think that's guitar murder. I think guitars have souls. I don't think any of that stuff's cool at all. Instruments have souls—why would you want to murder a guitar? I think it's pointless. Haven't you ever seen the Who, guys?"

Dale is a pretty easygoing person, so I'll never forget how adamant he was when he recounted his warning not to jump into his drum set. But they would never have done that—they respected him too much. Also, if Dale quit the tour, they'd be screwed.

Also on the bill for that tour: up-and-coming San Diego band Stone Temple Pilots.

At the Palladium in Hollywood, Kurt started the show by announcing, "We're Nirvana and we really don't particularly like heavy metal."

That Sonic Youth tour was pivotal. It's an unsung aspect of rock life that bands that tour together often bond closely. There's just something about seeing each other night after night, far from home. They catch each other's sets, loan equipment, trade musical ideas, go out on adventures together, all of this unseen by the public; the press never asks about it even though it's a huge part of being a touring musician.

Sonic Youth were already well connected, highly revered elder statespeople in the indie world; they'd carved out a great career even though they made challenging, uncompromising music. For Kurt, they were sophisticated, worldly New Yorkers whom he could learn a lot from and who could help him leave behind the stigma of the stump-dumb rocker dude from Aberdeen. In the liner notes for *Incesticide*, Kurt described the tour with Sonic Youth: "Totally being taken under their wing and being showed what dignity really means."

So when Sonic Youth gave Nirvana the seal of approval, it was a milestone: it meant Nirvana had been admitted to an exclusive club.

In particular, Kurt and Kim Gordon became close. Kurt clearly admired Gordon's cool and her great cultural sophistication; I'm sure Gordon found Kurt's sensitive aspects a welcome relief from all the men she was continually surrounded by. (She once wrote a great early Sonic Youth tour diary titled "Boys Are Smelly.") Gordon keenly sensed what was about to happen with Kurt and the band, which was why she urged Geffen to sign Nirvana.

###

Kurt and Tracy continued living together for over a month until Tracy could get enough money to get an apartment in Tacoma, which was closer to work. But Kurt wasn't at the apartment much. Usually, he was staying over at the home of Tobi Vail, one of only a handful of girlfriends Kurt ever had.

Unfortunately, Tobi Vail didn't want to be interviewed for this book. I gathered that it was still complicated between her and Kurt, and I bet she wisely didn't want to get mixed up in the monumental turmoil around the band or appear to be exploiting her connection to Nirvana. She also might well have figured that discussing their relationship might cause some domestic difficulties for Kurt. And besides, few people want their romantic relationships dissected in the media. The bottom line is, Tobi Vail is a far more key figure in Kurt's personal and artistic evolution than this book was able to convey.

Only twenty years old at the time, Vail had been embedded in the local, regional, and national underground punk community for years before Kurt met her. She was encyclopedic about the music and her well-developed punk ethos of inclusivity manifested in things like promoting all-ages shows and supporting women in bands.

The year before, she'd started a feminist/music fanzine called *Jigsaw*. As she wrote in an early issue: "it's becoming more and more clear how limited we are by our world . . . of capitalism and mass culture and 'you're the boy and I'm the girl' mentality . . . and we accept those limitations and live within them without being aware of the possibilities." Now think about, for instance, all the times Kurt was photographed wearing a dress.

Vail played in various bands, including drumming with Calvin Johnson in the Go Team. She'd been a DJ at KAOS since she was fifteen years old. Kurt often mentioned brilliant underground UK bands such as Young Marble Giants, Kleenex, Delta 5, the Raincoats, and Marine Girls—all bands that Vail championed.

All of this must have been life-altering for Kurt: Tobi Vail was yet another person who expanded his view of the world, an invaluable source of cultural information. Imagine what it must have been like to be twenty-three years old and in love with such a person.

Kurt says he slept with a total of two women on all of Nirvana's tours. Perhaps he had learned a lesson from an incident that occurred on the band's second US tour. After realizing that their audience at a sleazy dive in Iowa was mostly "frat jock people," Kurt downed a big jug of Long Island Iced Tea during a particularly shambolic set. Afterward, they all stumbled over to someone's house and spent the night. Kurt met a girl. "We had sex in the van in front of the house and I woke up in the morning to the sound of breaking glass," Kurt says. "It turned out to be her boyfriend with a hammer, smashing out the windows of the van. We were stark naked, covered in glass, wondering what we should do. He was walking around the van screaming 'Bitch, bitch! I'm going to kill you!'

"But then he took off."

Kurt had been looking for a dynamic and artistic girlfriend like Tobi. She had her own fanzine and was busy helping to start the riot grrrl movement, a group of young women dedicated to promoting female empowerment through music, fanzines, and eventually, the national media, with her friend Kathleen Hanna. Through Tobi, Kurt began to investigate feminism and other social and political causes. "I thought I was in love again," says Kurt, "and it was just wishful thinking."

That might be some revisionism. It sure seems like Kurt was very much in love. But there was bad blood between Courtney and the riot grrrl community, and I think Courtney was very jealous of Tobi, so Kurt couldn't really be candid with me about Tobi.

In 1991, in the fanzine of the same name, Bikini Kill singer Kathleen Hanna wrote a riot grrrl manifesto, declaring that "girls constitute a revolutionary soul force that can, and will change the world for real." Hanna decried "bullshit like racism, able-bodieism, ageism, speciesism, classism, thinism, sexism, anti-semitism and heterosexism" and anticipated the now widely embraced concept of intersectionality. ("Eat meat, hate blacks, beat your fuckin' wife / It's all connected," Hanna wrote in the insert for the Bikini Kill compilation *The First Two Records*.) This is all when she was in her early twenties.

(Kurt picked up on those ideas. In his journals, he wrote, "Classism is determined by sexism because the male decides whether all other isms exist. . . . In order to expand on all other isms, sexism has to be blown wide open.")

Riot grrrl railed against normalizing physical, verbal, and emotional violence against women, body shaming, and patriarchy. Underlying it all was the certain knowledge that it was folly to believe, as many did at the time, that women had finally attained equality and thus feminism was no longer necessary; by aggressively debunking that, riot grrrl was a key instigator of what became known as third-wave feminism.

With the idea that the punk rock community was a microcosm of society, riot grrrl took the punk DIY ethic—very much including its confrontational aspects—and applied it not just to music and zines but to consciousness-raising and activism, eventually spinning off chapters around the world. One of the goals was to create safe spaces for women, both figuratively and literally: at Bikini Kill shows Hanna would announce, "All girls to the front!" effectively displacing the oppressive male-dominated mosh pits that would invariably form at punk shows.

A couple of months after the Smart sessions, Chris called up Butch Vig and asked him if he'd be interested in producing a major label record with them at some point. Vig said sure.

Meanwhile, back at Sub Pop, Jonathan Poneman wanted another Nirvana single. "Dive," the B-side, was culled from the Vig sessions. "Dive" reprised the best elements of *Bleach*—the grinding guitar sound, the high, desperate growling vocals, the deliciously leaden riff. It was pop music, but it was very, very heavy pop music. "Dive in me!" Kurt wailed. For the A-side, Kurt wanted to take advantage of the fact that TAD was in the studio with Jack Endino and record a song while TAD was on dinner break. Tad Doyle vehemently disliked the idea, but Endino managed to talk him into it. In one hour on July 11, 1990, they did the basics for "Sliver," using TAD's drums, bass, and guitar.

"Sliver" featured drummer Dan Peters of Mudhoney, who were on hiatus while guitarist Steve Turner decided whether he wanted to pursue a graduate degree. The band auditioned a couple of drummers before Peters, already a veteran of many Seattle bands, an affable fellow known for his fleet and powerful

Anarchy reigned at the Motor Sports show. © Charles Peterson

stickwork. He'd heard that Nirvana was looking for a drummer and bumped into Shelli at a bar and asked if she'd mention he was available.

The July 7, 1990, issue of the UK music weekly *Sounds* ran a quick story with the headline "Mascis to Join Nirvana?" and very dubiously claimed, "Sources close to both Nirvana and J Mascis told *Sounds* that Mascis had auditioned for the Seattle band and 'really wants to play with Nirvana.'" Mascis is Dinosaur Jr's singer-guitarist, but he also happens to be a really good drummer—so good, the story goes, that Kurt invited him to join after a July 1989 show at Maxwell's in Hoboken, New Jersey. But Dinosaur Jr was about to release one of their best singles ("The Wagon") and was gearing up to sign with the major-distributed Sire Records—Mascis just wasn't going to join another band.

They started playing with Peters soon after. "It definitely felt good to play with someone who was rhythmically competent," says Kurt. "But it wasn't quite perfect."

"Rhythmically competent" is a tremendous understatement: Dan Peters played, and still does, with massive kinetic energy combined with a sublime thuggishness à la the

The Amplified Come as You Are

Stooges' Scott Asheton. But being an excellent drummer doesn't mean you're the right drummer for a particular band; there has to be chemistry, a certain ineffable *something* that happens when everybody hits the downbeat, an almighty swing, a "pocket." You know it when you hear it. And Kurt and Krist weren't hearing it with Dan Peters. Actually, as it turned out, they just plain could not hear Dan Peters.

At the Motor Sports show, the band lacked the heaving, oceanic groove they had with Chad Channing. That's "the pocket," and Kurt and Krist realized it was missing. They'd find it again—and then some—with their next drummer.

For practice, Kurt came up to Seattle from Olympia and Chris came from Tacoma and they practiced in Peters's truly grungy rehearsal room in an industrial building in south Seattle (First Avenue South and Spokane Street) known as the Dutchman, the very room where countless bands have rehearsed before and since, among them early bands such as Bundle of Hiss, Feast and Room Nine, as well as Screaming Trees, TAD, Love Battery, and 7 Year Bitch. If grunge had a birthplace, this was it. Rehearsals were brief and to the point, and little was said.

I visited the Dutchman once, to see Mudhoney practice when I was writing a story about the Seattle scene for *Rolling Stone* in early 1992. It was on a grim, remote stretch of the bleak industrial district south of downtown Seattle, under the West Seattle bridge overpass, surrounded by warehouses, light industry, garages, and salvage yards. Huge trucks lumbered down the streets at all hours; a freight train line was just down the street.

In his 2012 book *How Music Works*, David Byrne proposes that the spaces in which music is played influence how the music sounds. The Dutchman definitively confirmed that theory. The place was indeed "truly grungy": festooned with rat's nests of sketchy electrical wiring, and held up by cheap, rotting walls lining a claustrophobic hallway that led to equally claustrophobic rooms full of dirty cables and world-weary musical equipment, every surface seemingly lightly encrusted with the sort of damp, mossy filth characteristic of the Northwest. It's hard to imagine that any other sound could have come out of that thoroughly glorious place.

Sadly, the Dutchman was destroyed by a fire in 2009. It's currently an empty lot.

As far as drums went, Kurt and Chris were of the "bigger is better" school, while Peters had a great-sounding but small drum kit that couldn't keep up with the sonic onslaught. "I'd be in the practice space with them and the amplifier was turned up to ten," says Peters. "They'd always be going, 'I can't hear that bass drum.' Yeah, well, no shit you can't hear the bass drum—*I* can't even hear the bass drum!"

One day Kurt and Chris brought Peters a huge but dilapidated drum set to play. Particular about what he played, Peters would take only the bass drum. "If I knew that they were really that serious, I would have pursued another drum kit somehow," says Peters. "But I wouldn't play this big hunk of shit they wanted me to play."

Peters began to see the writing on the wall.

Still, he did play on "Sliver," a key track in the Nirvana repertoire. Like many of Kurt's songs, "Sliver" seems to be autobiographical. It's about a boy who is left with his grandparents for the evening while his mother goes out. He can't eat, he doesn't want to play, he just wants to go home. He falls asleep and wakes up in his mother's arms. Even the cover of the single is a picture of a transparent man, as if to say that the song within enabled the listener to see right through Kurt.

They had written it with Peters one day at practice. It came together within a matter of minutes, with Kurt coming up with the lyrics—in typical fashion—just before they recorded it. "The chemistry was definitely there with Danny, Chris, and I," says Kurt. "We could have ended up writing some really good songs together."

It was a bit of an experiment. "I decided I wanted to write the most ridiculous pop song that I had ever written," says Kurt. "It was like a statement in a way. I had to write a real pop song and release it on a single to prepare people for the next record. I wanted to write more songs like that."

Kurt believed he had to "prepare people" for his next musical move. He was thinking ahead and he was thinking big.

Kurt was listening to a lot of pop-oriented music at that point, including the legendary Seattle garage band the Sonics and the Smithereens; he was also delving deep into the R.E.M. catalogue.

It's the most literal lyric Kurt has ever written. "For some reason, it's one of the easiest songs for people to comprehend because it's that way," he says, implying that he doesn't understand why people don't grasp his more abstract songs just as easily. "That's why I choose not to write that way. I don't like things that are so obvious."

The only elusive aspect of the song is the title, which Kurt says he picked because "I had a feeling that if I called it 'Sliver,' most people would call it 'Silver.'" Kurt is still very pleased with everything about the track. "It has a massive naïveté to it," he says. "It was done so fast and raw and perfect that I don't think we could capture that again if we decided to rerecord it. It's just one of those recordings that happened and you can't try to reproduce it." It had that

The Amplified Come as You Are

Poster for the fateful Motor Sports show.

Nirvana at the Motor Sports show. Barely visible is Danny Peters on drums. Note the undersized drum set. © Charles Peterson

childlike quality that Kurt loved in the bands he heard on K Records, like Beat Happening and Young Marble Giants.

Many, including Wendy, believe the song is autobiographical, but Kurt says he doesn't recall being afraid of going to his grandparents' house. He may be disingenuous here, because the real point of the song is the anguished cry as the child is reunited with his mother.

Kurt loved his paternal grandparents, Iris and Leland Cobain. Bev Cobain told *People* that Iris "was the only person who gave him unconditional love."

Kurt insisted that the title had nothing to do with the song and that he just liked the word "sliver" because it could easily be confused with the word "silver." That's a great example of Kurt's impressionistic approach to words. "It wouldn't matter if we were speaking in tongues," he said with a little chuckle, to the BBC2 TV show *Rapido* in November 1991. "It's a universal language." But "Sliver" could easily be a nickname for a skinny little kid, perhaps bestowed by a loving relative, a thought that brushes against the song very nicely. Or maybe the title is a comment on the brevity and simplicity of the song itself, all of two minutes and eleven seconds long.

The song also pointed toward a new songwriting direction. The song was grungy enough, but it was also very tightly composed, a very "pop" song, as opposed to the "rock" riff-oriented music the band had played thus far.

The Amplified Come as You Are

(Tacked onto the end of the seven-inch version of "Sliver" is a hilarious snippet of conversation between Jonathan Poneman and a freshly awoken and very hung over Chris Novoselic. Chris recorded the exchange by accident on his answering machine one afternoon.)

"Sliver" isn't just a great song, it's key to understanding Kurt. The narrator is a kid whose parents go out for the evening, leaving him with his grandparents. He's upset about it—he kicks and screams and pleads for them not to go. It's a downright primal sentiment: the fear of abandonment. We've all experienced it; we all understand that feeling, and yet few, if any, rock songs have addressed it in the context of childhood.

Kurt usually favored a constellation of imagery over linear narrative, but "Sliver" is a straightforward story, the exception that proves the rule.

Over and over, the kid pleads to be taken home but eventually falls asleep—and then wakes up in his mother's arms. For a small child, there is no more idyllic place to be, a place of safety, warmth, and love. As someone who was continually depressed, in physical pain, and despising his physical and social surroundings, Kurt craved that feeling deeply and sought it in various ways. Tracy, his first real girlfriend, was kind of a mother figure. And, as mentioned earlier, Courtney resembled Wendy in some respects. But heroin was also a quick and very dirty route to that same sensation.

Peters played one gig with Nirvana, a September 22, 1990, show at the Motor Sports International and Garage, a former parking garage (now demolished) at Minor and Howell streets. Nirvana headlined over the Dwarves and their one-time mentors, the Melvins. With fifteen hundred customers, it was their biggest show in Seattle at that point. The band debuted several songs from the Vig demos, including "Pay to Play," "Imodium," and "In Bloom." There was no stage security at all, so people would climb up and dive off, but not before accidentally marring almost every song by knocking over a mike or bumping into a musician. It was just nuts.

In the audience was Dave Grohl.

Something big was going on. The Melvins were originally the headliner at the Motor Sports show, but at the last minute the promoter moved Nirvana into that spot. At around fifteen hundred people, the sold-out crowd was much bigger and crazier than it had ever been, and a lot of them were sporting Nirvana T-shirts. The production was so professional that there were even photo passes and backstage passes; there were virtually no photographers onstage for the opening bands, but then a bunch jumped up for Nirvana's set. The "Sliver"/"Dive" single had been released three weeks earlier, and it demonstrated that Nirvana was making dramatic artistic advances. The Motor Sports show was a major turning point for the band. Often, people only realize something like that in retrospect, but this time they realized it even in the moment.

In a now-all-too-familiar fashion, Kurt and Krist avoided the uncomfortable conversation with Dan Peters to inform him that he was out of the band.

As Keith Cameron reported in *Mudhoney: The Sound and the Fury from Seattle* (2013), Dave helped Peters, the guy he was replacing, put his drums in the Nirvana van after the show, then rode with the band down to Krist's house in Tacoma the next day. The cover story was, he was Krist's friend, crashing at his place for a while. Dave looked on as Nirvana did an interview and photo shoot with Peters at Krist's house for a *Sounds* cover story on the occasion of Nirvana's upcoming UK tour—a tour that Kurt, Krist, and Dave all knew Peters was not going to be on.

chapter seven

"ARE YOU HUNGRY?"

"YES"

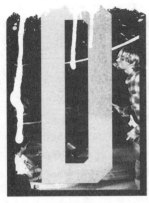

avid Eric Grohl was born on January 14, 1969, in Warren, Ohio, to James and Virginia Grohl. His father was then a journalist for the Scripps-Howard newspaper chain, his mother a high school English teacher. Dave has a sister, Lisa, three years older than he is. The Grohls left Columbus, Ohio, and moved to Springfield, Virginia, when Dave was three. When he was six, they divorced. "My mother and father were pretty much at other ends of the spectrum—he's a real conservative, neat, Washington, D.C., kind of man and my mother's more of a liberal, free-thinking, creative sort of person," says Dave. He says the divorce didn't affect him much, perhaps because he was so young at the time.

In the '70s, Jim Grohl served as special assistant to Ohio senator Robert Taft Jr., a Republican. According to Dave, he was also "one of the principal speechwriters for the Republican National Convention." Jim later became senior vice president of the United States Savings and Loan League, a lobbying organization for the banking industry, and a DC political consultant. So yeah, he was fairly conservative.

Dave was raised by his mom, whom he adores. "She's the most incredible woman in the world," he says, obviously filled with pride. "She's so great. She's strong, independent, sweet, intelligent, funny, and she's just the best."

Raising two kids on alimony payments and a schoolteacher's modest income was hard. "There were tough times when we'd eat peanut butter and pickle sandwiches for dinner," Dave recalls.

As a kid, Dave appeared professionally in a Washington theater company, but his main love was music. He formed a little duo with his buddy Larry Hinkle called the H.G. Hancock Band when he was ten. They'd write songs and Dave would play a one-stringed guitar while Hinkle banged on pots and pans.

Dave started playing guitar when he was twelve and took lessons for a couple of years. He'd write songs about his friends or his dog and play them into a boom box, then play the tape back over the stereo while he recorded the drum parts back onto the boom box.

That was also how he made the first Foo Fighters record: playing all the instruments himself.

Eventually, he got sick of lessons and just played in neighborhood bands doing the typical Rolling Stones and Beatles covers. Dave hadn't yet discovered punk rock, although he'd already gotten a taste of new wave from the same B-52's appearance on *Saturday Night Live* that Kurt had seen. He had gone out and bought the requisite checkered Vans as well as records by the B-52's and Devo, but nothing prepared him for the time he visited his cousin Tracey, who lived in Evanston, Illinois, in the summer of 1982, when Dave was thirteen.

When Dave and his sister Lisa came to the door, Dave's aunt called Tracey downstairs. "And Tracey starts coming down the stairs and she was *totally punk*," says Dave. "Bondage pants and chains and crew cut and we were like 'Wow! Tracey's punk now!'" Tracey took Dave and Lisa to punk shows all that summer, seeing shows by bands like Naked Raygun, Rights of the Accused, Channel Three, and Violent Apathy. "From then on we were totally punk," says Dave. "We went home and bought *Maximumrocknroll* and tried to figure it all out."

Naked Raygun and Rights of the Accused, a classic Chicago punk bill, was the first punk rock show—and the first rock show of any kind—Dave ever saw. "It was the best time I'd ever had doing anything," he told the *Chicago Tribune* in 1996.

Just as importantly, it turned out that Tracey (who wasn't actually a cousin but the daughter of one of Dave's mom's oldest friends) was the lead singer in a punk rock band called Verböten with three other kids, who ranged in age from eleven to fifteen. She brought Dave to a rehearsal in the basement of her family's home. "I couldn't believe these kids my age were playing this style of music and writing their own songs," Dave continued. "Jason [Narducy] was playing this guitar that looked bigger than he was. It was a huge revelation: 'I can do this, too!' From then on, I was a changed man."

This was very different from playing in classic rock cover bands. "I was just amazed and intrigued by this underground network that you could join, and the intensity of the music that you could play along with," Dave added.

Tracey played punk singles from her massive collection for Dave, including records by now canonical DC hardcore bands like Minor Threat, S.O.A., Void, Bad Brains, and the Faith. Those bands weren't from New York or Hollywood or some fantastical Valhalla where only rock stars lived, they were from Washington, DC—literally just down the road from Dave. When he got back home to Virginia, he resolved to track down the DC punk scene and proceeded to catch shows by all of them.

In 2020, thanks in part to Dave's mention of them in his 2014 documentary TV series *Sonic Highways*, Verböten became the subject of a musical: *Verböten: A Story About How Punk Saves Lives*.

Punk agreed with Dave. He liked "just being a little punk shit running around town and being a little derelict," he says. "I suppose that was half the attraction—being a slacker." The other half was the extreme energy of the music. "I was super-hyperactive," Dave says (although not hyper enough to get put on Ritalin).

The solidly middle-class people of Springfield were more tolerant of punk rock than the folks in Aberdeen. Dave always had "good, cool" friends. He was popular enough to get elected vice president of his freshman class at Thomas Jefferson High School in Alexandria, Virginia. Before he did the morning announcements every morning over the school intercom, he'd treat the whole school to a little blast of the Circle Jerks or Bad Brains.

Like Chris and Kurt, Dave was a stoner in high school. "I smoked too much pot," says Dave sadly. "That's the only thing that I really kick myself for doing because it seriously burned me out—bad. From the time I was fifteen to twenty, I smoked four or five times a day and a lot. Every day of my life. You just get so burned out. You don't feel burned out when you're smoking it but once you stop you realize, 'Oh, I lost something here.'"

A lot has been said about the fact that all three members of Nirvana were children of divorce. But perhaps not enough has been said about the fact that all three had difficult relationships with their fathers. Kurt's father neglected Kurt in favor of his new family; Krist's father was very tough on him, sometimes physically. Dave's father, who had been an accomplished classical and jazz flautist before moving on to his political career, criticized Dave for his lack of studiousness, scoffed at his music, and implied that he wasn't a dedicated musician. Boys who grow up like that often feel they have something to prove.

Pot began affecting his grades, so he and his mother decided that he would attend Bishop Ireton, a Catholic school. Meanwhile, he had decided that the drummer in his "bad punk" band, Freak Baby, was so lousy that he could play better. He'd sit down at the drums and bang around a little after practice, but most of his self-education on the drums came the classic way. In his bedroom, Dave would pull up a chair for a high-hat, a book for a snare, and his bed for tom-toms and play along to music by hardcore bands like Minor Threat, DRI, and Bad Brains.

When they kicked out the bass player in Freak Baby, the drummer switched to bass and Dave switched to drums. They changed their name to Mission Impossible and played fast hardcore punk, so fast that they eventually changed their name to Fast, which broke up around 1986.

Mission Impossible/Fast actually broke up in the summer of 1985, but not before a couple of important things happened. At age sixteen, Dave made his recorded debut with Mission Impossible on the six-band EP *Alive & Kicking* along with DC punk bands Marginal Man, Beefeater, and Gray Matter. The other was that former Minor Threat singer Ian MacKaye told Dave that he reminded him of one of the great punk drummers, the frenetic, explosive Chuck Biscuits (D.O.A., Black Flag). With that extremely flattering benediction, Dave had arrived. He became known throughout the scene as a loud, maniacally fast, and nearly out-of-control drummer. After Mission Impossible broke up—a couple of the guys were heading off to prestigious colleges out of town—Dave joined Dain Bramage.

Being a suburban stoner, it was only natural for Dave to get into Led Zeppelin. It was even more natural for him to start copping the classic licks of Led Zep drummer John Bonham. "I used to rip him off like crazy and then I figured out the weird stuttered kick drum in 'Kashmir' and that opened up a million new doors," says Dave. "You take pieces from other drummers and like the drummer from the Bad Brains to John Bonham to the drummer from Devo and it eventually becomes this big mush and that's me—just one big rip-off!"

After Fast, Dave was in a band called Dain Bramage that mixed hardcore punk with the sounds of adventurous pre- and post-punk bands like Television and Mission of Burma. "Everybody just hated us," says Dave. The dogmatic hardcore scene didn't take too well to outside influences (except for reggae) and Dain Bramage couldn't get many gigs because they weren't on the DC-based indie Dischord label, which was co-founded by Ian MacKaye of Minor Threat (and later, Fugazi) and was then the only game in town for hardcore bands.

As a joke, Dave originally put Bonham's three-circle logo on the front of his bass drum; later on, he got the logo tattooed on his arm, then variations of it on his wrist and then his other arm. He's also got a homemade tattoo of the Black Flag logo on his forearm that he made when he was thirteen.

To the original punks, Black Flag was supposed to be a refutation of dinosaur bands like Led Zeppelin, but to kids of Dave's generation a lot of that dogma was starting to become irrelevant—to them, it was all just cool music. It was OK to like both bands.

In truth, Dave's drumming with Nirvana didn't have much of Bonham's funkiness; what Dave did was play great, simple parts very hard, brilliantly supporting the songs and even the vocals. He himself was a singer and songwriter, so he knew what singers and songs needed.

Dave had long admired a local DC hardcore band called Scream, who had already put out several records on Dischord, and then he saw an ad in the local music paper saying that Scream was looking for a drummer. "I thought I'd try out just to tell my friends that I jammed with Scream," Dave says. He called, but the band never called him back because he was too young—and he had told them he was nineteen even though he was really seventeen. Finally, Dave wangled an audition, and after jamming a few times, Scream asked Dave to join the band. Dave said he was committed to Dain Bramage but a couple of months later he got back in touch with Scream and convinced them to take him on.

Dave might have been in Dain Bramage, but still, he was persistent enough to call Scream twice before they granted him an audition, and he learned the drum parts to every Scream song, including—thanks to snagging a tape of the demos—the songs from their as-yet-unreleased album. He rehearsed with them a few times before breaking the news to Dain Bramage. The timing couldn't have been worse: this was just a few weeks before Dain Bramage's first album came out, and there was no way the band could continue without Dave. Naturally, the other band members, two of his best friends, were angry and devastated. But Scream was one of the best bands in the area—who could turn down such an opportunity?

Scream wasn't part of the storied original DC hardcore scene from the late '70s/ early '80s—they were from Bailey's Crossroads, a small town in Virginia a few miles outside of DC. They didn't look or sound like the parochial DC punks, who once walked out of the room en masse when Scream opened for Minor Threat and D.O.A. because their look and sound didn't conform to DC punk's rigid standards. But this was when the major labels were starting to realize that indie bands could potentially sell a lot of records. The growing buzz about Scream suggested that they might be contenders.

Dave debuted with Scream on *No More Censorship* (released in August 1988 on the reggae-centric label RAS). Like so much hardcore of the time, the record took a political stand—the title refers to the culture wars then being waged by the Parents Music Resource Center.

Scream played hardcore with touches of pop-metal, leavened by shout-along choruses and wheedly-deedly guitar solos. On *No More Censorship*, Dave plays with great power and precision—he's already got incredible chops—but he also plays like the hyperactive eighteen-year-old that he was: impatient and busy. That approach fit Scream's music, but Dave went on to play with much more economy, poise, and musicality with Nirvana—a hectic attack just wouldn't work with Kurt's sturdy, simple songs.

Dave dropped out of high school late in his junior year. "I was seventeen and extremely anxious to see the world and play, so I did," Dave says. "I'm totally glad I did it." Dave plans to go to college someday, though.

Much later, when Wendy Cobain met Virginia Grohl in New York for Nirvana's *Saturday Night Live* appearance, they compared notes on their sons. "We were just amazed at how much these two kids are alike," says Wendy. "They're like twins that got separated somehow."

"I don't see that at all," Dave says at first, then he adds, "In some ways I can, because I remember the first time I went into the house where Kurt grew up and we went upstairs where his room was and there was stuff written on the walls—the brain with a little question mark—and I remember being stoned and drawing a little brain with a question mark in it in like seventh or eighth grade. When I saw that I thought it was kind of strange. And we're both total slobs."

In many ways, Dave and Kurt *were* very much alike: children of divorce, ex-metalheads, high school dropouts, raised by a single mom and alienated from their fathers, stoners prone to "derelict" behavior who became musicians and found kindred spirits in the punk rock community. Both were also driven artists. A key difference was that, aside from Dave coming from a somewhat more affluent, more stable, and certainly more well-educated background, he was "the most well-adjusted boy I know," whereas Kurt was not very well-adjusted at all.

Dave was supposed to go to night school, but he spent the tuition money on pot instead. He rehearsed with Scream for six months and then the band went on a two-month US tour in October of 1987.

He was still just eighteen years old.

"Touring with Scream was so much fun—it was a lesson in life," says Dave. "Learning to budget yourself on seven dollars a day. You had three meals—or two—and you have to somehow save up money or ask for the next three days' per diem if you want to buy pot. You can't buy cigarettes more than three times a week. If you do, you have to buy bargain brand. I'd never seen the country before and everything was just so fucking *punk*."

Dave became a big Melvins fan after seeing them open for hardcore bands in DC. When he read in *Maximumrocknroll* that they had re-formed after a brief breakup, Scream was on tour in Memphis. Dave had bought an Elvis postcard and happened to get Elvis's uncle Vester Presley to sign it. He sent it to the

The Amplified Come as You Are

Melvins in San Francisco and asked if they'd come to Scream's show there. The night before the gig, Dave found out that Scream and the Melvins were on the same bill. Dave befriended the Melvins and they swapped addresses and have corresponded ever since.

That's a great example of how small the indie underground world was at the time. Everybody knew everybody else. And when things are that small, some amazing connections can happen.

Back in San Francisco for another tour, Dave went backstage after a Melvins gig, where Kurt and Chris were hanging out. They were in town to rehearse with Dale Crover for the 1990 West Coast tour with Sonic Youth. "I remember [Kurt] sitting in this chair looking pissed," Dave recalls, while Chris was being exceptionally loud and boisterous. "Who *is* that guy?" Dave asked Osborne. He didn't wind up speaking to either of them.

Dave's sense of Kurt being antisocial and annoyed and of Krist being loud and boisterous only goes to show that first impressions are often correct.

During one of their forays down to L.A. to meet the labels, Kurt and Chris stopped in San Francisco to hang out with the Melvins, who told them there was a great hardcore band playing at the I-Beam called Scream. They went and were promptly knocked out by their drummer. "God, what a great drummer," Chris thought. "Wish he'd be in our band."

I screwed up the chronology there. The evening when Dave first met Kurt and Krist and the one when Kurt and Krist saw Dave play are one and the same. That was August 13, 1990, and they were in fact mostly in town to pick up Dale Crover before he started the brief West Coast tour with them, opening for Sonic Youth. Just forty days later, Dave was a member of Nirvana.

Kurt had actually seen Scream before, headlining in October 1987 at the Community World Theater in Tacoma. He hated it—they were too metal. It's amazing that Kurt agreed to see Scream again.

The thing is, *everybody* wanted Dave to be in their band. The beloved Richmond, Virginia, horror-metal band GWAR once invited him to join their hilariously gory circus. DC post-hardcore band Dag Nasty also reached out to him. Former Minor Threat singer Ian MacKaye had invited Dave to jam with him and his bass player friend Joe Lally for a project they were starting. Unfortunately, Dave didn't wind up jamming with MacKaye and Lally. That project eventually became the iconic post-punk band Fugazi.

Scream was so deferential to Dave's chops and star power that they broke with ironclad punk orthodoxy and gave him a three-minute drum solo every night, giving him the opportunity to do his best impression of John Bonham after many cups of coffee.

Dave recorded one studio and two live albums with Scream, who blossomed into one of America's most explosive hardcore bands, and toured the US and Europe until the middle of September 1990, when "girlfriend trouble" compelled bass player Skeeter to leave the tour suddenly. Stranded in Los Angeles with no money, Dave called his friend Buzz Osborne.

Osborne knew Kurt and Chris loved Dave's drumming and called Chris to tell him he'd given Dave his number. When Dave called, Chris was ecstatic, but he felt obligated to at least ask Dave a few questions before going any further. He was into the right bands and Chris invited him up to Seattle.

What actually happened was Dave called Krist, who informed him that they already had a drummer, Dan Peters, and they left it at that. Then, a few hours later, Krist called back. So it sure seems like Krist told Kurt about the call and they got to talking about whether Peters really fit in and whether they should replace him with that kick-ass drummer in Scream they'd seen a while back.

Krist started asking Dave what bands he was into. "Kurt's in the background going, 'Shut up!'" Krist is quoted as saying in the liner notes for the *Sliver: The Best of the Box* compilation. "'Why are you asking that shit? Tell him to get up here!'" Then Kurt got on the phone, and they proceeded to talk about . . . what bands they were into.

It turns out that Dave had some significant musical common ground with Kurt and Krist. As Dave told Paul Brannigan in *This Is a Call: The Life and Times of Dave Grohl*, "We kinda come from the same place. I love Neil Young *and* Public Enemy, I love Celtic Frost *and* the Beatles, and they were the same in that way . . . We all discovered punk rock and grew up listening to Black Flag but we also love John Fogerty. We were all little dirtbags who loved to play rock music. So it seemed like we might have a connection."

As Dave admitted to *Kerrang* in 1997, he "wasn't the biggest fan in the world" of Nirvana. In *This Is a Call*, Paul Brannigan writes that, at the Motor Sports show, Dave was more excited to see the Melvins. But in *The Storyteller*, Dave wrote that *Bleach* "had quickly become one of my favorites and stood apart from all of the other noisy, heavy punk records in my collection." Either way, hey, girls liked Nirvana, they had a major label deal, they seemed like cool people, and perhaps best of all, they kind of sounded like the Melvins. It sure beat being dead broke in Los Angeles with a band that was starting to disintegrate.

This guitar has seconds to live. Kurt at the Motor Sports show, September 22, 1990.
© Ian T. Tilton

It was a very difficult decision, abandoning his friends in Scream, so Dave called his mother for advice. "She told me there are times in life when you have to do what's best for yourself," Dave told the *Guardian*'s Tom Lamont in 2011. "Sometimes you just have to be selfish."

Dave had heard Nirvana for the first time during one of Scream's frequent European tours. "You look at the cover of *Bleach*," he says, "and you just think they're these big burly unshaven logger, drinking guys. They look kind of nasty on the front, almost like a metal band, but with this retarded weirdness about them." He thought they sounded a bit like the Melvins, which was okay by him.

Dave took apart his drums, fit all the pieces into one big cardboard box, and flew up to Seattle with only a bag of clothes. Kurt and Chris picked him up at

Sea-Tac Airport and began the drive to Tacoma. To break the ice, Dave offered Kurt an apple. "No thanks," Kurt replied. "It'll make my teeth bleed."

That wasn't the first awkward moment they had had. On the phone with Kurt before he headed up to Seattle, Dave mentioned a party he had gone to after a Scream show in Olympia. The band had bought a bunch of beer and the great disco music spilling out onto the street augured well for a happening bash. They arrived at the apartment to find about twenty people, with all the guys on one side of the room and all the girls on another. "They were total Olympia hot chocolate party Hello Kitty people," says Dave. The band stood around drinking beer and feeling awkward until suddenly someone turned off the stereo. "This girl comes in and sits down and plugs in this guitar and starts playing this total bad teen suicide awful music, 'Boys, boys / Bad / Die,'" Dave says. "And after every song everyone would clap and we were like, 'Let's get out of here!'" Dave had just begun insulting the "sad little girl with the bad fucking songs" when Kurt said, "Oh yeah, that's my girlfriend, Tobi."

Oops. Dave, then all of twenty-one years old, had come from a few years of living a hardscrabble punk boys club existence—he wasn't yet hip to the Olympia/riot grrrl thing. But he's a bright guy; he learned quickly. Olympia was a very industrious artistic community, with its own fanzines, art spaces, venues, handicrafts, and, of course, bands. Women played a major part, which was much different from the world where Dave had just spent some formative years. Consequently, the music in Olympia was very different, too—melodic, female-fronted underground UK bands such as the Vaselines, Young Marble Giants, and the Raincoats were central to the aesthetic. It's hard to imagine Dave coming up with a song such as "Marigold" without having lived in Olympia during this time.

Kurt was actually at the party and remembers that the members of Scream were making fun of everybody there. "They were real rocker dudes," says Kurt. "I hated them, I thought they were assholes." Kurt remembers Dave in particular. "He brought up this Primus tape from their car and tried to play it and everyone got mad at him."

It's difficult to understate the stigma of being a Primus fan at the time. They were an East Bay band with prog-rock chops and intricately "funky" beats; this was stuff for wisecracking stoner dweebs with peach-fuzz mustaches, the same kind of guys who had been into Frank Zappa twenty years earlier. Playing Primus at a party in Olympia was a huge faux pas, a turd in the sonic punchbowl.

The Motor Sports gig happened to be the night after Dave arrived. He was stunned by the size and enthusiasm of the crowd—the only other local show he'd seen that big was Fugazi in DC. In Seattle, punk rock had become big business. "It seemed like a local punk scene gone bad, in a way," says Dave. "I saw the Nirvana T-shirt stand—every fucking kid and their brother buying the 'crack smokin', fudge packin'' T-shirt. They must have sold two hundred T-shirts that night—that's *insane* for a local punk rock show.

"I didn't know what I was getting myself into at all."

Dave was not terribly impressed by Nirvana. "I thought they were all right," he says. "They didn't completely blow me away. The Melvins played before them and I was so into the Melvins that I was spent by the time Nirvana went on."

Actually, in 2005 Dave told *Rolling Stone*'s Austin Scaggs, "I didn't even watch them. I saw the first few songs and wound up outside talking to an old friend."

Still, the material seemed fun to play and besides, although Dave thought Danny Peters was "a fucking incredible drummer," he didn't think Nirvana sounded

From the *Sounds* shoot: Kurt smiles! Future Nirvana drummer Dave Grohl is at left. The can of sausage would reappear in the "Sliver" video two years later. No one knows why. © Ian T. Tilton

quite right with Peters. He was probably right—Peters is an excellent, hard-hitting drummer, but doesn't play in the heavy, Bonhamesque style that Nirvana requires. Peters played well at the Motor Sports show, but he didn't quite fit—it was like a man wearing a very nice hat that nevertheless didn't go with his suit.

Dave stayed with Chris and Shelli at first. The day after the Motor Sports show, Chris and Shelli threw a barbecue, during which Chris, Kurt, and Danny Peters did an interview for a cover story in the now defunct English music weekly *Sounds*. No one was to know they were auditioning a new drummer.

Danny Peters, Kurt, and Chris pose for a *Sounds* magazine photo shoot at Chris and Shelli's house the day after the Motor Sports show. © Ian T. Tilton

###

A few days later, Kurt and Chris auditioned Dave at the Dutchman. "We knew in two minutes that he was the right drummer," says Chris. "He was a hard hitter. He was really dynamic. He was so bright, so hot, so vital. He rocked." Dave was

The Amplified Come as You Are

steady, solid, tasteful, and definitely a hard hitter. When he played a roll on his snare, it sounded like the powerful chop of spinning helicopter blades; when he pounded on his gigantic tom-toms, they didn't make a tone so much as they exploded like rifle shots; his outsized cymbals fluttered like punching bags under his attack. Dave could also sing, giving the band the potential for live harmonies for the first time.

Given all we know now, that probably wasn't an audition and more like a first practice.

There's an old music biz saying that you're only as good as your drummer. Dave played great, no-nonsense parts with thunderous power and precision; that's exactly what Krist did, too; and that brawny rhythmic framework allowed Kurt to worry a little less about his guitar playing and focus on singing.

A rather drummerly but important distinction between Chad's playing and Dave's is that Chad used a double kick pedal; in other words, Chad played the bass drum with both feet, producing the rapid trills and cannon-fusillade beats most associated with speed metal. That gave Nirvana's music a connotation that Kurt wanted to leave behind. Dave used a single kick pedal, making for a more straightforward drumming style. Another distinction is that Chad played with a somewhat sloshy feel; Dave played more "on top" of the beat, punk-style, giving the music a more insistent, headlong drive.

And yes, having live vocal harmonies for the first time was huge.

Then there was the delicate matter of telling Danny Peters that he was out of the band after only a few weeks.

During an acoustic appearance on Calvin Johnson's KAOS radio show a few days later, Kurt revealed that they had a new drummer and that he hadn't even broken the news to Peters yet. "Who *is* the new drummer?" Johnson asked. "His name is Dave and he's a baby Dale Crover," Kurt answered. "He plays almost as good as Dale. And within a few years' practice, he may even give him a run for his money."

Kurt acknowledged the awkward situation with Peters. "Dan's such a beautiful guy and such a beautiful drummer," he said, "but you can't pass up an opportunity to play with the drummer of our dreams, which is Dave. He's been the drummer of our dreams for like two years. It's a bummer, a big bummer."

A tour of England had been planned. "Kurt called me up," says Peters, "and he said he thought they were going to go with Geffen and I'm like 'Cool.' Then I go, 'So what about this tour?' And he goes, 'Ahhh. Ummm. Well, ah, well . . . We got another drummer.' And I wasn't bummed at all. I kind of half-assed expected it and I was like, 'Oh, that's cool.' I wasn't sure how they were feeling because their

communication skills at that time were kind of not happening. I wasn't bummed at all. I'm still not bummed."

As we've seen, Kurt and Krist's communication skills had been "kind of not happening" for quite some time.

And it wasn't true that Dave had been "the drummer of our dreams for like two years"—he'd been the drummer of their dreams for a month or so.

And as Chris points out, "If he was going to join our band, that would be the end of Mudhoney. And we loved Mudhoney so much, we didn't want to be responsible for that."

"Dave suits them way better than I did," Peters admits. "He really does. To me, that's more important, too. He's got the heavy shit right there. He beats the fuck out of those drums. They definitely got the person that suited them better."

Peters went on to a short stint with Screaming Trees, then Mudhoney reformed and eventually signed with Warners in 1992. Peters says he's having a great time with Mudhoney, one of America's greatest rock & roll bands. "The only thing is," he says, "[Nirvana] put out one fuckin' killer record and I sure would have liked to play on it."

Krist was apparently being less than honest about not wanting to break up Mudhoney: according to Mudhoney guitarist Steve Turner's memoir, *Mud Ride: A Messy Trip Through the Grunge Explosion*, not long after Dave joined, they invited Turner to join the band. I think Krist was still trying to cushion the blow for Peters, years after the fact.

Peters still plays with Mudhoney, a great band that's made some of their most intense, fire-breathing records in recent years and continues to tour all over the world.

Meanwhile, Scream dissolved and the guitarist and the singer, brothers Franz and Pete Stahl, later formed Wool. In the summer of 1993, Dave joined Skeeter and the Stahls for a triumphant Scream reunion tour.

There were hard feelings when Dave left Scream, which Dave felt very bad about: they were a strong, very promising band, and Dave was close friends with Franz and Peter Stahl. But all involved patched things up pretty promptly: both Stahl brothers hung out with Nirvana in Los Angeles while the band recorded *Nevermind* and Dave made sure to wear a Scream T-shirt in the video for "Smells Like Teen Spirit."

And later, they patched it up some more: in 1993, Dave did that Scream reunion tour. In the late '90s, Franz played with the Foo Fighters and Peter was their tour manager. In 2011, the original Scream lineup recorded at Dave's studio in Los Angeles, and six years later, they remixed *No More Censorship* there and released it as *NMC17*.

Kurt and Chris had found a rehearsal space in Tacoma, a converted barn—it had brown shag carpet and a massive P.A. that made a loud hissing sound. They shared it with a slick bar band—students from the Guitar Institute of Technology, by Chris's guess.

Dave stayed with Chris and Shelli for a month, then moved in with Kurt in Olympia. The Cobain/Grohl house was knee-deep in corn dog sticks. "It was the most filthy pigsty I'd ever lived in," says Kurt (and that's saying a lot). They passed the time by shooting a BB gun, occasionally scoring a direct hit on the windows of the Washington State Lottery offices across the street.

Actually, it was just Krist who found the barn, via a classified ad in a local paper.

The place in Olympia was 114 Pear Street NE, the same address where Kurt had lived with Tracy. (It's often referred to as an apartment, but it was actually a house that had been divided into a few separate rentals.) As Dave observed earlier, one of the many things he and Kurt had in common was that they were "both total slobs." To give an idea of what it was like, Kurt once compared the chaotic set of the "Sliver" video, with its posters and flyers and other ephemera haphazardly scattered all over the place, to the Pear Street apartment.

There wasn't a lot to do besides rehearse, so Dave spent a lot of time writing his own songs on guitar and recording them on a four-track cassette machine. One of those songs was "Friend of a Friend," which was about Kurt and Krist: one character plays guitar alone in a quiet room, and the other wonders aloud whether he drinks too much. That song wound up on the 1992 cassette-only *Pocketwatch* album—credited to Late!, whose sole member was "Dave G." Dave later rerecorded another song on the album, "Color Pictures of a Marigold," with Steve Albini during the *In Utero* sessions, and as "Marigold," it became the non-LP B-side of the "Heart-Shaped Box" single.

An album of breakneck full-band alt-rockers (featuring Dave on all the instruments) with a few breathy acoustic-and-voice numbers thrown in, *Pocketwatch* was recorded in December 1990 and July 1991 and released on the Tool Set imprint of Simple Machines, the revered Arlington, Virginia, ultra-indie label. That was amid Nirvanamania, and Dave didn't want to be seen as riding the coattails of his own band, so he didn't promote the album; consequently, it remained obscure for a while before people realized that the drummer from Nirvana had made a solo record. The ensuing demand was so overwhelming—Simple Machines had to manually dub each tape themselves—that the label eventually deleted the cassette from their catalogue.

Around this time, Dave got deeply into Screaming Trees' singer Mark Lanegan's first solo album *The Winding Sheet*. "That was the soundtrack to my first six months in Olympia," Dave told *Rolling Stone* in 2005. "I listened to it every day—when the sun wouldn't come up, when it went down too early and when it was cold and raining. I was lonely. I'd listen to that record for reasons." Dave later cited *The Winding Sheet* as an important influence on Nirvana's *Unplugged* performance.

At the same time, Kurt was listening a lot to UK post-punks the Raincoats. The Olympia underground had been into the Raincoats since 1980, when the US branch of the UK-based Rough Trade record label sent a copy of the band's self-titled first album to KAOS. The Raincoats swiftly became foundational to the Olympia scene. "Everybody in Olympia knew about the Raincoats," Bikini Kill bassist Kathi Wilcox told Jenn Pelly for her 33⅓ book, *The Raincoats*. "The scene [Beat Happening leader] Calvin [Johnson] started was so obviously influenced by the attitude and philosophy of what they were doing." Sleater-Kinney guitarist Carrie Brownstein added, "Olympia just wouldn't have existed without them."

When Kurt first found the Raincoats, he was "extremely unhappy, lonely, and bored," as he wrote in the liner notes for a reissue of the band's self-titled 1979 debut album. "If it weren't for the luxury of putting on that scratchy copy of the Raincoats' first record, I would have had very few moments of peace." Those last few words give an indication of the internal strife Kurt was experiencing; music was one way to bring about a psychological cease-fire.

Dave describes the apartment as "small, cluttered, dirty, smelly." Six-foot-tall Dave slept on a five-foot couch. He slept in the same room as Kurt's tank and the clicking of the turtles' shells against the glass as they tried to escape would keep him up at night. "It just felt so weird," says Dave. "The last two and a half *years* have been pretty weird.

"There wasn't a lot to do," Dave continues. "There was a lot of time just spent sitting in the room totally silent reading or just totally silent doing nothing, staring at walls or going downtown and seeing a ninety-nine-cent movie or shooting BB guns in the backyard." Kurt and Dave began going to sleep at six in the morning as the sun was coming up and waking as the sun was going down, never seeing sunlight.

Remember that Dave was the guy who wanted to play Primus tapes at hipster parties. So when he arrived in Olympia, he felt like "an alien," he told the *Guardian*'s Eve Barlow in August 2019. "I remember this friend of Kurt's—a guy called Slim Moon—looked at me and said, 'You're a rocker...' I was like, 'Is that bad?!' I felt really alone."

The two barely spoke. The conversation rarely got past "Are you hungry?" "Yes."

Still, Kurt became more social after Dave moved in. "Kurt sort of came out of his shell," says Slim Moon. "He was around more, he seemed happier with his life.

He was hanging out with actual Olympians." Being around so many artistic people seemed to have an energizing, inspiring effect on Kurt; in Olympia, he could express himself without inhibition or fear of rejection. As a highly creative person, Kurt yearned to be around other creative people. In Olympia, he appreciated that he was appreciated.

Kurt had been going out with Tobi Vail since before Dave moved in. She was a couple of years younger than Kurt and had no intention of settling into a long-term relationship. "I was definitely looking for somebody I could spend quite a few years with," Kurt says, even though he was only twenty-three at the time. "I wanted that security and I knew that it wasn't with her. So I was just wasting my time and I just felt bad about it." By late 1990, that fact was becoming painfully apparent, and that's when Kurt says he broke up with Tobi.

I pointedly said Kurt "says" he broke up with Vail because I didn't completely believe he wasn't the dumpee. From what I can figure out, she broke up with him, which would explain why Kurt was, as Dave says here, "just a mess." So it seems like this was another example of Kurt lying to retaliate against an antagonist—or an attempt to appease his wife.

"He was just a wreck," says Dave, "just a mess." But Kurt insists that it wasn't strictly because of Tobi. "It was just that I was tired of my life, basically," he says. "I was tired of living in Olympia with nothing to do. All during the time that Tracy and I were breaking up, I wanted to move to Seattle. I knew that I was long overdue for a change. I didn't have any extreme thing I could do to just get out of it right away. It wasn't like all the other times where I could have a fight with somebody and get kicked out of their house and have no choice but to do something else.

"I was just tired of not finding the right mate," Kurt says. "I'd been looking all my life. I just got tired of trying to have a girlfriend that I knew that I wouldn't eventually spend more than a couple of months with. I've always been old-fashioned in that respect. I've always wanted a girlfriend that I could have a good relationship with for a long time. I wish I was capable of just playing the field, but I always wanted more than that."

###

The rides in the van to Tacoma for practice had already been quiet enough, but then Kurt stopped talking completely. Finally, after weeks and weeks of this, they were driving home from practice one night when Kurt broke the silence by saying, "You know, I'm not always like this," adding that he would eventually recover from the breakup. "I just kind of said, 'Oh, that's cool,'" Dave says. "But I was thinking to myself, 'Oh, thank God!'"

They practiced from ten o'clock to one in the morning almost every night over a four- or five-month period. The band's chemistry was quickly falling into place. "We felt like we could do whatever we wanted to do," Dave says. "There weren't any restrictions and it got weird and jammy and we'd do these noisy new wave noise experimental jam things. We'd always start off the practice just jamming. We'd set up and plug in and jam for twenty minutes on nothing at all." Out of the jams sprang countless songs, but they'd soon forget them or lose the tapes they recorded them on. "There were probably thirty or forty songs we had written that are just gone," Dave says.

"We practiced in a barn," Dave said in his keynote address at the 2013 SXSW music convention. "Every day. It was all that we had. There was no sun. There was no moon. There was just . . . the barn." That's because the place had no windows. Sometimes they'd turn off all the lights and play in the glow of the amps.

Jamming clearly brought Kurt, Krist, and Dave closer together musically—improvising together teaches the members of a band about each other's idiosyncrasies and go-to tendencies; it builds trust and makes the musicians coalesce into a telepathic unit. This was a formative time; it's when Kurt, Krist, and Dave really became a band.

After a few weeks, Dave played his first show with Nirvana at the North Shore Surf Club in Olympia. The show had sold out on one day's notice and Dave was so amazed that he called his mother and sister about it. They opened with a cover of the Vaselines' "Son of a Gun." Or at least they tried to—they blew a circuit twice before someone realized all the amps were on one line. It was a frenzied show—Dave played with such force that he broke his snare drum. "I picked it up and held it in front of the audience to show them that we have a new drummer who's very good," says Kurt.

"Kurt and Chris knew—and everybody else knew who saw them play—that they were only a hint of what they could be until Dave joined the band," says Slim Moon. "He just knew how to play drums and he understood their music. Chad just never got it and the guys before Chad never really got it. Danny was a great drummer but he just wasn't right."

Then they went over to Europe for a tour with L.A. rockers L7, ostensibly to promote the "Sliver"/"Dive" single, which didn't actually come out until a month after they left. At London's Heathrow Airport, they met tour manager Alex Macleod. Macleod and Dave had met on a Scream tour and they hadn't exactly hit

The Amplified Come as You Are

it off. **The working papers for the tour listed Danny Peters as Nirvana's drummer, so Macleod was surprised to see Dave coming through Customs at the airport. "Oh, fuck," thought Dave. "Oh, fuck," thought Macleod.**

Alex Macleod was, and surely still is, a very intense Scotsman. While you do not want to get on his bad side, he's a very intelligent and thoughtful man, a consummate professional, and fiercely loyal to his clients. He was perfect for Nirvana and an unsung hero in their story.

That was a good tour for Dave—there was a huge buzz on Nirvana in England, which was incredibly exciting in itself, not to mention rock-solid validation for quitting Scream. The band even sold out the two-thousand-capacity Astoria Theatre in London. And, as the icing on the cake, he and Jennifer Finch, the bass player from opening band L7, began a romance.

But they quickly made amends, partly out of necessity and partly because they shared an appreciation for what Macleod calls "inane, senseless humor."

Along for the ride were soundman Craig Montgomery, monitor man Ian Beveridge, and a lot of equipment. They also had a VCR and two tapes—a Monty Python episode and *This Is Spinal Tap*, which had long since become standard equipment on any tour bus.

They played to packed houses of about a thousand people a night, winning rave reviews from the all-important UK music weeklies. Kurt only half-sarcastically told Keith Cameron in the October 27 *Sounds*, "I don't wanna have any other kind of job, I can't work among people. I may as well try and make a career out of this. All my life my dream has been to be a big rock star—just may as well abuse it while you can." He added that the band was exploring a more pop style of songwriting—"We figured we may as well get on the radio and try and make a little bit of money at it."

When Kurt said, "All my life my dream has been to be a big rock star," he was being "half-sarcastic"—but he was also being half-sincere. And there's the rub.

At this point, the band had not officially informed Sub Pop that they were talking to major labels; the two sides communicated with each other via the press. Keith Cameron memorably called it "the weird shadowplay that currently passes for a relationship between the two parties." In other words, their communication skills were still kind of not happening.

In that same interview, Krist bemoaned the fact that so many Americans were glued to the TV watching *The Cosby Show* or *Lethal Weapon*. And Kurt gratuitously chimed in,

"Everybody's got their own form of heroin," which was simultaneously a coy hint about what he was actually doing and a weak attempt to justify it.

Nirvana's UK publicist Anton Brookes recalls that Kurt was very confident that he would soon realize his dream. "I remember Kurt saying that the album was going to go Top Ten and there were these tracks that were going to be massive as singles," Brookes says. "You could see in his face that he totally believed that. He *knew* it."

Granted, for every ten million musicians who predict massive success for themselves, approximately one of them comes anywhere near achieving it. But Kurt was an astute student of pop culture archetypes and a powerfully intuitive person. He told Keith Cameron in that *Sounds* interview, "We're one of those bands that break you in, that eases the middle class into wearing leather eventually!" He proved to be exactly correct.

Meanwhile, John Silva at Gold Mountain Management in L.A. had recently begun calling up the band and offering his expertise; Chris began consulting him informally on business matters. Gold Mountain, founded by industry veteran Danny Goldberg, counted decided nonpunks such as Bonnie Raitt and Belinda Carlisle as clients, but they also had Sonic Youth. And since whatever Sonic Youth did was by its very nature cool, Gold Mountain was cool by Nirvana. And since Thurston Moore was raving about Nirvana to Gold Mountain, the feeling was mutual. Goldberg was still kicking himself for passing on Dinosaur Jr even after Moore raved about them and he wasn't going to make the same mistake twice.

It was Krist who was consulting with John Silva; Krist was doing a lot of band business work at this point, but it was also becoming more than he could handle.

It was somewhat unfair to call Belinda Carlisle a "decided nonpunk," seeing as she once played drums for the Germs, one of the punkest of punk bands. But those days were long gone, and by this time, she was singing straight-up Top 40 pop.

In November, Gold Mountain flew the band down to L.A., and met with Goldberg and Silva, a hip, bright, and aggressive young manager who had worked with several alternative bands including Redd Kross and House of Freaks. Silva was in touch with the underground enough to have amassed a gigantic seven-inch indie rock singles collection; he'd even shared an apartment with the Dead Kennedys' Jello Biafra. Chris liked the fact that Goldberg was also the head of the Southern California chapter of the ACLU; Dave dug that Goldberg had been a publicist for

Led Zeppelin in the mid '70s. After a meeting with Goldberg and Silva, Kurt and Chris left and called Silva from the lobby of the building to say they were going with Gold Mountain. They would have told him in person, they said, but they were late for another major label schmooze.

Mudhoney also met with John Silva, in 1991, at a restaurant in Los Angeles. The band's singer Mark Arm recalled in *Everybody Loves Our Town*, "He positioned himself so that he could see this TV screen showing MTV. And he kept his eyes up there—he wouldn't even look at us and focus, and then, all of a sudden, the 'Smells Like Teen Spirit' video comes on and he just starts laughing maniacally and is like, 'Look at that!' You could see the dollar signs rolling in his eyes. . . . Get us as far away from this guy as possible."

But Nirvana had made a good call with Silva. The music business can be a very tough, cutthroat place, and if you're a young, relatively unknown band that doesn't have much leverage or business savvy, it's good to have a pit bull on your side. Silva had the advantage of having plenty of experience in the indie underground (and his then-girlfriend Lisa Fancher ran the fine indie label Frontier Records), so he had a strong grasp of where Nirvana was coming from. Even better, he was Sonic Youth's manager, so he was cool.

Silva helped keep Sonic Youth on DGC for nine albums and eighteen years despite the fact that the band never came anywhere close to having a hit. But Sonic Youth wasn't signed because anyone thought they were going to move a lot of units—it was in large part because they were a magnet band. In other words, their hip cachet would attract more commercial artists. Sonic Youth's prestige surely played a role in snagging cool indie artists such as Beck, Urge Overkill, Boss Hog, and Girls Against Boys. But with Nirvana, the magnet band approach paid off in a colossal way.

Sleep had become Kurt's favorite pastime—he often claimed to be a narcoleptic and to this day, he usually wears pajamas, probably to make sure he's properly dressed just in case Mr. Sandman should come knocking. "I'd sleep just to get away from the pain," Kurt explains. "While I was asleep, my stomach wouldn't hurt. Then I'd wake up and curse myself that I was still alive."

One day, Kurt was up at the Gold Mountain offices, moping around. "What the fuck are you moping about?" asked John Silva.

Kurt replied, "I'm *awake*, aren't I?"

"I just like to sleep," Kurt says. "I find myself falling asleep at times when I'm fed up with people or bored. If I don't want to socialize and I'm stuck in a social situation, like backstage or being on tour in general, I just sleep throughout the day. I would prefer to be in a coma and just be woken up and wheeled out onto the stage and play and then put back in my own little world rather than deal with . . . For so many years, I've felt like most of my conversation has been exhausted, there's not much I can look forward to. Everyday simple pleasures that people might have in having conversations or talking about inane things I just find really boring, so I'd rather just be asleep."

"I've got narcolepsy," Kurt claimed to Al and Cake of *Flipside* for the May–June 1992 issue, adding to his already lengthy litany of largely self-diagnosed disorders, "and I can see how someone would think I was nodding off when I'm just falling asleep."

Narcolepsy is a very rare condition—most likely, he seemed to be nodding off because he *was* nodding off. But he did sleep a lot, and, as noted earlier, excessive sleep is a classic sign of depression. So is saying there's not much you can look forward to and not being able to enjoy "everyday simple pleasures." And, for that matter, cursing yourself for being alive. Some people just didn't have the emotional intelligence to recognize warning signs like this; some were in denial. I was in the former camp. Even at age thirty-one, I had a lot of growing up to do.

Apparently, someone was on the case though. "Over the last few years of his life, Kurt saw innumerable doctors and therapists," Danny Goldberg told *Rolling Stone*'s Neil Strauss in the immediate aftermath of Kurt's death. "He was a walking time bomb, and nobody could do anything about it."

With lawyer Alan Mintz shopping around the band to all the major labels, Gold Mountain on their side, and a colossal buzz that just kept growing, Nirvana became the object of every major label A&R person's desire from coast to coast. The band was very wary of the slick, big-city corporate label types. At the fancy restaurants they'd get taken to, Kurt would just eat the expensive food and not say a word, while Chris would usually get quite drunk. It was essentially a milder version of their first meeting with Jonathan Poneman. But this time, they made sure they were nice enough to the labels so that they would get asked back to dinner a few more times, which, after all, was the point. "We felt like snotty little hot-shit kids," Dave says. "We felt like we were getting away with something."

At first, the band was confused. Why was everyone so interested in a punk rock band from Aberdeen? For one thing, bands such as U2, R.E.M., and Jane's Addiction were beginning to score gold and platinum records. "Alternative rock" was the new industry buzzword. The canned, lightweight pop then dominating the charts—Paula Abdul, Milli Vanilli, etc.—was making the major labels some quick money, but the labels knew they had neglected to cultivate artists with long-term potential. Alternative bands fit the bill nicely and the best of them had an important thing going for them—a large and loyal fan base. Just like Nirvana.

Other indie bands were being courted, too, like Dinosaur Jr, fIREHOSE, and Teenage Fanclub.

Part of what attracted the major labels was that the American indie underground had a ready-made pool of road-tested talent. There was no doubt that musicians such as the Replacements' Paul Westerberg, Soul Asylum's Dave Pirner, and Grant Hart and Bob Mould from Hüsker Dü were top-shelf songwriters with killer bands—and there was a whole lot more where that came from. On the fiscal side, the leading indie bands, their labels, and the rest of the indie infrastructure had already done the resource-intensive, time-consuming grunt work of developing grassroots fan bases. Major labels could swoop in and take advantage of that and use it to, as they say in the music industry, take it to the next level. Maybe.

And besides, it simply was time for one of popular music's periodic changings of the guard. It was just a question of who was going to lead it.

The vast majority of the indie bands that the major labels signed were commercial failures, but then the entire industry was predicated on the assumption that 80 percent of signings would lose money and that the big artists made up for all the duds. A precious few alternative bands did join pioneers such as R.E.M., Faith No More, and Jane's Addiction and became big, consistent sellers—not just one-hit wonders but the whole reason the music industry stays afloat: perennial catalogue sellers. Besides Nirvana, there was Soundgarden, Pearl Jam, Green Day, Nine Inch Nails, and others, making what, in retrospect, was likely rock's last commercial heyday.

After a while, Kurt, Chris, and Dave began to understand all this and started thinking that they might actually be in a position to be a moderate commercial success—enough to make a living at it, anyway.

The band flew to New York to check out Charisma Records and Columbia Records. Dave was homesick, so he flew to New York on a record label's tab and then caught a shuttle down to DC. At Columbia, they met label president Don Ienner, who told them, "Listen, men, I'm not going to dick you around. We want to turn you into stars." Actually, that's precisely what they wanted to hear—Kurt and Chris were afraid that they were going to be treated as a fringe band that no one at a major label would pay any attention to. But Columbia seemed "too Mafiaesque, a little too corporate," Kurt says. They liked Charisma, even though the label saw fit to make a special "Welcome Nirvana" video that was playing as they walked into the conference room.

Later on in the week, Dave rejoined the band in New York as they continued their whirlwind tour of the various labels. Kurt was so quiet and Chris was so

talkative that many label execs assumed that Chris was the leader of the band. This turned out to be an excellent way of separating the wheat from the chaff.

Dave thought the whole thing was pretty silly. "Basically, all I did was try to figure out how you become an A&R person," he says. "Each one of them, I would ask, 'So what did you do before you became an A&R person?' Every one of them had worked at Tower Records."

The band visited one major label where a loudmouth exec bellowed across his vast desk, "What do you guys want?"

"We want to be the biggest fucking band in the world," Kurt deadpanned.

"Now that's what I like to hear!" boomed the suit. "None of this dickin' around! None of this building from building blocks, brick by brick! Fuck it! That's great!"

"The best thing about the major label hunt was the collection of A&R people's business cards that you got," says Dave. "So when you went into shitty little lounges or taverns, you kind of drop it to the person that's performing there and give them the impression that you're an A&R person from a major label and you're interested in their act. You kind of slide it to them and say 'Give me a call.' So all those A&R men we dealt with are probably still getting calls from lounge bands all over Tacoma."

Like Dave said earlier, they were acting like "snotty little hot-shit kids."

With Alan Mintz as their legal seeing-eye dog, they visited several other labels, where their music would mysteriously be playing in nearly every office. At Capitol in L.A., they met a promotion man. "He's this good old boy from Texas, looks like he would like to beat my mom up," says Kurt. "I just wanted to dance on top of his desk with a dress on and piss all over the place."

Kurt was surely alluding to a then-legendary, now-forgotten incident from March 1991, in which Inger Lorre, the singer for alt-rock band the Nymphs, incensed by Geffen A&R exec Tom Zutaut's decision to delay the release of the band's album, retaliated by standing on top of Zutaut's desk—and urinating all over it. "I pissed on his Rolodex, his phone, the photo of his wife, everything," Lorre told LA Weekly in 1999. "But instead of screaming at me, he started to cry."

But this little fantasy of Kurt's also explicitly harks back to the "mean huge wife-beater" who was in a relationship with Kurt's actual mom when Kurt was a kid. As for the dress, flaunting his feminine side was Kurt's go-to for taunting macho Neanderthals, as he demonstrated during his appearance on MTV's Headbangers Ball.

Kurt thought he'd be provocative and sport a dress onstage during the December 1991 Red Hot Chili Peppers/Pearl Jam tour. "I was at the height of freaking out about playing big places," he told MTV News in October 1993, "and I was convinced that a lot of people out there in the audience, you know, a lot of macho people, would freak out about it and it would create a little controversy." But nobody cared—a little new to the game, Kurt had underestimated how tolerant (or blasé) the mass audience was.

"He asked me, 'So on that song "Polly," are you *beatin'* that bitch?' I said, 'Yes, I am.' Then two other big jock radio programmers walked into his office and said, 'Hey, we got two tickets to the Lakers game!' And they all stood up and started cheering. We knew this wasn't the label for us."

Still, they went out to dinner with another Capitol label exec that night. "Just bring us some food, just bring us all the food you have," he ordered the waitress impatiently. "Put it on this table. I don't care what it is." He began talking about spending a million dollars to get Nirvana out of the Sub Pop contract.

A million dollars. For a week, Kurt was seriously thinking of pulling the Great Rock & Roll Swindle—sign the contract, take the million dollars, *and then break up*. The Sex Pistols had achieved a similar feat not once but twice. Kurt would rant about the idea to Chris. "We've *got* to—it would be such a cool thing to do," he'd say. *"It would be so rock & roll."* Unsure whether this was even possible, Kurt broached the subject with Mintz, who just thought he was kidding.

The Great Rock & Roll Swindle was a disjointed, virtually unwatchable movie filmed in 1978, starring members of the Sex Pistols (except for Johnny Rotten, who had quit the band and appears only in documentary footage). It's a highly stylized fictional depiction of the Sex Pistols story, the actually plausible central conceit being that the band had been formed specifically to scam the music industry out of huge amounts of money and not to make galvanic, world-changing rock music. It's easy to see how this idea appealed to Kurt: a classically punk cover story for signing to a major label.

The way Gold Mountain saw it, it had come down to two labels: Geffen and Charisma. The way Nirvana saw it, it came down to two labels, too: Geffen and K. "We were really close to signing with K Records," Kurt reveals. "Those were the two we were choosing." The idea was, they'd pull the swindle, break up, change their name, and go to K. "I thought a million dollars was more money than anyone could ever have," says Kurt. "I thought a million dollars would support us and the record label for the rest of our lives, which isn't the case at all, now that I made a million dollars and spent a million dollars in a year."

Kurt wasn't really considering signing with K. One of the big reasons Nirvana wanted to leave Sub Pop was because of their relatively lackluster distribution; K had far worse distribution than Sub Pop. Maybe that story was just another indie-cred fantasy aimed at the Olympia crowd.

Eventually, the Great Rock & Roll Swindle fantasy subsided. Because so many labels were interested in Nirvana, they were in a good bargaining position when it came to negotiating a contract. Geffen wasn't offering the most money of any of the band's suitors, but Geffen already had Sonic Youth, and Kim Gordon was urging them to sign with Geffen. And all along, Gold Mountain had been steering the band toward Geffen because they knew the label would work hard at the surely long, hard task of breaking Nirvana—the label had already done well with Sonic Youth, selling 250,000 copies of their major label debut, *Goo*. Geffen also had two key players: director of alternative music promotion Mark Kates and marketing exec Ray Farrell, both of whom had spent years in the indie world before moving to a major label.

So they went to Geffen. "We just figured it was all just a crap shoot anyway," says Chris. Sonic Youth's A&R man, Gary Gersh, signed the band. Gersh had first seen the band with Kim Gordon and Thurston Moore at the April 1990 Pyramid show in New York. He had been sufficiently impressed to give them a call later. After talking with them and hearing the Smart sessions tape Gersh was even more impressed. In Nirvana, he heard "the energy and the simplicity and the aggressiveness of the Who." In Kurt, he saw a gifted songwriter with impeccable instincts about the direction he wanted his band to go. Gersh was savvy enough to be able to explain the band to the label, and just as importantly, hip enough to explain the label to the band.

There was one little hitch with the Nirvana signing: noted hardcore/skatepunk/hip-hop photographer Glen E. Friedman had fronted Scream some money so they could record a demo and had Dave under contract as a member of Scream, prompting a legal dispute that was quietly resolved.

The band got a $287,000 advance, which was swiftly decimated by taxes, legal fees, the management's cut, and debts. Instead of the big dough, they had gone for the strong contract, including full mechanical royalties if and after the album hit gold. No one could have guessed it at the time, but in retrospect, abandoning a higher advance in favor of an elevated royalty rate was a brilliant move, making the band millions of dollars they wouldn't have gotten otherwise.

That advance is about $570,000 in 2023 dollars. That would be a huge advance today, but back then, at peak music industry, it was relatively modest.

Mechanical royalties are payments based on sales of physical formats or streams. Since Nirvana sold tens of millions of records after *Nevermind* went gold (that's 500,000 copies), full mechanical royalties amounted to what is known in the industry as "a shit-ton of money."

Then there was the matter of that darned Sub Pop contract. The then-struggling indie label received an initial $75,000 buyout fee (half of which came out of Nirvana's advance), a reported two points (2 percent of sales) on the next two records, and even got the Sub Pop logo on the back cover of every copy of *Nevermind*. The arrangement took a bite out of the band's income, but it also almost single-handedly resuscitated Sub Pop. "I don't necessarily regret it now because I enjoy knowing that I'm helping Sub Pop put out some really good music," says Kurt.

"I don't doubt that for a minute," says Poneman, "had we not had that agreement, Bruce and I would probably be washing dishes at this moment."

Poneman wasn't kidding: up until then, Sub Pop was bouncing one-hundred-dollar checks.

In 1995, Pavitt and Poneman finally made that big major label deal: they sold a 49 percent stake of the label to the Warner Music Group for a reported twenty million dollars. Pavitt left the label the following year, uncomfortable with the corporate alliance and the overall direction of the label.

Sub Pop became one of the preeminent independent labels of the 1990s, 2000s, and 2010s and may well thrive through the 2020s. It's staggering to think that, but for this one stroke of luck, the label might have gone out of business in the early '90s.

Poneman is still at Sub Pop. Pavitt DJs, is a music software entrepreneur, and published *Sub Pop USA: The Subterranean Pop Music Anthology 1980–1988* and *Experiencing Nirvana: Grunge in Europe, 1989*, a book of his photographs of Nirvana during their European tour that year—the one when Kurt had his meltdown onstage in Rome. Neither of them ever had to resort to washing dishes for a living.

Sub Pop released one last Nirvana record, a split single featuring Nirvana and the Fluid. Kurt felt Nirvana's version of the Vaseline's "Molly's Lips" was ragged and called up Jonathan Poneman and asked him not to release it, but it was part of the buyout deal. Etched into the run-out groove of the record was a single word: "Later."

While the band members waited for their advance money to come through, Gold Mountain doled out a thousand dollars a month for each band member, barely minimum wage. Still they had to pawn instruments just to keep themselves fed. Sometimes they'd go down to the Positively 4th Street record store in Olympia and sell T-shirts. "You get thirty-five bucks and you're so happy," says Dave, "because you don't have to eat corn dogs that night—*you can have a Hungry Man Dinner!*" The band didn't formally sign a contract until just before recording *Nevermind*.

###

In November 1990, Dave was down in Los Angeles sitting in with L7 at a Rock for Choice benefit. He called Chris to ask him to wire some money and they were just about to hang up when Chris suddenly said, "Wait a minute. I gotta tell you something. Kurt's been doing heroin."

"What?" said Dave, shocked. "How did you find out?"

"He told me," Chris said. "Don't tell him that I told you."

When Dave came back home, Kurt mentioned he'd done heroin and Dave tried to stay cool about it and just asked what it was like. "It sucked, it's stupid," Kurt replied. "It makes you feel gross and bad. I just wanted to try it."

"Kurt said he wouldn't do it again and I believed him," Dave says. "It seemed so innocent. It seemed like a kid sticking a firecracker in a cat's butt and lighting it off for the hell of it. It didn't seem like anything at all."

It should be noted that sticking a firecracker in a cat's butt and lighting it is not in fact innocent and would actually be a disturbingly psychopathic thing to do.

One thing I learned from writing this book was that drug addicts can be very good con artists. They'll lie about their addiction so that nobody bothers them about it and will find all sorts of ways to justify those lies. Heroin is very, very powerful stuff.

It's just amazing that, as broke as they were, Kurt somehow found the money to buy heroin. Where there's an addiction, there's a way.

"The whole winter that Dave and I spent together in that little apartment was the most depressing time I'd had in years," Kurt recalls. "It was so fucking small and dirty and cold and gray every fucking day. I almost went insane at one point. I just couldn't handle it. I was so bored and so poor. We were signed to Geffen for months and we didn't have any money. We ended up having to pawn our amps and our TV, all kinds of stuff, just to get money to eat corn dogs. It just felt really weird to be signed to this multimillion-dollar corporation and be totally dirt poor. All we did was practice. It was the only thing that saved us. Even that got repetitious after a while."

And so Kurt had sought refuge in heroin. He had been wanting to do it again and finally found a dealer in Olympia. He did it about once a week, not often enough to get a habit. Not even Dave knew he was doing it. "It's weird, because with someone like Kurt, who's a sloth anyway, how are you to know?" he says.

It's telling that Dave was going through exactly the same thing as Kurt was, right down to living in the same house, and, unlike Kurt, was thousands of miles from home, and yet he didn't succumb to heroin like Kurt did.

One might well wonder how Dave could not have known that his own housemate was doing heroin. But, as stated, heroin addicts can be excellent con artists and hide it really well. And if you've never been around someone who does heroin—or done it yourself—you might not recognize the signs, which can be pretty subtle, depending on how much the person is using.

Before a January 1990 show in Olympia, there was a big rumor going around town that Kurt was doing heroin. So he turned up at the show with fake track marks drawn on his arms. That was Kurt's go-to trick for deflecting the gossip: no one who made exaggerated light of such things could possibly have done them. Kurt used that MO a lot, as we'll see.

No one in the band knew until the night that Kurt called Chris. Chris had gotten extremely worried and hung up. A little while later, he and Shelli called back and told Kurt that they loved him and they didn't want him to do drugs. "It was nice," Kurt says, the tone of his voice implying that he appreciated the gesture, but it wasn't enough to get him to stop.

"I told him he was playing with dynamite," says Chris. "It bummed me out. It was shocking. I didn't like it at all. I just don't see anything in that shit. I just told him that's the way I feel." After that, Kurt tried to hide his drug use, but Chris always knew. "I knew he'd hang around these certain people and it was 'Oh, Kurt's getting high,'" Chris says.

By that time, Kurt and Tracy had gotten back in touch and they went together to see Tobi Vail's Riot Grrl band Bikini Kill at a party in Olympia. "He kept nodding off and whatnot in the car on the way there," says Tracy. "He used to fall asleep, but he'd never fall asleep *that* fast." On the way to another party that night, Kurt asked if they could stop at his house so he could go to the bathroom. After a while Tracy went up so she could go, too. After fifteen minutes she heard a big crash in the bathroom. "So I go in the bathroom and he's kind of passed out on the toilet with one sleeve rolled up and I pick him up and he starts laughing and

Chris at the Commodore Ballroom in Vancouver, April 1991. © Charles Peterson

Chris and Kurt demonstrate their onstage chemistry at the Commodore Ballroom.
© Charles Peterson

then he nods off instantly and then he laughs again. I said, 'Kurt, what the hell are you doing?'"

Kurt probably did some heroin to allay his anxiety about being in a social situation, especially one involving two ex-girlfriends in the same room. And he knew Tracy's protective tendencies very well, so getting obviously high might also have been a passive-aggressive red flag: "See how high I am? Save me!" It wouldn't be the last time he'd pull something like that. It also wouldn't be the last time a partner of his found him collapsed in the bathroom after he'd OD'd on heroin.

"How did you know I did it?"

"Look at you, Kurt," Tracy said. "You've got one sleeve rolled up, there's a spoon in the sink, you're passed out on the toilet, and there's a bottle of bleach on the floor. You never clean *anything*—why else would you have a bottle of bleach if it wasn't for your needle?"

"At that time," says Tracy, "I didn't know it was going to go as far as it did. I don't think he did it when we were going out, as far as I know." Kurt told Tracy that heroin made him really social. "He felt like he could go out and have a good time and talk to people and not feel uncomfortable," she says.

"The funny thing is, when he was getting all these tests for his stomach, he actually came home one time from the hospital and he said, 'They tried to give me another blood test and they already gave me four tests.' He walked out of there because he said he would almost faint when they tried to draw blood because he couldn't stand the needle in his arm."

On New Year's Day of 1991, the band went back to the Music Source, where they had done the *Blew* EP sessions, and recorded several tracks with soundman Craig Montgomery, completing two, "Aneurysm" and "Even in His Youth," both of which later appeared as B-sides and on *Incesticide*.

"Even in His Youth" sounds a familiar theme: "He was nothing . . . Going nowhere / Daddy was ashamed . . . Disgrace the family name." So there's Kurt's old friend shame again.

Gersh thought the band should rerecord the seven songs from the Smart sessions and suggested several relatively fancy producers, including Scott Litt, who had worked on R.E.M.'s breakthrough records, longtime Neil Young producer David Briggs, and Don Dixon, who had produced R.E.M., the Reivers, the Smithereens, and many other bands.

At one point, Kurt told the Seattle music paper *Backlash* that Vig would be the main producer, but they'd use other producers for the songs the band deemed "commercial."

Briggs and Dixon actually flew up to Seattle to meet the band. Dixon made the final cut, and tentative plans were made for him to produce and Vig to engineer. But then something fell through. Some say that rumors that the band had received an astronomical advance had fooled some producers into pricing themselves out of the job, but the band was really holding out for Vig all along. Vig, a supremely nice guy, simply knew where they were coming from, musically and philosophically, better than anyone else.

Earlier in the book, I noted that Butch Vig is "immensely nice," and that really can't be said enough about him. Also, after recording with Vig in Madison, Kurt and Krist were comfortable working with him. But maybe the bow I neglected to tie up was the fact that such a pleasant fellow could get such nasty but well-articulated sounds—listen to Killdozer's *Little Baby Buntin'* (1987), Die Kreuzen's *Century Days* (1988), or Feedtime's *Suction* (1989) for hefty doses of impeccably wrought aggro. Along with people such as Jack Endino, Spot, Steve Fisk, Steve Albini, Don Zientara, and Rick Harte, Vig was one of the really talented and hardworking producers who enabled American underground rock in the '80s. He'd earned his twenty-four-karat indie cred. Sonically, temperamentally, and politically, Butch Vig was a really good fit for Nirvana.

Vig had never done a major label project and Gersh initially bridled, but came around to the idea after figuring that even if Vig didn't get the right sounds during recording, they could do the time-honored thing and "fix it in the mix." So Nirvana got their way—this time. Vig got the call just a couple of weeks before recording was to begin.

The band sent him some rehearsal tapes they made on a boom box. The band played so loud that the sound was wildly distorted, but Vig could make out some great tunes. Vig already knew most of the songs from the Smart sessions, but there were a few new ones, too, like "Come as You Are" and "Smells Like Teen Spirit" that sounded like they had a lot of promise.

So, basically, the Geffen brass said, *Yeah, sure, knock yourself out, use your little indie rock producer—if it doesn't turn out well, we can always hire a pro to tweak the mixes*, which is exactly what wound up happening. The label would take that view with the album after this one, too—but with different results.

"We knew that the stuff we were coming up with was catchy and cool and just good strong songs," Dave says. "We kind of could tell that they were really great. We didn't expect what happened to happen, but we knew it was going to be a really good record."

The April 17 show when Nirvana debuted "Smells Like Teen Spirit." Says Nils Bernstein, "Everybody went crazy."
Poster by Mark Bendix

chapter eight

VERSE, CHORUS, VERSE, CHORUS, SOLO, BAD SOLO

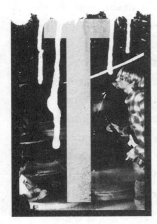

he band formally signed with Geffen on April 30, 1991. Soon after, Kurt called his father out of the blue and told him the big news. He said he was going to go down to Los Angeles to record in a few days, and that he was very excited about everything that was happening. They talked for over an hour, just catching up. Finally, Don told Kurt to stay in touch, they said goodbye, and hung up the phone. And then Don Cobain cried.

Chris and Shelli drove their Volkswagen van with all the band's equipment in it down to L.A. Kurt and Dave had decided they were going to drive down, too, in order to experience the romance of the open road. They took off a few days early in a beat-up old Datsun, looking forward to the adventures ahead. But the car overheated every fifteen minutes or so and it took them three hours to go a hundred miles. So they limped back to Tacoma, parked the car in a quarry, and pelted it with rocks for half an hour before driving it to Chris's house, where they picked up their trusty white Dodge tour van. They stopped in San Francisco and stayed at Dale Crover's house for a few days before setting off for L.A., going straight to the Universal Studios tour as soon as they arrived.

In the days before the sessions began, Vig and the band fine-tuned some of the arrangements at a rehearsal studio. All the new material was very promising, but the first time they played "Teen Spirit," the normally low-key Vig began pacing around the room with excitement. One night, Chris got a little plastered and commandeered the studio-wide intercom system and broadcast heartfelt words of encouragement to his fellow musicians throughout the rehearsal complex, including people like Lenny Kravitz and Belinda Carlisle. "Okay, you motherfuckers!" Chris hollered. "Get your ass in gear!"

Next, they went to a drum rental place and selected a brass snare for Dave. It was the loudest one they had. The employees had nicknamed it "the Terminator."

They stayed in furnished apartments in a nearby building called the Oakwood—"It was so gross with this mauve and powder blue," sniffs Chris. Naturally, they trashed the place, breaking a coffee table and a framed painting of flowers. "We were just in L.A. and for lack of anything to do," Chris explains. "It's fun having a party—there doesn't have to be any reason or any kind of anxiety or anything. It's just fun to go crazy."

Courtney Love. © Charles Peterson

Soon, a woman with the improbable name of Courtney Love began stopping by the Oakwood to see Kurt.

Courtney had seen Nirvana open for the Dharma Bums at the Satyricon club in Portland, Oregon, in 1989. Watching Kurt on stage, she thought to herself, "He's got Dave Pirner damage, but he's way cuter." She thought he was "hot in a Sub Pop rock god sort of way." After the set, as was his custom, Kurt wandered away from the stage area in order to get out of packing up gear. He walked by Courtney's table, sat down, poured himself a beer from her pitcher, and glared at her. She glared back.

"I thought she looked like Nancy Spungen," Kurt says, chuckling. "She looked like a classic punk rock chick. I did feel kind of attracted to her. Probably wanted to fuck her that night, but she left." They talked for a little bit and he gave her a few stickers he had made that had Chim-Chim and the Nirvana logo. "I put them all on my suitcase," says Courtney, "and I didn't even like his band."

This was a pretty difficult thing to confirm in 1993, and I went with the independent testimony of the two people directly involved. But there's some question as to whether this actually happened. Nirvana did support the Dharma Bums at a show at Satyricon on January 21, 1989. And Kurt and Courtney both told me about the incident in separate interviews, and their stories were identical, so they would have had to both anticipate the question and then coordinate their answers—to what end?

As Courtney said in the *Sassy* article: "I *saw him play* in Portland in 1988. *And then I met him* at a show about a year, or something, ago." (Italics mine.) But in the same interview, Kurt says they met at a May 17, 1991, Butthole Surfers/L7/Redd Kross show in Los Angeles. And in an interview conducted for *Montage of Heck*, Courtney said she had a crush on Kurt—"He was gorgeous, I mean, he was beautiful"—during the 1991 summer

The Amplified Come as You Are

festival touring season, before "Smells Like Teen Spirit" was released but well after the buzz about Nirvana had exploded.

"I really pursued him," Courtney told *Sassy*, "not too aggressive, but aggressive enough that some girls would have been embarrassed by it. I'm direct. That can scare a lot of boys. Like, I got Kurt's number when they were on tour, and I would call him. And I would do interviews with people who I knew were going to interview Nirvana, and I would tell them I had a crush on Kurt. Kurt was scared of me. He said he didn't have time to deal with me. But I knew it was inevitable."

Kurt added, "I would just like to say I liked Courtney a lot. I wasn't ignoring her. I didn't mean to play hard to get. I just didn't have the time, I had so many things on my mind."

In *Everybody Loves Our Town*, Babes in Toyland drummer Lori Barbero said that Courtney called her in October 1991 and asked her to meet her in Chicago "because Nirvana's playing." That would be October 12, 1991, at the Metro, with Nirvanamania well underway. And Barbero said she introduced Kurt (who was twenty-four at the time) and Courtney (who was twenty-seven) that evening, adding, "She broke up with Billy [Corgan] that night." And apparently Courtney then followed or accompanied Nirvana to Minneapolis.

The Chim-Chim sticker that Kurt gave to Courtney at the Satyricon.

Courtney had had a crush on Kurt ever since. Asked to describe her attraction to Kurt, something rare happens—Courtney Love is at a loss for words. "I don't know," she says, suddenly girlish, almost blushing. "I feel embarrassed. I just thought he was really beautiful. He was really cool and he had really beautiful hands. He was really beautiful. I can't explain it."

It's true—Kurt did have notably beautiful hands: they were certainly a man's hands but kind of alabaster and feminine, like a Michelangelo sculpture. Michael Stipe felt the same way: the only photograph he ever took of his friend Kurt was of his hands.

A couple of years older than Kurt, Courtney was also the product of a broken home and parental neglect, and like Kurt had an itinerant childhood, although while Kurt had bounced around tiny Grays Harbor County, Courtney's travels had spanned several continents. Her mother took her from L.A. to New Zealand to work on a farm, then they moved to Australia and back to the States, where Courtney eventually wound up in an Oregon reform school. She supported herself as a stripper during her teens, traveling from Portland to Japan to Ireland; by 1981, she was hanging out in the then-explosive Liverpool scene with post-punk luminaries like Julian Cope of the Teardrop Explodes and members of Echo and the Bunnymen.

She sang in an early incarnation of Faith No More in San Francisco and later moved to Minneapolis and formed a short-lived band with Jennifer Finch and Kat Bjelland called Sugar Baby Doll (Finch went on to form L7, Bjelland now leads Babes in Toyland). She landed a bit part in *Sid and Nancy* and later co-starred in the abysmal 1987 post-punk spaghetti western *Straight to Hell*, which featured the Pogues, Joe Strummer, and Elvis Costello. She founded the band Hole in March of 1990. She was already well known—some would say notorious—on the indie circuit.

In the course of writing a book about Nirvana, one inevitably comes across all sorts of unflattering stories about Courtney Love, some of which might even be true. She did not appear to be widely popular in the indie community. I didn't bother to pursue or verify any of these stories except as they pertained to, as the subtitle of the book puts it, "the story of Nirvana." I just wasn't going to veer off course, no matter how sensational that rabbit hole might have been.

Around December of 1990, Courtney and Dave became friendly through Dave's former girlfriend, Jennifer Finch. "She was fun to talk to because if you were bored, you could spend three hours on the phone," Dave says of Courtney. "It was funny because I'd never talked to anyone who was so entertainment business-wise or L.A.-wise as Courtney. It was kind of neat to have a conversation with someone who you could picture being behind a desk at *US* magazine or something."

There's the ultra-small world of the indie rock nation at that time: Courtney's ex-bandmate used to date the guy who played drums with the guy Courtney had a crush on. It was practically inevitable that Courtney and Kurt crossed paths.

After Courtney revealed to Dave that she had a crush on Kurt, Dave told Courtney that Kurt liked her, too, but she didn't quite believe it. Still, she gave Dave a package to give to Kurt—little seashells and pine cones and miniature teacups and a tiny doll, all packed into a small heart-shaped box. Courtney swears that if she hadn't forgotten that he never replied, she wouldn't have bothered chasing him anymore.

Kurt and Courtney met again at a Butthole Surfers/Redd Kross/L7 show at the Palladium in Los Angeles in May of 1991, shortly before the band began recording *Nevermind*. They were instantly attracted to each other. Courtney chose to express her attraction by punching Kurt in the stomach. He punched her back, then he leaped on her and they began wrestling. After a little while, Courtney got up, kicked Kurt, and walked away. "It was a mating ritual for dysfunctional people," Courtney cracks.

In three months, Hole would release its debut album, *Pretty on the Inside*. A harrowing, confrontational, and fearless dissection of childhood damage and feminine self-hatred, the record began with Courtney snarling, "When I was a teenage whore . . ." and went on from there. The English music press were already raving about the band and Courtney in particular; journalists fell all over themselves for an interview with this brash, outspoken, and devastatingly witty American. The album was a longtime UK indie chart entry after its debut in August of 1991.

Although many would soon come to believe—and still do—that Courtney was a gold-digger, she insists she didn't think Kurt would ever be anything more than a revered cult figure when she began chasing him. "I thought I was going to be more famous than him," says Courtney. "That was pretty obvious to me." The way she looks at it now, marrying Kurt Cobain was a bad career move.

There is no doubt that Courtney likes attention. But much of her grandstanding can be seen as an effort to assert herself, to avoid getting outshone by Kurt's brilliant star. Imagine the situation where the spouse who wants to be famous is overtaken by the spouse who never wanted to be. Of course, Courtney would eventually achieve her own kind of fame—or infamy—her name becoming a household synonym for a delinquent mother.

At that time, anyway, it did not seem "pretty obvious" to anybody but Courtney that she would ever be more famous than Kurt. It wasn't going to happen with *Pretty on the Inside*, which just wasn't fit for mass consumption. Courtney simply wanted to be famous very, very badly.

Much of Courtney's "grandstanding" was simply because she's voluble, unlike Kurt. It was a lot like band interviews, where Krist, garrulous and outgoing, did a lot of the talking. When Jonathan Poneman interviewed Kurt and Courtney for *Spin* in December 1992, Courtney did most of the talking. This was a year after the relatively obscure *Pretty on the Inside* and a year and a half before the release of *Live Through This*. At that point, Courtney was basically famous for being famous.

While Courtney may have been pegged as a delinquent mother, Kurt was a delinquent father—he was a heroin addict. It's just that he wasn't the one who was photographed smoking while pregnant.

Courtney happened to live only a block away from the Oakwood and she stopped by a few times. Chris didn't pay her much mind. "She was some loud girl," he says. "I'd never heard of her before."

But Kurt was interested. "We bonded over pharmaceuticals," Courtney says. "I had Vicodin extra-strength, which was pills, and he had Hycomine cough syrup. I said, 'You're a pussy, you shouldn't drink that syrup because it's bad for your stomach.'"

Stuff like this is why I needed that copy of the *Physicians' Desk Reference*. Courtney was encyclopedically knowledgeable about pharmaceuticals—she knew that Hycomine and Vicodin contain the same opioid, hydrocodone.

Kurt called her up at five in the morning on the pretense of asking if she had any drugs. Courtney said no and made a date with Kurt for the next day. He stood her up and then kept his phone off the hook so she couldn't call. "I couldn't decide if I actually wanted to consummate our relationship," he explains, smiling.

"She seemed like poison because I'd just gotten out of the last relationship that I didn't even want to be in," says Kurt. "I was determined to be a bachelor for a few months. I just had to be. But I knew that I liked Courtney so much right away that it was a really hard struggle to stay away from her for so many months.

It was harder than shit. During that time that I attempted to be a bachelor and sow my oats and live the bachelor rock & roll lifestyle, I didn't end up fucking anybody or having a good time at all." He decided to concentrate on making the album.

"She seemed like poison." Maybe that was part of the attraction.

As far as the "relationship that I didn't even want to be in," that would sure seem to be an attempt to appease Courtney, who remained very jealous of—or at least competitive with—Vail and indeed Bikini Kill and the riot grrrls in general; she wrote a scathing song about them ("Olympia," aka "Rock Star," from Hole's 1994 *Live Through This*) and even as recently as 2019 was bad-mouthing the Bikini Kill reunion.

###

They recorded in May and June of 1991 at Sound City Studios in suburban Van Nuys, California. The studio had seen better days in the '70s, when Fleetwood Mac had recorded *Rumours* there. Other previous clients included Ronnie James Dio, Tom Petty, Foreigner, the Jackson 5, Rick Springfield, Crazy Horse, Ratt, and even Kurt's childhood hero, Evel Knievel. It had a big drum room, a great old Neve mixing board, and the rates were reasonable. The original budget was about sixty-five thousand dollars including Butch Vig's services—a mere pittance in major label terms. For that amount of money, they could afford to scrap the whole thing if it didn't work out and start all over again.

By this time, Sound City was a bit of a '70s relic. As Krist so evocatively described the place to *Rolling Stone*'s Chris Mundy in January 1992, "It was like a time machine. It was like an old pair of corduroys that was starting to wear out."

That Evel Knievel album was released in 1974, Sound City's heyday, and is mostly spoken word but does contain two songs with lyrics by the legendary daredevil. He speaks over schmaltzy strings on one of them, "Why?" which was released as a single. These lines from the song sound a lot like Kurt's attitude toward drug use: "For you to do what I do is not right," Knievel piously intones. "But for me, it's not wrong."

I left it out at the time so as not to incriminate Kurt, but an anonymous source told me that Kurt actually stole the master tapes for the Evel Knievel album from Sound City.

Kurt gives part of the credit for the quality of the album to the fact that they were back in sunny L.A. "It was really nice to all of a sudden find yourself in a totally warm, tropical climate," he says. "I don't think it would have turned out nearly as well if we did it in Washington."

Verse, Chorus, Verse, Chorus, Solo, Bad Solo

Producer Butch Vig tuning Dave's drums during the *Nevermind* sessions.

Vig would make them comfortable by just hanging with them in the studio and not pushing them into the recording booth as soon as they walked through the door. And he tried to keep them out of the control room.

They'd work eight to ten hours a day, sometimes blowing off steam by playing covers of old '70s favorites such as Alice Cooper, Black Sabbath, and Aerosmith—the musical equivalent of comfort food.

Dave hit the drums so hard that they had to change the heads every other song. Although they're played with vastly more power and precision, Dave's drum parts on songs that appeared on the Smart sessions are very close to what Chad had played. "Chad wasn't the most solid drummer and he wasn't the most consistent drummer but he came up with really really cool stuff," Dave says. "I like the way he plays—the stuff on *Bleach*, it's almost drunken."

It's cool that a meticulous and technically gifted player such as Dave could appreciate another drummer's "drunken" style. When Nirvana was inducted into the Rock & Roll Hall of Fame in 2014, Dave graciously thanked most of the preceding Nirvana drummers,

The Amplified Come as You Are

including Chad Channing, who inexplicably wasn't invited to sit at Nirvana's table or join them behind the podium. "If you listen to a song like 'In Bloom' [and here he imitated the bludgeoning drum entrance from that song], that's Chad," Dave said to the roomful of industry heavies. "When I joined the band, I had the honor of playing Chad's parts, so Chad, thank you very much for allowing me to play your drum parts; I appreciate that very, very much."

Kurt's punk ethic was even stronger than Vig's, apparently, because Kurt would often refuse to do a second take. Vig had to figure out how to get him to do a second take and often would roll tape even when Kurt was warming up, just in case he got something usable.

Kurt had worked out his vocals so well that they barely varied in phrasing and intensity from one take to the next, so Vig would often take advantage of this consistency and mix the two takes together, especially on choruses for that extra sing-along effect. (That's Dave singing the high harmonies on "In Bloom," however. He had trouble hitting those stratospheric notes, but if he'd blow a take, he'd just take a drag on his cigarette and try again. Many takes later, Vig got what he wanted.)

With instrumental takes, if they didn't get something right away, they'd just move onto something else—after two or three tries, it was often a matter of diminishing returns. "I wanted him to double his guitars on some of the songs, especially on choruses," says Vig, "and he didn't really want to do that. My logic was, 'When you guys play live, it's just so incredibly loud and intense—it's larger than life and I'm trying to use some of these things I know in the studio to make you guys come across that way on record.' A lot of times, he'd go, 'I don't feel like doing that right now,' but for the most part, when I asked him to do stuff, he'd eventually do it. There weren't any major arguments or anything, but I could tell when I was pushing him a little far and he didn't want to do something. A couple of times, he just put his guitar down or walked away from the mike and said, 'I don't want to do it anymore.' And I knew I wasn't going to get anything else out of him."

There's a school of thought that says that recording is inherently artificial and that it can never truly capture the sensation of hearing the band live. So the idea is to use artificial means to emulate, but not duplicate, the "incredibly loud and intense . . . larger than life" sensation of live performance with techniques such as reverb and doubling vocals and guitars. Kurt didn't like doubling vocals but Vig had a very effective line he'd whip out: "Every time he'd resist, it was just, 'John Lennon did it,'" Vig said in the "Nirvana: Nevermind" episode of the *Classic Albums* documentary series, "and he'd go, 'OK.'"

Kurt probably felt techniques like that were dishonest, or at least not punk, if only because so many of the bands he idolized simply couldn't afford to record like that. (Then again, the Sex Pistols' *Nevermind the Bollocks*, a punk record if ever there was one, was assiduously overdubbed.) Yet he was still, deep down, that Aberdeen kid with big rock dreams, so he'd eventually do what Vig asked. And then later, when the album came out, he'd complain about how slick it was.

On "Territorial Pissings," Kurt ignored Vig's protests and plugged his guitar directly into the mixing board—no amplifier—in the style of countless low-budget punk records of the late '70s and early '80s. The song was recorded in one take. In the intro, Chris sang a bit of the chorus to the Youngbloods' altruistic late-'60s hippie hit, "Get Together." "They just said, 'Sing something,'" says Chris, "so I did it in one take. It just kind of happened. I wanted to put some kind of corny hippie idealism in it. But it wasn't really that thought into. I *like* that Youngbloods song.

"Maybe it was about lost ideals," Chris says. "Like, what happened to those ideals? 'Everybody get together, try to love one another.' And then there's 'Territorial Pissings.' Maybe some baby boomer will hear that and wonder, 'Hey, what happened to those ideals?'"

The Youngbloods' 1967 hit "Get Together" has been called "the hippie national anthem"—in the late '60s, it was covered by bands with names like H. P. Lovecraft, Jefferson Airplane, and the Sunshine Company . . . you get the picture. And Krist *was* kind of a hippie, and he probably did kind of like the song, and it was just the kind of 45 you'd find in a thrift store. But it would never have occurred to a baby boomer to mock this beloved souvenir of the Summer of Love—only a Gen Xer would, which is one big reason why Krist's eleven-second vocal solo is a defining generational statement even if it's a throwaway joke. Actually, it's a defining generational statement *because* it's a throwaway joke.

Or maybe it wasn't a joke. Krist sang that snippet of "Get Together" to call out the hypocrisy of "corny hippie idealism." The more progressive baby boomers had long since abandoned the peace-and-love philosophy of their idyllic, entitled youth and become the "Me Generation"—and then, after that, they became something even worse: yuppies. A 1984 *New York Times* article noted how boomers were backing Ronald Reagan over Walter Mondale by a margin of fifty-four to thirty-seven. So Krist was asking a great question: "Hey, what happened to those ideals?"

Kurt *liked* "Get Together." The song, he explained to the Brazilian newspaper *O Globo*, "speaks of people who join together to be cool and try something new, the ideal contrast to the macho men I'm portraying in 'Territorial Pissings.' We didn't mean to be offensive to the guy who wrote it. The idea of being positive and causing change in society and the world was appropriated by the media, who turned it into something ridiculous, a caricature."

Although the members of Nirvana probably didn't know this, "Get Together" was also the first hit for a budding twentysomething music mogul named David Geffen, who would one day own Nirvana's label.

The year after *Nevermind* was released, the first baby boomer president would proceed to build a massive carceral state, escalate the war on drugs, single out an obscure Black female rapper as a political punching bag (the infamous Sister Souljah incident), gut welfare, deregulate various industries, and embargo Iraq, causing the deaths of hundreds of thousands of children. So much for boomers and peace and love.

Vig says that "Something in the Way"—written just a week before it was recorded—was probably the most difficult song on the album to record. They tried it a few times with the rest of the band playing along, but it didn't work. Finally, Vig called Kurt into the control room and asked how *he* thought the song should go. Kurt sat down on the couch with his nylon-string acoustic guitar and sang the song in a barely audible whisper. "Stay *right* there," Vig said as he dashed out to the office and told them to turn off every phone and every fan and every other machine in the whole place. Vig recorded the song that way, with the levels cranked up as high as they could go to catch Kurt's voice—it's so quiet that you can practically hear Kurt's tongue sliding over his teeth as he sings. Later, they added bass, more vocals, and drums. "We had to keep yelling at Dave to play wimpy," says Vig. "He'd start playing the song lightly and halfway through the first verse he'd be playing pretty hard. His natural inclination is to attack the drum kit. He finally got it, but I think it almost killed him to just tap his way through."

Some of the lyrics were completely finished, but many others weren't, and Kurt would ask the others which line they liked best—sometimes, the lines would give the song widely different meanings, like when "Pay to Play" became "Stay Away." He'd also try different melodies.

The phrase "pay to play" was surely a reference to hair metal–centric Sunset Strip clubs such as Gazzarri's, the Roxy, and the Whisky, who had a "pay to play" policy in the '80s and '90s: if bands wanted to do a showcase set, they had to buy a number of tickets from the club in advance. The clubs could get away with this because so much of the music industry was based in Los Angeles, and there was intense competition among the bands for the attention of label scouts. It was exactly the kind of music biz chicanery that pissed off Kurt.

Kurt made the title/chorus change from "Pay to Play" to "Stay Away" at the last minute—between takes, actually. The change is a good insight into Kurt's lyric-writing process: it suggests that maybe the point wasn't completely what the words meant but the number of syllables and the consonants and vowel sounds they contained. Not only is it an easier phrase to scream, but Kurt surely realized that a lot more people—and probably he himself—could relate to someone screaming "stay away!"

Apparently, the whole Sunset Strip metal scene continued to annoy Kurt—Nirvana later recorded a song called "Gallons of Rubbing Alcohol Flow Through the Strip," which, after some dismal junkie rambling, rolls around to the idea of flooding the Sunset Strip with rubbing alcohol and setting it on fire, incinerating the big-haired metal musicians who ruled the clubs there.

Just a few weeks before recording was to start, Kurt showed a riff to the band and they jammed on it for the better part of an hour, playing with dynamics and different arrangements until it became a song, which Kurt titled "Smells Like Teen Spirit." Chris didn't especially like the song at first. "It was just one of the songs we did for the record," Chris says. "I remember when we first did it, it was nothing special. But after it was recorded, I thought, 'Hey, this is really good. It really rocks.'" Right away, both Chris and Kurt heard one of their influences in the song. "The Pixies," says Chris. "We saw it right away. Both of us said, 'This really sounds like the Pixies. People are really going to nail us for it.'"

Although they almost threw away the song, no one ever did nail them for sounding like the Pixies, although much comment was later made that the song bore more than a passing resemblance to Boston's 1976 hit "More Than a Feeling."

Those are primordial rock chords, dating back to at least Richard Berry's "Louie, Louie" (1957) and on through the Wild Ones' "Wild Thing" (1965) and a million other classic songs. Kurt was just moving barre chords around the neck of the guitar, as he did with so many Nirvana compositions. There's even a very similar riff in the chorus of the Pixies' "U-Mass" but that song was released the same week as *Nevermind*, so it's unlikely that Kurt could have ripped it off.

Kurt's lack of guitar technique was one of the punkest things about him. Punk rock was revolutionary partly because it rejected the idea that technique was important—instead, it's ideas and inspiration and passion that count, and it's possible to convey those things with even the barest amount of technical skill. Lots of musicians could play their asses off, or make highly polished recordings, but if the music was empty, then it meant nothing—and at the time punk exploded, the charts were filled with music like that.

Punk's rejection of technique—not just musical technique but recording technique and big-budget live performance—is a symbolic rejection of a privileged elite that tries to dictate culture. The Olympia crowd embraced this idea profoundly; Beat Happening could barely play their instruments and yet made several great records and helped to ignite an entire subculture.

"I'm worse at what I do best / And for this gift, I feel blessed" is an interesting line. Maybe it means that having limited chops meant that he'd never even be able to descend into the self-indulgent claptrap that punk decried. Or maybe it means that being a good musician with poor technique helped him to stumble into creative discoveries, such as using chords that don't technically belong in the key of the song, which Kurt did often. Kurt told *Guitar Player* that he actually liked Fender Mustang guitars precisely because "They're designed terribly . . . But I like it," he said. "That way, things sound fucked up and I stumble onto stuff accidentally. I guess I don't like to be that familiar with my guitar."

As Kurt acknowledges earlier in the book, punk rock freed him to lower his expectations. And that had a resonance for a generation that was continually told that it could never measure up to the previous one.

Once Chris and Dave had finished their basic tracks—which was a matter of days—they were done. Kurt was kept busy doing vocals, playing guitar overdubs, and writing lyrics, sometimes delaying production for precious hours until he found the right words. Kurt wrote most of the words for "On a Plain" minutes before he sang them. The "Don't quote me on that" line came from a dumb little running joke they had that week. "Someone would say something like 'Where's the mayonnaise?'" Dave recalls, "and someone else would answer, 'It's in the fridge, but don't quote me on that.'"

"But don't quote me on that" is a banal little phrase, but it resonated for a reason that Vig and the band might not have been able to quite put their finger on. That's the kind of thing Kurt loved to pluck out of the air and put in his songs.

"On a Plain" is the song with the lines "It is now time to make it unclear / To write off lines that don't make sense." And that was Kurt's modus operandi with lyrics: throw in some glints of autobiography but also unrelated lines to induce vivid but unpredictable associations, bringing the song into realms that can't be conventionally parsed. This, again, was the collage effect.

Verse, Chorus, Verse, Chorus, Solo, Bad Solo

It was more important to Vig that Kurt sing the songs with conviction rather than good diction. That wasn't a problem, however—once Kurt decided on finished lyrics, he sang so hard that he could often do only one or two vocals before his voice gave out and he'd be done for the day. His voice audibly goes to pieces on "Territorial Pissings."

It would be easy to claim that many of Kurt's lyrics were frivolous because they were written down at the last minute. But composing doesn't necessarily mean writing something down: those words might have been forming in his head for quite some time, which is composition, and it was only an impending recording session that compelled him to commit to them at the last minute, as it had with *Bleach*. That's just how creative people often work.

But even if he made it all up on the spot, so what? Don't discount the potential genius of improvisation. Ever listened to John Coltrane?

The thing is, his journals, and even the few lyric sheets included in this book, reveal that Kurt worked on the lyrics well in advance. For instance, the lyrics for "Lithium" and "Dumb" that he played solo acoustic on Calvin Johnson's KAOS radio show in September 1990 are virtually identical to the recorded versions. And yet at the start of the show, he claimed that he "just wrote most of the lyrics this evening."

"In the car on the way up here?" Johnson asked.

"While I was driving with one foot," Kurt replied. "I try to be as spontaneous as possible." But not really.

Kurt didn't know any dealers in L.A., so instead of doing heroin, he drank codeine cough syrup constantly during the sessions, not to mention a half of a fifth of Jack Daniel's every day. He wanted the cough syrup for the opiate, but it also helped preserve his voice. Unfortunately, he ran out of it by the time he was to start doing vocal tracks. There were a few days when he could do only one or two takes before his throat gave out entirely, which upset Kurt a lot. (He still takes cough syrup on tour for his chronic bronchitis. "It's the only thing that saves me," Kurt claims.)

Ten minutes and three seconds after the last chord of "Something in the Way" faded away came a surprise track. Although it never had an official name other than perhaps "The Noise Jam," the track has come to be known as "Endless, Nameless." They'd been playing variations on "Endless, Nameless" for months before the *Nevermind* sessions. At the end of practice, Kurt would tune his guitar way down and they'd just bang away, making caterwauling feedback noise and occasionally drifting into the song's main riff.

The guitar Kurt smashed during "Endless, Nameless."

The cough syrup Kurt was drinking was the aforementioned Hycomine, which contains the opioid hydrocodone, not codeine. One of the side effects of hydrocodone is feelings of extreme happiness or sadness, which is probably not something you want if you're bipolar to begin with. As Butch Vig told *Billboard* in 2016—and in various other interviews over the years—Kurt had "mood swings": he "could be engaged and fully committed and articulate and then a light switch would go off and he would just go sit in the corner and shut himself down."

When the session for "Lithium" began going awry, Kurt asked Vig to keep the tape rolling while the band tried an experiment. He went out into the studio and began flailing his guitar and screaming into a microphone as the band followed suit. Even Kurt isn't sure what he's screaming, but he believes it's along the lines of "I think I can, I know I can." Audible on the track (right around 19:32 on the CD) is the sound of Kurt smashing his guitar. Afterward, they realized that was the only left-handed guitar he had that fit the track, so the sessions were over for the day. They did a quick mix of the song and figured they'd find a place for it. Due to a technical error, "Endless, Nameless" didn't make the initial pressing of *Nevermind*.

I now realize he was being sarcastic and evasive: he simply isn't singing "I think I can, I know I can"—basically, he's singing the exact opposite of that: if the transcriptions of the lyrics are correct—and it sure sounds like it—he's actually screaming things like "Death and violence . . . No más, mama . . . Death is what I am." If those are anywhere near accurate—it's hard to tell because Kurt is screaming so incoherently—"Endless, Nameless" is basically a harrowing suicide threat.

It is downright bizarre to smash a guitar in a recording studio; it just doesn't happen. "I've never seen so much rage in someone in the studio that came out that instantaneously," Butch Vig said in *Everybody Loves Our Town*. "It was scary to watch him play that song. I'm not kidding."

By all means listen to "Endless, Nameless" and then spin the Butthole Surfers' "U.S.S.A." from 1987's *Locust Abortion Technician*.

The ten minutes of silence after "Something in the Way" was the band's way of playing with the new CD format, just like the Beatles put inscrutable messages in the run-out groove of *Sgt. Pepper* or put "Her Majesty" at the end of *Abbey Road*. Kurt had done something similar before. When he and his buddy Jesse Reed shared their studio apartment back in Aberdeen, Kurt took a ninety-minute blank cassette tape, wound it forward to nearly the end and recorded himself saying in a scary voice, "Jesse . . . Jesse . . . I'm coming to get yooooooo . . ." As they were getting ready to go to bed he popped the tape into the stereo, hit "play" and turned the volume down low. Forty minutes later, a voice said "Jesse . . ." and Reed sat up startled. "Hey, did you hear that?"

"Hear *what*?" Kurt replied, smirking to himself in the dark.

Hidden bonus tracks were a big fad in the '90s, as musicians realized that, with eighty minutes of time available on a CD, you could insert long periods of silence after the final listed track and then tack on a surprise track—preferably one that starts with a loud, startling sound. Bands had certainly included hidden bonus tracks before, but after *Nevermind*, the practice exploded: Pearl Jam did it, and so did Beck, the Lemonheads, Sheryl Crow, Korn, Mudhoney, Live, Green Day, Mr. Bungle, Urge Overkill, the Pet Shop Boys, Cracker, Afghan Whigs, Meat Puppets, Primus, Stone Temple Pilots, Nine Inch Nails, and many, many others.

One night during the sessions, Chris got picked up on a driving while intoxicated charge in Los Angeles. He guzzled the last bit of liquor just as the cop was

walking toward his car. With no money in their pockets, Kurt and Dave walked several miles back home, while the police took Chris to the city jail and then the county jail. When he was put in the holding tank, he tried to look as tough as he could so no one would hassle him. "There was fifty guys crammed in this cell," Chris says. "You open the cell door and boom—the heat hits you from all the people in there."

Immediately, a small, dapper black man with a withered arm and an unlit cigarette strode up to Chris and rasped, "Heymanyougotanymatches?"

"What?"

"Yougotanymatches?"

"No," Chris replied.

"There's like fifty guys in there with these cigarettes and nobody has a fuckin' match!" Chris chuckles. "It was totally quiet, except when somebody would walk in and that little guy would say, 'Yougotanymatches?' Finally this guy walked in with matches and they all just lit up like crazy, smoke is filling the room."

After sixteen hours in stir, Chris was bailed out by John Silva. Chris eventually got off with a fine and had to attend a series of seminars where victims of drunk drivers told their horrific stories.

###

Vig had started to sense something was going to happen with the record. All sorts of people had somehow gotten wind of the project and were asking him for tapes.

###

Kurt had three or four untitled songs and song fragments that were very melodic and not as heavy as most of the other material. A&R executive Gary Gersh remembers a conversation he had with Kurt where "We thought, let's not put it on this record because we don't want to make this record look like—they weren't finished, first of all—but the jump from an independent label to a major was like some big huge commercial sell-out or something," Gersh says. "Let's make the artistic jump as gradual as you feel comfortable with." Which is A&R-speak for "It's going to look like you're selling out if you put these pop songs on the record." So, once again, as he had on *Bleach*, Kurt had to adjust his recordings to the tastes of the marketplace.

Verse, Chorus, Verse, Chorus, Solo, Bad Solo

Kurt was walking a fine line between adjusting his recordings to the tastes of the marketplace and adjusting them to preempt criticism from the indie community. He was wary of how his peers and core fans would react to Nirvana's jump to a major label and didn't want to lose the uncompromising indie kids the way Hüsker Dü and Soundgarden had lost him.

Those three or four lighter, melodic songs were very likely "Pennyroyal Tea," "Dumb," and "All Apologies," all of which wound up on *In Utero*. Imagine what *Nevermind* would have been like if they had dropped harder songs such as "Territorial Pissings" and "Stay Away" and instead included "Pennyroyal Tea" and "All Apologies." Likewise, imagine *In Utero* without those quieter songs.

So, as with *Bleach*, "We wanted to try to please people at first, to see what would happen." And look what happened.

Although Gersh says he "always" stopped by the studio and was "a little bit therapist, a little bit referee," both Chris and Kurt say he barely showed up at all. In fact, Dave got so worried that Gersh wasn't around that he thought Gersh had lost his enthusiasm for the project. He even went so far as to place a worried phone call to John Silva, who assured him that most bands would kill for such a hands-off A&R person.

By everyone else's account, Gersh would often stop by the studio after the band had gone home, and Vig would play him rough mixes. Astutely, Gersh had chosen not to meddle, and by doing so, he had built up enough credibility with the band that when he had to step in and take charge at a certain very delicate moment in the recording, the band respected his ideas.

Vig was going to mix the record, too, but because the recording had gone behind schedule, the four or five days that were supposed to elapse between recording and mixing so that Vig and the band could rest their ears had evaporated. Vig finished recording and went straight into mixing, but the mixes didn't turn out well—they were flat and lacked power, especially in the drums.

If a recording of Dave Grohl playing drums lacks power, then, yeah, one might want to step back and reconsider a few things.

Gersh noticed Vig was tired and took the opportunity to call in veteran mixer Andy Wallace, who had done terrific work on Slayer's *Seasons in the Abyss*. Although the band was skeptical, they "just went along with the game," as Chris puts it.

Actually, the decision to call in a new mixer was a mutual one between Nirvana, Vig, the label, and Gold Mountain, and Gersh submitted a list of suggested mixers to the band.

Kurt passed on names like Scott Litt (who had mixed and produced albums by R.E.M., Patti Smith, and the Replacements) and Ed Stasium (the Ramones, Living Colour, the Pretenders) and settled on Andy Wallace.

Kurt was wary of being associated with metal but damn, *Seasons in the Abyss* does sound really good. Wallace had also mixed other killer-sounding albums including Run-DMC's *Raising Hell*, the Cult's *Electric*, and Sepultura's *Arise*. (He went on to mix classic early-'90s ragers like Screaming Trees' *Sweet Oblivion*, Helmet's *Meantime*, and Rage Against the Machine's self-titled debut album.)

It had become pretty standard to bring in someone like Wallace. Leading indie bands like the Replacements, Soul Asylum, and R.E.M. who had skipped to major labels had gone for radio-friendly sounds and commercially oriented producers and mixers in an attempt to get their music to play to the mainstream, with varying commercial and artistic results. This wasn't out of the ordinary. Alt-rock was already sounding pretty slick.

This was also Vig's major label debut and he may have overcompensated slightly. "That record is pretty hacked up," Chris says. "Some songs were pretty straight ahead but a couple of songs were electronic sleight of hand. It's a really produced record." Occasionally, Vig would have to stitch together several different parts to get a complete performance, but the lion's share of slickness came from Andy Wallace. Vig's mixes sound positively naked in comparison to the final result. Wallace sweetened the sound, filtering the raw tracks through various special effects boxes, cranking out about one mix a day.

Between extra lodging, extra studio time and Wallace's fee, calling in Wallace doubled the budget of the record, which was still comparatively modest.

The original recording budget for *Nevermind* was about $65,000, but according to *Guitar World*'s Alan di Perna, it wound up costing about $130,000 (about $283,000 in 2023 dollars). And that was pretty typical for the first album by an alternative rock band—no one was expecting the record to go multiplatinum.

The band wasn't wild about Wallace's presence. "We'd get in and he'd play us his mix and he wasn't too kind to suggestions," Dave recalls. "He did a lot of tweaking of the drums, making them more digital-sounding. Everything had a produced weirdness. All we wanted to do was record these songs and get a record out because it had been so long since *Bleach* and we'd been playing these songs and they were great and we were excited and we wanted to record them before we got totally sick of them, which we already were. So it was just like, 'Let's get it over with.'"

Wallace probably wasn't wild about the *band's* presence either. It's not difficult to imagine how such a seasoned, successful veteran would downplay the band's input, especially a young band without any experience making major label records.

Part of the reason the album sounds so slick is the fact that the room miking of the drums didn't work out well, and so Wallace used digital reverb to fix the sound and further pumped up the drums with equalization and some samples that he blended in behind the kick drum and the snare. "He gave some real wide stereo separation using some doubling and delays on guitars and things," says Vig. "He put a little bit of gloss on the voice but I don't think he went too far with it. If anything, we wanted to make sure the mixes still sounded fairly organic." For all the studio tricks, Wallace didn't use as much as most pop albums.

Listening to the album now, it sounds as if the music were a jagged stone encased in Lucite. "That's Andy Wallace," Kurt says, adding that Geffen loved it that way because they were used to records like that. It was all for the best anyway, according to Kurt, "because it sold eight million records and now we're allowed to do whatever we want. It was part of the plan that we had to try to get on the radio and get our foot in the door and be able to do whatever we want for the rest of the time we're a band."

"We tried to have a fine line between being commercial and sounding alternative," says Chris.

"Looking back on the production of *Nevermind*, I'm embarrassed by it now," Kurt says. "It's closer to a Mötley Crüe record than it is a punk rock record."

So the fancy recording was "part of the plan" and yet "I'm embarrassed by it now."

It takes a whole lot more than just getting on the radio for a band to have the freedom to do whatever they want—they have to sell millions of copies, and no one could have anticipated that for Nirvana (except maybe Kurt). *Of course* Kurt was obligated to renounce the sound of *Nevermind*—no matter how relatively raw sounding the music might have been, his punk rock ethos meant he'd have to disavow an album that sold so phenomenally well.

#

During the recording, Kurt and Dave had seen a documentary on underwater birth, and Kurt mentioned it as a cover idea to Robert Fisher, an art director at Geffen. Fisher found some pictures of babies being born underwater but they were too graphic, so they settled for a stock photo of a swimming baby. Kurt joked they should add a fish hook with a dollar bill on it, and the idea stuck. Then

it transpired that the stock house that controlled the photograph wanted $7,500 a year for as long as the album was in print, so Fisher got underwater photographer Kirk Weddle to go down to a pool for babies and take some more shots.

The band chose one of five different photographs, with a shot of five-month-old Spencer Elden emerging as the winner. The only thing was, the baby's penis was quite visible. "If there's a problem with his dick," Fisher said, "we can cut it off."

As a journalist, you just live for quotations like that.

Some people in the Geffen/DGC sales department did worry that the traditionally conservative chain stores might object to the penis and Fisher even went so far as to begin preparing a cover with the penis airbrushed out. Kurt had anticipated some outcry as well, and had already composed some copy to put on a sticker over the problematic member. It read, "If you're offended by this, you must be a closet pedophile."

Spencer Elden's penis stayed on.

There was only slight umbrage taken at the naked infant. In April of 1992, a city code enforcement officer allegedly advised the Wild Planet record store in Ventura, California, to cover the baby's penis on a poster they had in the window. They used a pink Post-it note. "It's just weird that anybody should have a problem with a baby," says Chris.

What's missing from this picture? The alternate artwork for the *Nevermind* cover.
Photo by Kirk Weddle, courtesy Geffen Records

There were many different interpretations of the cover. Some thought the baby represented the band, and that swimming toward the dollar bill represented their sell-out. But the image probably appealed to Kurt because it echoed his ideas about recapturing his innocent childhood bliss; like many of his paintings, the cover symbolized the very moment when that bliss would begin to disappear. More overtly, the image also signaled a departure

Outtakes from the infamous underwater photo session.
© Kirk Weddle

from the acquisitive, yuppie '80s, a rejection of the materialism which backfired into junk bond scandals, corrupt savings and loan institutions, and a whole lot of repossessed BMWs. When the book of the '90s is written, the cover of *Nevermind* should be on the first page.

Sadly, that era of short-sighted greed and self-obsession lasted a lot longer than the '90s.

The interpretation that the baby on the cover represented Nirvana itself, grasping for the major label dollar, would make sense given Kurt's predilection for exaggerating things he feared he would be accused of—as he did with the name of his Creedence Clearwater Revival band, the various mocking references to selling out in their bios, T-shirts, and stage banter, even the fake track marks on his arm at the show in Olympia.

Then there was a photo shoot with Michael Lavine, who had flown out from New York. During the shoot, the band passed a bottle of whiskey around until they were all quite stewed. "Hurry up, take the photo before I pass out," Kurt begged Lavine.

Later on, the group did an underwater photo session in a pool with Kirk Weddle to play off the cover concept. The shoot turned into a Spinal Tap–style fiasco. "It was really stormy the weekend before and the pool got really clouded up," says Fisher, "and the pump broke two days before so the water was really cold and Kurt was really sick and they were hating being in the water. It was kind of a nightmare. Kurt had a hard time—it seemed like he had a real buoyancy problem—he'd kick and thrash and he'd still be on top of the water. He just couldn't submerge himself." Fisher eventually had to make a composite of three different shots to get something usable. The photo appeared in an ad campaign.

It's strange that Kurt couldn't manage to submerge himself—recall his former job as a swimming instructor.

The photo on the back of the album is from when Kurt was in a "bohemian photography stage" and features the ubiquitous Chim-Chim. Behind Chim-Chim is the meat-and-diseased-vagina collage that Kurt put on his refrigerator back in Olympia. Close inspection of the photo reveals a picture of Kiss a little bit above Chim-Chim's head.

The band's bio contained some hilarious whoppers. "Cobain, a sawblade painter specializing in wildlife and landscapes, met Novoselic at the Grays Harbor Institute of Northwest Crafts," the bio said. "Novoselic had a passion for gluing seashells and driftwood on burlap and, he remembers, 'I liked what Kurt was doing. I asked him what his thoughts were on a macaroni mobile I was

Kurt catching
forty winks by
the pool.
© Kirk Weddle

working on. He suggested I glue glitter on it. That really made it!' The incident
formed the basis of Nirvana's magic."

Later in the bio, Dave explains his first encounter with Kurt and Chris. "They
wore berets, sunglasses, sandals and had goatees. Chris walked around with
these poetry books by Rod McKuen and Kurt would do interpretive dances while
Chris recited."

"Our songs have the standard pop format: verse, chorus, verse, chorus, solo,
bad solo," Kurt said. "All in all, we sound like the Knack and the Bay City Rollers
being molested by Black Flag and Black Sabbath."

Those last two sentences were among the only accurate things in the entire bio. It was
pretty cheeky to put out a jokey press bio for their major label debut album, but no one
expected Nirvana to become as huge as they did, with the press and public hanging on
the band's every word. Instead, it would be taken seriously by countless mainstream
journalists who assumed that a press release from a massively popular band would be
at least vaguely truthful.

The joke backfired. "Yeah, it was funny," Kurt told me, "but it also added to the Sub
Pop redneck image which really wasn't something we were very fond of." Still, it was
useful for sorting out which interviewers were on the ball and which believed anything
they read in a band bio.

From the Michael Lavine session done toward the end of the *Nevermind* sessions.
© Michael Lavine

To his regret, that bio was also the seed of the feeling that Kurt didn't much like his own audience. "No one, especially people our own age, wants to address important issues," it quoted him as saying. "They'd rather say, 'Never mind, forget it.'"

Saw blade art really is a longtime staple of American rural folk art, especially in the Northwest, where used circular saw blades are naturally abundant. And the handicrafts angle ties in with the milieu Kurt wrote about in "Swap Meet." Krist dressing up like a beatnik and reciting poetry was actually not too far from the mark.

Rod McKuen was a cultural phenomenon in the late '60s through the '70s: a hugely bestselling, if critically savaged, poet, he was to poetry what Kenny G is to jazz. "His poetry is not even trash," wrote the former US poet laureate Karl Shapiro. As a 2015 NPR obituary put it, McKuen's work was "the cheeseburger to poetry's haute cuisine."

Still, McKuen had the last laugh: he won a Grammy, got two Oscar nominations, wrote countless bestselling books, was a guest on all the big talk shows, owned a hugely successful record label, and wrote songs that were recorded by Barbra Streisand, Frank Sinatra, Madonna, Waylon Jennings, Dolly Parton, Chet Baker, Johnny Cash, and Dusty Springfield, among many others.

Nirvana could probably relate to McKuen, though: poetry is the underground indie rock of literature—you're supposed to make niche art, and if you're lucky, barely survive on it. But not McKuen—he got very rich from his poetry and paid dearly for that. "The most unforgivable sin in the world," McKuen once said, "is to be a best-selling poet."

The Nirvana-McKuen connection resurfaced when Nirvana covered "Seasons in the Sun," which was McKuen's maudlin rewrite of a Jacques Brel song, "Le Moribond" ("The Dying One.") And much later, the connection resurfaced again . . . kind of. In a 2006 documentary on his life, the seventysomething McKuen claimed, "I did some writing with Kurt Cobain." But that does not seem to be true.

MELVIN
NIRVANA
DWARVES
DERELICTS

LL AGES! $8/$10

SAT
22
SEPT

chapter eight and a half

IT FELT AS IF
WE COULDN'T
BE STOPPED

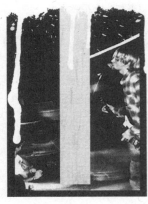

n mid-June, right after the record was finished, they landed an opening slot on a quickie eight-date West Coast tour with Dinosaur Jr. Shelli worked at the T-shirt stand. As the tour wound through Denver, L.A., and Santa Cruz, it began to seem like people were more excited about Nirvana than the headliner.

With an identical power trio lineup and burly, loud music that foregrounded powerful melodies, Dinosaur Jr was as stylistically close to Nirvana as any band of the time; Kurt admired Dinosaur Jr and especially its leader J Mascis, who, like Kurt, quietly maintained great control over virtually every aspect of his band.

In August, Nirvana opened for their heroes, Sonic Youth, on a European festival tour. "That was a wild tour," Chris says. "We got in a lot of trouble. Busting stuff up. Drunk, getting kicked out of clubs." Chris would know. He missed Shelli and he was homesick, and he'd get very drunk and disorderly on the tour. Eventually, John Silva called Shelli and asked her to talk to Chris. It worked a little bit, but finally, Shelli simply flew to Europe and kept Chris company, earning her keep by working at the T-shirt stand again.

Sonic Youth had made sure that their new favorite band was on the tour, smoothing the way for Nirvana with promoters and generally making sure they were well taken care of. They were by the side of the stage at every show, checking them out. If Kurt jumped off the stage, Sonic Youth's Thurston Moore would often be the one to haul him back up again.

Mostly, it was an idyllic time. Various members of Nirvana, Sonic Youth, and Dinosaur Jr all hung out together and laughed and drank and gossiped and talked about music and no one was a global superstar yet. Nirvana was playing festivals for the first time. They were curious and enthusiastic about what lay before them. "The most exciting time for a band is right before they become really popular," Kurt says. "I'd love to be in bands that just do that every two years. Every time I look back at the best times in this band it was right before *Nevermind* came out. It was awesome. That's when the band is at its best—they're really trying hard and there's so much excitement in the air you can just taste it."

Fender Frontline's Chuck Crisafulli asked Kurt about the relationship between composing songs and performing them live. "The real core of any tenderness or rage is tapped the very second that a song is written," Kurt replied. "In a sense, I'm only recreating the purity of that particular emotion every time I play that particular song. While it gets easier to summon those emotions with experience, it's a sort of dishonesty that you can never recapture the emotion of a song completely each time you play it." Maybe that's what he was referring to in "On a Plain": "The finest day that I've ever had / Was when I learned to cry on command" sounds like it's about the ability to sing with emotional force even when not actually experiencing the emotion that prompted the song—or, as singer-songwriter Freedy Johnston described the recording process, "trying to cry with the red light on."

Likewise, successful musicians are expected to simulate the purity of their original inspiration night after night in a grueling, endless *Groundhog Day* of identical arenas, mind-numbing interstates, and soulless chain hotel rooms.

A lot of artists are like that—the process of creating is mainly what excites them. Recall how Kurt would make those cool sculptures at his place in Olympia and then destroy them rather than put them on display. Those sculptures were finished; they served no purpose anymore. Imagine completing a crossword puzzle and then admiring it every day for years. Maybe that's why Kurt would intentionally screw up songs: to try to keep them in the present, in a state of creation rather than a state of reproduction.

As the great composer and bassist Charles Mingus put it to journalist Nat Hentoff, "I'm trying to play the truth of what I am. The reason it's difficult is because I'm changing all the time."

The band drank a lot. Part of their contract specified one bottle of vodka and one bottle of Glenfiddich at every show. Dave didn't actually drink much at first, but Chris would drain the Glenfiddich and Kurt and his buddy Ian Dickson, whom he brought along for the ride, would split the vodka. Eventually, even Dave broke down and would swig on a bottle of red wine during the drumless "Polly." "You stick all this free alcohol in front of people night after night and you get bored waiting around and you think, 'Oh, maybe I'll have a drink,'" says tour manager Alex Macleod. "And things go downhill from there."

Early in the tour at England's mammoth Reading Festival, Courtney, Kat Bjelland, and Kim Gordon were sitting in one of the trailers backstage, drinking whiskey and talking about Kurt. Filmmaker Dave Markey, shooting footage for what would become the documentary film *1991: The Year That Punk Broke*, stuck a camera in the door and Courtney stared straight into the lens and said, "Kurt Cobain makes my heart stop. But he's a shit," and walked away.

Turns out that that "he's a shit" comment was not in *1991: The Year That Punk Broke* or any of the outtakes that I can find. Dave Markey confirms this.

It would have been unseemly for Courtney to say that since, at the time, she was swanning around with Billy Corgan—as Thurston Moore gleefully exclaims for Markey's camera, "Courtney is in love with the singer from Smashing Pumpkins!" Not that people don't become attracted to people who aren't their partner—especially Courtney, who acknowledged to journalist Craig Marks for his 1994 *Spin* profile of her that, until she met Kurt, she had a "cheating problem."

So where did I get the "he's a shit" thing? Sometimes I get things wrong—but I never make things up. But I just can't remember where I saw this footage. One possibility is that Courtney fed the story to me. But then where would I get the visual imagery of "star[ing] straight into the lens" and walking away? I may never know the answer. And that really bothers me.

And then at least three other Nirvana-related books repeated the apparent error and gratuitously introduced their *own* errors.

Later, Courtney, Kurt, Mudhoney's Mark Arm and Dan Peters, and *Melody Maker* writer Everett True were indulging in some innocent backstage vandalism. Peters flung a big bottle of oil and it leaked, dousing Courtney's face and hair. Embarrassed, she ran away in tears—it reminded her of the humiliation she used to feel in school. That night, they were all watching Iggy Pop's set by the side of the stage and Kurt whispered in Courtney's ear, "I would never have picked on you in high school." "It was like he had ESP or something," says Courtney.

Kurt admits to plenty of bruises for his efforts, but he says he never really hurt himself by hurling his body into the drum set until he slightly dislocated his shoulder at Reading that year. "I have this protective shield around me that stops me from getting hurt," he half jokes.

"I would never have picked on you in high school." Of course, Kurt had been picked on in high school, too. He knew exactly what was going through Courtney's mind because he'd experienced it himself. That's one of the things that bonded them.

Aside from dislocating his shoulder at the 1991 Reading Festival, it really is kind of amazing that out of the scores, maybe hundreds, of times he violently hurled himself into the drum kit, Kurt apparently never broke something or impaled himself on a cymbal stand. During an interview with MTV after the Reading set, he repeatedly used that arm and said, "Whoops, I'm supposed to be hurt," cavalierly downplaying a fairly serious injury. That was the aspiring stuntman in him—or testament to the charmed, impervious state he reached through playing music.

By this time, the band had sorted out their talking point about signing to a major label. "What's wrong with a band that has good music, like Sonic Youth or Dinosaur Jr, to be readily available to people to buy—like, totally promoted—instead of most of the garbage that's out there," Krist told MTV News. "It's a crime, the total sappy junk that's pushed down people's throats."

At that same interview, Kurt took the opportunity to do a little myth construction. When asked, "What were you listening to growing up?" Kurt replied, "First it was the Beatles and then it was punk rock. That's about it." Of course, that wasn't "about it" at all—once again, Kurt had completely elided his metal roots.

By the time of the 1992 Reading Festival, they had gotten it down to a science, piling up the equipment with special care, then knocking it all down with gleeful malice for a good fifteen minutes after every show.

"It got to the point where it was like, people see the 'Lithium' video and that's three minutes of the ultimate Nirvana experience—we're rocking out, the crowd's going nuts, shit's getting broken—this is what it's like to see Nirvana play," says Dave. "From then on, everywhere we go, we walk offstage and we haven't smashed anything and people are like, 'What's your problem? Where's *Nirvana*?' So then it got to the point where it became a parody where everybody expects us to do this, so you might as well make fun of it. So you set things up and you set this on top of this and set this over there and do everything methodically."

The instrument smashing had become like playing the same songs over and over again: "a parody where everybody expects us to do this."

Later on the summer '91 festival tour, Kurt, Chris, Dave, Courtney, her then-boyfriend Billy Corgan of Smashing Pumpkins, and a few others went out to a club in London. Kurt boasted to Courtney, "I'm going to be a rock star soon."

"You are not."

"Yes I am. I'm going to be a big rock star. I'm going to buy antiques—really *expensive* antiques for my *wife*."

This all makes sense—Kurt, self-conscious about his provincial lack of refinement, trying to impress the far more cultured Courtney by touting something as stereotypically "classy" as "expensive antiques."

That night, Kurt went home with two English girls, very out of character. "I hope you get *fucked*!" Courtney called out to him as he left. As it happens, he didn't.

Nirvana played a Belgian festival called Pukkelpop, which translates as "Zit-pop." Nirvana's set began at eleven in the morning, but that wasn't too early for the band to get drunk before the show. "And," as Alex Macleod says, "things went downhill from there."

The band switched around all the name tags on the dinner tables backstage, so that the Ramones and their entourage of twelve were seated at a table for two which was meant for then-Pixies leader Black Francis and his girlfriend. Even John Silva got into the act and started a food fight.

Kurt was walking around with a Black Francis name tag stuck to his chest all day and by seven o'clock in the evening had built up quite a head of steam. While Black Francis played his solo set, Kurt spied a fire extinguisher by the side of the stage and started hosing down Black Francis. A horde of security men dashed toward Kurt as he dropped the hose and ran for his life.

As Sonic Youth once put it, "kill yr idols."

One country where Nirvana didn't do as well as it could have is Germany. During the European summer festival tour with Sonic Youth, they played a show in Bremen. A woman from the German branch of MCA, Geffen's parent company, stopped by and presented the band with a garbage can with a talking basketball hoop on it that made a crowd noise after every basket. It was filled with candy and American magazines and had a cheerful little card that read "Welcome to Germany and MCA!"

By this point, the band was fully dedicated to completely destroying their dressing room every night of the tour. The German MCA rep walked in after Nirvana's set to witness the band, falling-down drunk, trashing their dressing room and throwing all her gifts all over the place. Meanwhile, sometime during the show, Sonic Youth's Kim Gordon had found the note on the garbage can and written "Fuck you!" on it. The MCA rep saw this and assumed the band had written it to her; then Chris shot off a fire extinguisher. As Alex Macleod puts it, "It all went downhill from there."

It's no accident that one of Macleod's favorite phrases was "it all went downhill from there."

Later that evening, while sitting in the tour bus doing interviews, Kurt was playing with a lighter and managed to set the curtains on fire. They quickly doused them with some water, but seconds later, the same MCA rep knocked on the door and was greeted by Kurt, who was enveloped in a cloud of putrid smoke from the curtains; she walked off in a huff (somehow the English music press reported that the band had burned down their bus).

That night they got an apoplectic phone call from John Silva. "You guys have got to take it easy! What did you do?"

"We thought we were dropped," Dave says. "We were going 'All right, we got our advance and we've already been dropped! *Wooooo!*'"

Kurt's Great Rock & Roll Swindle fantasy had almost come true without anybody even trying.

The band got drunk before their set at the final show of the tour in Rotterdam. Chris climbed up the P.A. stack at the end of the set, with his trousers around his ankles and a bottle in his hand. Security ran onstage and hauled him down while Kurt trashed everything in sight. One of the security men took a swing at Chris and a brawl broke out right on stage. Chris eventually got thrown out of the venue and came back and started a fight with the promoter.

As it turns out, the description of Krist's antics is just a tiny patch on what actually happened.

Some backstory that I didn't know was that at this festival Nirvana had to play a smaller second stage, separate from their friends Sonic Youth, who played the main stage. To add insult to injury, the Smashing Pumpkins, whom nobody seemed to like, inexplicably got to play the main stage. It didn't help that Kurt and Billy Corgan's artistic rivalry might also become a romantic one. Understandably, Nirvana was a bit peeved about all this.

Since this was the final show of the tour, the members of Nirvana got hammered before they played.

As they close with "Negative Creep," Kurt throws his guitar right at Dave, who dodges the missile and keeps playing. But then Kurt jumps onto the drum riser, stands on the snare drum, and knocks over the entire kit, then begins bashing the bass drum with a cymbal stand, as Dave takes the mike and in a stagey announcer voice, bellows, "Thank you! Thank you! You've been a really wonderful audience! No, thank you!"

Then Kurt spreads his arms, pretending to be a bird and "flies" right into a massive amplifier, which falls over, narrowly missing his arm; he starts bashing his head hard into the speaker grille. Krist has been playing some doofy little tune on the bass the whole time—until Kurt tackles him, whereupon Krist does his patented high-altitude bass toss and actually catches it.

For some reason, the PA system is now playing giddy Greek folk music.

Kurt continues his rampage; not to be outdone, Krist lies down on the stage and pulls down his trousers while Kurt continues to smash everything in sight with a cymbal stand.

Then a bunch of security guys, dressed all in white and looking like, fittingly, orderlies from a psychiatric hospital, march onstage and start to manhandle Kurt. One of them puts his hands around Kurt's neck, and Alex Macleod jumps right in and single-handedly barks them all away without even touching them. (As stated, he was an excellent tour manager.) Kurt continues to trash the equipment until, eventually, one of the security guys gently walks him off into the wings. It's actually really uncomfortable to watch: they weren't just destroying their instruments, their music, and their connection to their fans; they were seemingly destroying themselves.

###

The band went home for a while, then went down to L.A. to shoot the "Teen Spirit" video. Kurt worked up a treatment for the video, which originally included vignettes resembling something out of the Ramones movie *Rock 'n' Roll High School*, or perhaps more like *Over the Edge*, an excellent 1979 movie about a band of crazed juvenile delinquents who smoke pot, drink, and vandalize a Southern California suburb. In the finale, their parents hold a meeting at the high school, but soon the local kids lock them inside, smash their cars, and set the building on fire. "That [movie] pretty much defined my whole personality," says Kurt. "It was really cool. Total anarchy."

Over the Edge was widely released in 1981, when Kurt was fourteen, just like a lot of the kids in the film. Set in a bland, remote community somewhere out west, it's basically a teen revenge fantasy: cool, alienated kids versus abusive cops and oblivious parents. Acting out against neglect and boredom, virtually every kid in the movie does drugs, trashes stuff, or both, just like in Aberdeen—and countless other towns all across America.

Kurt must have loved the movie from the opening shot, whose crawl text begins, "In 1978, 110,000 kids under 18 were arrested for crimes of vandalism in the United States" and soon gives way to a scene of two teenage boys shooting a BB gun at a police car. Some graffiti scrawled on the side of the high school says "Jocks are fags," and the soundtrack featured Cheap Trick, the Cars, and the Ramones. The movie ends (spoiler alert) in a spectacular act of mass violence involving the destruction of the high school. Clearly, someone had made a movie just for Kurt Cobain.

The video was shot for a modest $33,000 on a Culver City, California, soundstage made up to look like a high school gym, or what Dave fondly calls a "pep rally from hell." The janitor was played by Rudy Larosa, who was actually the janitor in director Sam Bayer's apartment building. Kurt had envisioned another type of gym—"It looked too contemporary," he says—and the backdrop bugged him, too. It reminded him of those bland backdrops used in aspirin commercials or Time-Life infomercials.

Kurt had other ideas for the clip—he wanted all the kids to run outside and start smashing things up and ruining cars. He wanted to have everyone in the audience come down and empty out their wallets into a big bonfire. He wanted to have a bonfire inside the gymnasium and burn some effigies. The last shot of the video, in which the janitor walks by a bound-and-gagged principal, was originally part of a larger scenario, but it got axed early on in the editing process.

Pretty much everything in the preceding paragraph is taken from *Over the Edge*.

The scene in the video actually involved a bound-and-gagged *schoolteacher*, not a principal, and it was part of a larger scenario that Kurt personally asked to be eliminated in the editing process.

Kurt had written a treatment for this video that was fairly close to what was actually filmed. The original plan was to start with the band strolling through a mall, throwing money in the air as shoppers scramble to snatch it up, then smashing up a jewelry store in an act of "anti-materialist fueled punk rock violence." Then the action moves to what actually got filmed: a high school pep rally with anarchy symbol–sporting cheerleaders and a custodian, the scene descending into glorious chaos.

The custodian and the cheerleaders were symbolic. In a journal entry made somewhere around this time, Kurt outlined his rationale for signing with a major: it was a way to subvert the status quo and foment revolution. "We can pose as the enemy to infiltrate the mechanics of the system to start its rot from the inside," he wrote. "It's an inside job—it starts with the custodians and the cheerleaders," in other words, with oppressed groups such as working people and women.

The "too contemporary" gym and the generic gray backdrops—which really were a staple of '90s mainstream television commercials and documentary interviews—are another example of the band's rough-and-ready punk rock sensibility colliding with major label sheen. In that light, the "Smells Like Teen Spirit" video is an analogue of *Nevermind*'s gritty core and glossy finish.

"The band now has an image: the anti-gluttony, materialism and consumerism image," Kurt wrote in his journals, "which we plan to incorporate into all of our videos." But that ambitious agenda pretty much began and ended with the video for "Smells Like Teen Spirit."

The cheerleaders were Kurt's idea. "But I wanted really ugly overweight cheerleaders," he says, "and a couple of guys, too, just because I'm sickened by the stereotypical prom queen."

Bayer vetoed the ideas. The band nicknamed him "Jethro Napoleon." "He's got a little Napoleon complex," Kurt says of the diminutive Bayer. "He was just so hyper, such a rocker guy. I just couldn't believe it. I couldn't believe we actually submitted to that."

Later, somewhere on the touring trail, Kurt and Krist were interviewed by MTV Europe backstage at a festival.

Interviewer: [Video] is a medium that is difficult for a band to have control over because the video is in the hands of the director.
Krist: Not with Kurt Cobain around.
Kurt [sarcastically]: Yeah, I'm a little Napoleon.

But, "Jethro Napoleon" is precisely what Nirvana called Sam Bayer—another example of Kurt altering the facts so he could attack an antagonist and aggrandize himself.

At one point during the shoot Bayer shouted, "All right, I'm going to lose my audience right now if everybody doesn't shut up!" And everybody in the audience went, "*Oooooo*," openly laughing at Bayer and heckling him. "It was just like we were in school," says Kurt, smiling. "He was the mean teacher."

"But by the end of the day," Kurt says, a mischievous sparkle in his eye, "we were having fun."

Kurt wanted everyone to come down from the bleachers and mosh. Bayer didn't like the idea but Kurt eventually talked him into it. And anarchy did eventually reign on the set. "Nobody knock anything over until I tell you because I want to get good close-up shots of it," Bayer told the assembled crowd, which had gathered after the band had announced just the day before on KXLU, a local college radio station, that they needed an audience for their video shoot. But after hours and hours of sitting around just watching the tedious goings-on, the audience was ready to explode. When they finally got to come down out of the bleachers, everybody started flipping out and knocking things over and running amok. People were mobbing Kurt and stealing Chris's guitar and Dave's cymbals. "Once the kids came out dancing they just said 'Fuck you,' because they were so tired of his shit throughout the day," Kurt says. The video's sense of joyous rebellion was for real.

Chris was having fun the whole time. He had brought a liter of Jim Beam to the set and had that and some pot with his friends during the lengthy waits between takes. Halfway through the shoot he passed out, then woke up just in time for the next take.

Kurt didn't like the edit Bayer had done, so he personally oversaw a new cut of the video. Over Bayer's protests, he added the next-to-last shot, a close-up of Kurt's face. It was a brilliant move—throughout the video, Kurt had come off as an intense but shy character, hiding behind his hair. It amounted to a tease, and the close-up was the payoff—he was not bad-looking (if he would only wash his hair).

For all its "alternative" overtones, "Teen Spirit" has all the classic elements of video: pretty girls in revealing clothes, kids dancing the latest dance and flaunting the latest fashions, the requisite dry-ice fog, guys with long hair playing guitars—kids getting off on kids' music. The point was that for the first time, the trappings were updated for a new generation—the flannel shirts, the moshing, the tattoos and anarchy symbols. The correlation with Nirvana's music—not stylistically trailblazing yet powerful and classic—is clear.

To give an idea of their schedule at the time, the morning after the shoot, they took a red-eye from Los Angeles to London, got directly onto a bus to Wales, then a ferry to Ireland, and played ten shows in twelve days in five countries, plus photo shoots and interviews. By September 3, they were in London, where they played their third session for BBC DJ John Peel. They were completely exhausted. And on that Peel session, it sounds like it.

Then came the infamous *Nevermind* release party, September 13, 1991, at Seattle's trendy Re-bar club. The band was told it would be a low-key affair and that they could invite their friends. They arrived to find the walls of the club plastered with Nirvana posters. They had to schmooze with all kinds of dull music biz types and endure hearing their album played twice in a row. Kurt especially found all the attention embarrassing, especially in front of his Olympia friends.

Because of Washington state's harsh alcohol laws, there wasn't any hard liquor available, so someone smuggled in a half gallon bottle of whiskey and hid it in the photo booth, where those in the know retired for a quick snort of Jim Beam. Soon everyone was quite plowed. They got DJ Bruce Pavitt to ditch *Nevermind* and play the trashiest new wave and disco music they could find.

Nevermind Triskaidekaphobia, Here's Nirvana

On Friday the 13th, join Nirvana and DGC Records for a release party in honor of Nirvana's DGC debut album <u>Nevermind</u>.

Friday, September 13
Re-bar
1114 Howell
Seattle, WA
(206) 233-9873
6:00 PM to 8:00 PM

Edible food, drinks, prizes you might want to take home, a few surprises, people to meet, the band to greet....But nevermind all that, the important part is the music. Hear <u>Nevermind</u> in its entirety and loud.

This invitation admits you and a guest only, and must be presented at the door. Space is limited. 21 & over with I.D.

DAVID GEFFEN COMPANY
© 1991 The David Geffen Company

After the band finished ripping all the posters off the walls, Chris heaved a tamale at Kurt and Dylan Carlson. Kurt remembers retaliating with a salvo of guacamole. ("Actually, it was a Green Goddess herb dip," corrects Nirvana fan club president Nils Bernstein, who catered the party.) Soon, food was flying everywhere, with no regard for the industry geeks whose suits were getting splattered with food. And that was when Nirvana got kicked out of their own record release party.

Who among us hasn't mistaken Green Goddess herb dip for guacamole? It's perhaps worth noting that party caterer Nils Bernstein, after a long career as a beloved music publicist, is now a very successful food writer.

They all piled into a Cadillac that Geffen/DGC Northwest promo woman Susie Tennant had rented for the occasion and the party raged on into the wee hours of the morning at her house. As everyone was leaving, Bruce Pavitt was down on the street, sitting on the curb and puking into the gutter as he waited for a cab. Kurt took this opportunity to lean out the window and pelt him with eggs.

Oh, sweet revenge. Only Pavitt denies it actually happened. So that's one more example of Kurt making up a self-serving myth to retaliate against a perceived antagonist. Some gratitude for DJing the party!

That party at Susie Tennant's place raged deep into the night. One highlight was Kurt finding a slingshot that Geffen had used as a promotional item, loading it up with one of Tennant's lipstick tubes, and firing it through the glass of a gold record award for their labelmates, pop-metal band Nelson.

As with the in-store appearance coming up, the band was embarrassed by the trappings of being on a major label, not to mention being overwhelmed by the adulation of fans, and proceeded to get wasted and out of control in an apparent attempt to blot the whole situation out of their minds.

Everyone knew they had a good album, but the plan was that if the management worked really, really hard and the label worked really, really hard and the band worked really, really hard, then maybe—just maybe—they could have a gold record by September of 1992.

The band got an inkling of things to come at an in-store appearance at Beehive Records in Seattle's University District. The band played a set to a packed house and afterward were besieged by autograph seekers. "There were all these weird, fawning people," recalls Dylan Carlson, who happened to work there. "These three guys from the Green River Community College radio station,

Kurt was talking to them and telling them about Bikini Kill and how they should listen to them. These three guys didn't want to hear that. They just wanted to talk to Kurt and to touch Kurt and get an autograph." Then a couple of "geeks" (Kurt's word) whom Kurt remembered from Montesano showed up. "I realized that if people you went to high school with—especially in Montesano—were aware that I was a rock star in Seattle, then it was getting kind of big," Kurt says. Afterward, Chris, Kurt, Dave, and a small group of friends retreated to a bar and got promptly and thoroughly trashed.

Then it was off to Toronto to begin a headlining tour, which kicked off September 20, four days before *Nevermind* was released. Along for the ride on different legs of the tour were opening bands the Melvins on the East Coast and Canada, Das Damen and Urge Overkill in the south and Midwest and Sister Double Happiness on the West Coast. For the occasion, Kurt put a sticker on his guitar that read "VANDALISM: BEAUTIFUL AS A ROCK IN A COP'S FACE" ("Corn on the cops! Corn on the cops!").

As he watched Kurt get off the plane, tour manager Monty Lee Wilkes remembers thinking to himself, "There's something not right about this guy."

A guitar with that "VANDALISM: BEAUTIFUL AS A ROCK IN A COP'S FACE" bumper sticker appears in a lot of photos of Kurt. The sticker was made by the Feederz, a deeply provocative Phoenix, Arizona, punk band. "Vandalism: beautiful as a rock in a cop's face," delivered in singer Frank Discussion's ethereal falsetto, is the opening line of the Feederz song "Gut Rage" from their 1983 album *Ever Feel Like Killing Your Boss?* (which also features the immortal "Burn Warehouse Burn": "Sorry, mom, can't do my chores / It's too much fun setting fire to stores").

The Feederz specialized in media pranks, which they called "anti-public relations." A classic was sending out a letter to every student in a certain Arizona school district, on the Arizona Department of Education letterhead, that began, "Well, school is boring. It's no secret that a lot of you feel that you are wasting your time here. You feel you are spending years of commuting to the boredom of school to prepare yourselves for a life of dull, meaningless tasks. But that's the way life is, and that's the way it has always been." One can only imagine how much Kurt loved stuff like this.

And it's very likely that Kurt thought the same. Right off the bat, Wilkes's "rock dude" poodle haircut marked him as something of an outsider. "I don't fit into that whole scene," Wilkes says. "I'm organized, I'm clean, I wear clean clothes every day, I take a bath once a day. They don't like me."

Chris rocking the Beehive record store. Looking on are Susie Tennant (white shorts) and Dylan Carlson (to her left). © Charles Peterson

I feel a little bad about how I portrayed Monty Lee Wilkes. He was, by all accounts, a consummate professional; he just got dealt a very challenging, very thankless hand by being Nirvana's tour manager at the very peak of their bad behavior, not to mention the peak of Nirvanamania.

For years, Wilkes had performed similar duties for the Replacements, so he was pretty unimpressed by Nirvana's antics; he'd already seen it all, and then some. That probably accounts for one story about him: on tour one night, Nirvana trashed the TV in their room. Wilkes scolded them, and Kurt protested that they would have done the classic bad-boy rock band thing and heaved it out the window—but they couldn't get the window to open. To which Wilkes replied, "Yeah? Well, a *real* punk band would've thrown it *through* the window."

In retrospect, it seems like Wilkes's resolute, all-too-compromising professionalism was yet another unwelcome reminder to the band that Nirvana was now literally serious business.

Wilkes was very good at his job and went on to mix live sound for Prince, Britney Spears, the Beastie Boys, Björk, and many others. For decades, since the '80s, he was also the front-of-house mixer for the legendary First Avenue club in Minneapolis.

The Amplified Come as You Are

Monty Lee Wilkes died of cancer in 2016; he was only fifty-four. He is one of the few nonmusicians to earn a star on the wall outside First Avenue, up there with Prince, R.E.M., James Brown, Radiohead, the Kinks, U2, Fela Kuti, and . . . Nirvana.

There seems to be little doubt that the guys in the band delighted in giving Wilkes a hard time. "Everything you fix," says Wilkes, "a guy like Kurt goes and deliberately unfixes it because he's a cutie pie, you know?" The running joke among the crew was to see whether Wilkes was wearing the same shirt he was the previous day, because that meant he'd been up all night taking care of all the screw-ups the band had created. Furthermore, the beleaguered Wilkes was not only the tour manager of an extremely chaotic tour, he was also the tour accountant and production manager, besides being the soundman for the first half of the tour and the lighting designer for the second. "Toward the end of that tour," he says, "I was throwing up blood from being stressed out."

"Everything you fix, a guy like Kurt goes and deliberately unfixes it." It's easy to glide right by that line, but "unfixing" things wasn't simply Kurt being an asshole—as ever, he deliberately sabotaged things to keep it interesting, to keep things in a state of becoming, as opposed to boring old completion.

One of the Who's early managers, Kit Lambert, once explained the band's instrument smashing to veteran English rock manager Simon Napier-Bell: "The purpose of success is to have something substantial to wreck, and the ultimate triumph is to create a magnificent disaster."

Wilkes carried around a road case which unfolded into a portable office, complete with Macintosh desktop and laptop computers, fax, modem, printer ("always loaded with paper," he boasts), office supplies, books, forms, and a telephone. Wilkes denies claims of color-coded paper clips. "Funny joke," he sneers. "That's completely untrue." He does, however, cop to the color-coded pens. "I'm a very organized person," he explains.

One of the things that had made Kurt and Chris unhappy with Sub Pop was the fact they did only a handful of interviews the whole time they were on the label. They mentioned this to the Geffen/DGC publicity department, who proceeded to arrange up to a half-dozen interviews a day for each member of the band while they were on tour. After two months of journalists asking things like "Why did you sign to a major?" or "Why did you put a baby on the cover of the record?" it became a grind.

"We did so many interviews blindly, just walking into radio stations and doing unnecessary interviews with metal magazines, anything," says Kurt. "It

was a nice education to make us realize we have to know what magazine we're doing an interview for before we just blindly do it." Two months later, all those magazines came out at once, producing a gigantic Nirvana media blitz. "We thought that most of these interviews would just die off into obscurity," Kurt says. "We thought we needed to do all these interviews to maybe sell a hundred thousand records."

They'd ferret out which interviewers were on the ball by seeing who fell for the bogus stories about Kurt and Chris meeting in arts and crafts class. Once they found a sucker, they'd go to town.

Once a band gets to a certain level, touring isn't just the same old tedium. It's the same *new* tedium. Now, on top of everything else, it's waking up early for a radio station appearance, dealing with meeting all the people at the station, and answering the same interview questions day after day; it's doing meet-and-greets with fans, meeting local reps from your label, and being nice to them no matter what they're like or how tired, hungry, or sick you are; it's doing press interviews, which are grueling whether the interviews are good or bad. This is all particularly exhausting if you're an introvert under a microscope.

Kurt and Dave roomed together during the tour and one night, Dave was in bed watching TV when he heard Kurt giggling and giggling in the bathroom. Finally, Dave asked, "What are you *doing*?" Kurt had shaved off all of his goatee except for the mustache. When he walked out of the bathroom to show Dave, he was still giggling, but he stopped long enough to share the joke. "I look like my father!"

Early in the tour, an MTV News crew showed up to do a shoot on the band before soundcheck in a bar adjacent to the Axis club in Boston. To help things along, someone had provided a Twister game and a can of Crisco vegetable shortening. Chris got into it the most, stripping down to his jockey shorts (dark blue) and slathering himself with the Crisco before starting the game. They had just started when Chris suddenly pulled up the Twister board and threw it away, then wiped the grease off his body with an American flag that happened to be hanging on a nearby wall—some of the gook had found its way down the crack of his butt and so he wiped it from there, too. An ex-Marine and his beefy buddies who happened to be looking on took exception to Chris's taste in toilet paper and began screaming at him and Chris had to be escorted out of the club.

On that day, September 24, 1991, *Nevermind* was released and 46,251 copies were shipped to stores around the country.

###

After a Pittsburgh show, there was a dispute about T-shirt sales with the promoter. The band trashed their dressing room—nothing new—and left. Later, in the wee hours of the morning, two agents of the city arson squad banged on Monty Lee Wilkes's door and began questioning him. It seems someone had set a couch on fire backstage at the club and they seemed to think a member of Nirvana had done it. After a long conversation, Wilkes convinced the agents that the band had left the club by the time the fire was set. "It gave me a whole new outlook on the whole goddamn thing and it made me wonder just what the fuck I'd gotten myself into," says Wilkes.

Kurt and Chris at City Gardens in Trenton, New Jersey. © Stephan Apicella-Hitchcock

After a show at the 40 Watt Club in Athens, Georgia, the band staged a little mutiny. They were supposed to drive to Atlanta so they could do a press day, but instead refused Wilkes's pleas and partied at R.E.M. guitarist Peter Buck's house all night. Of course, it was Wilkes who got the brunt of John Silva's wrath.

By this time, the tour had picked up opening band Urge Overkill, a much beloved indie band from Chicago. The guys in Urge Overkill were blown away by the force of Nirvana's music, but also by their unstated yet clear message. "It was fuck the government, fuck the status quo and the stupid people," says the band's Ed "King" Roeser. "And you can extend the whole philosophy to antiracism, antisexism, antifascism, anticensorship, etc. Somehow that message got across to the people at these shows."

What a testament to Nirvana that those things came through in their music without their explicitly saying them.

Urge Overkill had several parallels with Nirvana. Steve Albini recorded two of their albums, including the indie classic *The Supersonic Storybook* (1991), and Butch Vig produced one (1990's *Americruiser*). Like Nirvana, they left a great regional indie (in Urge's case, Chicago's Touch & Go) and signed with DGC, where they released, as with *Nevermind*, a killer alternative rock album (1993's *Saturation*) that was much glossier and catchier than their previous releases.

But at that point, the two bands' fortunes diverged: *Saturation* wasn't terribly successful, and the indie community condemned Urge for going major; their now ex-friend Steve Albini called them "freakish, attention-starved megalomaniacs." The band got a little vindication in 1994, when director Quentin Tarantino put their cover of Neil Diamond's creepy 1967 hit "Girl, You'll Be a Woman Soon" on the *Pulp Fiction* soundtrack and it became a modest hit.

And then Urge Overkill echoed Nirvana again: after a second album for DGC (1995's *Exit the Dragon*), they quickly descended into a toxic haze of drugs and infighting and fell off the musical map. (The band restarted in 2004.)

Kurt audience-surfing at the Marquee in New York.
© Kristin Callahan/London Features

The Amplified Come as You Are

Courtney heard from the manager of the 40 Watt Club that Kurt couldn't stop talking about her. This was too good to believe. So she began calling Dave on tour. When they finished talking, she'd ask to speak to Kurt. After a couple of days, they began to really hit it off, and eventually, Courtney wouldn't even bother talking to Dave first.

Monitor man and drum tech Myles Kennedy was astounded by the force of Dave's playing. "Just by playing so hard, he'd break drum thrones," he says. "There were just piles of sawdust on the drum riser from his drumsticks. He was just an animal."

Dave at the Marquee.
© Kristin Callahan/London Features

A couple of times on Nirvana's final US tour, Dave let me sit directly behind him, out of sight, onstage. He hit very hard; with those lanky limbs, it was like his body was specifically engineered to hit drums with a high degree of impact. Even his kit, with its oversized drums and cymbals, was set up so he could hit it as hard as possible. He played with the blunt end of the stick, which is like playing with billy clubs, and they had to duct-tape the cymbal stands to the stage so he wouldn't knock them over.

Dave's drum set lasted about halfway through the tour, until an October 12 gig at the Cabaret Metro in Chicago when the band destroyed it after a particularly good set. "There was nothing left any bigger than a six-inch circle of wood from the kick drum," says Wilkes.

"That's just what happened when they got so much energy and emotion worked up playing their set that it was the only way they could come to a good close," says Myles Kennedy.

It Felt as if We Couldn't Be Stopped

By that point, Kurt had axed Dave's drums with his guitar so many times that there were gashes in the shells, and the kit was sounding really bad. Dave was desperate for a fresh kit but their tour manager kept putting off his pleas for a new one. Finally, they figured that if they completely destroyed the drum set, "the grown-ups" would surely have to buy them a new one. Unfortunately, it didn't work out that way, and Dave had to borrow opener Urge Overkill's kit for the rest of the tour.

It also happened to be the day that *Nevermind* debuted on the Billboard album charts at a respectable #144.

That night, Courtney showed up at a party after the gig. Legend has it that she and Kurt had sex up against the bar. "God," Kurt says with a laugh, "that's so disgusting. Right—everyone was around in a circle, watching us fuck. You've *got* to put it in the book that we didn't fuck." They did kiss for the first time and Courtney ran out to a pay phone to tell a friend in L.A. The rest of the night, they wrestled on the floor and threw glasses at each other. Courtney had a bag of lingerie with her for some reason and Kurt ended up modeling the contents. They got kicked out of the place twice.

Dave was asleep by the time Kurt and Courtney shambled drunkenly into Kurt and Dave's hotel room and started making loud and passionate love on the bed next to Dave's. "I tried to ignore it but I couldn't," Dave says. "I had. To leave. The room." He wound up knocking on soundman Craig Montgomery's door and sleeping there for the night.

###

Nevermind had begun blowing out of the stores immediately, but out on the road, no one in the band really realized what was going on. Weeks went by before someone told Kurt that the album was selling and MTV was playing "Teen Spirit" constantly. Kurt remembers an almost out of body experience when he first saw himself on television. "Jeez, do I really belong there?" he thought to himself. "I just looked so familiar to myself," he says.

"Jeez, do I really belong there?" Yes, he did. But Kurt just didn't look like all the other rock stars on TV. That was part of the band's charm: Kurt, Krist, and Dave looked like people you might actually know, which was a little revolutionary for the mainstream.

And what an interesting thing to say: "I just looked so familiar to myself." Maybe he meant that it was a strange sensation to watch television, where you're only used to

The Amplified Come as You Are

seeing people you don't know and see not only someone you know but see *yourself*. It's almost literally an out-of-body experience.

As the tour wound through places like Providence and Memphis and St. Louis, gradually, the promo people who would show up backstage at shows changed from the alternative marketing people to AOR (Album Oriented Rock) and even CHR (Contemporary Hit Radio, or Top 40). Radio was picking up in a big way and MTV was playing "Teen Spirit" during the day—not just on the channel's alternative ghetto, *120 Minutes*. The channel had even begun running the words to "Teen Spirit" across the screen as the video played.

That was a joke about Nirvana at the time: you couldn't understand the words. Of course, there was a long and great tradition of that in rock music, extending back from R.E.M. to the Rolling Stones to the Kingsmen's "Louie, Louie" to Fats Domino, and yet the people who crowed about this seemed to believe they were making some sort of original observation. Kurt did obscure the words a little, maybe to savor their sounds as much as their meaning, but the lyrics might also have been more difficult to hear because they were more imaginative and abstract, and thus less predictable, than standard mainstream fare.

Weird Al Yankovic made light of the mumbling phenomenon with his really funny "Smells Like Teen Spirit" parody, "Smells Like Nirvana": "What is this song all about? / Can't figure any lyrics out / How do the words to it go? / I wish you'd tell me, I don't know."

Like so many other children of the '80s, Kurt grew up on Weird Al. So when Yankovic called Kurt while Nirvana was on the set of their first *Saturday Night Live* performance, Kurt immediately gave permission for the parody. He knew that getting the Weird Al treatment, like playing *SNL*, was a sign that one had truly arrived in popular culture.

"We thought, 'Oh, he's going to tear us apart,'" Krist said to *Kerrang!* in 2019, "but then we saw the video, and just started laughing, it was really funny, really good."

The song and video ignited a big comeback for Yankovic, whose career had dive-bombed after his star turn in the 1989 comedy *UHF*, which dudded badly. The video was a huge hit on MTV, and "Smells Like Nirvana" reached #35 on the Billboard charts.

As Yankovic told *Spin*'s Christopher Weingarten, after the video came out, he found himself dining at a restaurant a few tables away from Kurt. He walked over and introduced himself. "I just profusely thanked him and said, 'Anything I can do for you, let me know,'" Yankovic said. "Kurt extended his hand to me and said, 'Polish my nails.'"

Meanwhile, a Christian-oriented L.A. band that had been called Nirvana since 1983 had issued cease-and-desist orders to radio and TV stations who were playing Nirvana's music and videos. Both bands can use the name. When Nirvana sued the local band for two million dollars for issuing the order, the matter came before a federal court in L.A. in mid-October. The L.A. Nirvana agreed to sell its trademark to Nirvana for fifty thousand dollars and to retract the cease-and-desist order.

There's probably an interesting explanation of why a Christian-oriented band named itself after a Hindu/Buddhist concept.

With each copy of *Nevermind* sold, the band began to have less of an idea of who their audience was. With the college/indie crowd, they had a pretty good clue—people who were fairly intelligent, politically progressive, nonsexist, non-macho, and very much musically discerning. Now their shows were filling with jock numbskulls, frat boys, and metal kids. Their skyrocketing sales meant only one thing to Kurt, Chris, and Dave—they were losing their community.

The band was less than thrilled with their newfound audience, and they weren't shy about letting anyone know. As Chris told *Rolling Stone*, "When we went to make this record, I had *such* a feeling of us versus them. All those people waving the flag and being brainwashed. I really hated them. And all of a sudden, they're all buying our record, and I just think, 'You don't get it at all.'"

"I found myself being overly obnoxious during the *Nevermind* tour because I noticed that there were more average people coming into our shows and I didn't want them there," Kurt says. "They started to get on my nerves."

The thing is, plenty of fans did meet Kurt's exacting standards—and they had to endure Nirvana's overly obnoxious behavior along with everyone else. And what message did "more average people" get from watching their idol act obnoxious? Did it encourage them to become more enlightened?

And while Kurt may have resented macho idiots, what is more definitively macho than smashing up stuff?

Accordingly, instrument-smashing reached an all-time high, and not just because they could finally afford it. "We were feeling so weird because we were being treated like kings," says Kurt, "so we had to destroy everything."

"We were being treated like kings so we had to destroy everything." That was ostensibly an expression of punk rock egalitarianism as well as the flip side of creativity: the equal-and-opposite urge to tear things down. But with Kurt, it seemed to be all balled up with self-hatred.

"I was obnoxious and showing my weenie and acting like a fag and dancing around and wearing dresses and just being drunk," Kurt continues. "I would say things like 'All right! Frat rock! Look at all these frat geeks out here!' I'm usually not very vocal on stage, but during that tour, I was a jerk. We were out of control."

Poor Monty Lee Wilkes. And it only got worse.

Kurt's particular high point came at an October 19 show at the Trees club in Dallas. His bronchitis had been acting up for the past week and he was quite ill. That day, a doctor visited the hotel and gave Kurt some potent antibiotic shots, but neglected to warn him not to drink that night. "I started drinking and I just felt *insane*," he says, "like I did a whole bunch of speed or something. I just wasn't very rational at all."

Kurt had been complaining all along the tour that he couldn't hear himself in the monitors, but no one seemed to be doing anything about it. He was losing his voice and it made performing miserable. "That night I just decided to do something about it," Kurt says. "I decided to throw a star fit."

The club was alarmingly overcrowded; people could barely breathe, let alone move. In the middle of a song, Kurt suddenly took off his guitar and started tomahawking the monitor board by the side of the stage. He broke his favorite Mustang guitar, but he also broke the monitor board. After a long delay as the crowd chanted "bullSHIT! bullSHIT!" they got the monitor to work again through one speaker and the band resumed the set.

Unfortunately, the monitor system belonged to the best friend of one of the bouncers at the show, a heavily tattooed, mohawked gentleman with, Kurt claimed, the regulation butt-crack peering above the back of his jeans. During "Love Buzz" Kurt jumped into the audience and although the bouncer made it seem as if he was trying to pull Kurt out of the audience he was actually holding him by the hair and hitting him. "I decided to get one good blow in before he beat me up after the show," Kurt says. "So I smacked him in the face with my guitar. He got a big gash on his forehead." The bouncer punched Kurt in the back of the head while his back was turned and Kurt crumpled; then he kicked him while he was down. In a flash, Dave vaulted over the front of his drum set; two roadies held the bouncer, rivulets of blood streaming down his face, while Chris stood between him and Kurt and told him to cool out.

Eventually, the band came back and played another half-hour. Someone had placed a wooden loading palette over the monitor board in case Kurt got any more wild ideas.

After the show, the bouncer was waiting outside for the band with a couple of his friends. "They all happened to be wearing Carcass and S.O.D. T-shirts," Kurt says, "like speed metal meatheads." "He was totally violent and macho," Kurt continues. "He was screaming, beet red with blood all over himself. 'I'm gonna kill you!'" The band took off in a cab, only to get caught in a traffic jam right in front of the club, like some nightmare version of *A Hard Day's Night*. The bouncer and his friends began thumping on the cab and eventually one of them kicked in a window and tried to grab Kurt just as the cab pulled away.

A little later, the cabdriver pulled over, took a joint down from his sun visor, and they all took a few tokes to calm down.

It might help clarify the picture to note that the bouncer was crouching at the lip of the stage, keeping people from stage diving, so he was in a position to yank Kurt back onto the stage—by his hair. The man was quite a bit taller than Kurt and possibly twice his weight.

Naturally, Kurt took the opportunity to denounce the bouncer and his friends as "speed metal meatheads."

Krist actually went to make sure the bouncer was all right, took off his shirt, and tried to wipe the blood off the man's face with it. There was almost a riot when the crowd thought that the band wouldn't return to finish the set.

After the show, the band got wind that the bouncer and some friends were waiting outside to beat them up. They had to get out of there quickly. Monty Lee Wilkes arranged for a cab to pull up to the back entrance to the club, and Kurt, Krist, and Dave dashed out the door toward the waiting car just as the bouncer and his gang spotted them and started sprinting toward the taxi. Someone slammed the door closed before Dave could get in and the cab sped off. "I may or may not have gotten a ride back with a cute girl," Dave wrote in *The Storyteller*, "getting into a car accident along the way."

Ironically, the first thing Kurt said into the microphone that evening was "Just don't hurt me, OK? Please don't hurt me. Don't hurt me."

In the meantime, *Nevermind* had jumped thirty-five places to #109.

Courtney had been popping up sporadically along the way. She seemed to have a positive influence on Kurt's mood. Even the crew noticed it. "I think that helped him deal with it a lot," says Myles Kennedy. "I think it gave him someone to talk to and someone to deal with it with—someone who wasn't in the band or the crew."

As the tour wore on, the van became more and more crammed with all manner of broken equipment and accumulated garbage. After a while, there was barely any room for people. During one drive, Wilkes remembers being forced to sit on the edge of a seat for hours on end. "I look in the back and there's Courtney and Kurt," says Wilkes, "curled up amid empty bags of chips and spilled beers and everything else."

"It was pathetic."

On the morning of October 25, Kurt and Chris taped an interview for MTV's heavy metal show, *Headbanger's Ball*, where "Teen Spirit" was the "#5 Skullcrusher of the Week." Kurt wasn't feeling too chipper—he hadn't had much sleep the night before and he was hung over as well. "I was sleeping just seconds before we aired," he explains. "Courtney and I had just stayed up all night drinking and fucking, so I had about two hours of sleep. It was during our romantic period."

Chris wore his usual duds—including nerdy deck sneakers—but Kurt donned a striking yellow organza dress and dark sunglasses. Although Chris did most of the talking, it was hard to take one's eyes off Kurt. "It's *Headbanger's Ball* so I thought I'd wear a gown," Kurt explained. "Chris wouldn't wear his tux. He didn't give me a corsage, either."

"At least I asked you out," Chris replied just a tad too effeminately, enough to prompt a nervous little laugh from metalhead host Riki Rachtman. "This thing has gotten pretty wild," Rachtman said, recovering nicely. "Everywhere you go, in all different types of the music scene, people really seem to be getting into Nirvana." "Everyone wants to be hip," Kurt cracked softly.

"Maybe they like the record," Chris offered.

Once again, here's Kurt working hard to distance himself from metal even while he was a guest on a TV show about metal. He could simply have refused to appear on *Headbanger's Ball*, but maybe being on MTV was still something of a thrill for the starry-eyed rock dreamer from Aberdeen, so he had it both ways, and wore a dress to signal that he didn't really want to be there—not unlike the T-shirt he would soon wear on the cover of *Rolling Stone* that said "Corporate magazines still suck."

Kurt stayed mum for most of the interview, acting semi-narcoleptic while Krist gamely fielded softball questions. Host Riki Rachtman—sporting an oversized hockey jersey and even more oversized metal hair—asked why they think the band has caught on so quickly. It was an impossible question to answer—especially by someone in the band—so it got a silly answer. "Because we have our big bandwagon," Krist explained, channeling his not-so-inner hippie. "We have a bunch of Clydesdale horses, multicolored horses, pulling it and people are just jumping on and it's kind of a Ken Kesey acid trip–type thing."

But Kurt might not have been *pretending* to be out of it, or exhausted from sex and drinking—in *Grunge Is Dead*, Rachtman claimed that Kurt was "smashed out of his ass—high on dope . . . I walk into my dressing room and he's there—lying face down on the floor."

But even just one month after the release of *Nevermind*, Kurt and Krist were already aware of the position they were in to spread the good word. Krist added that he hoped they could introduce "more mainstream type of people" to "the underground scene . . . That's kind of one of our missions."

That's why Kurt finally speaks up: "We like all kinds of stuff: Lead Belly, Bikini Kill, the Breeders, the Pixies, R.E.M., the Melvins . . . the Vaselines." It's a political thing, plugging fellow bands, giving back to the community that raised you—he learned that from Sonic Youth—and maybe a way of living down the shame of being mind-bogglingly popular.

So maybe that was why Kurt agreed to appear (to a degree) on *Headbangers Ball*. As he wrote in his journals, "We simply wanted to give those dumb heavy metal kids (*the kids who we used to be* [emphasis mine]) an introduction to a different way of thinking and some 15 years' worth of emotionally and socially important music [i.e., punk rock], and all we got was flack [*sic*], backstabbing and Pearl Jam."

Toward the end of the appearance, Rachtman hits the nail on the head: "Some of the songs [on *Nevermind*] sound like early real hard punk stuff and some stuff, I mean, almost reminds me of, like, a heavier Replacements." Kurt told me he'd never really listened to the Replacements, but it was still a good observation: a big part of Nirvana's charm was how the band distilled and synthesized sounds from the preceding decade of the American indie underground, remaking/remodeling them into something the MTV crowd could grasp.

###

By the time they got to the October 29 show in Portland, Susie Tennant took the band aside and told them, "Congratulations! Your record went gold today!" No one in the band cared all that much. "I didn't give a shit, really," Chris says. "Yeah, I was happy about it. It was pretty cool. It was kind of neat. But I don't give a shit about some kind of achievement like that. It's cool—I guess."

The Amplified Come as You Are

Monty Lee Wilkes says he had turned down a lucrative tour with another band after Nirvana invited him to go on their upcoming European tour. "We really want you to go, man," Wilkes says Chris told him. "You're the *best* road manager we've ever had and we want to keep you *forever*." Then, the night of the Portland show, three days before they were to leave for Europe, Wilkes was told he wouldn't be going.

There was no love lost there. "Chris is basically a drunken hippie," says Wilkes. "Kurt, he just doesn't say much—never *did* say much unless he wanted something." Wilkes feels a lot kindlier toward Dave, though. "Dave is the greatest," he says. "I just totally dig Dave. Great fuckin' guy, great guy."

Dave might have been the most well-adjusted boy that Wilkes knew. Dave could certainly act out with the best of them, but he was also professional and didn't put up with much nonsense, kind of like Wilkes.

A legendary homecoming show on Halloween at the Paramount in Seattle was filmed by DGC. Parts of it can be seen in the "Lithium" video and it may one day be edited into a full-length film. Opening were Mudhoney and Tobi Vail's band, Bikini Kill, who hit the stage draped in lingerie, with words like "slut" and "whore" written all over their bodies.

The big homecoming show had been booked that summer, before *Nevermind* was released, and Mudhoney, who had been the flagship band of Sub Pop and indeed the entire Seattle scene, was originally the headliner. "In '88, '89, Mudhoney would blow Nirvana off the stage," Bruce Pavitt told me for *Our Band Could Be Your Life*. "They were the great band. They blazed the trail for Nirvana." But now Nirvana, the Aberdeen band that none of the discriminating hipsters at Muzak had liked very much, was headlining the show. Kurt and Krist really looked up to Mudhoney; it must have been difficult to absorb all around.

The show was originally planned for the 1,800-seat Moore Theatre, but as Nirvana began to explode, the show was moved to the cavernous 2,800-seat Paramount Theatre. That was a really huge deal: big national bands played the Paramount.

Grunge was very, very male, which set an explosive context for Bikini Kill's bold and visionary provocations. Despite any lingering awkwardness between Kurt and Tobi Vail, Nirvana had been supportive of Bikini Kill from the start—they were the opening band the night Nirvana debuted "Smells Like Teen Spirit" at OK Hotel that April, just six months earlier—and it was surely Kurt who made sure they were on the bill at the Paramount. It was a signal that Nirvana still wanted to be part of the community. Bikini

Kill had existed for about a year by this point and had recently made their recorded debut with the eight-song cassette *Revolution Girl Style Now*. That summer, they'd recorded another EP with Fugazi's Ian MacKaye in Washington, DC, where they played a riot grrrl convention and a pro-choice rally on the National Mall, cementing a musical and social alliance with that city's politically activist punk community.

Nirvana was now in a short-lived sweet spot between indie fame and mainstream fame. After more than two solid months of touring, their show was pretty tight—that night at the Paramount, there was not a lot of messing around between songs; for the most part it was one right after the other. They were riffing hard, and sometimes it sounded like classic power trio rock—minus the guitar heroism and plus great, catchy songs. But the large film crew—$250,000 worth (nearly half a million in today's dollars)—was all over the stage and in the musicians' faces. "More cameras in here than a 7-Eleven," Krist quipped. Maybe it was because of the cameras, or the pressure of the show, or road fatigue, that it was merely a good Nirvana show instead of a great one.

Confronted with the limelight, Kurt was literally self-effacing, hiding his eyes behind an unwashed mop of hair. He said virtually nothing until the encores, when he introduced an early version of "Rape Me": "This song is about hairy, sweaty, macho redneck men . . ." he said, as a hearty but premature cheer went up in the crowd. He paused for a moment, waiting until the noise subsided, and added pointedly, "who rape."

For the occasion, there was a dancer at either side of the stage: Ian Dickson and Nikki McClure, two friends of Kurt's who had gone to Evergreen. Dickson wore a shirt that said "Girl" and McClure wore one that said "Boy," the kind of gender-bending gesture that was virtually unheard of in the boys' town of grunge. (Dickson, who remained close friends with Kurt, joined Dylan Carlson's band Earth for a while and went on to work at Sub Pop, where he was the IT chief, pioneering online commerce for record labels; these days he designs apps. McClure became an artist and acclaimed children's book illustrator.)

###

The band got one day's rest before setting off for a European tour on November 2, the day that *Nevermind* first entered the Top 40 at #35. The record was now selling at an amazing rate, certainly far exceeding the expectations of anyone at Geffen/DGC or Gold Mountain.

###

They played their first date of the European leg of the *Nevermind* tour at the Bierkeller in Bristol, England.

Every time they'd check into a hotel room, they'd switch on the TV and see the "Teen Spirit" video. The radio seemingly played nothing but "Teen Spirit." The press had gotten out of hand—they were doing between ten and fifteen interviews a day and every show was sold out. In Italy, a thousand kids who couldn't get a ticket simply rushed the doors and barged their way in.

At every step of the way, the shows were dangerously oversold, the stage cluttered with TV crews pointing cameras in Kurt's face as he tried to sing. "We resented it, so we turned into assholes," says Kurt. "We got drunk a lot and wrecked more equipment than we needed to. We just decided to be real abusive pricks and give interviewers a hard time. We weren't taking it seriously. We felt we needed to start averting the whole thing before it got out of hand. We wanted to make life miserable for people."

And after all, life was miserable for *them*, too. To begin with, the tour bus wasn't a sleeper; it was a sightseeing bus. There were no bunks, just seats, and the oversized windows let in light and noise. Their driver only made matters worse. In Europe, bus drivers must take breaks after a certain amount of time or distance, as measured by a device called a tachograph. The driver was very strict about this, earning him the nickname Tacho Bill. Tacho Bill would also get lost a lot, and soundman Craig Montgomery often wound up doing the navigating. Meanwhile, Bill would tap the accelerator instead of just cruising, so the bus lurched nauseatingly throughout the month-long tour.

For comic relief on the bus, they'd play a legendary prank phone call tape in which a man with a piercing New York accent verbally abuses everyone from florists to auto mechanics. After a while, it became the constant in-joke of the tour, and guests would be shocked as the members of the tour entourage would call each other "jerky" and "fuckface" for no apparent reason.

That was the Jerky Boys tape, a favorite in tour buses all across America at the time. Before the internet, instead of emailing MP3s, people would dub cassette tapes of things like celebrity bloopers and prank calls and pass them around to friends, and they'd go viral in an analogue kind of way. Another big hit on the Nirvana bus was the infamous Tube Bar tape, in which some unknown wise guy would call a workingman's bar in Jersey City and ask for people with names like Phil DeGrave and Al Coholic, whereupon the gravel-voiced owner of the bar would obligingly fly into a rage and call them a "yellow rat bastard."

Touring in Europe is always more exhausting because of the disorienting and rapid-fire changes in time zones, food, and language, not to mention the fact that bands have to deal with a different record company in every country. And there's more media—with every new country came a whole new set of TV stations, newspapers, and magazines. Often, the band couldn't refuse to do press because that would mean that, for instance, the entire nation of Denmark wouldn't have a television interview with Nirvana.

And sometimes it was just a matter of temperament. "This was a *punk rock* band," Danny Goldberg of Gold Mountain observes. "This was not a band of choirboys. Their moodiness got covered by the press this time, but it was nothing new."

###

Back in the States, Nirvanamania was rampant. The album was ascending the Billboard chart by leaps and bounds, going from #35 to #17 to #9 (Top 10!) to #4 and hovering around the Top 10 throughout most of November and December. People were flocking to the stores to buy it, critics debated the ambiguities and profundities of Kurt's lyrics, the underground scene began to talk of an indie revolution, you couldn't switch on MTV without seeing the "Teen Spirit" video, you couldn't go anywhere in Seattle without overhearing a conversation about the band's success, and everywhere, anyone who cared a whit about rock & roll was pondering what it all meant.

Kurt couldn't bring himself to acknowledge to himself what the hubbub was all about. "Obviously, I wouldn't want to allow my ego to admit that we're that great of a band, that we deserve that much attention, but I knew that it was better than 99 percent of anything else on a commercial level," he says. "I knew we were a hundred times better than fucking Guns N' Roses or Whitesnake or any of that shit. It just made me feel stupid because there are so many other bands in the underground that are as good or better than we are and we're the only ones getting any attention. It just made me feel sorry for everybody that was freaking out about it because it just seemed sad that we're one of the only bands like us that are being exposed to the mainstream."

In the wake of Nirvana's paradigm-shifting success, many underground bands did get mainstream attention, presumably some that Kurt felt were as good as or better than Nirvana, and yet they didn't attain anything near the level of success that Nirvana did.

Pop music success is a perfect storm of many factors, one of the most important being pure, dumb luck. And luck, good or bad, can be very difficult to comprehend or even accept: why me? (See: the Book of Job.) If you have low self-esteem and an overwhelming sense of shame, success can be difficult to embrace. Plenty of other musicians, though, would be just fine with it.

But you can only win the lottery if you buy a ticket. Or, as seventeenth-century English poet John Milton put it, "luck is the residue of design." And Nirvana had been designing: they toured hard and built up a following; they hired a powerful L.A. management firm, got a fancy record biz lawyer to represent them, signed to a major label, worked hard to make a killer record, got Andy Wallace to mix it, and made a fairly slick video for MTV. The pieces were in place. They just needed luck—and it happened to smile on them.

Then they hit on the idea of using their fame to promote bands that they thought were just as deserving. "We were pretty excited about it at first—we actually thought we could make a dent," says Kurt. "But the only thing that's happened since we became popular is the Lemonheads, a fucking alternative cover band, are now one of David Letterman's favorite groups."

In some ways, the Lemonheads were not dissimilar from Nirvana: a three-piece band led by a good-looking singer-guitarist, they had come up through the American indie community with abrasive but catchy punk-inspired songs. The Lemonheads signed to a major label right around the time Nirvana did and enjoyed a substantial industry buzz, so maybe there was a little rivalry there—especially since Gold Mountain also managed the Lemonheads. Also, Courtney sometimes hung out with Lemonheads leader Evan Dando, an indie heartthrob whom she rarely failed to note was "beautiful," so perhaps there was some jealousy on Kurt's part as well.

The "alternative cover band" snipe was a reference to the Lemonheads' indie breakthrough: a hopped-up 1989 cover of singer-songwriter Suzanne Vega's 1987 hit "Luka"; three years later, the band hit the mainstream radar screen with a cover of Simon & Garfunkel's 1968 classic "Mrs. Robinson."

The Lemonheads' second major label album, 1992's *It's a Shame About Ray*, was a decent record, just not as well produced or well written as, for example, *Nevermind*. It did eventually go gold, as did the 1993 follow-up *Come On Feel the Lemonheads*, but the Lemonheads fizzled under the strain of Dando's well-documented substance abuse.

Actually, many bands who have appeared in Nirvana's T-shirt collection have at least landed major label contracts: Flipper, Daniel Johnston, Eugenius, the Melvins, Wool, and Shonen Knife, among others. "But it's not so the bands can get signed," Kurt says. "It's so some idiot out in suburbia will try to look for their album."

With the exception of Shonen Knife, all of those artists were dropped after one album.

In Mezzago, near Milan, Shelli and Urge Overkill's Ed "King" Roeser had figured out a way to break into the hotel wine cellar by taking the service elevator. "They came up with a case of all these different kinds of wine and we drank just about every bottle," Urge's Nash Kato recalls. "The hotel, the next morning, it was like a vomitorium. You could hear it up and down the hall. I went into Chris and Shelli's room and they were hurling *together*, like as man and wife."

A couple of days later, *Nevermind* went platinum in the United States. Says Chris, "It goes platinum and we're all over MTV and it's like weird, like, now what? Where do we go from here? Are we going to be Led Zeppelin and the big band of the '90s or are we just going to fall apart or what?"

Both, as it turned out.

Since both were on tour in Europe at the same time, Kurt and Courtney renewed their telephone romance. "That's when we started really falling in love—on the phone," says Kurt. "We called each other almost every night and faxed each other every other day. I had like a three-thousand-dollar phone bill." Courtney skipped out on a Hole show just to hang out with Kurt in Amsterdam.

Hole's debut album *Pretty on the Inside* was released the same month as *Nevermind*, September 1991. The first single, "Teenage Whore," reached #1 on the UK indie charts, and Hole toured Europe several times in the second half of 1991, often opening for Mudhoney. The British music weeklies, ever-attracted to outrageous personalities who give good sound bite, were smitten by Courtney: "You know more about Courtney Love than you do about Robert Smith, Phil Collins or George Bush," crowed one *Melody Maker* profile. "She's made quite an impact." She definitely had—even though *Pretty on the Inside* was, by Courtney's own admission, "unlistenable." By the end of the year, Hole was being pursued by major labels.

Despite the riot of excitement going on in Nirvana's honor, Kurt still felt he led a humdrum existence and that Courtney was a way out. "Initially, I just wanted to add some excitement in my life," says Kurt. "I'd never met anyone so outspoken and charismatic. It seems like she is a magnet for exciting things to happen. If I just happened to walk down the street with her, someone might attack us with a knife for no reason, just because she seems like the kind of person that attracts things like that. And I just wanted to piss people off, basically."

"I have this thing about me, this catalyst, that brings out hate in people, and I wonder about it," Courtney told the *Los Angeles Times*' Jonathan Gold in August 1992. "I think I may have always worn it around me, I think it is why I was always picked on, which is why I don't blame anybody. No matter where I go, or what context I'm in, I seem to provoke people, and I enjoy it."

Kurt knew that with Courtney around, things would never be routine, for better or worse. The chaos kept things interesting. And it was often entertaining—unless you were her target.

If Kurt was constantly tearing down and building back up his life, throwing all the playing cards in the air, he wouldn't ever have to stop and take stock of what he'd done and what he'd become. And maybe that need became more urgent as he amassed a fame he realized he didn't really want and couldn't really handle. As with the instrument smashing, he had to keep upping the ante on self-sabotage.

Kurt would often get bored on tour. "The highlight of the tour usually ends up with Chris being really drunk and obnoxious and standing on a table and taking his clothes off," Kurt says. "Or we'll shoot off a fire extinguisher or something like that. I just wanted to do something that was really exciting. I wanted to try to start having an exciting life. I figured Courtney was the best option. I knew that there wouldn't be a single person in the Nirvana camp that would approve of it. Because they're all so fucking boring. Their lives are so normal. I hate to say it, but that's just the way I feel. Everyone that I know that we work with, there's not much punk rock going on. There's no one willing to take risks, like 'let's just take off.' It's always such a strict regimen—'Let's get to the show, let's play, let's eat dinner and go to sleep.' I just got tired of it."

What a curious thing to say, that Courtney was a means to an end (i.e., attaining "an exciting life")—as opposed to simply being attracted to her.

Courtney suited Kurt's image of himself as the "black sheep" of the band. "I was going off with Courtney and we were scoring drugs and we were fucking up against a wall outside and stuff and causing scenes just to do it," he says. "It was fun to be with someone who would stand up all of a sudden and smash a glass on the table and scream at me and throw me down. It was just really fun."

A powerful personality such as Courtney had an equally powerful effect on the entourage. "I think everyone was taken aback a bit at first," says tour manager Alex Macleod, chuckling. "She would appear and it was like a tornado coming. Everyone was tired and laid back and she would arrive and she would talk your ears off—she had so much energy, God knows how she did it. But she was good fun. She was amusing."

Dave, who is not a "morning person," began rooming with Macleod. But as the tour went on, Macleod acted more and more annoyed at Dave. Finally Dave couldn't stand it anymore and confronted him.

"What's your problem? What's wrong?" Dave asked.

"Fuck you!" Macleod shot back.

Apparently, whenever Macleod would try to wake Dave up in the morning, Dave would yell in his sleep, "FUCK YOU! LEAVE ME THE FUCK *ALONE*! THIS IS BULLSHIT!" then settle peacefully back into his pillow. Later, he'd go down to breakfast and wonder why Macleod was scowling at him.

The stress of the tour began taking its toll and by Thanksgiving, the band was starting to send S.O.S. calls to John Silva at Gold Mountain. "We were all tired," Chris says. "I'd be drunk. I got on this kick where I'd drink about three bottles of wine a night. I was all sick and coughing. I was pale, I had blue lips. Smoke hash, cigarettes, and fuckin' drink Bordeaux. 'Where's my Bordeaux?' I drank like three bottles a night. First bottle, that would be a primer. A few shows I barely remember playing."

Chris has a one-word explanation for his drinking. "Stress," he says. "I was stressed out. That was the only way I could cope with it."

Three bottles of wine is about fifteen standard drinks. That's a hell of a lot of drinks. Every night. And yet there was virtually no media outcry or even much internal alarm about Krist's drinking like there was about Kurt's heroin addiction, even though alcohol abuse can certainly destroy lives, too. Of course, alcohol is legal and socially acceptable—and it's pretty difficult to die suddenly from it unless you're doing something like driving a car or operating heavy machinery. On the other hand, heroin is sensationally stigmatized, profoundly illegal, and very easily lethal. It helped that Krist wasn't the leader of the band, so *his* substance abuse went uncriticized and perhaps simply taken for granted.

"It felt as if we couldn't be stopped—or we didn't know where it was taking us and we were just sort of along for the ride," Dave says.

Kurt's stomach had started acting up on the American tour. A chronic flu that lasted throughout the European tour brought on bronchitis and Kurt couldn't stop smoking his hand-rolled cigarettes. "I just remember being real miserable and starving and sick all the time," says Kurt. "I was constantly drinking cough syrup and drinking. My bronchitis acted up so bad that I was vomiting while I was coughing before shows a few times. I remember in Edinburgh, we called this doctor. I was vomiting and coughing into this garbage can and he couldn't do shit for me."

Even steady Dave was starting to crack. "I started getting afraid of flying, really bad," he says. "Weird things started freaking me out, like all of a sudden I became claustrophobic and I'd never been claustrophobic before.

"I was insane," Dave says. "I was out of my fucking mind. I was sick of playing, sick of it. I would get so freaked out during shows—and I still do. While we're playing, I will just get freaked out that I'm going to freak out and go insane and puke and vomit and faint and then a hundred thousand people will have to go home and I'll be personally responsible. That happens to me every time we play. I can't explain it—it's this weird thing that's been with me all my life—a bad, bad anxiety thing all my life. One time, somebody told me you could hypnotize yourself if you stare in the mirror for hours on end and I did and I did kind of hypnotize myself and it freaked me out for the rest of my life really bad, and it still does. I was like thirteen or fourteen.

"I don't know how to explain it and it's not as insane as it sounds," he continues. "All it is is an impending fear of going insane every minute of the day. It's not something you get scared of for five minutes and then it goes away. You're constantly thinking about how do you know when you've gone insane? Where is the point where you just snap and you're completely out of your mind? So on that tour, everything was so completely insane, everything was just going at a hundred miles an hour and it was intensified tenfold."

OK, so maybe Dave *wasn't* "the most well-adjusted boy I know." Maybe that affable exterior, the professionalism, the aversion to nonsense and drama, all stemmed from a deep-seated fear of totally losing his shit.

On December 5, the night before Nirvana played the Trans Musicales Festival in Rennes, France, Kurt and Courtney were lying in bed and they decided to get married.

The next day in Rennes, while Kurt stayed in his hotel room, Chris downed an entire bottle of wine at a press conference. Dave couldn't get a word in edgewise.

Needless to say, it came as a huge relief when the band decided to cancel the rest of the tour before they hit the stage at the Trans Musicales. "We were going to go to Scandinavia and it was going to be below zero and every flight was at six in the morning," says Chris. "It would have been a disaster, it would have been a fucking disaster. We would have fell apart, we would have freaked out. There would have been freak outs. It was better to go home and rest."

Before the nine-thousand-person capacity crowd, they opened with a silly, over-the-top version of the Who's "Baba O'Riley" with Dave on lead vocals. "I walked out there blitzed out of my fuckin' mind," Chris says. "And then I went home and had feverish delusions all night long. Laying in bed, thinking there was a ghost in the room or something. I just sweated all night long."

On that "Baba O'Riley" cover, Dave does sing a few lines but it's Krist who caterwauls, "Don't cry, don't grab your wallet, it's only major label wasteland." Clearly, they were very self-conscious about what had happened to them.

"I'd like to live off the band," Kurt had told the University of Washington newspaper a couple of years earlier, in 1989. "I can't handle work." But what if the band *becomes* work? What if it involves making business decisions and dealing with people who have desk jobs at large corporations and relentless touring and nonstop interviews? What then?

John Lennon, 1970: "It just happens bit by bit, gradually, until this complete craziness is surrounding you and you're doing exactly what you don't want to do with people you can't stand, the people you hated when you were ten."

After the tour, Kurt, Chris, and Dave went their separate ways. Chris and Shelli went house shopping and found a place. At first they were going to put down a modest down payment. Then the royalty checks started to come in and they decided they could put up half the money. Then the royalty checks really started coming and they simply bought their $265,000 home outright.

"Three days after it was over, you were in withdrawal from not playing and then you start wanting to play again," Dave says.

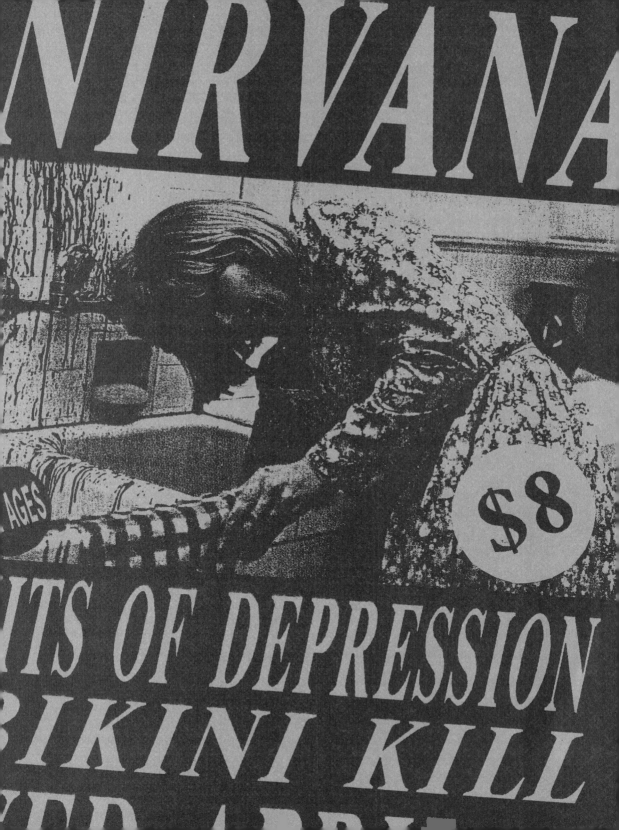

chapter nine

IT IS NOW TIME TO MAKE IT UNCLEAR

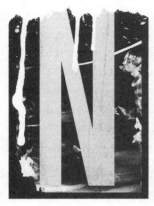*evermind* came without a lyric sheet. "I guess I wasn't confident enough," Kurt says. At first, he wanted to print some of his poems, then some "revolutionary debris," then nothing at all—no pictures or anything. At the last minute, he picked some lines out of the songs (and a couple that aren't in any of the songs) and ran them together into a poem.

In other words, he made a collage out of lyrics that were themselves collaged.

Kurt says "revolutionary debris" meant "all kinds of anarchistic, revolutionary essays and diagrams about how to make your own bomb." "And I just thought we better hold off on that," he says. "If we ever really want to do that, we'd be more effective if we gained popularity first. Then people might actually think twice about it, rather than us alienating everybody right off the bat. But once we started to get really popular, it was really hard to hold back. We played the game as long as we could."

Part of playing the game is going out to dinner with powerful music magazine editors and pretending to be friendly with them so they'll give the band an article or a favorable review. On one of these junkets, the band went out to lunch at a swank Beverly Hills eatery with *Rip* magazine editor Lonn Friend.

Before lunch, Kurt, Chris, and Dave visited Friend's office. "I looked up on his wall and I noticed that Lonn has a fetish," says Kurt. "A rock & roll butt fetish. He has to have all these pictures taken with him and up-and-coming bands where either he's naked or the bands have to drop their pants. He's pinching their butts. There are all these pictures of him with naked rock stars that have been in this magazine. He's in the bathtub naked and they're standing around him and it started to scare me."

"It was a disgusting scene because we were basically pimping our personalities to this person to see if he liked us before he decided to promote us," Kurt continues. "It was the most sickening thing I ever experienced. I just decided to not say a word and sit there and be pissed off and act really insane. The only words he said to me after he got up to leave were, 'Kurt, you shouldn't talk so much.' He was really offended, totally pissed off."

Sure enough, *Rip* didn't support Nirvana until it practically had to, at the height of Nirvanamania. When the band refused to cooperate any more with *Rip* after the magazine ran a special edition on the band without their permission, the letters page just happened to feature more and more anti-Nirvana screeds. "If we were smart," says Kurt, "we would have played the game a little bit longer to get the acceptance of the *Rip* readers, to where they liked us so much that no matter what we said, it wouldn't matter. But we blew our wad too soon. But at the same time, I feel sorry for those kids, I was one of them. You can't blame a fourteen-year-old kid for calling someone a fag if he's grown up in an environment where his stepdad has been saying that for years and it's an accepted thing that you're practically forced into."

That's an unusual admission from Kurt: that he was "one of them": a *Rip* reader, or at least a metal fan. And maybe he'd also been the kind of fourteen-year-old who hurled hurtful epithets at gay people.

Thanks to the First Amendment, *Rip* didn't need Nirvana's permission to run a special edition about them.

While oldsters called Kurt's lyrics incoherent, his Whitman's Samplers of images, ideas, and emotions fitted the short attention spans of channel-hopping kids everywhere. "I very rarely write about one theme or one subject," Kurt once told the *Seattle Times*. "I end up getting bored with that theme and write something else halfway through the rest of the song, and finish the song with a different idea."

Like the Pixies' Black Francis, Kurt didn't necessarily write his lyrics for linear sense. They're at their most successful when words and music collide to produce a powerful and distinct third sensation—"A denial, a denial" ("Teen Spirit"); "And I don't have a gun" ("Come as You Are"); "she said" ("Breed"); or even a good old "yeah," repeated thirteen times for emphasis in "Lithium." Most of the lyrics come from lines of poetry that Kurt writes in spiral-bound notebooks every night before going to sleep, so the impressionistic quality comes mostly from the juxtaposition of seemingly unrelated lines, rather than a stream-of-consciousness approach from word to word.

That state between waking and sleeping—called hypnagogia—can be conducive to creativity. As Kurt wrote in an early journal entry, "Just before I fall asleep and when I'm really bored I . . . lay [*sic*] down and think for awhile until I ~~subconsciously go~~ fall into a semihypnotic state of sub-consciousness."

The Amplified Come as You Are

"A lot of people don't realize," David Byrne told *Trouser Press* magazine in 1981, "that the sound of a voice, phrasing or phonetic structures are affecting them at least as much as the words. Usually lyrics that are a little bit mysterious, that don't quite come out and say what they mean, are the more powerful. They deal with things in a metaphysical way." That was Kurt's approach.

Black Francis's lyrics for the Pixies were nonlinear in a similar way to Kurt's and had to have been a big influence. In 1990, I interviewed Black Francis for *Musician* and received a revelation about songwriting—and creativity in general. I was trying to pin him down on how and why he wrote his powerful, impressionistic lyrics, but although he's one of rock's most articulate musicians, he was having a lot of trouble coming up with an answer. Finally, he just flung up his hands and said, "*I'm just trying to come up with a bunch of cool tunes*." And that's really all any songwriter—or any artist in general—is really trying to do: *make cool stuff*. Then other people can come along and analyze it.

Unsurprisingly, Kurt used collage to write his lyrics. "Almost all my lyrics have been cut-ups, pieces of poetry and stuff," Kurt told *Melody Maker* journalists the Stud Brothers in August 1993. "And the pieces of poetry are taken from poems that don't usually have meaning in the first place. They were cut-ups themselves. And often I'll have to obscure the pieces I take to make them fit in the song, so they're not even true pieces of poem."

That collage approach ran very deep in Kurt—not just with lyrics, visual art, and video, but even in the chords he played. Kurt "selected the chords in a manner consistent with the idea of non-functional harmony," wrote composer Vivek Maddala in a 2021 *Stereogum* piece about "In Bloom." As he did with words, scraps of paper, and snippets of videotape, Kurt juxtaposed disparate scales—like composers from Stravinsky to Public Enemy, he broke the rules of Western harmony. He popularized modal mixture as a key component of rock's harmonic vocabulary in the '90s.

So Kurt chose his chords the same way he wrote his lyrics: because they sounded good together, the laws of Western harmony be damned (if he even knew them in the first place). In other words, *he was just trying to come up with a bunch of cool tunes*. This approach not only helped make his songwriting unique and admired by fellow musicians, but it contributed to the ineffable quality that people can feel even if they don't know music theory.

And then Kurt knitted together those technically disparate chords with equally idiosyncratic melodies. There's a reason why the virtuosic jazz trio the Bad Plus covered "Smells Like Teen Spirit": there's a lot of interesting music in there.

The collage method of composition has a very arty pedigree: it harks back to the "cut-up" technique of the Dada art movement. In 1920, one of the founding Dadaists, writer and performance artist Tristan Tzara, published a recipe for cut-up poems: cut all the individual words out of a newspaper article, place the snippets in a bag, "shake it gently," pull them one by one from the bag, and write down the words. "The poem will be like you," he wrote. "And here are you, a writer, infinitely original and endowed with a sensibility that is charming though beyond the understanding of the vulgar."

"Charm beyond the understanding of the vulgar" was exactly what Kurt was going for.

But Kurt might well have gotten the cut-up idea from his hero William Burroughs. In the '50s, English multimedia artist Brion Gysin accidentally rediscovered Tzara's method and soon introduced his friend Burroughs to the idea. Burroughs used the technique in parts of his best-known work, the nonlinear 1959 novel *Naked Lunch*.

Kurt's cut-ups weren't random though—he fished through his notebooks and found things that he felt went well together, and out of that sensibility, some cohesive, powerful impressions emerged. That was why he could sing those words so passionately: because they meant something to him deeply. It also meant that he could add in some more direct sentiments and they would be safely muddled.

"You see, life *is* a cut-up," Burroughs told BBC interviewer John Walters in 1982. "Every time you walk down the street or look out the window, your consciousness is cut by random factors. And then you begin to realize that they're *not so random*, that this is saying something to you."

Bob Dylan was another fan of using cut-ups to construct ineffable imagery, and he had a good suggestion for how to perceive it: "The song is like a painting, you can't see it all at once if you're standing too close," Dylan told historian Douglas Brinkley for the *New York Times* in 2020. "The individual pieces are just part of a whole."

The effect is like a musical Rorschach test, but more importantly, they added up to very coherent ideas and emotions that you can comprehend conceptually. Of course, sometimes even Kurt got a little confused. "What the hell am I trying to say?" he sang on "On a Plain."

In his songwriting, Kurt deals in extremes and opposites that animate the songs. One of the most famously obscure couplets in "Smells Like Teen Spirit" was "A mulatto, an albino / A mosquito, my libido." But it's really nothing more than two pairs of opposites, a funny way of saying the narrator is very horny. The lyrics often loft an idea and then shoot it down with one little burst of cynicism. Even the music echoes the dynamic contrasts of the imagery. Many of the songs—"Smells Like Teen Spirit" and "Lithium" foremost—alternate between subdued, rippling sections and all-out screaming blitzkriegs, while the album

itself encompasses songs like the acoustic "Polly" and the majestic "Something in the Way" as well as primal scream workouts like "Territorial Pissings" and "Stay Away."

Kurt is smart enough to recognize that the dualities are a reflection of himself and perhaps his audience. "I'm such a nihilistic jerk half the time and other times I'm so vulnerable and sincere," he says. "That's pretty much how every song comes out. It's like a mixture of both of them. That's how most people my age are. They're sarcastic one minute and then caring the next. It's a hard line to follow." Few songs on *Nevermind* combine that mixture better than "Teen Spirit."

"It was basically a scam," Kurt says of the song. "It was just an idea that I had. I felt a duty to describe what I felt about my surroundings and my generation and people my age."

One night, Kurt and Kathleen Hanna from Bikini Kill had gone out drinking and then went on a graffiti spree, spray-painting Olympia with "revolutionary" and feminist slogans (including the ever-popular "GOD IS GAY"). When they got back to Kurt's apartment, they continued talking about teen revolution and writing graffiti on Kurt's walls. Hanna wrote the words "Kurt smells like Teen Spirit." "I took that as a compliment," says Kurt. "I thought that was a reaction to the conversation we were having but it really meant that I smelled like the deodorant. I didn't know that the deodorant spray existed until months after the single came out. I've never worn any cologne or underarm deodorant."

Courtney once insisted to me that Kurt never smelled even though he rarely bathed. But maybe love is nose-blind.

Kathleen Hanna told the story of that night at a performance at Joe's Pub in New York in 2010. In August 1990, a teen pregnancy center had just opened in Olympia. The thing was, "It was a right-wing con," Hanna said, "where they got teenaged girls to go in there and then told them they were going to go to hell if they had abortions." So one night Hanna went on a mission with Kurt: she was going to graffiti the words "FAKE ABORTION CLINIC" on the building while Kurt looked out. They fortified themselves with some whiskey and waited until the coast was clear. But instead, Hanna looked out while Kurt scrawled "GOD IS GAY" on the side of the building.

Then they went to a bar and drank some more. Then they got some forty-ouncers and drank even more at Hanna's apartment. They were pretty hammered at this point and ended up at Kurt's apartment, where Hanna vomited on someone's leg and later took out a Sharpie and wrote on Kurt's wall before passing out.

As it turns out, Hanna's bandmate Tobi Vail wore Teen Spirit deodorant, so Hanna was saying that Vail had marked Kurt with her scent—which is, ironically, a lot like the "territorial pissings" of various animals.

Six months later, Kurt called Hanna and asked if he could use one of the things she wrote on his wall as a song lyric, not knowing it was a brand name.

Virtually ever since he arrived, Kurt had been inundated with the Calvinists' discussions of "teen revolution" in Olympia coffee shops; after all, that's what bohemian people in their early twenties do—it's in the rule book. "I knew there was some kind of revolution," he says. "Whether it was a positive thing or not, I didn't really care or know."

The Calvinists would bridle at the comparison, but in many respects, teen revolution resembled the aims of the Woodstock Nation. It meant that young people were creating and controlling their own culture as well as their political situation, rescuing them from a cynical and corrupt older generation. The idea was to make youth culture honest, accessible, and fair in all respects—on the artistic side, on the business side, and even in the audience—making it the diametrical opposite of what corporate America had turned it into. After that, political change would be inevitable.

The concept of a "teenage revolution" dated back to the mid '60s. In November 1965, *KRLA Beat*'s Bob Feigel asked the Byrds' singer David Crosby, "What is your concept of the Teen Revolution?" And the twenty-four-year-old Crosby replied, "It definitely is a revolution and it definitely involves the teenagers and a great many more people than the teenagers. . . . The country isn't being run as they know and feel it should be. . . . They definitely want to change this and a lot of other things."

But the Olympia crowd was well aware that Crosby's generation, the boomers, had failed to foment a revolution. "A new generation formed the teenage nation," Calvin Johnson warbled on Beat Happening's 1985 "Bad Seeds." "This time let's get it right."

The Calvinists recognized an essential aspect of punk rock: it was about controlling your own media. If you didn't like what was on the major labels and commercial radio and the national magazines, then make your *own* music, start your *own* label, broadcast on your *own* radio station, publish your *own* fanzine. Don't let corporate interests determine your life: Do It Yourself.

Kurt didn't doubt that the Calvinists were earnest and he liked their ideas, but he also was dubious about their prospects. He found their altruism naive—they didn't seem to realize it was all a pipe dream. "Everyone seems to be striving for

Utopia in the underground scene but there are so many different factions and they're so segregated that it's impossible," Kurt says. "If you can't get a fucking underground movement to band together and to stop bickering about unnecessary little things, then how the fuck do you expect to have an effect on a mass level?"

A 2013 study by New York University researchers found that, while virtually everyone feels that they're different from other people, liberals feel this to a greater degree than conservatives do. And that would explain why liberals sometimes have trouble banding together and why people in institutions that depend on conformity, such as the military or law enforcement, tend to be conservative.

Kurt even felt that pressure was being put on Nirvana to help with the revolutionary effort. "I just felt that my band was in a situation where it was expected to fight in a revolutionary sense toward the major corporate machine," says Kurt. "It was expected by a lot of people. A lot of people just flat out told me that 'You can really use this as a tool. You can use this as something that will really change the world.' I just thought, 'How dare you put that kind of fucking pressure on me. It's stupid. And I feel stupid and contagious.'"

Kurt was very outspoken about personal-is-political issues such as racism, homophobia, and sexism. But that's difficult, especially for someone who doesn't have the knack for lowercase-p politicking like, say, Bono or Kathleen Hanna or Fugazi's Ian MacKaye. Kurt didn't sermonize from the stage; he just wasn't that type of person.

And yet Kurt was thinking about social revolution and his place in it. He considered incorporating "all kinds of anarchistic, revolutionary essays and diagrams about how to make your own bomb" into the artwork for *Nevermind*. And, as he wrote in his journal, probably sometime in 1990, he wanted to "design manifestos with ideas, contacts, recruits, go public, risk jail or assasination [*sic*], get employed by the target so its [*sic*] easier to infiltrate the system." Even though he never did any of those things, he helped pave the way for a bit of progress.

Krist was down with the program. "We're total leftists," he told the *New York Times*' Karen Schoemer on September 27, 1991, after Kurt failed to show up for the big interview with the paper of record. "We're going to demand the socialization of the music industry. Records are going to be free to everybody."

So "Teen Spirit" is alternately a sarcastic reaction to the idea of actually having a revolution, yet it also embraces the idea. But the point that emerges isn't just the conflict of two opposing ideas, but the confusion and anger that that conflict produces in the narrator—he's angry that he's confused. "It's fun to lose and to pretend" acknowledges the thrill of altruism, even while implying that it's plainly futile. "The entire song is made up of contradictory ideas," Kurt says. "It's just making fun of the thought of having a revolution. But it's a nice thought."

Part of embracing the revolution is blasting the apathetic types who aren't part of it. Even Kurt admits that his generation is more blighted by apathy than most. "Oh, absolutely," he says. "Especially people in rock bands who aren't educated. That's also an attack on us. We were expected to shed a minimal amount of light on our ideals, where we come from, but we're not even capable of that, really. We've done a pretty good job of it, but that was never our goal in the first place. We wanted to be in a fucking band."

Kurt was well aware that "Smells Like Teen Spirit" sounded like the Pixies. So it was a song about the futility of revolution using a formula that was a retread of something from the past, which is, fittingly for Nirvana's generation, very ironic. There seemed to be no hope: everything had been done before; there was no point in trying. Hence a generation that was, as Kurt scribbled on the song's lyric sheet, "neurotically lathargic [sic]."

And there he is, being self-deprecating about his lack of "education" again, and how inarticulate it made him, his band, and his entire cohort.

This was when crack was rampant; AIDS was still largely mysterious and virtually a death sentence; the Cold War flared up again but now with new, improved nukes; homelessness had increased dramatically; there were the first inklings of impending global environmental catastrophe via NASA climatologist Dr. James Hansen's 1988 congressional testimony that a long-term warming trend was underway and that it was probably due to the greenhouse effect; gruesome mass violence exploded in Bosnia and Rwanda; there was the Gulf War, the Challenger explosion, the apocalyptic L.A. riots, and so on.

On top of all that, the divorce rate had increased 45 percent over the course of the '60s, just as Gen Xers began being born; for better or worse, married people no longer stayed together "for the sake of the children." The daycare system hadn't caught up to the fact that more women were working, producing a generation of so-called "latchkey kids." Sure, boomers had endured the Cold War and Vietnam, but when they were young, the world had been their oyster—and, thanks to their unprecedented numbers and corresponding financial clout, it still was. The following generation had to toil in their shadow.

"As a smaller cohort following a giant one, the post-boomers are a hand-me-down generation," wrote Isobel Osius in a 1991 article in *American Demographics*, "one which will consistently experience neglect of their needs and priorities because they simply

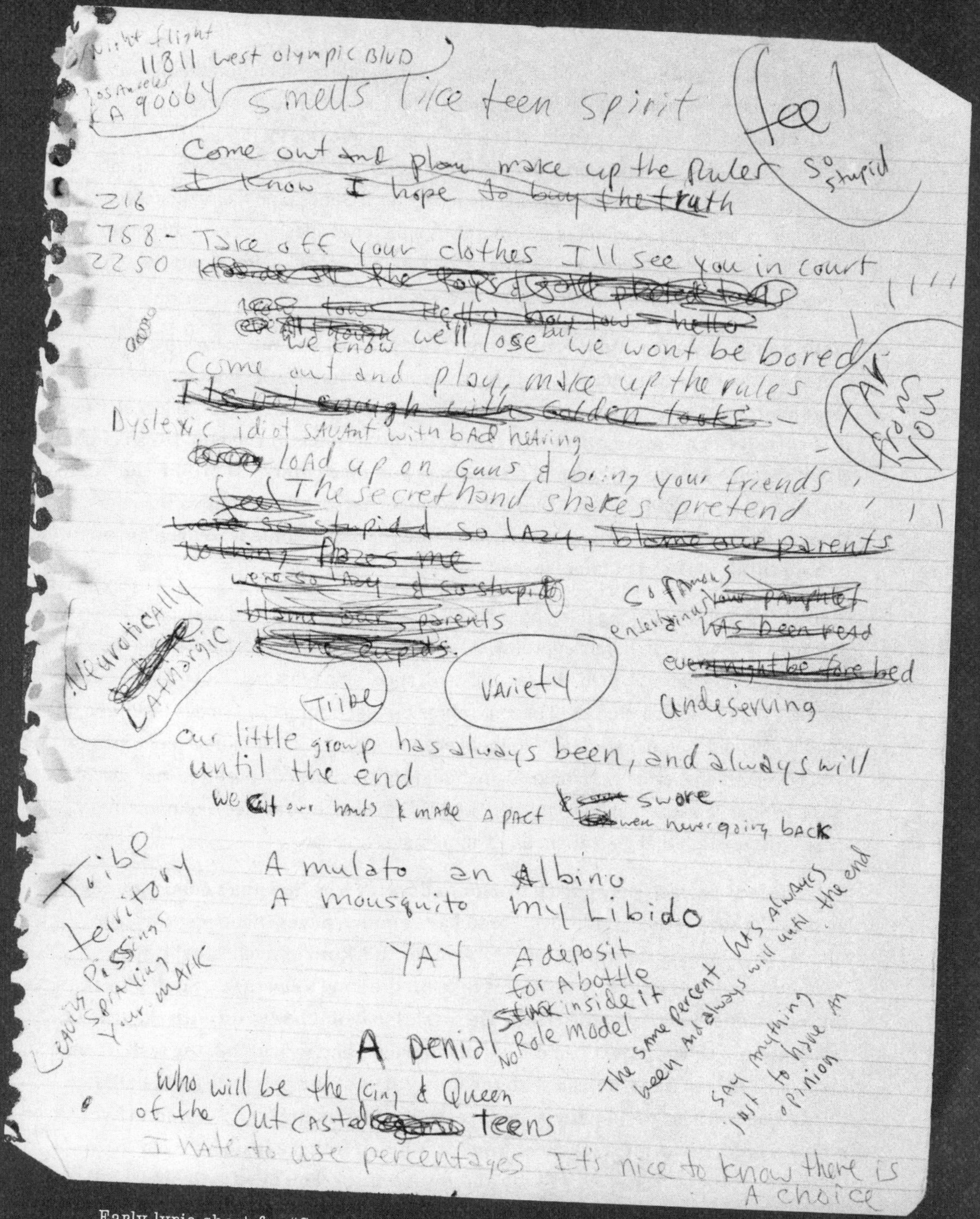

Night flight
11811 west olympic BLVD
Los Angeles
CA 90064

Smells like teen spirit

feel
so stupid

Come out and play make up the rules
I know I hope to buy the truth

216
758-
2250

Take off your clothes I'll see you in court

we know we'll lose but we wont be bored
Come out and play, make up the rules
Its bad enough with golden tools
Dyslexic idiot savant with bad hearing
load up on guns & bring your friends
The secret hand shakes pretend
were so stupid so lazy, blame our parents
nothing fazes me
were so lazy & so stupid
blame our parents

Neurotically
Lethargic

Tribe
variety

So famous
entertaining
your pamphlet
has been read
every night before bed
undeserving

our little group has always been, and always will until the end
we cut our hands & made a pact & swore we're never going back

Tribe
territory
Pissing
leaving spraying your mark

A mulato an albino
A mousquito my libido
YAY
A deposit for a bottle
stick inside it
No role model
A Denial

The same percent has always been and always will until the end

say anything just to have an opinion

Who will be the king & Queen
of the outcasted teens
I hate to use percentages It's nice to know there is
a choice

Early lyric sheet for "Smells Like Teen Spirit." "Who will be the King & Queen / of the outcasted teens."

don't have the numeric heft to effect change." That "hand-me-down" mentality was embodied by thrift store culture: reusing things the boomers had thrown away.

Generation X was so marginalized that the original term for them was postboomers—so, from the start, their identity was fundamentally defined by the fact that they weren't the generation before them. The term Generation X didn't become widely used until its first members were well into their twenties; and even then, the name still spoke of nonentity: X. The French call them Génération Bof. *Bof* is French slang for "whatever" or "blah." Or maybe "never mind."

"Teen Spirit" sounds violent—the drums clearly take a vicious pounding, the guitars are a swarming mass of barely contained brutality, the vocals are more screamed than sung. "I don't think of the song like that," Kurt says. "It's really not that abrasive of a song at all, really. It only really screams at the end. It's so clean and it's such a perfect mixture of cleanliness and nice candy-ass production and there were soft spots in it and there was a hook that just drilled in your head throughout the entire song. It may be extreme to some people who aren't used to it, but I think it's kind of lame, myself."

Granted, Kurt was posturing here, dutifully disavowing *Nevermind*'s glossy production, but years of listening to harsh, aggressive bands such as Black Flag, Hüsker Dü, the Butthole Surfers, Scratch Acid, the Jesus Lizard, and Celtic Frost had indeed inured Kurt and his peers to such a high level of sonic abrasion that a song like "Smells Like Teen Spirit" really did sound "candy-ass" to them even though it was far more violent than virtually anything else on pop radio. Mainstream kids had been exposed to that sort of music in small doses—maybe some Jane's Addiction here, a stray Replacements song there—just enough that it set them up to appreciate Nirvana.

Kurt's family turmoil may have had a lot to do with why Nirvana's music sounds so angry. "I'm sure it did," Kurt says, "but I have enough anger in me just toward society that I would definitely have looked for this kind of music anyhow."

Dave Grohl has a slightly different take on the song's message. "I don't think there was one, to tell you the truth," he says. "Most of it has to do with the title of the song, and that was just something that a friend had written on the wall. It was funny and clever. That, paired with the video of us at the pep rally from hell, I think that had a lot to do with it. Just seeing Kurt write the lyrics to a song five minutes before he first sings them, you just kind of find it a little bit hard to believe that the song has a lot to say about something. You need syllables to fill up this space or you need something that rhymes."

I'm not so sure about that. For one thing, the lyric sheet for "Smells Like Teen Spirit" proves that Kurt had been working and reworking the lyrics for quite some time. He even wrote down the word "yay," which sounds like an ad lib on the track but actually turns out to have been a premeditated lyric.

Kurt thought this stuff through carefully. "With the phrasing I allow myself," he wrote in his journals, "it isn't very easy to be lyrically prolific." The right syllables, vowels, consonants, and rhyme sounds were key. Kurt made sure to fit the words with whatever sound-event (i.e., the simultaneous stack of melody, harmony, rhythmic emphasis, timbre, and dynamics) was happening at a given moment, in addition to serving the vocal melody. Kurt was thinking not just about the song as a whole but about how each moment felt.

It's like something that Bob Mould, former singer-guitarist for one of Nirvana's forebears, Hüsker Dü, wrote in his 2011 autobiography *See a Little Light* (which I edited). He was working on his first solo album, 1989's *Workbook*, and had a breakthrough with his lyrics. "I was becoming more aware of the use of vocal sibilance and consonance," he wrote. "Sibilance functioned as percussion, and consonance worked when *s*'s landed on cymbals, and *t*'s and plosives and percussives landed in spots that fell in with the guitar. Now I was more in tune with the smaller details, the spaces between words and sounds."

"You're looking for that right word to occur at just the right place," Creedence Clearwater Revival leader John Fogerty told *American Songwriter* magazine in 2013, and "have the coolest-sounding word you could say because it was just a really cool word to say at that spot in the song. Like 'big wheel keep on toinin', proud Mary keep on boinin'.' What in the world is that? I don't know."

"Smells Like Teen Spirit" has a great example of this approach. When Kurt sings, "A denial, a denial," what does that mean exactly, or have to do with anything? We don't know but we feel it really deeply. And that's because of the way the words—not just their meaning but their sound and their melody—go with what's happening musically at that moment. Kurt did this all the time. It's one of the reasons his songs are so powerful.

Impromptu scribblings aside, one remarkable aspect of "Teen Spirit" was that unlike many previous songs of its type, it didn't blame the older generation for anything—it laid the blame at the feet of its own audience. That implies a sense of responsibility that didn't quite fit the slacker stereotype. Although "Teen Spirit" was a bold and provocative dare, Kurt feels he crossed the line into condemnation. "I got caught up in pointing the finger at this generation," says

Kurt. "The results of that aren't very positive at all. All it does is alienate people and make them feel the same feeling you get from an evil stepdad. It's like, 'You'd better do it right' or 'You'd better be more effective or I'm not going to like you anymore.' I don't mean to do that because I know that throughout the '80s, my generation was fucking helpless. There was so much right wing power that there was almost nothing we could do."

Kurt and Krist were dismayed by the apathy they perceived in their generation. And so the music and the shows were supposed to provide an example of passion, of caring about something, to provide inspiration. Essentially, they were enacting what theater theorist Jill Dolan calls "the utopian performative": "A hopeful feeling of what the world might be like if every moment of our lives were as emotionally voluminous, generous, aesthetically striking, and intersubjectively intense" as the performance they're watching. It's the idea that art can evoke the sensation of a better world, and that that sensation can prompt people to envision and create that world.

Krist did become politically active, but Kurt didn't go much further than speaking out about injustice because, I suspect, he didn't feel confident enough in his own intellectual abilities or political knowledge. Still, he had an enormous impact simply because so many people listened to what he had to say.

The '90s didn't start the moment the clock struck midnight on December 31, 1989. They started in November 1992, when Bill Clinton won the election, marking the end of twelve years of Reaganism. And maybe that's why Kurt says what he says in the following paragraph.

"I know that I've probably conveyed this feeling of 'Kurt Cobain hates his audience because they're apathetic,' which isn't the case at all. Within the last two years, I've noticed a consciousness that's way more positive, way more intelligent in the younger generation and the proof is in stupid things like *Sassy* magazine and MTV in general. Whether you want to admit that or not, there is a positive consciousness and people are becoming more human. I've always been optimistic, but it's the little Johnny Rotten inside me that has to be a sarcastic asshole.

"Introducing that song, in the position that we were in, I couldn't possibly say that I was making fun or being sarcastic or being judgmental toward the youth-rock movement because I would have come across as instantly negative. I wanted to fool people at first. I wanted people to think that we were no different than Guns N' Roses. Because that way they would listen to the music first, accept us, and then maybe start listening to a few things that we had to say, after the fact, after we had the recognition. It was easier to operate that way."

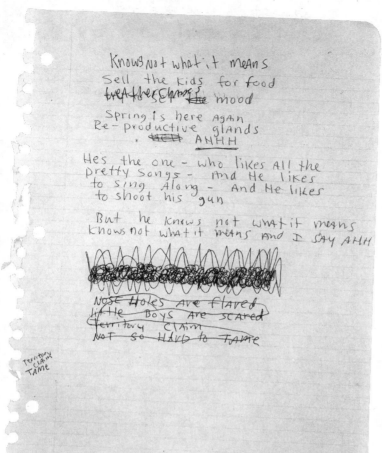

Early lyric sheet
for "In Bloom."

It's interesting to consider the idea that it would be punk for a punk band to make a popular record. And then, when they became astoundingly popular, it would be punk to make a *punk* record. But if they really wanted to fool people into thinking they were more mainstream than they really were, they would have worked much harder to act the part; as it was, the members of Nirvana were obviously misfits and malcontents.

Earlier, Kurt said he was outraged when people suggested that Nirvana smuggle in some subversive messages using their major label perch and "really use this as a tool . . . [to] really change the world." Now he's saying that that's what he was planning all along.

###

"In Bloom" was originally aimed at the dilettantes of the underground scene, the jocks and shallow mainstream types who had begun to blunder into Nirvana shows after *Bleach*. But remarkably, it translated even better to the kind of mass

Lithium

① ✱   I'm so happy because today I found my friends
     They're in my head

  ✱   I'm so ugly but thats ok cause so are you
     ~~And~~ ~~We~~ We broke our mirrors

     Sunday morning is ~~the~~ ~~da~~ every day for all I care
     And I'm ~~not sad scared~~ not scared
     Light my candles ^{in a daze} ~~~~ cause I found God
       Hey Hey Hey

     I'm so lonely but thats ok I shaved your head
     And I'm not sad

     And Just maybe
     I'm to blame for all I've heard but I'm not sure
     ^{excited}
     I'm so ~~lost in~~ I can't wait to meet you
     there - but I dont care

     I'm so horny thats ok my will is good
     ~~And I've got food to tie me over and~~
     ~~keep my mind on meeting you~~
     ~~And eat my friends~~ Again ~~and~~ Again

     I ~~liked~~ you   } I'm not gonna crack
     I miss you   }
     I love you
     I killed you

popularity the band enjoyed. The song mixes images of fertility and decay with a chorus about a gun-toting guy who likes to sing along to Nirvana's music, "but he knows not what it means." The brilliant irony is that the tune is so catchy that millions of people actually do sing along to it. It's also a good description of former band members like Jason Everman, Dave Foster, and Aaron Burckhard, who were honestly attracted to the band's music but didn't quite go along with Kurt and Chris's punk rock ethos.

"Come as You Are" sounds unlike anything else on the record—with its mysterious murky, aqueous feeling, it shows Kurt's metamorphosis from misanthrope to a more open-minded person. "I'm tired of people passing judgments on one another and expecting people to live up to their expectations," says Kurt. "I've done that all my life. I'm a Pisces and it's a natural thing for Pisces to be upset with people and expect them to be a certain way and then they aren't, so you're just mad at them all the time. I just got tired of it." The narrator admits that he's unsure how the other person will be, but is ready to accept the other person, contradictions and all. Furthermore, he adds that he won't be judgmental when the meeting occurs—"And I swear that I don't have a gun." It's a remarkably beautiful sentiment.

More dualities emerge as Kurt beckons someone to "Take your time, hurry up" and to "Come dowsed in mud, soaked in bleach." Kurt is full of opposites, too: masculine/feminine, violent/nonviolent, pop/punk. He's decided to accept it all, to come as he is. Perhaps instead of resolving the contradictions, he'll let them live together under one roof, sometimes warring, sometimes joining to produce a powerful third entity.

If only.

Once "Breed" builds up its hurtling momentum, Kurt wails "I don't care" half a dozen times, then "I don't mind" and finally "I'm afraid," saying about as much about the straight line between apathy, ignorance, and fear as needs to be said. "I don't mind if I don't have a mind" is merely icing on the cake.

The title of "Lithium" is an update on Marx's description of religion as the "opiate of the masses." Kurt says that the song may well have been inspired by Jesse Reed's family, the only born-agains he had ever had direct contact with. Kurt says he isn't necessarily antireligion. "I've always felt that some people should have religion in their lives," he says. "That's fine. If it's going to save someone, it's okay. And the person in that song needed it." The song is not strictly autobiographical, but it's easy to see a resemblance between Kurt's despair and loneliness in Olympia and the sorry state that the character is in. Kurt didn't find religion that winter of 1990, but he did find another kind of nirvana.

The Reeds weren't the only born-again Christians that Kurt knew. "I have this relative I really love a lot and she really inspired me because she was a musician," Kurt told *Flipside* in a 1992 interview, "and I used to go to her house all the time and she [became] really disillusioned with her life and became suicidal." The relative became a born-again Christian, which according to Kurt, saved her life.

"Polly" is based on an actual incident which occurred in Tacoma in June of 1987. A fourteen-year-old girl returning from a punk show at the Community World Theater was kidnapped by a man named Gerald Friend, who hung the girl upside down from a pulley attached to the ceiling of his mobile home and raped and tortured her with a leather whip, a razor, hot wax, and a blowtorch. She later escaped from his car when he stopped for gas. Friend was later arrested and eventually convicted and will likely spend the rest of his life in jail. Kurt's only embellishment to the story was the hint that the woman got away by fooling the rapist into thinking she enjoyed what he was doing to her.

I regret naming that odious monster. This was before it occurred to the media not to give any unnecessary publicity to criminals. As of 2023, Friend is in his eighties and still in prison.

Fighting rape and other forms of sexual violence was one of riot grrrl's key causes. "Polly" is testament to the huge influence that the movement had on Kurt's art and life.

There's a classic Appalachian murder ballad called "Pretty Polly"—recorded by the Stanley Brothers, Doc Boggs, Pete Seeger, and countless others—in which a man abducts a woman and then kills her. It seems to be more than a coincidence that the titles and themes of the two songs are so similar. It's entirely possible that one of Kurt's Olympia friends played him that song.

Rape is a continuing theme in both Kurt's interviews and his songs. It's almost as if he's apologizing for his entire gender. "I don't feel bad about being a man at all," Kurt says. "There are all kinds of men that are on the side of the woman and support them and help influence other men. In fact, a man using himself as an example toward other men can probably make more impact than a woman can."

The thing about "apologizing for his entire gender" was a ham-fisted hint that I knew something I wasn't saying, which was the following.

Two people close to Kurt told me that Kurt took sexual advantage of a "retarded" girl in high school, by which they meant that she was in a special-ed class. I hadn't asked;

they just brought it up. I didn't include it in the book because I'm not sure either of my sources was thinking about the fact that I was a journalist when they told me about it. Besides, it was just too dark. I buried it.

But then *Montage of Heck* had Kurt telling the story in his own words on a home tape recording he'd made. So now it's out in the open.

In Kurt's telling, it was consensual, and Kurt left before it went very far. Still, word spread around school about what happened, and he was publicly shamed. On the recording, Kurt says he "couldn't handle the ridicule" and claims he lay down on the local train tracks one night and waited for a passing train to run over him, but it went down another track.

Even if the railroad track story is apocryphal, it shows the power that shame had over Kurt.

I think the incident with that girl was a pivotal event in Kurt's life. When he encountered the riot grrrls in Olympia, who were so staunchly feminist, with a particular focus on sexual assault, his sense of guilt must have been overpowering. Not only did Kurt know he'd done something very wrong, but it was precisely the kind of thing all his new friends, the ones whose approval he wanted so much, were railing against. And it amplified the general sense of shame he already felt about himself. I wonder if he told anybody in Olympia about it.

And that might be one big reason why Kurt was so adamant about feminism: he was trying to live down what he'd done. He wasn't the first rock star to follow that paradigm. "I used to be cruel to my woman, and physically," said John Lennon in a 1980 *Playboy* magazine interview. "That is why I am always on about peace, you see. It is the most violent people who go for love and peace." Lennon wrote about it in the Beatles song "Getting Better": "Man, I was mean but I'm changing my scene." By railing against rape and sexism, Kurt was trying to change his scene, too.

He did penance ever after. So I think that's partly why the word "shame" appears in so many of his lyrics.

Although the title of "Territorial Pissings" blasts macho posturing, the song is frequently the occasion of the band's end-of-set instrument-smashing orgies. The lyrics are basically a handful of disconnected ideas which appealed to Kurt. He explains the opening words of the song ("When I was an alien . . .") by revealing that he always wanted to believe he was really from outer space. The fantasy, which he only recently stopped playing with in his mind, was that he was actually an alien foundling. "I wanted to be from another planet really bad," says Kurt. "Every night I used to talk to my real parents and my real family in the

It Is Now Time to Make It Unclear

skies. I knew that there were thousands of other alien babies dropped off and they were all over the place and that I'd met quite a few of them." For Kurt, the fantasy supported the idea that "there's some special reason for me to be here."

Believing that they're actually aliens is a fairly common fantasy for kids. But Kurt might also have been thinking about the 1980 Wipers song "Alien Boy," about someone who's persecuted because they're different.

He was a big fan of the Wipers, a Portland band led by singer-guitarist Greg Sage, one of the pioneers of the Northwest DIY punk movement; the band released some really great records: 1980's *Is This Real?*, 1981's *Youth of America*, and 1983's *Over the Edge* (there's that phrase again).

"Alien Boy" was actually written about an often homeless schizophrenic from Portland named James Chasse. In 2006, Chasse was brutally beaten to death by Portland police.

(Coincidentally, the creatures in Kurt's paintings look remarkably like artists' renderings of aliens which have appeared in everything from the *Weekly World News* to the cover of *Communion*, Whitley Strieber's allegedly nonfiction book about close encounters with beings from outer space.)

Communion: A True Story was still fresh in the popular memory when this book was first published, but these days it might help to know that *Communion* became a bestselling pop culture phenomenon when it came out in 1987. Strieber, who also wrote fiction (his novels *The Hunger* and *The Wolfen* were made into Hollywood horror films), wrote about being abducted by "the visitors"—who may or may not have been aliens—complete with bizarre and traumatic experiments on his body. Closely resembling the aliens in the 1977 movie *Close Encounters of the Third Kind*, the book's cover image, an artist's rendering based on Strieber's description of "the visitors" with their huge, black, saucer-shaped eyes, swiftly became the new canonical image of an extraterrestrial.

The song also proves that Kurt wasn't above penning a few lyrical clinkers—"Just because you're paranoid doesn't mean they're not after you" is a pretty hoary coffee mug adage.

In retrospect, maybe Kurt knew that and was quoting it sarcastically. It was, after all, the age of slacker irony.

"Never met a wise man, if so it's a woman." "The biggest piece of proof that I have is that there are hardly any women who have been in charge of starting a war," Kurt says. "They're actually less violent." By this time, one begins to wonder how

Kurt rationalizes being a man at all. His first response is revealing. "I don't know," he says. "Castration." Later on in "On a Plain," he is "neutered and spayed"; in "Come as You Are," he doesn't "have a gun."

Apparently, though, female leaders are no less violent than their male counterparts. The 2015 book *Why Leaders Fight*, by Michael C. Horowitz, Allan C. Stam, and Cali M. Ellis, finds "there is no difference at all between the average Risk Index (likelihood of starting armed conflicts) score for men and women." History shows plenty of female leaders willing to engage in war and violence: Indira Gandhi (India), Isabel Perón (Argentina), Tansu Çiller (Turkey), Golda Meir (Israel), Margaret Thatcher (UK), among others, going back to Catherine the Great. Still, it was a pretty provocative thing to say in 1992.

It's been pointed out many times that the first three songs on the album mention guns. "Dave Grohl's father tried to make an analogy about that," Kurt says. "Something about how I tie guns with my penis. I don't know why. I wasn't conscious of the fact that I mentioned guns three times. I've tried to figure out an explanation for it myself and I can't. I really can't." To paraphrase Dr. Freud, sometimes a gun is just a gun. But not this time.

Kurt's gun fixation didn't come out of nowhere: firearms were and still are particularly popular where he grew up. When I visited Aberdeen for the 1992 *Rolling Stone* cover story, the local pawnshops—which did a brisk business because of the area's economic downslide—were full of guns (and chain saws). It's not surprising that guns appeared in Kurt's songs. But maybe the gun imagery wasn't, as Dave's father theorized, Freudian phallic imagery but actually a presentiment, unconscious or not, of what would happen in a few short years.

On June 4, 1993, three months after I interviewed Kurt, Courtney called the police to their house, and Kurt was arrested on a domestic violence charge. The police found three handguns. He owned at least one gun when we did our interviews.

"Drain You" is a love song, or rather a song about love. In Kurt's universe, the two babies of the song represent two people reduced to a state of perfect innocence by their love. "I always thought of two brat kids who are in the same hospital bed," he says. The lyrics mix the utter dependence of infants with their narcissism—"I don't care what you think / Unless it is about me," one of them says. Although there is an obvious sexual connotation, the image of draining off an infection mainly has to do with relieving the other of bad feelings, like sucking out the venom from a snake bite. The medical theme—the song is rife with fluids, infection, and vitamins—would dominate the next album.

It turns out that "Lounge Act" was apparently very much about Tobi Vail—so much so that Kurt wouldn't put it in the set list if Courtney was at the show.

The title of "Lounge Act" came from the fact that "We just thought that song sounded like such a lounge song," says Kurt, "like some bar band would play." But the lyrics are nothing of the kind. "That song is mostly about . . . having a certain vision and being smothered by a relationship and not being able to finish what you wanted to do artistically because the other person gets in your way," Kurt says.

The line that goes "I've got this friend you see who makes me feel . . ." refers to some of Kurt's Olympia friends and the riot grrrl movement who inspired Kurt to surrender his misanthropy and break out of what he calls the "nihilistic monk world" that he had made for himself in his little shoebox of an apartment.

"Stay Away" undoubtedly began as an indictment of the Calvinist scene in Olympia, but in a broader sense, it could apply to any conformist clique— "Monkey see monkey do / I don't know why I'd rather be dead than cool."

This was a big theme for Kurt. "You're in high school again," he wailed on "School," and cliquishness appears again in "Smells Like Teen Spirit."

The title of "On a Plain" could be read as a pun, as in "airplane." Although he was otherwise miserable, Kurt had realized his dreams by the time he had written that song. He was getting flown to L.A. and New York because big record companies desperately wanted to sign his band. "I suppose it's some way of me saying I'm still complaining and bitching about things but I really have it better off than I had ever expected to be," Kurt admits.

Part of the lyrical motif of "On a Plain" is the construction of the song itself. "I'll start this off without any words," Kurt begins. He explains the line "Somewhere I have heard this before / In a dream my memory has stored" by saying that "I'd heard that bridge in some other song, I don't know what it is," Kurt says. "I'll find out some day," he adds, with enough sarcasm in his voice to imply that he means that the original author will slap him with a copyright suit. When he wrote "One more special message to go, then I'm done and I can go home," he meant that "On a Plain" was the last song that he had to write lyrics for.

"It is now time to make it unclear / To write off lines that don't make any sense." "That was my way of saying the first couple of lines seem like statements but they don't have any meaning," says Kurt. "I'm just making it obvious that there's really no meaning in it, so don't take it too seriously."

But perhaps he's protesting too much. "My mother died every night" and "the black sheep got blackmailed again" are loaded with personal resonance for Kurt. The former line sounds like a reference to Wendy's traumatic experience with her abusive boyfriend; Kurt often refers to himself as a black sheep. Make these points to him and he shrugs, laughs quietly, and mumbles, "I don't know . . ." After such revealing lines, "It is now time to make it unclear" seems like an attempt by Kurt to cover his tracks, as if he's given too much away.

Yeah, Kurt *was* protesting too much: "On a Plain" is a very autobiographical song, and it has *plenty* of meaning. "I got so high, I scratched till I bled" alludes to the fact that opiates tend to cause itching and rashes. Maybe "died every night" isn't a reference to physical abuse but to what the French call "la petite mort" and, to get a little Freudian, Kurt is expressing some Oedipal jealousy.

In light of all this, when he sings that it's now time to make things unclear and write lines that don't make sense, it seems like, to quote R.E.M., "Oh no, I've said too much."

An early lyric sheet for "On a Plain" bears out Kurt's description of culling bits and pieces of his writings for various songs: along with the chorus for that song and some discarded verses, it also includes the framework for the lyrics to "All Apologies."

For all his disavowal of most of the other songs on the record, Kurt does acknowledge that "Something in the Way" is about his experiences living under the bridge in Aberdeen. It's exaggerated for effect, though. "That was like if I was living under the bridge and I was dying of AIDS, if I was sick and I couldn't move and I was a total street person," he says. "That was kind of the fantasy of it."

Ironically, the one thing that Kurt claimed was autobiographical didn't actually happen.

###

Although Kurt roundly rejected the "spokesperson for a generation" tag, he will admit that the album did crystallize something about his peers. "Oh definitely," he says. "We're a perfect example of the average uneducated twentysomething in America in the '90s, definitely."

So there's another example of Kurt feeling self-conscious and self-effacing about being the provincial kid from Aberdeen and an insight into why he was drawn to more cosmopolitan people: Buzz Osborne, Krist, the Olympia crowd, Tobi Vail, the Seattle crowd, Courtney, Danny Goldberg, the members of Sonic Youth, and others.

And the twentysomethings are the generation that's been led to believe that they missed out on all the best times. "That's pretty much the definition of what we are, is punk rockers who weren't into punk rock when it was thriving," Kurt says. "All my life, that's been the case, because when I got into the Beatles, the Beatles had been broken up for years and I didn't know it. I was real excited about going to see the Beatles and I found out they had broken up. Same thing with Led Zeppelin. They'd been broken up for years already."

Because boomers were still dominating the media and popular culture, succeeding generations came to believe that they had missed the boat—everything good had already happened and anything else that followed was inferior. As Kurt wrote in his journals, "I feel there is a universal sense amongst our generation that everything has been said and done. True. But who cares. . . . It could still be fun to pretend."

And so, for instance, Kurt got compared to John Lennon. A lot. I've already done it here, several times, and in the 1992 *Rolling Stone* cover story, too: "If he can stand the heat, Cobain (extremely bright and unafraid to take provocative stands) may emerge as a John Lennon–like figure. The comparison with Cobain's idol isn't frivolous. Like Lennon, he's using his music to scream out an unhappy childhood. And like Lennon, he's deeply in love with an equally provocative and visionary artist—Courtney Love, leader of the fiery neo-feminist band Hole."

Comparisons like that are shorthand for helping people to understand an artist. But it denies the artist their individuality and unique creativity, and how those things speak to the moment the artist is in, and to their own unique audience.

And yet, as Kurt wrote in his journals, "John lennon [*sic*] has been my Idol [*sic*] all my life."

Ironically, Kurt himself became a go-to archetype for the next generation of media. For instance, many music journalists compared late underground emo-rapper Lil Peep to Kurt. (Lil Peep was "the scene's Kurt Cobain," wrote the *New York Times*' Jon Caramanica, making music that was "astonishingly gloomy and diabolically melodic.") There were plenty of similarities between Kurt and Lil Peep: depression (and maybe bipolar disorder), an absent father, drug abuse, hints of suicide, outspoken opposition to homophobia and sexism, overwhelming sudden success, an early death by his own hand, a death that people around him should have seen coming. Lil Peep himself was well aware of the parallels: he even had a song called "Cobain" and said, "I'd love to be the new Kurt Cobain." As the saying goes, don't wish for anything: you might get it.

But there's more to it than that. "I think there's a universal display of psychological damage that everyone my age has acquired," Kurt says. "I notice a lot of people a lot like me who are neurotic in certain social situations. I just notice that everyone in their early twenties have been damaged by their parents equally." Kurt describes a scenario in which his generation's parents grew up in the bland, conformist '50s and early '60s, then had kids just as the late '60s began. The onslaught of new ideas threw their old values into a tailspin and they reacted by drinking and doing drugs. And getting divorces.

"Every parent made the same mistake," Kurt says. "I don't know exactly what it is, but my story is exactly the same as 90 percent of everyone my age. Everyone's parents got divorced, their kids smoked pot all through high school, they grew up during the era when there was a massive Communist threat and everyone thought we were going to die from nuclear war, and more and more violence started to infuse into our society, and everyone's reaction is the same. And everyone's personalities are practically the same. There's just a handful of people my age, there's maybe five different personalities and they're all kind of intertwined with one another.

"I don't think our musical version of that is any different than any of the other bands that have come out at the same time we have," he continues. "I don't think we're more special as far as having that same kind of damage that our parents or our society gave us. It's the same. We got more attention because our songs have hooks and they kind of stick in people's minds. The majority of any bands you interview would have divorced parents. All these kids my age found themselves asking the same question at the same time—why the fuck are my parents getting divorced? What's going on? Something's not right. Something about the way our parents were brought up isn't the way it's supposed to be. They fucked up somewhere. They're living in a fantasy world. They must have done something wrong." Those are some tough thoughts to have, especially if, like Kurt, you were eight years old.

By the '70s, the boomers' youthful idealism had curdled in the wake of Vietnam, a massive oil crisis, and Watergate, not to mention the simple fact of getting older and willingly becoming ensnared in the system they had once condemned. Spirituality and a quest for freedom lapsed into hedonism. The boomers became known as "the Me Generation": greedy and self-obsessed, embracing what cultural historian Christopher Lasch called, in his acclaimed 1979 book of the same name, "the culture of narcissism." This was hardly a mindset well suited to raising children.

There was a lot of resentment from Gen X toward the boomers. "I like to blame my parents [*sic*] generation," Kurt astutely wrote in his journals, "for coming so close to social change then giving up after a few successful efforts by the media & government to deface the movement by using the Mansons and other Hippie representatives as propaganda examples on how they were nothing but unpatriotic, communist, satanic, inhuman diseases. and in turn the baby boomers become the ultimate, conforming, yuppie hypocrites a generation has ever produced."

Analyzing his own songs at length reminded Kurt of something. "I'm just starting to realize why I had such a hard time with interviews when this record came out," he said. "People were going through the songs and trying to get me to explain them and I just don't even have any opinions on them. They are all basically saying the same thing: I have this conflict between good and evil and man and woman and that's about it."

By "man and woman," Kurt wasn't referring to something as pedestrian as the proverbial battle of the sexes but more the battle between the archetypally masculine and the archetypally feminine that raged not just within Kurt but within society ever since there's been society. Kurt originally planned for the *Nevermind* LP to have "masculine" and "feminine" sides; it's pretty easy to guess which songs would have gone on each.

...with back...
...nd up on Guus & bring your friend...
The secret hand shakes pretend
...stupid so lazy. I blame our par...
...fazes me   so famous
...so lazy the so stupid   entertainment... HAS been
...our parents   every night...
...the stupids   Undeservin...

Tribe   Variety

little group has always been, and alway...
til the end   swore
...cut our hands & made a pact ...en never going

A mulato an Albino
    A mousquito my Libido

        YAY   A deposit
              for A bottle
              ...inside it
              No Role model   The same percent
                                been and always
A Denial

...ho will be the King & Queen
the Out casted   teens
              ...percentages It's nice t...

chapter ten

A CROSS-FORMAT

PHENOMENON

he massive success of *Nevermind* was a complete surprise, but in retrospect, there were plenty of warning signs. Copies of the Smart sessions tracks had been circulating throughout the industry and on bootlegs for well over a year before *Nevermind* came out, so industry tastemakers and music aficionados were already spreading the word about the band; the line for the *Nevermind* release party wound around the block. Nirvana's "CRACK SMOKIN', KITTY PETTIN'" T-shirts were very popular, providing massive amounts of free advertising. The band had done three US tours and visited Europe twice; they'd gotten the enthusiastic blessing of the influential UK music weeklies, not to mention the all-important Sonic Youth seal of approval.

Those Smart sessions tracks got spread around via cassette—copies dubbed one by one, in real time—so lots of people probably had crappy-sounding second- or third-generation dupes, and they still loved the music.

Kurt was remarkably savvy about Nirvana's marketability, anticipating its appeal with astonishing prescience. In November 1990, before *Nevermind* was fully written, much less recorded or released, he was talking, with no apparent irony, like a canny marketing guy to *Raw* magazine's Liz Evans. "We feel that we're diverse and accessible enough to try to infiltrate into more than just one market," he said. "We feel we can appeal to more than just the metal or the alternative rock market. We want to try to be mainstream, too. We want to reach the Top 40. Even if the whole of the next album can't get across to that type of audience there's at least a hit single or two in there."

Sub Pop succeeded because Pavitt and Poneman had studied the successes and failures of other indie labels and cannily exploited the infrastructure they had already built. In the same way, the infrastructure was already set up for Nirvana to succeed as well. Promoters and booking agents now knew how to deal with this new breed of bands, and several even specialized exclusively in them. Nirvana retained top lawyer Alan Mintz, who had built up expertise and contacts by winning excellent deals for Jane's Addiction, Toad the Wet Sprocket, and a host of other new bands; Nirvana saw Sonic Youth's satisfaction with Gold Mountain, Geffen, and even video director Kevin Kerslake, and eventually followed them to all three. R.E.M. opened up the doors at radio for the band; these days, Kurt even uses R.E.M.'s accountant.

By September 24, 1991, Sub Pop and grunge rock had begun to bubble their way into mass consciousness, but most consumers didn't know how to find the records, and the music wasn't being written up in the mainstream music press or played on big radio stations or MTV, so no one knew what grunge to buy even if they did find it. The miracle of major label distribution gave *Nevermind* a major leg up by making it one of the first grunge records—and that little Sub Pop logo made it official—to get distributed to the major record store chains, where anyone could (and did) buy a copy. Also, the album came out at the beginning of the academic year, when college radio programmers are energetically looking for material to beef up their play lists.

The music itself was a refinement and amplification of what bands such as Hüsker Dü and the Replacements had done, although at root it plugged into a collective consciousness of both Black Sabbath and the Beatles. And then there was that smooth production.

The rock audience was increasingly aware of this new music that spoke more directly to them—they just didn't know what to buy or where to buy it. That's where Geffen/DGC came in: they got Nirvana on the radio, as well as ads and stories in national magazines. Geffen parent company MCA's massive Uni Distribution Corporation distributed *Nevermind*; so if you wanted to buy it, it was definitely at a record store near you.

Nevermind was one of the first "alternative" records to sound good on the radio. Highly compressed—meaning the extremes of high and low volume were electronically limited—Andy Wallace's mixes were custom-tailored for mainstream radio, which is, after all, still where sales campaigns are won or lost. Compared to the usual raw alternative recordings, *Nevermind* sounded like a Bon Jovi record—the production sugar-coated the band's bitter punk pill.

Actually, the *mixing and mastering* sugar-coated the band's bitter punk pill, not so much the "production," i.e., the original tracking. Most of the radio-friendly fairy dust got sprinkled later in the process.

Compression reduces the dynamic range between the loudest and quietest parts of the music, so everything sounds louder. While there was some compression on *Nevermind*, it wasn't anywhere as extreme as when the "loudness wars"—an ever-escalating quest to have the loudest music on the radio—went so over the top that it began to audibly distort the music, as on the Red Hot Chili Peppers' *Californication*, Oasis's *(What's the Story) Morning Glory?*, and Metallica's *Death Magnetic*.

Steve Fisk, who produced the *Blew* sessions, feels that the record, with its heavily flanged bass and guitars and big, reverberant drums, sounds very much like an early-'8os British new wave record, hence what he calls "The Janet Theory."

On "Come as You Are," Nirvana was accused of ripping off a mid-'80s British post-punk record: "Eighties" by the excellent Killing Joke. But that song's riff resembles one in the Damned's 1982 song "Life Goes On." And goth godfathers Bauhaus had done a slow version of that same riff the previous year with "Hollow Hills." And then there's "22 Faces" (1984) by the obscure Norwegian band Garden of Delight. So yeah, maybe Fisk was right: it sounds like an early-'80s new wave record.

"When Janet was fifteen, she was really into the Smiths," Fisk begins. "They made her feel special about herself and she spent long hours in her room with her Walkman on and her parents couldn't bug her and those morbid lyrics really reinforced all that. When they broke up it was very hard for her. Then Morrissey went solo but all her friends got into it and it was very hackneyed."

"At maybe sixteen or seventeen she went into her British death gloom phase for real," Fisk continues. "Then she dyed her hair black and looked like Siouxsie, not understanding that it was a whole played-out cliché by that point. This is, like, 1986. It pissed off her parents and none of her friends were doing something that radical with their looks so it really made her feel good. Of course, that look came to the malls. And it got played out.

"Somewhere along the line she got onto the Sub Pop Singles Club. And she found some music that would really piss people off and she became Grunge Girl. Collectively, that demographic was spring-loaded for a new wave punk record like *Nevermind*.

"The lyrics are happy songs with sad lyrics—it's the Cure, it's Joy Division," says Fisk. "So poor Janet, she couldn't help but like it."

Kurt Cobain enjoys this theory very much. "It's probably true," he says, laughing.

Kurt laughed because he knew he'd been pegged: as he told the *Observer*'s Jon Savage in 1993, "I've always felt that there's that element of gothic in Nirvana."

The gothic really came out in Nirvana's November 1991 performance of "Teen Spirit" on the iconic BBC TV show *Top of the Pops*. *TOTP* policy had performers mime to a backing track, with vocals sung live. Naturally, Nirvana bridled at such fakery: amid a classically goth dry-ice fog, Krist and Dave made no attempt to pretend they were actually playing the song while Kurt sang in a lugubrious baritone that he later explained was a Morrissey imitation but actually came out sounding like Andrew Eldritch from '80s goth godfathers Sisters of Mercy.

###

The media made much of the fact that Bill Clinton was America's first baby boomer president, but boomers had already been dominating US culture for years—especially the music biz. Baby boomers control virtually every aspect of the mainstream music industry, guiding the signing of acts, radio airplay, press coverage.

So baby boomer totems such as the Rolling Stones, the Beatles, and Bob Dylan remain benchmarks; everything else is just a pale shadow. The boomers bombard the airwaves with classic rock. And when people get sick of hearing "Brown Sugar" for the 3,298th time, they slot in a "new" artist like the Black Crowes or the Spin Doctors who gladly caters to the same boomer standards, even as they claim to be "rebels."

But by the time *Nevermind* was released, a large new demographic had emerged. The twentysomethings hadn't been raised on *Let It Bleed*, the *White Album*, and *Blonde on Blonde*—those were oldies. Some called them the Baby Busters, but they actually outnumber the Boomers. And they wanted some music they could call their own.

Nevermind came along at exactly the right time. This was music by, for, and about a whole new group of young people who had been overlooked, ignored, or condescended to. As the twentysomething band Sloan sang in "Left of Centre," "I really can't remember / the last time I was the center / of the target of pop culture . . . I'm slightly left of centre / of the bullseye you've created / It's sad to know that if you hit me / it's because you were not careful."

That generation was well aware of their cultural second-class citizenship—and someone actually wrote a song about it: "Left of Centre" was from the 1993 debut album by the then virtually unknown power-pop band Sloan, who happened to be on Geffen, Nirvana's label. As of this writing, Sloan has gone on to make twelve wonderful albums and become a perennially beloved band, particularly in their native Canada.

Ultimately, it wasn't so much that Nirvana was saying anything new about growing up in America; it was the way they said it. It represented, as *Los Angeles Times* pop critic Robert Hilburn said, "the awakening voice of a new generation." This had all sorts of implications, from consumer marketing to political

demographics. It also marked the definitive end of the baby boomers, who prided themselves on their youth, as the sole arbiters of youth culture. A backlash was clearly in the cards.

#

As if there was any doubt, *Nevermind* proved once and for all that indie rock had completely turned in on itself and become far from the unifying force that rock began as. Just as Kurt took the gutsy step of exploring his pop gift, *Nevermind* forced the denizens of the indie world to consider whether they could like music that *everyone* could like and to consider the possibility that one of their own could make popular music that withstood an unspoken indie loyalty test. Some felt Nirvana's mere popularity disqualified them.

The concept is virtually passé now, but it's impossible to overstate the significance of "selling out"—compromising one's principles or art for the sake of pursuing money or fame—in the dogmatic indie community of the '80s and early '90s. The whole scene was predicated on the oceans of blood, sweat, and tears it took to build an infrastructure that enabled uncompromising musicians to have sustainable careers. If bands sold out, violating that social contract, they were ostracized and excluded; today, we'd call it "canceled." The Del Fuegos, Urge Overkill, and Butthole Surfers found out what that was like.

Kurt was very attuned to this. In the spring of 1992, he told *Flipside* that as a teen he "wrote off" Hüsker Dü as "corporate sell-outs" when they signed to a major label and released 1986's *Candy Apple Grey*. "I didn't even listen to the whole record," he said. "I just thought it was too commercial-sounding." Kurt had been the kind of indie snob that he was now afraid of offending. (*Candy Apple Grey* is much better recorded than previous Hüsker Dü albums, but it remains a raw, aggressive record and a forerunner of *Nevermind*.)

At the April 1991 OK Hotel show, before they set off to Los Angeles to record *Nevermind*, Kurt introduced the band by saying, "Hello, we're major label corporate rock sell-outs." (Even though they were so broke that they had to play the show for gas money.) After signing to Geffen, he changed the band's T-shirt slogan to "Flower-sniffin' kitty-pettin' baby-kissin' corporate rock whores." As ever, he was trying to neutralize charges of selling out by sarcastically embracing them.

Kurt had written on the toes of his sneakers: FUHGAWZ and FOOGAUZIE, a reference to Fugazi, the gold standard of indie integrity. He was probably making fun of Pearl Jam's Eddie Vedder for wearing a T-shirt that said "FUHGAWZ" and writing

"FUGAZI" in Magic Marker on his arm during a TV interview, but Kurt was also feeling his own need to pay fealty to the indie ideal.

(Pearl Jam walks the walk with eco- and worker-friendly merchandise sourcing, carbon-neutral touring, endless charitable work, and generous employee benefits.)

"When Nirvana became popular, it was a difficult transition," Dave told *Rolling Stone* in 2013. "You're in the underground punk scene with your heroes like [Fugazi's] Ian MacKaye or Calvin Johnson. You're desperately wishing for these people's approval, because it validates you as a musician. . . . He was afraid that the people on the scene wouldn't approve of where he was."

It was also "alternative" music that mainstream people could like, too. Suddenly, alternative rock wasn't just the province of jaded college kids—it began to reflect the social realities of a struggling, changing nation. *Nevermind* and the funk-and-roll phenomenon (the Red Hot Chili Peppers, Fishbone, Faith No More, etc.) then enjoying its first flowering renewed the inclusive power of rock. As Kurt came from working-class stock, the success of *Nevermind* was the ultimate expression of Sub Pop's populist ideals—it figures that the band came from an unlikely place such as Aberdeen, rather than Seattle.

Kurt and Krist were working-class—a relative rarity in indie rock, which was primarily oriented toward college types. With notable exceptions such as Hüsker Dü and the Minutemen, this was a milieu in which musicians' parents were music professors (Thurston Moore from Sonic Youth), environmental scientists (Steve Albini from Big Black), erstwhile heirs to great fortunes (Curt and Cris Kirkwood from Meat Puppets), *Washington Post* reporters (Ian MacKaye), kiddie show hosts (Gibby Haynes from the Butthole Surfers), and so on.

Not only was the music compelling and catchy, but it captured the spirit of the age. In one of countless articles on the emerging twentysomething phenomenon, the *Atlantic* magazine commented in a December, 1992, cover story that "This generation—more accurately this generation's reputation—has become a Boomer metaphor for America's loss of purpose, disappointment with institutions, despair over the culture and fear for the future." In that environment, it's no wonder that a song featuring a young man screaming with rage and pain could hit number one.

That *Atlantic* story, "The New Generation Gap," by Neil Howe and William Strauss, turned out to be a landmark in the cultural definition of Generation X.

Gen Xers' alleged embodiment of "America's loss of purpose" is why they were dismissively dubbed "slackers." The term "slacker"—"a person who avoids work or effort"—dates from the nineteenth century but gained new life in the indie world via Superchunk's classic 1989 single "Slack Motherfucker" and then the following year by Richard Linklater's era-defining film *Slacker*, about the bohemian underground in Austin, Texas. (As one of the film's characters puts it, "I may live badly, but at least I don't have to *work* to do it.")

The term "slacker" stuck because, like just about every generation, their elders thought they were lazy and apathetic. Except this time their elders were baby boomers, whose cultural clout was exceeded only by their chagrin that they were no longer young, and so slackers became both a media phenomenon and a punching bag. And that punching bag wouldn't, or couldn't, punch back: "Polls show them mostly agreeing that, yes, Boomer kids probably were a better lot, listened to better music, pursued better causes and generally had better times on campus," wrote Howe and Strauss. "So, they figure, why fight a rap they can't beat?"

The stereotypical slacker, though, was a bit more privileged than Kurt and could live with their parents after graduating from college and wait for something they actually wanted to do with their lives. Less fortunate Gen Xers didn't have that luxury: they had to get a fuckin' job. Or start a successful rock band.

Kurt screams in a code that millions can understand. He communicates in the same scattershot, intuitive way that his generation has been trained to assimilate and to express information, thanks to the usual litany of tens of thousands of hours of television advertising before they were even able to read, lousy schools, the glut of the information age, video games, etc. Kurt's lyrics make unusual sense of chaos. When he screams "a denial, a denial" over and over again at the end of "Teen Spirit," it's something that is understood on a deep level. And either you get it or you don't. It clearly draws the lines, even as it deals in universals. And it's one of the most transcendent moments in rock music.

###

The "Teen Spirit" single went out to radio on August 27, then it went on sale two weeks later on September 10. The single sold well but didn't immediately explode, but meanwhile, MTV accepted the video and a buzz was growing—the song was all over college and alternative radio.

"Teen Spirit" was not supposed to be the hit. The second single, "Come as You Are," was supposed to be the track that would cross over to other radio formats; "Teen Spirit" was the base-building alternative cut. "None of us heard it as a crossover song," says Gold Mountain's Danny Goldberg, "but the public heard it

and it was instantaneous. Right away, the then-emerging format of alternative radio began playing 'Teen Spirit.'" "They heard it on alternative radio," says Goldberg, "and then they rushed out like lemmings to buy it."

The song really was everywhere: grocery stores, passing cars, played over the PA between sets at rock shows. Everybody was talking about it. That kind of thing only happens a few times in a lifetime. And there's a good chance that, in an increasingly balkanized culture, it may never happen again.

In *Sing Backwards and Weep*, Mark Lanegan recalled lying on a bed in Kurt's hotel room, watching MTV while Kurt was on the phone, arguing about band business. Eventually, Kurt got so frustrated that he ripped the cord out of the wall. And then, "Teen Spirit" started playing on the TV. Kurt heaved one of Lanegan's boots at the TV, miraculously hitting the power button and switching it off. "In that same instant," Lanegan wrote, "we heard through the open hotel window a car rolling by three stories down blasting 'Smells Like Teen Spirit.' Kurt looked stricken. He groaned 'No way' and buried his head in the pillow."

It's hard to believe that a song can become a hit simply because it's very good, but this appears to be the case. "Every once in a while, a song *is* that powerful," says Goldberg. "And in their instance, they not only had a song that was that powerful— it combined with an image that was very attractive to a certain subculture."

MTV did not begin pumping the "Teen Spirit" video immediately. The video did receive a prestigious world premiere (making Nirvana the first debut act since Bart Simpson to be so honored) on *120 Minutes*, but only after Amy Finnerty, then a junior member of the programming department and a longtime supporter of new music at the channel, went into her boss's office and threw "a little tantrum." Thereafter, the clip languished in graveyard rotation until entering the Buzz Bin, where the video channel hypes new artists, on October 14, three weeks after the album was released. It stayed in the Buzz Bin for nine weeks, getting, as they say in the broadcast business, heavy phones. MTV market research revealed that "Teen Spirit" appealed to viewers across the demographic board.

Recall Kurt's prediction from almost a year before: "We're diverse and accessible enough to try to infiltrate into more than just one market," which helped with the "heavy phones," i.e., huge numbers of viewers calling MTV and requesting the video.

Goldberg says the album was virtually gold before MTV started playing the "Teen Spirit" video with any frequency. MTV, he says, was just a "multiplier." "It was really obvious that it was just the music—the song and the desire on the part of the audience for a band to emerge did it," says Goldberg. "R.E.M. maybe created that yearning, Jane's Addiction maybe created that yearning, but whatever it was, Nirvana was definitely in the right place at the right time."

###

Nevermind grossed $50 million for Geffen, not bad for an initial investment of $550,000. Still, no one rushes forward to take the credit. As Geffen president Ed Rosenblatt said to the *New York Times*, "We didn't do anything. It was just one of those 'get out of the way and duck' records." The phrase "Get out of the way and duck" is repeated over and over again like a mantra by Geffen execs. What they mean is that as records hit certain sales plateaus, different marketing approaches kick in; for the first million or so sales, *Nevermind* sold too fast for the marketing force to implement any approach. "It was almost disappointing how fast it was going," says Goldberg. "We were just trying to experience it because we knew it was a very rare occurrence."

Given the entire history of the music business, and indeed the entirety of human history, the success of *Nevermind* is notable if only for this one sentence: "No one rushes forward to take the credit."

The success of *Nevermind* was reminiscent of the massive word of mouth campaign that had launched Bruce Springsteen a decade and a half earlier. What happened to Nirvana has certainly happened before in less zeitgeist-defining instances—no one anticipated that Peter Frampton would sell over ten million copies of 1975's *Frampton Comes Alive!*, while Vanilla Ice's ten-times-platinum major label debut also came out of nowhere, garnering very little initial radio or MTV exposure and exploding largely through word of mouth.

Nevermind did eventually get some goosing, however. DGC added the record to cooperative advertising programs with record store chains, stepped up distribution of promo items like posters and mobiles, gave certain retailers a discount on the wholesale price of the album, and then gave them more time to pay for the ones they bought. Sales kept exploding.

Soundscan, a new system for charting records, was another factor. Based strictly on sales instead of an easily manipulated system of reporting, Soundscan revealed what people were actually buying, instead of what the major labels wanted people to buy. The *New York Times* reported that Geffen/DGC used

Soundscan as a marketing tool for *Nevermind*. Soundscan revealed that in certain markets, Nirvana was outselling Metallica four to one, information Geffen/DGC used to get Nirvana onto radio stations that were playing Metallica.

"Between September 24 and Christmas, it just had a life of its own," says Gary Gersh. By January, newsstands were packed with Nirvana stories and the January 11 *Saturday Night Live* appearance further pushed sales. By this point, *Nevermind* was selling over 300,000 copies a week—including 373,250 in the last week of December, as kids went out and spent their Christmas cash and gift certificates on the album all their friends were talking about. That was when Nirvana unseated Michael Jackson at the #1 spot on *Billboard*'s Top 200 Albums chart. The band was selling better than Garth Brooks, Metallica, U2, Guns N' Roses and Hammer.

Billboard magazine called *Nevermind* "a cross-format phenomenon," appearing on hard rock, modern rock, college, and AOR stations, and eventually CHR.

CHR airplay meant that Nirvana was definitively mainstream. On one hand, that was horrifying. On the other hand, now there was finally some good music on the radio.

Kurt wasn't the only one in the band who was conflicted about this. In *The Storyteller*, Dave recalled happily singing along to Top 40 hits as a kid but being of two minds about having a Top 40 hit himself. He'd been one of those zealous, self-righteous punk rockers, but "I also rejoiced," he wrote. "More and more people were showing up to share this music I loved and took so much pride in making and playing."

The fact that the album went to #1 was something of a freak, however. As luck would have it, U2 had decided to release its version of an art-rock record, Michael Jackson continued his artistic slide and Guns N' Roses saw fit to release two albums at once. "They went up against some bad competition, so it wasn't hard for them to do great," says Steve Fisk. "Whenever music gets bad enough, that creates a window of opportunity and shit happens."

To be fair, U2's *Achtung Baby* debuted at #1 and bore five hit singles; it wasn't just a massive record, it's a classic. Simultaneously, Guns N' Roses' *Use Your Illusion II* debuted at #1 and *Use Your Illusion I* debuted at #2, and they could have had much more of an artistic success if they had trimmed the dross out of both records and released a single album. Michael Jackson's *Dangerous* also debuted at #1; a global blockbuster, it's one of the bestselling albums of all time. But the public was beginning to look askance at Jackson's personal life, and with alternative rock on the ascent, Jackson and his highly processed music were beginning to feel passé. *Nevermind* has outsold all of them except *Dangerous*.

As Nirvana went out on a US tour of venues that were far too small for their skyrocketing sales, it created an effect not unlike the one created by putting out their first single as a limited edition of one thousand. It made the ticket that much hotter, ratcheting up curiosity about the group and boosting sales.

No one—the record label, management, concert promoters—anticipated Nirvana's massive success. Nor could they have. On one level, it must have been frustrating, since the band was probably losing all kinds of opportunities. But on another, it was a little terrifying—suddenly, everyone wanted a piece of them. It had become Nirvanamania, and there wasn't enough insulation between Kurt, Krist, and Dave and the churning madness around them.

That level of fame can be exciting and incredibly validating. But it can also be a nightmare. According to the Rolling Stones' Bill Wyman, his late bandmate Brian Jones once said, "It's all very nice, I suppose, to know you're appreciated, but it's also rather frightening." As early as 1964, Bob Dylan apparently felt likewise: "I once thought the biggest I could ever hope to get was like [folk icon Dave] Van Ronk, but it's bigger than that now, ain't it," author Anthony Scaduto, in the biography *Bob Dylan*, quotes him as saying. "Yeah man, it's bigger than that. Scary as all shit."

Some people are cut out for fame; some are not. The latter would include a depressed, drug-addicted high school dropout who was never told he would amount to anything. As Emily Dickinson wrote in her poem "Fame Is a Fickle Food," "Men eat of it and die."

The *Nevermind* phenomenon symbolized a sea-change in rock music. The so-called "hair farmer" bands—Poison, Warrant, Winger, etc.—that the Hollywood music establishment cranked out were perceived as mere entertainers, corporate employees, poseurs, fakes. And their substandard music and the pervasive sexism and machismo that invariably went hand-in-hand with it were getting very played out. And although they may have made a catchy song here and there, they didn't have any resonance.

"Overnight, glam metal had become not only superannuated but was deemed unmentionable and untouchable—and anyone tainted by the genre became equally undesirable," wrote Tom Beaujour and Richard Bienstock in their 2021 oral history of hair metal *Nöthin' But a Good Time*.

Rock culture was undergoing one of its periodic sea-changes. Krist makes a great point in *Of Grunge and Government*: "The old guard of big-hair bands touted a macho swagger packaged in a soft feminine look. Grunge was its symmetrical opposite. It broke through with sensitive introspection wrapped in aggression and facial hair."

The resonance thing is important. After musicians sell a ton of records, they begin to want something else. Just as the ultrarich eventually stop thinking about amassing money and instead covet power, successful musicians want cultural resonance: to *mean something*, to tap into deep societal veins and embody the zeitgeist, to come up with something profound and lasting. Very few get there.

Nirvana may have been the last rock band to achieve that, which is one reason why they continue to hold such a special place in the collective consciousness.

Part of the excitement was the excitement itself—it had been a long time since a rock band *mattered*, when an album seemed to define such a large and imminent cultural moment. There was something in the air and Nirvana turned it into music.

Buying a Nirvana album was something of a consumer insurrection. People were rejecting the old guard and going with what they felt instead of what a large and well-oiled hype machine was telling them to buy. People were choosing substance over image. It was a somewhat tenuous connection, but there was a feeling in the bones that something surprising was going to happen in the election that November.

The success of the album coincided with a general yen for "reality," encompassing things like MTV's *Unplugged* show, renewed interest in additive-free foods, the advent of network news segments that punctured the artifice of political advertising. "We weren't doing any posing and we weren't trying to be something that we weren't," Dave Grohl says. "It was sort of a package deal—you've got good music, you've got normal-looking people, just like Bruce Springsteen can sell out the Enormodome in New Jersey because he's 'a fuckin' average Joe.' I think it had a lot to do with something like that, maybe—people seeing normal people and appreciating that."

"Nirvana embodied the yearning for a moral universe that was more real and more sincere than what was going on in the conventional rock world at the time," says Goldberg, "and I think that resonates with a yearning in the culture for the post-Reagan set of values. There is a connection between their desire for authenticity and sincerity and ethics—it's a real commitment to an attitude that is very attractive. They convey a set of values that's egalitarian and ethics-driven and less macho, power-driven. All that stuff, combined with the musical genius, is what they are."

In the face of "fake news," Photoshop, Auto-Tune, highly processed foods, bots posing as people, and countless other artificial products, there will always be people who yearn for things that come from the heart and not from an algorithm or a test tube. Nirvana's music didn't become popular because the music industry promoted it; it became popular because people loved it. That's what Nirvana represents. It's another reason why Nirvana's legacy has lasted into the 2020s: they unfailingly kept it real.

###

Although Dave denies he is "Mr. Analysis," he has an excellent grasp of the circumstances which gave rise to *Nevermind*'s success. "There was a weird lull, a void in rock," he says. "If you looked at the Top 10 in the year before *Nevermind*, there was rarely any rock music in it except for bad heavy metal shit that no one could relate to. When our music came out, I think it was a combination of stoners, skaters, of derelict kids who saw a group of derelict kids playing music that sounded like we were pissed. And I think a lot of people related to that. And the songs were good songs. Kurt has a great voice. The songs were catchy and they were simple, just like an ABC song when you were a kid."

An unstated goal of rock music is to bug one's parents. But twentysomethings' parents were raised on rock & roll themselves, so the job had become a lot tougher than it was in the '60s. With its ravaged screaming, pervasive distortion, and bludgeoning attack, *Nevermind* fulfilled that goal admirably.

But beneath all that, there was no denying that the music was simply extraordinary. It captured all the energy and excitement of punk and applied it to songs that people could hum long after the album was finished playing. Unlike so many albums that consist of one or two singles and a bunch of filler, *Nevermind* is a really good album from front to back. You can put the CD on and listen to the whole thing and not skip over anything. "The key to Nirvana is the songs are great, truly great," says the fiftysomething Ed Rosenblatt. "I'm talking on a level with R.E.M., on a level with Paul Simon."

It is a massive compliment when a boomer compares a young band to Paul Simon.

Strangely, the press and the public don't think of him as such, but Kurt Cobain is a songwriter's songwriter. In one fell swoop, Kurt reclaimed pop songwriting from the convoluted, inbred freak it had become. This wasn't songwriting for its own sake, as practiced by the likes of Elvis Costello, Marshall Crenshaw, and Michael Penn, who lately seemed to take special pleasure in obscuring the very emotions they so very artfully claimed to convey. Kurt's music went simply and directly to the soul. His lyrics weren't tortured wordplay aimed at tickling the fancy of some jaded rock critic, the chord progressions weren't designed to impress a Juilliard student; instead, the words heightened the total sensation of the music. Like a cool guitar sound or a riff, they made it rock. The music was ingenious in its economy, the melodies were indelible.

Butch Vig chalks a lot of it up to Kurt's voice. "If you took all his songs and had someone else sing them, it wouldn't be the same," he says. "There's something in Kurt's persona that takes them to another level. There's mystery and passion and intensity and something that's almost otherworldly in his voice. You hear his voice and it conjures up some kind of image in your mind."

Nirvana songs are indeed not the same without Kurt's voice. But they're still great songs, so when other people sing them, they're great in other, new ways. Listen to Polyphonic Spree's joyous version of "Lithium"; Tricky's dark, dancehall-inflected "Something in the Way"; Sturgill Simpson's stunningly pensive "In Bloom"; neo-soul king Charles Bradley's Stax-ified "Stay Away"; or indie-folk musician Jessica Lea Mayfield's "Lounge Act." Jazz icon Herbie Hancock did a lovely version of "All Apologies," although Sinéad O'Connor's might just overshadow the original. That said, Post Malone's uncannily carbon copy–perfect Nirvana covers, live streamed on YouTube in April 2020, spread massive waves of life-affirming joy during the early depths of the pandemic.

It's a phenomenon that *Rolling Stone* critic Ralph J. Gleason once identified as the "yarrrrragh," a Gaelic word that refers to that rare quality that some voices have, an edge, an ability to say something about the human condition that goes far beyond merely singing the right lyrics and hitting the right notes. Semiologist Roland [Barthes] called it "the grain of the voice." Either you have it or you don't. Robert Johnson had it, Hank Williams had it; these days, it's people like Screaming Trees' Mark Lanegan and Kurt Cobain.

The "yarrrrragh" thing came from Gleason's review of Van Morrison's 1970 album *Moondance*. Interestingly, in *The Rolling Stone Illustrated History of Rock & Roll*, revered critic Greil Marcus elaborated on that thought with a reference to Kurt's beloved Lead Belly: "The yarrrrragh is Van Morrison's version of Leadbelly, of jazz, of blues, of poetry. . . . To Morrison the yarrrrragh is the gift of the muse and the muse itself." It is, Marcus adds, "a gift and a mystery and understood as such."

But each member brought something to the band. While Kurt's contributions are perhaps more obvious, Chris was for a long time the sole liaison between the band and the press, his business sense is indispensable and early on, his outspoken political sensibility helped to lend the band critical weight. Chris's onstage chemistry with Kurt is indefinable but clear. And not to be overlooked is his steadfast support of Kurt over the years in pursuing his musical vision.

It was Krist who demanded a contract from Sub Pop, helped fix Kurt's guitars and was always on the lookout for left-handed models in thrift stores, built out his basement so the band could practice there, found the barn in Tacoma where they later rehearsed, was the band's liaison with Sub Pop's in-house booking agent, explained Kurt's mood swings to outsiders, did most of the talking when they first met with Gold Mountain, asked Butch Vig if he'd be interested in producing their major label debut, kept an enraged and bloodied bouncer from beating the crap out of Kurt, and drove his Volkswagen van with all the band's equipment in it down to L.A. for the *Nevermind* sessions. Those are invisible, unglamorous tasks, but they were essential to the band's existence.

As Dave later told *Rolling Stone*, "Those two guys, together, totally defined the Nirvana aesthetic. Every quirk, all the strange things that came from Nirvana came from Krist and Kurt."

It can't be said enough: it might not have happened without Krist.

Dave's contribution to the band has largely been unsung. His powerful drumming propelled the band to a whole new plane, visually as well as musically. Try to imagine "Come as You Are" without the inspired cymbal bashing near the end that simply sends the track through the roof, the mighty snare rolls that machine-gun the band into the chorus of "In Bloom." Although Dave is a merciless basher, his parts are also distinctly musical—it wouldn't be difficult to figure out what song he was playing even without the rest of the music. His personal contribution is also essential. "Pretty much under every circumstance, David's the one who's rock-solid the whole time," says Alex Macleod. "He's a good influence on both of them."

"They've got it all, basically—great drummer, great singer, great image, great songs, great sense of the media, great live band," says Danny Goldberg. "It all kind of worked. They excelled in a half-dozen areas."

The album's impact was such that nowadays, industry pundits talk about the "post-Nirvana music business." One impact, as Matt Lukin puts it, is that after Nirvana, "The underground isn't as underground as it used to be."

Underground culture was transmitted through college radio, fanzines, word of mouth, cassettes sent through the mail, flyers on telephone poles, public access cable shows.

Then came MTV. Keen to fill twenty-four hours of airtime with new, hip content, MTV popularized indie and alternative musicians such as Hüsker Dü, Robyn Hitchcock, Faith No More, X, the Sugarcubes, XTC, Echo and the Bunnymen, and They Might Be Giants, bands who otherwise never would have made it onto national television.

But MTV had a homogenizing effect. In the early '80s, "people were inventing their own scenes because there was nothing else going on," Mudhoney's Steve Turner told me for *Our Band Could Be Your Life*. But once MTV aired nationwide, regional variations in things like slam-dancing, clothes, haircuts, and music began to disappear—everyone was imitating what they saw on MTV. "It went from each town having its own little story," Turner continued, "to it being kind of the same group of people in every town."

Nirvana's success also demonstrated to the music business the snowballing power of the indie network. Nirvana could not have broken without all the years of hard work by labels like SST, Twin/Tone, and Touch & Go, as well as bands like Sonic Youth, Black Flag, the Minutemen, the Replacements, and R.E.M., all of whom built a system by which kids could catch the indie buzz—outside of the influence of the major labels.

Consequently, labels began paying more attention to bands with a following— i.e., bands that people actually *liked*—rather than creating one out of promotional dollars. They ceded some—though hardly all—of the control of what gets signed and promoted to a grassroots level. As regional music scenes gained power, they began to decentralize the music business.

It shifted a fair amount of power from the corporate rock factions at the major labels to the people who had been following the indie rock scene. "There's no question that there's fifteen or twenty A&R people who can sign acts now who couldn't do that two years ago," says Goldberg. Those people began catching the next plane to Seattle and pretty soon any musician from the area with long hair and a flannel shirt could get signed for $350,000. At one point in early 1992, Northwest bands were getting signed at the incredible rate of one a week. The industry will be working all the bands that the new wave of A&R people is signing for years to come.

Most of those bands flopped on major labels and either broke up or went back to the indie world with their tails between their legs.

Part of the rocket fuel for the spending frenzy was the switch from vinyl and cassettes to CDs, which cost more even though they were cheaper to manufacture. There was a lot of money flying around.

Post-Nirvana, some hotly pursued alternative bands commanded a much higher advance than before. And since the labels didn't quite understand their music or their milieu, the bands were granted complete creative control.

As boomers get older, they buy fewer records. *Nevermind* heralded this changing of the music consumer guard. The major labels knew they had to begin addressing this emerging market. And that market suddenly became polarized between the people who would buy Def Leppard records, for instance, and those who wouldn't.

Mainstream radio got taught a lesson because a record caught on without it. And everyone knew it wasn't a fluke because *Nevermind* was an undeniably great record. And there was an army of like-minded bands right behind Nirvana.

By making a great album within the confines of a major label superstructure, keeping their integrity while acknowledging mainstream sonic tastes, Nirvana made a point. Perhaps the ultimate message of the success of *Nevermind* was that even one little band (or person) can make big changes in a large and seemingly immovable institution.

In fact, as history has shown time and time again, it takes the cooperation and hard work of many people to make changes in large and seemingly immovable institutions. Those changes were already underway, thanks to bands like R.E.M., Hüsker Dü, and Jane's Addiction, who had blazed the major label trail, and the inexorable groundswell of a new generation just entering its prime as consumers. With the right music at the right time, Nirvana was merely the figurehead for it all. As David Bowie once said, "It's not who does it first. It's who does it second."

But doing it second bothered Kurt: he was dubious about what had become of punk and Nirvana's place in it. "Punk Rock (while still sacred to some) is, to me, dead and gone," he wrote in the liner notes for *Incesticide*. "We just wanted to pay tribute to something that helped us to feel as though we had crawled out of the dung heap of conformity. To pay tribute like an Elvis or Jimi Hendrix impersonator in the tradition of a bar band. I'll be the first to admit that we're the '90s version of Cheap Trick or The Knack but the last to admit that it hasn't been rewarding."

As it had with virtually every other underground/avant-garde movement, the mainstream absorbed certain aspects of punk. But while there were commercial bands playing generically punk music, the punk ethos itself proved too virulent to be fully co-opted. Using DIY media to question and defy the status quo ultimately gave rise to radical eruptions such as 1999's World Trade Organization protests and 2011's Occupy Wall Street movement. True, those uprisings were largely quelled, but there's nothing more punk than fighting a war that you can't win.

Also, Kurt loved Cheap Trick and the Knack.

chapter eleven

SLAM-DANCING WITH MR. BROWNSTONE

Kurt and Courtney had done heroin together in Amsterdam for two days around Thanksgiving of 1991. "It was *my* idea," says Kurt. "I was the one that instigated it. But I didn't really know how to get it, so Courtney was the one who would be able to somehow get it. She would be the one who would take me to the place where we might have a chance of being able to find it. We only did it twice on the whole tour." They found a guy on the street who took them to the city's infamous red light district, where they scored. Later, they did some more in London.

Kurt's stomach pain had been driving him insane on the European tour, making him chronically irritable and antisocial. "A lot of the hatred would surface because I was in such a fucked-up mental state," he says. "I was so angry with my body that I couldn't deal with anyone socially. I was just totally neurotic because I was in pain all the time. People had no idea I was in pain and I couldn't complain about it twenty-four hours a day."

He says the pain made him suicidal, so he simply chose his poison. "I just decided I wanted to have a life," he says. "If I'm going to kill myself, I'm going to kill myself for a reason instead of some stupid stomach problem. So I decided to take everything in excess all at once."

It must have been intensely frustrating to be playing universally acclaimed, commercially successful music with an awesomely powerful band to huge crowds of adoring fans, only to have it all undercut by chronic, acute physical pain, which can also cause awful psychological damage.

That said, doing heroin isn't actually a life-affirming move.

And then there's "If I'm going to kill myself, I'm going to kill myself for a reason." What I learned, the hard way, is that people who commit suicide often basically tell you they're going to do it. Sometimes repeatedly. It's very difficult to say this, but when things got tough for Kurt, he'd often say, dejectedly, "I might as well blow my head off."

When you hear something like that, you don't think they're being literal. But they might be warning you. "I was a seriously depressed kid," Kurt told the veteran *Los Angeles Times* pop critic Robert Hilburn. "Every night at one point I'd go to bed bawling my head off. I used to try to make my head explode by holding my breath, thinking if I blew up my head they'd be sorry. There was a time when I thought I'd never live to see twenty-one."

(Another mournful example of this kind of foreshadowing is when the late Scott Hutchison of the Scottish band Frightened Rabbit sang about finding peace by jumping off Edinburgh's Forth Road Bridge on the band's song "Floating in the Forth"—some ten years before he apparently did just that.)

The only positive thing I can possibly salvage from that experience is to know to recognize it next time—and I hope the reader will, too. But I really hope there is never a next time.

In early December, when Kurt returned to Seattle after the tour and Courtney was still in Europe with Hole, he began hanging out with a recovering addict. He soon sweet-talked her into getting him heroin. At first, she'd cop for him only when she felt like it, but soon she was getting heroin for him every day.

Soon, Kurt and his supplier got a scare. "I *didn't* OD," he maintains. "She *thought* that I was OD'ing and so she started giving me mouth to mouth but I had just stood up too fast and fell down. She was giving me mouth to mouth and said I was turning blue but I wasn't out for very long at all—maybe half a minute. It was just kind of scary to her. She overexaggerated on it."

Turning blue after fainting from standing up too fast is highly unlikely. Either Kurt was bullshitting me or he'd actually convinced himself that that's what really happened—drugs do funny things to the mind.

Kurt eventually met the dealer and scored on his own. "I was determined to get a habit," he says. "I *wanted* to. It was *my* choice. I said, 'This is the only thing that's saving me from blowing my head off right now. I've been to ten doctors and nothing they can do about it. I've got to do something to stop this pain.'" He also admits there was the simple pleasure of getting high, but that wasn't the point.

"It started with three days in a row of doing heroin and I don't have a stomach pain," he says. "That was such a relief. I decided, 'Fuck, I'm going to do this for a whole year. I'll eventually stop. I can't do it forever because I'll fucking die.' I don't regret it at all because it was such a relief from not having stomach pain every day. My mental state just went totally up. I healed myself." Except for a long and profound relapse when he detoxed, the mysterious stomach pain has largely disappeared.

It was probably two weeks or so, but Kurt has little idea how long he was in Seattle or where he stayed before going down to L.A. "God, I don't even know," he says. "I wasn't there for very long. Jesus, where did I sleep?"

In the pines, in the pines, where the sun don't ever shine
I would shiver the whole night through

When Courtney came home to Los Angeles from her tour with Hole later in December, Kurt called and said, "Let's live together." They briefly lived in an apartment Courtney shared with Hole guitarist Eric Erlandson and another friend until it was made apparent that they weren't welcome because of their drug use.

They bounced from hotel to hotel, doing what Courtney calls "bad Mexican L.A. heroin." Kurt would do the lion's share of the drugs. Courtney never quite got the hang of injecting drugs, so Kurt would often shoot her up "whenever she'd beg me hard enough." She already had a dark little scar on the inside of her elbow from when other people had botched injections.

Kurt was notorious for the amount of drugs he could ingest. "Kurt was a gobbler," Courtney told *Spin*'s Craig Marks in February 1995. "If there were 40 pills, he'd take 40 pills instead of taking two pills and making it last a month."

What were those weeks like? "I don't really remember," Kurt replies, even though it's only a little over a year later. "I just remember us both being total slobs."

Heroin is a very seductive drug. It feels very relaxing, very comfortable. At low doses, it can make even the shyest user very social; high doses produce the phenomenon of "nodding out," when the user seems to fall asleep, even in mid-sentence. The high can last for ten hours, but the more you do, the less it lasts. It's a very insidious drug—it takes a while to become addicted, but once that happens, it suddenly becomes very uncomfortable to stop doing it. And then the cravings start. After a while, it becomes very hard to think clearly and to monitor and control the emotions, and often, the user isn't even aware that this is happening.

The same could be said about how heroin swept through the US around this time. It seemed to be everywhere in popular culture: heroin was practically a costar in a number of prominent films of the time, including *Drugstore Cowboy* (1989), *Pulp Fiction* (1994), *The Basketball Diaries* (1995), *Trainspotting* (1996), and even *Singles* (1992), the rom-com about the Seattle slacker/grunge scene.

"Heroin chic" was a bona fide fashion trend in the early '90s: a pale, emaciated look complete with lank hair and circles under the eyes. Models Gia Carangi, Jaime King, and Kate Moss were exemplars; Carangi and King really were heroin addicts.

But musicians were on the leading edge of this trend. In the wake of Kurt's death, celebrity drug counselor Bob Timmins told the *Seattle Times* that he wasn't surprised by musicians' fascination with heroin and other drugs, since they tend to be "pretty sensitive, emotional people. If most people feel things at a '10,' they feel things at a '12.' ... It's a pain reliever. It hides the demons and makes you feel insulated." In the '90s, many prominent musicians at least dabbled in the drug and wrote songs about the experience, including members of Red Hot Chili Peppers ("Under the Bridge"), Blur ("Beetlebum"), Everclear ("Heroin Girl"), Elliott Smith ("Needle in the Hay"), Stone Temple Pilots ("Interstate Love Song"), and Alice in Chains ("Junkhead" and many more).

Heroin chic became such a cultural phenomenon that President Bill Clinton felt obliged to speak out against it: "Images projected in fashion photos in the last few years have made heroin addiction seem glamorous and sexy and cool," Clinton said in a May 1997 speech. "And glorifying death is not good for any society."

Why did heroin flourish then? Every generation seems to have its signature drugs. Just as the shambling Yeti-rock of grunge was the antithesis of the geometric Day-Glo of '80s pop, heroin is the antithesis of the cocaine that was in vogue during the Reagan era. It's the difference between wanting everything to be like Saturday night and wanting it to be, as Kurt put it in "Lithium," like Sunday morning.

Cocaine amplified and ratified the previous generation's sense of invincibility and entitlement. But when an entire generation is told they're "slackers," it stands to reason that a fair-sized chunk of them will feel obliged to live up to the tag. Sub Pop made a virtue of this downtrodden status with a famous T-shirt that said "LOSER" in big block letters, a defining statement of slacker irony.

This generational zeitgeist colluded with some practical realities. Everyone knew that you could contract AIDS from sharing needles, but in the '90s, heroin became purer, which meant you could get high by snorting it instead of injecting it. That made it easier and more acceptable to use, and thus more appealing to different types of people. It wasn't unusual to see office types lining up with the rest of the junkies at the notorious open-air drug bazaars of New York's East Village and the Blade section of Seattle.

There are credible claims that the heroin problem in Seattle was no worse than it was anywhere else. But how to explain the high number of musicians who were heroin users in such a relatively small city: not just Kurt and Courtney but Andrew Wood from Mother Love Bone, Stefanie Sargent of 7 Year Bitch, Mark Arm from Mudhoney, Layne Staley and Mike Starr from Alice in Chains, Mark Lanegan from Screaming Trees, Kristen Pfaff from Hole, and countless others who aren't as well-known. (Often left out of the Seattle drug story are MDA/MDMA and Seattle's plentiful craft beer, with its high alcohol content; both played a major part in forming the community and its aesthetic.)

It was also enabled by a basic market factor: heroin was simply cheaper and more available, so more people bought it. Seattle is a port city for ships from Asia, one of the main sources of heroin, and a key distribution point for black tar heroin—a crudely refined form that can resemble sticky tar or little bits of coal—that comes up from Mexico and points south. Seattle was rife with black tar. It's like McDonald's food: *Why do so many people buy that crap?* Because it's cheap and it's everywhere. Combine that with the tenor of the times, Seattle's lagging recovery from the recession, and maybe the Northwest's depressingly overcast climate, and the conditions were ripe.

Just after Christmas, the band set off on a brief tour with Pearl Jam and the Red Hot Chili Peppers, who headlined. No one was happy about Nirvana playing second fiddle to the Peppers, but they had already committed to it during the chaos of the American tour. At any rate, Nirvana stole the show. For one thing, their album was number six with a bullet. And they had outstanding material—songs like "Lithium," "Teen Spirit" and "In Bloom." The best the Chili Peppers could muster was a cover of Stevie Wonder's "Higher Ground." Pearl Jam was just getting its act together.

The *Los Angeles Times*' Robert Hilburn covered the December 27, 1991, show at the Los Angeles Memorial Sports Arena. "What if you gave a concert and your special guest stole the show?" Hilburn wrote. "In what proved to be one of the year's most satisfying pairings, both bands turned in impressive, crowd-pleasing sets. However, the future may rest with Nirvana. That's because the Peppers may be deluxe party-givers but Nirvana—led by singer-songwriter Kurt Cobain—has more substantial and ultimately enthralling music."

The Chili Peppers tour is when Chris finally admitted to himself that Kurt was heavily into heroin, "He looked like shit," Chris says. "He looked like a ghoul." Chris knew he couldn't do anything about it. "I just figured it's his fucking trip, it's his life, he can do whatever he wants," he says. "You can't change anybody or preach some kind of morals or anything. What am I going to do? Nothing. So I just do my own thing."

Everyone assumed that Courtney had gotten Kurt to do heroin. "Everybody was blaming *her*," says Shelli. "She was the big scapegoat. If he wouldn't have hooked up with her, he would have hooked up with somebody else and done heroin. That's just the fact of the matter. It was easy to blame her at first—and looking back, that's what everybody did. They still do it. Just because she's loud and outspoken and has her own point of view . . ."

Blaming Courtney fit into the convenient stereotype of the domineering bitch and the henpecked wimp. For one thing, it's nearly inconceivable that someone could simply talk someone else into doing heroin—people who do heroin *want* to do it. And the fact is, Kurt had been doing heroin off and on for years by then; Courtney hadn't done it in three years. "[It's] such a fucking typical sexist stupid thing to say, so classic," Kurt says. "Man, when I got off the European tour, I went out of my *way* to get drugs every fucking day. On my own."

Chris was also struggling with his own demons. After a New Year's Eve show at the Cow Palace in San Francisco, he drunkenly hit his head on a low-slung heater element in a backstage passageway. He resolved to go on the wagon for as long as he could.

There's an Alcoholics Anonymous term, "find your bottom," for whatever low point it takes to finally compel you to get sober. For some, it's losing their job or their partner or their band; for Krist, it was hitting his head on a heater. I bet he's really thankful that that's all it took.

As a very directed, hardworking person, Dave must have been particularly annoyed by, as he says a little later in the book, "a drug that knocks us out and makes us look stupid."

###

The first press to acknowledge the heroin rumors was a January profile in *BAM* magazine which claimed that Kurt was "nodding off in mid-sentence," adding that "the pinned pupils, sunken cheeks, and scabbed, sallow skin suggest something more serious than fatigue." Soon, an item in the industry tip sheet *Hits* was hinting that Kurt was "slam-dancing with Mr. Brownstone," Guns N' Roses slang for doing heroin. The tidbit ran in a column written by Lonn Friend, the *Rip* magazine editor that Kurt had snubbed not so long before.

So that's when Lonn Friend turned himself into one of Kurt's many antagonists.

"By the end, it started to really suck because I started to get really paranoid because there were things being written about me being a heroin addict," Kurt says. "I just started getting paranoid that cops were going to bust into our house or I'd get pulled over and they'd recognize me, find my track marks and take me to jail. The biggest fear was detoxing cold turkey. I knew I'd probably die if that happened, because the cops wouldn't give a fuck—they wouldn't put me in a hospital, they'd just let me go cold turkey and I'd die in jail. So that was kind of scary. In the morning, I'd drive real cautiously to the drug dealer's house."

A lot of people around them struggled to understand why Kurt and Courtney were doing this to themselves. "It's like this," says Courtney. "'Hey, you know what? I just sold a million fuckin' records and I got a million bucks and I'm going to share it with you and let's get high!'"

Heroin still held an allure as a staple of rock culture. "That's the drug that makes you sleepy and happy," says Courtney. "That's the drug you do if you're in a fuckin' four-star hotel and you can order all the goddamn room service that you want and you can just lay in bed and drool all over yourself because you've got a million bucks in the bank. That's the drug you want to do if you want to be a kid forever."

"By the end"—as if he was no longer an addict. That was important to assert at the time, as we'll soon see.

Of course, few people who can order all the room service they want wind up lying in bed and doing so much heroin that they drool all over themselves.

But maybe heroin is the drug you do when you're in your mid-twenties and you suddenly feel immense pressure that you're not equipped to deal with. Maybe it's the drug you do when millions of people love you and you don't even love yourself.

The seductive combination of being head over heels in love and basking in the warm, embryonic comfort of heroin—away from the strains and responsibilities of being an internationally recognized rock star—must have been overpowering. "It was a love thing," Courtney says. "It was a drug/love thing. I met this person that's perfect for me, I'm in love. Even though it's not my million bucks, so what. Whatever. He's saying you can have it, so whatever, I'll just have his million bucks and let's just do some drugs. That's what it was about." If one of the reasons Kurt did heroin was in a misguided attempt to cope with his fame, perhaps Courtney used heroin to deal with Kurt's fame as well.

As Courtney said earlier, "I thought I was going to be more famous than him. That was pretty obvious to me." It's easy to see how someone who felt like that might have difficulty with being utterly eclipsed by someone else's talent and fame.

So there *was* an element of just wanting to get high. "There might have been in *her* eyes," Kurt says, who still maintains that he basically did heroin for its analgesic properties.

A denial, a denial.

###

They went up to Seattle for a while, then spent a week in San Francisco, oblivious to the fact that Kurt's band was the hottest, most talked-about group on the planet.

They must have been doing a *lot* of drugs because both Kurt and Courtney normally kept close tabs on their own press.

In the midst of all this, the unthinkable happened: *Nevermind* hit #1 on the Billboard album charts the week of January 11, 1992, topping U2, Guns N' Roses, and Garth Brooks, and even pushing Michael Jackson off the top spot. Besides hitting #1 in the United States, *Nevermind* also topped the charts in Belgium, France, Ireland, Israel, Spain, Sweden, and Canada, and went Top 3 in virtually every other major market in the world except for Italy, Japan, and oddly enough, the UK (although it did stay in the British Top 25 for months).

Meanwhile, the band was being wooed by Guns N' Roses and Metallica to appear on their joint US tour that summer. Despite some very high-level pressure, Kurt and the band refused. They'd never be caught dead playing with Guns N' Roses.

But Kurt didn't want to be seen playing with Metallica, even though he apparently still (secretly?) loved Metallica. "He came to one of our shows in Seattle [probably at the Seattle Center in May 1992]," Metallica guitarist Kirk Hammett told *Rolling Stone*'s Greg Prato in 2012. "We were playing 'Whiplash,' and he looked at me and kept punching the air with his fist and gave me a big thumbs-up sign. I was like, 'Cool, Kurt, I know you love this song. This one's for you!' . . . I was surprised at how much of a Metallica fan he was. He loved *Ride the Lightning*. He loved that album." But you won't see *Ride the Lightning*, or any metal at all, on any of the lists of essential albums that Kurt made.

Then the band went to New York to tape a live set for MTV and to play *Saturday Night Live* on January 11. When the car that had turned up at their hotel in Seattle turned out to be a limousine, Kurt and Courtney sent it back and asked for a more modest car. There were no smaller cars available, so the livery company sent another limousine. When all was said and done, Kurt and Courtney missed their flight.

By then, Kurt and Courtney had been doing heroin long enough to begin to get addicted.

The day of the *Saturday Night Live* taping, Courtney got Danny Goldberg to deliver five thousand dollars (a little over nine thousand in today's dollars) in hundred-dollar bills to their hotel room on the pretense that they needed it to go shopping. (Did they not have credit cards?) Instead, they went to the East Village and used the money to cop heroin.

Kurt nodding out at the Lavine session. © Michael Lavine

Early the next morning, Kurt apparently overdosed and likely would have died had Courtney not resuscitated him. Gold Mountain acknowledged what was going on, staged an intervention, and put off plans for an upcoming US arena tour.

"I remember walking into their hotel room and for the first time, really realizing that these two are fucked *up*," says Dave. "They were just nodding out in bed, just wasted. It was disgusting and gross. It doesn't make me angry at *them*, it makes me angry that they would be so pathetic as to do something like that. I think it's pathetic for anyone to do something to make themselves that functionless and a drooling fucking baby. It's like 'Hey, let's do a drug that knocks us out and makes us look stupid.' It's stupid and gross and pathetic for anyone to take it to that point."

("I went up to his room and Kurt came to the door in his underwear and Courtney, all I saw was a little piece of hair sticking out from underneath the covers," says Wendy. "There was like five deli trays, room carts with old food. And I said, 'Kurt, why don't you get a maid in here?' And Courtney says, 'He can't. They steal his underwear.'")

Although Kurt had been doing heroin for over a month, even his closest associates hadn't noticed until now. "I didn't realize that he was getting fucked up until *Saturday Night Live* just because I'm stupid and I just couldn't pick out something like that," Dave admits. "I'm naive and didn't want to believe it."

It's difficult to understand how Dave could have been naive about this; by now, his bullshit detector was extremely powerful. But maybe it was too huge and too depressing to acknowledge, especially as everything was exploding around the band. As he said, he just didn't want to believe it. Denial is a very powerful force.

There was at least one thing to be grateful about. "Thank God those two didn't do cocaine," says Dave, "because they'd be the biggest fucking assholes in the world."

It wasn't as if they were violent or irrational or any sloppier than they usually were. "Kurt was mostly just sleepy," says soundman Craig Montgomery. "They just seemed to be in a fog. They seemed not to care about much of anything, including their friends. That's the way it felt sometimes. They were in their own little world. And I'm sure they felt like the whole world was against them, too."

It was a vicious cycle: the more they did drugs, the more the world disapproved of them. And the more the world disapproved of them, the more they did drugs.

The day of their *Saturday Night Live* appearance, the band did a now infamous shoot with photographer Michael Lavine. Exhausted and having tanked up just beforehand, Kurt nodded out a couple of times in front of the camera. "I just blocked it out," says Chris. "I didn't give a shit."

A photo from that shoot graced the cover of the original version of this book. Kurt later told me he was bummed about that. That photo contradicted the line that Kurt was not as much of a junkie as he really was and endangered the whole idea that he was a worthy parent, which struck at what I came to realize was the whole purpose of the book.

Of the shoot, Kurt remembers "Dead silence. Dirty looks and dead silence. [Chris and Dave] weren't the type to confront anyone about anything. They were so passive-aggressive that they would rather give off bad vibes than talk about anything. I mean, what are they supposed to do? They're not going to be able to tell me to stop. So I didn't really care. Obviously to them it was like practicing witchcraft or something. They didn't know anything about it so they thought that any second I was going to die."

Lavine was terribly worried, too. "I asked him, 'Why are you doing this?' He said, 'It's the only thing that helps my stomach pain,'" says Lavine. "I didn't have enough guts to say, 'Kurt, that's a bunch of shit.'"

That night, the band played "Teen Spirit" and later, "Territorial Pissings," with the band trashing their instruments for a finale. Kurt took the opportunity to give some national exposure to an old favorite and wore a Flipper T-shirt he'd made at the Lavine shoot. During the closing credits, Chris kissed both Kurt and Dave flat on the mouth, just to annoy the homophobic rednecks back home, and all the other homophobes in their vast new audience. With twenty-five million people looking on, there was a lot of *bourgeoisie* to shock.

Krist took the high-visibility opportunity to plug some friends' bands, sporting a Melvins T-shirt during "Smells Like Teen Spirit" and then an L7 shirt for "Territorial Pissings." Dave borrowed the Melvins shirt for the latter song.

That performance of "Teen Spirit" might have been the most straightforward, error-free live version they ever played. Thanks to the show's powerful producer Lorne Michaels, not to mention the show's gruff, unforgivingly efficient crew, one did not mess around on *SNL*: famously, Elvis Costello, Fear, and the Replacements had all been banned from the show for insubordination. And, whether Kurt would admit it or not, appearing on *Saturday Night Live* was a career milestone, a universally understood signal that a band had arrived at the forefront of American popular culture, and he was not going to screw it up. Anarchy did reign, though, at the end of "Territorial Pissings," with an epic instrument-trashing finale.

Krist instigated the *SNL* kissing: first, he plants a passionate one on Dave. Then Kurt notices what's going on, looks pleasantly surprised, and gets in on the action. The show went out live, so there was no way to censor this grotesque affront to all that is right and good. For rebroadcasts, *SNL* edited in the closing scene from the rehearsal earlier in the evening, consigning the original ending to an Orwellian memory hole. Today, *Saturday Night Live* would probably circulate the clip on social media. Nirvana played a part in that cultural sea-change.

The next day, Kurt and Courtney did another shoot with Michael Lavine for a cover story in *Sassy* magazine, *the* monthly bible of hip teen girls (and certain

Kurt during the Australian tour. ©Neil Wallace

vampiric adults). "They were totally in love," says Lavine. "You couldn't separate them. They *are* in love—it's not like this fake thing. They have a genuine chemistry toward each other."

The April issue of *Sassy* put a kissing Kurt and Courtney on the cover. "Ain't Love Grand?" read the cover line. Without seeming to know quite what she was saying, writer Christina Kelly observes, "It's looking very *Sid and Nancy*."

Sid and Nancy is Alex Cox's 1986 biopic about late Sex Pistols bassist Sid Vicious and his late girlfriend Nancy Spungen, a sordid depiction of the ravages of heroin addiction that ends in murder. (In a mashup of art and life, Courtney badly wanted the role of Nancy Spungen but wound up being cast in a minor role.) So "it's looking very *Sid and Nancy*" could be quite a damning thing to say, but it's not clear whether Kelly was insinuating that they were junkies or just a raggedy-looking punk rock couple.

The thing was, at that point, it really was looking very *Sid and Nancy*—in the worst way.

Kurt brought a friend along on their trip to New York who would go out and score for them and then bring the heroin back to the hotel. Kurt gradually realized that the friend was a junkie, too, and was ripping them off. So once, he went down to Manhattan's notorious Alphabet City himself and bought some heroin on the street while Courtney waited in a nearby Indian restaurant. "People just wait in a line," Kurt says. "Lawyers, business people in three-piece suits, junkies, low-lifes, all different kinds of people."

These days, Alphabet City is fairly gentrified, and while it's still possible to buy dope there, you're more likely to score a pricey espresso or some CBD oil.

Meanwhile, his hopes raised, Don Cobain had been trying to contact Kurt again ever since Kurt called him just before recording *Nevermind*. "I don't know how many million times I tried to get ahold of him," says Don. "I called Geffen Records and Gold Mountain Management in Los Angeles, I called Sub Pop Records, I sent telegrams to *Saturday Night Live*, I sent letters to him and all the places where he'd been, tried to get ahold through his mom . . ." But he never heard back.

###

The rock & roll trail is littered with heroin fatalities: Sid Vicious, Tim Buckley, Janis Joplin, Andrew Wood of Mother Love Bone, the Red Hot Chili Peppers' Hillel Slovak, and more recently, Stefanie Sargent of the Seattle band 7 Year Bitch, who OD'd in 1992. "Those people did every drug in the book all at once," Kurt scoffs. "They get drunk and then they get high and then they die. I never drank—I learned that from junkies. You just don't mix alcohol and heroin at all or you'll die. It cuts down on respiratory twice as much. You pass out when you're drunk and you wake up and get high and there's no way you're going to survive that. Everyone I know of who's OD'd has gotten drunk. And it's been late at night, too."

Returning from New York, Kurt and Courtney moved into a modest apartment on Spaulding Avenue in the Fairfax district of Los Angeles. Their day-to-day existence was fairly routine. "I just got up and got drugs and listened to music and painted and played guitar," Kurt says. "That's about it. Watched TV. It was recuperation. I'd been on tour for seven months. I needed to do that."

"We went through a lot of blankets because you keep dropping your cigarette—it's pretty gross," Courtney says. "I threw all those blankets out."

Every morning, Kurt would drive to the home of one of their two drug dealers. To them, Kurt was just another customer. "They didn't care if I was a rock star or not," says Kurt. "They'd dealt to rock stars before." Kurt doesn't know how much he was doing in grams, but he knows he had a hundred-dollar-a-day habit.

Courtney had a very mild habit. "When I gave her drugs, I would do this much," Kurt says, indicating a large amount, "and I would give her that much," indicating a very small amount. "I was real selfish," he admits. "She probably had a twenty-dollar habit, if that. It was more psychological than it was physical."

Kurt says he never OD'd, although he did once get a case of "cotton fever," which happens when a stray strand of cotton gets into the needle and is then injected into the vein, producing an extremely high fever and an excruciating headache. Kurt went to the hospital and was given Benadryl, an over-the-counter antihistamine, which cured him. The rumor was that he had overdosed.

They grew paranoid. In the middle of the night, Courtney would think she heard an intruder and Kurt would take out the handgun that Dylan Carlson had given him and check it out. No one was ever there.

"I'm not against guns at all," Kurt says. "I own one. I believe in them for protection. I'm not as much of a hippie as some people would want me to be. I could blow somebody away easily, no problem, if I had to protect myself or my family. I actually kind of like them now. I'm thinking about buying another one."

Still, most people wouldn't have figured Kurt "And I swear that I don't have a gun" Cobain to be the proud owner of a firearm. "I wouldn't, either," Kurt says. "They're absolute evil things. I shot a gun with Dylan about a year ago. We went down to Aberdeen and went out in the woods and shot this gun and it was just such a reminder of how brutal they are, how much damage they can do to a person. It's a necessary thing—it's a defense weapon."

It's difficult to believe that, in the midst of a home invasion, a person who was regularly high on heroin could somehow manage to run through a multi-room apartment, retrieve a gun from a locked box, load it, and then fire it accurately before anyone was attacked.

According to a 2015 report by the Violence Policy Center, for every criminal killed in self-defense, there are two accidental gun deaths, thirty-four murders, and seventy-eight suicides. Those are not very good odds.

Kurt couldn't legally buy a gun himself: it's long been a violation of federal law for unlawful users of controlled substances to buy a firearm.

Looming ahead was a tour that went from California to Oregon to Australia, New Zealand, Japan, and Hawaii that was scheduled to kick off on January 24.

Courtney found out she was pregnant sometime around *Saturday Night Live*— whether before or after is unclear. Kurt and Courtney hadn't been using birth control, even though Courtney was mainlining heroin. Courtney calls that "a morality issue" and insists that she knew she'd quit if she discovered she was pregnant. "I was an idiot—what can I say?" she says now. "But I'm not immoral."

They had wanted to have a baby, but sometime in 1993, and certainly after they had finished with their dalliance with heroin. In the meantime, they thought maybe they'd get a little capuchin monkey. When they found out Courtney was pregnant, Kurt was ready to insist on an abortion because he assumed, like everyone else, that the baby would be born retarded or deformed. Courtney never even considered it. "We should breed," she thought. "It's better than buying a monkey."

"I don't promote having a fix-it baby, which is what I was—to fix their problems," Frances told *Rolling Stone* in 2015. "In the sense that their own families were so chaotic, that they wanted to create their own family as soon as possible. . . . It ended up being a million more times chaotic."

They consulted a teratogenic (birth defects) specialist who informed them that heroin use, especially if confined to the first trimester, was virtually harmless to the fetus if the mother's withdrawal wasn't too traumatic (there is a slight chance that the child may experience mild learning disabilities later on in life, however). Amazing but true. "But tell that to a middle American housewife," says Kurt. "You can't expect anyone to believe it."

That may have been the accepted science in 1992, but the latest findings from the Centers for Disease Control are that infants exposed to opioids during pregnancy "might be more likely" to experience a number of negative outcomes such as premature birth, poor fetal growth, and birth defects.

"We knew it really wasn't the best of times to have a child," Kurt says, "but we were just determined to have one. We figured we may as well do it now. It definitely would have been better on Courtney's part if she would have waited and put out her record a little while ago but, I don't know, I don't regret it now. Frances wouldn't be Frances if we had her later."

"I thought [having the baby] would probably be a good thing," says Danny Goldberg, "but I was also worried about the roller coaster that it puts you on, and when you combine *that* roller coaster with the roller coaster of massive success, you're dealing with one of the most complicated, stressful things that a human being can go through."

Kurt began to see the light at the end of his addiction. "I'm sure the awareness the baby was coming was a major factor," says Goldberg. "Having a kid is a big deal—it's one of the biggest things that happens to you. It's corny, but all different kinds of people, including punk rockers, do react that way."

"I didn't have a baby to stop doing drugs," says Courtney, "but I knew that I would continue to do drugs and my career would go to fucking hell and I wouldn't give a shit and I'd be one of those junkies that I've seen at N.A. meetings with track marks on their hands and neck."

"If I've ever seen Satan, that's it, because it's so insidious," says Courtney. "It breaks you down morally. It's very insidious. You have this angel that's really beautiful, it's not like this guy with horns, it's this beautiful angel who's promising you another heaven."

They entered the strange world of chemical dependency medicine. Various doctors competed for their business, as if they were another celebrity trophy to put on their wall. It was just like a bidding war.

Kurt knew he had to detox for the tour, so he and Courtney decided to detox together. A doctor checked them into a Holiday Inn and prescribed them various drugs to tide them through the three-day withdrawal period. Periodically, trusty Alex Macleod would stop by and make sure they were all right.

Kurt says detoxing was easy. "It wasn't a heavy drug addiction at all," Kurt says. "I'd only been doing it for a month straight and I'd just started to get addicted, probably that week that I got off of them. Withdrawals were nothing. I just slept for three days and woke up."

"I thought, 'Gee, if this is what detoxing is like, I could do this the rest of my life.' But once I got into a four-hundred-dollar habit and I detoxed off of that, it was a different story. A very different story."

But Courtney has a different take. "That was a sick scene because you get diarrhea and lots of sleeping pills and it was just vomiting," she says. "That was gross. That was a sick scene if ever there was a sick scene." As Kurt admits, "The bathroom didn't smell very good."

By the time of the "Come as You Are" video shoot, Chris and Dave hadn't seen Kurt since *Saturday Night Live*. They had heard secondhand that Kurt was going through detox. In Dave's words, "It was not something to be talked about." It was just two days before they were to leave for Australia.

According to Dave, Kurt looked "Bad. Gray. He just looked sad." And Kurt wasn't even using by that time. "That's why he looked so sad," says Dave. "Because he wasn't.

"I couldn't understand," Dave says. "If something like that is destroying somebody . . . I guess I don't understand addiction. Along with addiction comes denial or lies or deceit or paranoia, things that I just didn't understand. I understand them now a little better, but at the time, I didn't understand addiction and so I just thought, 'What the fuck are you thinking? Why are you doing this?'"

After the unpleasant experience with "Teen Spirit" video director Sam Bayer, Kurt had gone hunting for a new director and discovered Kevin Kerslake, who had done clips for Iggy Pop, Mazzy Star, Soul Asylum, and Sonic Youth. Kerslake's impressionistic, ethereal style didn't always suit the major labels, but Kurt now had the clout to choose any director within reason. So Kerslake it was.

Unable to come up with few visual ideas beyond playing off the album cover and including "a lot of purples and reds," Kurt let Kerslake conceptualize the clip. "I didn't care at that point," Kurt says.

"I didn't care at that point" is really saying something, since Kurt had exercised so much control over virtually every aspect of the band's presentation.

Nonetheless, Kurt's one-page storyboard for the "Come as You Are" video is remarkably close to the way things actually turned out. "Color scheme: 800% blue/purple," the band filmed in "fuzzy, warped, distorted" style, and footage of "sea monkeys" and "jellyfish" and "sperm" were all pretty much there. That was a testament to the clarity of Kurt's artistic vision and his determination, not to mention the clout he suddenly had as the figurehead of a phenomenally successful band. Kurt realized that everything to do with a band—not just their music but their clothes, haircuts, album art, merchandise, interviews, and videos, not to mention the myths they concocted about themselves—was part of their artistic conception. A rock band is what the Germans call a *Gesamtkunstwerk*: a comprehensive synthesis of different genres of art—ask anyone from the Beatles to Kiss to the Foo Fighters.

The follow-up to the "Teen Spirit" video was crucial—would they go with a similar approach or would they try to redefine themselves?

This was the height of the MTV era—videos were defining artistic statements, and their budgets were an indicator of how much the label was behind the band. They also helped sell records and concert tickets, and promote radio airplay.

Besides the color scheme, the only other thing Kurt wanted was for the band's faces to be obscured. That breaks an unspoken cardinal rule of video, but once again Kurt had the clout to get away with it. With Kurt's, Chris's, and Dave's faces obscured by running water, video effects, or shadows, the "Come as You Are" video pulled off the tricky feat of promoting a song without contributing to the overexposure of the band; Nirvana was seen and not seen. And the clip cemented their fame by exploiting the fact that everyone knew who it was anyway.

The approach also very conveniently disguised how awful Kurt looked.

"It is still hard for me to watch 'Come as You Are' knowing the state Kurt was in at the time," wrote Dave in *The Storyteller*. "Although our images are blurred by camera effects . . . I see a very clear picture of three people entering what would become a period of turbulence that we would feel for years."

It was the beginning of a long series of collaborations with Kerslake. "It turned out fine, it turned out great," Kurt says. "We finally found someone that shared the same vision as we do."

Kerslake came up with the idea of using projections of the band members in the background of many of the shots. They shot most of that footage in a park in the Hollywood Hills a few days before the main shoot. Kerslake encouraged the guys to "abuse the camera" and Kurt in particular was more than willing to comply.

The shoot went smoothly, but Kurt was clearly having a bad time of it. "It was strange because here's Chris and I running around this field having a great time, it's a sunny day," says Dave, "and Kurt just wasn't feeling too good." "I was on detox pills," Kurt explains, "so I wasn't very animated." Still, Kurt was able to swing on a chandelier for an hour, taking rests on a ladder between takes.

This surely appealed to the stuntman in Kurt, the kid who loved to jump off houses when he was growing up in Aberdeen. And perhaps it was an echo of his breakdown in Rome, when he swung from the rafters of the club and threatened to jump off the balcony.

When Kerslake came back to the band with his rough cut, Kurt, Chris, and Dave had surprisingly good suggestions. "They were all valid comments—artistically, they've all got really good taste, which is pretty rare for musicians," Kerslake says. "A lot of musicians hole themselves up in their room with their guitar and they don't have any feelers out to all the other aesthetic aspects of what is asked of them in this day and age. All the references that they talked about were revered artists, painters, filmmakers, stuff like that, so it was grounded in some artistic savvy."

One of their suggestions was to cut out the more goofy footage shot for the projections, in favor of more ethereal stuff. "That was the recoil from 'Teen Spirit,'" Kerslake says. The video aired in March and was a huge success, if not quite as successful as "Teen Spirit."

As noted earlier, the label thought "Come as You Are" would be the album's big single. Just goes to show you how much "the grown-ups"—or anyone, really—knew.

People in the band's inner circle began wondering if going on tour at that point was the right thing to do. "Everybody knew that it wasn't," says Dave. "Kurt knew that it wasn't, I knew that it wasn't, Chris knew that it wasn't. Maybe we didn't know within the first two days of the tour, but after a week and a half, sure, everybody knew it wasn't. Shows were all right, we got through the set every night. But if Kurt wants something, he'll do anything to get it.

"It took a lot of courage for him to do that tour," Dave adds. "He felt like shit, looked like shit, but he got over it. He worked it out."

The thing is, maybe it wasn't courage that made Kurt do that tour. Maybe it was kind of the opposite. Transcontinental deals had been struck, there were new territories to be conquered, and there was lots of money to be made. Canceling would have been inconvenient to a lot of people and an admission that Kurt had become so badly addicted to heroin that it was threatening his career and even his life. So maybe he just caved. It wouldn't be the last time.

In public, Kurt outspokenly touted the punk-rebel sensibility, but when it came down to it, he repeatedly yielded to outside forces. That must have troubled him deeply.

During the Australian tour, Kurt's stomach problem flared up worse than it had in years. The first few days, Kurt felt fine. Then suddenly, he was in intense pain. He was vomiting constantly and couldn't eat. He would call up Courtney, crying from the pain. At one point, he very nearly took the next plane home.

One day, Kurt says he was sitting on the steps of a hotel, wincing with pain, and Shelli walked up to him and said, "Kurt, I just hate to see you doing this to yourself. I can't stand to see you hurting your body like this."

"I just wanted to fucking punch her in the face because, just like everyone else, she just assumed that I was doing drugs," he says. "I was thinking, 'You fucking people have no clue how much pain I'm in all the time. It's from a natural thing that's in my body.' I couldn't believe it. I'll never forget those words because it just defined everyone's attitude toward me. Every time that I wasn't even doing drugs, they suspected that I was. They still do."

Tour manager Alex Macleod worried about Kurt, too. "I didn't like what I was seeing in someone I had so much respect and love for," says Macleod, "I was really scared, more than anything else, constantly. Scared of what he was going to do, who he was going to hook up with. It was kind of strange."

Slam-Dancing with Mr. Brownstone

399

Let's note how candidly people were speaking—even their loyal and tough-minded tour manager. It helped that they knew that Kurt had instructed the people around him to be very frank. They still didn't tell the whole story, but they told a shocking amount of it.

When Kurt suffered a particularly severe stomach pain attack, Macleod took him to a hospital emergency room, but not before mistakenly informing the doctors that Kurt was still detoxing from heroin. While he was on the examination table, Kurt says he heard one doctor snicker and say to another, "Oh, he's just a junkie, he's still coming off of drugs." Disgusted, Kurt walked out of the hospital and simply toughed out the pain.

Actually, Macleod did the right thing by telling the doctors that Kurt was detoxing since that notified them that they shouldn't prescribe him any painkillers that contained opiates. But it's entirely possible that the whole reason Kurt went to the hospital was to *get* some opiates, and when it became clear that that wasn't going to happen, he simply left and eventually found the "rock doctor."

He finally went to a "rock doctor" who had a picture of himself with the Rolling Stones on his office wall. Kurt told the doctor his stomach history and the doctor replied, "I know what your problem is," having been filled in by Macleod beforehand. "I think I'm going to get some kind of stomach medicine and the doctor just assumes that I'd just recently gotten off of heroin and I'm going through detox and I'm on tour," says Kurt, "so I'd better do what Keith Richards would have done and take methadone. It's called Physeptone in Australia, so I thought they were just stomach pills."

The Physeptone miraculously took away the stomach pain completely. Kurt couldn't wait to tell his doctor about these great new pills.

I kinda think that Kurt knew those weren't "stomach pills." That's why, a few paragraphs below, I said "he claims" he didn't know it was methadone.

On February 1, after dipping to #4 for a couple of weeks, *Nevermind* again hit #1.

They finished the tour, then played a show in Auckland, New Zealand, then off to Singapore for a day of press. When they arrived at the Singapore airport, there was a waiting mob of about 250 teenaged fans who waved "Welcome to Singapore" banners and chased after the band and grabbed at their hair. It turned out that this was standard practice in Singapore. The label had even printed an announcement of their arrival—including flight number and arrival time—in the newspaper and handed out the banners.

Kurt onstage in Australia.
© Mark Seliger

Then it was on to Japan, where Courtney joined the tour, and then Hawaii. By that time, Kurt was hooked on opiates again—without, he claims, even realizing it until he called his doctor and discovered what he was taking.

Kurt and Courtney got married in Waikiki, Hawaii, on February 24, 1992. At Courtney's insistence, the couple had already worked out a prenuptial agreement. "I didn't want Kurt running away with all my money," Courtney jokes (presumably).

The prenup wasn't at Courtney's insistence; reportedly, John Silva urged Kurt to do it.

Dave and his friend and drum tech Barrett Jones had both brought girlfriends to Hawaii, but Kurt and Courtney didn't want them there. "They all came from Seattle and they were all going to come back and say 'We were at Kurt and Courtney's wedding!' and lie about things," says Courtney. Besides, Kurt thought he might cry at the ceremony and wanted it to be as private and small as possible.

"Shelli and Chris were being really shitty to us and they thought I was doing all these drugs and I'm in Japan—how could I be doing any drugs?" says Courtney (then again, Kurt did have some Physeptone). Kurt had a crew member summon Chris up to his hotel room, where Kurt informed Chris that he didn't want anyone at the wedding who didn't want them to get married—meaning Shelli. Chris said if his wife wasn't going, he wasn't going either. "I don't regret it, I don't take it back one bit," says Courtney. "I can't see it happening with Shelli there at that point in time."

"It was *our* choice," Shelli insists. "It was weird because I knew what was going on and I knew that she was pregnant and I had a real objection to her doing drugs while she was pregnant," she says, then catches herself and adds, "Maybe at that point, maybe she was, maybe she wasn't. I don't know, but we all *assumed*. I didn't want to go because I knew if she was pregnant and doing drugs, I didn't agree with it and I didn't agree with Kurt being so fucked up all the time and I just decided I wasn't going to go." She says somebody talked her into going for the sake of band harmony. "Then we ended up not going because they didn't want me to go, which hurt my feelings," Shelli says. "Although things had gotten to a really bad point, I was still thinking that Kurt and I were still friends and that things could be worked out."

By the time they got to Hawaii, Kurt had run out of Physeptone and convinced a friend to bring him some heroin so he wouldn't start detoxing while he was there. Kurt was even high on heroin at his own wedding. "I wasn't *very* high, though," he explains. "I just did a little teeny bit just so I didn't get sick."

Present at the ceremony, on a cliff overlooking a beach, were Dave, Alex Macleod, soundman Ian Beveridge, Dylan Carlson and his girlfriend, and Nirvana guitar tech Nick Close. The bride wore an antique lace dress that once belonged to Frances Farmer and the groom wore green flannel pajamas. Everyone wore leis. A nondenominational female minister that Courtney found through the Hawaiian wedding bureau performed the brief ceremony. Kurt did cry, Courtney didn't. "It was very transcendent," says Courtney. "It was like being on acid. It was great. It was very much different than just being boyfriend and girlfriend. It's a good thing, I'm glad we did it."

Afterward, they got very depressed over the Chris and Shelli thing.

And Shelli and Chris got depressed over the Kurt and Courtney thing. "Kurt alienated us, but we alienated him, too," Shelli says, "just by not being upfront. Everybody was talking behind their backs. It was getting nasty and it wasn't fair. It's easy to gossip and it's easy when you have to spend every day with people and she was pregnant, I think, at that point and she wasn't being nice anymore and Kurt was not being nice anymore. The lines were being drawn and it was really stupid and there was no reason why it should have been like that. Everybody was just, 'You're just a bunch of drug addicts.' You alienate people by doing that."

Later, when the band was playing in Argentina in October of 1992, Courtney and Shelli finally talked it over. "I told her, 'Look, I never hated you,'" says Shelli. "She *thought* I hated her, so she treated me like 'you hate me, so I don't like you, either.' Then I started not liking her. It was a big misunderstanding."

Kurt was back on methadone for the *Rolling Stone* interview with this writer a day after he returned to the Spaulding apartment. He looked terrible and spoke even more quietly than usual. For most of the interview, he stayed under the bed covers in his pajamas, even though it was a particularly balmy L.A. evening. His complexion was bad, he could barely sit up in bed, and he said he'd been throwing up all day. His pupils weren't pinned, but it was pretty obvious that the guy had a monkey on his back.

We talked about the heroin rumors and he flatly denied they were true. "I had a responsibility," Kurt says now. "I had a responsibility to the kids to not let on that I did drugs."

That was a familiar refrain for Kurt, along with a massive helping of denial. "I DON'T TAKE drugs," Kurt told Al and Cake of *Flipside* in the May–June 1992 issue, "I HAVE taken drugs in my life and every once in awhile I may dabble in drug taking but I am definitely not a

Kurt giving it some attitude during Mark Seliger's *Rolling Stone* photo shoot in Australia, P.S.—wrong finger. © Mark Seliger

drug addict and I don't like to condone anyone using any kind of drugs. They're a waste of time. I think it's really lame for journalists to write and accuse me of taking drugs because kids are going to read that article and then they're going to do drugs because I do."

So it was actually *journalists'* fault that kids did drugs. If they'd only keep quiet about Kurt's heroin use, everything would be fine.

Even though he was bedridden, Kurt was ecstatic about his life. He was very much in love. "It's like Evian water and battery acid," Kurt said of his relationship with Courtney in the *Rolling Stone* story. And when you mix the two, according to Kurt, "You get love."

Rolling Stone had asked for an interview for a cover story and Kurt agreed, even though he's no fan of the magazine. "Every time I've ever picked up a *Rolling Stone*," he says, "I've gotten so disgusted and filled with so much rage that I ended up ripping it up. It's the epitome of yuppiedom. It's the perfect example of everything I hate. It's disgusting." Later, he got annoyed that the magazine pinched the "Smells Like Teen Spirit" tag for a cover piece on the execrable television series *Beverly Hills 90210.*

It just isn't believable that Kurt didn't read *Rolling Stone.* As Danny Goldberg made clear in his 2019 book, *Serving the Servant: Remembering Kurt Cobain*, Kurt paid a lot of attention to the music press. He certainly knew my writing, and I had mostly written for *Rolling Stone.* He was just posturing for the sake of the indie hipsters and, once again, making up something self-serving at the expense of a perceived antagonist.

Kurt claims he later forgot that he agreed to the story (plausible, considering his chemical state at the time). One morning during the Australian tour, he was awakened and told it was time for the *Rolling Stone* shoot. At first, Kurt refused, but then everyone from band members to the road crew urged him to go through with it. Then he began to try to think of something clever to put on a T-shirt that would keep the photo from being used. He hastily came up with "Corporate magazines still suck," a paraphrase of SST Records' slogan "Corporate rock still sucks." "It was a stupid little statement to *Rolling Stone*," Kurt says, "saying that you're not a hip magazine now just because you have a supposedly hip band on your cover."

Actually, it's *not* plausible that Kurt forgot that he agreed to the story. Back then, a *Rolling Stone* cover story was a huge deal. It just wasn't something you forget you agreed to. And, as Kurt acknowledged earlier in this book, it was a longtime dream to "be on the cover of magazines and stuff."

The taunting T-shirts were Kurt's way of having his cake and eating it, too: doing the interview and yet maintaining his precious indie cred.

Kurt told the *Advocate* that he decided to rebel against "pressure from my management and the band members" and "write something on my shirt that's offensive enough to stop getting our picture on the cover." But "Corporate magazines still suck" just wasn't terribly offensive—paraphrasing the SST Records slogan was just a secret message to the indie community. If Kurt had truly wanted to write something preemptive on his T-shirt, there were plenty of other options, such as his old standbys "God is gay," "Homo sex rules," or "Abort Christ."

"It wasn't necessarily to whatever his name is [*Rolling Stone* publisher Jann Wenner], like 'okay, let's see if you can put *this* on your cover.' I wasn't trying to make any kind of bold statement—it was just a joke. I didn't even really think about it. It was a decision made ten minutes before we did the photo shoot. It wasn't like I sat up all night and thought 'What should I write?' The funniest reaction to that is people taking it so literally—like I hate anything corporate, yet I'm on a corporate label. No shit. Obviously, I would wish that people would give me the benefit of the doubt to realize that I'm smart enough to understand that."

Actually, Jann Wenner was very amused by Kurt's T-shirt—in the way that truly powerful people can be amused by being insulted. And if he had objected to the words on Kurt's shirt, they could have easily been airbrushed out.

Actually, rock's magazine of record might have taken far more offense at another T-shirt Kurt had prepared just for the occasion. It portrayed a punk rock duck with the inscription "Kill the Grateful Dead."

"Kill the Grateful Dead" betrayed Kurt's clear familiarity with *Rolling Stone*, which, like the Dead, was founded in psychedelic-era San Francisco and as late as 1992 still had, infamously, not lost its attachment to musical icons of the '60s.

Once again, Kurt echoes Johnny Rotten's fateful "I HATE PINK FLOYD" T-shirt.

#

For all his iconoclasm, Kurt was well on his way to becoming the cliché of the wasted rocker. The success of *Nevermind* presented several difficult situations for Kurt. For one thing, a guy who loathed mainstream rock was now de facto *making* mainstream rock.

And a shy and reclusive man had gone from total obscurity to unwanted worldwide fame in three years. "Famous is the last thing I wanted to be," Kurt says. As the figurehead of the band, the brunt of the media spotlight shone on Kurt—his personal life and even his psyche were being relentlessly dissected in the media. The cover line on the *Rolling Stone* cover story read "Inside the heart and mind of Kurt Cobain."

Kurt openly resented his fame and most of his audience took that as a slap in the face. In turn, Kurt began to resent the prying of the press and his audience even more. "The classic reaction to someone who complains they're in the limelight is 'You made your bed, now you have to sleep in it. You're public domain now and everyone has a right to know everything about you,'" he says. "No

The Amplified Come as You Are

The cover shot
Rolling Stone
didn't use.
© Mark Seliger

one has any right to know anything about my personal life. If they want to
know about the music and how I try to write it, then that's fine. Of course, it
ties in with my personal life, but not as much as everyone thinks. I just always felt
violated and I don't agree with people who say they have a right to know. I have a
right to try to change that perception. I have a right to try to change people's way
of thinking about celebrities. It *should* be changed. It *should* be different. They
should be treated as human beings and their privacy should be respected."

Courtney felt that most people thought all rock stars lived like Kris Phoenix, the
protagonist of Jackie Collins's 1988 novel *Rock Star*, with his two mansions, seven cars,
and supermodel girlfriend. To make sure I got the point, she sent me a copy of the book.

Stardom means a tremendous loss of the kind of privacy that most people take for
granted. But Kurt wasn't having it, ostensibly because of his punk rock ethos, which was a

pretty revolutionary attitude. Previously, a certain amount of prying by the media was mutually understood to be the price of fame. Kurt just didn't accept the explanation that "that's just the way it is." And that was very punk rock, in the sense of questioning the status quo.

How could someone who had literally gone from rags to riches be unhappy? But Kurt was in good company: as Jimi Hendrix once told talk show host Dick Cavett, "The more money you make, sometimes the more blues you can sing." Maybe Kurt's protests were sometimes received poorly because they struck at the heart of the materialism of American culture—maybe money and possessions didn't actually make you happy. Some people just didn't want to hear that.

After Kurt, more celebrities became open about their ambivalence about fame. Later, thanks to the advent of things like social media and the cellphone camera, that ambivalence, and the damage done by fame, became easier to understand.

In the August 28, 1993, issue of *Melody Maker*, music journalist duo the Stud Brothers challenged Kurt: although Kurt resented having his personal life scrutinized by the public and the press, Kurt himself was fascinated with the personal life of star-crossed actress Frances Farmer.

"That's true," Kurt replied. "I don't know how I'm gonna get myself out of this."

He eventually decided that musicians' personal lives just shouldn't be scrutinized as closely as, for example, politicians' professional lives. The interviewers asked if he didn't have some sort of responsibility to his fans.

"I have a responsibility to not promote a negative lifestyle," Kurt said, reciting a now-familiar spiel. "I tried to hide it as long as I could. The main reason was that I didn't want some 15-year-old kid who likes our band to think it's cool to do heroin, you know?"

The Stud Brothers closed the piece on an ominous note: "It's not easy being a living legend. And living legends seldom learn to live with it."

Meanwhile, *Nevermind* was in the Top 3, and it remained there until mid-April.

At the apartment on North Spaulding, Kurt did his best to avoid tempting Courtney by shooting in a locked closet in an extra room down the hallway where he kept his heroin and his needles and his spoons and his rubbing alcohol. "I knew I was tempting her all the time," says Kurt. "I was high all the time. I just had to keep doing it. I didn't have it out of my system. I knew if I quit then, I'd end up doing it again for at least the next couple of years all the time. I figured I'd just burn myself out of it because I hadn't experienced the full junkie feeling yet. I was still healthy."

But that's not the way addiction works. You don't "burn out of it" or "get it out of your system"—the more you do, the deeper it sucks you in. Everyone knows that.

Heroin tends to make people really sleazy. There's a joke:

The Amplified Come as You Are

Q: What's the difference between an alcoholic and a junkie?
A: Both will steal your wallet. But the junkie will offer to help you find it.

"I didn't find myself just sitting in the house and nodding off and sleeping," Kurt says. "I was always doing something artistic. I got a lot of paintings done and wrote a lot of songs.

"It was a lot less turbulent than everyone thinks," says Kurt. "It was pretty boring."

Boredom, it turns out, was kind of blissful; Kurt was eager to find a respite from all the tumult and pressure of Nirvana's immense success, and opiates provided it.

Artistically, it was a fertile time for Kurt—he painted a lot and wrote many of the songs which appeared on *In Utero*. "I did all my best songs on heroin this year," he says. But he was falling out of touch with the band and Gold Mountain and he and Courtney were quickly falling into sweet oblivion. "Those guys went off into their own world and they were kind of thought of as vampires because they'd be gone and sleep all day," says Chris.

If Kurt wrote all his best songs that year, they didn't wind up on *In Utero*: although "Serve the Servants" and "Heart-Shaped Box" are top-shelf Nirvana, songs like "Very Ape," "Radio Friendly Unit Shifter," and "Tourette's" just do not rank among his most superlative songwriting—it's surely no coincidence that the band rarely performed "Tourette's" and "Very Ape" live. Kurt wrote "Scentless Apprentice" with the band, and he wrote "Pennyroyal Tea," "All Apologies," "Rape Me," and "Dumb" long before. He was kidding himself—and me, since I didn't know when those songs were written.

The attentive grunge aficionado will note the allusion to *Sweet Oblivion*, the 1992 album—one of the best of the '90s—by Screaming Trees, whose singer Mark Lanegan was one of Kurt's close friends as well as being a fellow heroin addict. Doing heroin is a kind of self-annihilation, as in Lou Reed's junkie narrator in the Velvet Underground's "Heroin," who wants to "nullify my life . . . Then thank God that I'm as good as dead." Or, as the famed British polymath Bertrand Russell wrote in his 1930 book *The Conquest of Happiness*, "Drunkenness is temporary suicide . . . a momentary cessation of unhappiness." That's a dark nirvana.

I had Kurt sign a release form for the interviews for this book, and for his mailing address he wrote "hell on earth." In the February 1992 issue of *Rip* magazine, writer Katherine Turman asked Kurt, "What is nirvana to Nirvana?"

"Total peace after death," he answered.

They barely spoke for five months, even at rehearsals.

But Chris was very upset about what was happening to his old friend. He would rant at Dave or Shelli, "Kurt's a fucking junkie asshole and I hate him!" Chris was angry with Kurt, he says, "Probably because I felt like he left me. I was really concerned and worried about him and there was nothing I could do about it. I was just taking my anger out on him.

"It was hard to understand," says Chris. "I couldn't get over the whole hurdle of heroin."

And who could blame Krist—heroin is a very high hurdle.

Again, note the incredible candor. Krist was saying these things not just while the band still existed but while its existence was becoming increasingly tenuous. And he was saying these things knowing not only that they would appear in print, but that his friend would read them. It's really difficult to imagine a band in this media-savvy day and age opening up so completely.

Part of the problem was that, as usual, Chris didn't confront the problem with Kurt directly. "We've never really communicated very well when there's been a problem between us," Kurt says. "We never talk about it, we just let it pass. We've never confronted one another about things that piss each other off. During the time that I was doing drugs, I did notice that people weren't calling as much but I also made it clear to everyone that I wanted to take a break. I remember Dave called up one day real hostile and asking me if I wanted to even be in the band anymore because we were getting pressure from everyone to go on tour and I decided I didn't want to be on tour this year because I needed a break."

Unlike many of Kurt's unflattering recollections, this one has the ring of truth. Dave often spoke of how, unlike Kurt, he could walk around in public fairly easily because he was "just the drummer," and yet he didn't seem to grasp Kurt's predicament: not only was Kurt the face of the band, he was a new father and desperately needed to kick a deep and abiding heroin addiction, along with other very formidable personal issues. Kurt also needed some downtime so he could work on new songs for the band to play and record. But Dave had no patience for drama and just wanted to get back on the road, where he'd existed for virtually his entire adult life.

Ironically, even though Dave got nightmarishly burned out on touring, "Three days after it was over," as he says earlier, "you start wanting to play again." Kurt, on the other hand, was not that guy.

And so Kurt was put in the awful position of turning down work, which affected everyone in the Nirvana organization: the rest of the band, their management, their crew, and everyone from merchandise vendors to booking agents.

"I don't know how much heroin Kurt was doing because I never saw him," Chris says. **"I never saw Kurt fucked up on heroin. I never went to his house. I saw him high a few times, but never really a fuckin' mess. I never saw that. That's just what I heard or what I assumed. He was down in L.A. I'd never go down to L.A., I'd never go to his house. I didn't want to go. Because I was afraid of what I might see. A lot of my perspective was secondhand."**

Like a lot of bands, Nirvana was founded on friendship, so when Krist and Kurt started to drift apart personally, it was a severe strain. For all Krist's goofy wildness, he was still also a very sensible person and helped to ground Kurt when things got crazy. Now all Kurt had was Courtney, and she was not as good at grounding Kurt when things got crazy; in fact, she was sometimes the reason things got crazy in the first place.

When Krist said, "I was afraid of what I might see," he probably spoke for a lot of people around Kurt: avoid confrontation, just get on with things, and maybe the problem will just go away. That's denial. I did that, too—I was dimly aware that Kurt was doing heroin more than he admitted; I just didn't want to dig into it. It would have jeopardized my book. And I feared the wrath of their management and legal team, especially after seeing what happened to would-be Nirvana biographers Britt Collins and Victoria Clarke. (More about that soon.) It would have betrayed the trust Kurt had for me—but was it really trust? Or was it faith—faith that he could play me, or at least that I would look the other way? Was it my place as a journalist to rat him out? Did I even know how to deal with such information responsibly and constructively? I just kept writing my Nirvana biography and left out the more sensational "Kurtney" stuff.

Dave wasn't as affected as Chris was by it all. "We do depend on each other for certain things, but for the most part, we're really removed from each other—far removed," Dave says. **"As close as we may seem sometimes, it's not like bosom buddies. It's not like a business thing where we talk to each other because we're in the same band—we're friends but we're not best friends or even great friends. So I don't know if it let me down or not because I didn't feel like I'd invested so much in the relationship anyway that I was being robbed."**

Krist and Kurt not only started Nirvana together, they also basically grew up together. They had been very close for years before Dave joined. And it wasn't all that long after Dave joined that the band exploded, disrupting whatever relationship he had with his former roommate Kurt. Nor did Dave have any desire to get swept up in all the turmoil. As far as I can tell, he and Krist, for somewhat different reasons, did not step up to Kurt and talk frankly with him about his drug problem. Until it was too late.

"As far as us getting together and playing music, it never really affected the band," Dave says. "When it started affecting the band's reputation, I got a little more upset."

Because he didn't feel close enough to Kurt, Dave didn't feel it was his place to step in. "With something as touchy as that, if you see someone doing something like that to themselves, the first thing you want to do is tell them, 'Look—stop.' But how do you go to someone you're friends with but at the same time, you don't feel as close to. You don't feel like it's your place."

Dave, even more than Chris, managed to stay out of the fray. "It's weird, because there are so many people that work with the band that don't really have anything to do with me," Dave says. "Basically, all I do is I walk up on stage and I play drums. And then afterward, I go home. There's just so much that goes on that I don't even know about. In a lot of ways that can be a blessing, but on the other hand it makes you wonder about your importance."

That last line is key. Wondering about your own importance isn't very sustainable when you know you have a lot more to offer: Dave could sing and play guitar and was writing his own songs—but understood that those songs would never appear on Nirvana records. The only real solution would be to start your own band. Maybe, knowingly or not, Dave was telegraphing that here.

Kurt didn't want to go out on tour again and have his stomach act up again, and besides, he wanted to be with Courtney throughout her pregnancy. Career-wise, it couldn't have come at a worse time. If Nirvana had toured the United States that spring—and an extensive US arena tour was planned for April and May—*Nevermind* would have stayed at the top of the charts for even longer than it did.

Chris, for one, didn't care. "We toured for three years," he says. "The tour just seemed like a lot more pressure, anyway. Before, we were just vagabonds in a van, doing our thing. Now you've got a tour manager and a crew and it's a production. You've got schedules and shit. It used to be, 'Stage time's at six o'clock.' And we could say, 'Fuck it, we're going to buy records.' We'd be on an adventure. And now it's a circus."

Gradually, the ice broke between Kurt and Chris. "Kurt and I would have these cool talks," says Chris. "Every once in a while we'd call and talk about

things and I'd really feel better about a lot of things, just through talking. You don't talk for a while and you just sit around and all these ideas pop into your head and you start believing them."

###

Later, a video sonogram revealed a normally developing baby (a picture of Frances in utero graces the insert of the "Lithium" single). "Oh God, it was incredible," Kurt says, suddenly aglow. "It was one of the most amazing things. It wasn't just a picture—it was a video, so you could see her moving around. It was the first time we realized she was a living thing. You could see her heart beating." While he was watching the footage, Kurt swears he saw Frances give heavy metal's familiar forefinger-and-pinky Satan salute.

It can't be said enough that whenever Frances entered the room, or even came up in conversation, Kurt would visibly light up. The joy of parenthood seemed to bypass those parts of his brain that kept him down and instead went straight to some powerful, primal place. That child literally made him happy.

###

In March, Tori Amos released a piano version of "Teen Spirit" on an EP. "Every morning when [Courtney and I] woke up we'd turn it up as loud as we could and dance around like a *Solid Gold* dancer," says Kurt, wearing his best poker face. "It felt really weird because the neighbors were listening. Maybe they thought I was an egomaniac, but I was really just miming the song and dancing around. It's a great breakfast cereal version."

Then came a bitter dispute over publishing royalties that came the closest to breaking up the band as anything ever has. Like everyone else, Kurt didn't expect that the band would sell millions of records. To avoid a potentially divisive situation in which he would have gotten an overwhelming slice of a very small pie, leaving the other two rather poor, he agreed to split royalties for music writing equally with Chris and Dave, even though he writes, by his estimate, 90 percent of the music.

"I write the songs, I come up with the basic idea, and then we work on it as a band," says Kurt. "Most of the time that I'm asking Chris and Dave their opinion, it's just to make them feel a part of the band. I always have the ultimate decision."

But once the album took off so phenomenally, Kurt changed his mind and asked for a more representative publishing split—not, he says, because of the money, which is relatively negligible (Kurt says the difference comes to about $150,000). "I realized how much more pressures are on me and how I deserve a little bit more because I'm the lead singer, all these perspectives are being written about me, I have to take all that pressure," says Kurt. "And I have to deal with the pressure of writing the songs. I don't care if someone else gets the credit for it but I should at least be financially compensated for it."

Needless to say, the difference ultimately came to quite a bit more than $150,000.

In 2011, Dave told Paul Brannigan for *Drum* magazine, "We'd always start rehearsals with a jam, an open, free-form jam, and a lot of the songs came from that." So that might have been the basis of Dave and Krist's claim to co-writing.

In a mutual *Rolling Stone* interview in 2019 with Ringo Starr, Dave said, "I had one person, who will remain nameless, say to me once, in a publishing dispute, 'Yeah, but drumming isn't songwriting.' And I said, 'Fuck you! Why not?'"

Dave and Chris had no qualms with that, and it does seem reasonable—Chris and Dave would still make plenty of money. But when Kurt asked for the new arrangement to be retroactive to the release of *Nevermind*, they erupted. Kurt, they argued, was virtually taking money out of their pockets. The uproar lasted only one week in March, but it nearly split the band.

"Chris and I were just like, 'If this is any indication of how much of a dick Kurt is going to be, then I don't want to be in a band with someone like that,'" Dave says. Meanwhile, everyone with a vested interest in the band was urging Chris and Dave to back down. "Everybody was saying, 'Let him have this one because the band will break up. You guys could make fifteen million dollars next year. Just let him have this one,'" Dave says.

There's another instance of Dave talking about leaving the band.

Music publishing is often an intense point of contention in bands. If a record sells well, it can mean that the songwriter buys a Ferrari while the rest of the band members are still driving used subcompacts. R.E.M. and U2 split their songwriting royalties equally, no matter who contributed to the song; this means that the principal songwriters have sacrificed many millions of dollars, but it's also no coincidence that both those bands lasted for decades.

On the phone one day, Kurt said to Dave, "I can't believe you guys are being so greedy."

"Whatever," Dave replied disgustedly, and Kurt hung up on him.

"At the time, I was ready to fucking quit the band over it," says Kurt. "I couldn't believe that [they were] giving me so much shit about this." Kurt eventually got his retroactive split—75 percent of the music writing royalties. The bad feelings still simmer.

###

Kurt checked into Exodus, a rehab program favored by rock stars. "It was disgusting," says Kurt. "Right away, these forty-year-old hippie long-term-junkie-type counselors would come in and try to talk to me on a rock & roll level, like, 'I know where you're at, man. Drugs are real prevalent in rock & roll and I've seen it all in the '70s. Would you mind if David Crosby came in and said hello? Or Steven Tyler?' Rattling off these rock stars' names. I was like, 'Fuck that. I don't have any respect for these people at all.'"

Kurt stayed for four days in his tacky, hospital-like room, reading in his uncomfortable bed. Then he abruptly left before his treatment was completed. "I was feeling all right," he says. "I thought it was over and then I ended up trying to detox at home because it wasn't quite over like I thought it was." He sweated it out for a few more days. Then he and Courtney went up to Seattle and Kurt got high. By the time they returned to L.A., he had a habit again.

Courtney spent more time with her guitarist Eric Erlandson in order to stay away from Kurt. She would occasionally go to the nursery at Cedars-Sinai and look at the babies to strengthen her resolve to stay clean.

More about this later.

###

In July, the "Lithium" single was released, with the B-side containing a live version of "Been a Son" and a previously unreleased track called "Curmudgeon." It also contained, at long last, all the lyrics to *Nevermind*. Soon after, the "Lithium" video aired. A fairly routine collage of footage from the big homecoming concert at the Paramount the previous Halloween and footage from the film *1991: The Year That Punk Broke* (the shot of Kurt taking a running leap at the drum set is from the 1991 Reading Festival; he dislocated his arm). Although it was enlivened by Kerslake's neat trick of using the more violent footage during the quiet parts of the songs and vice versa, it was something of a disappointment from a band and a song that promised so much. Some of the problem might have been that due to his drug habit, Kurt was simply not up to the job of helping to conceptualize a video, but he and Kerslake had actually been brainstorming for a much more ambitious project.

Kerslake says it was to be an animated film about a girl named Prego who lives in a house in a forest. One day, she finds a big pile of eggs in her closet and puts them in a train of three wagons that she wheels through the forest until she comes to a king's castle. By that time, all the eggs but one have cracked and she takes that egg and carries it up to the king's throne and places it on a large book that's on his lap. He's asleep, but when he awakes, he opens his legs and the book slides between them and closes on the egg. When Kurt and Kerslake discovered that the animation would take four months to do, they went with the easily produced live collage.

Meanwhile, the band had set out on a two-week tour to make up the dates they had canceled the previous December in Ireland, Northern Ireland, and Scandinavia, as well visit France and Spain. "It was pretty insane," says Dave of the tour, "and there was a lot of crazy shit going on and it was bad and it was not fun."

Part of the problem was the fact that the band had grown to dislike outdoor festivals, where they would often play in daylight, with the open air eating up the sound from the monitors and the wind blowing the P.A. sound all over the place. "I think the whole band realized we weren't having a good time anymore," Kurt says. Dave remarked to *NME* writer Keith Cameron that for the first time, he didn't even know the names of the crew members. The major label shit was hitting the punk rock fan.

But that was the least of it. Kurt was still using and worse still, his stomach was erupting again. To make it through the tour, Kurt skirted miles of red tape by getting some methadone pills from a "quack doctor" and then got some more from an AIDS patient that another doctor hooked him up with.

The morning after a June 22 Belfast show, Kurt collapsed in convulsions over breakfast. "I forgot to take my methadone pills that night before I went to bed," Kurt says. "I woke up with withdrawals. My stomach was so bad that I decided if I took methadone then I would just puke it up so I had them take me to a hospital so I could get some morphine." Allegedly the ambulance driver had phoned all the tabloids and the rumor started that Kurt had OD'd, despite the fact that, as Kurt points out, it's pretty tough to get heroin in Belfast. The official word from the Nirvana camp was that Kurt had a bleeding ulcer brought on by "junk food."

After that, Kurt got the hairy eyeball from nearly everybody on the tour. "I didn't do anything but forget to take my methadone pills the night before and had to be rushed to the hospital—big deal," Kurt says. "Dave could have hurt himself in a fucking jock accident. Chris could have fallen off the stage drunk that night." The specter of the incident hung over the rest of the tour. The band had been stonewalling on the heroin issue for months; now, it was obvious that word was going to get out sooner or later.

"I had to be rushed to the hospital—big deal." What a remarkable thing to say.

Bad vibes rattled around the entourage. For one thing, Courtney was six months pregnant and in full hormonal swing. For another, "Everybody was tired of me doing drugs," Kurt says, "even though I wasn't doing drugs, I was on methadone. I couldn't do anything but ignore it. All I could do was say fuck you to everyone. It's my problem and they shouldn't be so concerned with it. I could point fingers at everybody else and tell them that they're drunks. They've bought the same drug hysteria propaganda that has been going on in the United States since the Reagan years. They don't understand it, they've never done it, and so they're afraid and it creates bad vibes."

Someone with the outsized personality of Courtney, who was also the wife of the leader of the band, can indeed spread bad vibes throughout the small, hermetic community of a tour. It must have been very difficult to be on the road while with child.

"I wasn't doing drugs, I was on methadone" might sound a little nonsensical but for two things: (1) prescribed methadone keeps an addict out of the dangerous pursuit of illegal drugs, and (2) properly dosed, methadone does not produce a high.

It's unnecessary to point out all the denial and rationalizations and whataboutism and yet more denial in the rest of what Kurt said here. But it does give an idea of how combative he had become with almost everyone around him, both during the time he was discussing and at the time he did the interview.

It wasn't like Kurt and Courtney didn't have a sense of humor about it all— they would check into hotels as "Mr. and Mrs. Simon Ritchie," the real name of Sid Vicious.

And there's another example of Kurt's attempts to mock the drug rumors by sarcastically embracing them—this time, by adopting the pseudonym of a suicidal heroin addict who had an abrasive and opportunistic girlfriend.

Sassy wasn't the only magazine to make the comparison to Vicious and Spungen—as one anonymous "industry insider" said in the *Vanity Fair* piece, "Courtney and Kurt are the nineties, much more talented version of Sid and Nancy."

Gold Mountain hired a couple of professional "minders" to keep an eye on Kurt and Courtney. The day after the incident in Belfast, the band was in Paris for a show at Le Zenith. Kurt walked out of his hotel room to get some food and noticed one of the minders sitting in the room right next to his, facing his open door, just waiting for Kurt to try to leave. "I was being monitored by two goons," Kurt says, "and I was going out to have some *fish*. I wasn't looking for drugs at all. I had methadone, I was fine. I had absolutely no desire to do drugs but I was being treated like a fucking baby. They were turning this band into everything it wasn't supposed to be."

Indignant, Kurt and Courtney packed up their belongings, sneaked out of the hotel, and checked into another without telling anyone where they were until the next day. "They were eating their shit, they were so afraid of what was going to happen," Kurt says.

Food was also a problem, although Kurt had long ago learned to bring his own cereal and canned goods. "There's never any good food in Europe," he claims, raising eyebrows all the way from Paris to Rome.

"During the time that everyone thought we were on massive drugs and Courtney was injecting turkey basters full of heroin straight into her stomach," Kurt says, "the whole thing was no one knew anything and they were so spineless and afraid to ask us anything."

Yet another example of deflecting the drug rumors through exaggeration: Kurt intended "injecting turkey basters full of heroin straight into her stomach" to make what he called Courtney's "twenty-dollar habit" look mild in comparison. And note that he didn't actually deny they were doing drugs; all he said was that nobody asked them about it.

Seeing as "Dave at least listens and he's not very judgmental," Kurt opened up to him about what was really going on. "Dave's practically the only person I've ever really talked to about any of this shit," Kurt says. "Chris was massively judgmental—all he did was give me bad vibes all the time and dirty looks."

Fans like to think that their favorite bands are like the Monkees—living together, sharing good times and bad, and generally knowing everything about each other. But the fact of the matter was that Nirvana wasn't such an intimate, tight-knit group anymore. Granted, it may have been for his own good, but once Shelli began going on tour, Chris didn't hang out with the band as much anymore, then Courtney came along with Kurt. "We weren't doing things together anymore," Kurt says. "Before, we were going out and hanging around every night because we were best friends and we didn't know anybody else. Slowly, everybody started getting a mate and we wouldn't be in the same hotel rooms and everything like that. Before, we stayed in the same hotel room."

In their hit '60s TV show, the four Monkees shared a home. The thing is, *successful rock bands aren't actually like the Monkees*—they don't all live together. Often, band members don't even hang out that much. That's a sensible survival tactic: they're cooped up together on the road and in the studio so much that it's just healthy to spend as much time apart as possible so they don't get on each other's nerves. And then, after a certain degree of success, they don't even hang out on tour either, and mostly see each other at photo sessions or onstage. That's what was happening to Nirvana, and it was unfortunate because of Krist's invaluable gift for keeping Kurt grounded.

Because no one directly asked Kurt what was going on, even the inner circle thrived on rumor, infuriating Kurt and alienating everyone else even further. "I can't stand people who don't confront anyone," Kurt says, seemingly oblivious to the fact that he himself is a prime offender in this regard. "If you have a problem with somebody, you should just flat out ask them. They would never do that. They would just get on the bus and it was bad vibes—you could just see it radiating off of them. It just festered in my mind how spineless these people are, how they don't know what the fuck is going on at all but they're all *assuming* and they're in my *own fucking band*."

Of course, Kurt could have just cleared the air by calling a meeting and telling everyone what they so clearly wanted to know.

Chris feels it was a vicious cycle fed by both sides. "When he isolated himself, people would react to it, but he isolated himself to react to people's reactions," says Chris. "It just degenerates into bullshit."

"I was way more miserable during all the tours that I was vomiting every night and not eating and being totally straight," Kurt says. "I was way more of a bastard and a negative person. They couldn't be around me half the time. I was just looking straight ahead and concentrating on not puking all the time that it was hard for anyone to communicate with me. But when I started doing drugs, I was feeling fine—and happy for the first time in a long time. I was hoping that everything would be fine with them, but simply because I was doing drugs, it created more problems even though I was finally relieved."

Having a euphoric effect, heroin will give users an illusion of happiness. In *Sing Backwards and Weep*, Mark Lanegan wrote that heroin "had quieted the cyclone storm of my own voice in my head, constantly tearing me down, telling me what a shit heap I was. Most importantly, heroin had erased the myriad collection of endless worries that had kept me awake all night most of my life. It had freed me from feeling anything: loss, heartbreak, regret, grief, resentment as well as the burning hatred and disgust I felt not only for myself but also for other people I thought had wronged me, real or imagined. When dope enveloped me in its golden glow, all that melted away like springtime snow."

But, needless to say, heroin is also an extremely dangerous drug—not just because of its effects, but often because of the people and situations you have to deal with in order to get it. And if Kurt were to be caught with heroin, particularly in certain countries where they toured, he could have spent a lot of time in prison.

In Spain, Courtney experienced some mild contractions and became terrified that she might give birth prematurely. "Of course," says Kurt, "she had them right before we had to play a show so I had to play a show wondering if Courtney's going to die or if she's going to have a baby." After the concert, Kurt raced to the hospital. "It was the most groaty, disgusting hospital I've ever seen—dirt on the walls, the nurses were screaming in Spanish at Courtney, telling her to stay down," Kurt says. They moved her to a clinic, where they called their obstetrician, who believed there was no serious problem, but advised them to take the next plane home, just in case. "We had to buy two seats in first class so Courtney could lay down," Kurt says. "Of course, it got reported as two *rows*."

In early July, Kurt and Courtney came back from the tour to discover a major disaster. With the idea that a burglar wouldn't think of looking there, Kurt had put his favorite guitar and more importantly, several tapes and notebooks full of poetry and song ideas in the bathtub. But while they were gone, a plumbing problem had filled the bathroom with sludge, ruining everything—the guitar, the tapes, and the notebooks.

They soon found a new apartment, a comfortable two-bedroom in a relatively low-rent ("Right down the hill was a crack street," says Kurt) neighborhood in the Hollywood Hills, near the Hollywood Bowl, with a sweeping view of the hills. Kurt simply started writing all over again.

Meanwhile, yet another band named Nirvana—a British group that had enjoyed one minor hit in the '60s—filed suit for sole rights to the name in the UK. But when it was pointed out that Nirvana had been popular in Britain for over two years and they had done nothing about it, the case was dropped.

The UK Nirvana debuted in 1967 with one of the first concept albums: a work of quasi-Baroque psychedelia-lite called *The Story of Simon Simopath*: *A Science Fiction*

Pantomime. It's a fluffy precursor to the concept albums that fellow English bands the Zombies (*Odessey and Oracle*), Small Faces (*Ogdens' Nut Gone Flake*), and the Pretty Things (*S.F. Sorrow*) would do the following year.

Nirvana UK were good sports: in 1996, the band's principals reunited and did a dainty synth-pop version of "Lithium" that wouldn't have sounded out of place in 1984.

Also in July, Hole signed to DGC for a reported million dollars in a deal even richer and more favorable than the one Nirvana got. A *Newsweek* article on the onslaught of so-called "alternative" band signings in the wake of Nirvana quoted one industry maven as saying that "Sleeping with Kurt Cobain is worth a million dollars." DGC denies this had anything at all to do with the signing. Off in the distance is heard incredulous laughter.

At that point, although the band had been acclaimed in the influential UK music press, Hole had released one low-selling, resolutely untuneful album. But in the post-*Nevermind* music industry, all bets were off about what was commercial.

Except for the methadone he took on the summer tour, Kurt did heroin for months, for almost the entire pregnancy. Meanwhile, he was having to do more and more just to get the same kick, eventually working up to a four-hundred-dollar-a-day habit. He couldn't get up any higher because that was the maximum his bank's cash machine would dispense in one day.

Kurt, as Courtney said, was a "gobbler." He did drugs in huge quantities and consequently built up a gigantic tolerance. That's something to remember when considering the conspiracy theories around his death.

"I ended up doing a hundred-dollar shot in one shot and not even feeling it, hardly," he says. "I was just filling up the syringe as far as it could go without pulling the end off. At that point, it was like, why do it?" The next step would have been to start doing speedballs, the mix of cocaine and heroin which had killed John Belushi. With the baby imminent, Kurt checked into Cedars-Sinai on August 4 to detox, spending a total of twenty-five days there.

"He looked at killing himself on the one hand or living on the other," says Danny Goldberg. "He decided to live."

Hole guitarist Eric Erlandson visited Courtney and Kurt throughout the ordeal. "He totally saved our lives during that whole time," says Kurt. "He was the only piece of reality, the only calm person who was there as an example of what

Slam-Dancing with Mr. Brownstone

421

life could be like afterward, once this crazy shit was over with." In gratitude, they put Erlandson in their will.

To be or not to be—that was the question that Kurt had to answer. For the time being, anyway, he chose the former.

Erlandson did not come away from the experience unconflicted. Read his 2012 book *Letters to Kurt*, a cathartic collection of fifty-two poems and essays that form a loving but angry elegy for his close friend.

Except for Erlandson, no one visited Kurt in the early stages of his rehabilitation. "I was in a really vulnerable emotional state, which is the first ten days of detox when you're really fucked up and crying all the time," Kurt says. "It messes with your mind so much—it's like a never-ending acid trip. That's exactly what detox is like. It's like being on the heaviest dose of acid and not coming off of it for ten days, never sleeping. Time just stands still and anything will affect you emotionally—anything you read or see on television will make you cry. So it actually wouldn't have been a good time because I would have burst out crying in front of them, anyhow.

"I didn't get any support from anybody the first two times I tried, either," he continues. "No one came to visit me or call me or anything. This time I demanded that someone come and visit me so I felt like I had some friends. So eventually [Chris and Dave] came down."

"It was good to see him but it kind of bummed me out to see him in such bad shape," says Chris. "He was on some kind of medication, lying in bed, and I was thinking, 'Fuck, so this is where all this got you.'"

One day, Dave and Chris stopped by to discuss whether they were going to play a benefit to fight Oregon's infamously homophobic Proposition 9, play a homecoming concert in Seattle to benefit the anticensorship Washington Music Industry Coalition, or appear on the MTV Video Music Awards. They decided to do all three.

While Kurt was detoxing and Courtney was waiting for the baby to be born, a profile of Courtney appeared in *Vanity Fair*.

Kemchewa
Dear
NIRVANA is a three piece from
the outskirts of Seattle WA.
Kurdt-Guitar/Voice and Chris-bass have
struggled with too many undedicated drummers
for the past 3 years. performing under
such names as: Bliss, throat Oyster, Ted Ed Fred etc. for the last 9
months we have had the pleasure to
have Chad-drums under our wings and
develop what we are now and always
will be NIRVANA.

3 regularly broadcasted cuts on KCMU
Seattle College Radio (also KAOS olympia)
Played with Leaving Trains, Whipping Boy,
Hells Kitchen, Treacherous Jaywalkers &
countless local acts.
Looking for: EP or LP We have about
15 songs Recorded on 8 Tracks at
Reciprocal studios in Seattle.
Willing to compromise on material (Some
of this shit is pretty old) Tour any-
-time forever) hopefully the music will seek for its
Please Reply THANK YOU   Area code
                                        (206)
352-0992 114 N PEAR olympia VA. 98506

chapter twelve

ALL WE DID WAS CRY

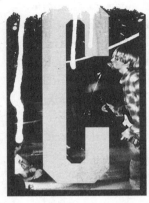ourtney originally did the *Vanity Fair* story believing that it would be a mostly flattering piece on her and her music. She was overlooking the fact that her band had only released one extremely modest-selling independent label album a year before, a point of little import to *Vanity Fair's* upscale readership. This bit of hubris blinded her to the fact that the article was being done by Lynn Hirschberg, well known for her unflattering celebrity profiles. Courtney thought the article would put her on the map.

It did.

She was used to an adoring UK music press that understood her sardonic, sarcastic sense of humor, didn't ask hard questions, didn't do much investigation, and kept secrets in exchange for the favor of a hip musician. Lynn Hirschberg had no such allegiances.

Courtney says the story was arranged when she was still using. "Had I not done drugs, I would have been lucid enough to see that *Vanity Fair* was going to stitch me up—what *else* were they going to do with me?" she says, adding that she thought that a hostile article in the "conservative" *Vanity Fair* would probably translate into a study in outlaw cool to the rock community.

It was pretty convoluted reasoning to think that an unflattering profile in a major national magazine could generate indie cred. For all her rage about the *Vanity Fair* piece, it was to her credit that Courtney did admit she'd been a fool to do it.

The interviews for the piece occurred early that summer. But, thanks to the long lead times of national glossies, it wouldn't come back to haunt Kurt and Courtney until late August.

The article appeared in the September 1992 issue. One of the many controversial aspects of the piece was a photo of a quite pregnant Courtney naked from the waist down in a bit of see-through lingerie. No big deal, but it turned out she had been smoking a cigarette in the photograph, and that editor Tina Brown had ordered it airbrushed out.

According to the Centers for Disease Control, tobacco use during pregnancy "increases the risk of health problems for developing babies, including preterm birth, low birth weight, and birth defects of the mouth and lip."

Courtney says they had done a marathon photo session for the piece, going through dozens of rolls of film and several costume and set changes. At one point, in the middle of changing costumes, she says she just happened to have a puff on a cigarette, and photographer Michel Comte just happened to be right there to capture it. She is, however, smoking in at least one other picture in the session. After the article appeared, magazines all over the world were clamoring for the unairbrushed photo. Courtney claims she and Kurt bought the pictures back for fifty thousand dollars, a price she calls "blackmail."

But that was the least of it. The piece described Courtney as a "train-wreck personality" who "isn't particularly interested in the consequences of her actions." It strongly hinted that she had introduced Kurt to heroin, although that was not the case. Hirschberg quoted various unnamed "industry insiders" who "fear for the health of the child," without mentioning whether these industry insiders had done any studies in teratogenic medicine.

Music biz executives probably aren't the most credible authority on the subject of embryonic development. It would have been infinitely better to consult a specialist in maternal fetal medicine.

Some of the article's more damaging assertions may have been true, it's just that there were enough errors to sow some legitimate skepticism about the piece overall.

Then there were insinuating little lines like "Courtney stamps out her cigarette, rummages through her purse, and heads off to the bathroom." While Courtney herself brought up rumors that she and Madonna "were shooting heroin together," that she had had sex onstage, and that she was HIV-positive, Hirschberg winkingly added, "None of these statements is true, although the live-sex thing is a very persistent rumor."

In addition to all that, Hirschberg was partial to wiggly statements such as "many believe she introduced Cobain to heroin" and "reportedly, Kurt didn't do much more than drink until he met Courtney." Hirschberg couldn't confirm either statement because they weren't true: Kurt was on record—in my *Rolling Stone* cover story, for instance—as saying that he'd started doing heroin long before he even met Courtney.

But far more damaging was one quote in the piece. After a description of how she and Kurt went to Alphabet City to score during the *Saturday Night Live* visit, Courtney added, "After that, I did heroin for a couple of months," which meant that she had done heroin long after she knew she was pregnant. Courtney vigorously protested that she had been misquoted; Hirschberg maintained that she had the tapes.

Although the article seems to conclusively paint Courtney as a conniver, various factual errors throughout the piece would seem to compromise Hirschberg's accuracy. For instance, she wrote that Danny Goldberg was a vice president at Polygram Records, when in fact he was a vice president of Atlantic. Hirschberg maintained that Kurt and Courtney first met "eight or so years ago," which would have put Kurt in high school. The piece perpetuated the gold-digger theory by saying that the next time Courtney met Kurt after their first meeting in Portland, "Kurt was a star," which was not true. Hirschberg also misreported an easily verified story about the bidding war over Hole.

In 2011, Courtney told Maer Roshan of the now-defunct addiction and recovery online magazine the *Fix*: "When my doctor informed me I was having a baby, I knew I had to get clean real quick. I checked in to a hospital to detox."

Most unfortunately, the piece also seemed to completely miss Courtney's sardonic sense of humor. This is a woman who, in the course of a delicate conversation about the whole "was she or wasn't she" controversy, can come out with a deliberately sarcastic line like "If there is ever a time that a person *should* be on drugs, it's when they're pregnant, because it sucks" without considering how it would look in print. Spend even a little quality time with Courtney and it's clear that an exchange she had with Kurt about firing Dave was purely facetious.

If *Nevermind* was a success because the band was in the right place at the right time, the *Vanity Fair* piece found the Cobains at the wrong place at the wrong time. Besides the nation's continuing drug hysteria and a misguided Republican crusade for "family values," the story also tapped into America's sudden guilt about what it had done to its children over the past decade. Suddenly, the US media became fixated on child abuse stories, from the kids who were left "home alone" while their parents vacationed in Mexico to the poor little Long Island girl who was shackled for days in an underground bunker. A mom who had allegedly done heroin (not to mention smoked cigarettes) while pregnant pressed some powerful buttons.

At the time, countless stories in the media decried the phenomenon of "latchkey kids"—children who had to look after themselves while their parents were at work—and relentlessly parroted the phrase "home alone." The latter was, of course, a reference to the hit 1990 comedy of the same name, essentially about a neglected child fighting for his safety; the film had clearly struck a cultural nerve.

"I wouldn't have thought that I could be dwarfed or squashed or raped or incredibly hurt by a story in that magazine," Courtney says. "But the power of it was so intense. It was unbelievable. I read a fax of it and my bones shook. I knew that my world was over. I was dead. That was it. The rest of my life. Not only was I going to walk around with a big black mark but any happiness that I had known, I was going to have to fight for, for the rest of my life. It shouldn't be that way, but I exposed myself to it. Had I not taken drugs in the first place, I would have been lucid enough to know what she was about, I wouldn't have been candid, I would have figured out where I fit in the scheme of the *Vanity Fair* world."

Hubris is the sin of pride or dangerous overconfidence; in ancient Greek mythology, when humans were too proud, or defiant of the gods, the gods retaliated, bringing about the person's downfall. Courtney's decision to do the *Vanity Fair* profile was an attempted star turn by someone who was not (yet) a star. And the gods reacted accordingly. With perfect irony, it was in a magazine called *Vanity Fair*.

Courtney likes to think the story was some kind of set-up—perhaps commandeered by *Vanity Fair* darling Madonna, whose new record label, Maverick, she had recently spurned, and loudly.

But a simpler explanation is that Courtney made for good copy—she was an outspoken woman with a checkered past who happened to be married to the rock star of the moment. While they maintain it is a pack of lies, even the Cobains acknowledge that Hirschberg's piece was at least an entertaining read—and the worst thing that ever happened to them.

Courtney checked herself into a hospital, she says, "because I was going to go crazy. I was going to take drugs. I've never been a person to take drugs in a crisis. I usually take drugs when I'm happy. I felt really like killing myself. I was eight and a half months pregnant. I couldn't kill myself so I checked into a hospital for two weeks before the baby was born."

So maybe Courtney checked herself into a chemical dependency unit without actually being chemically dependent on anything, but just worried that she might relapse. Maybe that's how she was able to get the very unusual opportunity to visit the Cedars-Sinai neonatal unit even though she had not yet given birth.

Meanwhile, Kurt was detoxing and, once again, in enormous pain. Unable to eat, he was placed on an IV and got weaker and weaker for a time, then rallied. His rehabilitation was slowed by the fact that he was occasionally given morphine to kill the stomach pain. He saw a battalion of gastrointestinal specialists who took X-rays, upper GI's, lower GI's, CAT scans, etc. He was weak. He was ready to snap. "He'd been crying for weeks," says Courtney. "It was nothing *but* crying. All we *did* was cry. It was horrible."

At first, Kurt didn't understand the implications of the *Vanity Fair* story. "It was obviously upsetting," he says, "but I was in such a vulnerable state of mind and my mind was so clouded from getting off of drugs that I would have rather just let it pass for a while, but Courtney was so upset about it. She was about to have a baby—she wasn't in a clouded state of mind at all."

Gradually, it dawned on Kurt what the story was doing to his and Courtney's reputation. "One day I snapped out of it and realized how awful it was," he says. "It was definitely affecting our livelihood and our image and everything to a real extreme." And since the *Vanity Fair* piece was based largely on unnamed "inside sources," they had to deal with the profound disappointment and paranoia that arose from the fact that some of their most trusted friends and associates had betrayed them.

They tried very hard to find out who those sources were. Despite their strong suspicions, they didn't succeed in confirming anything.

"We'd already been turned into cartoon characters by then and it justified everything—all the lies and rumors that had been going around," says Kurt. "I just found it amazing that someone could get away with something like that, that she couldn't go to jail for it or get busted somehow or sued. I thought we'd be able to sue her, but it's a matter of having the millions of dollars to fight in court with [*Vanity Fair* publisher] Condé Nast, who would support her."

"I just decided, 'Fuck this, I don't want to be in a band anymore. It just isn't worth it. I want to kill [Hirschberg],'" Kurt says. "'As soon as I get out of this fucking hospital, I'm going to kill this woman with my bare hands. I'm going to stab her to death. First I'm going to take her dog and slit its guts out in front of her and then shit all over her and stab her to death.'" He was too weak to do that so he says he considered hiring a hit man, then calmed down a bit and thought about asking David Geffen to pull some strings to get Hirschberg fired or else he'd quit the band. None of this ever happened.

Kurt sent a handwritten letter to David Geffen about the *Vanity Fair* story, claiming he was so upset about it that he was breaking up Nirvana.

Kurt very humbly introduced himself as "the lead singer, guitar [*sic*] and songwriter for the band NIRVANA," as if Geffen wasn't well aware of who he was. (I bet he added "songwriter" because the publishing squabble with Krist and Dave was still on his mind.) He bluntly reminded Geffen that "I've made your company a lot of money."

The Hirschberg piece, he said, "has forced me to decide on breaking up my band."

"The article suggests," Kurt continued, "that Courtney and I have been [*taking* or *doing*, it's not quite legible] heroin continuously throughout her pregnancy which is not true." That was a very lawyerly way to put it: *technically*, Kurt had not done *heroin* continuously—he'd also done various other opiates—and he had probably gone off them at various times during the pregnancy, so it wasn't, strictly speaking, "continuously."

Hole, Kurt helpfully added, was also on Geffen's label DGC—as if David Geffen wasn't already well aware of this, too—and "is a very important band to be heard especially my wife's openess [*sic*] and embrace of womens [*sic*] rights and homosexuality." Kurt seemed to be trying to ingratiate himself here—widely understood to be gay, Geffen came out a few months later.

Then Kurt prevailed on Geffen, an extremely wealthy and powerful man, to weigh in. "After you read the article (I hope) something may be done about it. . . . The person who wrote the article Lynn Herschberg [*sic*] must have her karma broken. Some way. It's either her or me. . . . At this point fuck NIRVANA."

Kurt was bluffing. He wasn't really going to break up the band, he was just threatening to, in the naive hope that David Geffen would somehow lean on Lynn Hirschberg, with whom he had no ostensible connection.

Geffen, a tough-minded but famously nurturing man, wrote a very gracious letter back. "The press have a way of sabotaging your privacy. The thing you have to remember is that these things pass and people quickly forget about articles of this type," he wrote. "Please know that I am here if you need me. This should be a time of joy and celebration and I realize it's been difficult. I'll help you get through it any way I can."

That was very kind of Geffen, and very wise, but he was wrong: certain people didn't quickly forget about that article, and it would soon have devastating consequences.

Kurt still gets scarily angry when the subject of Lynn Hirschberg's story comes up. "She'd better hope to God that someday I don't find myself destitute without a wife and a baby," he says. "Because I'll fucking get revenge on her. Before I leave this earth, she's going out with me."

"I don't have hate in my heart for anybody," Courtney told the *Fix* in that 2011 article, "but [Lynn Hirschberg is] more responsible for my husband's death than anyone." Of course, Kurt was more responsible for his own death than anyone.

###

On the morning of August 18, 1992, Courtney began to go into labor. She stunned her doctors by picking up her IV and slamming out of the room. She marched over to Kurt's room, clear across the hospital, and screamed, "You get out of this bed and you come down now! You are not leaving me to do this by myself, fuck you!" She came back to find that the hospital security force had "gone apeshit." Kurt was still groggy from a dose of sleeping pills and in extreme pain, but managed to get himself down to the delivery room a little later.

At seven forty-eight in the morning, Frances Bean Cobain was born. She weighed seven pounds, one ounce, and according to the Cobains she was perfectly healthy.

Kurt didn't witness his own daughter's birth. He had passed out. "I'm having the baby, it's coming out, he's puking, he's passing out, and I'm holding his hand and rubbing his stomach while the baby's coming out of me," says Courtney. "It was pretty weird," she says, laughing darkly.

"I was so fucking scared—it was probably a classic case of what the typical father goes through," says Kurt, who was still hooked up to an IV and in the midst of rehab. "I was just so weak and sick and afraid that something was going to happen to Courtney or the baby."

A press release from Gold Mountain a few days later aimed to refute all the speculation about Frances. "The infant is in good condition, is feeding well and growing at the normal rate expected for a newborn," the statement said, adding, "The vicious rumors that Frances was suffering any withdrawals at the time of birth are completely false, and in fact, she has not suffered any discomfort since delivery."

If their baby was a boy, they were going to name it Eugene, after Eugene Kelly of the Vaselines. When they found out that they were to have a girl, they thought of Kelly's partner in the Vaselines, Frances McKee. At the time, they weren't thinking of Frances Farmer, the Hollywood actress who was blacklisted and hounded into insanity in the '50s, but Kurt now wishes that was the reason. He adds that the word "bean" has cropped up in both his and Courtney's lives many times, but mostly they came up with the name after noticing that Frances actually looked like a kidney bean in her early sonograms.

###

Tarnished reputations turned out to be only the beginning of the *Vanity Fair* controversy.

Even Kurt and Courtney's lawyer, Rosemary Carroll, believes that the *Vanity Fair* article prompted the Los Angeles County Department of Children's Services to begin taking action against them. The agency must have seen the *Vanity Fair* piece—(both Carroll and the Cobains claim it was stapled to the top of the report on them). The story was so well publicized that the agency could not ignore it, even though Courtney had allegedly detoxed almost immediately after learning she was pregnant. Whether anticipating pressure from higher-ups or even public outcry, it's not outside the realm of possibility that the agency was virtually obligated to hassle this rock star couple.

Late in Courtney's pregnancy, Children's Services threatened to relieve Kurt and Courtney of custody of Frances. At a hearing in Family Court, where rules of evidence are relaxed, Children's Services used the *Vanity Fair* article and what later proved to be a spurious urine test to argue that both Kurt and Courtney were multiple substance abusers and therefore did not deserve to have custody of their child. The judge agreed and ordered Kurt to go to yet another detox center for another thirty days, even though he was completely clean after his stay at Cedars.

But that was the least of it. Two weeks after their daughter was born, Kurt and Courtney were forced to surrender custody of Frances to Courtney's sister Jamie. For a month after that, Kurt and Courtney were not allowed to be alone with their own daughter.

Kurt genuinely believes it was a conspiracy. "It was all a total scam," he says. "It was an attempt to use us as an example because we stand for everything that goes against the grain of conformist American entertainment. It was a witch hunt. It was an outright Frances Farmer case where we were being mistreated beyond belief. Social Services literally took the *Vanity Fair* article and Xeroxed it and then took that pee test that Courtney took in the first trimester of her pregnancy and used that as an excuse to take our baby away."

Although Nirvana represented a sea-change in the music industry, with implications for the culture at large, it beggars belief that some nefarious entity targeted Kurt and

Courtney for the crime of going against the grain of mainstream American entertainment. This all happened partly because Courtney said and did some sensationally ill-advised things in the presence of an unsympathetic journalist for a national magazine. But that's something that almost any loyal husband would find difficult to admit. It wouldn't be the last time that someone screwed up badly and their spouse blamed it on a vast conspiracy.

Granted, this was all happening during one of conservative culture's periodic moral panics. Just one day before Frances was born, right-wing firebrand Pat Buchanan made an infamous speech at the 1992 Republican National Convention. "There is a religious war going on in this country," Buchanan proclaimed to the assembled conventioneers, "for the soul of America. And in that struggle for the soul of America, Clinton and Clinton are on the other side, and George [H. W.] Bush is on *our* side."

His party, Buchanan thundered, stood against a woman's right to choose, against women in military combat units, against same-sex marriage, and against "the raw sewage of pornography that so terribly pollutes our popular culture."

So, on top of some bad decisions, Kurt, Courtney, and Frances were also just the victims of bad timing.

No one knew this was happening except for a very close inner circle of the Nirvana organization. Given that the couple was fighting for the custody of their own baby—and that a magazine article was virtually being used as evidence—their extreme reactions to subsequent bad press start to become more understandable.

Courtney still becomes distraught when telling the tale. Toward the end of her account of the *Vanity Fair* fiasco, this tough, seemingly indomitable woman begins to cry openly. "It's one thing to ruin your credibility or to be publicly humiliated but they took our *baby* away and there was nothing wrong with her," she says, sobbing. "I did *not* do drugs during my pregnancy after I knew I was pregnant. I went and got all the help I could fucking get. I went to every doctor in town. I have medical records to prove it and they just fucking tortured us."

It seemed hopeless—doctors, government agencies, the press all were against them. At one dark moment, they took out Kurt's handgun and considered taking their own lives.

It's excruciating to come across all the references to suicide in this book. But things like that can be difficult to see when you're right in the thick of it.

"It was just so humiliating and it just felt like so many powerful people were out to get us that it just seemed hopeless," says Kurt. "It didn't seem like we'd ever win. It was amazing. We were totally suicidal. It's not the right time for a woman

trying to get rid of the hormonal problems of just having a baby and me just getting off of drugs and just being bombarded with this. It was just too much." But in the end, they put down the gun.

The next day, the band flew to England to headline the closing night of the 1992 Reading Festival. The English press was running with rumors that the band was breaking up because of Kurt's health. Kurt says the rumors were completely unfounded. "No, it was classic, typical English journalism," he says wearily. "Sensationalism. I have absolutely no respect for the English people. They make me sick. I thought I'd never say anything racist in my life, but those people are the most snooty, cocksure, anal people and they have absolutely no regard for people's emotions. They don't think of other people as humans at all. They're the coldest people I've ever met."

Dave was worried about Nirvana's future. Kurt was living in Los Angeles, and Krist and Dave in Seattle, and they were barely talking. Their one rehearsal before the big Reading show went badly. "I really thought, 'This will be a disaster, this will be the end of our career for sure,'" Dave told the *Scotsman* newspaper in 2009.

Kurt took a lot of grief for that remark about "the English people." He later explained that he only meant English *journalists*, but the fact that he added, "I thought I'd never say anything racist in my life" would seem to indicate that he meant the English people as a whole. (And note the upcoming remark about "limey" bands.)

Kurt had personally programmed the bill for that day, purposely leaving out "lame-ass limey bands." The festival organizers originally balked at including the Melvins and Screaming Trees, but Kurt threatened to pull out of the festival if they weren't included. Also on the all-day bill were old friends like L7, Mudhoney and Eugenius, as well as Pavement, Nick Cave, and the Bad Seeds, and the uproarious ABBA tribute band Bjorn Again.

The Reading Festival organizers balked at Screaming Trees because of an incident earlier that summer. According to Mark Lanegan in *Sing Backwards and Weep*, the Trees were scheduled to play during the day at Denmark's Roskilde festival in late June, with Nirvana headlining that evening, but Kurt was "fighting dopesickness" and asked the Trees to play last—after Nirvana. As great as the Trees were, that was a thankless task. "I had tried to argue with him as he lay uncomfortably under a blanket on a couch, being administered to by a doctor, in his dressing room," wrote Lanegan. But Kurt had made up his mind.

During the Trees' set that night, a "beyond shitfaced" (his description) Lanegan couldn't hear himself in the monitors and began hurling equipment into the pit, damaging some expensive television cameras. Then he threatened to punch out the roadies who tried to stop him. It was ugly. Screaming Trees were banned from the rest of the European festival season, a massive blow to their career. It's a testament to Kurt's clout that he managed to get them on the bill at Reading.

It rained all day and festival goers wallowed in the traditional Reading mud bath. At last, it was Nirvana's turn to play. Kurt rolled out on stage in a wheelchair and wearing a hospital gown, as a poke at all the rumors about his bad health. Yet less than a week before, he had vomited and then passed out onto a cot as his daughter was being born; the day before, he had contemplated killing himself. At any rate, Nirvana played a glorious show—an eight on a scale of ten, by Kurt's reckoning. Tens of thousands of English voices turned virtually every song of the hour and a half set into a gigantic sing-along. The band played with staggering power. Rumors of Nirvana's demise had been greatly exaggerated.

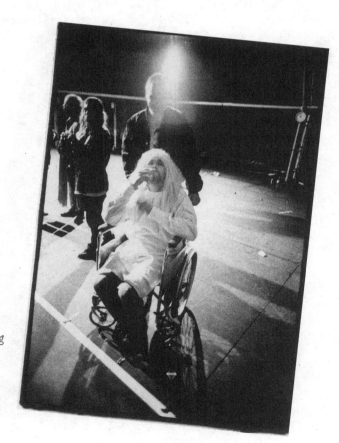

Kurt getting wheeled
onstage at the Reading
Festival, 1992.
© Charles Peterson

All We Did Was Cry

435

Kurt at Reading '92.
© Charles Peterson

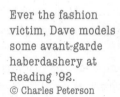

Ever the fashion
victim, Dave models
some avant-garde
haberdashery at
Reading '92.
© Charles Peterson

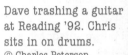

Dave trashing a guitar
at Reading '92. Chris
sits in on drums.
© Charles Peterson

There's another example of Kurt trying to deflect the all-too-accurate drug rumors by making light of them through exaggeration.

That day, a bunch of us press types were escorted to a tight little space at the very back of stage right, amid the myriad large black boxes that rock music gets transported in. We stood there the whole day, watching from behind the bands—including the Melvins, Screaming Trees, Pavement, L7, Teenage Fanclub, Mudhoney, and Nick Cave—as they played to the proverbial sea of humanity.

It had been rainy and windy earlier in the day and the grounds—normally a cow pasture—were muddy. And so, all day, people amused themselves with the wholesome pleasure of throwing manure-infused dirt clods at the stage. L7 got pelted pretty badly during their set, which was plagued not just by technical issues but by the downright enmity of much of the crowd. Eventually, singer-guitarist Donita Sparks had had quite enough. So she squatted down, reached into her shorts, pulled out her tampon and flung it into the audience. That was awesome, but perhaps even more awesomely, the tampon came flying back a few minutes later, landing on the stage, where it remained for the rest of the set. Afterward, a stagehand swept it away with a push broom, along with a large pile of fetid dirt clods.

There was a long break after Nick Cave. We waited and waited for Nirvana in the humid English night, which was heavy with anticipation and scented with the smell of thousands of bodies, manure, and the acrid stench of toxic bonfires made from piles of Styrofoam cups and plates. Finally the lights went down. And there was Nirvana.

In a hospital gown and a ridiculous blond wig, Kurt was rolled onto the stage in a wheelchair by his friend and Nirvana's longtime staunch supporter, British music journalist Everett True.

Kurt got up from the chair haltingly, stepped to the microphone, and in a theatrically shaky voice, sang the first line of "The Rose," the title song from the 1979 film. "Some say love, it is a river . . ." he whined and then pretended to collapse to the floor.

It was actually a pretty serious joke. Always pay close attention to Kurt's choice in covers. *The Rose* is about a troubled rock star who is a recovering heroin addict and desperate to take some time off but is bullied into staying on the road by a ruthless and greedy manager. In the end, the rock star, lonely and exhausted, dies of a drug overdose. (It might also be worth noting that Kurt's beloved Mudhoney covered "The Rose" on 1988's *Sub Pop 200* compilation.)

Once again, Kurt was smokescreening by exaggeration, only now it was on a very big stage.

The band began to play. It was extremely powerful. That sea of faces was bouncing up and down in huge, rolling waves as they pogoed in the light pouring off the stage.

Huge clouds of steam rose from the audience; it looked like a vast human forest fire. Some freaky guy was onstage with the band, dancing like a blissed-out rag doll, doing what everybody in the crowd wished they had the room to do. Nirvana played with an oceanic force, truly rocking the way that waves do, a powerful, inexorable, heaving energy. The music was transcendent. It was the greatest rock concert I have ever seen.

It does seem like Kurt didn't want to play Reading. Or at least maybe he shouldn't have, given that he'd been contemplating suicide a few days earlier, not to mention the fact that he'd become a father just twelve days before.

Still, the controversy surrounding the band would not go away. The two main UK music weeklies arranged for cover stories on the band at the time of the European make-up tour earlier that summer. *Melody Maker* **agreed to run their piece, by the band's longtime friend and supporter Everett True, just after the interviews took place, while the** *NME* **agreed to run their piece to coincide with**

The stage after Nirvana's triumphant set at Reading '92. ©·Charles Peterson

Reading six weeks later. Nirvana also required that the piece be written by Keith Cameron, who had developed a good relationship with the band through doing profiles on them ever since the *Sounds* cover story back in the summer of 1990. While True had glibly skirted around the controversies, in the *NME*, Cameron confronted the myriad rumors with the wounded tone of a disillusioned fan, which is precisely what he was.

After interviewing the band at a show in Valencia, Spain, Cameron wrote that the band, or at least Kurt, had begun to behave like the self-indulgent dinosaurs they had disdained and displaced, missing soundcheck for unexplained reasons, making themselves difficult to be interviewed and photographed, and very likely, doing hard drugs. The piece ran through the litany of drug-related rumors, many of which, as it turns out, were not far off the mark. "They've begun to blow it all via smack, the biggest sucker punch of the lot," Cameron wrote. "From nobodies to superstars to fuckups in the space of six months! That had to be a record." Cameron wrote that when he asked about the heroin rumors, Kurt made him check his arms for needle marks. Of course, there were none because he was on methadone by that time.

Methadone, of course, is generally taken orally. Remember, addicts are sneaky.

But the real target of the piece, with its "LOVE WILL TEAR US APART" headline, was Courtney. The piece quotes one crew member who referred to Courtney as "The Wicked Witch of the West," while someone else on the tour recalled Kurt as being a nice guy, "BC—'Before Courtney.'"

Cameron even laid into Janet Billig, who had recently joined Gold Mountain to work with Nirvana and Hole. "Her role on this tour is like a cross between wet nurse and human sponge," wrote Cameron, "indulging whims and soaking up all of Courtney's excess bullshit." Courtney, Cameron concluded, is a "Grade A pain in the arse." The band was on the verge of breaking up, and it was all her fault (Cameron now admits he was influenced by the *Vanity Fair* article).

Cameron bumped into Kurt and Eric Erlandson at the traditional post-show wingding at the Ramada hotel in Reading. Kurt scolded him for the piece, then Erlandson poured a glass of vodka and lime juice on his head. They walked away, leaving Cameron literally to cry on the shoulder of *NME* photographer Steve Double. "I wrote what I thought was a sensitive piece," he says. Cameron remains *persona non grata* with the Nirvana camp.

"If there's any sense of me feeling betrayed in any way by Nirvana, which there really probably isn't, it's that reality as I discovered it on that day in Spain," says Cameron. "This was a band that totally inspired me. They'd been the most meaningful musical event in my life, ever. And they became this cliché that your favorite bands just don't do, at least not mine. I was shocked at that reality."

Stories like that weighed on my mind as I wrote this book. I'd worked my ass off on it and had developed a good rapport with Kurt and virtually everyone else. I didn't want that all to come tumbling down. But one of the things one learns as a journalist is that you're never totally sure what will set off your subject—it could be the big, obvious bombshell or it could be some seemingly negligible incident that somehow turns out to be very touchy. So you could write what you were sure was, in Keith Cameron's words, a "sensitive piece" and still get a drink poured over your head. I did my best to observe Kurt's request: "Just tell the truth." Even if I left out some inconvenient truths.

But Cameron was right: Nirvana had quickly and perhaps inevitably fallen into some classic rock star tropes . . . or traps. Pointing that out pressed Kurt's buttons because of his acute self-consciousness about how the underground community perceived him. By that time, Kurt's old friend Slim Moon, along with Tinuviel Sampson, had started an Olympia-based indie label very significantly called Kill Rock Stars. If Kurt was becoming precisely what his friends were rejecting, maybe they would reject him, too.

Days later, Nirvana played the 1992 MTV Video Music Awards show.

The band was told they could play whatever song they wanted during their performance, which would kick off the ceremonies. At soundcheck the day before the show, the band played a then-unrecorded song called "Rape Me" and another new song provisionally entitled "New Poopie." The next day, perhaps because of the title of "Rape Me," perhaps because it wasn't a hit, perhaps because the show's organizers thought they had made a deal with Gold Mountain, MTV insisted that Nirvana play "Teen Spirit."

"New Poopie" was the working title for "Tourette's." Although it was far from the best song on the upcoming album, Nirvana planned to hit the VMAs with a pretty ferocious tune, an effective way to proclaim their new tone and direction.

Hours before show time, Nirvana decided they weren't going to play.

Then the band began to ponder the repercussions of the move—MTV could fire their best friend and ally at the channel, programmer Amy Finnerty, if she didn't manage to convince them to appear, and could blackball other Gold Mountain acts including Sonic Youth and the Beastie Boys, and perhaps even other acts on

Geffen/DGC. Suddenly, Nirvana found themselves forced into the world of high-stakes corporate rock—and they had to deal with the situation in a matter of hours.

In an interview not long afterward with the hilarious and irreverent travel magazine *Monk*, Dave provided corroboration: "We found out that if we were to do anything but 'Lithium,'" he said, "a good friend of ours, who works at MTV, would have been fired."

Then MTV said it was "Teen Spirit." Or "Lithium." Or else.

"We didn't want to fuck everything up for everyone so we decided to play 'Lithium,'" Kurt says. "Instead of bowing out and keeping our dignity, we decided to get fucked in the ass. It would have hurt us worse than it would have hurt them if we actually had gone through with it."

Once they got on stage for the live telecast, Kurt sang and played the first few bars of "Rape Me," "just to give them a little heart palpitation." He succeeded. As soon as Kurt started playing the offending song, MTV VP Judy McGrath let out a startled little scream and dashed toward the control room. Just as they were about to cut to a commercial, the band launched into "Lithium."

Amy Finnerty has since given a different account of what happened in the control room: When the band started playing "Rape Me," McGrath decided not to cut to a commercial and burst out laughing when they segued into "Lithium."

Ironically (and surely, it was deliberate), the opening guitar riff of "Rape Me" sounds exactly like the one that begins "Teen Spirit," the song MTV originally wanted Nirvana to play. But starting right off with the words "rape me" not only achieved the desired effect of giving MTV execs cardiac arrhythmia, it expressed how Kurt was feeling about the whole situation. "I'm a turd . . . I'm so retarded," he sang on the final verse of "Lithium." Then he threw his howling guitar behind the drum riser, tried to tip over the enormous amps until it became apparent that they might fall on him, and duly hurled his scrawny but seemingly impervious body into the drum set before walking off the stage.

As the song ended, Chris threw his bass high in the air and missed catching it. The butt end hit him square on the forehead. He writhed on the floor for a moment then ran off stage somewhere. For several tense minutes, no one could find Chris. Was he staggering deliriously around the Universal lot? Was he lying unconscious somewhere? Eventually Alex Macleod found him. He was lounging in the ready room with an ice pack on his head and a champagne bottle in his hand, chatting with former Queen guitarist Brian May.

The band didn't want to go onstage to accept the award for Best Alternative Music Video, so it was Kurt's idea to have a Michael Jackson impersonator come up and accept for them. Except for Kurt's suggestion that he introduce himself as "the King of Grunge," the impersonator improvised a speech, which was greeted by a confused silence out in the audience. No one got the concept. "I wanted it to be used as a reminder that I'm dealing with the same thing," says Kurt. "All rock stars have to deal with it. It's the fault of the fans and the media."

The band didn't have any other celebrity impersonators prepared when they won their second award, for Best New Artist, and Kurt initially refused to go up to the podium, but friends and associates convinced him that if he didn't go up, people would talk. "I was just kind of nervous up there," Kurt says. "When we played, I didn't look out in the audience and realize how big it was. And once I got up there, I realized millions of people are watching and it's a really big place and these lights are really bright and I don't want to be here, this is really stupid. I just wanted to leave right away."

Kurt managed to thank his family, his label, and the band's "true fans." Then he paused a moment, fixed the camera with a soulful gaze, smiled, and said, "You know, it's really hard to believe everything you read." Chris spoiled the moment by bellowing into the microphone, "Remember Joseph Goebbels!" but Kurt had made his point, even though most people in the audience had no idea how much it meant to him.

Krist was revealing what a history buff he was: Joseph Goebbels was, of course, the Nazis' propaganda chief, who had a gift for manipulating the newly blossoming media of radio and film with powerful propaganda. So Krist was trying to amplify Kurt's point—but it likely went right over a lot of heads.

But with that one little smile, Kurt struck a major blow for his tarnished image. In terms of PR value, the MTV appearance was the equivalent of eight months of touring. Before an audience of millions of people, the band reminded people of why they liked Nirvana in the first place.

But the day was far from over. Also on the bill was Pearl Jam, whom Kurt had been skewering in the press for months, although he jokingly denies there had been a full-blown feud. "No, I just happened to express my feelings toward their music, that's all," he says with a little smirk.

But it wasn't just their music—Kurt felt that the band was a bunch of hypocritical sell-outs. Two members of Pearl Jam—Stone Gossard and Jeff Ament—had been in Green River, the first band to put out a record on Sub Pop. Kurt's friend Mark Arm had quit the band and formed Mudhoney because he felt that it was going in an overtly commercial direction, largely because of Ament, who was among the first of the early Sub Poppers to openly declare he wanted to be a professional musician.

The thing is, *most* members of the Seattle music community wanted to make their living from being musicians. It just wasn't cool to say they wanted to be *stars*. But, in some compartment of Kurt's mind, he wanted to be a star, too.

Back when Mudhoney's Mark Arm was in Green River, he had famously butted heads with his bandmates over their "careerism" and courting of major labels. I'm guessing that Kurt targeted Pearl Jam partly as a virtue signal of his allegiance to Arm and the indie die-hards of the Seattle music community. Former Green River member and now Pearl Jam bassist Jeff Ament agreed: "Basically [Kurt] was just saying what Mark had said a few years previous," he told Keith Cameron for *Mudhoney: The Sound and the Fury From Seattle*. "I think a lot of that was just Kurt mimicking Mark—which I think he did a lot." Arm later reconciled with his former Green River bandmates, and Mudhoney opened for Pearl Jam on several tours.

"I know for a fact that at the very least, if not Stoney, then Jeff is a definite careerist—a person who will kiss ass to make sure his band gets popular so he can become rich," Kurt claims.

And Jeff Ament was also a jock, an all-state basketball player in his native Montana. "Jocks have completely taken over music," carps Kurt. "That's all there is nowadays is muscular bicep Marky Mark clones. It's pretty scary. And just to get back at them, I'm going to start playing basketball."

Pearl Jam also played into one of Kurt's pet peeves: jocks. In fact, Pearl Jam was originally named after professional basketball player Mookie Blaylock. ("Really unselfish; great shooter; great fundamentals," Jeff Ament explained to the *New York Times*.) They even titled their debut album *Ten* after Blaylock's jersey number. Very uncool.

Marky Mark, along with Ashey Ace, Scottie Gee, Hector the Booty Inspector, and DJ-T—collectively known as Marky Mark and the Funky Bunch—were a somewhat inauthentic Dorchester, Massachusetts, hip-hop group that enjoyed brief but great success, albeit precious little critical acclaim, in the early '90s. Marky Mark, who moonlighted as a Calvin Klein underwear model, later went on to a successful acting career as Mark Wahlberg.

Pearl Jam had assumed the look and some of the sound of "grunge rock," or just enough to ride the commercial wave. It was a calculated—and highly successful—attempt to dress up the same old corporate rock in tattered flannel shirts and

Doc Martens boots. Also, the band's label spent enormous amounts of money in promoting a band with no indie-style grassroots following—it was another case of major labels burying the indie rock revolution with money. All this annoyed Kurt to no end. He began sniping at Pearl Jam in the press.

In the January 1992 issue of *Musician* magazine, Kurt had declared that the members of Pearl Jam were going to be "the ones responsible for this corporate, alternative and cock-rock fusion." "I would love to be erased from my association with that band," Kurt said of the band in the April 16 *Rolling Stone* cover story. "I do feel a duty to warn the kids about false music that's claiming to be underground or alternative. They're just jumping on the alternative bandwagon."

But by that time, he had decided to at least forgive Pearl Jam's immensely likable singer, Eddie Vedder. "I later found out that Eddie basically found himself in this position," says Kurt. "He never claimed to be anybody who supports any kind of punk ideals in the first place."

So the real villains weren't people who never touted punk ideals—it was the opportunists, the poseurs who hitched themselves to the indie community but didn't emulate its values. The villains were also those who originally embraced those ideals and then betrayed them. *Someone* had to police these people.

Vedder was standing around the backstage area at the MTV Awards show when out of the blue, Courtney walked up to him and slow-danced with him as Eric Clapton played the elegiac "Tears in Heaven." Kurt walked over and butted in. "I stared into his eyes and told him that I thought he was a respectable human," Kurt says. "And I did tell him straight out that I still think his band sucks. I said, 'After watching you perform, I realized that you are a person that does have some passion.' It's not a fully contrived thing. There are plenty of other more evil people out in the world than him and he doesn't deserve to be scapegoated like that."

As noted earlier, passion was one of Kurt's most cherished values—he couldn't have paid Vedder a higher compliment. Kurt surely also recognized his colleague's artistry— Eddie Vedder is an excellent rock singer.

Which is where Axl Rose comes in.

Backstage, Courtney spotted Rose and called him over to where they were sitting with Frances. "Axl, Axl!" she said. "Will you be the godfather of our child?" With several bodyguards looming behind him, Rose leaned over, his face reddening beneath a thick layer of makeup, and pointed his finger in Kurt's face. "You shut your bitch up or I'm taking you down to the pavement!" he screeched. The Nirvana entourage exploded in laughter, except for Kurt, who made as if he was about to hand Frances to Courtney so he could stand up to Rose. But instead he glared at Courtney and said, "Shut up, bitch!" and they all exploded some more.

Rose's then-girlfriend Stephanie Seymour broke an awkward silence by innocently asking Courtney, "Are you a model?"

"No," replied Courtney. "Are you a brain surgeon?"

There was a little background to this dust-up: Courtney had ripped on Rose in the *Vanity Fair* article. And Nirvana had rejected Rose's invitation to open on a Guns N' Roses tour. So this whole episode was quite a slap in the face for Rose, especially in front of his girlfriend.

I can't remember why I said Seymour asked that question "innocently." By then, Seymour had been a professional model for nearly a decade and surely knew most people in the business or was at least able to know a colleague when she saw one. But maybe she was trying to defuse things by complimenting Courtney on her appearance. Or maybe she really was just being nasty. Either way, Courtney chose to inflame an already tense situation.

When the band returned to their trailer, waiting for them was the formidable Guns N' Roses entourage, veritable sides of beef. Kurt dashed into the trailer to make sure Frances was all right while Chris was surrounded. They started pushing him around. Guns bassist Duff McKagan wanted to personally beat up Chris, but a crowd began to gather and the confrontation dissolved. (Guns N' Roses refuses comment on the incident.)

In a 2002 interview with the Internet Nirvana Fan Club site, Nirvana's beloved guitar tech Earnie Bailey told a funny story about Kurt at the 1992 VMAs:

After Nirvana played "Lithium," Kurt went below the stage, where Axl and Elton John's two pianos were mounted on a hydraulic lift awaiting their duet. Kurt spit up some pretty nasty stuff upon the keys of what he thought was Axl's piano, but when the pianos arose for the duet's intro to "November Rain," Elton was seated at the piano whose keys Kurt had spat upon. I'm not sure which was funnier, Kurt's horror at what he had done, or the sight of Elton John hammering away on that piano.

Rose may have been angry at Nirvana for spurning his offer to open on the Guns N' Roses/Metallica tour that summer. They'd even turned down his request to play at Rose's thirtieth birthday party. There may be an unspoken jealousy at work, too. The two have similar backgrounds and have similar audiences, yet Kurt is everything Rose is not—a gifted singer and a peerless songwriter, articulate and sensitive. The two bands had often been pitted against each other—early on, the English music weekly *NME* had pronounced Nirvana "the Guns N' Roses it's OK to like."

Rose was such a fan that he had even put a Nirvana baseball hat in Guns N' Roses' "Don't Cry" video, but he just didn't get it. Before a Guns N' Roses show at Madison Square Garden in December 1991, the band's cameramen zoomed in on women in the audience until they lifted their shirts up, broadcasting the signal to giant video screens around the arena. The mostly male crowd stomped and hooted its approval while the other women in the audience looked embarrassed, disgusted, or giggled nervously. And what was playing during this loutish video rape? "Smells Like Teen Spirit."

Perhaps the enmity comes from the fact that the two bands are competing for roughly the same vast audience of frustrated, damaged kids. "I don't feel like I'm competing at all," Kurt says. "I've said in public enough times that I don't give a fuck about his audience." But Kurt and Rose hate each other with an almost brotherly intensity, as if they're flip sides of the same coin. "We do come from the same kind of background," Kurt says. "We come from small towns and we've been surrounded by a lot of sexism and racism most of our lives. But our internal struggles are pretty different. I feel like I've allowed myself to open my mind to a lot more things than he has.

"His role has been played for years," says Kurt. "Ever since the beginning of rock & roll, there's been an Axl Rose. And it's just boring, it's totally boring to me. Why it's such a fresh and new thing in his eyes is obviously because it's happening to *him* personally and he's such an egotistical person that he thinks that the whole world owes him something."

Still, Kurt admits Nirvana could learn a thing or two from Guns N' Roses. "They fuck things up and then they sit back and look at what they fucked up and then try to figure out how they can fix it," he says, "whereas we fuck things up and just dwell on it and make it even worse."

###

Don Cobain showed up uninvited at the September 11 show at the Seattle Coliseum, a benefit for a local anticensorship organization called the Washington Music

Industry Coalition. Along with his son Chad, Kurt's half-brother, Don got past the ticket-takers by showing his driver's license with his name on it. He asked to get backstage, but nobody ever got back to him, so he stood around and waited. Finally, he discovered the room where the after-show gathering was. "Somebody opened the door and there he was so I just walked right in." Kurt introduced his dad to Courtney, Frances, and Chris. Don had already found out that he was a grandfather from an item in the newspaper.

Don surveyed the typical backstage scene—the bleak cinder-block walls, the sycophantic hangers-on, the depressed and dissipated post-concert vibe. "I felt sorry for him," says Don. "What a life. Didn't look that glamorous to me."

"Well, it's been a long time," said Don. It had been seven years.

"Jeez, you look old," Kurt replied.

"It was really hard," says Don of the meeting. "Really, really hard.

"I asked him if he was happy and stuff," Don says, "and he said he was happy and he said he didn't have much money and I said 'Well, are you having fun?' He said he was and I said 'Well, okay then.' I didn't know what to say because it was real hard. We hugged a couple of times and I said to just keep in contact." Don hasn't heard from Kurt since. "I guess he's been busy and stuff."

Some say Don just came out of the woodwork because his son suddenly became rich. "That's the feeling I got from his mom and different people," he says, "but I don't give a shit. I haven't got any money, I don't give a shit about money. I wish *I* could do something for *him*, because really, I don't think I ever have. I just want to wish him well. If he can make something of himself, then go for it. I just keep waiting and waiting for him to come around."

Kurt officially ended all the speculation about his drug use by admitting in a September 21 profile by veteran *Los Angeles Times* pop critic Robert Hilburn that yes, he had done heroin for "three weeks" earlier that year. After the Physeptone episode, he went into detox again, took a month to straighten himself out, "and that was it." Of course, that wasn't quite it, but it was still a major admission which went oddly unnoticed in the mainstream music press, perhaps because everybody was already sure it was true.

When he did the interview, Hilburn didn't know that Kurt and Courtney were fighting for custody of their daughter. He found out the day after it ran and called up Danny Goldberg, who had known Hilburn for many years and had set up the interview. "I feel I

Nirvana at the Seattle
Center Arena.
© Charles Peterson

was used," Hilburn said. Then, according to Goldberg's book, after a long, awkward
pause, he added, "Well, I guess if I'm going to be used at least it's to help a genius."

**Kurt told Hilburn, "The biggest thing that affected me was all the insane rumors,
the heroin rumors . . . all this speculation going on. I felt totally violated. I never
realized that my private life would be such an issue."**

That's it: *he never realized that his private life would be such an issue*. But, as David
Geffen warned Kurt, "The press have a way of sabotaging your privacy." It's really
difficult to come to terms with the fact that the media and the public are prying into your

personal business; after all, you're just you, the same you that you've always been—but now your every move is scrutinized and publicized. Sure, you have a lot of money, but you can't go out and pick up a quart of OJ at the supermarket without people staring at you; you can't go for a walk in the park with your partner on a sunny spring day without a bunch of people taking your picture; you have to stop and cheerfully sign a bunch of autographs when you really need to go take a piss; you just generally have to be on your guard in public at all times. Things most people take for granted are now impossible for you. And it might be like that for the rest of your life. It's overwhelming even to think about.

Kurt was painfully self-conscious about not being well-spoken or well-educated—and "now I have these people so concerned with what I have to say and what I do at all times," he said in a February 1993 interview in the *Advocate*, "that it's really hard for me to deal with that."

And the scrutiny is even more frightening when you're in regular possession of controlled substances. Then there could be the colossal shame of being arrested and tried and maybe imprisoned. The media circus would be horrendous and unimaginably degrading. Being a parent made that prospect yet more frightening.

And it wasn't just that the press was violating Kurt's privacy. It had almost taken away his daughter. Losing custody of Frances traumatized Kurt and Courtney, as it would any parents. Not to mention the massive public humiliation, the shame, of it. Imagine you're in your mid-twenties, you have your first baby, and then you see that story in the *Globe*—not about some distant, untouchable celebrity but about *you*, *your* wife, and *your* child. Again, it's impossible to get your head around it.

The raft of hostile press had only begun with the *Vanity Fair* article—it continued with things like a horrendous article in the *Globe*, a supermarket tabloid, which ran a story with the headline "ROCK STAR'S BABY BORN A JUNKIE," along with a disturbing picture of a crack baby. "THEY'VE GOT MONEY & FAME BUT NO DAMN HEART," the subheadline added. After a few more articles like that, Chris, Shelli, and Dave dropped their resentments and fears and supported Kurt, Courtney, and their newborn baby. "We all rallied together and it was cool," says Chris. "That's when things really turned around. Things hit rock bottom and they rebounded."

"I think they appreciated that people came to their side," Chris adds, his voice breaking with emotion.

They've got money & fame but no damn heart

ROCK STAR'S BABY IS BORN A JUNKIE

Nirvana singer's pregnant wife boasted they took heroin — now tiny tot pays the shocking price!

Singer Kurt Cobain has also battled drugs, says an insider

Tragic Francis Bean Cobain is going through agonizing withdrawal. She will suffer shivering, cramps and muscle spasms — just like this drug baby

Rocker mom Courtney Love was totally incoherent at the hospital, the source says. "She was spaced out"

BY ROBIN JAMES

THE drug addict rocker wife of Nirvana singer Kurt Cobain has given birth to a tragic baby junkie, a source close to the couple reveals.

Little Francis Bean Cobain was born three weeks premature fighting for her life, with mom Courtney Love's $100-a-day heroin habit eating away inside her, the insider says. Doctors at Cedars Sinai Hospital in Los Angeles immediately put the tiny tot on a special rehab program.

"The baby had to go cold turkey, helped along by sedatives. She will go through withdrawal like anybody else coming off a powerful drug," says the insider.

"At the moment, she is high on methadone, a heroin substitute. Slowly, the doses will get less and less. She will suffer cold sweats, shivering, cramps and muscle spasms, but she should live.

"She's lucky she is in Cedars Sinai, which is one of the best hospitals in the world for treating babies like this. In many other hospitals, her chances of survival would be slim indeed."

Platinum-blonde Courtney — whose hubby Kurt has also battled drug problems — outraged America when she boasted she was still taking heroin even though she was pregnant.

But just two weeks before her child was born, she checked into the hospital to try and kick her drug habit, says the insider. Courtney was so rowdy, she had to be moved to a special area.

"For an expectant mother, she was not acting responsibly," the source says.

'Confused and disruptive'

"She was on a $100-a-day heroin habit, and was even doubling up on the prescription methadone she was buying on the black market.

"She was confused and disruptive. Both the drug treatment and the gynecology units refused to take her, saying she was too tough to handle.

"Eventually, she was taken to six south-west, an area specializing in kidney failures, where her baby could not be monitored fully. Courtney was a real handful. She was so spaced out she had no idea what she was doing.

"It seemed so weird to see a heavily pregnant woman behaving that way. Normally, they are so cautious.

"But Courtney was totally incoherent. You couldn't make out what she was saying and she couldn't understand what you were saying. Her room was a complete pigsty with clothes strewn everywhere and food all over the walls and floor.

"She would demand food, eat some and then throw the rest against the wall.

"She didn't know what was happening. She would even leave tips for the nurses on her food trays, thinking they were waitresses. She was still smoking, but compared to the other ways she was abusing her body, the smoking was minor.

"When her rock and roll friends came around, they would sit around cross-legged and chant.

"A few times, there was a frantic alert after she wandered off barefoot in her nightgown."

QUANTUM LEAPS INTO KENNEDY KILLER'S SHOES!

Quantum Leap's Scott Bakula

Lee Harvey Oswald

● QUANTUM LEAP star Scott Bakula will be gunning for John F. Kennedy in the shocking season opener when the time machine puts him in Lee Harvey Oswald's body.

The astounding story line was developed by producer Don Bellisario, who met Oswald while they were both in the Marines.

The *Globe* article.

###

Kurt is anxious not to appear to endorse heroin. "At the end of the last couple of months when I was doing four hundred dollars' worth every day, I was definitely noticing things about my memory and I knew that eventually my health would start getting a lot worse," he says. "It sounds like I don't regret it and I don't, but that's because I used it as a tool. I used it as a medication to get rid of a pain. And that's the biggest reason why I did it. In that sense, I don't regret it, but anybody else who's going to get addicted to drugs are obviously going to fuck up their lives eventually. If it doesn't take a year, it will be next year. I've seen it happen with every person that gets strung out. Drugs are bad for you. They *will* fuck you up.

"I just knew that I would eventually stop doing them and being married and having a baby is a really good incentive but most people don't even have that and also I'm a rich, millionaire rock star and I have a lot of things to keep right now. I have a lot of reasons to not do drugs. But try telling that to a person that feels like they don't have anything. When you're on a poverty level and you're addicted to drugs, you'll start turning tricks and you'll start ripping people off and find yourself in jail—those are all the negative things that go along with drug addiction.

"When you have more than four hundred dollars to spend a day, and you're pretty much pampered by living in this place that you know you don't have to worry about rent, you have a car that runs well and all that stuff, it's really easy to be a successful drug addict," he says. "But most people who are going to be influenced by the fact that I did drugs are going to be average people who have a job and can barely make ends meet."

Kurt realizes how all this sounds—that it was okay for him to do drugs, but nobody else. "But I'm saying that eventually, if I would have kept doing drugs, I would have lost everything, just like anyone else would have," he says. "I was able to be a successful junkie for a year, but if I kept going, I would eventually completely fuck my body up and ruin every relationship that I had and lose everything. I'd lose my friends and my family and all my money, everything—if I kept doing it. And I always knew that, too."

This was yet another big anti-drug speech that Kurt felt obligated to give, in order to excuse his addiction. He should have kept it at "Drugs are bad for you. They *will* fuck you up." Instead, he was still trying to justify his addiction. He spoke of it here in the past tense, but he was still using. He was living a lie. He did keep doing it. And he did lose everything.

Courtney is also penitent. "I lived out my little rock & roll fantasy," she says. "I just wish I hadn't gotten into so much trouble for it."

Actually, it's not penitence if your only regret is that you got caught.

chapter thirteen

THREE NICE, DECENT, CLEAN-CUT YOUNG MEN

he rest of 1992 found Kurt and Courtney still jousting with their detractors while the band tried to resume business as usual.

In October, Courtney's old Liverpool friend Julian Cope took out an ad in the music press, ostensibly to promote his new EP. At one point in a lengthy rant, he declared, "Free Us (The Rock 'n' Roll Fans) From Nancy Spungen—Fixated Heroin A-Holes Who Cling To Our Greatest Rock Groups And Suck Out Their Brains . . ." Cope, like everyone else, had assumed he knew exactly what the story was; it was also a rather sexist attack from the otherwise self-righteously feminist Cope, who later said of Courtney in Britain's *Select* magazine, "She needs shooting and I'll shoot her."

Julian Cope was lead singer of the great English post-punk band the Teardrop Explodes and went on to a successful solo career; he met Courtney at a Teardrop Explodes show in Dublin in 1982 and was so taken by her that he gave her the keys to his former flat in Liverpool. Just seventeen, she promptly found herself in the midst of Liverpool's second great rock era, with Echo and the Bunnymen, Wah!, Orchestral Manoeuvres in the Dark, Frankie Goes to Hollywood, Dead or Alive, and the Teardrop Explodes ruling the English post-punk scene.

According to Cope's 1994 autobiography *Head-On*, Courtney brought a lot of hallucinogens to Liverpool and shared them liberally. "She was a wild, wild girl," wrote Dead or Alive leader Pete Burns in his 2006 book *Freak Unique: My Autobiography*. "She was responsible for the whole change of the musical climate in Liverpool due to her distribution of Superman LSD tabs which Julian and the Bunnymen and all that crowd were dropping and going on a transcendental Jim Morrison experience."

The Cobains also felt under fire from a planned Nirvana biography by two British writers, Victoria Clarke and Britt Collins. Kurt and Courtney allege that Clarke and Collins allowed interview subjects to believe they were working with the band's approval, claimed to have slept with Dave or Kurt, and even interviewed James Moreland, Courtney's first husband (the marriage lasted a matter of days); the way they see it, the book was shaping up as an excuse for a tawdry hatchet job on Courtney. Gold Mountain tried to put the kibosh on the book by sending out a letter to prospective interviewees asking them not to talk to Clarke or Collins.

Kurt smiles again! © Charles Peterson

According to Gold Mountain, the pair apparently did not succeed in formally interviewing anyone even remotely connected with the band.

According to Clarke, she and Collins pitched a book about Nirvana to the band's UK publicist Anton Brookes and manager John Silva, who were OK with the project. Nirvana allowed Clarke to follow the band on a few European dates in June 1992 while Collins did research in Seattle. The book, tentatively titled *Nirvana: Flower Sniffin', Kitty Pettin', Baby Kissin' Corporate Rock Whores*, was to be published the following summer.

Clarke told *Select* magazine that everything was fine until she asked to interview Courtney. It made perfect sense to interview Courtney for a book about Nirvana, but it infuriated Kurt.

Also, Clarke must have suspected that Kurt's collapse in Belfast wasn't brought on by "junk food," and Gold Mountain surely realized this.

Clarke was asked to leave the tour; Nirvana withdrew all access to the band and their friends, family, and associates. But, understandably, neither Clarke nor Collins wanted to abandon the book, so they kept working, even though Gold Mountain had warned everybody the band knew not to talk to them.

The backlash against Clarke and Collins was daunting; anytime their names came up, Kurt and Courtney would practically tremble with rage and say all kinds of vile things about them. I did not want to be on the receiving end of anything like that.

Clarke did get some media mileage from some threatening messages that she said Kurt and Courtney had left on her answering machine in late October. Clarke said the first calls came late one night from Courtney, but they were comparatively civil compared to Kurt's. The next night, he began a message, then hit the machine's two-minute limit and called back—nine times. "If anything comes out

The Amplified Come as You Are

in this book which hurts my wife, I'll fucking hurt you," Kurt said, sounding, as *Select* euphemistically put it, "tired, confused, very upset." "I love to be fucked, I love to be blackmailed, I'll give you anything you want, I'm begging you, I'm on my knees and my mouth is wide open. You have absolutely no fucking idea what you are doing . . ."

"Tired, confused, very upset" is the sort of euphemism that journalists, particularly British ones, use when they want to hint that the person was intoxicated.

After the *Vanity Fair* story broke, Collins interviewed Lynn Hirschberg, which *really* set off Kurt and Courtney, and that's when they left those phone messages. (How did they know that Collins had interviewed Hirschberg?) Clarke gave the answering machine tapes to *Entertainment Weekly*, and the story was picked up by the *Los Angeles Times*, the *New York Times*, and various UK newspapers.

Oh, but it gets worse. On December 5, Clarke went out to the L.A. nightclub Raji's and thought it would be a good idea to chat with Hole guitarist Eric Erlandson and drummer Patty Schemel. Then Kurt and Courtney walked in. Courtney, Clarke alleged, hit her on the head with a cocktail glass, drawing blood, and then dragged her across the floor of the club as Kurt looked on. A bouncer soon broke it up. A March 1993 article in *Select* said that Clarke went to Cedars-Sinai hospital and was diagnosed with a mild concussion. (In a 2011 blog post, she said, "I was not seriously injured, mainly shocked and bruised.") Clarke also said that the doctor who examined her at Cedars-Sinai told her he had been present when Courtney gave birth there earlier that year. (It's unclear why an ER doctor would also have attended a birth.) Clarke told *Select*, "He said, 'There's a couple of things I'd like to tell you but I can't because of medical confidence. But if you sue them, call me, I'll be a witness'" (which, if true, would seem to be a breach of medical ethics).

According to Clarke, both she and Courtney reported the incident to the Los Angeles Police Department, and it went to court in February 1993. Clarke's attorney Albert Dworkin handled the case for free; perhaps coincidentally, he also happened to be Axl Rose's attorney. The judge dismissed the case, and Clarke did not file a civil suit.

[On the answering machine recording] Kurt went on to call the two writers "parasitic little cunts," adding, "At this point I don't give a flying fuck if I have this recorded that I'm threatening you. I suppose I could throw out a few hundred thousand dollars to have you snuffed out, but maybe I'll try it the legal way first."

The *New York Times* quoted Gold Mountain's Danny Goldberg as saying, "Kurt absolutely denies the notion that he or any other member of the band made any such phone calls."

"In my opinion, either this is a prank that someone has played on these women," Goldberg added, "or this is something they are fabricating to publicize an unauthorized biography."

In *Serving the Servant*, Goldberg admitted that he knew it was Kurt's and Courtney's voices on those tapes. "I never had any regret about trying to cover up for them," he wrote. "I was doing my job and standing up for my client. However, I was worried that Kurt and Courtney were out of control and were hurting themselves." He did what any loyal friend and manager would have done. But what a terrible position to be in.

Kurt, however, doesn't deny that it was his voice on the tapes. He sounded homicidal, he says, "Because I want to kill them." By the truly terrifying look on his face—jaw muscles visibly knotted, eyes darkened—one gets the idea that he really means it. "Obviously, I have a lot to lose right now so I won't be able to do it," he says, "But I have all the rest of my life. If I ever find myself destitute and I've lost my family, I won't hesitate to get revenge on people who have fucked with me. I've always been capable of that. I've tried killing people before in a fit of rage when I've gotten in fights with people. It's definitely a character flaw, to say the least, but I feel so strongly about people unnecessarily causing negative things to happen to people for no reason."

Kurt at an early October show at the University of Washington at Bellingham, opening for Mudhoney. © Charles Peterson

This is eerily similar to what he said about Lynn Hirschberg: "She'd better hope to God that someday I don't find myself destitute without a wife and a baby. Because I'll fucking get revenge on her. Before I leave this earth, she's going out with me."

"I don't enjoy people fucking with my family and carrying on the tradition of lies and slander," he continues. "I don't deserve it. No one deserves it. We've

Chris at the Bellingham show
on October 3, 1992.
© Charles Peterson

been scapegoated more than any fucking band I can think of in the history of rock, to my knowledge. People fuck with us and they want dirt and they want to lie about us and I just don't understand it. I've never really tried to do anything scandalous in my life. When people unnecessarily fuck with me, I just can't help but want to beat them to death."

The late-'60s Rolling Stones—particularly Mick Jagger, Keith Richards, and Brian Jones—were harassed by the police, relentlessly hounded by the press, and imprisoned for drug offences after high-profile trials. The politically radical late-'60s Detroit proto-punk band the MC5 was surveilled by the FBI and the US Army; their manager, John Sinclair, was sentenced to ten years in prison for the possession of two marijuana joints. The Sex Pistols were denounced by the press and violently attacked by street gangs. And, from the very top, the US government tried for years to deport outspoken antiwar activist John Lennon, who was also surveilled by the FBI. But one can't blame Kurt for feeling that way. He was only twenty-five, he was a new father, and he was going through living hell.

The undeniable creepiness of the answering machine tapes reveals that despite the great happiness he's gained with his wife and baby, Kurt still harbors a dark and seemingly bottomless well of anger and alienation. It's not as if Kurt is a complete pacifist. He says that when he was living with the Shillingers, he got in a fight with a guy who was picking on him at a party. "I picked up a stick and started beating him with it and I couldn't stop," he says. "It was disgusting. It was a really scary reminder of how violent I can be when I really want to hurt somebody. It actually felt good, I was actually laughing about it." His victim got a concussion and lapsed into a brief coma. "I was really upset about it afterward, for a long time," Kurt says. "Especially after I saw him when he got out of the hospital."

I wonder if this really happened—he might have been telling a tale in order to seem threatening to his current enemies.

The hypocrisy of the phone calls—the sexism, even misogyny—is profoundly disillusioning. When Kurt rails against sexism and rape, it now begins to seem like a desperate attempt to stifle something ugly within himself, rather than merely standing up for what's right. It looks very, very bad. "I don't care," Kurt says. "I'm a firm believer in revenge."

That bit about stifling something ugly within himself was another oblique reference to the episode with the girl from the special-ed class in high school.

When it's revealed that at the time, Kurt and Courtney were still fighting for custody of Frances and that any unflattering press that came out about them might jeopardize the proceedings, the phone calls do begin to make a little more sense. But only a *little* more. On the whole, the answering machine tapes—along with Kurt's defense of them—present a very disturbing side of Kurt. "Fine," he says. "I don't care. I guess I *am* unbalanced in that part of my psyche. I wouldn't hesitate and if I ever do see [Collins or Clarke] in public, I'm going to beat the fucking shit out of either one of them. If they can get away with doing that much damage to me and my family, then I can sit in jail for a few months for battery. I don't really care at this point."

A few weeks later, Kurt had simmered down. "I don't ever talk like that," he maintained. "That's the first time I've ever been so vicious and so sexist and weird. I just wanted to seem as extreme and irrational as possible to scare them. For all I care, they are exactly those things. I don't feel bad about saying any of that stuff because they *are* cunts. Men can be cunts, too."

Still, I'll never forget the rage that filled Kurt when he talked about this incident. His eyes literally became a darker shade, like a storm was gathering in an electric blue sky.

Kurt believes their scare tactics worked by scaring Collins and Clarke into toning down their book. Ironically, though, publishing industry scuttlebutt has it that discreet legal pressure from Gold Mountain could have gotten publisher Hyperion Books to shelve the project quietly—but after Collins and Clarke made the answering machine tapes public, Hyperion could not be seen as having backed down under pressure. Ironically, as of this writing, the book had not reached the stores in the US.

I read a typeset manuscript of the Clarke and Collins book. I could see why Nirvana and Gold Mountain were so upset about it. For one thing, the book, ostensibly about Nirvana, included a lengthy and scathing profile of Courtney—easily thirty pages. Her ex-husband (of five days), "Falling" James Moreland of the band Leaving Trains, said some very unflattering things, as did Hirschberg and several other journalists (many of whom Collins and Clarke then proceeded to slight in the course of the manuscript).

There was an even longer section composed of a strange semifictional conversation with the band in dialogue form—"A jumble of disparate quotes stitched together," wrote Amy Raphael in *The Face*, "it is both intentionally and unintentionally comical." And then there was a chapter full of misguided musings about punk and alternative rock, often quoting Pogues leader Shane MacGowan, who happened to be Clarke's longtime partner (and a fellow cast member with Courtney in *Straight to Hell*).

This all understandably set off alarm bells.

After threats of lawsuits by Nirvana's legal team, the UK and US publishers abandoned the Clarke-Collins book. An Irish publishing house offered to print it—but then the person who headed up the publishing house died. To date, *Nirvana: Flower Sniffin', Kitty Pettin', Baby Kissin' Corporate Rock Whores* has not seen the light of day.

Many years later, Clarke apparently gained some empathy for her tormentors—the hard way. She had by then married MacGowan and had received a manuscript of a Pogues biography. "It was deeply unflattering, about both of us," Clarke wrote in a 2011 post on her website. "After reading it, I was upset and angry for several days. Just the very thought that someone is scrutinizing your life and writing about you can be hurtful. I wondered what it must have been like for Kurt and Courtney, knowing that Britt and I could have been writing something that would affect their child, as well as them? Would I have been angry enough in their position to threaten the writers? Quite possibly!"

In reading *Serving the Servant*, I discovered how *Come as You Are* came to be: the idea was to bigfoot the Clarke and Collins book. In November 1992, Danny Goldberg wrote a letter to Kurt and Courtney saying, "Courtney's original idea is still the best, to get someone you trust to write an authorized book, preferably a writer of some stature (Danny Sugerman, Everett True, Michael Azerrad, etc.), and it will dwarf an unauthorized one written by amateurs." (By "authorized," he meant with the band's cooperation.)

And that's when Courtney called me.

###

On October 30, four years to the day after Kurt first smashed a guitar at a modest dorm party at the Evergreen State College, the band played a nearly sold-out show at the fifty-thousand-seat Velez Sarsfield Stadium in Buenos Aires, Argentina. They had hardly practiced, their enthusiasm was low, and they played badly. They had done it for the money and it showed. They vowed never to make the same mistake again.

Part of the agreement was that Nirvana could choose their opening act. They went with Calamity Jane, a virtually unknown all-female band from Portland, Oregon. The overwhelmingly male crowd hated them. From a seat in the highest tier at the far end of the stadium, Kurt watched in disgust as within a minute's time, virtually the entire crowd was chanting "Puta madre!" at the band and throwing lighters, beer cans, dirt clods, coins and whatever else they could find onto the stage. "It was the largest display of sexism I've ever seen at once," Kurt says.

Kurt jams with Mudhoney at an early October show at the Crocodile Cafe in Seattle. Singer Mark Arm does the swim. © Charles Peterson

Chris knew what Kurt was going to do and tried to calm him down. But Kurt was determined to sabotage the show. The first thing they played was an improvised jam, which deteriorated into a fifteen-minute feedback fest from Kurt, with brief breaks when he would stop to glare at the crowd. Between songs, Kurt would tease the crowd by beginning to play "Teen Spirit" and then stopping. After a perfunctory set, they played a definitive version of "Endless, Nameless." "It was so intense," Kurt says. "There was so much emotion in it and feedback was coming out of my guitar just perfectly. I was manipulating it better than I ever had. It was really a great experience. It was really fun." They never did play "Teen Spirit."

The members of Nirvana, Krist wrote in a tour diary for *Raw* magazine, were "pretty disappointed with the crowd and went on stage with a bad attitude.... The novelty of playing these 30,000-capacity stadiums has worn thin."

But it was, in fact, a very good show. They started with a rockin' three-minute improvisation, with Kurt howling, "Shit on the stage . . . I'll shit anywhere," raging at an audience that didn't realize they were being raged at. The "fifteen-minute feedback fest"

Dave at the Crocodile.
© Charles Peterson

was in fact "Endless, Nameless," it was actually about *ten* minutes long, and it came at the *end* of the show, as usual. And yeah, it *was* a pretty cool version.

Kurt defaced "Come as You Are" by singing nothing but "hey, hey, hey" through the first verse, and there was a brief, silly jam featuring Dave on a toy drum kit, but that seemed more out of fun than spite. Kurt forgot how to start a couple of songs, so Krist had to show him—in front of fifty thousand people. They didn't play "Smells Like Teen Spirit," apparently as punishment for the audience for being abusive to Calamity Jane.

The show was very far from "perfunctory"—they played a mostly ferocious eighty minutes, and it's a good example of how powerful Nirvana could be. That version of

The Amplified Come as You Are

"Endless, Nameless," Krist wrote in the tour diary, "was actually one of the best versions of that song we've ever done, with us just totally jamming and playing off each other, toying with dynamics. I was in musical bliss. . . . 30,000 people, I hope, got to share with us for ten minutes the reason why we are in a band."

But before that was the Calamity Jane debacle. The popular Argentinian band Los Brujos opened the evening with their typically theatrical set—they were a strong live band, and the crowd knew and loved them and were surely proud and excited that an Argentinian group was sharing the stage with the big American band. Then it was Calamity Jane's turn to play.

Calamity Jane was an extremely obscure band even in the United States, not to mention Argentina—it's quite possible that not one person in that stadium knew who they were. And so when Calamity Jane came on, the audience naturally grew restless: they'd been amped up by Los Brujos, they were impatient to see Nirvana, and now some band they'd never heard of was playing raucous, shambling, thoroughly unfamiliar, thoroughly arena-unfriendly punk rock songs, sung in English. That's when all the cans, dirt, spit, and abuse began to fly.

Calamity Jane managed to play two or three songs before smashing their guitars in frustration and walking off the stage, frightened, angry, and humiliated.

It didn't need to happen. Kurt—and it was surely Kurt—arranged the bill so that it inordinately featured this little-known band from Portland. Nobody suffered for this miscalculation except Calamity Jane: they were too broke to replace or even fix their broken guitars, the check for the show didn't arrive for months, and the band was completely demoralized. Their show at Sarsfield stadium was the last Calamity Jane ever played.

My guess is Kurt exaggerated to me how much he screwed up the show to make himself appear more chivalrous toward Calamity Jane. He actually would sabotage a stadium show much more severely a few months later, and for the worst reason.

###

The "In Bloom" video reached MTV in late November, about a month after it was shot. At first, Kurt had an idea for another film, this time a surrealistic fable about a little girl who is born into a Ku Klux Klan family and one day realizes how evil her parents are. Like the aborted "Lithium" concept, it was too ambitious, so Kurt came up with the idea of parodying an appearance on an early-'60s TV variety program à la *The Ed Sullivan Show*, which was essentially the dawn of rock video. He asked Kevin Kerslake to find authentic cameras from the period. Kerslake dug up some old Kinescopes to shoot the video with.

Spontaneity was key, and there was no script. Kurt aimed to keep it simple. "That's how things should happen," Kurt says. "Just do whatever you can instead of some long, drawn-out script, acting and practicing your moves." The philosophy would carry over into the making of the band's next album. Unlike most video shoots, even the most low-budget, they ran through the song only five times. Despite the feeling that they are performing in front of a huge television studio audience, there were only a handful of people on the modest soundstage.

That's Doug Llewelyn, the *People's Court* post-trial interviewer, as the host (coincidentally, Llewelyn's first job was on *The Ed Sullivan Show*).

One of the earliest hit reality TV shows, *The People's Court* had its first run from 1981 to 1993. People who had filed cases in small claims court instead agreed to let retired judge Joseph Wapner decide the case in a Los Angeles television studio made up to look like a courtroom. Some of the cases, the *Los Angeles Times* wrote, involved "a cat that was supposed to have been dyed blue to match its eyes but came out pink. . . . Or the woman who bought a birthday cake for her daughter for $9 and discovered it was moldy, but the baker would refund only $4.50."

It was cheesy, dumb, and kitschy, just the sort of thing that Kurt would thread into his video montages.

In 1989, a *Washington Post* poll found that 54 percent of American adults could name Wapner as the judge of *The People's Court* but only 9 percent knew who the chief justice of the Supreme Court was.

They dressed up in ridiculous Beach Boys–style suits, although Kurt thoughtfully brought along some dresses for himself and the band, just in case. Chris cut his hair for the occasion and he liked it so much he kept it that way. The glasses Kurt wore made him dizzy. They also made him look very much like his father did at his age.

The cuts to the amped-up kids in the audience make them look like conformist freaks—they're so "normal" they're weird. The great mainstream masses look weird to the band, instead of vice versa. It's quite a leap from the "Teen Spirit" video, where the audience members were the band's peers and even went so far as to dance and mingle with the band. In "In Bloom," the audience is separated from the band not only by space but also time.

Of course, the kids in those early-'60s audiences would become the baby boomers of today. The "audience as freaks" idea, says Kurt, "was kind of an attack on what those kids turned into. I'm sure the majority of them turned into yuppies. It was kind of a dis on their generation, the whole *Rolling Stone*

The Amplified Come as You Are

Kurt onstage at the Seattle Center Arena. © Charles Peterson

generation. There was nothing wrong with those kids at the time—they were totally innocent and into rock & roll. Now they're in control of the media and the corporations and they're cranking out the very same shit that they used to despise. There are still Fabians and the Monkees, but at least the Monkees had good songs, instead of New Kids on the Block."

The video lampooned the idea of manufactured pop idols like Fabian and the Monkees; it was also an ironic comment on the fact that Nirvana had attained similar status. "These three fine young men from Seattle," the announcer declares, "are thoroughly all right and decent fellas." The slicked-back hair, the nerdy suits, and the band's stiff, repressed movements highlighted the absurdity of the notion of squeaky-clean pop idols and the uncompromising moral standard they were expected to live up to. By wearing dresses and destroying

Three Nice, Decent, Clean-Cut Young Men

the set, they are literally trashing that idea. "Let's hear it for these three nice, decent, clean-cut young men!" Lewellyn says to the audience at the end of the clip. "I really can't say enough nice things about them!"

The humor of the clip was also quite strategic. With all the rumors about the band over the previous year, a few laughs were simply good PR. "I'd just been so tired for the last year of people taking us so seriously and being so concerned with what we do and what we say that I wanted to fuck off and show them that we have a humorous side to us," Kurt says. "It's always been there, but a lot of people have misread it, not understood it."

The humor had an edge though. Kurt was anything but squeaky-clean, and the audience knew it, and he knew the audience knew it. In one cut of the video, shots of the band in wigs and dresses, goofing off with their instruments, alternate with the polite '60s-era sequences. As with the "Teen Spirit" video, it descends into chaos.

The original plan was to first send MTV a cut of the video with the '60s pop idol motif all the way through. The highlight came when the camera came in for a close-up for Kurt's guitar solo—instead of the guitar, the shot shows the top of Kurt's bobbing head the whole time, only to cut to the guitar just as the solo ends. After that version ran awhile, they planned to release the version where the band changes into dresses halfway through, which would have made for a neat surprise.

Unfortunately, the MTV "alternative" show *120 Minutes* insisted on debuting the video, and Kurt doubted they'd get the humor of the all-pop idol version, so they went with a third version, which was all dresses and destruction, thereby killing the gag. (The planned first version never did air.)

On December 15, *Incesticide* was released. Ever since the *Nevermind* sessions, the band had planned to issue an "odds and sods" album of live tracks, B-sides, and selections from the January 1988 Crover demo, basically to beat the bootleggers and to give fans good sound quality for less money than a bootlegger would charge. Then Sub Pop announced that *they* were planning a Nirvana rarities album, too. With typical Sub Pop candor, it was tentatively titled *Cash Cow*. Having two Nirvana rarities albums was a bit much, and pooling the material would produce a definitive collection, so Gary Gersh made a deal with Sub Pop. This way, the band would have more control over the final product—from music to artwork—and distribution would be far superior to what Sub Pop could muster.

And, this way, sales wouldn't be split between two competing rarities albums, which was the real point of the deal. It was also a great set-up for their next album, reclaiming

Nirvana's gritty American post-punk roots after the radio-ready sheen of *Nevermind*. "Some of the stuff [on *Incesticide*] is kind of wild," Krist told me for a *Rolling Stone* piece previewing the record. "Maybe the next step we'll take, because the pendulum is swinging back in that direction, won't be that much of a shock."

The album shows off the extremes the band has been through; from the grinding, nearly tuneless chain of riffs called "Aero Zeppelin" to the fully realized pop of "Sliver," from the flagrantly Gang of Four–ish sounds of "Hairspray Queen" to the cover of Devo's "Turn Around," the collection contains all the elements of the Nirvana sound. It's all there—Nirvana synthesized '70s hard rock, punk-pop, new wave like Devo and the Knack, and what Kurt calls "new wave" (Butthole Surfers, Saccharine Trust, Big Black), etc., into a unique voice. "It does explain what kind of a band we were when we first started—obviously a Gang of Four and Scratch Acid rip-off," Kurt says.

The final track, the mighty "Aneurysm," demonstrates how Dave's juggernautic beats helped turn Nirvana from an interesting indie group into a world-class rock & roll band. The track also points the way toward the more experimental elements of the next album.

"Turn Around" and the Vaselines covers "Son of a Gun" and "Molly's Lips" had all been broadcast on John Peel's BBC-1 radio show in October of 1990. All three had been included on *Hormoaning*, a much sought-after Japan- and Australia-only EP released to coincide with the early-1992 tour there. "Stain" hailed from the *Blew* EP and "Been a Son," "(New Wave) Polly" and "Aneurysm" from a 1991 session for Mark Goodier's show on BBC (a better version of "Aneurysm," recorded by Nirvana soundman Craig Montgomery, appeared on *Hormoaning* and as an extra track on the "Teen Spirit" CD single).

The cover, a painting by Kurt, is incredibly revealing. In it, a damaged baby clings to a skeletal parental figure which seems to be ignoring the baby. It looks longingly at some flowers. They are poppies. Typically, Kurt denies the tableau has any significance. "It's just the image I came up with," he says. The poppies, he says, came from a postcard that just happened to be lying on his floor.

It's still a damaged infant, neglected by its parent, gazing at a poppy flower, which is where heroin comes from. In that light the painting is autobiographical. Maybe Kurt didn't realize that. But even if he did, he wouldn't have admitted it.

The painting well fits Kurt's friend Dylan Carlson's learned assessment of the major theme of Kurt's paintings: "Innocence and authentic vision beset upon by a cruel and uncaring universe. Artists continuously attempting to extract beauty from the world and being unable to because of being denied a beatific relationship with the world." A bit academic, but right on the mark.

Kurt's original liner notes included a strongly worded broadside directed at Lynn Hirschberg, but the brass at Geffen/DGC deemed them "pretty harsh" and asked him to tone them down. "I just went into the *Vanity Fair* and media scam," Kurt explains. "It was really negative, although it was very truthful. It came straight from my heart and I really felt that and I still do. Anyone looking back on it would see complaining. No one has enough empathy for me or Courtney to look beyond that and realize that it should be a legitimate complaint."

This is the paragraph that got cut from Kurt's liner notes for *Incesticide*:

The biggest "fuck you" of my life goes out to the self-inflated, indefensible, florid and pompous lies set down by Lynn Hirschberg and any lemming that followed her knowing how evil and how full of shit her story was. I think it's very sad that we can't move onward in the history/ demise of rock music instead of assigning me/us/my wife these ridiculous, archetypal, retro-rock roles to live out. We are decent, ethical people—we take no delight in being involved in blatant sexism, treachery, or scandals made up off the top of someone's head. And now, as a result of Ms. Hirschberg's personal and unhealthy obsession with me/us/my wife, we are having to deal with the betrayal and harassment that stems from the "inside sources" and aspiring groupie "writers" who surround us now like celebrity worshipping jackals moving in for the kill. I have learned one thing from this and not much else—the life of a failed groupie (i.e. someone with no self-respect but a hugely sociopathic need to be near to and accepted by successful people, whether the objects of their obsessions like them or not) is a very sad and dangerous thing. I'd really like to thank those of you in the media who saw this for what it was and did not sell us down the river for the sake of a "story," who didn't dirty our music with things that have nothing to do with music or, for that matter, reality.

The notes are typical of Kurt's two-fold nature. They begin in a celebratory mode, plugging favorite bands like the Raincoats in an extended anecdote, then Shonen Knife, the Vaselines, Sonic Youth, Mudhoney, the Breeders, Jad Fair, Fits of Depression, etc. The tone shifts as Kurt launches a brief defense of Courtney, "the supreme example of dignity, ethics and honesty." Soon, he is sending "a big 'fuck you' to those of you who have the audacity to claim that I'm so naive and stupid that I would allow myself to be taken advantage of and manipulated" and telling the homophobes, racists, and sexists in their audience to "leave us the fuck alone!"

Added to the broadsides against his generation in "Smells Like Teen Spirit" and remarks made in virtually every interview he'd done, the missive seemed to cement Kurt's reputation as a man who held a nearly bottomless disdain for his own audience. "He needs a PR makeover," Courtney says of Kurt. "It's like he's a snob and he's too good for everybody. If I was a kid, I'd spend my twenty dollars on Alice in Chains and the Chili Peppers because they *like* me—I'm not good enough for Kurt."

Courtney was very savvy about the rock audience, and this is a good example of the unchecked honesty Kurt mentioned above. But lots of kids craved the approval of someone as cool and judgmental as Kurt—just as Kurt craved the approval of the hipster leaders of the indie community. If you're insecure, as teenagers often are, you yearn to be validated by people who are cooler than you are.

Nirvana got an inkling of their new audience in January 1991, the day after a US-led coalition began the Gulf War by bombing Iraq. That evening, Nirvana headlined a benefit for draft resisters at Evergreen. When Krist gave a brief antiwar speech, a few knuckleheads shouted, "Shut up and play!" That was a foreshadowing: now some of their fans were the type who would yell "shut up" at someone who was speaking out against war.

Of course, *Incesticide* is not a complete anthology of Nirvana's non-LP output. Left off the album were the excellent "Token Eastern Song," an outtake from the *Blew* sessions, a staggering cover of the Wipers' "D-7," which rounded out *Hormoaning*, "Even in His Youth," a cover of the Velvet Underground's "Here She Comes Now" done for the Community label, the remaining two tracks from the Crover demo, "Pen Cap Chew" and "If You Must," and the "Lithium" B-side "Curmudgeon," not to mention any number of live tracks recorded at the Halloween 1991 show at the Paramount in Seattle.

With the "In Bloom" video still on MTV and the possibility of Nirvana burnout quite real—*Nevermind* had been out for fifteen months by that point—Geffen/DGC elected not to push *Incesticide*, merely letting fans discover it for themselves. Vague plans for a single and video of "Sliver" were lofted and shot down. The album went gold the following February.

Today, fully promoted releases by major artists struggle to get even halfway to a gold record (500,000 copies). *Incesticide* went gold in two months.

Meanwhile, Gold Mountain's Nirvana hype machine managed to get a story in *Spin* magazine, a fluffy interview with Kurt and Courtney by Sub Pop's Jonathan

Poneman which neglected to reveal that Poneman had a substantial financial stake in his subject's latest release (as the last remnant of the buyout deal, Sub Pop got a cut of *Incesticide*). Of course, the real point of the story was the cover shot. Although the headline trumpeted "Nirvana: Artist of the Year," the cover featured a heavily airbrushed Cobain family portrait with Mom and Dad proudly cradling a perfectly normal-looking baby. It was aimed directly at Children's Services.

Kurt and Courtney did the *Spin* interview in mid-September, not long after the Reading Festival and the star-crossed MTV Video Music Awards appearance. The idea was to talk to a friendly interviewer who would portray them as decent, loving parents in order to impress Children's Services, the media, and the public. Poneman, a kindly, thoughtful person, and no doubt keen on burying any hatchets that still existed between Sub Pop and Nirvana, was down with the program. As the introduction to the interview duly noted, Poneman was "a longtime friend" of Kurt and Courtney; the whole thing was a fluff job, starting with the flattering family portrait on the cover.

The article's subheadline began, "Kurt Cobain and Courtney Love have weathered a media storm this year, fueled by rumors of the couple's prenatal indulgences." But they weren't "rumors," they had been reported in a major magazine with a diligent fact-checking department. And "indulgence" is quite a euphemism for heroin addiction. And, by Courtney's own admission, those "indulgences" weren't just "prenatal" either.

"As a curmudgeonly reporter," Poneman wrote, playfully acknowledging that he was actually wielding very little journalistic skepticism, "I detect excessive attention and doting on the child, with Kurt and Courtney willfully contributing to their kid's happiness." And that was the crux of the piece: to show that Kurt and Courtney were good parents. Everything else was window dressing.

On the raw tape before the interview begins, Kurt expresses annoyance that both Bono and Perry Farrell are also sporting his trademark bug sunglasses. He cared about these things. (But Kurt had probably borrowed the look from Mark Arm, who sported similar shades on the cover of Green River's 1988 album *Rehab Doll*.)

Frances, says Courtney, was "guaranteed a 100 percent perfect childhood. We knew we could give her what we didn't get: loyalty and compassion, encouragement. We knew we could give her a real home and spoil her rotten."

They hammer the wholesomeness a little more: "I just want to have kids by the same person and stay with the same person," Courtney continues.

"You sound like Phyllis Schlafly," Poneman replies, referring to the outspoken antifeminist of the '70s and '80s who crusaded against the Equal Rights Amendment.

"Do you concur?" Poneman asks Kurt.

"Yes," he says, "I'm really old-fashioned."

Spin obligingly edited out some vaguely edgy things they said, particularly about the baby. For instance, when Poneman asks Kurt and Courtney who Frances looks like, Courtney says, "she has my *real* nose," and then Kurt quips that if it had been a boy, they would have given him a nose job when they got him circumcised.

On the tape, Courtney says that MTV threatened Nirvana that if they played "Rape Me" at the Video Music Awards, all their management company's other acts and Hole would suffer and they would fire friends who work at MTV.

"Can I print this?" Poneman asks, incredulously.

"Yes," says Courtney.

"Sure," says Kurt.

Spin didn't print that.

Spin didn't print this either: "If we find ourselves having to compromise anymore, just for the sake of our child . . ." Kurt says. "We've done it once—we did it for the VMAs—and I've never felt more of a whore in my life. And if I ever find myself in that kind of a position again, I'll . . ." I'm afraid I know exactly how he was going to finish that sentence. But he thought better of it, surely mindful of the authorities, and cut himself off.

"I couldn't possibly do it, there's just no way," he continues. "And if I have to resort to quitting my band and putting out my own records from home . . . and pretending to be some sort of cult figure and selling a thousand records a year, that's fine, I'm prepared for that. . . . In fact, I might even look forward to that."

"But," Kurt adds, "at this point I'm still really excited about this band. I like playing the music with them still."

But the real reason why playing the VMAs was an awful compromise wasn't just because MTV wanted them to play "Smells Like Teen Spirit."

It's because Kurt was in rehab when the invitation to play the VMAs came in. On the tape, Courtney says that Kurt was warned that if Nirvana didn't play the Video Music Awards, it would be blamed on his drug addiction, which could mean that they would again lose custody of Frances. So he did it, very reluctantly.

Strangely, the published interview omits Courtney's flat-out denial that they were still doing drugs. "We certainly don't do it now," she tells Poneman. "It'd almost be living up to something to do it now. It would just be a joke. It wasn't a mistake to do it either. We don't regret doing it except that . . ."

And Kurt chimes in, ". . . it was publicized."

"Journalists," he angrily explains, repeating a now all-too-familiar theme, "are doing *more* damage by influencing kids with writing these articles."

In 2014, journalist Andrew Beaujon did a piece for the journalism website Poynter about *Spin*'s coverage of Kurt, Courtney, and Nirvana, including the Poneman interview. "There's no journalistic ethics at all there!" said former *Spin* editor Craig Marks, laughing. "We were purely a PR mouthpiece for Kurt and Courtney at that time."

Marks called the decision to do the interview "a jaw-dropping error in all of journalistic integrity" but said that "in order for Kurt and to some extent Courtney and Nirvana to have faith in *Spin* and to view us as sympathetic to them and their music, we felt it was worth doing that."

It should be noted, Marks added, that music journalism "was a two-magazine universe" (along with *Rolling Stone*) at the time, as far as *Spin* was concerned. "*Spin* at that point, generationally, culturally, economically, needed its Bob Dylan," and so "we probably went overboard in sucking up to [Nirvana]."

Despite what Courtney claimed, it's almost certain that Kurt was still doing heroin at that time. The introduction to the *Monk* magazine interview, which happened around the same time as the *Spin* interview, noted of Kurt, "He sits on a couch, sweat beading on his face. He looks fragile, sensitive and intense." It's not hard to read between the lines there. After the interview, Kurt asked one of the *Monk* writers, Michael Lane, for a ride home. They wound up making several stops around downtown Seattle. "At each of the stops, Kurt would disappear for a few minutes, and then pop back to the car," wrote *Monk*'s James Marshall Crotty in 2001. "After the final stop, Michael noticed something different: a smile, a relaxation, a sense of peace."

The popularity of the lighthearted "In Bloom" video couldn't have been better timed to take the edge off the controversies swirling around Kurt and Courtney. Newspapers all over the country reported that on December 29, Courtney had filed a suit regarding the leak of her medical records to the *Los Angeles Times*. Many papers reported that she was merely suing Cedars-Sinai hospital for releasing the records, but according to a published report in the *Los Angeles Times*, the suit also named Courtney's physician and alleged medical fraud and negligence, invasion of privacy, wrongful disclosure of medical information, and negligent and intentional infliction of emotional distress. The suit was settled out of court in April of 1993.

The public didn't know it, but the battle to have free and clear custody of Frances still raged on. Frances now lived with Kurt and Courtney, but the couple had to submit to regular urine tests and a social worker had to check up on them periodically to make sure they were raising their child in an acceptable manner.

It's now a matter of public record, but a reliable source close to the band told me at the time that Kurt cheated on those urine tests. That's the kind of thing I kept to myself. I was just not going to pursue it and perhaps be responsible for them losing their child again, maybe for good.

Kurt says he and Courtney spent a million dollars in 1992—$80,000 went to personal expenses, $380,000 went to the taxman; they also bought a relatively modest house for $300,000. "The rest of it was because of Lynn Hirschberg," he says, referring to the legal bills they piled up in their efforts to keep Frances and defend their name. "That bitch owes me something."

Of course, they also spent a whole lot of money on doctors and drugs.

chapter X

IT'S ANGER, IT'S DEATH, AND ABSOLUTE TOTAL BLISS

fter all that's happened, it's not surprising to hear that Kurt has found that being a professional rock musician is not quite what he imagined back when he was banging out his raunchy punk rock songs all alone in his bedroom in Aberdeen. "It's become a job, whether I like it or not," he says. "It's something that I love doing and would always want to do, but I have to be honest—I don't enjoy it nearly as much as I used to when I was practicing every night, imagining what it would be like. It's nothing like what it was like the first couple of years of actually playing in front of a few people, loading up the van and going to a rock show to actually *play*. The privilege of that just can't be reproduced after doing it for ten years. The same feeling is not there."

Kurt cited that same sentiment—"I don't enjoy it nearly as much as I used to"—in his suicide note. That's a lot different from what he said in the *Spin* interview, but that particular day, maybe he meant it. Or maybe he was trying to seem upbeat for the benefit of Children's Services.

By that point he had actually only been playing shows with Nirvana for just under six years (and not, as he said, ten). But it probably seemed like an eternity.

Kurt was hardly the first musician to reject fame. In the late '60s, at the peak of his celebrity, Scottish folk-pop star Donovan bought three islands in the Inner Hebrides and planned to start an alternative community there. Fifty years earlier, English composer Gustav Holst, having achieved great success with his orchestral suite *The Planets*, fled from fame, turning down awards and avoiding interviews. (He carried preprinted cards that read "I do not hand out my autograph.") Classical music critic Alex Ross wrote of Debussy, "For a man accustomed to thinking of himself as a loner, the fame was disconcerting." Plenty of other rock musicians have disdained the spotlight—Scott Walker, Mark Hollis (Talk Talk), Eddie Vedder, Jeff Mangum (Neutral Milk Hotel)—but none were quite as famous, or outspoken about it, as Kurt.

Despite Kurt's disparaging Grateful Dead T-shirt, he actually had a lot in common with the Dead's leader Jerry Garcia. Like Kurt, Garcia resisted all the attention and power that came with being the figurehead of a really huge, culturally resonant band. "I did a lot of things to sabotage it," Garcia said in an interview clip in the Grateful Dead documentary *Long Strange Trip*. "You don't want to be the king, you know?"

But the boomer icon and the Gen X icon had more than that in common. They were both iconoclasts who came out of an egalitarian countercultural musical community, were fundamentally formed by its values, and went on to experience such immense fame that they became alienated from that community, so idolized that they couldn't appear in public.

Like Kurt, Garcia deeply believed that people should think for themselves and was pained that the audience was hanging on his every word. "That," Garcia's bandmate Phil Lesh said in *Long Strange Trip*, "just drove him nuts."

Despite the fact that they desperately needed a break to regain their health and ponder how to sustain their creative life, both musicians kept touring in no small part because their respective bands had become unstoppable business machines, with lots of people dependent on them.

Both Garcia and Kurt tried to find solace in heroin. Like Kurt, as journalist Nick Paumgarten said in *Long Strange Trip*, "[Garcia] had something in him that embraced his own self-destruction." Both men, essentially, committed suicide, although Garcia's route was decades-long while Kurt's was very quick.

"I'm surprised to get as excited about it as I do still," he continues. "Sometimes I'm just blown away that I can enjoy it as much as I do when we have a really good show. I'm feeling really good and loose, it really doesn't matter if the crowd is into it or not. I don't judge it by that at all because usually the crowd is the same wherever we go. It has to do with my mood usually—if I feel relaxed and I really want to play, it just happens to be that time of day when I would have wanted to play if I didn't have to play a show, then it usually goes really well and I appreciate it a lot."

What goes through Kurt's mind as he performs on stage? "It's just a mixture of every emotion that I've ever experienced," he says. "It's anger, it's death, and absolute total bliss, as happy as I've ever been when I was a carefree child running around throwing rocks at cops. It's just everything. Every song feels different."

That association of anger, death, and bliss says it all, just as the most idyllic, joyous childhood pastime Kurt could imagine was assaulting authority figures—"Corn on the cops!" That's the "negative ecstasy" I mention early in the book. And the sweet oblivion.

Playing live was certainly one way of tapping into that feeling. "Being in a band is hard work and the acclaim itself just isn't worth it unless you still like playing," Kurt wrote in his journals. "And I do god how I do love playing live."

So all the wailing and flailing and intense, distorted volume are not quite what they seem. "People see energy like that and screaming, people see it as a negative

The Amplified Come as You Are

release, like we've got to get it out of us or we're going to kill somebody," Dave says. "But I'm happy when I play this music. It makes me really happy. Maybe when I was thirteen or fourteen I was mad at Springfield, Virginia, and things just rubbed me the wrong way. It's just fun to make noise and the bigger the noise, the funner it is. So the more noise you've got going, the better you feel."

It's called catharsis. Dave understood that not just on a musical level but also on a deeply personal level. It's one of the reasons he was so great with Nirvana: he was naturally down with the concept.

The only times Kurt feels real anger on stage is when the monitors aren't working well, which often precipitates instrument smashing or abrupt stage exits. "If I can't hear myself, I cannot have a good show," he says. "I can't fake it. I feel like a fool. The audience doesn't deserve to be witnessing this when I can't hear myself because I'm not giving it 100 percent. I can't stand there and pretend I'm having a good time when I'm not. So I feel like I'm cheating the audience when that happens." Nowadays, the band can demand and receive whatever they want in terms of sound equipment.

That bit about being able to hear himself ought to inspire a much deeper appreciation for the person responsible for the sound onstage: the oft-unsung monitor engineer. They're by the side of the stage, out of sight, and they don't usually have the prestige of the house sound engineer, but the monitor engineer can make or break a show.

It's easy to fake it if you're doing something phony. Not so much when the music comes from deep down inside. As country great Loretta Lynn told the *New York Times*' Jon Pareles in 2016, "You put your whole heart into a song when you're hurting."

If only Kurt had heard and heeded the words of early-'60s topical/protest folk icon Phil Ochs and his song "Chords of Fame":

> So play the chords of love, my friend
> Play the chords of pain
> If you want to keep your song
> Don't, don't, don't, don't play the chords of fame

Ochs knew what he was talking about: ravaged by years of mental illness, alcoholism, substance abuse, self-loathing, and grief, he hanged himself in 1976 at age thirty-five.

Despite what he said before, Kurt is very aware of the vibe from the audience. "A lot of times I'll be going through the motions and I'll look up at the audience and realize that they're really enjoying themselves and that makes me happy," he says. "It's quite a sight to see that many people pogoing at once. Definitely one of the only things that our band has introduced to rock & roll is gathering that many people in one place to pogo."

He was serious about that: gathering great numbers of people to pogo is a great metaphor for Nirvana's popularization of punk rock. Pogoing, the simple act of hopping up and down to loud, fast music, is one of punk's foundational gestures. Just about anyone can do it, and it's really fun. But more significantly, pogoing can be a gateway: once you've seen that light, there's no telling what else you can feel capable of doing.

There's a reason the band has lasted through all the trials and tribulations, and at the very core of it is the solid relationship between Kurt and Chris. Just as it's tempting to fit Kurt and Courtney's relationship into a stereotypical framework, the same could be said for Kurt and Chris. To be sure, there are elements of Mutt and Jeff—the short, high-strung one and the big, steady sidekick. Chris usually is more levelheaded about business decisions. It's Chris who calms Kurt down when he gets flustered by anything from a belligerent bouncer to a lousy monitor mix.

But they complement each other perfectly. "Sometimes Kurt will be quiet and Chris will be loud, other times Kurt will be loud and Chris will be the one trying to keep things in control," says Tracy Marander. "It's almost yin and yang in a way."

"We've always had enough respect for each other to figure out what irks one another beforehand, what little personality defects that bother each other, and try to stop them before it turns into a fight," Kurt says. "We've never spoken mean words to each other. It's really weird. It's not because we love each other so much—we both think of each other as hypocrites and there are things about each other that I'm sure we despise—but there's no point. We just have this common knowledge that there's no point in fighting with one another because for the sake of the band, it's an irrelevant thing."

But what Kurt was describing *is* love—in the sense of remaining close friends despite being very aware of each other's shortcomings. Not fighting might have been for the sake of the band, but the band was founded on Kurt and Krist's friendship.

The one complaint Kurt has about Chris is that Chris's sense of humor drowns his out. "He's really a funny person," Kurt allows. "He's real clever in an almost inane

Kurt and Krist sleeping at JJ Gonson and Sluggo's place in Watertown, Massachusetts, July 1989. Photo by JJ Gonson.

way—the things that he says are just so asinine at times that they're hilarious. They make me laugh. But I feel like he restrains me from joining in on this sense of humor and actually contributing to it. I'm allowed to laugh at things that he says, but for some reason, I'm not allowed to be funny on the same level as he is."

Truth be told, Kurt just wasn't nearly as funny as Krist. In 2009, director Bobcat Goldthwait explained to Geekscape's William Bibbiani why he cast Krist in a poignant cameo with Robin Williams in *World's Greatest Dad*. "I called Chris up and I said, 'I want you to be in this scene.' He goes, 'Why?' And I said, 'Because you're funny.'"

Kurt, Krist, Dave, and Pat Smear did an interview with MTV's Kurt Loder in Minneapolis in December 1993. Krist is drinking from a seemingly bottomless glass of wine, and the more hammered he gets, the more he barges in on every question, always getting the first word but almost always spouting glib silliness. The new guys, Dave and Pat, speak very little, mostly when spoken to. And Kurt, the leader of the band and someone whom the MTV audience would want to hear talk about pretty much anything, barely gets a word in edgewise.

At one point, Loder asks, "What was the first music you heard that turned you on?" Krist immediately goes off on a rap about UK glam-poppers the Sweet's 1975 hit "Ballroom Blitz." It's a funny reply, but Kurt doesn't get to talk, and it sure would have been interesting to hear his answer to the question.

Later, Loder asks what they think about the latest uproar about Michael Jackson. (Recently, Jackson's sister La Toya had publicly accused him of being a pedophile.) Speculating about the private lives of celebrities was a topic that Kurt had strong feelings about and he starts to say something: "We have no right to even . . ." and then Krist bigfoots him again, slurring a little, almost spilling the wine out of his glass. Once Krist has said his piece, Kurt mumbles, "I just feel really sorry for him."

Then again, with Kurt getting so much of the attention, it's only fair that Chris grab some of the limelight with his easy sense of humor. "Yeah," Kurt says, "but it sucks to have to be around somebody where you can't be yourself 100 percent. When me and Dave are together and Chris isn't around, it's totally hilarious. We're just playing off one another and it's really fun and I enjoy it. But when all three of us get together, Chris is in the middle and Dave and I are on the side. I take all the serious questions and Chris makes all the smarmy comments and funny things. And Dave is in the middle of both of us. You don't know *where* he stands."

But of course Kurt is usually too shy to be funny around large groups of people. "Everybody knows if Kurt smiles, it lights up the fucking room, because he usually doesn't," says Dave. "I don't know if he's really unhappy or if he's always been unhappy or if he just doesn't know how to be happy. When we'd shoot BB guns in the backyard or throw rocks at cars from the roof of the house or shoot out the windows at the lottery building with a BB gun when we were trying to quit smoking and we had nothing better to do, you'd see the laughing, funny, ha-ha-ha Kurt come into play, which a lot of people don't see."

Most people have never seen that side of Kurt, except the "In Bloom" video or perhaps a few choice scenes in *1991: The Year That Punk Broke*. "A lot of people think he's always the quiet-bitter-angry-confused little pixie, but he's not," Dave says. "I don't even know him that well and I know that much."

Kurt isn't the only one who's felt overwhelmed. "For the first year of me being in the band, there was just no reason at all for me to be at interviews," Dave says. "Chris is really politically motivated and really bright. He has a lot to say even though he sometimes gets spasms of the brain and can't spit out what he means to say. He really was the king of the interview and Kurt always had the beyond-clever snaps of wit. And I was like a paperweight."

How interesting that, even after three years of being in a band with him, sharing an apartment, countless van rides, cigarettes, rehearsals, and hotel rooms, Dave could say of Kurt, "I don't even know him that well."

It was no accident that you didn't know where Dave stood. He was the new guy, and he didn't feel comfortable saying much even though he was possibly the most well-spoken member of Nirvana. As he says earlier, Nirvana was Kurt and Krist's brainchild; both Jason Everman and Chad Channing learned that the hard way. Dave was just the drummer. That wasn't quite the case, but that's how he often felt.

So, in interviews with the three of them, Dave might quietly interject comments, but very rarely, always aware that the camera was mainly trained on Kurt. Often he'd fiddle with something—a cigarette or a nearby television, for instance—or just stare off to the side, making it abundantly clear that he had checked out of the conversation.

Earlier, Dave acknowledges that he wasn't part of a lot of business discussions either. That all must have been frustrating for him—as we now all know, Dave is an alpha type, smart, articulate, and outgoing, comfortable with being the focus of attention. In professional situations, Dave knows how to work the room: he remembers people's names, maybe drops a little personal tidbit about them, earnestly chats them up, then efficiently moves on to the next person. But he barely needed to use those people skills while he was in Nirvana, so he largely kept his own counsel.

But there was another reason why Dave tried to keep the band at arm's length as much as possible: "There's people that you meet that you know aren't going to be around forever," he told Q magazine in 2006. "I kind of prepared myself mentally for that and disconnected just to protect myself."

Although Dave is much more socially integral to the band than any other drummer has ever been, Nirvana is still not exactly the Three Musketeers, all for one and one for all. "Chris and Kurt are unlike any people I've ever met before," Dave says. "They're hard to understand and they're hard to really feel like you're getting along with them, like you can really sit down and talk to them. Some people you can hit it off with immediately and you can talk about anything. With Chris and Kurt, I always felt so different from them. They'd known each other for a long time and sort of had the same sense of humor. Only recently—and this is just barely—did I feel like I really know them more and really felt like I was in the band."

"I don't feel like the new guy anymore, but I don't really know if I feel *vital* to the band," Dave continues. "You're joining a band that's had five drummers before—you might as well be on an hourly wage.

"It was kind of strange—and it still is, too," he says. "It's weird because I've always felt expendable. If they were tired of me being in the band they could always find another drummer, so I've always had that in the back of my mind. It's understandable—I don't think that drums in the band are of such importance that one person's style would really make a difference. A drummer like Dale Crover, you can tell when Dale is playing in Nirvana because he's the best drummer in the world. I've always thought if things didn't work out, they could always get Dale.

"It's not an apocalyptic thing, but I've never had a feeling of real security.

"Playing with Chris and Kurt is really great and we really do have something that nobody else has and I realize that," Dave says. "When I say that they could get any other drummer, it's true, but there is a chemistry between the three of us. I hate flattering myself by saying that the band wouldn't be the same without me, but deep down I know it's true—it would be different. Sure, someone else could play the stuff that I'm playing and someone could play as hard as I play. Anybody could do what I do—it's no big deal, but there is a chemistry that clicks sometimes.

"With Chris and Kurt, there's never really any reassurance," Dave says. "It's never like, 'Wow, that was great!' It's like, you just do it." On the other hand, he feels that part of the magic of their collaboration lies precisely in the fact that they don't communicate with each other very well. "No one really says anything," he says, "so when we write a song, the arrangement just falls together—it's not so conscious. We don't decide 'We need a bridge *here*.' It just sort of happens."

An MTV interviewer at the 1991 Reading Festival asked, "Do you think anything has changed on *Nevermind* from *Bleach*? You're better songwriters or better musicians . . . ?" And, as Kurt jokes that they could now hire studio musicians if they wanted and Krist gives some goofy answer about *Nevermind* being like a mixed-up teen, Dave's face falls: neither of his bandmates had the presence of mind to mention that, between the two albums, an absolutely killer drummer had joined the band and played a major part in propelling their music to a whole new level.

Dave to *Rolling Stone*'s Austin Scaggs in 2011:

I can't think of one show that I ever played with that band where we walked offstage and said, "That was great." Never one. Only two times did I get any reassurance from Kurt. Once when I joined the band, in 1990, we were drunk at some disco in England, and Kurt came up and said, "I'm so glad you're in this band. I'm so glad you're down-to-earth." I was like, "Wow!" The next time was in late '93 or early '94 when I came home and turned on my message machine and had a message from Kurt that said, "Y'know, I was just *sitting here listening to* In Utero, *and your drumming is so awesome. You did such a great job!" I was like, "Wow!" Those two things were spread out by about four years [laughs].*

(It was actually a little under two and a half years, but the point still stands.)

###

Success has driven the three apart to a certain extent. "We get along well, the three of us, and at times it was sort of palsy-walsy, but never too much," Dave says. "Kurt and I used to spend every minute of the day with each other. We became really close, as close as we could get, I suppose, when we lived in Olympia. Then after that, we kind of got distant again. Things get crazy and you kind of want to get away from it all."

What's it like to be famous? "The only thing I can think of is paranoia—it makes you feel like someone's watching you," Kurt says. "It really isn't as hard as I thought it would be—or as hard as it seemed like it was at first. I used to resent people for recognizing me. I'd blame *them*. 'Don't fuckin' look at me. What the hell are you looking at?' You can't blame them for looking. But it *is* annoying."

Yet for all his outspoken abhorrence of fame, Kurt now wants to have another crack at it. "It's not that I like it any more, it's just that I'm getting familiar with it," he says. "I know how to react when people stare at me. I don't feel quite as paranoid as I did. I could probably learn to live with being famous. It doesn't mean that I've given in and I actually enjoy it, I just have a better attitude toward it than I did before."

Although Chris and Dave do it all the time, going out in public is a somewhat different proposition for Kurt. Because he is the frontman, because he is reclusive, because of the drugs, and because of the formidable mystique around his music, a Kurt spotting, even in Seattle, is the talk of the town. He's learning how to deal with getting ogled.

"Most of the time I'll smile and let them know that I understand that they recognize me, because I'd do the same thing if I recognized a star," he says. "If they keep staring and they're being obnoxious or if they snicker or something like that, I give them a dirty look or ask them what their problem is or confront them about it. Lots of times, people have just laughed in my face when they recognize me. I couldn't believe it. I can understand it now. Like a sarcastic thing—'Look at that fucking idiot!' 'It's *him*! Ha-ha!' Those are the people that I really like to deal with because I'll walk right up to them and start drilling them with questions, like what's their problem. They are just amazed because they

think of me as someone who wouldn't confront them and when I do, they clam up and turn beet red and run away sometimes."

In 1991, it was virtually unheard of for an artist who had punk rock roots to go platinum. There were R.E.M. and U2, but their fame had accumulated gradually enough that they could get somewhat acclimated to it. But for Nirvana, fame this sudden was uncharted territory; Kurt didn't have many role models for how to navigate this bizarre situation.

Confronting pesky strangers would have been some true punk rock attitude. One aspect of punk was that the bands were no better than the audience and didn't deserve to be put on a pedestal. But people saw Kurt as a cartoon, a figure on a TV screen— even when he was standing right in front of them, waiting in line to get a burger and fries. (I once saw this happen at the McDonald's at the corner of Sixth Avenue and Westlake in Seattle.) Were he to have confronted people who hassled him, it would have been like the television talking back, Kurt bursting through the screen and into their faces. Sure, some people would run away and some would be pissed off. But all of them would have changed their attitudes, if only a little bit.

People expect celebrities to brim with a constant supply of good cheer, something that Kurt rarely seems to do. It can make for some awkward situations. "Most

The Amplified Come as You Are

people think if I look at them and I don't smile, that I'm pissed off, so I go out of my way to make it look like I'm enjoying myself," Kurt says. "I usually *am* enjoying myself. I'm hardly ever depressed any more, so it's a lot easier to be able to do that."

He *was* depressed, of course. Maybe he said that for my benefit, maybe he said that for the benefit of Children's Services, maybe he was trying to convince himself of it, maybe all of the above. But he found it soul-destroying to pretend that he was enjoying himself.

Kurt also has to fight another perception. Rock stars just aren't supposed to have chronic health problems. Many believed that Kurt's stomach problem was merely a "stomach problem"—a euphemism for a heroin habit (and occasionally it was). But he really does have intense, chronic stomach pain. "I've seen it, I've been there," says Chris. "I've been there when he's had his major episodes and it's terrible because there's nothing you can do."

Kurt has seen countless specialists for his stomach—nine in the first part of 1993 alone—who remain baffled as to what his problem might be. Ulcers have been ruled out. Besides opiate-derived analgesics, the only effective cure Kurt has found is performing on stage, when a massive endorphin rush kills the pain.

Ironically, Kurt's condition may have something to do with his agonized wail. Or vice versa. Asked to pinpoint the source of the pain, he indicates a spot just below his breastbone—it also happens to be exactly where he says his scream originates.

"There's been so many times when I'll be sitting there eating and having massive pain and no one even realizes it," Kurt says. "I'm so tired of complaining about it. It hurts on tour so often, I have no choice but to go about my business. After a show, I have to try to force myself to eat. I'm sitting in my hotel room, forcing myself to eat, taking a bite, and drinking water and doubling up and puking. Halfway through the European tour, I remember saying I'll never go on tour again until I have this fixed because I wanted to kill myself. I wanted to fucking blow my head off, I was so tired of it. There's no way I'm going to live like that. It turned me into a neurotic freak. I was psychologically fucked up. I was having a lot of mental problems because I was having chronic pain every single day."

Imagine how frustrating it must have been to feel such intense pain and no doctor could figure out the cause—and a lot of people didn't believe you were experiencing it at all.

It scarcely needs saying how chilling it is to read the words "I wanted to kill myself. I wanted to fucking blow my head off..." Kurt was obsessed with a horrific videotape of R. Budd Dwyer, the disgraced Pennsylvania state treasurer who shot himself to death at

Kurt's illustration on the back of Sonic Youth's *Whores Moaning: Oz '93 Tour Edition* EP.

a televised press conference in 1987. (Back then, that sort of thing got passed around on bootleg VHS tapes; Rapeman had a song about the incident called "Budd.") Kurt's artwork for an Australia- and New Zealand–only 1993 Sonic Youth EP was a crude drawing of a woman sticking a gun in her mouth. Then there was the awful February 1994 photo session with him sticking a gun in his mouth. Apparently, he had begun to visualize his own death.

Heroin was one way of killing the pain, although Kurt subsequently found a legal and relatively safe remedy for his condition—Buprenex, a mild synthetic opiate which he injected directly into his stomach during an attack. Often he would go a week without resorting to the drug, but when he did something stressful, like playing a show or shooting a video, he'd do it several times a day. Recently, a doctor diagnosed his stomach pain as a result of a pinched nerve in his spine, brought on by his scoliosis. The physical therapy he's getting for his back seems to be working and Kurt says he's glad that he isn't dependent on a chemical for his well-being anymore. Nowadays, he eats better food and even does push-ups and sit-ups before going to bed. He actually looks forward to touring again.

Circa June 1993, Kurt wrote in his journal, "I was introduced to a medicine called bubrenorphine [sic] which I found eleviates [sic] the pain within minutes. . . . I've been on an increasingly smaller dose of it for nine months and haven't had a single stomach episode since."

Buprenorphine was originally prescribed to treat acute pain; doctors later realized that it was also a way to wean addicts off of heroin. So it was kind of a miracle drug for Kurt. And since it was prescribed, he didn't have to go to a public clinic for methadone, which, as a public figure, he surely didn't want to do. Unfortunately, in 1993, buprenorphine hadn't yet been approved for physicians to use in treating opioid addiction.

In *Serving the Servant*, Danny Goldberg mentioned that Kurt had begun seeing Dr. Robert Fremont, who was what was then called a "chemical dependency" specialist in Hollywood, and often worked with celebrities. Goldberg wrote that Kurt deeply appreciated Fremont's compassion for him. Fremont prescribed Kurt plenty of Buprenex (a brand of buprenorphine)—but then Fremont died in the summer of 1993. "Courtney told me," Goldberg wrote, "that Kurt wept when he heard the news." Fremont's death meant that Kurt's Buprenex supply dried up since no other doctor would prescribe it. And so he eventually, inevitably lapsed back into heroin.

By "nowadays," I was referring to the spring of 1993, when I was finishing up the book.

Another stumbling block for Kurt is the public's perception that he is a frail, passive person who has little idea what he is doing. "In addition to everything else, he is a literal genius about what it is to be a rock artist," says Gold Mountain's Danny Goldberg. "It's not something that he has not thought about." Goldberg tells a story about Kurt at the MTV taping back in January 1992, while he and Courtney were bingeing on heroin.

"Kurt's just wiped out and he looks terrible and he says, 'I want to see it back,'" he recalls. "So they play back about fifteen different takes of four or five different songs. He just sat there and said, 'That's no good.' 'That one's no good.' 'That one you can put in "The Year in Rock" but I don't want it on regularly.' 'That one is the one you put on *120 Minutes*.' 'After a week I only want this one repeated.' He could barely walk across the room, but they were all exactly the right decisions and it was not like anyone else's opinion mattered. When it comes to the professional product of what Nirvana is, he makes all of those decisions and he makes them from a place of tremendous consciousness."

Kurt is also savvy about publicity. Everybody who was anybody was backstage at the 1991 Rock for Choice benefit in L.A.; Perry Farrell was there, even Axl Rose was there. In a crowded hallway, Kurt mentioned to Danny

Goldberg that journalists had been asking the band a lot of political questions and missing the band's sense of humor. Kurt had figured out that they were being prompted by a specific paragraph in the band's bio and asked Goldberg if it could be removed. Goldberg was very impressed. "I've *never* had an artist—or a manager or a publicist—pick up within a month the effect of a bio on the types of questions being asked and *then* figure out how to edit it to skew it slightly differently," he says, marveling.

Goldberg likens Kurt's savvy to John Lennon's, recalling a celebrated 1970 *Rolling Stone* interview with Lennon in which he revealed things like the fact that the Beatles always took care not to release a record at the same time as the Stones. At the time, fans were shocked by such conscious manipulation, but, as Goldberg says, "You don't become the Beatles by accident. And you don't become Nirvana by accident, either."

For much more on Kurt's savvy about his career, by all means consult Goldberg's *Serving the Servant: Remembering Kurt Cobain.*

The John Lennon comparisons trouble the Cobains, if only because of what that makes Courtney. She once greeted a visitor to the Cobains' hotel room by saying, "Okay, you want to see Yoko Ono? Here goes." Whereupon she proceeded to pick up the phone, call Gold Mountain on Nirvana business, and positively excoriate whatever hapless person was on the other end of the line.

I was the visitor. I was just being formal there—it's an old-school journalistic custom not to use the first person singular.

"Sometimes Kurt just doesn't feel like saying stuff, so he has her say it for him," says Goldberg. "When Courtney does that, it's because he has asked her to do it. It's a terrible mistake if anyone ever thinks that she does things on her own. Sometimes, he just would rather not talk, so he'll have her call. But the idea that she could make him do anything that he doesn't want to do is just so absurd. You can't get this guy to drink a glass of water or walk across a room to turn over a cassette or do *anything* he doesn't want to do. He is one of the most willful people I've ever met in my life. Sometimes I think he'll just ask her to be the bad guy."

Many wonder why Courtney should be involved in her husband's business affairs at all. "Because I'm too lazy to deal with it," Kurt replies. "I'll just bend over and help them slip it in my ass. I forget about things all the time and everyone takes advantage of that. If it wasn't for Courtney going out of her way to just take care of things without even asking me sometimes—obviously I would allow her to do it anyway—it's mainly for the benefit of our baby so we can make sure we have some money in the next ten years. I'm just too lazy. I decided a couple of years ago that I wasn't going to deal with the business side of it. Now I have to. I'm getting better at it. I'm learning from her."

It's just funny to note the apparent contradictions between what Goldberg said and what Kurt just said. Kurt was "one of the most willful people" Goldberg had ever met in his life and yet Kurt said, "I'll just bend over and help them slip it in my ass." When Courtney berated someone on Kurt's behalf, Goldberg said, it was because Kurt had asked her to do it; on the other hand, Kurt said she did it "without even asking me sometimes."

Perhaps the truth was somewhere in between, but we do know about Kurt's avoidance of confrontation. In the past, he would just not say anything at all and trust that the other person had somehow gotten the unspoken message, or Krist would be the go-between. But now Courtney was doing some of that work, and she was not always the soul of diplomacy.

Goldberg cites his experience as a publicist with Led Zeppelin. Although Jimmy Page was a quiet man, he ran Led Zeppelin with an iron fist—it just wasn't his fist. When he didn't like something that was going on, he'd just mention it to manager Peter Grant and Grant would do whatever yelling was necessary. "I'm not saying that Courtney has got the same relationship that Peter had to Jimmy," Goldberg says, "I'm just saying that people who are quiet are not necessarily passive."

Despite the bit of nuance Goldberg added at the end, it seems that Courtney had the same relationship to Kurt that Peter Grant—an infamously intimidating, even violent, man—had to Jimmy Page.

Often, Courtney is simply looking out for the man who is her husband. "If they're on tour and he's got a terrible stomach and there's a certain kind of food that doesn't give him stomachaches and they go into a dressing room somewhere and that food's not there and he's going to be doubled over in pain, she does make a big scene," Goldberg says. "But she has nothing to do with things like who's producing the record or what the songs are or whether they tour or don't tour.

"Honestly, she's not very involved," Goldberg continues. "She's just very visible—you can't miss her when she's in a room. She's loud and she's forceful and she's flamboyant."

But there's so much more to a band's decision-making than artistic choices—it's a very multifaceted business. And a "loud" and "forceful" voice will certainly color all the band's interactions, and not necessarily for the better.

For instance, if the food backstage is not right, it's the tour manager's job to make it right. And Nirvana had an excellent tour manager. The singer's wife making a big scene about it just does not help resolve things in a productive and professional manner.

Even Kurt admits his wife can sometimes be a social liability. "She'll confront people even when there's no point in confronting them," Kurt says. "There'll be someone who's obviously a sexist jerk but you have to be around this person because you're working with them at this time and there's really no penetrating this person, you know they're a lost cause, but she'll go out of her way to confront him and make a bad scene in front of all these people just to let him know, 'Don't fuckin' bullshit me at all.' She didn't make a dent in this person at all. But still, it's her duty to do things like that. Even though it doesn't make anything better, it still needs to be done. I'll just leave the person alone. That's the difference between her and me—she's definitely a fighter."

The need to call people out on their wrongdoing, even though it's futile or even self-destructive, recalls one of the punkest lines in human history, from Black Flag's "Police Story": "Understand: we're fighting a war we can't win."

And besides, fighting can be entertaining. At the end of the 1992 *Rolling Stone* cover story, Kurt told me he hoped that his audience would discover the underground through Nirvana's music. I replied that, for the most part, that seemed pretty doubtful. "Yeah," Kurt said, "but it's fun to fight. It gives you something to do. It relieves boredom." And then he laughed a little laugh.

Naturally, Courtney makes for a formidable business adversary. "I will ask my management to do something for me twenty times," Kurt says, "and finally Courtney calls up and screams at them and it finally sticks in their brain. They get off the phone and they go, 'What a cunt!' But the thing gets done." Of course, the question is, at what cost?

Courtney is extremely intelligent and does not suffer fools gladly. The slightest misstep, even in the most casual of conversations, is often rewarded with a withering comment—or worse. But Kurt is no fool, either. He readily acknowledges that his wife's brusque personal style hurts far more often than it helps. "She's totally abusive to people and she doesn't even realize it, she's so

used to talking that way," Kurt says. "And a lot of times she unnecessarily jumps to conclusions. And that's her downfall. That's why she doesn't get taken seriously." Even he admits they fight nearly every day.

It's been said that if Courtney were a man, her extreme forwardness and caustic manner wouldn't earn her any flak at all. But even Kurt agrees she'd get it no matter what sex she was. "I remind her of that almost every day," he says with a sly chuckle, their latest spat probably still fresh in his mind. "She admits it and she tries really hard but there's this chemical in her mind that just won't allow her to think before she freaks out on people. A lot of times, someone deserves it, though."

It's an interesting situation for such a sensitive person as Kurt. "Well, I'm not as sensitive as most people probably think," he says, defensively. "There are so many positive qualities about her that it doesn't even matter. She's already getting a lot better at it. It just takes people a long time to change their ways. It's the only character flaw she has is that she jumps the gun too fast."

This is the same quality of love I mention earlier regarding Kurt and Krist: the other person's bad qualities—the ones that alienate some people, or even *most* people—just aren't important. Hence Kurt's concession that "there's this chemical in her mind that just won't allow her to think before she freaks out on people" and yet feeling that "there are so many positive qualities about her that it doesn't even matter." *That's* love.

Remember this when thinking about Kurt and Courtney, or indeed any couple in love: don't ever wonder "what does he/she see in him/her?" Because *you will never really know*.

That said, sometimes those negative qualities can eventually become a dealbreaker.

Although tension still flares between Courtney and the other members of the band, things are definitely looking up. Many say Courtney has been changing for the better, especially after Frances was born. "She has definitely become a person who admits she's wrong," Kurt says. "It usually takes two or three examples before she will admit it, but she does. She isn't *that* pigheaded."

The Courtney factor still dogs the band. The idea persists that Courtney controls Kurt, that she is sapping his talent, that she will break up the band. Call it the Delilah Complex. But she simply is not the monster that much of her recent press has painted her to be. It wasn't for nothing that Kurt said, "Don't believe everything you read." But thanks to the ripple effect of the *Vanity Fair* profile, it has become increasingly difficult to portray Courtney Love as anything but a horror without seeming to be a stooge or a liar. And while Courtney isn't above reproach, it's obvious that there's a considerable sexist force behind the attacks on her character.

Courtney was very entertaining: outrageous, widely knowledgeable, acidly candid, rapid-fire loquacious. But Kurt's line in "Heart-Shaped Box" about being "drawn into your magnet tar pit trap" was exactly right: consort with Courtney—back then, anyway—at your peril.

Kurt is hardly optimistic about the future. "No matter what we do or how clean we live our lives, we're not going to survive this because there are too many enemies and we threaten too many people," he says. "Everyone wants to see us die. We might just keep going just to spite those fuckheads. They've already treaded past the most offensive part, which is attacking my family, and that could go on for years, but there's going to be a time when I'm not going to be able to deal with it anymore, when my daughter is old enough to realize what's going on. She's already going to be twelve years old and start reading all this old press and ask, 'Hey, did you really take drugs when I was a baby?' It's going to be a hard thing to convince her of all the things that aren't true."

It's troubling to read things like "we're not going to survive this . . ." and "there's going to be a time when I'm not going to be able to deal with it anymore." As with so many other statements in this book, it's frightening and obvious—in retrospect. But at the time, it just seemed less like threats and more like blowing off steam. They were yet more of those melodramatic statements that one just sort of tuned out, or at least toned down, because they were too disturbing to take literally.

What an odd thing to say: "We might just keep going." As if it was more likely that they wouldn't.

Kurt probably said those last two sentences with Children's Services in mind as well as Frances.

"There are some amazing things that have happened that I'm so blessed with, but there are so many damaging things at the same time," Kurt says. "I should be completely rehabilitated as far as my bad attitude—at this point, if everything had gone fine, I would be so much of a happier person, my humor would have started to come out more.

"I used to be a pretty funny person, always going out of my way to look on the funnier side of life, but I've withdrawn back into a bad attitude. I'm sure it will just be a matter of time because the positive things—the baby and the wife—are so great, they're so etched in my life as being positive things that I'm blessed with

and grateful for that if people just keep their fucking mouths shut and stop the accusations, in a couple of years, I'll probably be okay. But I just don't see it ending. Just yesterday, another fucking article came out . . ."

"But I just don't see it ending."

Dave is more than happy to be the least visible member of Nirvana. He doesn't even want to do interviews anymore. "One," he says, "because I'm too lazy and two, because why does everyone want to know what I have to say? What's the big deal? It's like one-two-three-four, I play drums and that's about it. I'll put my face on the record and go home at night and clean the house. I just want to lead a normal life. I don't want to be the drummer of Nirvana for the rest of my life, so I lay low.

"It's such a blessing to play in the band and see and do everything that we've done, and not pay the price that a lot of people have to pay," says Dave. "I take pride in leading the most simple life of anybody in the band because I don't do much, other than be happy. There's so much that goes on with Kurt and Courtney that I can't keep up with."

"I just don't want to be David Grohl of Nirvana for the rest of my life," Dave had told *Rolling Stone*'s Chris Mundy. "It's like the kid who got caught masturbating in the bathroom of high school. That's the only way he's ever known." And that was in January 1992, only months after *Nevermind* came out.

Monk magazine, 1993: So, honestly, how long do you think this Nirvana thing is going to last?
Dave: I give it a couple more years.

Dave was thinking ahead, which was incredibly shrewd and pragmatic, especially for a person just into his mid-twenties and playing in the most celebrated rock band on the planet. A lot of musicians would have reveled in that staggering success and maybe thought it would last forever. But Dave was more savvy than that. Perhaps it was skepticism he'd gained from his bitter experience with Scream or his ambition to do his own thing, but he sensed that either Nirvana wouldn't last or that his time with the band was limited.

Given Dave's strong singing voice, ability to play the guitar, and songwriting prowess, not to mention all the hints he readily provided in this very book, it wasn't difficult to see where things were heading. "He had his sights on what he is today the second he was in Nirvana," Dave's former girlfriend L7's Jennifer Finch told Mark Yarm for *Everybody Loves Our Town*. "Central figure, songwriter. When he was the new guy in the band, the A&R people would come around and he'd slip them his demo."

Dave knew how to look out for himself. For instance, even though he knew it would harm close friendships, Dave had left Dain Bramage to join Scream, and then he left Scream when the band was on the ropes and signed on with a promising major label band that he wasn't even sure he liked that much. But, like his mom said, "there are times in life when you have to do what's best for yourself. Sometimes you just have to be selfish." If only for the sake of self-preservation.

As far as envisioning a musical career after Nirvana, Dave was proven right beyond anyone's wildest dreams—except perhaps his own. The Foo Fighters have sold tens of millions of albums, won fifteen Grammys, were inducted into the Rock & Roll Hall of Fame, and fill stadiums all over the planet. And they may well turn out to be The Last Big Rock Band.

Here's Nirvana

**On Friday the 13th,
join Nirvana and DGC Records
for a release party in honor of Nirvana's
DGC debut album Nevermind.**

Friday, September 13
Re-bar
1114 Howell
Seattle, WA
(206) 233-9873
6:00 PM to 8:00 PM

chapter fourteen

THINGS THAT PISS ME OFF

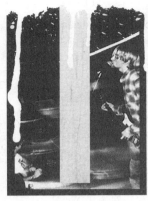

n 1993, Nirvana began to return to business as usual.

In January, the band played two huge shows with their old friends L7 in Brazil early in the year, the first on the sixteenth at Morumbi Stadium in São Paulo and another show a week later at the seventy-thousand-seat Apoteose Stadium in Rio de Janeiro.

The band was in peak form. The São Paulo show, according to Alex Macleod, was "punk rock heaven, baby." Just for the occasion, they played "Rio" by Duran Duran, with Dave on bass and vocals, Chris playing guitar, and Kurt behind the drums. Later, they played a seemingly endless version of Terry Jacks's insipid 1974 bubblegum hit "Seasons in the Sun." Flea from the Red Hot Chili Peppers played the "Teen Spirit" solo on trumpet.

"Punk rock heaven" is one way of putting it. "A pathetic debacle" is another. I didn't realize that Macleod was being facetious.

According to a Brazilian paper, before the show, Kurt gobbled a bunch of Valium. That would explain why he played and sang erratically throughout the show—in front of about 110,000 people. (And, as the late Alice in Chains bassist Mike Starr told Mark Yarm in *Everybody Loves Our Town*, "Kurt had taken me to the bathroom, him and Courtney, and we shot up all night.")

The band hadn't realized that the festival was sponsored by a cigarette brand, which must have particularly frustrated Kurt, who was already mortified by the idea that he was promoting bad habits to his fans. The shows in Brazil turned out to be Nirvana's very public rejection of stadium shows and everything that goes with them.

The set started with Kurt playing "School" much too slowly; Dave and Krist kicked in at the right tempo, saving the day. "Something in the Way" became a cacophonous dirge as Kurt mocked his all-too-adoring audience by making up nonsense lyrics, echoing his remarks at the stadium show in Argentina by changing one verse to "I could shit on stage / You would eat it up." And things went downhill from there. Midway through the set, Kurt broke apart his guitar.

But they weren't through: they switched instruments—Dave on bass and vocals, Krist on guitar, Kurt on drums—and desecrated Queen's "We Will Rock You" and "Seasons in the Sun." They went on to butcher a succession of '80s new wave hits: Duran Duran's "Rio," Kim Wilde's "Kids in America," the Clash's "Should I Stay or Should I

Go," Tommy Tutone's "867-5309/Jenny." It's funny to realize that Kurt Cobain knew those songs just as well as anyone else his age.

Granted, sometimes the hijinks were amusing but mostly it was a spectacle so sad that it was disturbing. It was like they were a band of amateurs playing someone's drunken basement party, not a world-class rock group playing a stadium in front of a small city's worth of people.

"Is everyone having a good time tonight? *Rock and roll!*" Kurt barked with caustic sarcasm.

During a ridiculously extended "Scentless Apprentice," even the band's resolutely even-keeled guitar tech Earnie Bailey succumbed to the chaos and playfully bowled a cantaloupe onto the stage toward Kurt. Kurt picked up the cantaloupe and mashed it into the strings of his guitar, making an ugly, guttural sound, his hands and the guitar dripping with juice.

Krist and Dave played as solidly as possible in an attempt to salvage the evening. But even Krist had his limits. At one point, he disgustedly threw his bass all the way across the stage at Kurt and stormed off—Krist must have been *really* pissed off if he did that—and was only convinced to come back because if they didn't play at least forty-five minutes, they'd get their asses sued and possibly start a massive riot.

The next day, Bailey turned the ballroom of the hotel where Nirvana was staying into a sprawling workshop and diligently repaired all the gear they'd destroyed.

That show might have been punk rock, but it was not "heaven" in any way. It was quite the opposite, in fact. Brazilian reviewer Marcel Plasse wrote that when Kurt trashed his guitar and amplifier, it was "as if he were attacking himself or his band." The show itself, Plasse added, "was the abyss staring back at anyone who stared into it."

A week later at another gigantic stadium show in Rio, it was more of the same. During "Scentless Apprentice," Kurt staggered around the stage, playing caterwauling nonsense for six minutes. As if it weren't apparent enough that this was a big fuck-you to the crowd, he spat on the lenses of two cameras that were projecting his face on giant screens, then apparently exposed himself to a third. The expression on Kurt's face as he looked into the camera was really unsettling, an almost psychotic glare. This wasn't irreverent rock & roll abandon, it was just very troubling.

An unsigned review in *Raw* magazine called the show "a sad display of excess . . . I left after 'Teen Spirit' with the horrible premonition that this might be the last time Kurt plays his paean to youth culture. . . . All in all, a thoroughly depressing experience. He's too good to go like this."

Nirvana had recorded a cover of "Seasons in the Sun" at a demo session with their soundperson Craig Montgomery while they were in Brazil, testing out songs for the upcoming record (including a fantastically caustic, shambling, and catchy number called "I Hate Myself and Want to Die").

In case anyone missed the autobiographical resonances in his choice of cover song, Kurt ad-libbed a verse at the São Paulo show: "Goodbye, Papa, please pray for me / I was the black sheep of the family / And I know I was a really big fuck-up / And I couldn't hold a job at McDonald's / And you ousted me at the age of sixteen / I was on the street and I had nowhere to go."

So there was Kurt, very publicly railing at his father all those years later and hinting at his own imminent demise—to a vast crowd of people who didn't understand what he was saying.

Back home, Kurt became his own publicist and personally arranged for interviews with the *Advocate*, a national gay magazine, and *Monk*, a roving magazine written by two guys in a Winnebago who travel around America and focus on a different city in each issue.

The *Advocate* piece was a master stroke. It encouraged Nirvana fans to buy a gay-oriented magazine. And it exposed the band to an audience that doesn't tend to go for rock bands like Nirvana.

That was such a clueless thing for me to say. *Of course* there were plenty of gay people who liked rock bands such as Nirvana. But, as Pansy Division singer Jon Ginoli points out in *I Found My Friends*, "People thought gays weren't making or listening to that kind of music, because almost no one playing it was out of the closet."

This was around the birth of queercore—in 1992, the hilariously raunchy and, yet, deep down, deadly serious and very brave gay punk band Pansy Division covered "Teen Spirit," retitled it "Smells Like Queer Spirit," and "queerified" the lyrics: "Hello, hello, hello homo . . ." (Also on the single were: "Fem in a Black Leather Jacket" and "Homo Christmas.") On the single's sleeve, the

Kurt and close personal friend Ren Hoek at the *Advocate* shoot.
© Charles Peterson

band wrote, "With kisses to Nirvana: no superstar American rock band has ever before had the guts to take such an overtly pro-gay stance. Right on!"

Funnily enough, Pansy Division bassist Chris Freeman had attended Aberdeen's high school, several years before Kurt did. Fittingly, Freeman told *Spin* magazine in 2011 that in Aberdeen, he "[got] beat up routinely."

Kurt made it clear that Nirvana shows were a safe space for gay people. And that was truly visionary. It might seem pretty mundane now, but back then, rock stars defending gay people was very rare and very bold. Aside from the music, it's one of Kurt's greatest legacies.

In the interview, Kurt mentioned that he had thought he was gay for a brief time in high school, and added, "I'm definitely gay in spirit, and I probably could be bisexual." Somehow that got translated by several major newspapers, as well as the entire Gannett newspaper chain, into a statement that he was a "practicing bisexual" and that "this was just fine with his wife."

The Amplified Come as You Are

In February, Kurt designed a custom guitar for Fender—a cross between a Jaguar and a Mustang. A limited run for his use only was planned, but in the spring of 1993, a consumer edition was being considered.

Kurt created the Jag-Stang the same way he created his music: with collage. He cut up photos of two of his favorite guitars, the Fender Jaguar and the Fender Mustang, and taped together the pieces. Even the name of the guitar is a collage.

At the start of the third week in February, the band traveled to Minnesota to record their new album with producer Steve Albini.

Of course, there had long been plenty of speculation about how Nirvana would follow up their blockbuster major label debut. But the band had known pretty much what they were going to do for a very long time. A few days before *Nevermind* was released, Krist told Canada's MuchMusic, "Next time around we're going to choose a different path because it's such a well-worn path. We did that go-to-Hollywood trip," he said, alluding to the fact that they'd recorded *Nevermind* in a legendary studio in Los Angeles.

"I have a pretty good idea," Kurt said in my *Rolling Stone* cover story. "I think both of the extremes will be on the next album—it'll be more raw with some songs and more candy pop on some of the others. It won't be as one-dimensional." He was right: while the instrumentation and recording style were relatively one-dimensional, the songs ranged from the "raw" to the "candy-pop," from "Scentless Apprentice" to "Dumb."

Kurt had the basic ideas for most of the songs by the time he and Courtney had left the Spaulding apartment in the summer of 1992. They just needed structure, which was worked out in rehearsals with Chris and Dave. Early versions of three of the songs—"Rape Me," "Dumb," and "Pennyroyal Tea"—had been kicking around on bootlegs since just after *Nevermind*. Kurt had wanted to begin recording the album that summer, but all three members lived in different cities and they weren't in close touch; besides, Kurt and Courtney were about to have a baby.

In fact, the band members were not in close touch because there was a lot of tension among them, primarily because of Kurt's heroin addiction and his cocooning with Courtney, as well as perhaps lingering resentment over the revised publishing split.

Kurt had always wanted to record with Albini, ever since he first heard Big Black, an incendiary, tremendously influential Chicago trio on Touch & Go Records that combined nasty guitar textures, bilious, nasal vocals, and the incessant pounding of a drum machine to induce visions of urban rage and paranoia. Albini went on to a thriving, even legendary, career recording (like Jack Endino, never **producing**) various bands like Helmet, Superchunk, PJ Harvey, and even EMF, as well as countless underground heroes, such as the Jesus Lizard and Tar.

For more on the origin story of Steve Albini and Big Black, I humbly recommend my book *Our Band Could Be Your Life: Scenes from the American Indie Underground 1981–1991*, which includes a chapter on Big Black.

But Kurt was particularly after the drum sound he had heard on two Albini projects—the Pixies' epochal 1988 album *Surfer Rosa* and the Breeders' excellent 1990 album *Pod*. It's a natural, powerful sound produced with canny microphone placement rather than phony sounding effects boxes. It reminded Kurt of the drum sound on Aerosmith's 1976 *Rocks* album.

In particular, Kurt was looking for a great room sound—rather than existing in a generic sonic space, he wanted the instruments, particularly the voice and drums, to sound like they were in a dynamic acoustic space. Quiet sounds don't react as powerfully with a room as loud ones; the louder the sound, the more you hear the room, which is a great psychoacoustic cue to indicate volume and aggression. Using some clever studio technique, David Bowie and producer Tony Visconti brilliantly exploited this phenomenon on "Heroes," where you hear more room sound the louder Bowie sings.

Aerosmith's *Rocks* is a great album, by the way. For an example of the drum sound Kurt was thinking of, listen to "Nobody's Fault."

After Big Black, Albini fronted the unfortunately named thrash band Rapeman. Within indie rock circles, a reputation as a misogynist seems to dog Albini, which would make him an odd choice for Kurt. "That's what I've heard from people, but I just thought until I meet him, I don't really care, because if he turns out to be an asshole, I'll at least use him for his recording abilities," Kurt says. "Definitely a few sexist things leaked out of him, but that's just the scene he's in. There's a few misogynists that I admire like William Burroughs. Brion Gysin is a total misogynist and I like his writing. I hate people for being misogynists and I would choose not to be associated with them but sometimes they produce some good work. They just have a flaw that they need to work on."

There is possibly no band name that Kurt could have found more objectionable than Rapeman. It was named after a superhero (for lack of a better word) in a Japanese adult comic book. Several of the band's shows were picketed purely because of the name. "It was the typical motley alliance of housewives and lesbians," Albini said, with his then-characteristic lack of propriety. (He's long since matured into a thoughtful, righteous human being.)

They were a great, ferocious band, though, and not at all, as I erroneously called them, "thrash"—more like the dawn of post-hardcore. Formed in 1987, Rapeman was Albini on guitar and vocals with the incredible former rhythm section of one of Kurt's favorite bands, Scratch Acid: bassist David Wm. Sims (who would soon co-found another of Kurt's big favorites the Jesus Lizard) and drummer Rey Washam.

If you can manage to get past song titles such as "Coition Ignition Mission," "Kim Gordon's Panties," and "Hated Chinee," their 1989 album *Two Nuns and a Pack Mule* is one of the best of the decade. The 1988 *Budd* EP is also excellent. Rapeman broke up in 1989.

"I learned a long time ago that if you're too strict about things and you cut yourself off from people who have those tendencies, you're limiting yourself," Kurt says. "There are things that can be learned from people like that. And why not try to persuade them into thinking differently rather than just banning them, putting a veto on them, and not having anything to do with them. All it does is make them resentful and they won't even think about the things that they do wrong."

So there we have it: Kurt Cobain wasn't interested in canceling people. Maybe because he had a personal interest in the possibility that anyone can be redeemed.

So, misogynist or not, Kurt was eager to get Albini, or more specifically, the Albini sound. "That sound is as close to the sound that I hear in my head that I've ever found," he says, "so I just had to do it."

For months before the band contacted him, rumors had been circulating that Albini was to produce the next Nirvana album. At last he sent a disclaimer to the UK music press stating that "the appearance in the press of this mistake fosters the impression that I only work with bands who've been on television. This is not the case!" Days later, Gold Mountain contacted Albini.

This was the man who once told a friend that he thought Nirvana was just "R.E.M. with a fuzzbox." "I thought they were an unremarkable version of the Seattle sound," Albini admits. "I thought they were typical of the bands of this era and of that locale."

It's an opinion he still holds, so one wonders why Albini would take the assignment. The way he puts it, it was a mission of mercy. "This is going to sound kind of stupid," he says, "but in a way, I felt sorry for them. The position they were in, there was a bunch of bigwig music industry scum whose fortunes

Things That Piss Me Off

depended on Nirvana making hit records. It seemed obvious to me that fundamentally they were the same sort of people as all the small-fry bands I deal with. They were basically punk rock fans, they're people that were in a band that came up from an independent scene and it was sort of a fluke that they got famous."

The members of Nirvana truly believed themselves to be the peers of all the underground bands Albini worked with. Acknowledging that they were also world-famous cultural icons created massive cognitive dissonance.

"It seemed that they understood doing things the way I usually do them and they would appreciate making a record like that," Albini continues. "But if I didn't do it, they weren't going to be allowed to make a record like that by the record company or by anyone else who worked with them. Any other producer that would work with Nirvana, for a start, would rob them, would want to get a lot of money out of them. And they'd probably be banking on making a hit record, in which case he would be making a record that he thought fit the mold of the hit singles record, not a powerful, personal punk rock record, which is the sort of record I got the impression they wanted to make."

In addition to a $24,000 studio bill, Albini's fee was $100,000, but unlike virtually any other producer, Albini refused to take points (a percentage of sales) on the album. "I just think that taking points on an album is an immoral position—I cannot do it, I think it's almost criminal," says Albini. "Anyone who takes a royalty off a band's record—other than someone who actually writes music or plays on the record—is a thief."

Albini didn't want the album to sound anything like *Nevermind*. "It sounds like that not because that's the way the band sounds," he says, "but because that's the way the producer and the remix guy and the record company *wanted* it to sound."

Once again, Kurt finished writing most of the lyrics within days of recording his vocals, culling most of them from notebooks full of poetry.

Booking themselves in as "The Simon Ritchie Group," the band recorded and mixed the entire album in two weeks at Pachyderm Studios, located about fifty miles south of Minneapolis in the middle of the Minnesota tundra. It's a favorite haunt of Albini's, where he has produced the Wedding Present, PJ Harvey, Killing Joke, Failure, and others. Clients stay at a large house which Chris described as "Mike Brady meets Frank Lloyd Wright." The studio is a separate building about a hundred yards through the woods. The spacious wood-paneled main room where they set up the drums had a large window that looked out onto the snowy Minnesotan winter. The Neve mixing board had been used to make AC/DC's *Back in Black*.

Albini had his own studio in Chicago, where he'd recorded many of Nirvana's favorite records, but Pachyderm was in small-town Cannon Falls, Minnesota, where it would be difficult for Kurt to find drugs. I'm sure Pachyderm was sold to the band as a place where "the grown-ups" wouldn't visit and interfere, and to their credit, they didn't. It probably didn't hurt that Pachyderm was also where Albini had recently recorded *Rid of Me* by Kurt favorite PJ Harvey—Kurt and Courtney had gotten hold of an advance tape of the album and talked about it all the time. The sonic similarities between *Rid of Me* and *In Utero* are no accident.

The band had made it abundantly clear to DGC and Gold Mountain that they didn't want any interference with the recording—they'd learned at least one lesson from *Nevermind*. They didn't even play any work tapes for their A&R man Gary Gersh, a pretty cheeky maneuver, to say the least. But Nirvana now had enough clout that Geffen wouldn't dare reject the album—or would they? "If they do, they know we'll break up," says Kurt. "Fuck, we made them fifty million dollars last year."

For most of the two weeks it took to make the album, it was just Albini, Kurt, Chris, Dave, and assistant engineer Robert "Bob" S. Weston IV.

Also present was Pachyderm apprentice Brent Sigmeth and hired chef Carter Nicole Launt. As Launt told Keith Cameron for *Mojo*, "Krist was a vegan, so no dairy and no meat. Kurt, he had a little erratic schedule of eating. He liked frozen pizza and he would get up in the middle of the night and make himself something. Dave was kind of the all-American eater. Nothing too strange!"

Although it was ostensibly a low-budget project, Albini says the band was not above typical indulged rock star behavior. The band didn't actually show up with their equipment and instead had it shipped, then wasted the better part of three days waiting for it to arrive. Albini says the band wanted someone to Fed Ex a boom box to them instead of just going out and buying one; when Kurt began having trouble tuning his guitar, they wanted to fly in their guitar tech Earnie Bailey. "When you've got millions of dollars, maybe you go a little crazy and start doing stuff like that," says Albini.

But once they actually started recording, it went very quickly and they completed all the recording—basic drum, bass, and guitar tracks, guitar solos,

and vocals—in about six days. Kurt says they could have done the whole album in a week if they had really wanted to.

They recorded live—meaning bass, drums, and guitar all at once—and kept virtually everything they laid down. Kurt added another guitar track to about half of the songs, then added guitar solos, then vocals. This time, he didn't run out of cough syrup before it was time to sing.

I'd bet that the cough syrup was Kurt's old favorite Hycomine, or something like it, to tide him over while he was out in the middle of nowhere.

"It was the easiest recording we've ever done, hands down," says Kurt, who had anticipated at least some disagreements with Albini. "I thought we would eventually get on each other's nerves and end up screaming at each other. I was prepared to have to live with this person who was supposedly a sexist jerk, but he was surprisingly helpful and friendly and easy to get along with."

Personally, Albini was pleasantly surprised by all three band members. "Kurt is actually quite normal," Albini says. "He's been through a lot and you can tell that it's beaten up on him. He's kind of sallow and a little bit somber and melancholy but I think he's melancholy because he's in a situation that he thinks is not as pleasant as it should be, considering all the attributes—he's got a lot of money, he's famous, he's in a successful, popular rock band, so things should be going fairly easily for him and they're not. That's a dichotomy that he's uncomfortable with and I think he's coming to accept it."

It would be easy to let that word "sallow" go right by, but it's a dog-whistle word often applied to heroin users to describe their jaundiced complexion.

But while Kurt was indeed dissatisfied with wealth and fame, he was "somber" and "melancholy" because he was a depressive.

"He is an intelligent guy—he doesn't come off that way," Albini continues. "He plays dumb occasionally to try to get people to trip themselves up. Also I think he thinks it cool to be naive and dumb. But I think he's an intelligent guy and he's handled it better than most people. He still has a healthy suspicion of the other big shots in the music industry. A lot of people in his position would have completely converted and gone to the position where 'They're people just like us and I give them all the credit I would give you.' I think he recognizes that most of the players and movers and shakers in the music scene are real pieces of shit."

"Probably the easiest guy to deal with of them all was Dave Grohl," Albini says. "For one, he's an excellent drummer, so there's never any worry whether he's going to be able to play. His playing was rock solid and probably the highlight of my appreciation of the band was watching Dave play the drums. He's also a very pleasant, very goofy guy to be around."

Albini respected Chris as well. "If he listens to something and he doesn't like it," he says, "he will say that he doesn't like it but he's adult enough that he can say, 'Well, this is the sort of thing that might grow on me. I'll let it sit there for a while before I veto it.'" Albini also feels that Chris has to do a fair amount of "mopping up." "Like if Kurt doesn't know how to plug in his guitar and tune it, for example, and Chris does, he doesn't make a big deal about it," Albini says. "Chris will just run in there and take care of it."

That's a great encapsulation of Kurt and Krist's relationship. Kurt really depended on Krist. Krist was a much better musician, technically, so he could show Kurt how to do things—like how to play their own songs in the middle of a huge stadium show. But Albini was exaggerating—Kurt knew very well how to plug in and tune a guitar.

As Albini himself insists, he's more of an engineer than a producer—he gets sounds rather than arrangements. So although he had his own opinions, Albini encouraged the band to decide what was a good take and what wasn't. "If he would have had his way, the record would have turned out way raunchier than it did," Kurt says. "He wanted to mix the vocals at an unnecessarily low level. That's not the way we sound good."

But putting the vocals relatively low in the mix was one of Albini's signature moves: it gives the effect of someone trying to holler over a very loud rock band, which is pretty much how it goes when a rock band is actually rehearsing. And on Albini's recordings the drums are typically very loud, which is also pretty much how it goes when a rock band is rehearsing. These were key traits of the classic Albini sound—and Kurt and everyone else fully knew this at the outset. Albini and the band were on a collision course, but no one would acknowledge it. And that would eventually lead to fireworks.

Albini was confident that Kurt knew what he was doing. "Generally speaking, he knows what he thinks is acceptable and what isn't acceptable," says Albini. "He can make concrete steps to improve things that he doesn't think are acceptable. After the fact, when he's in a vacuum, when he's back at home, occasionally he gets a little too overcritical and introspective about things. But while he's actually doing it, he's very efficient."

The idea was to go for a natural sound. "The last Nirvana album, to my ears, is sort of a standard hack recording that has then been turned into a very, very controlled, compressed radio-friendly mix," says Albini. "That is not, in my opinion, very flattering to a rock band."

The all-important drum sound was achieved with virtually no electronic chicanery—just a lot of microphones placed around the room to pick up the room's natural reverberance. If you've got a good drummer, a good drum set, and a good-sounding room, you're home free. "Dave Grohl's an amazing drummer," says Albini. "If you take a good drummer and put him in front of a drum kit that sounds good acoustically and just record it, you've done the job."

Kurt's vocals also had few effects. Instead of electronically doctoring the vocal tracks to make it seem like they were done in a nice, resonant room, Albini simply recorded the sound of someone singing in a nice, resonant room. "On the last album, there was a lot of double-tracked vocals and stuff, which is a hack production technique to make vocals sound 'special,'" Albini says. "It's been done so much over the last ten years that to me, that now sounds ordinary. That's now a standard production trick. To hear just the sound of a guy singing in a room—which is on the new album, it's just one take of Kurt singing in a room—that sounds so different from what else is out there that it sounds like a special effect."

In Utero is the equivalent of an acoustic album—but it gets back to basics in a way that isn't as forced and obvious as the "unplugged" trend. This is Nirvana's version of the stereotypical indulgent follow-up album—they're doing exactly what they've always dreamed of doing. Usually, that means two double-length CD's full of filler and overinflated wankery, the budget ballooning with university marching bands, legions of chanting Gyuto monks and months and months of time wasted in the studio. Instead, Nirvana recorded the follow-up to a quadruple platinum album in two weeks on a vintage twenty-four-track analog board.

The astute rock nerd will have noted that "the budget ballooning with university marching bands" was an allusion to Fleetwood Mac's fine but infamously self-indulgent 1979 album *Tusk*, whose title track features the University of Southern California's Trojan Marching Band recorded by a mobile studio that was rolled onto the field at Los Angeles's Dodger Stadium. The album's budget was several million of today's dollars.

The Gyuto monks, a Tibetan Buddhist order based in rural India, have guested with both the Grateful Dead and Van Halen. Their music is fantastic—check out *The Perfect Jewel: Sacred Chants of Tibet* (Smithsonian Folkways Recordings, 2010).

Of course, some would say they made a low-budget album out of some sort of indie rock guilt complex. "We didn't make a raw record to make a statement at all, to prove that we can do whatever we want," Kurt insists. "That's exactly what we've always wanted to sound like." Many have contemplated such a move, but no one has ever actually done what Nirvana did. Kurt covers himself, though, because even the most "new wave" songs have hooks, such as the spiraling ascending riff on "Scentless Apprentice," the wrenching, Zeppelinesque breaks in "Milk It."

And as far as modest recording strategies go, Nirvana was not the only one. A low-tech, low-profile approach had already begun sweeping—or rather, resweeping—underground rock in the early '90s. As a reaction against the cold, digital CD and the cynical, greedy way it was foisted on the public—and as a cost-cutting measure—Nirvana favorites such as Pavement and Sebadoh became proponents of "chimp rock," or "lo-fi," as this crude approach to recording became known. Ever with their eyes on the horizon, Sonic Youth purposely recorded their *Dirty* album (1991) with plenty of distortion and at a lower than usual tape speed for even lower fi.

Sonic Youth didn't use a lower tape speed for "lower fi"—it was to capture a certain quality of low- and midfrequency sounds. As for distortion, that had always been a quintessential color in the Sonic Youth palette.

Dirty was recorded with the same producer (Butch Vig), mixer (Andy Wallace), and mastering engineer (Howie Weinberg) as *Nevermind*. Obviously, that was more than a coincidence. "We were sort of maybe looking forward to the insanity of the Nirvana thing happening," Sonic Youth singer-guitarist Thurston Moore admitted to author Alec Foege for *Confusion Is Next: The Sonic Youth Story*, "but it didn't happen." Maybe they should thank their lucky stars it didn't.

Lo-fi became really hip through at least the end of the decade, not just with Pavement and Sebadoh, but other popular indie bands such as Guided by Voices, Liz Phair, and Beck. (Daniel Johnston, R. Stevie Moore, Jandek, and Half Japanese, among others, had already been there for years.) It played to the indie world's yen for authenticity—there was no expensive studio trickery to gloss up the music.

Lo-fi reclaimed the filth and fuzz—the grunge, if you will—that had helped to make rock music so exciting in the first place. And this was music for the generation of diminished expectations; big-ticket production values signified lofty professional aspirations and corporatism that just didn't resonate with the indie sensibility.

Despite the name, lo-fi didn't mean just low audio fidelity; it could also mean extraneous sounds like a squeaking chair or a car honking outside, or just less-than-slick performances. That was the sonic analogue of everything else in that community: homespun photocopied fanzines, staticky low-powered radio stations, amateur record labels, ramshackle venues, and so on. The flaws were *inclusive*, a signal that anybody—or at least anybody who was inspired—could do it. It was kind of aspirational—even if it wasn't actually true that anybody could do it *well*, it at least gave the feeling that they *could*, which is empowering, as opposed to the passive consumeristic appeal of commercial music.

On the musicians' side, lo-fi/DIY meant that there was more studio time to experiment, to take chances. And without a lot of money invested in production, there wasn't as much urgency to be commercial, so the musicians didn't have to compromise creatively just so they could sell more records.

(Back then, DIY was lo-fi. But in the digital era, musicians can make pristine multitrack recordings with a wide array of effects and powerful mixing and editing tools. There isn't much excuse for low fidelity anymore, except as some sort of affectation or signifier.)

The approach isn't confined to cheap equipment or primitive recording techniques—a first-take, best-take philosophy is part and parcel. Besides making the music more spontaneous—when you think you're only going to get one take, you try harder—it's also a dare: Can the music stand without layers of studio gloss? As they began to get into the no-fi ethos, *Nevermind* became even more repugnant to Kurt, Chris, and Dave than it already was. Rock history will probably record *In Utero* as a giant step back to the future.

To be clear, *In Utero* was certainly not lo-fi—they used a great mixing board, an excellent-sounding room, some extremely high-end microphones, and an exacting, highly experienced engineer—but it was a very straightforward recording, nowhere near as tricked-out as *Nevermind* was, and was largely first takes.

So *In Utero* signaled that Nirvana had seized the means of production, that they weren't swinging for the commercial fences, and that they were making exactly the music that they wanted to make, free of interference by the big, bad major label, which was precisely what made the ensuing non-scandal about the record so juicy.

As far as *In Utero* being "a giant step back to the future," well . . . it's true that after *In Utero*, several big bands did work with Albini, including Bush, Manic Street Preachers, and Robert Plant and Jimmy Page. But not many quadruple-platinum bands went on to record harsh, aggressive albums that featured mostly first takes and few overdubs.

###

A little over a week into the recording, Courtney flew in, basically because she missed Kurt. Albini says she tried to butt in on the proceedings, but he won't say exactly what the problem was. "I don't feel like embarrassing Kurt by talking about what a psycho hose-beast his wife is," says Albini, "especially because he knows it already."

I had always thought Albini had devised that piquant, now oft-quoted epithet "psycho hose-beast," but it's from *Wayne's World*, which had come out the previous year.

I now wonder if maybe Albini was right, and Courtney really just came to meddle in the recording. Kurt was only gone for two weeks, much shorter than most tours, so it's not like they'd been separated for long. It's pretty clear that Kurt didn't ask her to come and was powerless to stop her. Anybody would realize that inserting oneself into such an intimate and remote situation, and on such a tight timetable, would be disruptive no matter how mellow and unassuming they were.

A big reason why they recorded at Pachyderm was so they'd have no distractions. But it sounds like Courtney was nothing *but* distraction: as Carter Nicole Launt told Keith Cameron, "I think [Courtney's presence at Pachyderm] was stressful for Kurt. I think she put a lot of pressure on him and wasn't always as approving of the way the songs were. She was very critical of his work, and actually was kind of confrontational with people there. Yeah, it definitely was stressful."

This reminds me of something in my April 1992 *Rolling Stone* cover story: "Whenever Love walks into the room, even if it's to scold him about something, he gets the profoundly dopey grin of the truly love struck." Why would someone interrupt an interview for a cover story in a major national magazine to scold their spouse in front of the reporter?

The first thing Courtney said to *Select* interviewer David Cavanagh before a June 1992 concert in Belfast was "I'm Courtney, hi. I married someone more famous than me." Then Cavanagh related a little dialogue Courtney had with Kurt:

"See, you've gotta make sure, when you go out with a guy in a band, his band should be smaller than your band . . ."

"Yeah!" snorts Kurt. "And you fucked up and went out with someone in the Beatles!"

"Yeah!" she shouts. "But there was a point where we were almost peers . . ."

"We were," he nods, "at one time. For about a month."

"FUCK YOU!!!!" She storms out.

In the extras on the *Montage of Heck* DVD, Courtney is asked to describe her plans for herself when she was younger. She replies, "I'm going to be a movie star and a rock star, too," then repeats that exact sentence three times in a row for emphasis, adding, "I was just a pure ball of ambition."

As she admits in an interview for *Montage of Heck*, "I coveted his success," which would explain her meddling and needling as expressions of an envy that it took her a very long time to overcome. Courtney told the *Los Angeles Times* in 2021, "It's taken me a couple of decades to realize that not only am I not as good a songwriter as Kurt, but nobody is."

"The only way Steve Albini would think I was a perfect girlfriend," Courtney replies, "would be if I was from the East Coast, played the cello, had big tits and small hoop earrings, wore black turtlenecks, had all matching luggage, and never said a *word*."

Eventually, Courtney and Dave got into a huge spat, but no one will talk about it.

The mixing was done in under a week—quick by the band's standards, but not for Albini, who was used to mixing an entire album in a day or two. If a mix wasn't working out, they'd all goof off the rest of the day and do things like watch the complete series of David Attenborough nature videos or go in for a little pyromania. "Steve was really into lighting his ass on fire," says Kurt. "He'd pour rubbing alcohol on his ass and light it on fire. He likes to do that," Chris spent most of his spare time working on a magazine article about his latest visit to Croatia.

It was actually high-grade alcohol used to clean studio equipment, and don't try this at home, kids. At one point, Dave poured some on his baseball hat, lit it on fire, and walked into the lounge, where Albini was catching a nap. "Steve! My head's on fire!" Dave exclaimed. Albini opened his eyes, calmly appraised the situation, and then went back to sleep. The partially incinerated hat is still on display at Pachyderm.

Dave had plenty of time to light his hat on fire because he recorded all his drum parts in three days. For the next eleven days, he had virtually nothing to do except the occasional harmony vocal. And it would probably always be like that for every Nirvana album. That had to be frustrating for the type of person who would soon go on to be the lead singer, guitarist, and songwriter for a blockbuster rock band.

At one point during the recording, Kurt drew a simple but evocative caricature of the band on a drum head. "When you see Kurt do something like that, you think about the way Kurt writes songs," Dave says. "They're so simple and so to the point and so right. Something that would take me an hour to explain, Kurt would

sum up in two words. That's something he has that I've never seen in anyone else."

They also used their spare time to make prank phone calls and record them for later delectation. Kurt had gotten a message from Gold Mountain that Gene Simmons from Kiss wanted to talk to him. Albini "just happened" to find the number sitting by the studio phone and decided to call Simmons and pretend to be Kurt. It turned out that Simmons wanted Nirvana to play on a planned Kiss tribute album and even offered to co-write a song with Kurt. Albini also called Eddie Vedder and pretended to be legendary producer Tony Visconti (David Bowie, T. Rex, etc.). "Your voice really speaks to me," said Albini, who offered to get Vedder in with "a real band" to do some recording. Vedder bought it, but said he'd rather just make a home recording and sell it for five bucks a throw.

They called Evan Dando of the Lemonheads on tour in Australia and told him that Madonna was on the line, and to please hold. Dando bought it hook, line, and sinker, growing more and more anxious the longer he waited on hold. "I'm going to start beating off!" he says at one point on the tape. Gradually, he gets more and more impatient. Finally Albini, saying he's Madonna's assistant, tells Dando that Madonna will have to call back.

The capper was a call Dave made to John Silva to fill him in on how the project was going— "Things are going really bad," Dave says solemnly. "Chris was throwing up blood last night . . ."

To celebrate the completion of the record, they had a listening party and sat around and smoked cigars, except for Kurt, who stuck to his trusty Winston Lights.

So what does Albini think of *In Utero*? "I like it far more than I thought I was going to," he allows. "I like this record way more than I've ever liked a Nirvana record. I find myself listening to it of my own free will, occasionally."

Kurt's drumhead doodle, made during the *In Utero* sessions. Courtesy J. Mario Mendoza

"I think it's a far better record than they could have made under any other circumstances," Albini continues. "Is it one of my top ten favorite albums of all time? No. Is it in my top one hundred albums? Maybe."

This is actually fairly high praise from Steve Albini. He's heard a lot, likes little of it, and can tell you exactly why, in the most acerbic and persuasive terms.

Kurt admits his lyrics are hard to decipher. "I slur and run words together a lot," he says, "and I have a fake English accent sometimes." This time, Kurt might actually consent to print his lyrics. "I really like them, there's really nothing that's embarrassing about them so I might print them this time," he says. "I'd rather do it now than read reviews and have these idiots write the wrong lyrics in."

Besides the pedestrian fact that it's their third album, the classic causes of the sophomore jinx did not apply to *Verse Chorus Verse*. Often, when bands get famous quickly, they fall into the easy life, disconnected from what inspired them in the first place. This was clearly not the case for Kurt or indeed Chris and Dave, for that matter. The material for follow-up albums is typically thrown together on the run during a lengthy tour that often ends a week before recording begins. That didn't apply either—Nirvana didn't tour for most of 1992 and into 1993, so Kurt had plenty of time to develop material.

I refer to the album as *Verse Chorus Verse* because that was its working title.

The thing is, many of the best songs on *In Utero* are actually older, pre-*Nevermind* material. Kurt was apparently having trouble writing new songs, even with substantial downtime. That was surely due to drugs but also to all the distractions of success and fame and the *Vanity Fair* debacle, not to mention mundane things like being married with a child and moving house a few times.

Also, as mentioned earlier, the plumbing disaster in his Los Angeles apartment destroyed a bunch of notebooks and cassette tapes. Who knows how many great songs were lost in the muck.

But Kurt's expressions of pain, which once tapped into the mass consciousness so perfectly, may now be less relevant. Just when the country is starting to feel optimistic again, here comes Kurt with a huge sack of woe. And the cause of his pain is no longer something that everyone can relate to. Most people are not familiar with the sensation of being publicly pilloried because of their drug use. Months before the album was released, it remained to be seen if Kurt had

translated his personal experience into a universal feeling, as he has done in the past.

Even if Kurt was howling about his own problems on *In Utero*, the music communicates on a much wider, deeper level. Decades later, it's still powerful because it does what all Nirvana music does: transcend pain by expressing it to an almost ecstatic degree. As social theorist Jacques Attali wrote in *Noise: A Political Economy of Music*, music is "the organization of controlled panic, the transformation of anxiety into joy, and of dissonance into harmony."

Kurt was a true rock believer: he once traded a fan a broken guitar for a new one, and on his busted-up guitar, he wrote: "If it's illegal to rock and roll, then throw my ass in jail." That was some dumb-ass catchphrase from the '70s or '80s—but deep down, Kurt meant it. That was one of the refreshing things about Nirvana: for a sardonic generation drowning in skepticism and irony, rock music was fast becoming a cynically created and promoted product that didn't move anybody at all, but Nirvana reminded people that it was possible to take back the catalyzing power of music and, by extension, maybe take back other things as well.

The day the band returned to Seattle after recording *In Utero*, Kurt gave me a cassette of the mixed but unmastered album so I could write about it for the book.

Kurt was really trusting me. Sometimes, unscrupulous people slipped advance tapes to radio stations, who then "premiered" the album before the release date. Or sometimes the tapes got bootlegged. An advance tape of the next Nirvana album was just radioactively hot.

The next day, Kurt called: could I bring him a copy of the new Lead Belly biography (*The Life and Legend of Leadbelly* by Charles Wolfe and Kip Lornell) I had told him about? Sure, although why was he asking me and not sending someone out to get it?

I didn't have a car, so Krist said he'd drive me. That evening, we pulled into the driveway of Kurt's house in Matthews Beach. I got out, but Krist stayed in the car. And then he did something odd: he took out a flashlight, held it next to his head like a miner's lamp, and shined it out the window. Later, I asked him why he did that. He said it was so Kurt couldn't see who was in the car. I guess Krist just wanted some distance from his bandmate after being cooped up with him for two weeks in rural Minnesota.

Kurt came to the door, grabbed the book out of my hand, and demanded, "Where's the tape?"

I said it was stashed in my travel bag at the place where I was staying.

"I thought you said you wouldn't let it out of your sight!" The tendons were sticking out of his neck, and he was kind of barking at me; he'd never raised his voice at me before. What was about to happen? It was tense, scary.

To be specific, the tape was in the laundry pocket of my bag, tucked in with some socks and underwear. Not even the people I was staying with knew I had an advance tape, and besides, they were not only dear friends of Kurt, but they had a vested interest in the tape not leaking.

He'd trusted me with that tape just the day before, but now, he was in an almost hysterical, paranoid panic. It turned out my nemesis at Nirvana's management company had heard about it and kicked up a fuss. I assured Kurt the tape was safe with me and that I would never in a million years violate his confidence. He sternly warned me not to leak the tape, then I walked back to the car, very rattled.

I got in the car and told Krist what happened. He didn't know I had an advance tape, but he totally understood and told me not to worry about it. Krist is such a good guy.

The next day, I got a fax at my hotel from my nemesis: "I can not [sic] stress to you enough just how inappropriate and dangerous this is." But it was neither inappropriate nor dangerous: I needed the music to write the book, and my nemesis was well aware that I knew and kept many other confidences about Nirvana. It was crazy.

Later that week, I was over at Krist's house when he gave a cassette tape of *In Utero* to Sonic Youth's Thurston Moore. That June, three months later, Sonic Youth played a show at the Academy, an old theatre in Times Square, with openers the Breeders and St. Johnny. Before Sonic Youth's set, some music played very, very quietly on the PA, almost inaudibly, at a truly ambient level. I realized it was *In Utero*. But nobody else in the audience knew that, months before its release, they were hearing one of the most eagerly anticipated albums of the decade.

It was a classic Thurston prank, part puckish and part a reflection of the band's fascination with celebrity—he was invisibly bragging that he had the tape. But it pissed me off: I'd gotten that angry scolding from Kurt for no good reason, and now, Thurston was playing the music *in public*.

The lyrics aren't as impressionistic this time—they're more straightforward, which is not to say they're as literal as "Sliver" or "Polly." A medical theme runs through most lyrics, expanding the vocabulary of "Drain You." Virtually every song contains some image of sickness and disease and over the course of the album, Kurt alludes to: sunburn, acne, cancer, bad posture, open sores, growing pains, hangovers, anemia, insomnia, constipation, indigestion. He finds this litany hilarious. "I'm always the last to realize things like that, like the way I used guns in the last record," he says. "I didn't mean to turn it into a concept album."

Long before *In Utero*, "Mexican Seafood," recorded in January 1988 at Reciprocal, established the blueprint for Kurt's morbid litany of ailments. As he sings in one verse,

"Now I vomit cum and diarrhea . . . With a toilet bowl full of a cloudy pus."

Once again, the record is a product of Kurt's opposing sensibilities. On the one hand, as Courtney says, "He chews bubblegum in his soul." But that deeply held pop instinct has an equal and opposite reaction. "Sometimes, he may be his own worst enemy in terms of thinking something is too hooky or too poppy," says Butch Vig. "I think maybe that's one of the reasons they wanted this new record to be really intensely brutal sounding."

The music reflects some powerful opposing forces in Kurt's life; the rage, frustration, and fear caused by his and Courtney's various predicaments and the equally powerful feelings of love and optimism inspired by his wife and child. That's why *In Utero* takes the manic-depressive musical mode of *Nevermind* to a whole new extreme. The Beatlesque "Dumb" happily coexists beside the all-out frenzied punk graffiti of "Milk It," while "All Apologies" is worlds away from the apoplectic "Scentless Apprentice." It's as if Kurt has given up trying to meld his punk and pop instincts into one harmonious whole. Forget it. This is war.

Amazingly, Kurt denies it to the bitter end. "I don't think of it as any harsher or any more emotional than the other two records," Kurt says. "I'm still equally as pissed off about the things that made me pissed off a few years ago. It's people doing evil things to other people for no reason. And I just want to beat the shit out of them. That's the bottom line. And all I can do is scream into a microphone instead," he adds, laughing at the futility of it all.

That is the perpetual state of the empathetic person: baffled and enraged at man's continual inhumanity to man. It's also the state of the person who has had inhumanity perpetrated on them. In Peter Bogdanovich's 2007 documentary *Tom Petty and the Heartbreakers: Runnin' Down a Dream*, Tom Petty reflected on his own upbringing, with a mother who died young and a verbally and physically abusive father: "When I look back on it," he said, "I sort of turned that anger into ambition. There was an extreme rage in me, that from time to time, would show its head through a lot of my life. Any sort of injustice enraged me. I just couldn't contain myself." And now think of how angry and ambitious Kurt was, and how outspoken he was about injustice—injustice against women, people of color, LGBT folks, and other oppressed groups. Maybe it was because he had a pretty good idea what it felt like. (Perhaps not coincidentally, Tom Petty also became a heroin addict.)

Let's not downplay the value of screaming into a microphone. One of the beauties of music is that it can convey things that are too difficult or too uncomfortable to say in mere words. For instance, people make mixtapes for their lovers or call in to radio stations and ask them to dedicate a song—because not everyone has the ability to express exactly how they feel. Kurt had that rare gift for expressing things that a lot of people feel but are unable or unwilling to say out loud or even articulate. And he did know that. He was just being self-deprecating there.

It was a really sweet moment when he said that bit about screaming into a microphone to me. I still smile when I read those words because that's when I knew that Kurt understood the effect his music had on the world.

Kurt had a little more time to work on the lyrics for *In Utero* than he did for *Bleach* and *Nevermind*. "I swear the lyrics I wrote on those last two albums were so rushed," Kurt says. "They were absolute last-minute, quick-fix, taken from poems. Most of the lines that I took from poems had to be rearranged to fit the song phonetically, so they don't have much personal meaning at all, really."

"There's definitely some pieces in there that reflect on my personal life," Kurt says, "but really, they aren't as personal as everyone thinks they are. I would *like* them to be more personal. The *emotions*, the songs themselves are personal. I can't do it—I've tried to write personally and it just doesn't seem to work. It would be too obvious. Some things that you could read in could fit into anyone's life that had any amount of pain at all. It's pretty cliché." Of course, it isn't cliché—it's just that once again, Kurt rightly won't reveal just how personal this album is, if only to encourage different interpretations.

Kurt worked on the lyrics, as he says later in the book, until "I like them enough to where I'm not embarrassed to sing them." In other words, until he thought they were *good*— and what you think is good is called your aesthetic, and your aesthetic is based on a particular set of principles and values. Kurt was intimately in touch with his aesthetic and doggedly clung to it, and that's why his music communicates so powerfully and clearly.

Just as he wrote lyrics in collage fashion, dipping into old notebooks for bits of ideas, maybe that was how Kurt put together *In Utero*—adding older songs into the mix because they collaged with the other new material to produce a strong overall impression of what he was feeling. (Or maybe it was because he hadn't written enough good new songs.) His explanation of "Rape Me" a few paragraphs ahead is a great example of this.

But even Dave acknowledges that the lyrics are loaded with personal meaning. "I guess just knowing what has happened in the past eight months and listening to

some of the lyrics and knowing what they're pertaining to is kind of strange," Dave says, "because there's a lot of spite, a lot of 'Fuck you' or 'I've been fucked over.' And a lot of lines that refer to money or legalities or babies. The hit I get off of that is very weird. It's intense but at the same time it just seems like Kurt feels like he's backed up against a wall and he's just going to scream his way out. A lot of what he has to say is related to a lot of the shit he's gone through." And it's not so much teen angst anymore. It's a whole different ball game: rock star angst. At the same time, the lyrics are similar to the first demo they'd done.

"There are a lot of lyrics to this record whereas with *Nevermind*, there was a verse and a chorus and it was usually repeated," says Dave. "But on this one, there's a lot of lyrics and with a lot of lyrics comes a lot to say. So you kind of figure that Kurt has something to say."

"Sometimes the lyrics on *In Utero* are really creepy," Krist told Keith Cameron in 2001. "I listen to 'em now and it's like—why didn't I hear that back then?" It's a recurring theme in this story: hindsight is 20/20.

"I really haven't had that exciting of a life," Kurt protests none too convincingly. "There are a lot of things I wish I would have done, instead of just sitting around and complaining about having a boring life. So I pretty much like to make it up—I'd rather tell a story about somebody else."

Kurt likes to talk about his "boring life," but there's no doubt that he's merely being disingenuous. For one thing, the year before the recording of *In Utero* was hardly Dullsville. "No, it wasn't," he says, "but if I were to write some songs expressing my anger toward the media, it would really be cliché and everyone's expecting that, so I'm not going to write a single fucking song, I'm not going to give anyone the pleasure. I would be easily able to write a song and it wouldn't be so obvious that I would come out and say 'Fuck the media.'"

"Rape Me" would seem to be about just that. "I wrote that before this happened, but it could easily fit in," he concedes. "It was actually about rape. That was what it initially was supposed to be about, but now I could definitely use it as an example of my life for the past six months or year, easily."

Kurt wrote *most* of "Rape Me" before he got caught in the media's glare—but not all of it. The version of the song on *Live at the Paramount*, from October 1991, didn't have a bridge—"My favorite inside source . . . Appreciate your concern / You'll always stink and burn." He surely added that in the wake of the *Vanity Fair* debacle. Now "Rape Me" described what he was going through. Now he could sing that song with a force that he couldn't have before. Now it definitely belonged on the album.

Here's another John Lennon reference: in 1968, Yoko Ono made a disturbing seventy-seven-minute conceptual art film called *Rape* in which a camera crew pursues an ostensibly random woman on the street; at first, she plays along, but the cameraman follows her relentlessly, invading her personal space. She becomes increasingly terrified, winding up lying on the floor of her apartment, hiding her face. It was, in the words of Beatle associate Peter Brown and Steve Gaines's 1983 book *The Love You Make: An Insiders Story of the Beatles*, "a metaphor for the media's treatment of [Ono and Lennon]." Not long after the film was made, Lennon and Ono entered into a heroin cocoon together to shelter from the media's merciless intrusions and scorn.

Kurt had written "Rape Me" on an acoustic guitar at the Oakwood as they were starting to mix *Nevermind*. Although the song addresses an issue that Kurt has long felt strongly about, it has certainly taken on a new cast since the savaging he and Courtney endured. It seems to be addressed to all the journalists who assailed the couple, all the fans who bothered Kurt for his autograph, all the people who wanted to squeeze whatever they could out of Kurt and the band without thinking about the personal toll it was taking. "Yeah, it could, it definitely could," he says.

The song is perhaps the ultimate statement of resignation from someone who's been beaten so badly already that it doesn't matter anymore. "Rape me, my friend" is an invitation to a public that doesn't realize its adoration is hurting its object. "I'm not the only one," Kurt wails, meaning Courtney and Frances, too. The "Teen Spirit" reference in the opening guitar strum is no accident. Like the chorus of "In Bloom," it packs a powerfully ironic musical joke—"Teen Spirit," after all, is the song that started the whole thing.

This reminds me of something in Jon Savage's excellent Joy Division oral history *This Searing Light, the Sun and Everything Else*. The band's singer Ian Curtis hanged himself in 1980, and the incident underscored the fact that genius worship can be toxic: as Curtis's widow observed, "People admired him for the things that were destroying him."

That wasn't the first time Kurt used that same chord shape and progression. But he had to be aware of the similarity; the intro wasn't on an early demo and it was clearly intended to heighten the self-referential force of the song.

"My favorite inside source," Kurt sings on the bridge, "Appreciate your concern / You'll always stink and burn." The lines are a not so opaque reference to the manager of a Seattle band, who patronized Kurt about his addiction and whom

the Cobains believe was a key anonymous interviewee for the *Vanity Fair* article. They even sent the manager a Christmas card last year that read, "To our favorite inside source."

Kurt says that "Milk It" is a really good example of the direction the band had been moving toward in the six months before recording. "We've been trying to write new wave songs," he says, "something that's aggressive and weird and experimental but still has . . . It's still not going any farther out of the boundaries than we've gone before but it's *different*. It's a really good mixture of sounding like a punk rock band yet being melodic—or at least memorable."

The thing is, "Milk It" bears an all-too-close resemblance to a song from the Melvins' fantastic 1991 album *Bullhead*. And the Melvins' Buzz Osborne agreed: "Of course I like this song!" he told MP3.com in 2011. "Of course I like it, because it's a total, TOTAL ripoff of a song I wrote called 'It's Shoved.'" That kind of thing speaks of creative drought.

The song contains yet another metaphor for a codependent relationship, this time expressed in even more chilling terms. "I have my own pet virus," Kurt sings, his voice trembling with dread, "Her milk is my shit, my shit is her milk." The song explodes into the chorus, "Doll steak, test meat," at once nonsensical and hellish, delivered in bursts of hysterical rage.

"I just tried to use a medical theme—viruses and organisms and stuff," Kurt says of the lyrics. "Just wordplay, images." But surely it's not "just wordplay, images"—Kurt couldn't just sing a page out of the phone book with the same passion and conviction. "Yeah, I could," he insists. "That's practically what it is. That's what those lyrics *are*. But I think they're written cleverly enough, I like them enough to where I'm not embarrassed to sing them. In general, it's about my battle with things that piss me off. And that's the theme of the whole album— with every album I do, actually."

"Scentless Apprentice" came together during the rehearsals for the album and marks a watershed for the band. First, Dave showed Kurt the guitar riff which forms the backbone of the song. "It was such a cliché grunge Tad riff that I was reluctant to even jam on it," Kurt says frankly. "But I just decided to write a song with that just to make him feel better, to tell you the truth, and it turned out really cool." Kurt brought in the ascending hook line and Chris devised the second section and then Kurt arranged it all. It was the most collaborative song the band has ever done.

"I think most of the reason that song sounds good is because of the singing style and the guitar parts that I do over the top of the basic rhythm," Kurt says.

"But hell, that was great—he came up with the beginning of the song and we worked off of that and that was really different. We've never done that before." They split the music royalties evenly.

You just have to chuckle a little bit at Kurt's condescension: basically, "He made up this cliché riff and just to make him feel better I managed to turn it into something cool." But Kurt was legitimately looking for new ways to make music: not just thinking outside the verse-chorus-verse paradigm but also in terms of process. The idea was to keep surprising and challenging himself in much the same way the cut-up method did.

At an MTV interview on September 24, 1993, Kurt said of "Scentless Apprentice," "Dave came up with the drum beat . . ."

"And the riff," Krist interjected, bowing his head in an interesting show of body language.

"And then he showed me the riff," Kurt continued. And at that moment, Dave rubbed his thumb and forefinger together in the universal sign for money—the publishing contretemps was apparently still fresh in his mind.

"I was thinking, this is kind of boneheaded," Kurt said. "And we worked on it and it turned out great." Talk about microaggression.

It's ironic that Kurt dismissed it as "a cliché grunge Tad riff"—five years earlier, when Kurt first showed "School" to Krist, "I said, 'Oh my god, that is the most Seattle fucking riff I'd heard in my life,'" Krist recalled to *Guitar World* in 2001. "It was the quintessential grunge song."

"Scentless Apprentice" was inspired by Patrick Süskind's 1986 novel *Perfume*, about a maniacal perfume maker in pre-Revolutionary France who has no scent, yet his acute sense of smell alienates him from society. Perhaps this is a character Kurt can relate to. "Yeah, more so a few years ago," he says. "I felt like that guy a lot. I just wanted to be as far away from people as I could—their smells disgust me. The scent of human."

Although it's an identical sentiment, the hysterically screamed chorus of the song—"Go away, go away"—makes the raw wails of "Stay Away" sound mighty tame in comparison.

The main riff is indeed pretty meat-and-potatoes but that bone-simple ascending vocal/guitar line redeems everything. In effect, Kurt devised a hook that clinches the song. Kurt was a Public Enemy fan—maybe he borrowed that hook from the squealing, upward saxophone glissando in PE's "Rebel Without a Pause."

It was ingenious of Albini to remove all the reverb on the vocal and add distortion as Kurt screams "go away"—it suddenly sounds like he's imprisoned in a small closet full of coats and blankets, just horrific.

The song is basically a recap of *Perfume*—a ripping read, by the way—but, as Kurt acknowledged, it's impossible not to read the outcast antihero of the book as a stand-in for Kurt. The line "electrolytes smell like semen" seems like a non sequitur but it's still apt olfactory imagery, and as someone who had been admitted to the emergency room several times, Kurt might well have been familiar with the smell of electrolytes.

In the final verse the narrator imagines himself dead, his corpse fertilizing the soil for mushrooms; the gases from his decomposing body turn into perfume. "You can't fire me because I quit," he adds. ("If there's one line in any song that gives me the chills," Dave told *Mojo* many years later, "it's that one.") And then the final line: "Throw me in the fire and I won't throw a fit" seems to be another reference to executing witches. But is it a declaration of defiance, that he won't let his tormentors see him writhe? Or is it a declaration of resignation, that he'll willingly be incinerated?

Kurt explains "Heart-Shaped Box" by saying, "Every time I see documentaries or infomercials about little kids with cancer I just freak out. It affects me on the highest emotional level, more than anything else on television. Anytime I think about it, it makes me sadder than anything than I can think of. Whenever I see these little bald kids . . ." He stops and pauses for half a minute as his face reddens and his eyes well up with tears. "It's just really sad," he finally manages to say.

That was the only time I saw Kurt cry. We were sitting in his living room, doing an interview in front of a TV with the sound off, as it usually was around that house. A commercial for a childhood cancer charity came on, with footage of little bald kids gazing into the camera. After he said those words, Kurt began weeping.

That moment put a few things into focus. Here was a profoundly sensitive person, and that sensitivity was key to what made him such a great artist. Also, he cherished the blithe bliss of childhood and couldn't bear the thought that terminally ill children were cruelly deprived of that all-too-fleeting moment in life. I also realized that he was comfortable enough with me that he could cry.

What should I do? Comforting him would have been crossing a professional line, so I paused the tape recorder and averted my gaze toward the TV, pretending to be interested in whatever was on the screen, while Kurt composed himself. After a few moments, I asked him if he wanted to keep talking, and he said yes, so we continued the interview. But something had changed between us. I just really felt for the guy.

Things That Piss Me Off

Kurt came up with "Heart-Shaped Box" at the Spaulding apartment, where Courtney had laid out her extensive collection of heart-shaped candy boxes in the front room. Kurt has always liked heart-shaped boxes, too, but he insists they don't have too much to do with the song. "Most of the lines in it are just from [different] poems anyway," he says. "I just thought they painted a good picture, every line. But the basic idea of the song is about little kids with cancer."

He forgot about the song for a while, then picked it up again at the Hollywood Hills apartment. The band tried it out several times but nothing came of it. "I was just so tired of them relying on me to come up with everything all the time," Kurt says. "During those practices, I was trying to wait for Chris and Dave to come up with something but it just turned into noise all the time." But one day, they were jamming on some ideas when Kurt decided to give the song one last try. "I just all of a sudden wrote the whole song as we were jamming on it," he says. "I came up with the vocal style instantly and it just all flowed out real fast. We finally realized that it was a good song."

Despite Kurt's emotional description, the song seems not to be about little bald-headed kids with cancer at all. It seems to be about Courtney. "Meat-eating orchids forgive no one just yet" and "I wish I could eat your cancer when you turn black" would appear to refer to his wife's storm-cloud disposition while lines like "Throw down your umbilical noose so I can climb right back" and being "locked inside your heart-shaped box" describe an almost horrific dependency. But the biting sarcasm in the chorus shows signs of an imminent psychological jailbreak—"Hey, I've got a new complaint," Kurt sings, "Forever in debt to your priceless advice."

Maybe the "forever in debt to your priceless advice" line isn't about Courtney—maybe it's about *everybody* who gave him advice he didn't ask for, which probably happens a lot when you're famous.

Kurt does project—and cultivate—an air of childlike vulnerability and naïveté which can coax others to coddle him. The K Records ethos may be an inspiration for that air, but it may also be a way of rationalizing it. The members of the band, and Kurt very much in particular, have become very dependent on others to insulate them from the realities of their career, attracting the inevitable coterie of hangers-on from the press, radio, and other media who somehow feel charged to "protect" the band, proud of their possession of closely held secrets, sure they're helping Kurt by shielding him from the cold, cruel world. Then again, Kurt has always had someone who would take care of him, from Wendy to Tracy to Chris and Dave to Courtney.

That was a two-way street, obviously—to widely varying degrees, the band members enabled it. After all, they were only human, and it's hard to say no when someone comes along and gives you a sympathetic ear in the middle of a hurricane and they're really helpful, always there when you need them, never asking anything for themselves. And then one day you wake up and realize you've forgotten how to order takeout.

To a certain extent, I was one of those people: for a time, I had Kurt's trust and friendship, as well as Krist's, and it was easy to be intoxicated by that. Being accepted into such an intensely rarefied circle *is* intoxicating—there's no better word for it because not only does it make you feel a sort of high, it makes you do things you might not have done if you were sober. And it's like an addiction, too: not just because you'll sacrifice other aspects of your life in order to maintain it but because of how bad you feel when it's suddenly gone.

"Serve the Servants" is a typical smattering of different themes. One of them is the aftermath of Nirvanamania, beginning with the opening lines, "Teenage angst has paid off well / Now I'm bored and old." "That's obviously the state I feel right now," Kurt says. "Not really, but I may as well make some sarcastic comment on the phenomenon of Nirvana." "Self-appointed judges judge more than they have sold"— people who criticize Kurt and the band without knowing what it's like to be in their position. The "Get Courtney" movement also makes another appearance—"If she floats then she is not a witch." The line refers to a test used to see if someone was a witch— the town wise men would weigh down the hapless suspect with rocks and throw her in a well. If she sank, she wasn't a witch. Unfortunately, she was also now dead.

"Serve the Servants" also contains a very direct and personal message to Don Cobain that will be heard from Iceland to Australia, from Los Angeles to London. "I tried hard to have a father / but instead I had a dad / I just want you to know that I don't hate you anymore / There is nothing I could say that I haven't thought before." The fourth line is a rather cruel thing to say—that Kurt won't tell his father what he really thinks of him. The lines got put in at the last minute. "They just happened to fit really well," says Kurt.

Kurt was withholding dialogue with his father, not telling him how he felt, and just expecting him to intuit it, as he had with so many other people in his life.

Those lines closely recall what Kurt said earlier in the book: "I never felt like I really had a father." They also recall what Don Cobain said earlier, too: "He's like me—don't say anything and maybe it'll disappear or something. And don't explain."

Along with some photos he sent me, Don included a letter he wanted me to give to Kurt. I didn't read it and just duly passed it along and never heard anything about it again. I guess Don didn't even know how to contact his son. But he did try to reach out. It was just heartbreaking.

"I just want him to know that, that I don't have anything against him anymore. But I just don't want to talk to him because I don't have anything to share with him. I'm sure that would probably really upset him, but that's just the way it is.

"But that's not what the song was originally about," Kurt says. "I mean, none of the songs are about anything when I write them. That's pretty much one of the only things that would be personally tied with me."

"The legendary divorce is such a bore," he adds at the end of the chorus. Kurt is growing tired of the well-publicized idea that his parents' divorce made a traumatic impact on his life. "It's nothing that's amazing or anything new, that's for sure," he says. "I'm a product of a spoiled America. Think of how much worse my family life could be if I grew up in a depression or something. There are so many worse things than a divorce. I've just been brooding and bellyaching about something I couldn't have, which is a family, a solid family unit, for too long. I've grown out of it now. I'm glad that I could share it with kids who have had the same experiences, but overall it's sad that if two people choose to marry and have children that they can't at least get along. It amazes me that people who think they're in love with one another can't even have enough courtesy to their children to talk to one another civilly when they see each other even once in a while when they pick the kids up from the visit. That's sad, but it's not more my story than it is anyone else's."

The first thing you hear on *In Utero* is Dave counting in the song by clicking his sticks together—something that's usually edited out on a commercial album—immediately serving notice that this is a raw, authentic recording. And then there's a gigantic dissonant chord on the guitar, a gnarly declaration of chaos. From the opening moments of the record, it's made abundantly clear: this is not going to be like *Nevermind*.

Despite Kurt's earlier protestations, "Serve the Servants" is absolutely autobiographical: he told me that the phrase "serve the servants" referred to feeling obligated to do whatever "the grown-ups" and other music industry types asked (or forced) him to do—such as playing the 1992 Reading Festival and the MTV Video Music Awards and probably a million other things, large and small. He was paying these people to serve him, not the other way around.

"Serve the Servants" covers Kurt's ambivalence about fame, media persecution of Courtney, his difficult childhood, his poor relationship with his father, the relentless scrutiny of his personal life. The song is an open book.

But Kurt was right: divorce *was* a lot of people's story. And he could communicate that feeling in a way that a lot of people understood.

It's true that there are lots of worse things than having divorced parents. But that doesn't mean it's not harmful. Children of divorce can experience all kinds of social, psychological, academic, economic, and even physical deficits. In his suicide note, Kurt pretty much cited his parents' divorce as a crucial turning point in his life: "Since the age of seven"—when they began to split—"I've become hateful towards all humans in general."

###

Kurt tended toward lengthy titles for the new songs, basically as a reaction against the way so many so-called "alternative" bands use one-word titles for song and album titles. "It's a cop-out," says the guy who named his first three albums *Bleach*, *Nevermind*, and *Incesticide*. "Ooooh, just think of the irony in this word, 'cartoon,'" he mocks. "There are so many angles on it."

It really was a thing at the time: there was Stone Temple Pilots' *Core*, Alice in Chains' *Dirt*, Sonic Youth's *Dirty*, Pearl Jam's *Ten*, Smashing Pumpkins' *Gish*, Helmet's *Meantime*, all six Jesus Lizard albums from *Head* to *Blue*, and countless others.

Then there were all the one-syllable band names: Tar, TAD, Cows, Paw, Pond, Scrawl, Mule, Slint, Seam, Bush, Clutch, Gaunt, Hum, Dwarves, and, of course, Hole, among many others. A couple of years later, the *Onion* duly immortalized the phenomenon with the headline: "Hip New Alternative Band Has One-Word, One-Syllable Name."

Hence "Frances Farmer Will Have Her Revenge on Seattle," written in honor of the Cobains' patron martyr, many of whose persecutors remain in Seattle to this day. "In her false witness / We hope you're still with us" is a clear message to the fans about the Hirschberg piece in *Vanity Fair*, while the next line, "To see if they float or drown," repeats the witch-test imagery in "Serve the Servants." The song ends on a note close to Kurt's heart—revenge. "She'll come back as fire / To burn all the liars / And leave a blanket of ash on the ground."

"I guess that's my way of letting the world know that bureaucracy is everywhere and it can happen to anybody and it's a really evil thing," Kurt says. "The story of Frances Farmer is so sad and it can happen to anybody and it almost felt at a time that it was happening to us, so there is a little personal part but it's mainly just exposing the Frances Farmer story to people.

"Seattle is supposedly this perfect, utopic place," says Kurt. "Judges and heads of state were part of this conspiracy to put her in a mental institution, give her a lobotomy, and she was gang raped every night she was there and she had to eat her own shit and she was branded a Communist because she wrote a poem when she was fourteen entitled 'God Is Dead.' They just fucked with her all the time. From the time she was fourteen to when she was a star, they just constantly had her arrested for no reason and totally ruined her reputation by writing right wing lies in magazines and newspapers and stuff and it turned her insane, turned her into a barbiturate addict and alcoholic and she got a lobotomy and ended up being a maid at a Four Seasons and eventually died. There are a lot of very important people in Seattle involved in that conspiracy and they're still alive today, sitting in their nice fucking houses."

Although Farmer's tale is even more dire than Kurt and Courtney's, their stories are quite similar. "I expect a lot of these titles and little lines in some of the songs to be read as totally personal," Kurt says, "but there are other angles on them, too. I would rather focus on the Frances Farmer story; it just so happens that there are similar things involved in our story."

Kurt seemed to be a little fascinated with coprophilia: there's that line in "Milk It" ("Her milk is my shit, my shit is her milk") and then his ad-libbed line at the São Paulo show: "I could shit on stage / You would eat it up." Or a few pages from now, when he says of his record label, "They're going to eat my shit." Earlier in this book, Kurt says of some minders who lost track of him and Courtney, "They were eating their shit, they were so afraid of what was going to happen." This from the fellow who furtively said "poo-doo!" into the tape recorder as a four-year-old and later titled his first demo tape *Fecal Matter*. In his journals, Kurt decried journalists who "insist on coming up with a second rate freudian evaluation on my lyrics." But it was difficult to resist that tack when he served up the poo-poo on a platter.

Kurt recommended that I read *Shadowland*, William Arnold's 1978 biography of Frances Farmer; it was largely the basis for this song, not to mention the basis for Kurt's rage about Farmer's fate in general. The book opens with a distressing scene of Farmer getting a lobotomy. The thing is, it's since been discredited that Farmer had a lobotomy; in fact, much of *Shadowland* has been debunked, and the author himself eventually admitted that it was "fictionalized." The book is now considered a "biographical novel." Consequently, very little of what Kurt says here about Farmer is actually true.

But it's easy to see why the true parts of Frances Farmer's life story resonated with Kurt and Courtney. An acclaimed stage and film actress in the mid '30s through the early '40s, Farmer, a Seattle native, was an intelligent, strong-willed woman who battled with writers, producers, and directors over the flimsy roles she was given—and so she was deemed "difficult." And she paid dearly for it.

Farmer was also an alcoholic who abused amphetamines. In 1942 she was arrested for drunk driving and then for a parole violation related to the DUI. Soon she was diagnosed as a schizophrenic—which she disputed—and her mother committed her to mental hospitals through most of the '40s, a hellish experience, particularly since she was sent to the violent prisoners' ward. After Farmer was released in 1950, she went back to Seattle and worked for a short time at the city's famous Olympic Hotel (which Kurt did rightly identify as part of the Four Seasons chain at the time). Later, she moved to Indianapolis and hosted a popular daily afternoon movie show on local television. She died in 1970, only fifty-six years old.

The similarities with Courtney are obvious but Kurt could surely relate to Farmer, too. As one synopsis of the 1982 biopic *Frances* put it, "Torn between new-found success and intense feelings that she does not deserve the riches and fame she gains from the phoniness of Hollywood, Frances butts heads with studio executives."

In 1958 on the TV show *This Is Your Life*, Farmer explained her psychological collapse: "So much had happened to me when I became first successful as an actress, many agonizing decisions arose that I had to make and I just wasn't mature enough and didn't have time enough to be able to make them without time and peace to think, and I didn't have it, and I had a nervous breakdown." That sounds familiar, too.

"I miss the comfort in being sad"—Kurt is not used to happiness, a condition which he turned into a whole song in "Dumb."

Kurt wrote the main outlines of the Beatlesque "Dumb" during the summer of 1990, just before the band signed with Geffen and debuted it on Calvin Johnson's KAOS radio program that fall. "I think I'm dumb or maybe just happy," Kurt sings. "I just tried to use some confusion theme," he says. It's just interesting that being happy would prove confusing.

"Kurt Cobain will never find an inner peace," wrote Amy Raphael in a September 1993 *Face* magazine profile of the band. "He will always be leaning on the self-destruct button in a way that's become almost masochistic. Like he's been on the edge for so long that he's addicted to hatred, misery and frustration."

Few of Kurt's lyrics capture that truth any better than "I miss the comfort in being sad." Being depressed can become one's default state and so routine, so familiar, that it's difficult to cope with feeling any other way. "I miss the comfort in being sad" is one of the most poignant lines Kurt ever wrote.

Although it was written long before the fact, the verse which goes "My heart is broke but I have some glue / Help me inhale and mend it with you / We'll float

around and hang out on clouds / Then we'll come down and have a hangover" makes for a good synopsis of his and Courtney's months in the drug wilderness; distraught after breaking up with Tobi, he sought refuge in heroin with Courtney, then paid the consequences afterward.

Those were actually *years* in the drug wilderness.

The eagle-eared will notice that the song's chords are similar to those of "Polly."

Kurt also wrote the anthemic "Pennyroyal Tea" in the apartment on Pear Street during the bleak winter of 1990, after the band signed. "Dave and I were screwing around on a four-track and I wrote that song in about thirty seconds," says Kurt. "And I sat down for like a half an hour and wrote the lyrics and then we recorded it."

Pennyroyal is an herb known for its medicinal properties, one of which is an abortive, but only in lethal doses. "I thought that was a cool image," says Kurt. "I've known girls who tried to drink it because they thought they were pregnant. It's a cleansing theme where I'm trying to get all my bad evil spirits out of me and drinking pennyroyal tea would cleanse that away. You have to drink gallons of it and I heard it doesn't work very well. I've never found herbs to ever work for me—anything. Ginseng and any of that other shit is all a bunch of hippie left-wing fascist propaganda."

The song sure seems to be another psychological autobiography. The narrator bemoans his "very bad posture" (recall Kurt's scoliosis), indulges in self-recrimination, takes various medicines to deal with stomach ailments—and wants to "still the life inside of me" while yearning for a life in the "afterworld."

Kurt thought "Pennyroyal Tea" could be a hit. It had been scheduled to be the next single from *In Utero*, but DGC canceled it after his death. Maybe it was because of the song's death-haunted imagery. Or maybe it was because of the title of one of the single's B-sides: "I Hate Myself and I Want to Die."

"Very Ape" used to have the working title, "Perky New Wave Number." "I really didn't have any idea what the song is about," Kurt says. "It's kind of an attack on men in a way and people that have flaws in their personality and they're real manly and macho." The "King of Illiterature" line is probably a reference to the way Courtney chides Kurt about not being well read.

Remember Los Brujos, the band who opened for Nirvana at the stadium show in Argentina? At the time, they had an Argentinian hit with "Kanishka." Compare that song with "Very Ape." It's like what Kurt did with "Scentless Apprentice" and "Milk It," and probably with "Radio Friendly Unit Shifter," which resembles Public Image's 1978 "Annalisa": adapt someone else's riff and put your own spin on it. That's nothing new in music, but here it seems like another instance of someone who apparently didn't have enough new ideas.

It might seem peculiar that someone wouldn't know what one of their own songs was about, but maybe Kurt sincerely didn't know. Or maybe he just didn't want to say. Admittedly, it's a difficult song to parse except to note that it seems to be about embodying opposites—the singer is "buried in contradictionary lies" and is both "very ape" and "very nice," kind of like his music. And himself.

A couple of lines apparently refer to his provincial background. "I'm too busy acting like I'm not naïve" seems to be a sarcastic swipe at himself and his awe of hipsters. "I take pride as the king of illiterature" recalls Kurt's long-standing self-consciousness about not being as cultured as he wanted to be.

"Out of the ground, into the sky / Out of the sky, into the dirt" might be a typical non sequitur, just one of those elemental images that Kurt could drop into a song and imbue with emotional impact. But it does bring to mind a pop Icarus: the trajectory of an ordinary person who flies too high into the cultural stratosphere and then fatally crashes to earth.

"Contradictionary" and "illiterature" are typical examples of Kurt's zest for portmanteau, or combining two words into one. Other examples: the album title *Incesticide* and song titles such as "Sappy" (Kurt's combination of "sad" and "happy"), "Anorexorcist," "Vendetagainst," "Erectum," and (kind of) "Aero Zeppelin." Even Kurt and Courtney themselves got portmanteau'd as "Kurtney." Portmanteau is a kind of collage, yet another example of it in Kurt's art.

On the face of it, "Tourette's" has nothing to do with anything. "I just babbled," Kurt says. "I didn't make any sentences or any words, I just screamed." An early lyric sheet for the song merely printed the words "Fuck shit piss." But the title recalls something Kurt said about all the negative press he had been getting. "All my life, I've had a bad attitude and it does me no good to become even more of a bitter person because of stuff like this," he said. "I just don't know how I can do it. I was starting to get a good attitude again and I'd been validated as a musician and a songwriter and everything and all of a sudden I'm this massive scapegoat. I have this attitude that makes me look even more like an asshole. There's a big threat of me turning into this crazy street person. Some eighty-year-old guy with Tourette's syndrome, cursing his head off, telling the whole world they're fucked."

As we've seen, Kurt was fascinated by mental disorders. Tourette's syndrome is a neurological condition characterized by physical or verbal tics, sometimes obscenities.

Maybe the song implies that he would eventually be driven to madness, incapable of anything but spouting profanity, but Kurt was probably annoyed by the fun some critics made of his indistinct vocals and impressionistic lyrics. So "Tourette's" could well be another example of two of Kurt's tendencies: reacting to his press (as in "Token Eastern Song") and fending off attacks on himself by exaggerating them to the point of absurdity. Maybe the artistic conceit of "Tourette's" was that, rather than carefully composed collages of words meticulously matched to the music, Kurt's lyrics were really just the product of a neurological disorder.

But the song is not his best work, and Kurt knew it—see next paragraph.

The title of "Radio Friendly Unit Shifter" is obviously a reference to _Nevermind_. "A blanket acned with cigarette burns" harks back to the scene at the Spaulding apartment, while "Use just once and destroy / Invasion of our piracy" is yet another reference to harassment by both a fickle public and a hostile, invasive press. Yet even Kurt acknowledges that the song is a throwaway. "It could have been better," he says. "I know we could have had a few better songs on the album."

As Courtney says earlier in this book, "We went through a lot of blankets because you keep dropping your cigarette—it's pretty gross. I threw all those blankets out."

"Use just once and destroy" is a variation on "Use once and destroy," which is printed on syringes to prevent disease transmission from used or discarded needles—so that's partly a drug reference as well as a metaphor for the way the media treats some celebrities as disposable.

The song does contain the very plaintive, poignant lines "I do not want what I have got" and "What is wrong with me?" but the song is, let's face it, filler, and the lyrics are more of a hodgepodge than most—although "Find, find your place / Speak, speak the truth" is solid advice even if Kurt never really achieved the former and didn't always do the latter.

###

Surely the confessional lyrics of "All Apologies" have some personal meaning for Kurt. "It really doesn't have any relevance at all," he says, as usual. "The song isn't about anything, really." He did dedicate the song to Frances and Courtney onstage at Reading in 1992, though. "I like to think that that song is for them, but the words really don't fit in relation to us. I wrote it for them but none of the lyrics really expose anything. The feeling does, but not the lyrics." The feeling, Kurt says, is "Peaceful, happy, comfort—just happy happiness." And the way Kurt

sings "Yeah, yeah, yeah, yeah" after the second chorus, it's hard not to feel the same thing.

"All Apologies" features cello, an instrument that had started to become a staple of alternative rock even before Nirvana used it on "Something in the Way." It may well have started with R.E.M.'s 1988 major label debut *Green*, then former Hüsker Dü singer-guitarist Bob Mould's album *Workbook* from the following year. (Both records featured cello player Jane Scarpantoni, who became the go-to rock cellist of the '90s and beyond.) After *In Utero* and *Nirvana Unplugged*, the cello became ubiquitous in '90s alternative rock, featured by Therapy?, the Beastie Boys, Helmet, Silverchair, Fuel, Luna, Soul Asylum, the Cranberries, Bush, and many more.

It's interesting that Kurt differentiated between the "feeling" of a song and the literal sense of its lyrics. For him, they weren't necessarily the same thing. "Words suck," Kurt wrote in his journals. "I mean, every thing has been said. . . . WORDS aren't as important as the energy derived from music, especially live. . . . Music is ENERGY. A mood, atmosphere. FEELING."

Two of Kurt's favorite bands, R.E.M. and the Pixies, had famously enigmatic yet evocative lyrics. He was on the same page as R.E.M. bassist Mike Mills, who told NPR in 2008, "I don't always probe too deeply into the lyrics. I don't need to. As long as they take me somewhere and they make me excited to play the song, that's really all I need."

"I personally don't care what my favourite bands' music is about," Kurt told *Melody Maker*'s Ann Scanlon on the bus ride to the Reading Festival in 1991. "I mean, they could be speaking in tongues and it wouldn't matter to me as long as it sounds good."

In fact, another master of nonlinear lyrics named one of his band's albums *Speaking in Tongues* for that very reason. "As long as the words aren't crap, it's the musicality of the words that hits you first," David Byrne told *Uncut* in December 2006. "If I'm writing words, I try to say something, but I realise that it almost doesn't matter. If you can say something, that's an extra bonus." I think Kurt would have agreed. He was mostly trying for something synergistic, weighing the overall *feeling* of the combination of word meanings, word sounds, and music. It's why nonsense lines like "aqua seafoam shame" and "all in all is all we are" work in this song, and even the meaningless words have a certain power: those "yeah-yeah-yeahs" at the end of the chorus—not ad-libbed but expressly written into the lyrics—tap into an entire '60s-worth of "yeah-yeah-yeahs," from "She Loves You" to "Helter Skelter."

"I wish I was like you, easily amused" seems to key into the same sentiment as "Dumb."

In an early draft, probably written circa 1990, "All Apologies" certainly sounds like a breakup song. And the recorded version *still* sounds like a breakup song, reworked, recycled, and repurposed for a different relationship: "everything's my fault / I'll take all the blame / aqua seafoam shame." He's saying, true to character, that he doesn't want a confrontation and that he's ashamed of how things turned out.

It could be that Kurt didn't get around to finishing the lyrics by the time they recorded the song and "aqua seafoam shame" was just a placeholder for the vowel and consonant sounds, as well as the meter, that Kurt wanted for the line. Or maybe, as stated earlier, "aqua seafoam" is an oblique reference to the typically pastel confines of a hospital or rehab center.

"Choking on the ashes of her enemy" is a pretty clear reference to Courtney—quasi-biblical imagery of incinerated foes, as in "Gallons of Rubbing Alcohol Flow Through the Strip" and "Frances Farmer Will Have Her Revenge on Seattle."

So yes, "All Apologies" may have been for Courtney and Frances, but not in the way it may have seemed. It may have been a farewell.

"I always manage to write a couple of happy songs," he says, "but then there are lots of neutral songs, too, that sound angry but really aren't anything."

So an angry sound is just a starting point, a status quo. Kurt laughs when it's suggested that his natural state is one of agitation. Not unlike the music of Dinosaur Jr's J Mascis, whose laid-back vocal persona exists against a constant backdrop of angry, teeming distortion. "That's not really a character he plays—he *is* that person," says Kurt. "God, I wish I could get away with that because I've always thought I was really close to J Mascis as a person, personality-wise—just quiet and talking with a cigarette voice, but I couldn't sing like that. I have a different side to me that's really hyperactive."

I once blurted out to Dave the dumb idea that it must feel good to get his aggressions out on the drums. But, as he says in this book, it wasn't about aggression—hitting the drums ferociously hard was just fun and made him feel happy. Brutal music was just Nirvana's default mode, the music they were raised on, as it was for so many of their peers, which is how they could come up with an indisputably hard rocker and call it "Lounge Act" because they thought it sounded like "a lounge song like some bar band would play."

Like Mascis, Kurt appears passive, yet both control virtually every aspect of their band's music and image. It galls Kurt to realize that most people aren't conscious of this. "I just can't believe that people wouldn't listen to this music and think a little bit more highly of me than they do," he says. "I come up with every idea for everything we do, practically. Everything. It's mind-boggling and it's a lot of pressure. It just pisses me off to see on the back of the *Bleach* album, 'art direction by Lisa Orth' and everyone thinks that Lisa Orth came up with that picture and the idea and the way it was all set up. I came up with the whole idea and they get credit for it. I don't need it to feed my ego, I just want people to know that I can do other things than just the music."

###

Originally, the album was going to be called *I Hate Myself and I Want to Die*. Ever since the Australian tour, the phrase had been Kurt's standard answer whenever someone asked him how he was doing. After a few weeks, the title was ruled out. "That's pushing it too much," Chris says. "Kids would commit suicide and we'd get sued." Kurt meant the title as a joke. "I'm tired of taking this band so seriously and everyone else taking it so seriously and trying to read into things," he said. "Basically that's what all our songs are about—confusion and I hate myself and I don't want to live, so I thought it was really appropriate."

That comeback, "I hate myself and I want to die," is a lot like Kurt's answer earlier in the book when Nirvana's manager asked him, "What the fuck are you moping about?" and Kurt replied, "I'm *awake*, aren't I?" As ever, the clues were hiding in plain sight.

Kurt had apparently changed his mind about what his songs were about: they weren't, as he said earlier in this book, "all basically saying the same thing: I have this conflict between good and evil and man and woman and that's about it." Now they were mainly about self-hatred.

Later, Kurt tried to dismiss the title as a joke about himself, telling *Rolling Stone* when he was interviewed in October 1993, "It was totally satirical, making fun of ourselves. I'm thought of as this pissy, complaining, freaked-out schizophrenic who wants to kill himself all the time. 'He isn't satisfied with anything.' And I thought it was a funny title."

"That [title] pretty much defines our band," Kurt continued. "It's satirical and it's serious at the same time." Granted, being simultaneously satirical and serious is a good summation of a wide swathe of '90s youth culture. But he probably just realized that he'd given away too much with that title and was now just trying to cover his tracks. It was really yet another example of Kurt trying to smokescreen the truth by spoofing it.

There's no apparent humor, ironic or otherwise, in the song of the same name, recorded during the *In Utero* sessions. It repeats now-familiar masochistic imagery: "Even if you have a cold still / You can cough on me again / I still haven't had my full fill." The character in the song endures all sorts of abuse and victimhood. And then there's that disturbing repeated refrain: "End it someday."

Allegedly, "I Hate Myself and I Want to Die" was left off *In Utero* because, as Kurt told journalist Jim DeRogatis, it would have made it seem like "it's nothing but a noise record." "It was just such a typical, boring song," he continued. "We could write that song in our sleep. There was no point to putting it on the record." But one can say with almost objective certainty that it's still better than several songs on *In Utero*. And it's difficult to believe his dismissal of the song: obviously, at one point he thought enough of it that he not only wanted to include it on the record, he wanted to make it the title track of the album.

Or maybe he got talked out of it on legal or moral grounds. Krist's worries about being sued had some very serious precedent. Among other things, he was surely alluding to an infamous 1990 lawsuit—just three years earlier—against Judas Priest that claimed that the band's 1978 album *Stained Class* album contained subliminal messages that caused two young Nevada men to enter into a fatal suicide pact. The judge dismissed the case, but not before the incident caused the band a lot of stress, profound heartache, and immense legal bills.

Then the title was changed to *Verse Chorus Verse*, a sarcastic comment on the standard pop song framework that Kurt says he is tiring of. "I would hate to keep rewriting this formula," Kurt says. "It's a formula. I've mastered this. It's over, as far as I'm concerned, but I know I can probably write a couple more albums like this and be happy with it, but less and less happy every time we do one. Then again, I thought that before I recorded this record and now it turned out exactly how I wanted it to and I'm really proud of it."

Kurt's songwriting was deeply rooted in convention—popular music's verse-chorus-verse archetype has been in place for a very long time. Structurally, Nirvana songs aren't all that different from '50s- and '60s-era Brill Building pop, Tin Pan Alley tunes of the 1890s, nineteenth-century songwriter Stephen Foster ("My Old Kentucky Home," "Oh, Susanna," "Beautiful Dreamer"), and songs from even further back. It's difficult to imagine Kurt breaking out of that paradigm, but this is one of several quotations in the book that show an artistic restlessness. It sure would have been cool to see where Kurt would have gone next.

But by late May, the album's title had changed to *In Utero*. Kurt had noticed the phrase in some poetry that Courtney had written and decided that it fit the album art perfectly. Of course, it also fit Kurt's conception of earthly bliss. He didn't care if people thought it was too close to the embryonic imagery of the cover of

their previous album. The artwork, all conceptualized by Kurt and executed by *Nevermind* designer Robert Fisher, teems with feminine imagery. The front cover features a transparent woman, the female counterpart to the "Sliver" single cover but winged like some Greek goddess (the feminine symbols sprinkled throughout can be decoded using a book called *The Woman's Dictionary of Symbols and Sacred Objects*). For the back cover, Kurt arranged an assortment of plastic fetus models and other body parts, lilies, and orchids on a rug at his house (the photograph is by Charles Peterson). "I always thought orchids, and especially lilies, look like a vagina," Kurt says. "So it's sex and woman and *In Utero* and vaginas and birth and death."

The name Nirvana, the title *In Utero*, and the title *Nevermind* (as well as the amniotic scene on the album's cover) all speak of a blissfully innocent, serene state. But the back cover of *In Utero*, a brutal and lurid collage of fetuses and internal organs, looks as if something barged into a nursery and committed a heinous act of carnage.

It was either Kurt or Courtney who specifically referred me to *The Woman's Dictionary of Symbols and Sacred Objects* by Barbara G. Walker for decoding the symbols on the back cover of *In Utero*. I didn't follow up on it, but I should have—it turns out that Kurt had hidden a very interesting story there.

If you were to consult *The Woman's Dictionary of Symbols and Sacred Objects* and match up the symbols on the back cover with their descriptions in the book, you'd eventually discover that virtually all twenty-one of them share one character in common: the ancient Greek goddess Demeter, the goddess of grain and, by extension, agriculture, plant life, and the general fertility of the earth. She's also a goddess of health, birth, and marriage.

Demeter is very sexual but also prone to powerful rage—when she gets angry, there are failed crops and famine. It sure seems like Demeter is a stand-in for Courtney.

Another interesting thing is that Demeter's daughter Kore, later called Persephone, was taken from her—abducted to the underworld by Hades (aka Pluto). Demeter desperately searched the world over to regain custody of her child. It's not difficult to see the story of Demeter and Persephone as an analogy for what happened with Kurt, Courtney, and Frances.

Demeter's emblem happens to be the poppy—because a species of poppy often grows in grain fields. From *The Woman's Dictionary*: "Legend has it that Demeter, in despair over the seizure of her daughter Persephone by Pluto, ate poppies in order to fall asleep and forget her grief."

chapter fifteen

THE GROWN-UPS

DON'T LIKE IT

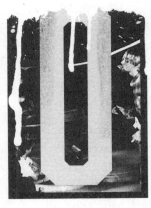

nce the album was completed, the band sent unmastered tapes off to Geffen president Ed Rosenblatt and Gary Gersh, as well as their lawyer and the inner circle of Gold Mountain. Kurt's description of their feedback was succinct. "The grown-ups don't like it," he said with a mixture of disappointment and disbelief. In fact, "the grown-ups"— management and senior label execs—*hated* it. Kurt says they told him the songwriting was "not up to par," the sound "unlistenable." There also seemed to be uncertainty whether mainstream radio would go for the Steve Albini sound.

Earlier in this book, even Kurt acknowledges that the songwriting was indeed not up to par. As far as being "unlistenable," it's true, *In Utero* didn't have the radio-friendly, unit-shifting sheen of *Nevermind*. But, from the start, everyone knew it wouldn't because everyone knew what Steve Albini's recordings sounded like: he specialized in raw, loud, brutal records—that was precisely why musicians hired him. The only surprising thing about any of this was that Kurt didn't seem to have anticipated "the grown-ups" reaction.

But more than swarming distortion and coruscating rage and angst, what some of "the grown-ups" probably heard was the sickening sound of evaporating raises, bonuses, expense accounts, and promotions.

"As it turns out," says Albini, "the record company would much rather they made an indulgent rock star album because then they'd have something to promote. And the band would be broke and the more broke the band is, the better it is for the record company, because then they can pull the strings more."

Later that year, Albini wrote a scathing, enlightening, controversial, and still oft-quoted essay about major label business economics for the *Baffler*, titled "The Problem with Music." Here's how it begins:

Whenever I talk to a band who are about to sign with a major label, I always end up thinking of them in a particular context. I imagine a trench, about four feet wide and five feet deep, maybe sixty yards long, filled with runny, decaying shit. I imagine these people, some of them good friends, some of them barely acquaintances, at one end of this trench. I also imagine a faceless industry lackey at the other end, holding a fountain pen and a contract waiting to be signed.

And it goes on from there, although not in such scatological terms, to rip on major label A&R execs, major label music producers, and, worst of all, major label recording contracts. After an accounting of a typical major label band's income and expenses, Albini concludes that "The band members have each earned about ⅓ as much as they would working at a 7–11, but they got to ride in a tour bus for a month."

He leaves the reader with these famous parting words: "Some of your friends are probably already this fucked."

It turned out that few people at Gold Mountain or Geffen really wanted the band to record with Albini to begin with, although the band was free to have their way. Faced with the disapproval of virtually everyone involved in Nirvana's career, Kurt thought he was getting an unstated message: scrap the album and start all over again—there was still plenty of time and the Albini sessions hadn't cost all that much, considering they were following up a quadruple-platinum album.

"I should just rerecord this record," Kurt sneers, "and do the same thing we did last year because we sold out last year—there's no reason to try to redeem ourselves as artists at this point. I can't help myself—I'm just putting out a record that I would like to listen to at home. I never listen to *Nevermind*. I haven't listened to it since we put it out. That says something. I can't stand that kind of production and I don't listen to bands that do have that kind of production, no matter how good their songs are. It just bothers me."

Friends of the band loved the record, however. As of early April, the band was determined to release the record as it was and damn the torpedoes—DGC would put the record out. "They're going to eat my shit," Kurt says. "Of course, they want another *Nevermind*, but I'd rather die than do that. This is exactly the kind of record I would buy as a fan, that I would enjoy owning. I couldn't be truer to myself than to put this out the way it is. It's my favorite production and my favorite songs."

But even right after returning from Minnesota—and before anyone else had heard the tracks—Kurt and Chris were beginning to worry about the bass sound, which they felt was too mushy and not musical enough, and the vocals on a couple of the more melodic songs, which were too low in the mix, the latter a common complaint leveled at Albini's productions. Still, those reservations took a backseat to their resolve to release an unvarnished, straightforwardly recorded album.

I was with Krist when he first listened to *In Utero* all the way through, driving back from Kurt's house after I dropped off the Lead Belly biography. He played a cassette tape of the unmastered album on the car stereo.

Krist spontaneously said that the bass could sound "more musical" on "All Apologies." By that, he meant that the bass sounded a little indistinct and not enough like a tuned instrument, which was a shame because it's a beautiful part. And sure enough, that was one of the issues the song's mastering specifically addressed.

Krist also thought the vocals could be a bit louder on "Heart-Shaped Box," and one or two other songs, and that wound up being addressed, too. (Mastering can pinpoint certain frequencies so precisely that it can boost a specific element, such as a voice.)

In hindsight, it's obvious that *Nevermind* was a strong rightward swing of the band's artistic pendulum toward pop, while *In Utero* leans more heavily on the arty, aggressive side which was showcased on *Incesticide*. "There's always been songs like 'About a Girl' and there's always been songs like 'Paper Cuts,'" Chris says. "*Nevermind* came out kind of 'About a Girl'-y and this one came out more 'Paper Cuts.' It's an artistic thing. The label's all freaked out about it. It's like, 'Shit, it's *art*—what are you going to do about it?'"

The record called the bluff of all the music biz pundits who hailed the triumph of "real music" over the processed pop that Nirvana had trounced. One or two of those pundits worked with Nirvana; *In Utero* forced them to put their money where their mouths were. "The thing about *Nevermind* was it just flew out the window," Chris says, "and now nobody can predict anything in the music industry anymore. They say there was a pre-Nirvana music industry and a post-Nirvana music industry, so we'll see how post-Nirvana the music industry really is."

Most directly, the music industry was post-Nirvana in that major labels soon signed lots of soundalike bands that they hoped would be the next Nirvana—but that sort of thing had happened at least since labels started signing Frank Sinatra clones in the '40s. For some listeners, Nirvana did provide a gateway to the kinds of bands that Kurt flaunted on his T-shirts. But for vastly more, it was just a gateway to bands that kinda sounded like Nirvana. Hence the likes of Sponge, Everclear, Silverchair, Matchbox 20, Creed, Collective Soul, Candlebox, Seven Mary Three, Live, 3 Doors Down, and Bush, many of whom sold quite a lot of records but didn't exactly predispose many minds to smashing the capitalist patriarchy.

Nirvana and the entire alternative rock phenomenon did serve notice that the major labels had gotten out of step with their audience and needed to sign more artists who actually spoke to people instead of marketing to them. The major labels obligingly applied that lesson to all sorts of genres in the coming years—not just with alternative rock but hip-hop and electronic music.

The band was prepared not to match the gargantuan sales of *Nevermind*— although *In Utero* was really *good*, it was not necessarily really *commercial*. "I expect this record will sell maybe half as much," Kurt predicts. "We've offended too many people within the last year." Dave doesn't think the album will do as well either, not that he even wants it to. "Not at all," he says. "I kind of think of it sometimes as a test. We're testing the limits. A record like *Nevermind* came along and it blew things apart and it changed a lot of stuff. By doing this, maybe the next big hit could be on an eight-track. A band from out of nowhere could have an eight-track recording of a great song and it will be on the radio. The Beatles and the Rolling Stones did it."

One day, sometime before the album came out, while Kurt was driving Pat Smear, Frances, and me to the Seattle Center science museum, he bet me that *In Utero* wouldn't sell more than five hundred thousand copies, which meant it wouldn't go gold. He was being melodramatic, but I gladly took that bet, which involved the loser surrendering the cardigan he was wearing at the time. *In Utero* went gold within a month of release. I never did collect that cardigan; Kurt later wore it at the *Unplugged* show.

In a sense, the band could afford to take a chance—since nobody knew exactly why the last album took off, how could anybody second-guess this one? Besides, Nirvana would likely take a pounding no matter what they did.

"It's the sophomore jinx—everybody's just waiting for us to fuck up," says Dave. "Everybody's waiting to tear this to shreds and say, 'The one-hit wonder.' I *know* that it's a good record. I know that people who like Nirvana will like this record. The seventy-five thousand people that were into Nirvana before *Nevermind* I think will like the record maybe even *more* than *Nevermind*."

So this isn't "career suicide." "No, although it will be thought of as that," Kurt says. "The album that brought them down to the gutter."

"These are the songs we came up with," says Chris. "If you don't make a raw album, you make another slick album and then people say, 'Oh, they just made a slick album so they can sell more records.' You can't win for losing. Let them say what they will—I did it my way.

"I told Kurt, 'If this record bombs and it doesn't do anything, there's still all those years we spent in the van and all the good times we had—we were happy back then and nobody can take that away from us,'" Chris says. "The music speaks

for itself, we put out good records. So what if we have to play fifteen-hundred-seaters. So what if Pearl Jam and Stone Temple Pilots keep going to all the music awards shows—we were never into that shit in the first place."

Kurt might have felt differently, considering the large bills he was now paying for legal fees and medical treatment, not to mention the care of his child, and unfortunately, drugs.

###

Albini had been impressed that Kurt, Chris, and Dave wanted to try to forge new creative ground instead of making a record that was just a retread of the successful ideas of their last record. "Frankly, that's all the record company wanted or expected, and to date, that's what they *still* want," Albini claimed a month or so after the album was completed. "What they don't understand is that it represents the band more accurately and it is more faithful to the band's vision of their record than a record made any other way would be.

"You could put that band in the studio for a year and I don't think they could come up with a better record," Albini continues. "I think that's as good as they're going to be. If that doesn't suit their record company then their record company clearly has problems that go beyond this record. The record company has a problem with the band. The sooner everybody involved recognizes that, the easier it will be on everybody."

"The people at the record company are clearly geniuses, right?" says Albini. "They put out Nelson—they know what they're doing. This is the record company that sued Neil Young for not being commercial enough. Those are the people that are telling the band they don't know what they're doing. If you have to rely on people like that as your barometer of quality, then you're in a lot more trouble than just having a bad record. It means you're a fool."

Albini was right: Geffen Records had some issues in the "artist-friendly" department. There was a lot of history to back him up.

At the time, after a couple of big hit albums and a very long professional relationship with David Geffen, superstar former Eagle Don Henley was suing to get off Geffen's label. And it had recently emerged that Geffen Records had sent the legendary Aerosmith back to the studio because the brass were not hearing any hit singles. (To the label's credit, the resulting album, *Get a Grip*, became Aerosmith's first #1 album and their biggest worldwide seller.)

Earlier, Neil Young had run afoul of the label. First, he'd made 1982's commercial flop *Trans*, a synthesizer album with highly processed vocals, followed by a country album that Geffen rejected. Then, when the label insisted on a guitar-rock album in the vein of Young classics such as *Zuma* and *Rust Never Sleeps*, Young gave them *Everybody's Rockin'*, a lightweight, oddly clinical rockabilly record. That was the final straw for Geffen: in 1983, they sued Neil Young for $3.3 million for, essentially, not sounding like Neil Young.

Young countersued, pointing out that his contract gave him artistic freedom, and the suit was settled; David Geffen himself apologized to Young, who put out two or three lesser records on the label before returning to his previous label Reprise, where he went on to release some of the greatest music of his storied career.

Kurt probably could have related to a song Neil Young recorded for Geffen called "Prisoners of Rock 'n' Roll" (from 1987's *Life*): "We never listen to the record company man," Young sang. "They try to change us and ruin our band."

"Literally, every other person involved in the enterprise that is Nirvana, besides the band itself, are pure pieces of shit," Albini rails. "Their management company, their record company, the A&R people, all the hangers-on, all the phonies that cling to that band as a bogus source of hipster credentials, everyone associated with the band—other than the band—I think are pieces of shit and I have no time for them.

"You know, after all this, I would be willing to do another Nirvana record," Albini said shortly after finishing the record. He would soon change his tune. "I enjoyed dealing with the guys, but I would not be willing to deal with their superstructure anymore—their management company or their record company."

On March 23 came good news. After months of legal battles, it was finally decided that none of the allegations made against Kurt and Courtney in Family Court were legally valid. The Cobains had already won legal custody of their daughter, but now, the Department of Children's Services would not supervise Kurt and Courtney's care of Frances any longer—no more humiliating urine tests, no more checkup visits from social workers, no more costly legal fights. The nightmare was over.

So that was the end of six months of living hell for Kurt and Courtney.

On April 9, the band raised over fifty thousand dollars at a benefit at the Cow Palace in San Francisco for the Tresnjevka Women's Group, an organization based in the Croatian city of Zagreb that assists rape survivors. As part of the vicious campaign of "ethnic cleansing," Serbian soldiers had been systematically

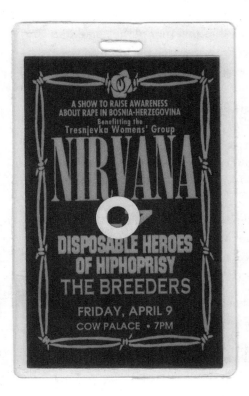
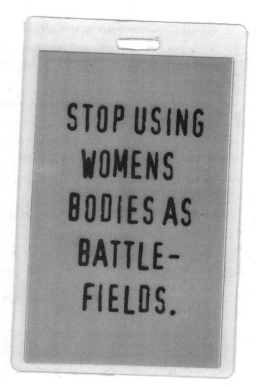

Backstage pass for the April 9, 1993, benefit show at the Cow Palace, where Nirvana debuted many of the songs from *In Utero*. Courtesy of the author.

raping Muslim women so that they would eventually have Serbian babies. The victims are often mutilated, their children murdered right in front of them.

The benefit was Chris's idea. "I was really pissed off by everything I'd been reading and nobody was doing anything about it," he says. After some initial encouragement from Courtney, he started putting together the show, which also featured the Disposable Heroes of Hiphoprisy, the Breeders, and L7.

Chris also helped lead protests against Washington State House Bill 2554, better known as the "Erotic Music Bill," which would jail record store owners for selling music that was judged "erotic" and therefore somehow damaging to minors. Back in December of 1991, Chris led a march and petition drive at the state capitol building in Olympia. MTV News and *Rolling Stone* picked up the story and the governor's office was inundated with letters from people who opposed the bill. But Governor Booth Gardner, who only recently had boasted in

The Grown-Ups Don't Like It

his 1992 State of the State address that he was "the governor of the home state of Nirvana, the hottest new rock band in the country," signed the bill into law.

It was repealed, although its sponsor is vowing to submit a modified version of the bill.

"There's a lot of rap music and rock music for that matter, Andrew Dice Clay, that's just fuckin' bullshit, it's just sexist crap," Chris says, "but you have to tolerate it. You have to tolerate hate groups, too, because that's the price of freedom of speech—you place your ideals above your feelings. I can't make the Ku Klux Klan illegal because I don't like it—I can't do that because they have the right to believe what they want."

Even though he's known as "the political one," Chris doesn't exactly relish the tag. "I want to depoliticize myself—I just don't want to be this rock & roll pundit," he says. "I don't want Nirvana to be a political band—we're a rock band and I'm a bass player. I just happen to be politically active."

Krist simply believed that any citizen can and should become politically active, no matter what they did for a living—even if it was, heaven forbid, playing music. And to his immense credit, he walked the walk.

A couple of weeks before *Nevermind* was released, Krist and Dave stopped by Seattle's KNDD for an interview with DJ Bill Reid. "Do you have political aspirations, Chris?" Reid asked.

"Maybe, someday," Krist answered. "But it would be too radical, it'll never go anywhere."

Krist always talked so knowledgeably and enthusiastically about current events and history that I got the feeling he might have been one of those kids who played the geopolitical board game Risk. But he learned a lot about geopolitics at school in his early teen years in Croatia—a very culturally and politically complex place—and from coming of age just as the conflicts in the former Yugoslavia were starting to explode.

Krist helped fight the so-called "Erotic Music Bill" by organizing meetings, attending press conferences, mobilizing fellow musicians, speaking on TV news shows, and even hauling a PA system for rallies in his van. It was a silly idea for a law—one wonders what would have happened if someone had released a song with lyrics from the Bible's "Song of Solomon": "Your stature is like a palm tree; your breasts are clusters of fruit / I said, 'I will climb the palm tree and take hold of its fruit.'"

Krist was also a strong advocate for legalizing hemp, an easy-to-grow plant that can be made into things like textiles, biofuel, animal feed, building insulation, rope, and biodegradable plastic. The effort eventually helped lead to the passage of the Hemp Farming Act of 2018, which made it legal to grow hemp in the US again.

But Krist's activism really took off after Nirvana ended, including forming JAMPAC (Joint Artists and Musicians Political Action Committee), which essentially used music to resist (in vain) the rapidly encroaching gentrification of Seattle; getting elected as a state committeeperson; and serving on the board of the Center for Voting and Democracy (now FairVote, where he was later appointed chairperson), which works for election reforms such as automatic voter registration and abolishing the electoral college. For years he was the head of his local grange. He also advocates very persuasively for ranked choice voting, which has started to catch on in the US.

Krist is a big believer in getting involved. "All those people on their blogs . . . they don't know about the real world," he told the Washington State secretary of state's website in 2008. "If you want to change things, you've got to get out and meet people. You gotta make things happen. If you're gonna suggest something, you ought to see how to do it."

###

Despite the band's determination to release the record exactly as it was, blemishes and all, they began to have serious doubts about it around the time of the benefit show in San Francisco. There was even some talk of going back into the studio and recording a couple of new songs, just to see what they would sound like. By late April, Kurt's enthusiasm for the album had plummeted drastically. "I don't know what it is, but it doesn't make me as emotional as it does listening to *Nevermind*," he said of the new album. "When I listen to *Nevermind*, I hate the production, but there's something about it that almost makes me cry at times. With this record, I'm just deadpan."

This is quite a switch from how excited he'd said he was about the new album. But that was Kurt: loud-soft, hot-cold, passive-aggressive. Regardless, he got over it and very passionately played those songs on tour.

The hope was that the album could be saved in the mastering process, when a last wave of the electronic wand can often subtly transform a record. After working with mastering wizard Bob Ludwig at his studio in Portland, Maine, Chris was satisfied with the results, but Kurt still wasn't sure. It wasn't *perfect*. Of course, that was part of the deal—you record *and* mix in two weeks with Steve Albini and you don't get pristine pop perfection, you get a raw, honest, warts-and-all rock record. It seemed that Kurt was in love with the *idea* of the low-budget philosophy, but not its actuality. Once again, his pop soul was at war with his rock sensibility.

The Grown-Ups Don't Like It

Then a brief story in the *Chicago Tribune* quoted Steve Albini as predicting that Geffen/DGC was going to reject the Nirvana album. An item in the influential *Village Voice* soon picked up on the story.

The story snowballed, gaining a media momentum all its own. A full-page piece in *Newsweek* further sensationalized the issue. The piece quoted unnamed sources, one of whom claimed to have heard the album but instead had merely heard some demos the band had recorded with Craig Montgomery during the Brazil trip. Writer Jeff Giles quoted Jonathan Poneman as saying that Geffen was "guilty of a complete lack of faith and respect for Kurt, Dave [Grohl], and Chris [Novoselic] as artists," yet Poneman says Giles left out a key qualifier just before that statement, along the lines of "If what I hear is true, then . . ." In a letter to *Newsweek*, the band claimed Giles got quotes by saying he was merely writing a piece about Albini, not Nirvana.

At the end of the piece, Gary Gersh states, correctly, that "Nirvana has complete control over what they want to do with their record." The piece should have noted that at the outset—but that would have poured cold water on the entire non-scandal. Nonetheless, Giles closed by scoffing, "Smells like corporate spirit."

Not long after the *Newsweek* article came out, I was discussing the controversy with someone who knew Nirvana very well; they unwittingly repeated, virtually word for word, one of the anonymous quotations. So I'm pretty sure I know who the unnamed source was. But I'll never tell—it was a private conversation, and besides, it would disappoint a lot of people.

"Most damaging to us is that Giles ridiculed our relationship with our label based on totally erroneous information," read the letter, which the band also reprinted in a costly full-page ad in *Billboard*. In a press release, Ed Rosenblatt vowed Geffen/DGC would release anything the band submitted, and, in a highly unusual move, David Geffen himself blew in an irate phone call to the magazine.

So Nirvana wanted to make nice with Geffen/DGC. Actually, they *needed* to. Geffen/DGC was probably legally obligated to release the album, but what the label was *not* obligated to do was *promote* it. That is key. A big part of running a major label is deciding how to allocate resources: what gets the grease and what doesn't. The execs make those calculations based on, among other factors, how they perceive the commercial viability of a record. Obviously, Geffen/DGC was going to promote a Nirvana album. The question was *how much* they would promote it. That's really what Nirvana was up against.

Luckily, Geffen wanted to make nice, too—they were well aware of the need to do damage control after the Don Henley and Neil Young debacles, and they weren't going to take the public relations hit of fighting one of the biggest, coolest, and most outspoken artists on the label, and throwing away all the hipness points they'd earned by signing Nirvana, Sonic Youth, and all the rest.

Stories in *Rolling Stone* and *Entertainment Weekly* soon followed as the controversy ballooned even more.

"Steve Albini takes the position that anything he thinks is good is good, that he's David Koresh [the infamous cult leader who had died during a massive FBI raid a few weeks earlier]," Danny Goldberg told *Rolling Stone*'s Fred Goodman. "He is God, and he knows what's good. And if the artist doesn't like it, then the artist is somehow selling out because they don't agree with his personal vision."

"Is Geffen's tinkering with the record just part of the standard artistic process?" *Entertainment Weekly* wondered, ignoring the well-documented creative control clause in Nirvana's contract, not to mention reality: Geffen wasn't tinkering with the record, the band was, and of their own free will.

"Did the band record an aggressively punk album," the piece continued, "and then get cold feet?" As if the members of Nirvana could write, rehearse, and record a set of songs and not quite realize what they were doing. It must have been very frustrating to have to deal with all the uninformed speculation about such a sensitive subject.

The truth of the matter was, the band had legitimately disliked some aspects of the Albini recordings from the start and had wanted to fix them; that their management and label wholeheartedly agreed made the band appear to be spineless pushovers and their associates to seem like greedy bullies (which is not to say that both Gold Mountain and Geffen/DGC weren't relieved when some changes were eventually made). The combination of Nirvana's clout with Geffen and the creative control built into their contract ensured that they could put out whatever record they wanted to, regardless of what anyone else thought.

Kurt issued a statement about the controversy: "We—the band—felt the vocals were not loud enough on a few of the tracks. We want to change that." And I can personally verify that.

The thing was, Nirvana were fairly vocals-forward—which is an approach more associated with pop music than rock, but when you have a truly great singer singing some catchy melodies, it makes sense to ensure that the vocals are up front.

It could have been a case of studio rapture: with their longtime hero Steve Albini at the mixing board, the band members may have been beguiled by the initial mixes and then come home and realized they weren't quite what they wanted. Or maybe they didn't like some aspects of the mixes from the start and, in typical Nirvana fashion, didn't confront Albini about them. Back then, Albini was a very difficult person to confront: doggedly dogmatic, impregnably self-assured, and ferociously articulate. Kurt, Krist, and Dave were probably a little intimidated by him.

The whole controversy, ignited by Albini's single broadside, was a by-product of sloppy, herd-mentality journalism. The one writer who got anywhere close to the truth of the matter was Jim DeRogatis of the *Chicago Sun-Times*. The headline to his story read "Flap Over Nirvana LP Smells Like Bogus Issue." In the piece, even Steve Albini conceded that he didn't *really* know what was going on with the album and that he had been speaking "largely out of ignorance."

"I don't feel that I've been included enough in the decisions made after we finished recording to have any real authority to speak about what's been going on with the record," Albini diplomatically told DeRogatis. "The last time I spoke with Kurt, the complaints anybody has with the record are small." And that was true.

Albini, it appeared, was also trying to have his cake and eat it, too—producing a major-label record for $100,000 and then disavowing the whole experience, thereby silencing cries of sell-out. This wasn't the first time he had done it, either. Albini had used similar tactics after doing major-label productions—or rather, *recordings*—for the Pixies and the Breeders. And no one pointed out that those avatars of indie credibility, Fugazi, had themselves rejected some recordings they made with Albini shortly before the *In Utero* sessions. Nobody had called *them* corporate stooges.

The band wanted to do some more work on a few songs, perhaps with R.E.M. producer Scott Litt, and remix at least a couple of tracks with, of all people, Andy Wallace. Albini vehemently rejected those ideas. He claimed he had a contract with the band that they could not remix or otherwise modify the album without his involvement. The fact that the band had not actually signed the agreement was immaterial, Albini claimed, since they had been proceeding with the project with that understanding. When Gold Mountain requested the master tapes, Albini at first refused to send them, then eventually changed his mind after a phone call from Chris. At the last minute, the band decided against working with Andy Wallace and instead decided to remix and augment "Heart-Shaped Box" and "All Apologies" with Litt.

Typically, Krist, not Kurt, made that call to Albini.

The squabble with Geffen was a really big deal at the time and, since this was pre-internet, it played out in the press over a month or so rather than a few days. Today, if even the coolest band wanted to rework some tracks from the album they'd just recorded with even the coolest producer, no one would care. But early-'90s alternative rock presented itself as an uncompromising antidote to the phony tripe the labels had served up for years. Its philosophical roots were in the very dogmatic indie community, which had set a high and strict ethical bar. So Nirvana, who identified with and so assiduously championed the indie underground—and had so outspokenly censured other bands (well, one band in particular) for being "careerists"—had set itself up for accusations of hypocrisy for the slightest misstep.

In fact, indie cred was so valuable that some major labels created "fake indies"— labels that appeared to be independent but were actually owned by major labels. The idea was to establish some authenticity and grassroots followings for bands before moving them to the major label they'd actually been signed to. Seed Records, for instance, was a front for Atlantic Records; Elektra had Egg Records. (Note the telling commonality in the label names.) Smashing Pumpkins had no indie cred to speak of but shrewdly latched onto the Sub Pop train, releasing a single for the label in December 1990; the band was the object of a major label bidding war and signed to the Caroline label, which was actually a quasi-indie subsidiary of the major label Virgin Records, where they released their second album.

It was a particular cultural moment. The indie community had been founded as a platform for artists who would never be signed to major labels. But now this same music had to contend with the paradox of being a genre originally intended for a very narrow audience that was now being sold to the very widest audience. As the *In Utero* flap reveals, the transition was awkward and painful.

There were even more profound implications. Deep down in American punk's DNA, especially with the more political hardcore bands, was the conviction that, ultimately, the mass media were dumbing down the culture as a mode of social control; therefore, bands who signed with major labels were succumbing to much larger, nefarious forces than just uncool record companies. (In the most blatant example, EMI, Capitol, and Virgin were once part of a corporation that made missiles and other weapons of mass destruction.) But could this music subvert the corporate ogre from the inside? That was Kurt's pipe dream.

In early May, Litt and the band worked at Bad Animals Studios (owned by the Wilson sisters of Heart) in Seattle and remixed the two songs, with Kurt adding acoustic guitar and Lennonesque backing harmonies to "Heart-Shaped Box." The rest of the album was left as is, although by remastering, they managed to

sharpen up the bass and boost the vocals by some 3 dBs. So much for the Big Sell-Out.

"Heart-Shaped Box" was going to be a single; it had to sound right. So Kurt did the extra work on "Heart-Shaped Box" (and "All Apologies")—no one had to tell him to do it, and certainly none of "the grown-ups" had the musical expertise, not to mention the chutzpah, to tell one of the most gifted rock musicians of his generation that he should add acoustic guitar and vocal harmonies; those were canny artistic decisions.

Now that they all live in the same town, band morale is at an all-time high. Kurt, Chris, and Dave visit each other at home and hang out and listen to music, just like the old days. Late in March, while Courtney was on a quick English tour with Hole, they all met at Kurt's house to look at archival footage for a long-form video and to shoot a video for "Sliver" with director Kevin Kerslake.

For the "Sliver" video, Kurt dragged out several years' worth of dolls and knickknacks from a storage space that hadn't been opened since before recording *Nevermind*, then set it all up in his garage so that it looked just like his old apartment back in Olympia. The band set up and rocked out, with Frances in a chair by her father's side. Kerslake manned the Super 8 camera while standing on a chair for the adult's-eye-view effect. Later, Kurt cut some armholes in a big piece of cardboard, placed Frances in front of it and put his arms through it, holding her up so it looks like she's standing up on her own, dancing like a go-go girl.

MTV accepted the video in mid-May, but, because of its rules about product placement, required that the band cut out a few frames of footage that featured a collage of the logos of *Maximumrocknroll* and *Better Homes and Gardens* magazines. Unfortunately, those frames also contained a little message Kurt had written: "INDIE PUNX STILL SUCKS."

Those few frames are now back in the video, and it's easy to see why Kurt included the *Better Homes and Gardens* cover: it lists a story with the title "Celebrating at Grandma's House." The video is loaded with blink-and-you-missed-it Nirvana signifiers.

Of course, Dave was miming to Dan Peters's drumming.

The "Sliver" video showed the band in peak playful form, but even if spirits are high, the question remains as to whether the band will be a lasting proposition or just another flash in the pan. Internally, there are still many possible

The Amplified Come as You Are

flashpoints: Kurt's desire to play with other people, the limitations he sees in Chris's and Dave's playing, Dave's alienation from the band, the Courtney factor. Breakup rumors have long dogged the band; although it's getting to be like the boy who cried wolf, Kurt is always threatening to quit.

"I know we're going to put out another record after this one," Chris says. "We'll play it by ear. I don't think we're going to go on and on. I think when the consensus is like 'yeah, this thing's pretty much reached its course,' I think we're going to know. But I know now that it's not over. And I never did during that whole pissed-off time. It's just going to come naturally. We're all going to get the hit, like yeah, this is it. Maybe we'll take a sabbatical that will never end, I don't know. We've put out four albums—four albums is a pretty good stretch for a band. How many bands put out four good albums without going on to be the Scorpions or Rolling Stones or whatever?"

It's strange to ponder the possibility of the band lasting out the decade. "I don't want it to, but it might," Kurt says. "It all depends on how the songs are. I was surprised to find us working together as such a unit lately." But Kurt isn't sure how much more the three of them can accomplish musically. "I would love to be able to play with other people and create something new," he says. "I'd rather do that than stay in Nirvana. I don't want to keep rewriting this style of music, I want to start doing something really different."

In an August 1993 interview with Canadian television's MuchMusic, Kurt said that *In Utero* "is like the closing of the chapter of the formula we've been using. . . . Our tastes are just changing so rapidly that we're really experimenting with a lot of stuff and it might get too indulgent and be really embarrassing for the next album but . . . this is the last chapter of three-chord grunge music for us."

Kurt was self-conscious about the relatively conventional and rudimentary formal nature of his work to date—remember, the title of *In Utero* was almost going to be *Verse Chorus Verse*—and there's no question he would have explored new musical directions. "I love change," Kurt told *Sassy* magazine's Christina Kelly around the same time. "All the bands I respect the most have changed with every album. I can't stand to hear the same format, where after three or four albums you know exactly what to expect. That's boring, and that's why those bands lose their audience" (although Kurt enjoyed great bands such as the Ramones, Motörhead, and AC/DC, who didn't appreciably change their sound and maintained and even increased their following).

Kurt definitely wanted to evolve, but it seemed uncertain whom he'd do that with. "Whether I will be able to do everything I want to do as a part of Nirvana remains to be seen," he told Chuck Crisafulli for *Fender Frontline* magazine. "To be fair, I also know that both Krist and Dave have musical ideas that may not work in the context of Nirvana. We're all tired of being labeled. You can't imagine how stifling it is."

It's a parlor game to speculate about the music Kurt would have gone on to make, but maybe he provided a clue in a December 1993 *Rolling Stone* interview: he wanted to make music with more subtlety and "a lot more structure," he said. "It's a really hard thing to do, and I don't know if we're capable of it—as musicians." But Kurt could easily have found musicians to play what he wrote. Krist is a versatile player, but Dave might not have been a part of that—Kurt wished Dave could play with more finesse and sensitivity. In *The Storyteller*, even Dave acknowledged that at the time, he "only knew how to play the drums one of two ways: on or off."

History might well provide a guide to what Nirvana—or Kurt—might have gone on to do. Artists such as the Beatles, Joni Mitchell, Talking Heads, Prince, Radiohead, and Wilco began by making fairly basic music and then, as their musicianship and expertise in the recording studio improved, started doing much more adventurous, highly arranged work—and their audience happily followed them.

As Kurt says later in this book, "I want to do more new wave, avant garde stuff with a lot of dynamics—stops and breaks and maybe even some samples of weird noises and things."

"I know what the next Nirvana recording was going to sound like," R.E.M. lead singer Michael Stipe told *Newsweek* a few months after Kurt's death. "It was going to be very quiet and acoustic, with lots of stringed instruments. It was going to be an amazing fucking record." Stipe added that he and Kurt, who was a big fan of R.E.M.'s haunting, beautifully orchestrated 1992 masterpiece *Automatic for the People*, were planning on working on some music together when Kurt died. No mention of Krist and Dave.

At one point, Kurt pondered dispensing with the whole band thing. "It might be nice to eventually start playing acoustic guitar and be thought of as a singer-songwriter, rather than a 'grunge-rocker,' you know?" he told interviewer Martin Romance around the release of *In Utero*. "Because then I might be able to take advantage of that when I'm older and sit down on a chair and play acoustic guitar like Johnny Cash or something and it won't be a big joke, but who knows?" At the time, Cash was sixty-one years old; it's strange to consider Kurt thinking about being sixty-one.

There were other artistic directions he might have taken. Recall the jarring sound collages he made in Olympia, and with digital recording and sampling technology exploding just a couple of years after his death, who knows what he could have come up with.

Kurt could have opted out of the grind of making studio albums, doing press, and touring and just made DIY albums at home. He said it himself during the *Spin* interview:

The Amplified Come as You Are

"If I have to resort to quitting my band and putting out my own records from home . . . and pretending to be some sort of cult figure and selling a thousand records a year, that's fine." He could have been thinking of the reclusive outsider avant-folk-blues musician Jandek, who self-released literally scores of crudely played and recorded albums, starting in 1978, before making his first known live appearance in 2004. One of Kurt's favorite songwriters, Daniel Johnston, did something similar, too (until Kurt's advocacy helped to land Johnston an ill-fated major label deal). Every once in a while, he could have recorded a "big" album and made some serious money.

But there's the question of whether Chris and Dave can keep up with him. "I don't know," Kurt says. "I really don't know." Kurt thinks that Chris doesn't practice enough and that Dave isn't an imaginative enough player. Yet they have always come up with good touches that really complete a song—Kurt loves the bass line Chris dreamed up for "Heart-Shaped Box"—but Kurt now wants the collaboration to take place earlier in the songwriting process. "I get really frustrated sometimes when we're trying to write a song because I'll sit there and play a riff for a long time and just listen for Chris and Dave to try to come up with something else to help change the song or go into another part and they've hardly ever done that," Kurt says. "They don't take the lead and they're always kind of following."

It's hard to imagine Kurt relinquishing that much creative control over the songwriting. I wonder if this was an empty gesture on Kurt's part, outwardly inviting Krist and Dave to participate in the songwriting process but knowing that, for perhaps different reasons, neither of them ever would.

Monk magazine asked Krist if he wrote music. "I write a little bit," he replied, "but not for the band. Because I can't sing." His stuff, he added, is "kind of campfire guitar-pickin'."

"I was in awe of Kurt's songs," Dave told *Guitar World*'s Alan di Perna in 1997. "And intimidated. I felt it was best that I keep my songs to myself."

Of course, for the longest time, that's exactly what Kurt wanted, and Chris and Dave were more than willing to oblige. Now, Kurt waits for the other two to take the initiative without letting them know that's what he wants. But someone with that kind of imagination would almost have to be a songwriter himself. Dave writes fine songs on his own, but there's only so much a drummer can do. "Chris could be a songwriter if he actually wanted to," Kurt says. "If he had been working on his songwriting for the last few years, he'd probably be up to the level right now where he could help write half of a song for every riff that I come up with and it would be really great."

Then again, all the best bands are dictatorships. "Yeah, that's true," Kurt says. "But I would love to find people that could write songs and write them with them. That's why it's so easy to play songs with Courtney—every time we jam on something, we write a great song. It's weird. Because she's a person who takes command and isn't afraid to be the leader. And when you've got two leaders together, it takes a lot of pressure off both people. I've always wanted to have another person in the band that could write songs with me." Hence the occasional mutterings from Kurt's direction that he might start a band with Mudhoney's Mark Arm or Mark Lanegan from Screaming Trees.

It's difficult to envision Kurt working in a sustained, meaningful way with either Arm or Lanegan—recall, for instance, how the Jury fell apart because no one could decide who should take the lead. But they might have collaborated on a one-off single now and then.

"I know we won't break up within this year," Kurt says. "I guess I just have to take it one year at a time."

In the *Rolling Stone* piece back in April of 1992, Kurt predicted very accurately what the next album would sound like—"It'll be more raw with some songs and more candy pop on some of the others," he said. "It won't be as one-dimensional." So what might the album after *In Utero* sound like? Kurt thinks it will be an extension of the ideas in "Milk It" and "Scentless Apprentice." "I definitely don't want to write more songs like 'Pennyroyal Tea' and 'Rape Me,'" he says. "That kind of classic rock & roll verse-chorus-verse, mid-tempo pop song is getting real boring. I want to do more new wave, avant garde stuff with a lot of dynamics— stops and breaks and maybe even some samples of weird noises and things—not samples of instruments. I want to turn into the Butthole Surfers, basically."

Of course, the Butthole Surfers have already done the Butthole Surfers quite successfully. "Yeah," Kurt says, "but it would be our version of it. We won't be able to escape the pop sensibility that we have. It's ingrained in our marrow— we'll never be able to get rid of melody and singing, so I want to try to take a pop song and extend it and have weird mood swings in the middle of the song, where it doesn't just follow this typical rock & roll formula. I'm tired of it."

Kurt doubts the band will have any lasting influence, say, twenty years from now. "Fuck no," he says. "It's sad to think what the state of rock & roll will be in twenty years. It's already so rehashed and so plagiarized that it's barely alive now. It's disgusting. I don't think it will be important any more."

He was so right about the future of rock music. In fact, twenty years after he said those words, rehashing had become an entire aesthetic of rock and pop music. Music critic Simon Reynolds wrote an entire thought-provoking book about that phenomenon called *Retromania: Pop Culture's Addiction to Its Own Past*. And Kurt turned out to be correct: by that time, rock wasn't nearly so important anymore.

By the late '90s, one of the very few remaining big rock bands would be led by one of Nirvana's former drummers. And while they don't particularly rehash or plagiarize, the Foo Fighters do embrace and very outspokenly celebrate a traditionalist approach to their music, their shows, and how they record.

It could be argued that Nirvana was a rehash: a concoction of classic rock, the Beatles, and American punk and post-punk, played by boys with guitars. It was commercially successful not just because it was catchy but also because it synthesized things that a lot of people were already at least vaguely familiar with. It spoke very vividly to a new generation of listeners, partly because of the musical palette it drew from and partly because it ineffably captured a set of widespread feelings, the zeitgeist.

Kurt was wrong about Nirvana's influence though: to this day, there are people in Nirvana-inspired bands who weren't yet born when Kurt died—or even when the self-titled best-of album came out in 2002.

There's a difference between influence and inspiration. A band's influences are who they sound like. But a band's *inspirations*—the artists who galvanize them to make music in the first place—may not sound like the band at all. (Kurt and Dave being inspired by the B-52's is a great example.)

Not many bands imitate Nirvana anymore, but that's not a very meaningful index of Nirvana's legacy. The animating idea of Nirvana wasn't really to see what happened if, as Kurt put it, you mixed the Beatles and Black Sabbath—really, it was to make music that was true to yourself and to play it with all the passion you possibly can. That recipe can and does come out a lot of different ways: the rapper MIA was inspired by Nirvana, and she sounds nothing like them; same with rappers Lil Wayne and Kid Cudi (who wore a Virgil Abloh–designed floral-print sundress in tribute to Kurt for his 2021 appearance on *Saturday Night Live*). So were musicians as diverse as new music composer Tyondai Braxton, pop singer Lana Del Rey, avant-rock band Dirty Projectors, folk-rockers the Avett Brothers, Radiohead, Post Malone, and countless others.

I'm not sure Kurt would have been too impressed by musicians who were *influenced* by Nirvana. But he would have been proud of any musician who truly was *inspired* by Nirvana, no matter what kind of music they made, as long as they were, you know, passionate about it.

"It's just mathematics, that's all rock & roll is," Kurt says. "Everything's based on ten. There's no such thing as infinity—it repeats itself after ten and it's over. It's the same thing with rock & roll—the neck is that long on a guitar, there are six strings, there's twelve notes, and then it repeats. It can only go to a certain point and it got to that point ten years ago. And there will be another band just like the Black Crowes twenty years from now, doing a version of the Black Crowes doing a version of the Faces."

"It starts getting watered down every five years," Kurt observes. "Kids don't even care about rock & roll as much as they used to, as the other generations have. It's already turned into nothing but a fashion statement and an identity for kids to use as a tool for them to fuck and have a social life. At that point, I can't really see music as having any importance to a teenager, really."

But rock music had *always* been a fashion statement and an identity for kids to use as a tool for them to fuck and have a social life. The thing is, there was a golden span of time when it was also more than that. That era was coming to a close with Nirvana. And Kurt knew it. Today, rock music, and perhaps most music, is increasingly a lifestyle accessory embodied by the corresponding playlist, which might verge on the idea Kurt outlines next.

Of course, many people are quite content with the notion of rock & roll as nothing but a social and sexual soundtrack, but Kurt thinks it will eventually be superseded. "I think they'll use sounds and tones and use it in their virtual reality machine and just listen to it that way and get the same emotions from it and then go to a party—there will be a virtual reality machine there with a whole bunch of headphones and if you want to talk to people and listen to the virtual reality machine you can do that or you can go into the bedroom and fuck and drink, but actually I think virtual reality machines will get you high. Technology will be that good. And then there will be virtual reality junkies and you'll find them dead on their couch from OD'ing."

Rather than "virtual reality," Kurt actually meant visual stimulation devices along the lines of Brion Gysin's Dreamachine, only much more technologically sophisticated. But the technology he describes also sounds a lot like multiplayer gaming, which really did become a form of social interaction.

By now, a lot of musicians might be pondering solo albums. Chris, who also happens to play some wicked guitar and banjo, says he'd like to do one someday, except he'd issue it on a ten-inch record only. He says he's already got some material—a surf song, some beat poetry. "It's going to be heavy humor," he says.

Sadly, the "heavy humor" album never happened (although surely somewhere there is a bootleg consisting only of Krist's stage banter). Krist did form a band called Sweet 75 with Venezuelan singer Yva Las Vegas, and they released a record on Geffen in 1997 with not much success. A few years later, Krist formed Eyes Adrift with Meat Puppets guitarist Curt Kirkwood and former Sublime/Long Beach Dub Allstars drummer Bud Gaugh. They released a self-titled album on SpinART Records in 2002 and did some touring, but that band also fizzled. In April 2022, Krist's new band 3rd Secret released a self-titled debut album of "art-folk/grunge." Besides old pals drummer Matt Cameron and guitarist Kim Thayil from Soundgarden, the band includes guitarist Bubba Dupree (who was formerly in the celebrated '80s hardcore-metal band Void and played in Dave Grohl's 2004 Probot project) and singers Jillian Raye (of Krist's other band Giants in the Trees) and Jennifer Johnson. Jack Endino co-produced and mixed the album.

Dave says he'd like to play guitar and sing in a band someday. "Drums get kind of boring after a while," he admits. He's been quietly piling up material at Laundry Room Studios, playing all the instruments himself. First, he lays down the drum part without any other accompaniment, then adds bass, guitar, and vocals. One of the outtakes from *In Utero* was a touching, indelible song Dave wrote called "Marigold," and there's more where that came from.

It was uncanny how Dave recorded. The drums usually do go first, but the drummer plays along to a guide track played by the rest of the band, which they replace after the drums are done. But, as the songwriter, Dave had the guide track in his head—he didn't need to hear it played out loud.

Needless to say, there was indeed more where that came from, and Dave did go on to play guitar and sing in a band someday.

"No," Kurt says, "I thought about recording stuff on a four-track and releasing it, but I wouldn't release it as a Kurt Cobain solo thing—I'd make up a name for it and try to be as anonymous as possible. I really like the idea of low-fi recordings and to throw out something that hasn't been worked on as feverishly as I would a Nirvana project."

Kurt says he's going to start his own label and call it Exploitation Records. "I'm just going to record street bums and retarded people and people with deformities and mental deficiencies," he says, "and I'm going to have a picture of that person on the front of the album and it's going to be a low-fi recording and it's just going to be for novelty reasons, for collector geeks to buy for twenty dollars apiece. I'm not really exploiting the people on the records, I'm exploiting the people who buy them, because there's going to be a twenty-dollar price tag on all of them. There will be a limited edition of five hundred of the Singing Flipper Boy."

I guess the unhoused and mentally disabled people were a metaphor for Kurt, who was "exploited" by his record label. But the concept was also a poke at his own deification—people would blindly buy and praise anything he was associated with. He was mocking the same people who said to him, "good show, man!" even when it had been a bad show. Or, as he told a stadium full of fans in Argentina, "I could shit on stage / You would eat it up."

Every label needs a distributor and Exploitation Records will be distributed through one Kurt Cobain. He says he'll simply take a box of records along with him on tour and sell them to record stores at every stop along the way.

Kurt also says he wants to rerelease all of Nirvana's releases on vinyl, except remastered by recording the sound from boom box speakers so it sounds just like a low-fi punk rock record or a bootleg, with appropriate cover art. "It's just for my own punk rock fantasy of thinking that maybe if *Nevermind* came out this way, it would sound better," he says. "It would only be for me to have a box of them."

The way Kurt looks at it, Exploitation Records might turn out to be a much-needed source of income. "It's too bad because I spent almost all the money I made off *Nevermind* fighting for my child because of the insane rumors created by the media and now I don't have anything to live off of for the rest of my life," Kurt says. "If this record doesn't sell—you have to sell eight million records to make a million dollars and the average middle American family makes more than a million dollars in a lifetime—I'm not going to be set for life. I'm going to have to get a job in ten years."

And that's where the book originally ended. It's probably fitting to end on a note of melodrama and exaggeration—even if Kurt never released another note of music, he'd have been set for life, and he knew that. But he couldn't have known that in 2006, twelve years after his death, *Forbes* would name him the highest-earning dead celebrity— ahead of Elvis Presley, Peanuts creator Charles M. Schulz, and John Lennon—pulling in an estimated fifty million dollars that year, thanks in part to Courtney selling a 25 percent stake for the rights to his work to a music publishing company.

I purposely ended the book like that because it suggested a sequel. What can I say, I was being optimistic.

final chapter

A SAD LITTLE SENSITIVE, UNAPPRECIATIVE, PISCES-JESUS MAN

Kurt Cobain, Los Angeles, May 23, 1991. © Michael Lavine

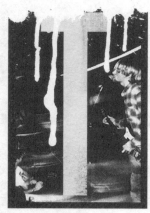

his chapter was written after Kurt's death, as an addition to the book. The publisher, Doubleday, felt that the book should acknowledge what had happened, and I agreed. After all, all complete biographies end in death, or at least the end of the band.

Over the course of writing this book, I got to know Kurt Cobain pretty well. You can't spend that much time with a person and not become friendly, especially when that person has told you his entire life story. After this book came out in October of '93, we stayed in touch. We'd hang out when the band came to New York for a TV appearance, sometimes I'd fly to Seattle to see everybody, and for two one-week stretches, I tagged along on Nirvana's final US tour in late '93. In between, Kurt and I would hold marathon phone conversations every couple of weeks. Sometimes we'd talk about whatever music we were listening to, sometimes we'd gossip a little, sometimes we'd talk about the upheavals in our lives, but always, Kurt would complain very candidly about his career.

I don't claim to have been Kurt Cobain's exclusive confidant or anything, but he trusted me enough to vent about all sorts of things. Every once in a while, the phone would ring in the wee hours of the morning. I don't think he considered the time difference from Seattle to New York, or maybe he figured that everyone else was as nocturnal as he was—but I always anticipated that he was in a crisis and I didn't want to be in a position where I had ignored the call. In *Sing Backwards and Weep*, Mark Lanegan writes about his deep regret that, one day in early April 1994, "I [had] not responded when he was calling out for my help." Kurt killed himself a day or so later.

So I'd roll out of bed, trudge into the living room, pick up the landline, and talk with Kurt in a groggy haze—sometimes for a couple of hours.

Usually he'd want to rail about management or the label or the band. One of his pet peeves was the definition of "net"—what the band was paid after expenses, a figure Kurt always found dubious. He trusted that whatever he told me wouldn't go anywhere. And after he'd gotten it all off his chest, he'd suddenly realize that he'd been talking completely about himself, pause, and ask, "So how are you?" I'd tell him, and the funny thing was, he gave great life advice. And we'd also talk about music or whatever else was on our minds. I wish I could remember specifics, but like I say, I was half asleep for these conversations. I just remember them very fondly.

Things were fine between us until Kurt fell into a coma after ingesting a reported fifty tablets of Rohypnol, a powerful depressant, and some champagne in a hotel in Rome during the band's last tour in March of '94. It didn't dawn on me that this was a suicide attempt until much later (I should have known immediately—see page 393 of this book). In the meantime, I spoke to CNN and to a reporter I knew at *People* magazine about it. This definitely upset Courtney and perhaps Kurt, too, although his mom assures me Kurt didn't care. I'll never know for sure.

Rohypnol pills are individually wrapped in bubble packs, so Kurt would have had to methodically open each of them. He knew perfectly well what he was doing. And when he woke from the coma, his first words to the hospital staff were "fuck you"—he was angry that he'd lived.

He knew not to mix drugs and alcohol. And I *knew* he knew that. But I didn't put it together that he'd attempted suicide, and no one at Gold Mountain told me about it—they weren't about to share such news with a journalist. I was an idiot.

In my heart of hearts, I had known that my being a journalist and my friendship with Kurt were on an inevitable collision course. I just thought I could provide some responsible commentary on what happened. But maybe I shouldn't have done it. At any rate, I never spoke to Kurt again.

It hardly makes me feel better, but I later learned that virtually everyone close to Kurt had a similar story: Something went terribly wrong right at the end and, as a result, their grief for him is riddled with the same crippling mixture of confusion, regret, and guilt.

###

If his music was any indication, it shouldn't have come as a surprise that Kurt's end was so sudden. After all, not one Nirvana song ends on a fade-out.

Maybe that was a little glib, but it was meant as a tribute to Kurt and the band: fade-outs can be cool, but it's a point of pride among some songwriters to figure out a definite ending for a song.

Also, when this book was written, there actually was a released Nirvana song that fades out: "Negative Creep." Still, that's quite a feat for a band with four albums.

And just as his music played loud against soft, aggressive against melodious, the violence of Kurt's death contrasted with its quiet aftermath. On an uncharacteristically sunny Saturday afternoon, the day after his death was announced, a dozen or so young fans gathered in the small park next to the house, where someone had set down some candles and flowers. Everybody spoke in hushed tones. There was no music—no boom boxes played, nobody strummed Nirvana tunes on an acoustic guitar; there was just an eerie stillness, a deafening silence that hung over a strange, haunted scene.

But there were more representatives of the media than fans hovering around the sprawling, gray-shingled Cobain home overlooking Lake Washington. On hand were MTV, *Entertainment Weekly*, *First Person with Maria Shriver*, *Details*, and a gaggle of local media. Several photographers skulked through the undergrowth that covered the hill behind the house, poking their cameras over the fence for a view of the two-story garage where it all happened. Uniformed security guards with microphones and headsets guarded the driveway, occasionally dipping the yellow police-line ribbon for arriving family and friends. "This is sick," said one guard to another as he surveyed the scene. "It's only a house."

I flew out to Seattle as soon as I could after the news. *Rolling Stone* paid for my trip without even expecting me to write anything. I wish I could remember who OK'd that, because it was very, very kind.

Because of the CNN and *People* interviews, I had become persona non grata. So I stood by the side of Lake Washington Boulevard and watched as Kurt's friends stepped over the police ribbon and walked into the house.

I was friends with Peter Buck's then-wife Stephanie Dorgan; their home overlooked the Cobain home, so I made my way there. She and Peter were very kind and welcoming to me, and I'll never forget it. For a little while, we stood and watched as someone walked around the backyard with Frances in their arms. R.E.M.'s drummer Bill Berry had just become seriously ill, and Peter was talking about it on the phone for a long time and was really concerned. It could not have been a weirder, worse day for them. Peter very kindly gave me a ride back into town.

I felt like an idiot for doing those interviews—well, far beyond an idiot since I was brutally beating myself up for it and still am to this day. But I also thought that the punishment was almost pathologically cruel—everyone knew that Kurt and I had become friends. I'll never know for sure who made sure I wasn't invited to the memorial, but I have a pretty good idea: my nemesis, the same person I had to hide the *Physicians' Desk Reference* from a year and a half earlier.

The day after the memorial, I called Krist—as soon as he heard my voice, he said, "*Where were you?*" He was pissed that I was excluded. That day, he took me on a long walk in the Washington woods along with Pat and a friend of Krist's, and that was my closure. Krist is good people.

That's all a very unhappy blur. It's even painful to come back to it all these years later. Stuff like this scars you, permanently. But maybe you learn something from it, too.

With so much media and so few fans, many of those mourning in front of the house attained a widespread if fleeting celebrity. The mascara-stained face of young Renae Ely made CNN, *Newsweek*, and the front page of the *Seattle Times*. Although many fans were quite ready to talk to the media, Seattle scene insiders were another story. Or rather they were no story at all. In a remarkable show of unity, the key players in the Seattle scene closed ranks decisively and refused to talk to any press. After not one, not two, but three waves of intensive media exposure, they had all learned some hard lessons. The media blackout in the wake of his death very effectively protected the privacy of Kurt's friends and family. If only he were alive to see how well it worked.

Sub Pop briefly considered barring the press from its long-planned sixth anniversary party at Seattle's Crocodile Cafe that Saturday night, but then realized the media would simply write a story about how they couldn't get in. Still, cameras were not permitted inside the club, so partygoers were greeted by a small media army on the sidewalk outside. Reporters thrust microphones in people's faces and asked, "Why are you here?" In the wake of suicide, the question gained an existential force.

Some had been calling for the party to be canceled, claiming it was disrespectful. But going ahead with the party was the best thing to do. As Sub Pop's Bruce Pavitt said at Kurt's memorial service the following day, "The most important things in our lives are our friends, our family, and our community." The Seattle scene was founded on a strong sense of community—community gave rise to the music, nurtured it, kept its most successful members grounded, and provided solace in the face of calamity, as when Mother Love Bone's Andrew Wood died of a heroin overdose in 1990, when 7 Year Bitch guitarist Stefanie Sargent fatally overdosed in 1992, when the Gits' singer Mia Zapata was murdered in 1993. And so gathering at the Crocodile, a popular musicians' hangout where Nirvana played the occasional surprise gig, was downright necessary. Still, very few partygoers talked about what had just happened.

Small clutches of journalists gathered and did a lot of well-lubricated soul-searching about the ethicality of what they were doing; were we guilty of exploiting a sad story or were we documenting an important historical event? The fact that many of us had so much affection for Kurt compounded the problem painfully while the media blackout by the insiders drove it even further home. The rise of tabloid journalism had soured us on our own jobs, but it had also soured Seattleites on journalists, making them, in the words of one insider, "instant assholes."

A new Sub Pop band called Sunny Day Real Estate, soon to release their debut album, played in the music room while we all talked in the back bar. Later, Jonathan Poneman came up to me and asked if I'd seen their set. I said I hadn't, and Jonathan told me that it had been "life-affirming," which was quite a thing to say in that moment. I don't regret having those heart-to-hearts with my colleagues, but I sure could have used some life-affirming music that night.

Said Charlie Campbell of Pond, a Sub Pop band from Portland, Oregon, "Some woman from some magazine called me up and I didn't even know the guy. I just wanted to say, 'This is exactly the kind of conversation that killed the poor guy.'" "One of our own has been taken away from us by outside forces," adds Ron Rudzitis, singer-guitarist for Seattle's Love Battery. "There's some resentment."

Ron, a very nice person, was also in Room Nine, one of the earliest Seattle bands of that generation, and was a mainstay of the community. He was expressing the consensus of his peers: that the press had hounded Kurt to his death.

Someone had to take the fall for what happened, and it couldn't be Kurt—he was beloved and blameless.

On an overcast Sunday afternoon, while Kurt's friends and family attended his memorial nearby, a candlelight vigil was held in a park at Seattle Center, in the shadow of the Space Needle. The tented stage bore a modest collection of flowers and other offerings. A bootleg single of "Lithium" bore a note which began, "This song gave me strength during a difficult breakup . . ." A small bouquet of flowers also contained a miniature plastic shotgun.

Before about seven thousand grieving fans, a minister intoned, a poet recited, a trio of local DJs reminisced, a crisis counselor pitched, and a DJ read a bittersweet letter from Kurt's uncle Larry Smith, Don's second wife's brother, about his memories of Kurt as a teenager.

Smith began by noting that his grandfather thought a lot of Kurt and enjoyed his company very much.

One time Gramps invited Kurt along on one of our steelhead fishing trips. We were spread out a few hundred feet apart along the Wenatchee River. All of a sudden we heard this horrendous combination of screaming, warbling, and yodeling from Kurt, who was upstream and out of sight. Gramps told me to run up there and help

Kurt who must have hooked into a big fish. When I reached Kurt he didn't even have his line in the water. When I asked him what was going on he just looked at me with those piercing eyes and a huge grin and he said, "I'm just trying to thicken my vocal chords so I can scream better."

Kurt didn't fit the general mold of society in a logging town and so he was beaten on by people who didn't understand him. One day I heard he was in a fight a few blocks away. When I ran to the scene, the fight was over, however I heard from a friend that Kurt was assaulted by a burly 250-pound logger type. Evidently Kurt did not even fight. He just presented the bully with the appropriate hand gesture every time he was knocked down until the bully gave up. [This got a big cheer from the crowd.]

This is exactly the attitude I described earlier, about the kid I used to know who would bloody his own nose when bullies would pick on him. It's one way to fight a war that you cannot win.

It's also worth noting that Kurt spent quality time with—take it slowly, now—his father's second wife's grandfather on fishing trips hundreds of miles from home. It sounds like maybe Kurt was welcomed into his father's side of the family a bit more than he let on.

A wonderful picture comes to mind. When I peeked out the window into the yard, there was Kurt with some kind of contraption on his head that resembled a tin-foil hat, sneaking around the yard followed by a half a dozen laughing toddlers. Kurt had that million-dollar grin on his face and I could tell he was definitely in nirvana. I guess you could say he was the Pied Piper of compassion.

I hope that these little examples of happiness will show that even though Kurt experienced pain in his teenage years, he still did not let that pain stop him from loving life as fully as he could. We should never condemn Kurt for leaving us. We should instead look inward and thank him for loving us enough to share his feelings with us. Let us all learn that no amount of pain should ever stop us from loving life. We must all maintain respect for the significance of our own lives as well as for the lives of others.

But the most powerful messages were from two people who weren't there. In their taped speeches, Chris and Courtney sent two very different messages. Chris made a brief but wonderful statement about the egalitarian punk rock ethos that Kurt stood for.

On behalf of Dave, Pat and I, I would like to thank you all for your concern at this time. We remember Kurt for what he was—caring, generous, and sweet. Let's keep

the music with us. We'll always have it, forever. Kurt had an ethic toward his fans
that was rooted in the punk rock way of thinking. No band is special, no player
royalty. If you've got a guitar and a lot of soul, just bang something out and mean
it. You're the superstar, plugged into the tones and rhythms that are uniquely and
universally human: music. Heck, use your guitar as a drum, just catch a groove
and let it flow out of your heart. That's the level that Kurt spoke to us on—in our
hearts. And that's where he and the music will always be, forever.

And it was really great of Krist to remind us: Kurt was flawed, but he was also caring, generous, and sweet. He could be funny, too. Qualities like that get lost in our memory of him. That's especially true of documentary accounts, which tend to emphasize Kurt's dark side at the expense of the other facets of his humanity—maybe no one believes that an audience will buy the idea that someone can be vengeful and deceitful *and also* caring, generous, and sweet. The thing is, no one is a cartoon, which is a point I tried to make with this book.

"No band is special, no player royalty" was one of Kurt's core beliefs, and that refreshing rejection of hierarchy sets up another foundational Kurt ethos: just play your music with "a lot of soul . . . and mean it. . . . Let it flow out of your heart."

Courtney's typically rambling message was a loving tirade, full of the affection and anger, resentment and pity that everyone felt. It reduced much of the crowd to tears, leaving virtually the entire 7,000-person assembly shuddering with emotion. Courtney being Courtney, she couldn't help interjecting her own rejoinders. While they occasionally seemed overly bitter and even of questionable taste, like any good artist Courtney was only being honest; she reflected the deepest feelings of everybody there. It was a sort of dialogue, so I'll present it that way.

Courtney: I don't really know what to say. I feel the same way you guys do. But if you guys don't think that when I used to sit in this room when he played guitar and sing and feel so honored to be near him, you're crazy. Anyway, he left a note. It's like a letter to the fuckin' editor. I don't know what happened. I mean, it was going to happen. But it could have happened when he was forty. He always said he was going to outlive everybody and live to be a hundred and twenty. I'm not going to read you all the note because it's none of the rest of your fuckin' business. But some of it is to you. I don't think it takes away from his dignity to read this considering that it's addressed to most of you. He's such an asshole. I want you all to say, "Asshole" really loud.

Crowd: *Asshole!*

"It's like a letter to the fuckin' editor." Even in his suicide note, Kurt was carefully orchestrating his media strategy. But the note had one final editor: Courtney.

Courtney: This note should be pretty easy to understand. All the wording's from the Punk Rock 101.

Courtney skipped over this, the first sentence of the note:

Speaking from the tongue of an experienced simpleton who obviously would rather be an emasculated, infantile complain-ee.

So there's Kurt's typical self-blame about being uneducated and uncultured.

Complaining about being emasculated is an interesting thing to say, coming from a man who so famously championed his feminine side. But who was in a position to emasculate and infantilize Kurt and make him a "complain-ee"—in other words, someone who is complained about?

Kurt: Over the years, it's my first introduction to the shall we say ethics involved with independence and the embracement of your community, has proven to be very true. I haven't felt the excitement of listening to as well as creating music along with really writing something for two years now. I feel guilty beyond words about these things. For example, when we're backstage and the lights go out and the manic roar of the crowd begins, it doesn't affect me the way in which it did for Freddie Mercury [Courtney laughs], who seemed to love and relish the love and admiration from the crowd . . .

"I want to quit when I'm not having fun anymore," Kurt told Jerry Culley for the January 10, 1992, issue of *BAM*. "Especially if I wasn't writing good songs anymore." For the most part, he really hadn't written much in the previous two years—most of the best songs on *In Utero* were old, and most of the new ones were riffs that were jammed into song form.

Note also the little story below about Kurt admiring Pete Townshend on TV in his hotel room in New Orleans. Kurt was convinced he didn't have the passion anymore and was only going through the motions—he wasn't able to, as Krist put it, "mean it" and "let it flow out of [his] heart." For someone whose art was so completely entwined with who he was, this was devastating. He was, to cite a recurring theme, "guilty beyond words" about it.

Courtney: Well, Kurt, then so fucking what—then don't be a rock star, you asshole.
Kurt: . . . which is something I totally admire and envy. The fact is, I can't fool you, any one of you. It simply isn't fair to you or to me. The worst crime I can

think of would be to pull people off by faking it, pretending as if I'm having 100-percent fun.

Courtney: No, Kurt, the worst crime I can think of is for you to just continue being a rock star when you fucking hate it. Just fuckin' stop.

Easier said than done. As Sinéad O'Connor once posted on Twitter, "[The] music business is a very unforgiving place for artists who need to postpone due to emotional or mental health issues." Kurt saw only one way to get off the treadmill.

Kurt: Sometimes I feel as if I should have punched a time clock before I walk out on stage. I've tried everything within my power to appreciate it and I do. God, believe me, I do. But it's not enough. I appreciate the fact that I and we have affected and entertained a lot of people. I must be one of those narcissists [Courtney gives a bitter little laugh] who only appreciate things when they're [gone]. I'm too sensitive.

Courtney: *Awww.*

Kurt: I need to be slightly numb in order to regain the enthusiasm I once had as a child. On our last three tours I had a much better appreciation of all the people I know personally and the fans of our music. But I still can't get out the frustration, the guilt, or the empathy I have for everybody. There's good in all of us and I simply love people too much . . .

Courtney: *So why didn't you just fuckin' stay?*

Kurt: . . . so much that it makes me feel too fucking sad, a sad little sensitive, unappreciative, Pisces-Jesus man.

Courtney: Oh shut up, bastard.

Kurt: Why don't you just enjoy it? I don't know.

Courtney: Then he goes on to say personal things to me that are none of your damn business, personal things to Frances that are none of your damn business.

Kurt: I had it good—very good—and I'm grateful. But since the age of seven, I've become hateful toward all humans in general only because it seems so easy for people to get along and have empathy . . .

Courtney: Empathy?

Kurt was seven when his parents began to split. So "the legendary divorce" was not such a bore after all—in the waning minutes of his life, Kurt admitted that it was in fact a crucial part of the story.

Kurt: . . . only because I love and feel for people too much, I guess. Thank you all from the pit of my burning, nauseous stomach for your letters and concern

The Amplified Come as You Are

during the last years. I'm too much of an erratic, moody person and I don't have the passion anymore. So remember . . .

He actually wrote "baby" and not "person." Again, Courtney purposely omitted a reference to Kurt being infantilized.

Courtney: And *don't* remember this because this is a fuckin' lie.
Kurt: . . . it's better to burn out than to fade away.
Courtney: God, you asshole.

Gotta agree with Courtney there. Kurt, of course, was quoting the famous line from Neil Young's "My My, Hey Hey (Out of the Blue)." What a way to sign off from a life—sarcastic literally to the very end. The thing is, in that song, Young was talking about the *rock & roll spirit* burning out, not life generally. But maybe Kurt equated the two.

Poor Neil Young, having that on his conscience. "When he died and left that note, it struck a deep chord inside of me," Young wrote in his 2012 autobiography, *Waging Heavy Peace*. "It fucked with me."

Another line in "My My, Hey Hey" might have been more apt for Kurt: Young's pithy summation of the cost of stardom, "They give you this, but you pay for that."

Kurt: Peace, love, empathy, Kurt Cobain.

The word "empathy" was underlined twice. His name was in the smallest lettering of the whole note.

Courtney: And then there's some more personal things that are none of your damn business. And just remember, this is all bullshit. And I want you to know one thing. That '80s tough love bullshit, it doesn't work. It's not real. It doesn't work. *I should have let him, we all should have let him have his numbness, we should have let him have the thing that made him feel better, that made his stomach feel better. We should have let him have it instead of trying to strip away his skin. You go home and you tell your parents, don't you ever try that tough love bullshit on me*—because it doesn't fuckin' work. That's what I think. I'm laying in our bed, and I'm really sorry. I feel the same way you do. I'm really sorry, you guys. I don't know what I could have done. I wish I had been here. I wish I hadn't listened to other people. But I did. Every night, I've been sleeping with his mother and I wake up in the morning and I think it's him because their bodies are sort of the same. I have to go now. Just tell him he's a fucker, OK? Just say, "Fucker, you're a fucker." And that you love him.

###

Much later, Courtney visited the site of the vigil with her old friend Kat Bjelland of Babes in Toyland, and distributed some of Kurt's clothes to whatever fans still remained.

The speeches ended and the crowd was directed to move to the huge fountain nearby, where a sound system played an audio tape of Nirvana's recent MTV *Unplugged* appearance. Dozens of kids leaped into the forty-foot jets of water to great cheers from the crowd, which still must have numbered around five thousand. When the bowl-like fountain was turned off, it became a circular amphitheater, with people singing along to the music at the top of their lungs, cheering after every song as if they were at a real concert. Many knew the *Unplugged* show so well that they even sang along to the two rather obscure Meat Puppets songs.

In the fountain people danced, hugged strangers, did the Wave, threw Frisbees and batted around condom balloons, dogs ran around. But when the security detail tried to disperse the crowd once the music was over, they rebelled. A chunky kid with dyed-blond hair burst through the circular human chain the guards had made to push kids out of the bowl, and dozens followed, cheering and dancing, then defiantly mounted the fountain's central dome like the Marines at Iwo Jima. When a policeman waded into the crowd to eject the chunky barrier-basher, people began chanting "Fuck! You! Fuck! You!" and pointing at the cop until he gave up and walked away. Kurt would have loved it.

I said Kurt would have loved it because maybe Nirvana's inherent message of constructive subversion had reached some of his audience after all. There was really nothing wrong with those kids playing in the fountain—it was just that it was against the rules. So, as a group, they decided to reject the rules. And that was anarchy in the true and best sense.

###

When I began this book, I told my grandmother I was writing a biography of a rock band. The very first thing she asked me was, "Do they do drugs?" I had to reply that yes, I was pretty sure one of them did. "But that doesn't necessarily make him a bad person," I told her. That was a tough concept for a lot of people to grasp. But Kurt was a really nice person. He could be cranky and moody and stubborn, but those shortcomings were far overshadowed by his better qualities.

As I write these annotations and reflect on what others have discovered about Kurt in the intervening years, I'm not as sure about Kurt's essential blamelessness as I was when I wrote the book. Then again, maybe I should trust my own direct impressions of the man at the time rather than impressions filtered through thirty years, as well as other people's portrayals clouding my own memories. And drug addiction will certainly bring out the worst in otherwise good people. In retrospect, I think that to a certain extent I was sold a bill of goods, that Kurt and Courtney were performing for my benefit, just as they did for Jonathan Poneman and Robert Hilburn. And that makes me a sucker. I would like to think that, as I've grown older, I've also grown at least a little wiser.

Obituaries and other press accounts centered on the "tormented rebel" and the "troubled voice of a generation." In death as in life, few if any simply talked about Kurt as if he were a real person. This is the Kurt Cobain that I knew.

At five-seven, 125 pounds, Kurt was slight, painfully thin; he'd wear several layers of clothes under his usual cardigan and ripped jeans just to appear a little more substantial. His complexion was often bad, which was due just as much to a lack of sun and a strict diet of frozen dinners as it was to his pharmaceutical intake. It was amazing that such an insubstantial body could produce such a soul-rending sound, just like it's amazing that a tiny eight-pound baby can make such a piercing wail.

In Kurt's journals, he pasted in an illustration of his head from a comic book about Nirvana. Below the neck, though, Kurt drew in an emaciated weakling. He might well have had some body image issues.

Aside from some underwater photos to promote *Nevermind*, one of the few times Kurt ever felt comfortable enough to show his more or less bare chest, arms, and legs was when he wore a slinky little dress at the January 1993 show in Rio de Janeiro.

He had discovered what this fragile frame could withstand several times already, but what tormented Kurt wasn't merely physical. All that talent and charisma packed into such a brittle little package recalled Robert Fripp's description of Jimi Hendrix as a thin wire with too much current running through it. It was a horrible, unspoken piece of common wisdom among close friends and fans alike—Kurt wasn't long for this world. Every minute spent with him was precious.

It was well known that fame did not sit well with Kurt Cobain. There were a lot of good reasons why and not simply that he was a shy person. Kurt needed to monitor every aspect of Nirvana. If the T-shirts weren't just right, it cut him to the quick; his reputation as an artist hung on every frame of every video the

band made not because he was a control freak but because his art was his life. That was obvious to anyone who heard, really heard, the music. Kurt was able to oversee his career for a long time, probably longer than he thought he could, but by the time of *In Utero*, the Nirvana organization had definitely sprawled too far.

That's not a knock on Gold Mountain. It's just that early on, the band was basically a small business—and then very suddenly it became a very big business. Kurt and Krist used to oversee every aspect of the band, but eventually, they had to delegate a lot of important tasks to people who didn't necessarily share their sensibility.

In his classic *The Devil's Dictionary* (1911), Ambrose Bierce defined "famous" as "conspicuously miserable." Kurt lived that out to a tee. As Krist so succinctly summed it up in a 2013 *Rolling Stone* interview, "He wanted to be a rock star—and he hated it."

One aspect that Kurt vainly tried to keep tabs on was the press. Realizing that interviews were another facet of his art, and justly traumatized by the *Vanity Fair* debacle, Kurt was hypersensitive to his portrayals in the media. The slightest nuance could send him into a fit of panic. He once called in the wee hours of the morning, pleading for me to delete something from this book. "If you keep it in," he said, "I might as well just blow my head off." It was a list of his fifty favorite albums.

This was his answering machine message: "Michael, this is Kurt. Hi. Do *not*, whatever you do, for your *life*, don't print that Top 50 records [list]. Because there are too many that I left off and I think I'd piss too many people off by not putting their record on. If it goes in the [book] then I might as well blow my head off, OK? It's something I may have to explain later but *it's caused a lot of problems in my household* [emphasis mine] and it's ree-fucking-*diculous*, I can't believe it. So whatever you do, don't print it, OK? Thanks."

Over the phone, Kurt later confessed to me that the reason why he was so upset about that list was because Courtney was chastising him for including too many hipster indie bands and largely ignoring the uncool bands that had been so formative for him in Aberdeen: no Queen, the Cars, Black Sabbath, Cheap Trick, AC/DC, Kiss, Led Zeppelin, the Beatles, all bands he had loved and that had an undeniable impact on the music Nirvana made. The list was revisionist image-making intended to burnish his indie cred. And Courtney called him out on it.

Kurt complained constantly about the media prying into his personal life, but unfortunately the often painful (albeit not always truthful) candor of his music extended to his interview style. The man seemed not to be familiar with the phrase "no comment." He answered every question I asked him for this book and openly told me things which I had to beg him to take off the record.

I don't know why I put it that way, "beg him to take off the record." That makes no sense—as long as it was on the record, it was my choice whether to use what Kurt or anybody said in interviews. But in all the hours that we spoke, he never once said to me, "This is off the record." (Or, ha-ha, "Don't quote me on this.")

One thing he told me that I left out of the book—but is now a matter of public record—is that he smuggled a dealer into his room at Cedars-Sinai while Courtney was there to give birth; he nearly fatally overdosed right there in the hospital. Printing that would have caused a world of trouble and I wanted no part of that.

But his privacy wasn't the only casualty of Kurt's celebrity. Iconoclastic as he was, Kurt couldn't help living out at least one other cliché of success—he lost contact with most of the people he came up with. None of his friends had money; their entire creative and social lives, even their grunge fashion (an oxymoron if ever there was one), were based on poverty. He knew his wealth distanced him from his old pals and skewed their relationships. When he bought a Lexus in the winter of '93–'94, peer pressure made him trade it back in and stick with his trusty old gray Volvo with the one bald tire.

Kurt was still friendly with Dylan Carlson, as we know. He was still friendly with Mark Lanegan, too. But they were drug buddies. Courtney encouraged some stable, drug-free friends from Kurt's past, including Charles Peterson, to hang out with him, but understandably, nobody was keen to venture into such a dark situation.

Indeed, friendship is one reason Kurt stayed in the band. Chris and Dave were two of the best, most loyal friends he had left. And he couldn't deny the power of the music they made together. Even when his stomach was excruciating, he said the pain would go away during a performance because of the endorphin rush the music created in him. That's why he sometimes hurled himself into the drums at the end of a show—to prove that he was feeling no pain. That he had reached nirvana.

"In the midst of my own tiny personal troubles," Leonard Cohen once told *Rolling Stone*'s Mikal Gilmore, "I turned to the thing I knew how to do and I made songs out of it, and in the making of those songs, much of the pain was dissolved. That is one of the things that art does, is that it heals."

But in the last year of his life, Kurt was clearly growing apart from the thing he loved most. He knew he had to reinvent his music. *In Utero*, Kurt conceded, was virtually a remake of *Nevermind*, only recorded indie-style. As Kurt once pointed out, the Beatles went from "I Wanna Hold Your Hand" to *Sgt. Pepper* in just three

years. Kurt was capable of such staggering artistic progress. The fact that there now appears to be no other musician who could say the same is just another facet of the tragedy.

Despite what I said before, maybe Kurt's music might not have changed dramatically: he was a very rudimentary musician, technically speaking. ("I'm the guitar anti-hero," he told *Fender Frontline* magazine. "I can barely play the things myself.")

Maybe—with the help of a collaborator—he would have been capable of creating a canonically "ambitious" record like *Sgt. Pepper* or *OK Computer*. But, like Neil Young and Bob Dylan—with some notable if sometimes ill-fated exceptions—he might well have simply continued to write songs in roughly the same vein he always did, but in different contexts and different moods, not to mention different phases of his life and times, and that might well have been enough.

At the April 9, 1993, show at San Francisco's Cow Palace, Kurt arrived to find a large entourage filling the dressing room. He slouched in a folding chair against the white cinder-block wall. There was another chair right next to him, but nobody would just plop down and talk to him. So I did. He smiled, said hi, and plunked Frances down on my lap. We chatted about *Speed Racer*, one of his favorite TV shows. He sang me the theme song as several self-appointed minders eyed us worriedly.

One or two Gold Mountain employees just could not abide the fact that Kurt and I had become friends. They deeply mistrusted any member of the press, with absolutely no ability to understand that some journalists have integrity or, you know, empathy. Since they were such suspicious people, I was surprised that they weren't Machiavellian enough to realize that if I burned Kurt, I would never have any connection with him again. It felt insulting to be constantly presumed guilty. If they had anything to do with it, I would have been far, far away from this cozy scene. But Kurt liked me, so there was nothing they could do about it.

That night, Kurt changed what side of the stage he played on, from his usual stage left to stage right. "It kind of makes it interesting again," he explained. It seemed a bit trivial at the time, but hindsight says otherwise.

On July 23, 1993, the band played another high-pressure gig, an unannounced show at the Roseland Ballroom in New York for New Music Seminar attendees. Things went well, despite the finale, a painfully anticlimactic acoustic set. Two months later, Nirvana made its second *Saturday Night Live* appearance. Backstage, Alex Macleod tried to clear the dressing room, which was crowded with friends. "No, the more the merrier," Kurt quietly asserted. Everybody stayed just where they were.

Not many accounts of that well-documented show talk about the acoustic mini-set. It just didn't go over well—people just wanted to mosh. Kurt was painfully aware of this, as he noted during a September 24, 1993, interview with MTV.

Kurt: We had one day before we left to practice our acoustic set. Which explains why it sucked so bad.
Krist [surprised and disappointed]: You think it sucked?
Kurt: I think a lot of people thought it sucked. I didn't hate it *that* much.

That experience might partly explain why Kurt was stressed out about the band's appearance on *Unplugged*. But the great success of *Unplugged* trained Nirvana's audience to appreciate music in a quiet, acoustic mode; Nirvana could easily have done an entire tour that way.

Backstage at *SNL* was Anthony Kiedis from the Red Hot Chili Peppers. I got the sense that Kiedis was there specifically to support Kurt in his sobriety; at the time, Kiedis was several years into being clean after a heroin addiction. He and Kurt went into a quiet little huddle that everyone instinctively knew not to intrude on. RuPaul stopped by, too—he was in street clothes and looked kind of preppy. He was personable and charismatic, and everyone kind of gravitated to him when he walked in the room.

In October, Nirvana began their first US tour in two years. On second guitar was Pat Smear, formerly of L.A. punk legends the Germs. Pat bolstered Kurt's powerful but sometimes erratic attack with chunky, propulsive chording and passionate lead work, as well as a genial and energetic stage presence. Pat also found himself another, perhaps more crucial role—radiating a remarkably upbeat brand of cool, he rarely failed to lift Kurt's spirits.

Pat is such a sweet guy. He would smile throughout the shows, which is not something any previous member of Nirvana had really ever done. He found the joy in the music and projected it to the audience. At the December 1993 MTV interview, MTV News anchor Kurt Loder asked about Pat's effect on Nirvana's stage dynamic. "I look over and I see Pat's smiling face and it just gives me a bit of hope, you know?" Kurt said, gazing fondly at Pat. "It makes me feel good."

Pat's sweetness was all the more remarkable considering what he had gone through. He'd been the guitarist in the Germs, one of the original Los Angeles punk bands, the ne plus ultra of punk in many people's eyes, debauched exemplars of ecstatic cacophony and surprisingly sophisticated lyrics. As such, Pat had seen a lot of darkness, culminating in the 1980 suicide by heroin overdose of the Germs' brilliant but deeply troubled singer Darby Crash, only twenty-two years old.

The interview also features this exchange:

Loder: I wanted to ask you what it's like playing with these guys. As opposed to playing with your previous group [the Germs].

Pat [smiles coyly]: Oh, it's kind of the same.

Kurt [in a jokily resentful voice]: You mean you call me Darby?

Pat [smiling]: No, it's not the same problem.

Loder [genuinely concerned]: Oh gee, I hope not. I hope that's not true.

But nobody could lift Kurt's spirits like Frances, who traveled with Kurt while Courtney recorded Hole's new album. Frances was almost literally the light of Kurt's life—whenever she was around, Kurt's face would brighten, a rare grin would spread across his face, and the entire room filled with his joy.

Maybe it was just because he was the focal point of a huge rock band and so everyone was acutely attuned to his vicissitudes, or maybe it was that ineffable phenomenon of charisma, but Kurt's mood really did pervade any room he was in. "He was one of those special people," Polly Harvey told Rock's Backpages in 2004. "There was a light inside him that you could see. He had a charisma that went beyond his physical presence."

The band had resolved to make roadwork pleasant—they picked their favorite bands to open, including the Breeders, the Butthole Surfers, Chokebore, Come, Half Japanese, Meat Puppets, Mudhoney, and Shonen Knife. They indulged in two band buses, nice hotels, a chef, and a masseur. They booked plenty of days off and brought along wives, fiancées, and friends. Maybe that's why they played the most consistently amazing concerts of their career, transcendent shows where you almost felt your feet weren't touching the ground.

Halfway through the tour, a day off at an isolated hotel two hours from Boston had left everybody stir-crazy. Dave found out that the legendary punk-pop band the Buzzcocks were playing in Boston, so a bunch of us drove down to catch the set. Few at the club noticed the diminutive figure in the Holden Caulfield hunting cap; those who did simply smiled at him. Backstage afterward, the Buzzcocks kept saying what an honor it was to meet Kurt, but over and over he softly insisted, "No, it's an honor to meet _you_." Later, he hung out in front of the club, chatting with some punk rock kids who simply treated him as a peer—they didn't even ask for autographs. Kurt was very happy.

The Amplified Come as You Are

Those kids were for-real, crusty punk rockers. They recognized Kurt as one of their own and vice versa. There was no celebrity-fan dynamic there; they were just hanging out. I really wanted to drift over and hear what they were talking about, but I would have ruined the vibe. The beautiful thing was, they probably weren't talking about anything interesting. Kurt was so comfortable chatting with those kids, so carefree and relaxed, just standing on the sidewalk outside of a club, smoking a cigarette and talking about the cool show they'd just seen. Like normal people do. This was precisely what the first punk, Richard Hell, was talking about when he wrote in his autobiography, "I was trying to . . . undermine this idea of 'rock star as idol' and have it be sharp-eyed kids talking to each other about what they saw." It's one of my favorite memories of Kurt.

Not everyone found him so approachable. Kurt's piercing blue eyes, his moodiness, the question of whether he was high or not, his fame, and especially his almost palpable charisma were extremely intimidating. But by ignoring all that and treating him normally, one could meet a kind, sweet man who listened sincerely, who was capable of dispensing thoughtful advice and comfort.

I discovered those things when I traveled with Nirvana on that tour for two weeks, partly to see the people who had become my friends, partly to see what were the greatest rock shows I've ever seen, and partly to escape some personal and professional crises. By the time the tour reached New Orleans in early November, I was in serious trouble and needed a sympathetic ear. From a pay phone on Bourbon Street, I made a midnight call to Kurt. He said to come over to his hotel room and we'd talk.

I arrived to find Kurt lying on his bed watching a TV broadcast of a Pete Townshend concert with the sound off. Ever the guitar showman, the aging Townshend sang and played with unqualified gusto. "Look at that guy," Kurt said. "His music isn't even that good anymore but he's still so passionate about it. I wish I still felt that way." I couldn't quite believe he meant it, so I let it drop.

Kurt was exhausted but still eager to talk; he spoke of his own history of failed relationships and creative lulls with a wisdom I didn't know he possessed. Then, at around 4 A.M., I was in the middle of a sentence when he just shut his eyes and drifted off to sleep. He wasn't high, he simply couldn't stay awake anymore. "Why'd you leave?" he demanded the following morning.

I really wish I'd stayed, and not just because I was hungry and we'd ordered some room service pizza that finally arrived after I left. But it would have been awkward to stay in his room while he was asleep.

A Sad Little Sensitive, Unappreciative, Pisces-Jesus Man

At tour's end in November, Nirvana appeared on MTV's acoustic music show *Unplugged*. Kurt was in great spirits, cracking jokes between songs and singing with a cathartic intensity worthy of the most highly charged arena show. He chose an unprecedented amount of covers and, revealingly, they were either about fame, death, or both. In Meat Puppets' "Plateau," there's little more than a bucket and a mop—more work—at the top. Another Meat Puppets tune, "Lake of Fire," pondered the fate of damned souls, while on David Bowie's "The Man Who Sold the World" Kurt intoned, "I thought you died alone a long, long time ago." "Don't expect me to cry for all the reasons you had to die," he crooned on the gospel standard "Jesus Wants Me for a Sunbeam."

"Jesus Wants Me for a Sunbeam" is not, in fact, a "gospel standard." Maybe I was thrown off by the fact that Kurt introduced it on *Unplugged* by saying that it was "a rendition of an old Christian song." It's actually a Vaselines song that vaguely alludes to a corny early twentieth-century American children's hymn called "I'll Be a Sunbeam." "Jesus wants me to be loving / and kind to all I see," goes one treacly verse of the waltz-time hymn, "showing how pleasant and happy / his little one can be."

In an apparent gesture of self-hatred, on the *Unplugged* release, Kurt retitled it "Jesus Doesn't Want Me for a Sunbeam."

That was the last time I saw Kurt Cobain. He hugged me goodbye.

Because Kurt and Courtney were very interested in floriography, or "the language of flowers," it's worth paying attention to which flower Kurt specifically requested to be strewn around the *Unplugged* stage. Most flowers have very formalized associations, some going back centuries: for instance, everyone knows that a red rose represents passionate love, or that the daisy represents innocence and purity. Kurt specifically asked for the stargazer lily. The stargazer lily was developed relatively recently, in the mid '70s, so it doesn't have much of a tradition, but I looked it up and one website says it represents "heaven on earth, or reaching a paradise in the afterlife." Which is maybe nirvana.

Actually, that wasn't the last time I saw Kurt. A few days later, I joined the *In Utero* tour in Atlanta, traveling with them through Houston, which is where I last saw him.

A six-week European tour began in early February and ended with the overdose in Rome on March 6. Having survived a suicide attempt, Kurt had to endure the abject misery of continuing to live a life he no longer wanted. The band returned home to Seattle. On April 8 came the news.

I think I might have been one of the first to know. Someone from CNN called me, told me a body had been found in Kurt's garage or greenhouse or something, and asked if I knew anything about it. I knew it had to be Kurt. The first person I called was my nemesis at Gold Mountain. They answered the phone, and I actually said, "I have some bad news. I think you should sit down."

I don't know what happened the rest of the day; I've blacked it out. I know a lot of news organizations somehow got my unlisted phone number, I did an interview with MTV, and then I flew to Seattle with no idea what I was going to do when I got there.

A few days later, a Seattle limo driver who had often squired Kurt around town remarked, "Nice young man. Very quiet. But I guess he had a lot of hurtin'." Hurtin' occupied most of Kurt's waking life. Between stomach pain, chronic bronchitis, and scoliosis, even his own body was a hostile environment.

I could also have thrown in addiction and the agony of repeatedly withdrawing from it. And then there was the hostile environment of Kurt's own mind.

It wasn't like Kurt didn't have a sense of humor about his own misery; on the release form he signed for this book, Kurt listed his address as "Hell on earth." Like most suicides, Kurt provided plenty of hints, virtually all of which were amply documented in the slew of media coverage after his death; a few more appear in this very book. In retrospect, those clues weren't cries for help, they were announcements.

Much was made of the fact that Kurt died at precisely the same age as Joplin, Hendrix, and Morrison, but Kurt didn't act out some hackneyed rock truism about living fast and dying young. When he said in his suicide note that "it's better to burn out than to fade away," it was his sarcastic way of showing that he knew full well how his death would look.

Kurt was the first rock musician of his stature to take his own life so deliberately, rather than simply fritter it away through misadventure. A local Seattle newscast that weekend called Kurt "one of rock & roll's latest victims," but rock & roll never killed anybody. His suicide was a personal decision and it probably would have happened anyway, fame or no fame, riches or no riches, talent or no talent. But to speculate on precisely why he did it is a pointless parlor game. Although Kurt was clinically depressed and suicide ran in his family, no one will ever really know why he did it.

In the wake of his death there was one image of Kurt that refused to leave my mind. It was from the Reading Festival back in the summer of 1992. Still wearing the full-length doctor's smock he'd worn during the show, Kurt walked off stage, hand in hand with a little boy who it turned out had terminal cancer and had wangled his way backstage. Kurt slowly descended the stairs from the stage as a lone Kleig light beamed down on him. All in white, his blond hair gleaming, he looked just like an angel, the boy a cherub. There was a horde of people all around Kurt, but somehow the light never hit them. No one made a sound. It was very quiet, especially after the thunderous noise of the show. The crowd followed him down an alleyway made by the backstage tents and then he turned a corner, still hand in hand with the little boy, and was gone.

epilogue

A DARK
CONSTELLATION

ery late one night in June 1993, there was a knock on my hotel room door. It was Kurt. I'd recently finished writing *Come as You Are* and my agent and I agreed that we should let him read the book, as a "courtesy"—publishing industry jargon for "he can read it but he can't make any changes"—just before advance versions went out to the press, so he could be prepared for the revelations it contained. But, given her famously combative tendencies, we couldn't let Courtney (or anyone else, very much including my nemesis) see it, so we couldn't mail Kurt the manuscript. Instead, I'd fly out to Seattle and have Kurt read the entire book in my presence.

Kurt completely understood why we had to do it this way—Courtney could make things very difficult, we all knew that. So I booked a room at the Warwick Hotel in downtown Seattle and flew out from JFK with a thick pile of paper.

The first night, I took out the printed manuscript and a box of the chocolate-covered butter cookies that we both liked and set the precious stack of paper on the little desk in the corner of the room by the windows. Kurt was sober at that time, and Courtney had ordered the car service driver not to make any detours. (Remember what happened when the writers from *Monk* magazine gave him a lift.) I can't remember how she got it to me, but Courtney slipped me a tiny note asking me to make sure Kurt didn't call any beeper numbers: "P.S. Xtra secret don't tell I wrote this." (Beepers, also called pagers, were a now-primitive remote-messaging device popular with drug dealers in the late '80s and early '90s.) He didn't call anybody, but I'm not sure I could have stopped him anyway.

Kurt sat right down at the desk and began reading. He smoked a lot and read very intently. I kicked back on the bed behind him and worked on an article or played solitaire on my laptop.

This was in the wee hours of the morning, and it was very quiet—the only sounds were distant gurglings in the hotel's plumbing or a quiet hum from the ventilation suddenly switching on or just Kurt turning pages. Occasionally, he'd mumble something like, "Yeah, yeah, this reads real good," or sometimes he'd chuckle at something funny or sigh at something painful.

A few times, he moaned, "Aw, do you have to keep that in?" I don't remember every passage he had trouble with, but one was about the onstage freakout in Rome in the autumn of 1989. Every time Kurt objected, I'd say yeah, it has to stay in, and I'd explain why, and he never pressed the matter. For one thing, that was our original agreement—

to do it any other way would be, as he had said, "too Guns N' Roses." He didn't have any choice in the matter, but it was validating to successfully make the case with him every time.

Very occasionally he'd point out a minor factual error, such as correcting the name of the aunt who gave him his first guitar.

On the first visit, he got about a third of the way through before he started to fade and had to call it a night. It must have been a lot to absorb: foremost, he was probably thinking about how this would play to the people who wanted to take his child away from him, but I imagine he was also looking at it as Nirvana's chief conceptualist, weighing how everything squared with how he wanted the band and himself to be perceived. I hadn't been rigorous about following up on his mythologizing, and that worked well for him.

In this book, in the time-honored manner of really big bands, the members of Nirvana were communicating to each other through the press. As Kurt read *Come as You Are*, he must have been learning a lot about what Krist and Dave really thought about him and about what had happened between them. But Kurt didn't let on about any of that as he read.

The September 24, 1993, MTV interview touched on this aspect of the book:

Kurt: We're really passive-aggressive people and we don't like to complain to each other very often. That's probably why we've survived.

Krist: We should go to therapy, all of us—sit down with a therapist . . .

Kurt: No way, we should bitch about each other in articles, separately.

Dave: Yeah, read [*Come as You Are*].

Kurt: I did a lot of bitching. I can't even finish that book. I really can't even finish it. Oh God, I hate myself.

Krist: I learned a lot from that book!

Kurt: I learned a lot from just the first two chapters: that I should just shut up sometimes.

Krist: It's a good book!

Kurt: It's well written.

Interviewer: You guys were extremely honest.

Kurt: Sometimes that hurts.

Kurt again claimed he hadn't read the book during a January 1994 interview with Nardwuar. "I've skimmed through it a few times," Kurt said. "But I've never read it from front to back." But, of course, he absolutely had. I watched him do it.

Kurt and I reconnecting over screwdrivers at the Reading Ramada before Nirvana's appearance at the 1992 Reading Festival. © Charles Peterson

The second night was the same thing: just me and a guy reading the book I wrote about him and his band, in a modest, dimly lit hotel room, punctuated by the slow rustle of paper and the occasional grunt of appreciation or soft chuckle or Kurt noting a minor correction. He said it was illuminating to read about his entire life in chronological order. Maybe he was seeing the patterns that it took me years to notice.

Sometimes he'd take a break, and we'd stand together in front of the floor-to-ceiling window overlooking Fourth Avenue, and just talk, eat cookies, and look down to the street, where little gangs of homeless kids, probably runaways, swarmed around taxis stopped at red lights, trying to wangle a few bucks out of the cabbies. We never talked about the book, just people we knew in common, music we were listening to, or maybe things that were in the news. Sometimes we just stared out the window at the city, without saying anything at all.

Kurt needed one more night to finish the book. A little before dawn on the third night, he turned over the last page, planted his palm on the top of the stack as if absorbing its vibrations, and took a long, pensive drag on his cigarette. Then he got up, walked up to me, and said, "That's the best rock book I've ever read." He hugged me and looked me in the eye: "Thank you," he said, and left the room.

Doubleday was stunned that Kurt had only a few minor factual corrections. They were expecting him to raise a fuss. What they were forgetting was that the most sensational things were said by Kurt himself. The guy knew what he was doing.

When I got back home to New York, Courtney called me, incensed. Kurt had told her that Steve Albini had called her a "psycho hose-beast." So I gave her the courtesy of a rebuttal. That's how I got her snappy riposte about Albini only preferring women who were "from the East Coast, played the cello," and so on. (I assume that was her description of whoever Albini was actually seeing at the time.) The next day, I received some flowers via messenger, accompanied by a little card apparently written in the hand of an older lady to whom Courtney had dictated the following message:

> We love you Michael—you mensch
> Courtney & Bean
> p.s. from Courtney: fuck Steve up the ass

I love how Courtney made it clear that the foulmouthed part wasn't from Frances.

After *In Utero* came out, Kurt did an interview with MTV and the offscreen interviewer asked him how I came to write this book. Kurt's answer: "He said, 'You want me to write a book?' And we said, 'Sure, go ahead.'"

That just isn't true. It all started when Courtney called and asked me if I was interested in writing a book. Kurt just wanted to make sure that no one would mistakenly think the book was authorized.

"We had absolutely no control over editing anything," Kurt continued. "He let me read it right before it went to print. He stood behind me looking over my shoulder as I read it, like, at four in the morning until, like, seven in the morning. By that time I was so delirious, I don't remember what I read. If there were inaccuracies, I wouldn't have been able to tell him at the time anyhow. But that's about as much control as we had over it."

It's true that nobody else had control over what I wrote. But the rest of it isn't true—Kurt was revising history, as ever. I didn't stand over his shoulder as he read, and it wasn't "four in the morning until, like, seven in the morning." Kurt would arrive around midnight or so—a time *he* chose, not me. And he certainly wasn't "delirious"—he was reading carefully enough to ask valid questions and point out little inaccuracies.

At first I was sort of hurt when I saw that footage, but then I realized what he was doing: this time, he wasn't revising history to make himself look good; he was doing it to make *the book* look good. (Although, sure, he intended the book to make him look good.)

By making the subject-biographer relationship appear more adversarial than it actually was, he was helping make sure the book was received as credible and independent, which it was.

When Kurt told me that an authorized biography would be "too Guns N' Roses," it wasn't just a snarky swipe at his nemesis Axl Rose. He was also saying, *I know this will be unflattering sometimes, but I also know you understand where I'm coming from, I trust you to tell the story as accurately as you can, and I'm not afraid of how that will make me look.* And, to his immense credit, he kept his word.

There's plenty of unflattering stuff in this book, and it just wouldn't have been credible if there weren't, and Kurt knew that, too. Maybe I pulled some punches, but looking back on it, it really is, as a *Billboard* review put it, "amazingly raw and candid." All the frankness and revelations in *Come as You Are* have become so familiar to people that maybe it gets taken for granted. But there's actually a lot of heavy shit in there.

I just should have made it clear in the book itself that *Come as You Are* was unauthorized, and defined the term. That would have preempted countless lazy, ill-informed references to it as an authorized biography.

Probably the best review I got was from Dave. I had sent the finished book to him, and a few days later, I came home to a cheerful message on my machine: "Hi, Michael, it's Dave Grohl! Thanks a lot for sending the book. I read it and I like it, I think it's really great. . . . Want you to give me a call because I'd like to talk. I'd also like to apologize for my cold behavior—I suppose that's just my, I don't know, standoffishness, but I was wary of what the press had done to us before."

I called him and he said, "It's a great book!" and then he added, with a mixture of gratitude and disbelief, "and it's all true!"

In July 1993, Nirvana was in town to play Roseland, the cavernous, now-defunct former dancehall in midtown Manhattan. It was during the New Music Seminar, a widely attended and much beloved music biz convention and an essential platform for promoting the forthcoming *In Utero*.

While he was in town, Kurt had a business dinner with a bunch of "the grown-ups" at a fancy restaurant on the East Side. He asked me to come along, I guess so he wouldn't be completely alone with the business types or maybe so I could see firsthand what he was always complaining about.

There were maybe eight of us, all men, sitting around a large, circular table; I sat directly across from Kurt, out of conversation range, but facing him, and I could see he was uncomfortable. He was withdrawn and not really responding to anything anyone said to him. Everyone just tried to pretend like nothing was wrong. They all ordered their food—appetizers and steaks and wine and things—but all Kurt ordered was a slice of cake. "That's all you're going to have, Kurt?" someone asked. Kurt just kind of mumbled.

At one point, Kurt excused himself to go to the bathroom. He was gone a long time. I considered, with an inward chuckle, the possibility that maybe he had somehow sneaked out of the restaurant and done a runner. That would have been brilliant. But after maybe fifteen minutes, just as I was starting to think maybe I should go check on him, he returned.

He was really high, heavy-lidded and dazed, nodding slightly. It was the first time I had ever been sure Kurt was high on heroin. A mutual friend of ours, a former heroin addict, had told me that the signs of being high can be so subtle that only a fellow heroin user could notice—call it junkdar. But even my innocent eyes could see now. Surely everyone else at the table could see, too, but nobody said anything or acknowledged it in any way.

Kurt got high at that dinner deliberately: it was a self-destructive protest.

The conversation simply continued around Kurt as if he were a senile grandparent. It wasn't just awkward, it was upsetting.

The ostensible purpose of the dinner, aside from dining at a fancy restaurant and putting the bill on an expense account, was to discuss some pressing business decision with Kurt. But he was in no condition to make any big decisions.

When the check was finally paid, everyone scattered, leaving Kurt by himself, standing alone out on the sidewalk, really stoned on heroin in a city he didn't know very well. So I walked him back to his hotel, holding on to his arm as if he were an elderly person in case he stumbled and making sure he didn't walk into other people or even traffic.

We made it up to his room, where Courtney was kicked back on the bed, reading a magazine or something. She was annoyed that Kurt was high—she'd been working hard to keep him away from drugs—and scolded him a little bit while he stood there sheepish and unsteady, mumbling halfhearted protests and denials. Then he flopped down on the end of the bed, and Courtney nonchalantly put up her feet on his back like he was a sofa cushion. So Kurt was definitely using heroin again. And, judging by Courtney's reaction, incidents like this were routine. Kurt was now sleeping, or something like it, and Courtney apparently had things under control, so I left them and headed down the hall to hit a little party the rest of the band and crew were having.

The band and crew party couldn't have been more different from the sad, quiet scene I'd just departed: there was all kinds of booze and horseplay and music blasting out of a boom box. But it was also terrifying in its own way. Not long after I arrived, one

The Amplified Come as You Are

of the members of the band stepped out the window and onto the broad ledge on the side of the building—many stories above the street—and started walking toward the next window of the room, maybe ten feet. I was petrified. He was hammered and rowdy, not the ideal condition for tightrope walking. I thought I was about to witness some horrific rock history. But he made it. Everybody in the room cheered. Then one of the crew tried it. And I was terrified all over again. But he made it, too. Then the guy in the band went a second time. By this time I was totally freaked out. He made it again. Thankfully, there were no more ledge walks. I made a beeline for the drinks table.

Courtney later told me that Kurt OD'd later that evening. He had been in the bathroom a long time, and it had gotten very quiet. Then Courtney heard a thud. So she opened the door—or tried to, since Kurt's unconscious body was blocking it from opening. Eventually, she got in. Kurt was turning blue. It was very scary. Word was sent out to the band's crew: pack up the equipment, there will be no show tomorrow. Because Kurt is dead. I'm not sure who resuscitated him or how, but he played the Roseland show the next night, and rocked.

"Things have got better," Kurt told Jon Savage during an interview the day of the show (July 22, 1993). "Ever since I've been married and had a child, within the last year, my whole mental and physical state has improved almost 100 per cent. I'm really excited about touring again. I'm totally optimistic: I haven't felt this optimistic since [before] my parents got divorced, you know." The night before, he had nearly died of a heroin overdose.

###

In September, Nirvana came back to New York for their second appearance on *Saturday Night Live*. While Kurt was there, I invited him to join me for a visit to the Museum of Modern Art—Kurt was a painter and I figured he might like to see some of the world's most famous artworks in person. He showed up with MTV exec Amy Finnerty, a member of Kurt and Courtney's trusted inner circle, and he generously paid for our tickets. Kurt radiated his usual ragged charisma, turning a few heads, but nobody bothered him as we walked through the museum. There was an exhibit of Robert Ryman's signature all-white paintings, and Kurt was unimpressed; he just did not have the intellectual grounding, or perhaps interest, in that kind of heady, elite art. But then very few people do.

We eventually arrived at Van Gogh's *The Starry Night*. People travel thousands of miles just to be in the presence of this hallowed work of art. As Kurt, a troubled genius, gazed on perhaps the greatest work of another troubled genius, it struck me how the painting's roiling blue waves, the way its beauty transcends its own darkness, seemed like a perfect analogue to Nirvana's music. I waited expectantly for Kurt's response to this quintessential landmark of Western culture.

"Huh," he murmured. "Cool."

We moved on.

###

I made some dear friends in the process of writing the *Rolling Stone* cover story and *Come as You Are*. After I finished writing the book, I'd fly out to Seattle sometimes, just to see them. On one of those trips, I visited Kurt. It was early October 1993, and the band was getting ready for the *In Utero* tour. Kurt invited me along to a practice. He said it would be boring, but then he thought everything about his life was boring. Of course, I was really psyched.

The band's practice space was in a loft building in a grim industrial area south of downtown. The long concrete-floored hallway leading to their room was lined on one side with cremation urns, which were manufactured in another space on the floor. It was late at night when we arrived, and the entire building was dead quiet. Nobody else heard Nirvana run down a set of songs from their new album.

By that point, Nirvana was one of the biggest bands in the world—but you'd never know it from their rehearsal space. The room was maybe six hundred square feet, with windows along the longer wall that looked out onto other industrial loft buildings. A very basic riser for the drum set was about as fancy as they got—there was just a modest PA just like tens of thousands of other bands have, some amps, and a couple of workaday Shure microphones. There was no soundproofing, no soundperson, no special lights, no fancy recording equipment, no well-stocked bar. A few mismatched chairs were strewn around the room, likely picked up at the local Goodwill, some cool Frank Kozik show posters hung on the wall, and there was a small fridge, but that was it as far as adornments. It could almost have been *your* band's practice space.

They fussed with the PA a little, just like every other band does before starting a practice, and then they were off, running down songs from *In Utero*. I wanted to dance to it like the guy onstage at Reading, but instead, I just tried to be invisible so they could practice without feeling as though they were performing for anybody. They sounded fierce. It wasn't the sound of a band playing in a big arena, with all the lights and a big-time sound system—it was just four musicians in a small room, playing some incredible rock music.

Kurt ran the show, giving very specific directions for each of the players. They'd run different passages of songs, starting and stopping until Kurt felt it sounded right. I guess that was what Kurt thought was boring, but it was really illuminating to see how much he called the shots and how exacting he was with music that appeared so rough-hewn.

Sometimes it was difficult to hear the flaws Kurt wanted to correct, but when they were fixed, everything audibly snapped into place. It was kind of uncanny.

Eventually they seemed to tire and lose focus. Krist picked up his accordion, and then Dave, seeing an opening, made a beeline for Krist's bass. Krist started playing Led Zeppelin's "Kashmir" on the accordion, and everybody else joined in. Now the drum set was unmanned. I'd been playing drums since I was a little kid, so I raised my hand and pointed to the drums; Dave very kindly waved me in. I sat down on the drum throne and began jamming on an instrumental version of "Kashmir" with Nirvana. I'm not a *great* drummer, but I'm pretty good, and I could tell they got a kick out of that. The jam mutated into a Gang of Four–ish groove, then gradually dissipated into nothingness, the way jams do.

I wish I could say that I gleaned some sort of priceless insights into the inner musical workings of Nirvana by jamming with them once for ten minutes or so, but really, I was just trying to keep it together, especially in front of such an outstanding drummer. Afterward, Dave said, "I thought, *sure, let him fuck around on the drums*," he told me, "but I didn't know you could really play!" He was being generous.

Then they called it a night, and we drove back home.

###

That November, Courtney decided that it would be good if I joined the tour for a string of dates—I was a relatively steady person, a little older, and thoroughly drug-free. She figured I'd be good company for Kurt on the tour, maybe help keep him on the straight and narrow. I don't know if I accomplished that—it wasn't like I spent all that much time with Kurt—but maybe just having me on the bus did a little bit to break up some of the usual tensions and boredom, and I guess I set a good example, for what it was worth, in terms of not getting fucked up. Their old friend UK music journalist Everett True was along for part of the ride, too.

Kurt and Pat rode in one bus, and Dave, Krist, and cellist Lori Goldston were in the other. That arrangement worked out well—Pat cheered up Kurt simply by being Pat, but also they both smoked and Dave and Krist didn't (or at least were trying to quit), so there was the smoking bus and the nonsmoking bus. And sometimes Courtney, Frances, and her nanny Cali joined the tour; Pat and Courtney had known each other for a long time, so that worked out well, too.

Some of the greatest shows on that tour were ones that were off the media radar. The Roseland show in New York is considered a landmark, but that's mostly because the national media were there. The thing is, Nirvana played even more transcendent shows on that tour in "secondary markets" like Bethlehem, Pennsylvania; New Orleans; and Williamsburg, Virginia—shows that were so good that it was positively spiritual, which really was the whole idea.

Dave hit the drums with such force that they kind of distorted. The soundman would beg him to tune his drums a little higher so they'd make a more pitched tone, but Dave liked their low, flappy feel and sound—it probably reminded him of the pillows he used to whomp on as a kid, before he got a drum set. And besides, it announced in no uncertain terms that some punk rock music was being very vehemently performed.

Krist is so tall that he had to link two guitar straps together to get his bass slung low enough. He played with a wonderfully brutal impact but also with a tremendous precision and musicality—his immaculate parts are absolutely crucial to the band's sound. Pat Smear is a natural-born killer rhythm guitar player who understood Kurt's music completely and gave Kurt the latitude to concentrate on his singing. They sounded great every night.

On that tour, the prank call tape of choice was *Shut Up Little Man*, a very dark series of surreptitious recordings of the arguments of two elderly, alcoholic, spectacularly foulmouthed San Francisco men, one gay and the other viciously homophobic, and frequently physically violent to each other. These days we'd call *Shut Up Little Man* edgelord humor. Throughout the Nirvana tour—on the bus, backstage, during meals—it was good sport to quote favorite lines from the tape. Out of nowhere, someone might growl, "I got a decent *dinner* ready! Nothing *happened* with the dinner! Because you *crucified* it!" "If you wanna talk to me, then shut your fuckin' mouth!" Or just "Shut up, little man!" And everyone would just break up, laughing.

But sometimes a dark cloud hung over the touring party. That was partly due to Kurt's mental and physical state—his mood, light or dark, pervaded any room. And a lot of that depended on whether he'd been fighting with Courtney. There were tensions within the band, too, although Krist and Dave were insulated from some of the drama by traveling on a separate bus. And even if they scoffed at it, everyone was feeling the enormous pressure of being in a huge band and the relentless journalistic scrutiny that came with it.

Kurt would vent about all of that stuff to me, and his anger could be unsettling. I stopped by his hotel room once, and he started very loudly yelling about firing Dave for being an unsubtle and unspontaneous player. The thing was, Dave was staying in the room next door. I hissed at Kurt: "He can *hear*!" "I don't *care*!" Kurt yelled back, more at the adjoining wall than at me. There was no way Dave didn't hear the whole thing. As it turned out, Dave was already well aware of Kurt's feelings: he told his biographer, Paul

Brannigan, that on a flight from Seattle to Los Angeles he overheard Kurt bad-mouthing his drumming two rows back. After they landed, Dave told Alex Macleod that he was quitting the band after the last scheduled show. Macleod talked him out of it.

A couple of times, when the tension got to be too much, I visited Pat Smear in his hotel room. Pat is a kindly and serene presence, always ready with a smile and a cheery greeting of "Hey, fucker!" He'd seen it all already—several times over—and nothing seemed to faze him. He brought a portable record player on tour so he could play music in his hotel rooms. Late one evening, we sipped red wine, and he played me a record he'd been obsessed with for many years: a bootleg of a 1972 David Bowie live show at the Santa Monica Civic Auditorium, and it was fantastically good. Pat had been a massive Bowie fan for a long time and was not only the one who suggested to Kurt that they cover "The Man Who Sold the World" for the *Unplugged* show but also figured out the chords of the song.

When we reached Dallas, Kurt called my room and asked if I wanted to walk around downtown with him, Pat, and Frances. We rolled out with Frances in her stroller. It was eerie—a weekday in the middle of the afternoon in a major city, and there were no people on the streets. Where was everybody? As a provincial New Yorker, I was baffled. But it was great for Kurt because he could walk around and not get hassled.

After wandering around for a while, we walked down a wide boulevard and suddenly found ourselves at the edge of a big, open space. An absolutely massive flock of birds circled above it—I later learned they were grackles—forming a gigantic undulating disk so vast and dense that the sunlight filtering through them was turned gray. It looked apocalyptic. Except for the occasional car, there was not another human being in sight. It quickly dawned on me that this was Dealey Plaza, the site of the John F. Kennedy assassination. There was the former Texas School Book Depository and, surprisingly close by, the infamous "grassy knoll." It was a weird, staggering moment. Just like everybody else who visits there, we checked out the scene of the crime, considering the angles and weighing conspiracy theories. Then Frances needed some baby supplies, so Kurt split off and went to a drugstore.

Sometimes, after the audience left the venue, Dave would go out onto the floor and look for change people had dropped. Obviously, he didn't need the money anymore, but it was a ritual, a holdover from his hardscrabble days with Scream.

My favorite memory of that tour, besides the actual shows, was in the most boring, un-rock & roll place imaginable. In the wee hours of the morning after an arena show in Houston, Jim MacPherson and Kim Deal from the Breeders—who were the opening band—Dave, and I all headed out to a twenty-four-hour laundromat, one of the unsung mainstays of touring life. The place was bathed in blinding fluorescent light; we were pretty much the only people in the whole place, and we were all punchy from being on tour. There might have been some beer involved. I wish I could remember some details, but it was just a joyful interlude of dumb horseplay and assorted inside tour jokes, letting off steam, relief at being away from the tour bus, the hotel, the venue, "the grown-ups," and just anything to do with rock music. I've never had so much fun doing laundry.

The next morning, it was time for me to leave the tour and come back to real life. Shelli Novoselic had a flight back home to Seattle that same day, so we headed off to the airport together. I would never see Kurt Cobain again. I sure wish I'd known that.

###

In the DVD extras from Grant Gee's excellent 2007 documentary *Joy Division*, there's an outtake with the band's former road manager Terry Mason. At one point he describes what happens virtually every time that people find out he used to work with Joy Division. "All the time, they're dancing around their humbug to ask me the big one. They always want to ask that, and it usually starts with the line '*I'm not a ghoul like the others*, but why did Ian kill himself?'" Mason says, his face exuding both grief and anger. "They think I'm going to tell them the deep and dark secret—everyone thinks there's some deep, dark, mystical secret. And there's not. He was a nice guy, got into a strange situation, and the only way he could think about [it], at that time, was to kill himself. Sorry, no secrets." And then, twenty-seven years after his friend's death, it looks like Mason might start to cry. But first he looks straight into the camera and firmly says, "Cut."

Over the years, hundreds of people have asked me why Kurt killed himself. Actually, what often happens is that they *tell* me why he killed himself. They have their opinions, despite never having met the man, and disregard, to my face, my own firsthand observations of Kurt if they don't confirm what they already believe. And very few of them are willing to acknowledge this simple, unsensational fact: Kurt had a dark constellation of well-documented risk factors for suicide, including truly inhuman levels of professional pressure, chronic severe physical pain, some sort of mental illness, a long family history of suicide, and a deep heroin addiction, not to mention the fact that opiates were likely diminishing his brain's ability to feel happiness or tolerate pain of any kind.

Not everyone who endures those things commits suicide, just as not everyone who smokes gets lung cancer; it just makes it more likely. Kurt really had the deck stacked against him. But, as noted several times here, that's a surprisingly difficult thing to realize in the moment and an even more difficult thing to confront head-on—that requires a *real* grown-up.

In Kurt's 1993 interview with Jon Savage, the conversation rolled around to the difficulty of having tough conversations with loved ones. "It's what I've done all my life: I've always quit jobs without telling the employer that I'm quitting—I just wouldn't show up one day," Kurt told Savage. "Same with high school—the last two months of high school, I quit. So I've always copped out of things, all my life." That's pretty much what he did by taking his own life: he just . . . copped out.

It's true, Kurt achieved wild success, the fulfillment of his dreams. But we tend to overestimate the ability of a good material situation to make us happier—for instance, it turns out that, after the initial euphoria wears off, winning the lottery won't actually make you a happier person. We all have a happiness set point that we tend to return to no matter what happens. Kurt had won the lottery, but he also had a very low happiness set point.

When author Hua Hsu was on NPR's *Fresh Air* in October 2022, talking about his book *Stay True: A Memoir*, host Terry Gross asked him about his Nirvana fandom and what his father said to him when Kurt died. His father, Hsu replied, said that "You have to have passion, you have to have belief—but you also have to figure out how to live."

Krist had known for a long time that Kurt didn't exactly have a lust for life. In Krist's interview with John Hughes for the Washington State website, he recalled an early tour when he was reading *One Day in the Life of Ivan Denisovich*, the 1962 classic by Russian dissident novelist Aleksandr Solzhenitsyn. Kurt asked him what the book was about, and Krist said it was about prisoners suffering in a miserable Soviet gulag in Siberia. "And he's like, 'Ah, and they still want to live?'" Krist recalled. "He was disgusted."

"So it kind of tells you what was going on," Krist continued, "[thought processes] distorted from heroin, drug-distorted, I don't know. . . . It's just personality or something."

It was definitely "personality or something." It goes without saying that manic depression is a serious risk factor for suicide. Don's cousin Bev Cobain (Kurt's first cousin once removed, for those keeping score) is a registered nurse with a certification in mental health and the author of *When Nothing Matters Anymore: A Survival Guide for Depressed Teens*. She didn't know Kurt, but she is on record as saying, "Kurt was diagnosed at a young age with Attention Deficit Disorder [ADD], then later with bipolar disorder."

"I was hyperactive as a child," Kurt told David Cavanagh in the June 1992 issue of *Select*, "and they gave me speed to counteract that."

If Bev Cobain was correct, that would explain why Kurt joked about manic depression so much: it was the same gambit—smokescreening by exaggeration—that he used for so many other things he wanted to downplay, from selling out to doing heroin.

There was suicide on both sides of Kurt's family. In 1913, his great-grandfather's sister, seventeen-year-old Florence Cobain, wanted to go to the movies, but her father wouldn't let her, so she shot herself in the chest with a rifle. She survived and lived to be ninety-four. (Oddly enough, this happened in Ellensburg, Washington, which is where both Calvin Johnson's and Kurt's close friend Mark Lanegan grew up.) One of Kurt's great-grandfathers on his mother's side attempted suicide with a knife—he survived but then died after he purposely reopened the wounds while he was in a psychiatric hospital. In 1938, when Kurt's grandfather Leland and his brothers Burle and Kenneth Cobain were young men, their father, John "Arthur" Cobain, a deputy sheriff who lived in Ellensburg, was sitting on a stool at the beer counter of a store in Markham, Washington, a few miles west of Aberdeen, when he apparently reached in his pocket for a cigarette and accidentally knocked his pistol out of its holster; the gun dropped to the floor and discharged, killing him. In 1979, when Kurt was twelve, Burle Cobain killed himself with a gun. Five years later, so did Kenneth.

I didn't know that history—the diagnoses or most of the family suicides—when I wrote Come as You Are, nor were they the kinds of things I even thought to ask about. All I knew was that I had the distinct feeling that Kurt would not live a long life. But what, if anything, could I do about it? Was it even my place to get involved?

At least once, I did get involved. I'm just not sure exactly when this happened, but one evening in 1993, I got a panic-stricken call from Courtney. She said Kurt had locked himself in a room in their house. He was distraught, she said, and had a gun and was threatening to use it on himself. She was terrified. So was I. I asked if I could speak with Kurt, but there was no way to get the phone to him. I could hear him yelling in the background. It was really, really scary. I told her to call the police and to keep me posted. Then I called one of Nirvana's managers. I told them what was happening, and that two such volatile people, who did drugs and had a small child, absolutely should not have guns. After a long pause, they replied, "I'll take care of it." I don't know if they did.

When Kurt really started spiraling down, I thought back to the time I visited his hotel room late at night in New Orleans, and we were lying on his bed watching a Pete Townshend concert. I'd been a huge Who fan as a teen, and I noted Kurt's respect for Townshend.

In late 1993, I was part of a team of people that was working with Townshend to develop a CD-ROM about the history of Tommy, the Who's classic 1969 rock opera. Townshend had helped his friend Eric Clapton recover from a heroin addiction many years earlier and was all too familiar with the catastrophic consequences of substance abuse. So I asked Townshend if he might have a word with Kurt about beating heroin. I gave him Kurt's phone number and hoped that he would call—and that somehow Kurt would listen.

"When Cobain was in deep trouble with heroin addiction in 1993," Townshend wrote in the Guardian nearly a decade later, "I met Michael Azerrad who had written Come as

You Are: The Story of Nirvana. Azerrad asked if I would contact Cobain, who was in constant danger of overdosing. I had chosen this year to give booze another gentle try after 11 years. When Azerrad approached me, I was not drunk, nor unsympathetic, but I did not make the necessary judgment I would make today that an immediate 'intervention' was required to save his life."

Neil Young wanted to reach out to Kurt. When Kurt died, Young wrote in *Waging Heavy Peace*, "I, coincidentally, had been trying to reach him through our offices to tell him that I thought he was great and he should do exactly what he thought he should do and fuck everybody else. I wanted to talk to him. Tell him only to play when he felt like it. And that would be good enough. Be true."

I'm sure Pete Townshend and Neil Young both wonder to this day what might have happened had they gotten through to Kurt. It might have helped, but in retrospect, anyone who does something as drastic as taking their own life is usually very determined, not likely to heed the advice of anybody, even people they revere.

But that's the kind of thing that haunts people who know people who have died by suicide: Is there something I could have done? Even thirty years later, I still ask myself that question. I tried, but maybe I could have—should have—done more. I was in my early thirties but still immature and naive. Maybe I wasn't so well suited to the task. And there were other people much closer to Kurt. In late March 1994, Dave and Krist threatened to dissolve the band unless Kurt went into rehab. There were interventions. But it was too late, he'd made up his mind. He'd already tried a few months earlier. And he'd probably made up his mind a very long time before that. It was only a matter of time until the slings and arrows became overwhelming.

In 2022, Tobi Vail told Damian Abraham for the *Turned Out a Punk* podcast, "I know there were people that cared, that were trying to help but, like, at the same time you can't, you can't save someone—you really can't, you know? Like, if they're going to self-destruct, they're going to self-destruct. It was unfortunate—like, it was really unfortunate—the way it all went down and it should not have gone down that way."

Kurt shouldn't have been touring. He should have been in therapy and working on staying clean. Instead, he was out on the road. Maybe he thought that "the grown-ups" wanted him to go out there and flog the product. He probably felt he needed to support his family. And the fans certainly wanted to see Nirvana.

Also, Kurt had lost a really crucial port in the storm: Krist. He'd begun to push Krist away back in late 1990, when Krist said he disapproved of Kurt's heroin use. They were never as close again. Things got a little better around the time they were rehearsing to record *In Utero*—there was the excitement about playing new songs, recording with Steve Albini, and just generally starting a new, more artistically liberated phase of the band. But by the time of *Unplugged*, they were becoming distant again. Kurt surrounded himself with his little family and his own set of friends, several of whom were drug addicts, and Krist didn't feel very welcome.

But something else really bad was going on with Kurt toward the end. As Dave told his biographer Paul Brannigan: "A lot of fucked-up shit went down that nobody knows about. And Krist and I have always kept quiet about a lot of what happened because it's a personal issue.... But there's some other things that happened long before [the late March 1994 intervention and Kurt subsequently going to rehab in Los Angeles] that made it clear that maybe we weren't going to be a band forever."

One can only speculate about what Dave was referring to, but some "fucked-up shit" made Kurt want to cancel Nirvana's final show, at Munich's Terminal Einz, on March 1, 1994—two days before he nearly fatally overdosed on a lethal cocktail of Rohypnol and champagne. "He had something going on," Krist told *Guitar World* in 2001. "There was something going on with him and his personal life that was really troubling him." That's all Krist would say on the matter.

In *Montage of Heck*, Courtney is asked if she ever cheated on Kurt. "I almost did one time and he knew it," she says. "The plan didn't ever go anywhere . . . nothing happened. I never cheated on him but I certainly thought about it one time in London. And I could have done it. And the response to it was, um, he took sixty-seven Rohypnols and ended up in a coma because I thought about cheating on him." Kurt "knew" of her "plan," Courtney said, adding, "that's how psychic he was?" But maybe he had an inside source.

On February 26, a few days before Nirvana's Munich show, Courtney's ex-boyfriend Billy Corgan and his band the Smashing Pumpkins completed a four-night stand at the Astoria in London. At the time, Courtney was in London to do press for the upcoming Hole album. Maybe that's a clue about who Courtney thought about cheating with.

As with the São Paulo stadium show, Reading '92, and *Unplugged*, Kurt tended to play very pointed covers, sending messages. Nirvana opened that Munich show with the Cars' 1978 hit "My Best Friend's Girl." Kurt had known and loved that song since he was a teenager, but it was the first and only time Nirvana played it live. Why did he choose that particular song at that particular time?

The narrator of the song has had his lover stolen from him. "She's my best friend's girl," goes the chorus, "but she used to be mine."

Sexual jealousy is a primal feeling, and even the *fear* of being cheated on induces feelings of humiliation. And recall Kurt's particular sensitivity about being humiliated: "I couldn't handle the ridicule," he said about the allegation that he had abused the girl from the special-ed class in high school, which allegedly prompted him to try to get run over by a train. "I am threatened by ridicule," he wrote in his diaries. "I've been told by doctors and psychiatrists that public humiliation is one of the most extreme and hardest things to heal yourself from," Kurt told *Melody Maker*'s the Stud Brothers in August 1993 (perhaps revealing that he had had in-depth conversations with psychiatrists, unless he was making it up). "It's as bad as being brutally raped, or witnessing one of your parents murdered in front of your eyes or something like that. It just goes on and on, it grinds into you and it's so personal."

In *Montage of Heck*, Krist recalled how angry Kurt was at the first press Nirvana ever got: a negative review of the "Love Buzz" single. "Kurt hated being humiliated," Krist explained. "He hated it. *He hated it*. If he ever thought he was humiliated then you'd see the rage come out."

Think about all the times the word "shame" appears in Nirvana songs.

Kurt searched for acceptance, stability, and family for most of his life. He'd found it with Courtney and Frances. "I guess getting married has a lot to do with security and keeping your mind straight," Kurt told *BAM*'s Jerry Culley. "I've never felt so secure in my life." But even the mere suspicion of being cheated on could have shattered that, producing—among a million other unpleasant emotions—humiliation and shame.

But this is crucial: killing yourself just isn't a rational response to suspecting you've been cheated on. Kurt was in a particularly vulnerable state, exhausted from touring, hopelessly addicted to heroin, and unsure as to the direction of his career and his life in general. And it turns out that Rome wasn't the first time Kurt had attempted suicide: as Courtney revealed in *Everybody Loves Our Town*, he'd tried it in December 1993, too. He'd left a note: "a list of reasons why he shouldn't be alive," Courtney said, "and how he could never stop doing heroin."

This can't be said enough: *It's absolutely wrong to blame Courtney*. Kurt would have found some other pretext to do what he did. I mean, it was going to happen.

It was only natural, though, for Courtney to feel guilty, just as we all did. For weeks after Kurt's death, she aired her grief on America Online bulletin boards. "Thank you for respecting the finest man who ever lived, that he loved a scum like me is testament enough to his empathy," she wrote. She told MTV News, "Everyone who feels guilty, raise your hand."

Surely everyone around Kurt has beaten themselves up about things they could have done, and it's likely that the closer they were, the more they beat themselves up. But there was nothing they could have done. As Danny Goldberg said of Kurt, "He is one of the most willful people I've ever met in my life."

###

But covering "My Best Friend's Girl" might not have been Kurt's only hint about marital strife. Kurt was painfully aware of the fallout from his parents' divorce: the bitter, open acrimony between Wendy and Don and the effect it had on their children. The last song Nirvana ever recorded suggests that maybe Kurt felt he was in danger of repeating his parents' mistake.

"You Know You're Right" was recorded during some troubled informal sessions in late January 1994. Although it cleaves to Nirvana's classic quiet, tense verse/explosive chorus dynamic, it's an uncharacteristically direct and internally consistent lyric. The narrator addresses a second person, seemingly saying, *Things have gotten irreparably bad, so let's just part peacefully, no hard feelings.*

The song is suffused with self-effacement and appeasement, the same as in what seems to be another apparent breakup song, "All Apologies," where he sang, "Everything's my fault / I'll take all the blame." In "You Know You're Right"—the implication being "I'm (always) wrong"—the narrator offers to "crawl away for good" from a relationship that had always had a bomb strapped to its chest. He feels relieved to have gotten it out in the open ("I'm so warm and calm inside / I no longer have to hide") and couches it all in biting sarcasm and self-loathing ("Things have never been so swell / I have never failed to fail").

"Oh God, it's hard to listen to," Dave told the *Guardian* in 2019. "Lyrically, it's heartbreaking. He was in a place we may not have recognised."

###

I can't count the times I've been asked, "Were you shocked when you heard the news?" And I always say the same thing: "Yes, I was shocked. But I wasn't surprised." There's a difference. Like many people, I thought I was prepared for it; I just didn't know when it was going to happen—it could have been days, it could have been decades. And then it happened. That's when you find out, the hard way, that you *can't* actually be prepared for such a thing. I don't remember much from the weeks and months after. I could outwardly function, but inside, I felt catatonic. I was profoundly grief-stricken for a few years. I beat myself up a lot about it. I can't even imagine what people who were close to Kurt went through; I just know it hit me really hard.

"The awful thing about suicide is, the person who commits suicide, their problems are over," as Joy Division bassist Peter Hook put it in *Transmissions: The Definitive Story of Joy Division & New Order*, a 2020 podcast about the band. "And yet yours, and everybody left behind—his family, his parents, everybody else, in every occasion—theirs is just beginning. And they last all your life."

Dealing with death is always difficult and strange, but it has its own unique difficulties and strangeness when the person who died was a public figure. When, say, a parent dies you can dole out the information at a rate you're comfortable with. You can tell friends and co-workers one at a time—or not at all. They offer their condolences, maybe share a memory of the person if they knew them, say a few supportive words, and that's it.

But when it's a public figure, everyone in the whole world knows right away. So you can't divulge the information at a rate that you're comfortable with. And if everyone knows that you knew the public figure, a lot of well-meaning people will reach out to you. Often, they have a parasocial relationship with the celebrity, an emotional investment in someone who did not know them. They tell you, unbidden, what that person meant to them. But they don't seem to understand that you actually knew and loved this person, and they knew and loved you, and that you're on a deeper level of grieving.

They invariably ask what the person was really like. And the more you explain it, the more the answer becomes a rote response, which in turn pushes the dead person further and further away from you, reducing them to a few pat, well-rehearsed anecdotes.

Then there are the people who tell you with absolute certainty that Kurt was murdered. They've seen a movie about it, or maybe they've read something on the internet, and they're absolutely convinced that something outlandish and highly improbable happened to this person who happened to be someone you deeply cared about. I understand the parasocial thing, and that they have trouble coming to terms with the fact that someone they felt such a close connection with would do this to them, so they're looking for someone else to blame. At first, I would patiently explain that the person was mortally depressed, that they had a number of risk factors for suicide and repeatedly telegraphed what they were going to do, and that real evidence to the contrary is nonexistent. But eventually, I realized that having to explain this stuff just made me very sad. So I would very candidly tell those people that they don't know what they're talking about and end the conversation.

When Bobcat Goldthwait cast Krist in *World's Greatest Dad*, Krist wanted to know what the movie was about. "It's about when someone dies," Goldthwait explained, "and people that don't really know them reinvent it and make it all about themselves and forget about the people who were really close to the person."

And Krist said, "I have no idea what you're talking about."

And then there was the media. In an episode of *The Larry Sanders Show* that aired after Kurt's death, Garry Shandling's character is reading the newspaper. "It turns out the electrician found Kurt Cobain's body two days after he was dead," he says. "Talk about grunge."

The mainstream news media were mostly clueless about Kurt, but by far the worst of it was the infamous commentary by crotchety *60 Minutes* regular Andy Rooney. "Everything about Kurt Cobain makes me suspicious," ranted that clueless blowhard. "This picture shows him in a pair of jeans with a hole in the knee. I doubt that Kurt Cobain ever did enough work to wear a hole in his pants. He probably had ten pairs just like these hanging in the closet—all with fake holes in the knee. . . . If [Cobain] applied the same brain to his music that he applied to his drug-infested life, it's reasonable to think that his music may not have made much sense, either." That was the only time in my entire life that I've ever been tempted to kick in my television screen.

Needless to say, sales of this book spiked in the wake of Kurt's death. I felt awful that I was financially benefiting from this horrific, heartbreaking thing. A wise friend reassured me, "Being a good journalist means being in the right place at the right time. That's what you did. Don't feel bad." That made me feel a little better, but not much.

It was just as well—I was so cripplingly depressed for the next few years that I couldn't work very much. I lived off that money. There's an effect they used to use in silent movies: the iris, where the picture closes up into a circle in the middle of the screen, surrounded by blackness. That's almost literally how I saw the world for a long time after Kurt died.

For many years, if Nirvana's music started playing somewhere, I'd quietly step outside until it was over—I never played it at home either. Hearing that music was just too emotional. It brought back such vivid, intense memories and all the feelings of regret. Vivid sensations of good times and bad ran through me like an electrocution. The music's very strength—that it's an open window to Kurt's soul—only reminded me of all the hints I'd missed, the things I could have done, things I shouldn't have done.

Then a few years ago, I was out at a loud bar in the East Village with some friends. The music was blaring. And some songs from *Nevermind* started playing.

Instead of stepping outside for a bit, this time, I stayed and listened. And you know what? Nirvana fucking rocked. Despite what happened, it's still life-affirming music. It made me feel better.

Up until then, I hadn't read anything about Nirvana either. I didn't want other people's reminiscences and speculation to muddy my own firsthand experiences. "Who put these fingerprints on my imagination?" Elvis Costello once sang. I didn't want someone else's fingerprints on my memories.

My ego also wouldn't let me read things that contradicted or denigrated things I'd written—and I knew there were plenty; it comes with the territory. And there was some dark stuff that I just did not want to know. Over the years, Nirvana fans would ask me what I thought about some bit of news about Kurt or some freshly discovered demo or even wanted to know about something in *Come as You Are*. And I just had nothing to say—I had put Nirvana completely out of my mind; I stopped following anything to do with the band the day Kurt died. I didn't want to go back there.

That was also partly so I could have plausible deniability. When Nirvana fans ask what I think about dubious documentaries like *Kurt and Courtney* and *Soaked in Bleach*, I can shrug my shoulders and say, in all honesty, "Haven't seen it." (I did see *Montage of Heck*, although only because fate virtually dictated it.) They're always a little flummoxed and disappointed by that—I'm supposed to be The Nirvana Guy. The thing is, when fans ask me questions about Nirvana, more often than not, they know more about the band than I do anyway. Or they just want to hear me confirm their preconceived notions.

But my strong desire to put my experience with Nirvana behind me was infinitesimal compared to how Kurt felt. "I wish nobody ever knew what my real name was," Kurt says earlier in this book. "So I could some day be a normal citizen again." That reminds me of a daydream I still have now and then. It's that Kurt's death was all a big fake. He just staged it so he could quit everything, run away somewhere, and start a new, anonymous life. In this fantasy, I spot him on the street: he's disguised somehow, maybe with a big beard and a baseball hat pulled down low, but his laser-blue eyes instantly give him away. He sees me, too, but we just nod at each other, smile, and keep walking.

###

But you know what? That's a bullshit ending. The "they're actually still alive" fantasy has been applied to everyone from Elvis to Tupac. It's a hoary trope, right up there with ending a story by saying "it was all a dream." The real happy ending would have been this: Kurt took as much time as he needed and did whatever was necessary to save his own life.

The interview tapes used for the writing of *Come as You Are: The Story of Nirvana.*
© Michael Azerrad

ACKNOWLEDGMENTS

These people gave me the precious gift of wisdom, inspiration or encouragement:

John Agnello	Steve Holtje	Bruce Pavitt
Elvira Asensi Monzó	John Hughes	Mark Pickerel
Dave Ayers	Jeffrey Michael Kauffman	Jonathan Poneman
Nabil Ayers	Dan Kaufman	Sadie Powers
Earnie Bailey	Matt Keating	Marianna Ritchey
Tom Beaujour	Emily Lee	Ben Schafer
Lisa Benger	The folks at LiveNirvana.com	Dr. Joshua Straus, MD
Karl Braun	Jen Long	Kurt Stream
Amy Dupcak Remland	Dave Longstreth	Chris Swenson
Matthew Elblonk	Ian MacKaye	Susie Tennant
Steve Fisk	Natalie Mason	Bruce Tracy
Don Fleming	Jonathan Meiburg	Jon Wurster
Danny Goldberg	Steve Michener	Mark Yarm
Abraham Gutman	Denise Oswald	Kelly Zutrau

A deep bow to: The great Robert Greenfield for writing a really cool book called *Ain't It Time We Said Goodbye: The Rolling Stones on the Road to Exile*, which was the inspiration for the "amplified" approach.

Great thanks to the following folks at HarperOne:
My editor, Biz Mitchell, for her patience, wisdom, and enthusiasm
Gideon Weil, for believing in this pretty much unprecedented project
Stephen Brayda, for being so into this idea and for liaising
Judith Curr, for believing in this project, too

Ghjulia Romiti, for being so helpful and cheery
Janet Evans-Scanlon, for figuring out how to visually present this thing
Trina Hunn, for looking out for me

A great big thank-you to my agents, Sarah Lazin and Laura Nolan, for their crucial help in making this book a reality, and for all their wisdom along the way.

And immense gratitude to my brilliant third cousin, Lawrence Azerrad, who designed the excellent cover of this book. By all means check out his stuff at https://laddesign.net.

Acknowledgments

SELECT BIBLIOGRAPHY

Arnold, William. *Shadowland*. New York: McGraw-Hill, 1978.

Attali, Jacques. *Noise: A Political Economy of Music*. Minneapolis: University of Minnesota Press, 1985.

Azerrad, Michael. *Our Band Could Be Your Life: Scenes from the American Indie Underground 1981–1991*. Boston: Little, Brown, 2001.

Brannigan, Paul. *This Is a Call: The Life and Times of Dave Grohl*. Cambridge, MA: Da Capo Press, 2011.

Cameron, Keith. *Mudhoney: The Sound and the Fury from Seattle*. London: Omnibus Press, 2013.

Cobain, Kurt. *Journals*. New York: Riverhead Books, 2002.

Collins, Jackie. *Rock Star*. New York: Pocket Books, 1988.

Erlandson, Eric. *Letters to Kurt*. New York: Akashic Books, 2012.

Gilmore, Mikal. *Shot in the Heart*. New York: Doubleday, 1994.

Goldberg, Danny. *Serving the Servant: Remembering Kurt Cobain*. New York: Ecco, 2019.

Hinton, S. E. *The Outsiders*. New York: Viking Press, 1967.

Hinton, S. E. *Rumble Fish*. New York: Delacorte Press, 1975.

Hughes, John C. and Ryan Teague Beckwith. *On the Harbor: From Black Friday to Nirvana*. Aberdeen, WA: Daily World, 2001.

Lanegan, Mark. *Sing Backwards and Weep: A Memoir*. New York: Hachette Books, 2020.

Lavine, Michael, with Thurston Moore. *Grunge*. New York: Abrams Books, 2009.

Malcolm, Janet. *The Journalist and the Murderer*. New York: Alfred A. Knopf, 1990.

McMurray, Jacob, ed. *Nirvana: Taking Punk to the Masses*. Seattle: Fantagraphics, 2011.

Novoselic, Krist. *Of Grunge and Government: Let's Fix This Broken Democracy!* New York: RDV Books/Akashic Books, 2004.

Pavitt, Bruce. *Experiencing Nirvana: Grunge in Europe, 1989*. Brooklyn, NY: Bazillion Points, 2013.

Pavitt, Bruce. *Sub Pop USA: The Subterranean Pop Music Anthology, 1980–1988*. Brooklyn, NY: Bazillion Points, 2015.

Pelly, Jenn. *The Raincoats*. New York: Bloomsbury Academic, 2017.

Peterson, Charles. *Screaming Life*. San Francisco: HarperCollinsWest, 1995.

Peterson, Charles. *Touch Me I'm Sick*. New York: powerHouse Books, 2003.

Prato, Greg. *Grunge Is Dead: The Oral History of Seattle Rock Music*. Toronto: ECW Press, 2009.

Reynolds, Simon. *Retromania: Pop Culture's Addiction to Its Own Past*. New York: Farrar, Straus & Giroux, 2011.

Savage, Jon. *This Searing Light, the Sun and Everything Else: Joy Division: The Oral History*. London: Faber and Faber Social, 2019.

Schemel, Patty. *Hit So Hard: A Memoir*. New York: Da Capo Press, 2017.

Soulsby, Nick. *I Found My Friends: The Oral History of Nirvana*. New York: Thomas Dunne Books, 2015.

Süskind, Patrick. *Perfume: The Story of a Murder*. New York: Alfred A. Knopf, 1986.

Tarver, Clay. "The Rock 'n' Roll Casualty Who Became a War Hero." *New York Times Magazine*, July 2, 2013.

Turner, Steve. *Mud Ride: A Messy Trip Through the Grunge Explosion*. San Francisco: Chronicle Prism, 2023.

Walker, Barbara G. *The Woman's Dictionary of Symbols & Sacred Objects*. San Francisco: HarperSanFrancisco, 1988.

Wheeler, Alice. *Outcasts and Innocents: Photographs of the Northwest*. Seattle: Minor Matters Books, 2015.

Wolfe, Charles and Kip Lornell. *The Life and Legend of Leadbelly*. New York: HarperCollins, 1992.

Yarm, Mark. *Everybody Loves Our Town: An Oral History of Grunge*. New York: Three Rivers Press, 2011.

Young, Neil. *Waging Heavy Peace*. New York: Blue Rider Press, 2012.

RECOMMENDED FILMOGRAPHY

Arkush, Alan, dir. *Rock 'n' Roll High School*. 1979.

Bogdanovich, Peter, dir. *Tom Petty and the Heartbreakers: Runnin' Down a Dream*. 2007.

Boyle, Danny, dir. *Trainspotting*. 1996.

Cox, Alex, dir. *Sid and Nancy*. 1986.

Crowe, Cameron, dir. *Singles*. 1992.

Kaplan, Jonathan, dir. *Over the Edge*. 1979.

Lindstrom, Brian, dir. *Alien Boy: The Life and Death of James Chasse*. 2013.

Linklater, Richard, dir. *Slacker*. 1990.

Racco, Mark, dir. *Live at the Paramount*. 2011.

Sillen, Peter, dir. *I Am Secretly an Important Man*. 2010.

Tarantino, Quentin, dir. *Pulp Fiction*. 1994.

Van Sant, Gus, dir. *Drugstore Cowboy*. 1989.

CREDITS

If you or someone you know is struggling
or in crisis, help is available.
Call or text 988 or chat at 988lifeline.org